DEATH AND DYING

DEATH AND DYING

A Bibliographical Survey

COMPILED BY
SAMUEL SOUTHARD

FOREWORD BY
THERESE A. RANDO

G. E. Gorman, Advisory Editor

Bibliographies and Indexes
in Religious Studies, Number 19

GREENWOOD PRESS
New York • Westport, Connecticut • London

Library of Congress Cataloging-in-Publication Data

Southard, Samuel.
    Death and dying : a bibliographical survey / compiled by Samuel
Southard ; foreword by Therese A. Rando.
      p.   cm.—(Bibliographies and indexes in religious studies,
ISSN 0742-6836 ; no. 19)
    Includes indexes.
    ISBN 0-313-26465-1 (alk. paper)
    1. Thanatology—Bibliography. 2. Death—Bibliography. 3. Grief—
Bibliography. 4. Terminal care—Bibliography. I. Gorman, G. E.
II. Title.   III. Series.
Z5725.S67 1991
[HQ1073]
016.3069—dc20   91-7222

British Library Cataloguing in Publication Data is available.

Library of Congress Catalog Card Number: 91-7222
ISBN: 0-313-26465-1
ISSN: 0742-6836

First published in 1991

Greenwood Press, 88 Post Road West, Westport, CT 06881
An imprint of Greenwood Publishing Group, Inc.

Printed in the United States of America

The paper used in this book complies with the
Permanent Paper Standard issued by the National
Information Standards Organization (Z39.48-1984).

10 9 8 7 6 5 4 3 2 1

CONTENTS

FOREWORD

"Dying," in the words of Küng, "means the physico-psychological events immediately preceding death, which are irrevocably halted with the advent of death. Dying then is the way, death the 'destination'."[1] Death as destination, whether intermediate or final, and dying as way have been accepted by societies and accommodated by religious traditions throughout history, but not always with the equanimity and understanding one might expect of an intelligent species. Death, of course, has as its corollary in the human psyche a drive towards hope, and in many ways the story of religious belief is the story of the search for balance between death and hope. An accurate and stable balance between the need to hope and the reality of death has never been achieved for long in the history of humanity; more often than not the pendulum seems to swing wildly from one extreme to the other, occasionally pausing somewhere in the middle.

"...The ultimate reality that looms up for everybody, inexorably, is the dark void of death. Nonetheless all human life, even that of men who do not believe in an afterlife, and reduce hope theoretically to dread, is penetrated by the notion of progress and hope."[2] Such a notion seems to have predominated in Western thought during the middle decades of this century, as the pendulum has swung well into hope and away from the reality of death. Science and medicine have made dying less painful and death less an unexpected end to youth or middle age. Segregated homes for "senior citizens," bloodlessly sterile hospital wards, "bereavement counselors" with

---

[1]Hans Küng, Eternal Life. Trans. by Edward Quinn (London: Collins Fount, 1985), p. 33.

[2]A New Catechism: Catholic Faith for Adults (New York: Herder and Herder, 1967), p. 467.

their carefully contrived masking of the dead—have all conspired to remove death and dying from the realm of normality and place it in a never-never land of unreality. Consequently, hope has been subject to few natural controls and for a time reigned supreme in the modern psyche. Gradually, however, political, social, economic, and a host of related worldly events—overpopulation, recurring crop failures, destruction of the environment, growing human suffering in the developing world— conspired to destroy this naive reliance on hope and to restore a realistic acceptance of death to its rightful place as a counterpoint to hope.

Throughout this changing ethos religions have not faltered in their awareness of death and the need to treat dying as a significant rite in existential terms. All religions have been united in their tacit recognition of the significance of death through ritualization of some sort and the concomitant role of pastoral care for both the dying and the living. In religious circles the perennially perplexing issue has been rather the nature of death and its ultimate significance, and at best lack of agreement has been the norm. In earlier days, for example, the Egyptian obsession with an afterlife as exemplified in elaborate embalming procedures was countered by a slightly later biblical insistence that man's fate upon death was simply to return to dust (Gen. 3:19). Even within a single religion there has been significant disagreement about the nature of death. The Old Testament shows the Hebrews believing on one hand that the dead descend to *sheol* and on the other hand that Yahweh will save man from *sheol*, not to mention at least a clear allusion to resurrection (Dan. 12:2) as man's fate after death—a belief that of course becomes paramount in Christianity. Thus the great religions that emerged in the Near East exhibit nothing like a common or necessarily compatible understanding of death.

At least the various religious traditions have not, like the secular world, sought to hide from the reality of death, and now that society at large has rediscovered this inexorable end of man there appears to be a common religious and secular acceptance that "death is served up piecemeal by life itself. A bitter disappointment, an affection which has cooled, loneliness, sickness, the brittleness of the body—these are all presages, cat's paws from the storms of death, like the cobwebs of July which are an early sign of autumn."[3] One consequence of this remarkable unity of acceptance and understanding has been a refreshing convergence and cross-fertilization of ideas; beginning in the early seventies with popular works like *On Death and Dying* by Kübler-Ross and *Life after Life* by Moody and continuing up to the present, religious and secular counselors have recognized that they have something useful to offer one another not only in understanding death and dying but also in counseling the dying and their families. Equally noteworthy has been the almost obsessive fascination with the nature of death and pastoral treatment of the dying. All of these factors have converged in recent years to result, among other things, in a massive burgeon-

---

[3]*Ibid.*

ing of the literature on death, dying and pastoral counseling; this in turn has motivated the preparation of this volume by Dr. Samuel Southard of Fuller Theological Seminary.

Through a forty year career as a practitioner and teacher of counseling and pastoral theology Dr. Southard has developed a unique perspective on the theology, psychology and pastoral treatment of death and dying. At the same time he has been able to draw upon the expertise of colleagues in the Association for Clinical Pastoral Education, the American Association of Pastoral Counselors, the Society for Pastoral Theology, and the medical profession. The result of all this has been the present volume, which is nothing less than a most thorough, detailed and wide-ranging guide to the literature on death and dying from a counseling perspective. From the first page of the table of contents to the last page of the index one is aware of the care and attention that has gone into preparing literature survey suited equally to the priest, counselor, scholar and student. Within this survey Dr. Southard carefully and judiciously selects literature related to every pastoral aspect of death and dying, ranging from biblical studies and eschatology to AIDS, from medical technology to support groups, from the will of God to euthanasia. While the bibliography is thus catholic in its treatment of appropriate topics, it is also judicious in its selection of items representing the several traditions, schools of thought, therapeutic styles and viewpoints related to the treatment of death and dying. There have been many bibliographies in recent years devoted to aspect of this field and to specific counseling practices, but none of them has surveyed the field in so unified and thorough a fashion as has Dr. Southard. Accordingly, this work both sets the standard for all future bibliographical works in its field and fulfills a valuable reference function in institutional and personal libraries. It is most gratifying to see discussions with the author over four years come to such abundant fruition.

G. E. Gorman
Advisory Editor
Charles Sturt University – Riverina

FOREWORD

It's not easy being a thanatologist in the 1990s. At least it *should not* be easy being a thanatologist in the 1990s. When it is, something is awry and something quite complex has been oversimplified.

In an era of increasing specialization in everything from medicine to sales, today's professional appears to be required to develop increased expertise in a focused area of decreased breadth. To be sure, there are many people—usually in these circumstances termed "consumers"—and movements that have rallied against such minimized perspective—for example, the hospice movement and wholistic medicine—yet the trend continues. Being considered a generalist at something is frequently taken to mean a lack of training, signifying one who is a "jack of all trades and master of none." To identify a good medical general practitioner in one's community often can be quite a task, notwithstanding the specialization of family practice, that is, the specialization of the general.

Unfortunately, the field of thanatology has not escaped this tendency to specialize. For example, there are now professionals who work exclusively with bereaved parents, and even solely with those who have lost a child at a certain age and under certain circumstances. This is not to say that increased discrimination within thanatology is unnecessary. Indeed, the mandate for it has been made clear,[1] and there is no dearth of arguments for the necessity to hone generalizations about dying, death, loss, grief, and mourning to accommodate the particular realities that reflect the following two incontrovertible facts: (1) Because of the idiosyncratic nature of experience, no two loss experiences—either predeath (i.e., dying and anticipatory grief) or postdeath (i.e., grief and mourning)—are exactly alike; and,

---

[1]Therese A. Rando, *Grief, Dying, and Death: Clinical Interventions for Caregivers.* Champaign, Il.: Research Press, 1984.

therefore, (2) different losses require different types of support and treatment interventions.

Sixty-two sets of variables have been identified to influence the dying of an individual and the anticipatory grief of his or her loved ones.[2] Combined under three categories, these include: three sets of psychological factors (characteristics pertaining to the nature and meaning of the person(s) and relationship(s) to be lost, personal characteristics of the dying patient or the anticipatory griever, and characteristics pertaining to the illness and type of death involved); three sets of social factors (characteristics of the dying person's knowledge and response to the illness and ultimate death, characteristics of the family and its members' responses to the illness and impending death, and general socioeconomic and environmental factors); and one set of physiological factors.

Correspondingly, in terms of postdeath grief and mourning, twenty-nine separate sets of factors influencing a person's response to loss have been identified.[3] These can be categorized into three broad realms: psychological factors (including factors pertaining to the nature and meaning of the relationship severed, the personal characteristics of the mourner, and the characteristics of the death), social factors, and physical factors. As can be seen, all these factors span a wide array of disciplines and inherently pertain to a host of broad-spectrum issues. A narrow focus just will not do.

What does all of this mean to the thanatologist? It means that even though two or more members of a family or social system undergo the death of the same beloved person, it is experienced in different ways because of the individualistic meanings and factors circumscribing the loss for a given mourner at a particular point in time. For the thanatologist—whether caregiver, academician, researcher, or student—this translates into the necessity of apprehending a variety of factors if maximal understanding and, ultimately, impact is desired. The demand exists to insure that any specialized focus or interest be placed into a more general, multidisciplinary context that can incorporate the factors delineated above that spawn the individual's response to loss. If this is not done, critical factors determining a person's idiosyncratic reactions to loss and unique needs for intervention can be overlooked, minimized, or, at worst, ignored. Therefore, despite any concentration of interest and/or practice, the more narrowed vision of the specialist is to be eschewed in favor of the development of a more wide-angled and inclusive perspective.

For this reason, the thanatologist must embrace, if not specific knowledge about, then at least sufficient sensitivity to, and awareness of, the multiple factors that impinge upon and influence the individual, and must be able to respond accordingly when appropriate. This is not easy, for it demands effort on the part of the thanatologist who must evaluate and take

---

[2]Therese A. Rando, ed., *Loss and Anticipatory Grief.* Lexington, MA: Lexington Books, 1986

[3]Therese A. Rando, *Grief, Dying, and Death: Clinical Interventions for Caregivers.* Champaign, IL: Research Press, 1984.

into consideration a host of influencing variables. It would be so much easier to ignore them. Yet, the relevance to dying, death, and loss of the dynamics from philosophy, theology, psychology, medicine, history, anthropology, political science, economics, education, and the arts—all of which combine to give rise to the unique constellation of factors circumscribing any dying person or mourner—must be not only appreciated, but also made manifest through the specific actions undertaken, the context provided, and the viewpoint maintained by the thanatologist in regard to that person.

Without a doubt, however, it is more difficult these days to respond to those contending with death because of the increasing demands of the psychosocial milieu. In earlier times, people were more homogeneous, deaths more natural, and mourning less complicated. Now, we witness a more pluralistic society with increasing populations of cultural minorities, with the types and manners of deaths increasing in violence and preventability, and with those forced to contend with it being less prepared, having fewer resources than ever before, and too often experiencing the sequelae of poor attachment bonds.[4] The aforementioned disciplines become more than mere abstractions when examined as factors influencing human response. They shape the hard realities of dying, death, and loss, and the myriad reactions to each—the stuff of the thanatologist. They also provide the context within, and the dimensions across, which the individual's needs must be determined. The unique situation of each person must be assessed and must form the basis for judgment and intervention. All dying patients are not alike; all bereaved do not have the same needs; all interventions are not equally effective.

It is in the recognition of these truths that Dr. Southard's extensive annotated bibliography serves the thanatological community so well. Herein all the related disciplines are integrated. Their practical relevance to the field is illuminated. The grounding of dying and death into these disciplines and the rooting of it in the diverse components of the rich tapestry of human life, anchors for us these events at the very same time that it frees them up from rigid compartmentalization and the Procrustean bed of myopia.

Breadth, mooring, and greater perspective are not the exclusive gifts of his contribution, however. Dr. Southard has also provided critical commentary with his annotations, thus supplying these three dimensions intratopically, in addition to the work as a whole. Comprehensiveness is enhanced through his inclusion of articles, chapters, monographs, and reports, along with books. The scenario for all of this is set in the book's superb and in-depth chronicle of the development and direction of thanatological literature. This is a choice synthesis of the origin and convergence of the multiple disciplines that effect and are affected by death and its ramifications, the personal influences upon those who have been most influen-

---

[4]Therese A. Rando, *Treatment of Complicated Mourning*. Champaign, IL: Research Press, 1991.

tial in the field, and the socio-historical contexts both forming and formed by all of this. This introduction alone is invaluable.

The thanatologist who recognizes the responsibility to understand dying, death, loss, grief, and mourning in the totality of the human context, with all of its variegated dimensions, has in this compendium a rich resource to point the way for doing just that. The multidisciplinary aspects of these events are identified, analyzed, and placed in proper conjunction with them. Those who want solely to delve deeper into a specific aspect of the field have at their fingertips an excellent reference guide. Thus, although it still is not easy being a thanatologist in the 1990s, because of all the generalist considerations and the multidisciplinary perspectives required, it just got a little bit easier thanks to Sam Southard.

Therese A. Rando, Ph.D.
Warwick, Rhode Island
December 1990

PREFACE

The reading of this bibliography will require the courage of a believer and the humility of a learner. I am a believer in research reports and in reflective essays on the subject of dying and death. This bifocal approach to thanatology requires courage to hold in tension the scientific and the philosophical/theological aspects of a subject which inevitably flows beyond our experience. On the one hand, empirical research depends upon our authentication of another person's experience, and that of us can really imagine our own death? We can only report the experience of observing the death of another, or we try as a dying person to explain that which others have not yet felt. On the other hand, philosophy/theology proposes meaning and purpose in death, which can be experienced in the present and shared in some community of faith between those who know the time of their death and those who do not.

But who is in our particular "community of faith" and how can we trust our lives to meaning and purpose that transcends our experience? These questions drive us to the humility of learners before the everlasting mystery of death and dying. The history of the subject and range of concerned disciplines of study are staggering. Only the arrogant and the ignorant can confidently assert that their "facts" or their "faith" provide all that we need to know about death.

With some courage I present in this bibliography a multidisciplinary outline on death and dying that seeks to be comprehensive without being exhaustive. With some humility forced upon me by four years of bibliographic study I present annotations that are representative of fields with which I have some acquaintance. The selections are not exhaustive, and perhaps not even judicious in any one discipline; and many chosen references will lead the alert reader to other sources beyond the range of this book. The very mention of a "field" is a limitation. Most of the references in this bibliography are by practitioners and researchers for others in their own or a related profession. Few of the annotations are of books for or by a dying person, a bereaved relative, or a person of any age or stage of health who wants to know more about death and dying. Happily, books for these audiences are now available in profusion.

What led to the selection of books and articles for this bibliography? It was the usual research trilogy: identify, classify, evaluate. First, I assembled a list of studies that were frequently cited in standard thanatology texts. This gave me some idea of pivotal empirical studies and reflective essays. Then I compared table of contents in standard texts to determine current topics for classification. Finally, I evaluated the contribution of a book or article as a building block in research or reflection and as a signpost of established facts or faith, and perhaps pointing the way to new knowledge about a very primitive problem.

My limitations in this approach will be obvious: almost total reliance upon English-language texts, especially from the United States; dependence upon more Western than Eastern philosophical and religious essays; ignorance of technical studies in medicine, pharmacology, mortuary sciences.

Some of my deficiencies have been remedied by authorities who have kindly assisted me: Therese Rando and Ed Dobihal corrected and expanded my original selection of topics; comments for and corrections of "Development" were provided by Robert Baird, Lucy Bregman, Herman Feifel, Paul Irion, Edwin S. Shneidman, Michael A. Simpson, Hannelore Wass; Michael A. Simpson provided medical and other references in his reading of my entire list of annotations; the advisory editor, G. E. Gorman taught me all I know about the preparation (and punctuation) of a bibliography. David Sielaff and Noel Taylor input and typeset the text, and corrected my errant attempts to turn a bibliophile into a bibliographer.

Each reader can also remedy my limitations by consulting other bibliographies (some of which are listed in Chapter 8) and requesting extensive and up-to-date listing from the National Library of Medicine and other computer-generated resources. Also, a complete listing of articles by leading authors, such as Parkes (4212) and Bowlby (3038) are available in some of their own works.

Some bibliographies will be useful in strengthening a conclusion of Steinfels that "We will not be able to speak with any wisdom about the future of death unless we have examined the past of death." With these sources we may also escape his scorn of those who think they have newly discovered death. He considers this to be ludicrous self-deception (Steinfels 2064, 5).

In an effort to show that we are not necessarily wiser than those who thought about death before, I have placed historical and anthropological studies first. Then there are sections on philosophy and theology, which may aid us to a perspective of death as a mystery of life rather than as a self-contained problem in positivistic research. The third and fourth sections on terminal care and grief will show the richness of clinical research and the importance of interdisciplinary collaboration. The following section on caretaking professions is short, because interdisciplinary study and practice has reduced the distinctives of professional guilds in thanatology. The next set of reviews are on education for death, both a reminder and a challenge that discussions about death must be discussions about life (Steinfels 2064, 6). The final sections are on literature and the arts, research, evaluation and bibliographies. These studies give us encouragement to believe (1) that we really have learned new ways to think about an old subject. The meditations of saints and the pontifications of professors are now open to empirical investigation. Facts are now as important as faith in research on death and dying. But (2) the "age of faith" provided perspectives that enrich empirical studies with mystery and humility before the great destroyer in this life, who is ultimately defeated by the acceptance of facts about life with faith beyond death.

DEVELOPMENT
AND DIRECTION OF
THANATOLOGY
LITERATURE

A narrative poem on death, *The Day of Doom,* was the first best-seller in America. First printed in 1662, it was a broadside of over 200 doggerel verses on death, doom, and judgment (Wigglesworth 1118). The pamphlet was literally read to pieces in Puritan New England. No copy of the first edition is known to survive.[1]

A hundred years later, the best-seller was "The Way to Wealth," a preface to *Poor Richard's Almanac* by Benjamin Franklin.[2] Dollars replaced death in the attention and intentions of an expanding, entrepreneurial nation.

The success orientation of America submerged but did not drown the publication of literature on death and dying. At least an interest in the afterlife continued. Almost five thousand items were in an 1864 publication of "Literature of the Doctrine of a Future Life, a catalogue of works related to the nature, origin and destiny of the soul." (Travis 2292, 15)[3] But the *study* of death was drowned until World War II. In a 1970 publication, Saffron wrote: "In America thanatology has had until very recent

---

[1]Perry Miller comments on the popularity of the poem, which was frequently reprinted until 1929. Perry Miller, *The Puritans*, vol. II, Rev., ed. (New York: Harper and Row, 1963), 585.

[2]Moses Coit Tyler *The Literary History of the American Revolution, 1763-1783* , II (New York: Barnes and Noble, 1987) 365. "The Way to Wealth" is printed in Sculley Bradley, ed., *American Tradition in Literature*, 4th ed. (New York: Grosset and Dunlap, 1974), 246-253.

[3]This is the number of an annotated work in the following chapters and the page of a citation.

times few rational students." (Saffron 1047, 333). A pioneering psychiatrist in the treatment of dying patients noted in 1955 that not only the speciality of psychiatry but also the whole field of medicine had neglected the problem of death. (Eissler 3456).

A professor of surgery, Roswell Park, called attention to this need in a 1912 article on "Thanatology," which was the first American use of the term. His was an emphasis on the biomedical study of nature and cause of death that would separate physics from theology. In the new scientific study there would be no place for vague notions of "the soul" (Park 1135, 1245).

A more eclectic and classical medical study was presented in 1935 by Alfred Worcester, *The Care of the Aged, the Dying and the Dead*. (Worcester 3158). As a student of Oliver Wendell Holmes, Sr., who combined medical and literary pursuits, Dr. Worcester wrote for medical students on the "art" of service to the dying and their families. Cicely Saunders considers this to be the classic in hospice therapeutics for that time and observes that "little was written before 1960" (Zimmerman 3409, ix).

During the period of American scientific silence and restrictions, English and European sociologists and anthropologists, were stimulated to study death because of field reports about "primative" peoples and the theory-building of Spencer (1255) and others. One special interest was the discussion of animism, a belief in spiritual beings among primitive peoples. An early and representative response in anthropology was Tylor's *Primitive Culture* in 1871 (1256). He posited friendliness or hostility of dead ancestors as the organizing center of religious beliefs and social customs of primitive peoples (Goody 1297, 15). These theories were criticized by Durkheim (1239) who also published a pioneering sociological study of suicide (3527). Another seminal study by W. Robertson Smith gave specific attention to the place of a deified father in death rituals (1253). The work was influential upon Freud who postulated a connection between fear of a murdered father and worship of supernatural beings (*Totem and Taboo*, 1246).

In other publications Freud continued an interest in the fear of death. His early distinctions between this sphere as a manifestation of neurosis and a realistic response to external danger (*Mourning and Melancholia*, 4301) was a central question for psychoanalytic writing on death before World War II and was revised in the influential study of widows by Bowlby in the 1960s (1168). Saffron concluded in 1970 that "contemporary studies in the psychology of death and death and dying are still dominated by the powerful figure of Freud." (1047, 332). At the same time, Saffron noted that medicine had paid little attention to death as a specific entity. The entry, "death," did not appear in the indices of the most widely read general histories of medicine (1047, 329).

American professionals with an interest in thanatology before World War II would need to look mainly at European and English studies in anthropology and psychoanalysis.

In the United States, the few professional publications on death were a continuation of psychoanalytic themes from Freud, pastoral or theological books of consolation, anthropological studies of primitive death rituals, or philosophical monographs on the treatment of death by some philosopher, such as Heidegger (Heidegger 2019; Kaufman 2054). The few popular works presented brave individuals, often children, who died sad but peaceful deaths (Steinfels 2066, 1).

In the 1960s, the number of books on death multiplied and also were read by a general audience. Kübler-Ross' *On Death and Dying* appeared in 1968 and sold half a million copies by the 1970s (1020). By 1970, the *New York Times Book Review* published summaries of eight books on death in one issue and there were references in the review to this "avalanche" and to a "death renaissance." By 1973 the *Accumulated Index Medicus* had over 100 titles on death, and courses on death education were initiated in medical schools and theological seminaries, and were beginning in colleges and adult education programs (Steinfels 2066, 1-2).

But publications on death and dying in the 1960s and 70s would not qualify for the cultural comprehensiveness that undergirded *Ars Moriendi* publications in the late Middle Ages when death seized the center of popular attention after the massive devastation of the Black Plague (Huizinga 1091; Rolfes 1098). For example, among the many specialties of psychology, interest in death and dying was found mainly in stress research and crisis intervention theory. Sociological contributions continued the nineteenth century study of mourning rituals in less differentiated societies. Where contemporary studies of death were published, they dealt primarily with either the influence of value judgments and forms of behavior upon the society or upon psychoanalytic issues in family constellation and personality dynamics. Theological studies were mainly confined to medical ethics and a few psychologically sensitive manuals for pastors on the funeral and immediate grief reactions. Individual coping with dying and grief was not a subject of philosophical, theological, or historical research (Spiegel 4015, 18-19).

Publications in the 1980s filled out neglected areas. The quantity of publications as well as the range of subjects increased. The medical bibliographer, Simpson, commented on the "deluge" of books on nuclear issues between 1980 and 1984 (Simpson 8039, x). Simpson notes that in the 1979 edition of his bibliography, 763 books were listed. His 1987 list has increased to 1700 books, most published since 1979 (Simpson 8039, ix). This does not include the surge of professional articles, which can be documented from 1845 to 1975 in the chronological bibliography of Fulton (8016) and the yearly specialized bibliographies such as *Bibliography of Bioethics* (Walters 8047).

The Nuclear Age as an Accumulation of Loss

What educated guesses are advanced to explain this ebb and flow of thanatology publications?

Gorer's "Pornography of Death" introduced readers and writers of the 1960s to correlations between Victorian prudery about sex and early twentieth century inhibitions about death (Gorer 1131). A Belgian observer of the American death scene, Godin (1266) made a similar observation. He found "a virtually non-existent field of investigation before 1965." Why? His first explanation was an omnipresent social silence on death. The generalized silence was part of the vagueness of an oppressive anguish in late nineteenth and early twentieth century European cultures.

His second explanation reinforced the first. Silence on the subject of death was appropriate for Western cultures that inhibited displays of emotion (Godin 7013, 224-225). His conclusions find some support in the investigations of Feifel, who found that terminally ill patients thanked him for open conversations about death, while medical personnel told him they "never" talked about death with patients and administrators refused his requests for research on death because it would cause "test toxicity."[4]

An eminent American observer of society, Talcott Parsons, attributed the denial of death to the success of public health agencies and a rising standard of living among Americans. The sharp decrease in premature and early deaths led the American public to feel that an active and healthy life was possible without preparation for or conversation about death. There is always resistance to the fact of death and it will not be accepted unless it is felt to be inevitable and uncontrolled. When pain is alleviated, as it is in many modern hospitals, people believe that the pre-awareness of death-suffering can be eliminated. Also, the inevitability of death was now so lessened from natural causes that increased attention was given to the avoidance of death that could be traced to "man-made" causes: accident, crime, war. It was optimistically assumed that these were preventable. Both social and medical control would keep death far away. The normal life cycle would not be prematurely terminated (Parsons 1141, 62).

A disregard of death at the conscious level was associated with both social forces and philosophical developments by Carbine. He quotes the observations of Berger that a new structure of consciousness can be detected in the post-industrial West. The institutional fabric has become incohesive, fragmented and progressively deprived of plausibility. Radical differentiation, technological change, and pervasive bureaucracy erode the reliability of institutions that formerly provided meaning and stability. The individual subjective experience remains alone. This presents modern humans with a "present-immediate" orientation in which the historical past is relatively unimportant and personal salvation is to be concentrated upon temporal concerns. Carbine uses the writings of Sigmund Freud, Erik Erikson, and Carl Rogers to demonstrate this shift toward a non-dimensional time that is based upon empirical reality in the present. Symbols of time in the past and in the future are now irrelevant (Carbine 2013).

---

[4]Herman Feifel, "Death," in *Tabooed Topics*, ed. by Norman L. Faberow (New York: Atherton Press, 1963), 10.

Feifel notes the sway of logical positivism as both a wholesome and a stultifying influence upon psychological studies of death. As a pioneer in clinical research on death, he reviews empirical findings and clinical perceptions of the field from 1955 to 1989 and describes perspectives from the death movement that contribute to the emerging adulthood of psychology.[5]

My summary conclusion is that personal security and salvation are now concentrated in the present experiences of an individual. The fear of death is destroyed (1) by the suspicion of the past in which humans were exhorted to find salvation from time and (2) by contempt for any thoughts for the future that would provide salvation beyond time.

These suspicions bring thanatology into the area of philosophy, anthropology, theology. Indeed, Hoffman (6001) and Veatch (3450) assert that critical questions for open debate about death are basically philosophical or theological rather than scientific.

The influence of a culture's philosophical theology upon awareness of and response to death was succinctly stated by a French anthropologist, Farbre-Luce: "In former days, men did not die."[6] He first observed that primitive peoples were continually reminded of the dead and destiny beyond this life in the signal events that were interpreted as signs of an ancestor's interference. Secondly, primitives belonged completely to a clan and death was taught as perfect integration with the clan forever.

The post-World War II upsurge of death awareness in the United States has probably not been due to primitive influences such as malevolent ancestors or hostile deities, although a 1988 Gallup poll reveals 77% of the American public believe that there is a heaven and most believe that they have a good or excellent chance of getting there. Fifty-eight percent believe that there is a hell and only 6% think they have a good or excellent chance of getting there.[7] God is not dead in the mind of the American public, but the *Day of Doom* dread of His eternal judgments has disappeared.

Why would literature on death and dying appear in such profusion when we seem to be conquering pain and dissolving any fear of future punishment? One reason for an open consciousness of death is a secure philosophical foundation in Heidegger, Kierkegaard, and other existential philosophers (Koestenbaum 2008, 7). Heidegger's philosophy of "being for death" fits a twentieth century preoccupation with the immediate experience of individuals (Heidegger 2019). This is suggested by Choron's survey of modern philosophical answers to death (Choron 1041). Existentialists provided new understanding of both death and life for thanatologists who sought some explanation for the mystery of suicide and the existential drain of professional commitment to dying people.

---

[5]Feifel, Herman, "Psychology and Death: Meaningful Rediscovery." In *American Psychologist* 45, 4 (April 1990): 537 - 543.

[6]Quoted in Godin 7013, 236.

[7]*Newsweek*, March 27, 1989, p. 53.

Existential philosophy, especially the despair of Sartre, was congruent with the agony of Vietnam, the assembling of facts about the Holocaust, the rise of violent crime, and the possibility of nuclear annihilation. At least one of the most popular writers on death mentioned this mood (although she was not in despair). Kübler-Ross, after reviewing social forms of megadeath concluded that "ultimately, it is the knowledge of our own potential destructiveness that forces us today to confront ourselves with the meaning of life and death." (Riemer 2339, 1). Also, there has been much professional and some public interest in Lifton's scholarly sociological and philosophical studies that connected the horrors of atomic warfare with our attitudes towards death (Lifton 1157, 1221).

Perhaps the manifest violence of the 1960s provided a "teachable moment" for professionals in many fields to show how a new focus upon death could bring the dark and light side of life together with both courage and compassion.

What was the new focus upon death and dying that illuminated the accumulation of loss in a society that buried death awareness under secular and religious assurances of success? Feifel's *The Meaning of Death* (1008) is credited by Godin as "the decisive factor in breaking the taboo." (Godin 7013, 226). The work was both comprehensive and heuristic. Philosophers and theologians joined with professionals in the natural sciences as contributors to this pioneering volume edited by a clinical psychologist. The publication of interdisciplinary studies or the awareness of contributions from various disciplines has characterized post-World War II publications in thanatology as contrasted with late nineteenth and early twentieth century tomes in which one anthropologist criticized the view of another or one psychoanalyst wrote a different interpretation of the death instinct from colleagues.

The work of Feifel and collaborators was also heuristic. It stimulated more study. As Godin notes, Feifel published at least one research study per year after the 1959 publication of *Meaning of Death* (Godin 7013, 227).

The interdisciplinary and heuristic quality of post-World War II studies were probably founded on mutual interest in empirical research. The "teachable moment" was the federal budget from presidents Truman through Johnson, which provided humanitarian support for many causes including studies of suicide, the trauma of widows, sharing of information among thanatologists, and myriad individual research projects. Publication was encouraged, for the publication of research reports opened the way to one grant and promised the renewal of another.

Authors who did not support their studies with empirical findings were soon downgraded by professional colleagues, even if their public impact was significant. An example would be the writings of Kübler-Ross. Her initial distinction of five psychological stages in dying grew out of a study of interviews with 200 dying patients, which were provided by clinical pastoral education students at the Chicago Theological Seminary. (Godin 7013, 229). Kübler-Ross neither sought to replicate and refine her initial findings, nor did she develop any ongoing interdisciplinary studies with chaplains.[8]

The Development of an Interprofessional Discipline

When we consider interdisciplinary cooperation and research publication as heuristic elements in a new view of death and dying, difficulties of definition arise. Kutscher and others found from a questionnaire to members of the Professional Advisory Board of the Foundation of Thanatology that varying professions favored a comprehensive study of death. Yet, in 1976 the Foundation of Thanatology had a definition that "omits fear of death (anticipatory grief), which should be included." (Fleming 6158, 303). Lindemann's influential and pioneering article on acute grief in 1944 introduced the term "anticipatory grief" (Lindemann 4044). In 1974 Schoenberg's, *Anticipatory Grief* contained contributions from many professions (4027). Feifel had noted in 1977 that "preparation for death" was one of the accomplishments since he headed the 1959 symposium, *The Meaning of Death* (Feifel 1008).

Why should definitions catch up with an expanding field? Both published research and clinical practice require some common understanding of the parameters of a field, viewpoints, theoretical issues, symptoms and treatment modalities. Pine, at a symposium on communication strategies in thanatology noted that "careful and thoughtful indexing" was necessary for the retrieval of thanatological research through computer file systems and documentation of terms. This was the key to retrieval. (Pine 6161, 322).

Pine also observes: "The definitions of dying and death are generally not so much established by the actual process through which people pass or their end result, as they are a result of the activities of those whose job it is to care for dying and dead patients" (Pine 6161, 323).

The importance of professional orientations also appears in David Sudnow's 1967 statement that death appeared as a taboo because of a widespread inability of the general public to readily define "dying" or "dead." Medical procedures and institutionalized activities shaped these definitions (Sudnow 3371).

The importance of professional care in relation to death can explain the powerful combination of definitions, clinical and research reports, and theory-building publications on more open attitudes toward death and dying. But how are we to account for the multitude of works since 1960 for the general public, the college student, the public school teacher, parents, children, siblings, widows—almost everyone with any concern for death except the widowers, about whom little is written and less is known? I think the public is more friendly to a variety of publications on death and dying because the meaning of "professional" is changing, and some of that change may be credited to the influence of thanatologists and their works.

---

[8]For criticisms of the division of dying into linear stages by Kübler-Ross, see Feigenberg (3206) and Schultz (3214), among others.

Consider for example *The Psychiatrist and the Dying Patient,* 1955, a pioneering and highly regarded study in the psychoanalytic tradition by Eissler. In one of the three major cases presented in the book he conceals the true nature of disease from a patient who had asked him for the truth. His answer "was instrumental in preservation of the patient's illusion of approaching recovery" (Eissler 3456, 207-209). Contrast that closed professionalism of the 1950s with Veatch's 1977 *Cases Studies in Medical Ethics.* Truth-telling in response to a request for prognosis from a patient is considered to be a requirement of professional ethics (Veatch 3461, 163). I think the difference of twenty years arises in part from the post-Vietnam emphasis upon patient rights, the evidence from hospice studies that terminally ill patients are quieter and require less medication when they control their own injections under medical supervision, references to "burnout" and other emotional involvements of the professional as a person in care of the dying, a spirit of exploration in studying a subject for which the professionals do not have answers for everyone and will soon succumb to some similar fatality. For example, Garfield's "Impact of Death on the Health-Care Professional" was an article in the second influential collection of Feifel, *New Meanings of Death* (Garfield 3106).

Thanatology was developing with a more open and humane awareness of "professional." This may be illustrated in the enumeration of topics for concern in this new specialty by a respected pioneer in thanatology and author of standard texts on suicide: psychological comfort of the person, the flow of love between patient and therapist as a person is dying, changes in treatment according to the shifts of mood and needs in the patient, acting as an advocate of the patient, the acceptance of limited goals because time for therapy is short and the patient is dying, an acceptance of what is appropriate to the patient rather than the standard of professional success that is desired by the therapist, a series of successive approximations of solutions at a pace set by the patient, a tolerance for periodic denial throughout the time of dying, a concentration upon psychological comfort rather than optimistic reassurance that the patient will get better, constant sharing of information with other hospital personnel, attention to relatives and friends who survive the patient, and dependence upon a psychological support system for the therapist as the patient becomes increasingly anguished by the prospect of loss. (Shneidman 3384, 210-214). This is a human, equalitarian approach to care that synchronizes with the assumptions of post-Vietnam youth culture.

Who was writing with such appeal to a post-Johnson and Nixon public? The comparatively young age of writers on the dying process is probably as significant as the emotional maturity of pioneers in the field of thanatology who were now approaching retirement. It was a winning combination. Worcester was 80 years of age when he published what Greene called "a priceless gem," *Care of the Aged, the Dying and the Dead* in 1935. Forty years later, authors that were continually cross-referenced in the study of the dying patient were 37-40 years of age, except medical internists who averaged 58 years and theologians, aged 65 (Greene 3127, 87).

The comparatively youthful authors developed a "second phase" of death studies that moved beyond efforts at controlling death into a deeper probe concerning the source of our attitudes towards death and the full implications of our attitudes. But, will professionals who obtained leadership in the field at age 40 continue into this additional challenge? Steinfels finds characteristics of this in essays in the symposium *Death Inside Out* that provide conclusions about the way the discussion of death must proceed: Death must be viewed as a mystery, not a problem, we will not be able to speak of any wisdom about the future of death unless we examine the past of death, death cannot be discussed profitably without a strong awareness of the underside of human nature and behavior, discussions about death must be discussions about life (Steinfels 2066, 5-6).

What have been the direction of articles from various disciplines on the subject of death and dying up to the time that Steinfels made his observations? Feifel in *New Meanings of Death* (1977) reviewed the twenty years since he gathered articles for *The Meaning of Death* (1959) and listed these representative accomplishments: (1) articles on the impact of death throughout the life-span of an individual, (2) a wide range of interest in clinical management with articles by psychologists, physicians, nurses, and health-professionals, (3) responses of family, (4) preparation for death, (5) death education, and (6) the impact of the hospice movement (Feifel 1008, 352-355).

The Span and Style of Life:
General and Historical, Anthropological, Sociological, Biomedical, Statistical Studies

The interdisciplinary, clinical, and research orientation of post-Vietnam literature on death and dying has not succumbed to debates between guilds on the question: "Which of us has the best or final answer?" Instead, writers are more inclined to consider a more existential problem: "What style of life will reduce our denials, our defensiveness, our anxieties, fears and despairs?" Such a question comes from clinical observations such as those of Weisman that in defense against an enemy that cannot be outwitted through good medical care, physicians may defend themselves with emotional isolation, standoffishness, intellectualized professionalism (Weisman 3384, 192-193).

Historical studies of death provide some alternative defenses. Thanatologists often look to the historical and cultural analyses of Aries (1039, 1040), which demonstrate the interrelationships of religion and culture in the shaping of attitudes and rituals in death and dying. This tradition of wide-ranging aspects of social history is seldom duplicated in American studies, but we are good at more provincial analyses of some period in American life that can be organized around a developing theme on death, such as Farrell's use of some of the same sources as Aries (public documents about death, funeral customs, cemeteries) to show how death was denied, controlled, and managed in one county between 1830 and 1920 (Farrell 1120).

Comprehensive studies of death and dying in the U.S. usually appear as textbooks that build a style of life and awareness of the life-span through incorporation of resources from social history, anthropology, philosophy and theology, sociology, psychology, the mortuary industry, and the arts/literature. Readers may be urged through questions at the end of chapters to develop a style of life that includes death through personal questions or group discussion (Wilcox and Sutton 1038).

Here are some American examples. Kalish, *Death, Grief, and Caring Relationships* (1017), is a rich source of social and psychological studies arranged around subjects that were most competently explored by American thanatologists. Historical and anthropological perspectives are missing. Philosophy and theology receive attention that is not accorded them in some other texts, but without references to the pastoral counselors who are most often cited in studies of death: Grollman (6112), Jackson (4296) and Irion (4386). Sticking close to the literature in which he has confidence as a social scientist, Kalish also gives minimal attention to ethical issues and explains, for example, "I won't go into the religious and political ramifications of abortion" (Kalish 1017, 247).

Wilcox and Sutton, *Understanding Death and Dying* (1038), seek comprehensiveness through selections from authors who demonstrate a variety of disciplines and the maturity of thought that will define thanatology as a distinct field of study. Multicultural, humanistic, and lifespan-perspectives appear in the short selections for each of the five chapters. Structured exercises, questions, and projects for further study encourage students to bring death into their own style of life.

But although the presentation of seminal excerpts from great thinkers and helpers has a fresh and penetrating quality, students are not presented alternative solutions to cultural, philosophical, theological, and ethical issues on death and dying. For example, the classic selection of Plato's description of Socrates' death is included without a balancing selection from the other major philosophical attitude—death is an enemy and we cannot be serene when our life-span is shortened. (Wilcox and Sutton 1038).

Wass, *Dying: Facing the Facts* (1036), chose in 1979 a number of authors who are competent to summarize and evaluate a wide variety of published sources on death and dying with an emphasis upon the facts of death, logic and cohesion. The book strengthens the stability of a growing field, but without the adventuresomeness of much attention to the study of anticipatory grief, which was just beginning to emerge through Pattison's "Living–Dying Interval" (Pattison 3161, 43-60), and Schoenberg's 1974 text, *Anticipatory Grief* (4027). Any references to the place of death in the span of Western civilization and the discussion of philosophy, theology, and ethics appear only as brief references in the writings of authors on more pragmatically oriented subjects. Ethical issues were part of a second edition in 1988 (1037).

Rando provides a series of volumes that progressively approach comprehensiveness in an appeal to varying audiences. Beginning with *Grief, Dying and Death* (1028), primary sources are summarized in one or two paragraphs that provide a sense of direction and contribution of a particular authority. But with these very satisfying summaries of primary sources on caregiving, civilization-oriented studies are either missing (nothing from Aries or Choron) or anthropological references like van Gennep are compressed into a sentence and the pastoral study of funerals by Irion is listed without a summary (Rando 1028, 173). However, in the next volume for caregivers, *Loss and Anticipatory Grief* (4026), a concentration upon one seminal category for the entire span of death and dying gives opportunity for more extensive discussion of civilization topics such as references to prayer in a chapter on clergy and some brief references to ancient sacred texts by Fulton. The difficulty of contextualization in an edited work can be seen in the chapter that is supposed to deal with both legal and ethical issues in terminal care, but which actually concentrates upon description of legal cases and procedures.

If we move from general surveys to specific clinical studies, American and English authors offer a rich source of material for the development of life-span and life-style approaches to death and dying (Capps 1335, Weenolson 1353).

Yet none of these texts have much place for the dark side of life that is the precursor of death. The ancient quaternity of sin, disease, death, and hell is found only in anthropological and cross-cultural studies of dying and death. Although Goody notes that the conclusions of Tylor (1256) and Frazer (1242) were bounded by "rationalistic positivism" (Goody 1297, 30) these "primitive religion" studies did give serious consideration to fear of ghosts, careful attention to the jealous ancestor for a year or more after death, mourning rituals that expunged a sense of individual sin and/or family shame. It seems natural that Freud should find kinship with these darker studies of death, for he located the death instinct in unconscious drives and thereby maintained a continuing sense of mystery and furtiveness in his discussion of death-awareness in life.

In contrast to some anthropological and cross-cultural studies, American analyses of death may seem superficial in the sense that a discussion of morbidity is bounded by positivistic assumptions about reality. Only that which can be observed in customs or behavior is worthy of serious comment. Sometimes that's all the evidence to be observed anyway in a population confident in the post-World War II era with success in this world. As Huntington and Metcalf observed: "The majority of Americans seem shaky in their faith in a Christian afterlife" (Huntington and Metcalf 4369, 189). But the authors' *Celebration of Death* does include discussions and representative bibliography on anthropological studies of primitive peoples. Here we find the relationships of symbols of death to divinity, the place of souls, ghosts, and the hereafter in rites of passage and death rituals.

Dark precursors of death appear more frequently in the Vietnam era as biomedical, psychological and sociological thanatology, which literature provide studies of unlimited technological violence and absurd death. These are the forces that stir our shadowy awareness of death as our inner destroyer, as in Lifton's *Death in Life* (1157).

Another appropriately scientific approach to signs of the shadow of death has been the competent and creative work on separation anxiety by Bowlby (1168), Parkes (4244), and others. These studies show how loss or the threat of loss will insert deathlike anxiety into crucial stages of the lifespan and deflect a child's ability to integrate trust into a developing style of life. These studies urge those who have been bereaved at an early age to give up the darkness that comes with continued internalization of a lost person and find new life and light in faithful relationships.

Parkes (4244), Glick, Weiss, and Parkes (1365) have painstakingly presented the tracks of death across the shattered lifestyles of widows. Here is where the hundred year old tradition of Western scientific medicine has provided instruments for the assessment of death's intrusiveness.

It is through studies in this tradition of morbidity and mortality that we recognize the neglected fact that some losses in life, such as divorce, may destroy more trust in self and others than the physical death of a spouse (Hyman 1366). The influence of divorce upon a trustful style of life is an invitation for writing on death and dying to go beyond sociological studies of relationships or psychologically bounded investigations of anxiety and fear. Writing in thanatology can now combine attention to the crisis of physical death with studies of the mini-deaths that are suffered throughout life and the way in which cultural and religious attitudes condition our perception of and responses to a multitude of losses.

With this broadened perspective, thanatology becomes open to the new learning of a very old perspective—consolation—by which the philosopher Boethius reconciled himself (and readers for a thousand years), to the multiple losses of the last days of crumbling Roman civilization (Gibson 1089, Reiss 1097).

The Meaning and Mystery of Death: Philosophy

Whether we contemplate the shattered dreams of a great empire or the pain of a personally depleting divorce, we are raising questions that are intimately philosophical. These may arise in caregivers as well as in those who are dying. Weisman raises several of them: "Is hope or despair determined only by whether we shall live or die? . . . How can we come to terms with death so that, as physicians should, we can offer more to those who have less?" (Weisman 3386, 193).

Would philosophers see this inevitable connection? Not necessarily so. Choron notes that "the most influential representative" of the "philosophies of life" movement in the early twentieth century, Bergson, makes only a passing reference to death in his major work *Creative Evolution* (Choron 1041, 209). Twentieth century philosophers were like physicians and other professionals in their silence on the subject of death. Wittgenstein, for example, is not mentioned in Choron's enumeration of contemporary philosophers who were significant in the study of death. Choron pays particular attention to the existential philosophies that were influenced by the philosopher-theologian, Søren Kierkegaard: Jaspers, Heidegger, Sartre, Marcel. The concern was with concrete individuality, the anguish, despair, and loneliness of the individual soul. This was the continuous theme of Kierkegaard (2007, 2021, 2028). The theme was more concentrated in Heidegger's contention that death is a way to "be." To know ourselves is to see ourselves as being-toward-the-end. This state of being becomes significant and purposeful when we define ourselves as beings who encounter others with care.

For Heidegger, "being" has an immediate, subjective state of awareness of our "non-being" This is the awareness of death, a realization that our uttermost possibility of existence can never be completely realized.

What is the existential answer? First, humans who are open to a deeper knowledge of the self in the present moment will question, contemplate, discuss, decide, do something. These are the characteristics "of taking care."

This kind of knowledge serves a different purpose from older philosophies (such as Boethius) in which abstract contemplation of absolutes brought intellectual solutions to the place of humans in the world beyond us. Existential philosophy provides a "caring" knowledge in the present time that provides for others even when we may be at cross purposes with them.

This is the second contribution of existential philosophy to thanatology. It is based on authenticity of the self that creates the possibility of sharing in the suffering of another.

We are receptive to the suffering of another because we have mutually experienced the fundamental mood of anxiety or dread of nothingness. This is the third characteristic of existential philosophy most fundamentally presented by Kierkegaard. It was given a specific direction toward death by Heidegger. It is more than a feeling open to psychological investigation. It is the very sign of human existence, an existence that is being thrown into death.

The fourth characteristic of Heidegger's philosophy of death is courage in time with no knowledge of eternity. This is a thrust toward the uttermost possibility of existence that we can conceive of with full knowledge that death will cut short our potential and defeat any speculation about the future.[9]

---

[9]The specific enumeration of these characteristics are my own, but they are founded on a reading of Heidegger's *Being and Time* (2019). Heideggar and other existential philosophers are considered to be "footnotes on Kierkegaard," John I. McNeill, "Reflections on the Interrelation of Death and the Human Meaning of Time." In Florence M. Hetzler and Austin M. Kutscher, eds., *Philosophical Aspects of Thanatology*, (2053, 167).

Of these four characteristics, courage was given the most specific coverage in a work of a philosopher-theologian, Paul Tillich. His *Courage to Be* was widely read by pastoral counselors and included in the bibliographies of thanatologists. He distinguished three types of anxiety: fate and death in ancient civilizations, guilt and condemnation in the Middle Ages, emptiness and meaninglessness in the modern period. Tillich affirms life in the modern period through courage to live fully without any literal guarantees of a future in heaven or any form of theological or psychological security that was offered to us in the past (Tillich 1190).

In another work of Tillich, *The Eternal Now,* the implicit influence of Heidegger upon thanatology appears in the definition of eternity as new meaning in the present. Eternity is no longer to be thought of as an endless future. We do not seek forgiveness for sins in order that we may enjoy an endless future. Instead, an existential emphasis upon the present allows forgiveness to flood us with new meaning because we are released from a dead past (Tillich 2022).

Are works in thanatology influenced by philosophy, especially existential types?[10] Usually the influence is implicit, which means that the attribution is uncertain or nonexistent. For example, a theologian, Branson, believes that the implicit philosophy of Kübler-Ross is ethical naturalism (Branson 3307). "Implicit" may mean similarity. Thoughts similar to those of Heidegger and other existentialists appear in many thanatological texts, especially those that emphasize anxiety. In *The Psychology of Death* Kastenbaum and Aisenburg are existential in the following ways: First, they distinguish between death anxiety and the fear of death. It is similar to Heidegger's distinction between the restless search for potential wholeness and a generalized, objective contemplation of the death of others. Heidegger's categories also appear in the authors' assertion that acceptance of our death-of-self will lead to self-awareness. This will be a leap of understanding toward non-being, very similar to Heidegger. Also, as in many other texts, there is a constant stress upon emotional factors in death, or, as Heidegger would phrase it, "being-as-present-at-hand" (Kastenbaum and Aisenberg 1018).

If thanatologists are interested in the connections of existential philosophy to their studies on death and dying, they may find many relationships described in Koestenbaum (1187) or they may observe a philosopher's mind at work in concentration upon studies of death in Steinfels and Veatch (3461) and Choron (1041). On occasion a thanatologist will combine existential philosophy with a particular school of psychology, as in Becker's use of the theories of Otto Rank (2194).

10"In response to Freud's pressing invitation to recognize a death instinct acting directly from within, a psycho-sociological interpretation of death is being organized and is giving fresh support to the philosophical theme of a being-for-death (Heideger)." (Godin 7013, 237).

The Journey of the Soul: Theology and Ethics

Thanatologists will also find a number of theological writings in which existential philosophy seems compatible with studies of death. A practical application of existential themes may be found in Neale (1193), a Protestant minister who wrote out of his experience in a department of psychiatry. He advocates an open awareness of the certainty of death without assuming knowledge of the time or mode of death. A variety of exercises are recommended for readers to increase their basic awareness of death, dispel fear and affirm life. Neale is heavily dependent upon psychoanalytic assumptions of death fears, fears which he considers to be a form of neurosis.

In keeping with the assumptions of Heidegger and Sartre, Neale gives no attention to traditional themes of judgment and eternal life. The assumptions may be similar to those of Kastenbaum and Aisenberg, who write in friendly fashion that interested readers will have no difficulty in finding texts in the belief in immortality. They recommend the anthropological contribution of Frazer and the philosophical works of Hocking, Lamont and Ducasse. Then they conclude: "fascinating as the topic may be, we will not linger here." (Kastenbaum and Aisenberg 1018, 102).

Why is there no lingering on immortality and similar themes? Late twentieth writers on thanatology do not seem interested in the hundred year old comparisons between modern religious rituals of mourning and primitive tribes in which guilty sons propitiate a murdered father, whose wives they have possessed (Freud, *Totem and Taboo*, 1246). Instead, they discuss data found in recent surveys, which show a diminished place for religion and ritual in death. Gorer noted that very few respondents to his questionnaire made any reference to judgment, God, Jesus, or the ministry of a clergyperson. He laments the lack of established rituals to support widows during grief (Gorer 1012, 110-116). Anthropologists find that Americans no longer have a service for the dead at home. Despite these findings, there is no suggestion that theology is irrelevant to intimate family living and crises. In fact, Huntington and Metcalf's *Celebrations of Death* encourage a return to theological instruction about death when they review "a continuous tradition of literature on how to die" in Western Christianity and criticize Neale's "almost Buddhist resignation." They offer a judgment that "the latest writers advise a sidelong glance in order to avoid psychological maladjustment" (Huntington and Metcalf 4369, 203).

Why a "sidelong glance"? In part the answer may be found in studies such as I have just cited by Gorer in which theological or philosophical themes are almost completely absent from questionnaires on death rituals, or in which religious people seem to be more afraid of death (Feifel 1206), less anxious (Kahoe 1208), or show no correlation between anxiety and belief in afterlife (Berman 1203). Such contradictory or weak correlations do not encourage depth analysis of theology in a new field that has gained credence through realism and pragmatism.

Of course some pivotal studies in thanatology gave more than a side-long glance to theology and philosophy. Feifel's early symposium, *The Meaning of Death,*1959, not only included contributions by existentially oriented theologians such as Tillich and Jackson, but also by philosophers such as Marcuse. The editor, Feifel, asked for research beyond the space-time limitations of positivistic science (1008, xvii). Few may have heeded his plea, for in *New Meanings of Death,* 1977, Feifel did not present research beyond the space-time limitations of positivistic science as one of the representative accomplishments of the twenty years since the publication of *The Meaning of Death* (1009, 353-355).

Traditional theological topics concerning death would probably find more place in modern thanatology literature if more researchers had responded to Feifel's challenge. One predominantly European response was the symposium edited by Godin, *Death and Presence: The Psychology of Death and the Afterlife,* in which the 1959 work of Feifel is praised (Godin 1266, 227). The studies assembled by Godin were primarily sociological and often drawn from Roman Catholic institution in Europe. It is not a source that has found its way into the mainstream of American thanatology literature.

When researchers, beginning with Feifel, did investigations on the relevance of beliefs about the afterlife for such psychological issues as anxiety and fear, conclusions showed weak or contradictory correlations (see, for example Feifel 1207). Researchers have sought to improve precision through more discriminatory instruments that measure intrinsic versus extrinsic religion (Minton and Spilka 1211) or develop death prospective instruments that specify salient attitudes such as loneliness-pain, indifference, unknown, forsaking dependence, and natural end (Spilka 1215).

Refinement of measurement and discriminating concept formation are some of the ways in which theology might become more salient in studies on death and dying. But one part of theology that stresses the traditional importance of preparation for death and eternal life will strain the ingenuity and boundaries of empirical research. This is the literature on a life of eternal joy and avoidance of eternal damnation that has been a theme of religious publication on death for thousands of years (Aries 1038, Jackson 1043, McGatch 1044). Although thoughts of heavenly reward had been well established since antiquity in both philosophy and theology (Simon 2310), hell began to decline in importance during seventeenth century theological discussions that presaged the religious tolerance, rationality and universalism of the late nineteenth century (Walker 2313). The nineteenth century saw Ritschl's devaluation of the Last Judgment in his presentation of rationalistic moralism (Martin 2299, 207) and the twentieth century theologians applied Bultmann's "demythologizing" to death and found no place for hell. (Bartsch 2105, Hick 2213, 2180).

Under the impact of theological, philosophical and cultural forces, existential theologians moved more toward Heidegger's philosophy of death.

Tillich is considered to be the "best example of this movement."[11] Doss refers to this movement as "theological reductionism," in which theological views of reality are limited to those categories verifiable within finite experience.

Twentieth century existential theology is congruent with many texts on thanatology, and existential theologians are usually represented in significant symposia, such as (Feifel 1009). Despite the lack of conversation between existential thanatologists and conservative theologians, some synthesis is possible as in Lepp's *The Challenges of Life* (2031). This Roman Catholic psychologist draws upon Kierkegaard and later philosophers to affirm courage for full humanity in the midst of anxiety, but without the absurdity and hopelessness that he finds in Heidegger. Since he also draws upon Augustine and Pascal, his work may meet the criteria of "theological realism" which Doss proposes as a "middle way." This is faith in a personal, loving Creator who is working out His purposes in the temporality and finitude of human existence. A more practical example would be the two works of Autton, an English hospital chaplain who not only reviews consolation literature from Boethius in the fifth century to Taylor in the seventeenth, but also shows an awareness of modern studies of thanatology in his discussions of pastoral care with the dying and the bereaved (Autton 3304, 4446). A theological symposium with much scholarly insight for thanatology would be Mills (1161).

There also is common ground between theologians and thanatologists in symposia on moral and professional issues of death and dying. First, there are publications such as those from the Center for Bioethics, Georgetown University, that bring together contributors from many disciplines around a broad range of ethical judgments in treatment of the dying (Beauchamp 3425). There are also reports of interdisciplinary discussion of moral differences concerning medical decisions such as those of a group convened by the Bishop of Durham as the London Medical Group (Shotter 3446). Some of the symposia are more philosophical, ethical, and historical than practical and personal, such as *Death Inside Out* (Steinfels 2066).

Second, there are individual works that review disputants on both sides of complex medical and ethical issues, such as *Birth and Death: Bioethical Decision-making* (Simmons 3447), or a symposia will bring together professionals with varying philosophical and theological viewpoints to discuss specific issues such as euthanasia (Horan 3473). On the other hand, theologians and medical ethicists are missing from such symposia as *Clues to Suicide* (Shneidman 3586) and his *On the Nature of Suicide* (3588).

Perhaps the theological and ethical aspects of thanatology would be more prominent in future publications that have more place for "wisdom." Entire sections of the Hebrew Bible (Job, Psalms, Proverbs, Ecclesiastes)

---

[11]Richard Doss, "Toward a Theology of Death," *Pastoral Psychology* 23 (June 1972): 17.

are classified by theologians and at least by one psychologist as "wisdom" literature because they faced this central question: "How do I keep myself from misfortune, especially from premature death?" (Crenshaw 2084, 193). The definition reappears in the writings of a life-cycle psychoanalyst, Erikson: "Wisdom, then, is detached concern with life itself, in the face of death itself" (Erikson 1338, 133). This kind of wisdom was the goal of Boethius and made "consolation" the philosophical resource of the dying from the fourth through the seventeenth centuries in Western Europe (Reiss 1097).[12]

Assessment and Alleviation of Loss: Clinical Studies of Dying and Death

Since the literature of thanatology in the last half of the twentieth century has not been characterized by separation between professional guilds or the building of comprehensive theories and philosophical schools of thought, it seems appropriate to classify the patient-oriented literature functionally by type of research and target population at risk.

The earliest population for sustained professional study were the physically healthy clients of psychoanalysts. In the first half of the twentieth century there were professional papers, articles, and books on the fantasies of death that neurotics reveal during psychoanalysis. Most of the articles considered some aspects of the philosophical theories of life and death that were published between 1912 and 1930 by Freud, such as "Mourning and Melancholia" (4312). Payne felt that this psychoanalytic literature represented the "most sustained medical tradition of interest in and writing about death and grief" until the 1950s (Payne 6160, 115).

Payne also notes the appearance in the 1950s of a series of studies that involved patients with cancer. Their emotional situation was investigated by psychoanalytically oriented psychiatrists, psychologists, and social workers, most of whom formed teams in general hospitals or cancer hospitals. The combination of psychoanalytic therapy with care of the physically ill patient was well presented by Eissler's *The Psychiatrist and the Dying Patient* in 1955. Feifel also represented this expanded definition of populations-at-risk in his study of attitudes toward death in both normal and mentally ill populations (Feifel 7011) and continued to investigate various populations in later studies.

In the 1960s, research studies of cancer and other life-threatening illnesses were stimulated by changes in treatment that were more appropriately designed palliative rather than treatment in hope of a cure. The writings of Saunders (3231), Hinton (3221), and Twycross (3234) represented this trend in the emerging hospice movement.

The hospice movement was one model for the interdisciplinary tradition of thanatology in treatment, research and publication. Another model

---

12A wise critique of the thanatology movement is offered by a pastoral theologian, Johnson (1140).

was the Foundation of Thanatology, which grew out of the Columbia College of Physicians and Surgeons, and provided interdisciplinary studies such as *Loss and Grief* (Schoenberg 5026).

As social workers, clinical psychologists, sociologists, and others began to contribute to studies and consequently to symposia, the population at risk broadened from healthy people with neuroses and unhealthy people with fear of death to the family of the dying patient and the bereaved relatives, especially the widow. The study of widows received strong support from the published studies of Bowlby (1168), Parkes (4244), Glick, Weiss, and Parkes (1365), Lopata (4240), and, in the 1980s, Worden (4358) and Raphael (1029). It is obvious from the many quotations of these works that Klass is correct in stating that the study of widows represented "the mainstream of research on grief" into the 1980s (Klass 4207, 193).

This group of studies was united not only in concentration upon one population at risk, but also upon a particular type of interaction, "affectional bonds." In early psychoanalytic literature it was theorized that infants learned the necessity of another human being to obtain food and that later development produced a similar dependency upon others for fulfillment of sexual drives (Weiss 4154, 40-41). Those who supplied these needs become objects of affection. When a "cathected" provider is lost to an individual, pain results and can only by diminished by emotional separation of the individual from memory of the loved one. This is the psychoanalytic view of the function of grief, but as Parkes noted in a review of the work of his colleague Bowlby, the investigations of widows showed that grief functioned to promote reunion. There was a continuing search for the lost loved one. This was seen by researchers as a consequence of many different types of loss, such as temporary separation of a hospitalized child from a mother. When there is a final loss through death, the intensity of pining and yearning for restoration decreases very slowly and only after repeated frustration as the mourner seeks to modify internal perceptions to fit the realities of an external absence (Parkes 4244, Bowlby 1168).[13]

Research expanded into the general area of loss and larger populations were sampled. Hyman noted that the early studies of widows were based on "small, sometimes biased samples of restricted, occasionally peculiar populations" (Hyman 1366, 7). Later studies by Parkes (4244) and Lopata (4240) included representative samples of widows that were larger and more heterogeneous (Hyman 1366, 7).

Studies of widows were expanded from interviews after the first year of bereavement (Glick, Weiss, and Parkes 1365) to longitudinal over a decade (Hyman 1366). The longitudinal involved a new type of research for thanatology, the survey of data collected from persons in national opinion polls that did not concentrate upon loss or grief. It was assumed that this reduced the influence of interviewers upon responses from widows. Hyman notes the implication for response bias of a "skillful psy-

---

[13]For comparative studies on these themes, see Klass (4207, 193-213) and Furman (3053, 233-296).

chiatrist" like Parkes who knows the symptoms of a patient or the grief of a relative "before he asks his first question" (Hyman 1366, 7).

The publication of longitudinal studies was not only an expansion of concern for populations at risk; it was also a broadening of concern for the meaning of care itself. Acute grief had been the principle concern of early medical, psychological, and theological monographs on treatment, of which the most influential was Lindemann's work with survivors of sudden loss, (4044, 4332). By the 1980s, treatment concerns had broadened to include anticipatory grief (Fulton 4020, Schoenberg 4027, Rando 4026), short and long term morbidity studies (summarized in Stroebe 1380) and specialized needs of grieving persons of varying ages and relationships with the dying and dead (especially Raphael 1029).

Also, the meaning of assessment and alleviation of loss was broadened. Early psychoanalytic preoccupation was with distinctions of mourning (normal grief) and melancholia (pathological grief) in Freud's "Mourning and Melancolia" (4312) and those who interpreted or challenged him (Meyer 1192). By the 1980s, many types of loss were enumerated throughout life, as in Mitchell and Anderson (4032), Oates (4516), Strom (4156).

There was also a deepening of concerns for those who had lost status because of death (Parkes 4244, Lopata 4240), hellish fires of war (Lifton 4066), the holocaust (see the bibliography in Simpson 8039), or aggression of men against women (Burgess 4157, Warshaw 4166).

The alleviation of loss also came to encompass more than medical specialties had considered. When Furman reviewed the "numerous and diverse" literature of various professions on mourning in 1974, the topics were those of a hospital or clinic staff who were alert to the needs of the bereaved, especially children: precipitating factors, recognition and acceptance of loss, internal means of adaptation, decathesis in children, process of internalization, affective responses, outcomes of mourning in adults, and a child's coping with the death of a parent. Furman organized clinical studies under such headings as: development of concept of death, child's response to loss of other loved objects, psychotherapy with children, adult pathology related to childhood mourning, and assistance with mourning (Furman 3053, 233-308).

Over the next 10-15 years, Furman would have needed a section that expanded "widow-to-widow programs" (Silverman 4245), life-span studies (Weenolson 1353), death of the environment, (Anglemyer 4130, Merchant 4143), self-help literature (Rando 4342), parent-child conversations (Grollman 4189), and books for children on loss (Donnelly 6108, Hickman 6115).

That last category, books for children, could demonstrate the impact of thanatology literature upon consciousness-raising in post-Vietnam American culture. During the sociological "fallout" of Vietnam, books about children and death proliferated. There had been clinical studies like those of Bowlby (3048), Bluebond-Langer (3047), and Furman (3053) before 1980. But in the 80s the popular writers from the 60s (Grollman 6112, Jackson

4190) were joined by hosts of others. Some of the newer popular works were personal testimonies to the initial and long term impact of a child's death (Claypool 4472). Others were books for children who were bereaved or who should begin to think about the place of death in life. The publications became so numerous that bibliographies were prepared with listings by recommended age for reading (Bernstein 8005).

Perhaps the consumer-friendly orientation of thanatology publications after Vietnam was a response not only to public readiness but also to the creative mix of disciplines in thanatology. The broadening impact of sociology and anthropology upon the concept of grief as loss might be illustrated in the relation of symbolic interaction theories to grief by Marris (1277) and Rosenblatt (4344). In addition to an emphasis upon a stable definition of situations, the theory deals with the importance of others in defining ourselves and our situations. Most of these definitions, difficulties, and reinforcements come through day to day interactions such as the comments and postures of those who are most intimately involved over a period of time with those who grieve. Such theory increases the relevance of personal testimonies for public awareness and professional alertness to the meaning of grief and mourning.

Although thanatologists are realistically wary of sentimental testimonies that appear in popular literature on grief, their own sentiments have not led to a retreat within the barriers of a guild. Instead, thanatologists have urged community courses on both the understanding of dying/death and care of the dying and bereaved (Leviton 6144, Shneidman 6148, Morgan 6088, Neale 6153).

Publications by professionally trained persons for a lay audience will raise concerns about appropriate communications skills. The sensitivity of the field of thanatology to this issue is presented in a volume of the Foundation of Thanatology on communications with patients, media, documentation, public and professional education, and technical definition of thanatology (Fleming 6158). Hopefully, the spirit of this writing will be similar to that of Nighswonger who considered terminally ill patients to be his "teachers." (Nighswonger 6159).

Interprofessional communication in thanatology is facilitated by the willingness of a wide variety of publishers to support studies of death and dying in discipline-specific professional symposia and general trade books. Publishing houses may support a series of books on general or specific topics in thanatology, but no one house is considered to lead all others in this expanding field.

;Professional journals in thanatology began to be published in the 1970s: *Advances in Thanatology* (formally *Journal of Thanatology*), *Death Studies* (formally *Death Education*), *Omega, Thanatos,* and others. Specialized topics in death studies included such journals as *Suicide and Life-Threatening Behavior* (formally *Life-Threatening Behavior*) and *Violence and Victims*. Public interest was recognized in popular magazines such as *Bereavement: A Magazine of Hope and Healing*. The growth of the field from year to year can be assessed through *Thanatology Librarian* and *Thanatology Abstracts*.

Thanatology in the 90s includes references to almost everything about this life—and something about the life to come.

Chapter 1

GENERAL WORKS:
SPAN AND STYLE
OF LIFE, ANCIENT
AND MODERN

1.1   GENERAL TEXTS

1001   Aries, Philippe. "The Reversal of Death: Changes in Attitude
Towards Death in Western Societies." In *Death In America*, ed. by
David E. Stannard, 134–158. Philadelphia: University of Pennsylva-
nia Press, 1975.

In a survey of literature on death from medieval times until the last
third of the twentieth century, the author concludes that death which had
been a familiar friend in previous generations has now almost disappeared
from the language. Credit for renewed public interest is given to Edgar
Morin in France, Geoffrey Gorer in England, Jessica Mitford and Evelyn
Waugh in America. See also Aries (1039), Gorer (1012), Mitford (1150),
Waugh (6046).

1002   Backer, Barbara A., N. Hannon, and N. A. Russell. *Death and Dying:
Individuals and Institutions*. New York: Wiley, 1982.

A comprehensive textbook relates individuals and institutions in
varying responses and styles of coping with death.

1003   Bugen, Larry A., ed. *Death and Dying: Theory/Research/Practice*.
Dubuque, Iowa: William C. Brown, 1979.

This book of readings for college students is organized to show
levels of understanding death: individual, family and group, community
and society. Thought questions are provided for each selecion. Varying

viewpoints are presented, as in Kübler-Ross' article on stages of dying and Bugen's article that questions "stages." Structural exercises are included for death education. The discussion is at the introductory level. For more complex discussions consult a text such as Kalish (1017).

1004 Carrington, Hereward. *Death: It's Causes and Phenomena with Special Reference to Immortality.* 1921. Reprint. New York: Arno Press, 1976.

This classic organization of material on death considers experiences, causes and signs of death along with mortuary topics such as preserving and disposing of the body. Philosophical and theological views are presented along with discussions of psychical research. Bibliography. See also Bloch (4362).

1005 Corr, Charles. "Selected Texts and Reference Books." In *Death Education II.* Ed. by Hannelore Wass, *et al.*, 251–286: Washington, D.C.: Hemisphere Pub. Corp., 1985.

See 8009.

1006 DeSpelder, Lynne Ann and Albert Lee Strickland. *The Last Dance: Encountering Death and Dying.* Palo Alto, Calif.: Mayfield Pub. Co., 1983.

As a basic text on death and dying, this attractively presented book covers the development of attitudes toward death, the way that children learn about death, the handling of death in health care systems, and the facing of death in times of life threatening illnesses. This is followed by sections on last rites, the attitudes of survivors, the death of children, medical ethics, law, disasters, suicide, concepts of immortality, near death experiences and the value of thinking about death during life. The perspective is anthropological and sociological with some references to psychological dynamics and scattered references to religious resources. "Further readings" are included at the end of each chapter. Index. See other texts: Kalish (1017), Rando (1028), Raphael (1029), Wass (1036), Shneidman (1032, 1033); for medical and nursing texts, see Garfield (3378); for a specialized emphasis on affective learning, see Wilcox (1038). See Leming (1024) for social studies.

1007 Enright, D. J., ed. *The Oxford Book of Death.* New York: Oxford University Press, 1983.

Through an international selection of prose and poetry that ranges from ancient Babylonia to America in the 1980s, emotions concerning death are arranged: the nature of death, human feelings toward death, suicide, graveyards and funerals, resurrection, immortality, the hereafter, the death of children, love and death, last words, and epitaphs.

1008 Feifel, Herman, ed. *The Meaning of Death.* New York: McGraw-Hill Book Co., 1959.

Ten years before there were over a hundred titles published each year on death and dying, this pioneer symposium included articles of philosophers, psychologists, theologians, and pastoral counselors in literature, art, and religion, the care of the dying, clinical and experimental studies. Contributions were made by such notable thinkers as Paul Tillich, Edgar Jackson, Karl Jung, Herbert Marceuse, Gardner Murphy. The book was prophetic in its call for more systematic study of death, the need for research beyond the space-time limitations of positivistic science, the opening up of a taboo subject in American society. See also Feifel (1009).

1009 Feifel, Herman, ed. *New Meanings of Death.* New York: McGraw-Hill Book Co., 1977.

Professional practice, current research and public policy are the dominating themes of contributions by authorities in medicine, psychology, anthropology, psychiatry, psychoanalysis, nursing, social work, education, funeral directing and the law. Some new perceptions of death (as seen by Feifel) are: death is directly related to all ages of life, the increase of medical specialization has left many persons to die emotionally and spiritually alone in hospitals, we are beginning to make room for expressions of anger, guilt, abandonment and relief during mourning, anticipatory grief is significant and helpful. In comparison with Feifel's 1959 volume (1008), the 1977 symposium shows the expansion and deepening of interest in the subject of death. Some of the representative accomplishments in twenty years were (1) articles on the impact of death throughout the life-span of an individual, (2) a wide range of interests in clinical management with articles by psychologists, physicians, nurses, and health professionals, (3) responses of family, (4) preparation for death, (5) death education, (6) the impact of the hospice movement. See also Feifel (1008).

1010 Fulton, Robert, ed. *Death and Identity.* Rev. ed. Bowie, Md.: Charles Press, 1976.

See 1146.

1011 Gentles, Ian, ed. *Care for the Dying and the Bereaved.* Toronto: Anglican Book Center, 1982.

In a multi-disciplinary approach this publication of the Anglican Church of Canada for a general audience has two objectives. One is to present up-to-date information about the relief of pain, palliative care of the dying in hospitals and at home, how to be a friend to the dying and to mourners, the mourning that follows abortion and the special issues of caring for dying children. More theoretical, theological chapters deal with the history of death and dying, euthanasia and theological reflections on holy dying. A sensible text for volunteers in training and church-community groups.

1012 Gorer, Geoffrey. *Death, Grief, and Mourning*. Garden City, N.Y.: Doubleday and Co., 1965.

This pioneering study by an anthropologist is based upon a questionnaire concerning death that was completed by 1628 persons in Britain, 1963. Three hundred fifty nine of these had lost a member of the family or a close relative within the past five years. Persons in this category were interviewed. 344 reported funerals or cremations accompanied by religious rites. Yet only 11 made some reference to Judgment and 15 to God or Jesus in their answers to the questionnaire. 14 made a spontaneous mention of their clergy person, and half of these were in Scotland. Only a few felt deeply about the method of disposal of the body. Customs of mourning had practically disappeared, although there were some psychological statements about mourning, such as restless sleep. Respondents seldom reported expressions of condolence from friends or neighbors, but a few reported and were grateful for evidences of concern. There was no one psychological pattern of mourning, but the author found that 9 of the 80 he interviewed to be in despair a year after death, which he attributed to the absence of any ritual or people to guide them. Brief references are made to the death of various family members. The author concluded that there was a connection between the denial of mourning and callous, irrational preoccupation with fear of death and vandalism. The Orthodox Jewish community stood alone as one which knew how to console a bereaved person on first contact after loss. Theories of mourning are discussed from recent literature, questionnaire and statistical tables. The author's "Pornography of Death" article, 1959, often cited in later literature is reprinted. He presents evidence of prudery in thoughts about death that were similar to "unmentionables" of the Victorian era: copulation and birth. (See for example Aries, 1001, Jackson 1133). Gorer's interpersonal approach went beyond the earlier preoccupation with intra-psychic conflicts as reported by Freud (4312) and Lindemann (4044). See also Eliot (1129).

1013 Grollman, Earl A., ed. *Concerning Death: A Practical Guide for the Living*. Boston: Beacon Press, 1974.

A work in the "classic" tradition of death that includes religion and philosophy. The first article on grief was written by a very practical mystic in the field of pastoral counseling, Edgar Jackson (4508). Protestant, Roman Catholic, and Jewish ways of death and mourning are given separate chapters. Other articles concern such pastoral issues as care of the dying person, the relationship of doctor and family, children and death, law, insurance, the coroner, funerals, cemeteries, cremation, organ donation, sympathy calls, letters, suicides, dealing with loneliness, death education. A helpful work for the general public. See Anderson (4460), Mitchell and Anderson (4032), Autton (3329).

1014 Hafen, Brent Q., Kathryn J. Frandsen. *Faces of Death: Grief, Dying, Euthanasia, Suicide.* Englewood, Colo.: Morton Publishing Co., 1983.

For a general audience this practical handbook surveys reactions to loss, stages of grief, learning to confront, euthanasia and suicide. The text is based upon research studies, without any critical evaluation of them.

1015 Hendin, David. *Death as a Fact of Life.* New York: W. W. Norton Co., 1984.

In a journalistic survey of popular questions concerning death, the author gives prominence to criteria of death, euthanasia and refrigeration of a body that is already pronounced dead (cyronics). Selected bibliography of popular and some professional articles.

1016 Hinton, John M. *Dying.* 2nd ed. Baltimore: Pelican Books, 1972.

A psychiatrist who spent many years in the care of the dying relies both upon material in his own field of psychiatry and related sociological, psychological and theological references. In thoughtful and straightforward prose the author presents many useful attitudes and techniques of care for the dying and the bereaved. Content includes a survey of attitudes toward death in ancient civilizations and mid-twentieth century, the struggle between awareness and denial during the physical and emotional distress of dying, the issues of speaking about death with dying persons and the prolonging or hastening of life, reactions to bereavement and a relationship between social expectation and inner feelings in adjustment to bereavement. The extensive bibliography indicates the emphasis of psychoanalytic studies in the area of death before 1970.

1017 Kalish, Richard A. *Death, Grief and Caring Relationships..* 2nd ed. Monterey, Calif.: Brooks/Cole Publishing Co., 1985.

As an introductory text on death for college students, the book draws upon a broad range of sources, which range from clinical studies to personal stories. As the title indicates, there is an emphasis upon caring relationships that include both the care of those who are dying and the attitude of caregivers and survivors. The first sections of the book are notable for a very basic development of the meaning of death in modern society and its impact upon individuals. A section on religion and immortality includes studies of the 1970s and 1980s on near death experiences. Other chapters deal with attitudes towards death such as fear and anxiety and the process of dying. Grief and bereavement are treated in terms of the process of grief, the social process of bereavement, and the meaning of bereavement at various stages of life. Preventative care is emphasized in the last chapters. References at the close of the book include professional articles and books. Well-balanced, but not as service-oriented as Rando (1028).

1018 Kastenbaum, Robert J. and Ruth Aisenburg. *The Psychology of Death*. New York: Springer Pub. Co., 1972.

The authors note that death anxiety and fear of death are different constructs. Fear has an object of attention, whereas anxiety does not. Also, fear of death may be fear of other things. A person may be thinking either about death of another or death of the self. The implication leading from death-of-self is self-awareness, which includes necessity, causation, time, finality and separation. It is a leap of understanding toward non-being. The book stresses emotional factors in death along with a consideration of cultural issues. Many references to published research. More philosophically sophisticated than most thanatology texts, with an existential emphasis. See also Heidegger (2019), Kierkegaard (2021), Macquarrie (2060), Wittgenstein (2071).

1019 Kastenbaum, Robert J. and Beatrice Kastenbaum, eds. *Encyclopedia of Death*. Phoenix, Ariz.: Orxy Press, 1989.

One hundred and thirty-two articles are provided on subjects that range from hospice care, suicide and grief to historical background on burial practices and the Black Death. Sources for additional information at the conclusion of each article. Some illustrations and cross-references. Strong emphasis on suicide and none on philosophy.

1020 Kübler-Ross, Elisabeth. *On Death and Dying*. New York: Macmillan Pub. Co., 1968.

In an impressionistic and humane report of her interviews and those of theological students with dying patients at the University of Chicago clinics, Dr. Ross (as she was known before publishers inserted a dash after her maiden name) presents five stages of emotional and physical reactions to impending death: denial and isolation, anger, bargaining, depression, acceptance. The consequent popular understanding of the stages was not substantiated by later research of Feigenberg (3200) Schulz (3208), Shneidman (1032); the ethical naturalism of the author is questioned by Branson (3307), McGill (2115), Miller-McLenore (2142). The work includes many sections of verbatim interviews and that proved very attractive to the general reading audience. The author closes with observations on the reactions of reluctance, rejection and some acceptance from varying professions to her first seminar on care for the dying. See also Ross (7021). The viewpoint of the author moved toward a vague existential phenomenology in *Death: the Final Stage of Growth* (1021). For more precise philosophical definitions of death and dying see Koestenbaum (2008) and Becker (2194).

1021 Kübler-Ross, Elisabeth, ed. *Death: the Final Stage of Growth*. New York: Simon and Schuster, 1975.

In an introduction to this symposium, Kübler-Ross presents death as an integral part of our lives which gives meaning to human existence. The following articles by other authors describe the relationship of organizations to dying, hope and reassurance, personal meaning in nursing of the dying, concept of death among Alaskan Indians, in Judaism, Hinduism, Buddhism. Pastoral care, funerals, the feelings of mothers and women, spouses are other topics. In a summary Mwailiu Imara describes the last stage of growth as an attempt to put death into some meaningful life pattern. See McGill (2115).

1022 Kutscher, Austin H., ed. *Death and Bereavement.* Springfield, Ill.: Charles C. Thomas, 1969.

An editor of several synopsia on thanatology has collected brief articles from experts in a variety of disciplines on the emotional and practical problems facing a bereaved person: anticipatory grief, relationships between those who minister to the dying and care for the bereaved, time when a person is willing to consider these issues during bereavement and the choices made by bereaved persons in the rearrangement of their lives. Annotated bibliography.

1023 Langone, John. *Death Is a Noun: A View of the End of Life.* Boston: Little, Brown, 1972.

This survey of death is written with young readers as well as adults in mind. Research reports, historical analyses and human interest stories are used to describe various attitudes to death, including the quest for immortality. Various philosophical and religious beliefs are presented and modern ethical issues are discussed. See also Langone (1148).

1024 Leming, Michael R. and George E. Dickinson. *Understanding Dying, Death, and Bereavement.* 2nd ed. Fort Worth: Holt, Rinehart and Winston, 1990.

Social thanatology is presented in this university text with the hope that students will both understand and cope with personal issues relating to an individual's ability to cope with the social and psychological processes of dying, death and bereavement. The work is designed also for a broad range of professional courses related to thanatology. Attention is given to relevance of learning by boxed inserts that present timely readings and articles to illustrate issues in the text, summaries of chapters that will serve as study aids to important points, discussion questions that are content centered, glossary, references, suggested readings briefly annotated. Chapters describe the social meanings of dying and death by age, religion, process, hospice care, biomedical issues, suicide, children, cross-cultural understanding, a history of bereavement and funerals in American culture, bereavement, legal and educational issues. References to many basic works are omitted, especially those that deal with clinical issues, religion and philosophy.

1025 Meyer, Charles. *Surviving Death: A Practical Guide to Caring for the Dying and the Bereaved.* Mystic, Conn.: Twenty-Third Publications, 1988.

An Episcopal hospital chaplain presents plain and sensitive advice for hospital care of the dying and close support of survivors. The author denounces the denial of death in church, community and medicine. He vividly exposes the myths with which patients, relatives and friends separate themselves from the impact of death or personal involvement with the dying. See Autton (3304, 4446).

1026 Miller, Randolph Krump. *Live Until You Die.* Philadelphia: United Church Press, 1973.

A Professor of Christian Nurture unites a classical tradition of moral and spiritual preparation for death with modern emphases upon psychological impact of dying and bereavement. The poetry of the soul and the precision of clinical studies are in his writings. For similar tone, see Nouwen (3318).

1027 Phipps, William E. *Death: Confronting the Reality.* Atlanta, Ga.: John Knox Press, 1987.

See 6155.

1028 Rando, Therese A. *Grief, Dying and Death: Clinical Interventions for Care Givers.* Champaign, Ill.: Research Press, 1984.

A researcher and counselor in the field of thanatology gives special attention to work with individuals and families during the grief process. This is followed by advice on issues faced in the dying process: initial diagnosis, treatment, control, patient reactions and defenses. Anticipatory grief and post-death mourning are described in detail. Exercises and case examples are included for use by caregivers who need to recognize the unique situation of each patient and family. The writing is as a college text that would be used for human service clinicians. Recommended as a service oriented guide. For more philosophical/theological issues in a college text, see Kalish (1017).

1029 Raphael, Beverley. *The Anatomy of Bereavement.* New York: Basic Books, 1983.

A psychiatrist in Australia organizes the bedside ministry around typical experiences of persons from childhood to old age. Each chapter includes some of her experiences as a psychiatrist, some research studies and specific suggestions for a general audience on the dynamics of grief and recovery. Extensive references to professional literature, and an index are provided. A comprehensive and compassionate text.

1030 Schoenberg, Bernard, *et al.*, eds. *Psychosocial Aspects of Terminal Care*. New York: Columbia University Press, 1972.

To increase the perspective of medical, nursing and other helping professionals with terminal patients, articles and reports from workshops are printed with the support of the Foundation of Thanatology. Clinicians discuss education, medical, pediatric and surgical care, along with articles on radiotherapy, psychopharmacology, social work, care of the elderly and oral care of the dying. St. Christopher's Hospice is described by Saunders as a therapeutic community. The pastoral use of the "seven last words" in terminal care is described by the chaplain of the National Institutes of Health, LeRoy Kerney.

1031 Shibles, Warren. *Death: The Interdisciplinary Analysis*. Whitewater, Wis.: Language Press, 1974.

A professor of philosophy seeks in this text to help students live better because they have discussed death and developed a philosophy for its meaning in life. There is a section on student responses to the course, followed by material on various philosophers, (especially existentialism), psychiatric, medical, sociological and religious analyses of death. There are short sections on death in art, psychic phenomena, various cultures, and the special problems of aging. Specific issues of merchandising methods, memorial societies and other aspects of the funeral industry are considered. Extensive bibliography. Research studies are largely confined to the bibliography.

1032 Shneidman, Edwin S. *Deaths of Man*. New York: Quadrangle Books, 1973.

From his experience with life threatening behavior, and from questionnaires, a professor of medical psychology examines the process of dying, the inner thoughts of those who are dying and of those who survive as mourners. Suggestions are made concerning an appropriate death in which one is able to tie together some of the loose ends of life and to face mortality. Questions are asked about the way in which some persons are in a state of mind that hastens toward death and the way in which some persons think simultaneously in ways that will maintain life but also hasten death. As a clinician, he observes frequent alternations between acceptance and denial in the dying process, rather than a sequential progression of Kübler-Ross stages (1019). The writings of Herman Melville on Captain Ahab are used to illustrate both the concepts of subintention and ambivalence.

1033 Shneidman, Edwin S., ed. *Death: Current Perspectives*. 3rd ed. Palo Alto, Calif.: Mayfield Pub. Co., 1984.

A professor of thanatology presents philosophical and clinical perspectives on quality of life for a dying person, a life span view of the survivors of death, the legal-ethical-moral aspects of death and suicide, and the emerging issue of "megadeath" which is prompted by the nuclear age. Contributions are made by historians, anthropologists, philosophers, sociologists, psychiatrists, and thanatologists. The contribution of religion is neglected, although there are some theoretical references in the article by Arnold Toynbee. There is an excellent annotated bibliography.

1034 Simpson, Michael A. *The Facts of Death*. Englewood Cliffs, N.J.: Prentice-Hall, 1979.

This practical book for families and helpers reviews what we know about the nature of death and dying, patients' rights, how to manage one's own death and to cope with the dying of another, death and children, suicide, how to cope with a suicidal person, and with one's own suicidal impulses; bereavement and grief, funerals, and how to plan one's estate and funeral. A pioneering presentation of clinical practice and research for the lay reader.

1035 Stephenson, John S. *Death, Grief and Mourning: Individual and Social Realities*. New York: Macmillan Pub. Co., 1985.

A sociologist provides an interdisciplinary approach to the understanding of death through the concept of the image as an inner schema through which humans understand an act in the world. The social context of American attitudes and behaviors surrounding death are the setting for the study. Ceremonies of death are discussed. The works of significant contributors to thanatology are briefly reviewed as the author considers various subjects in well-organized and plain style. For other psychological/ social commentaries, see Jackson (1043), Lifton (1221), Fulton (1146), Aries (1001, 1039), Marris (1277).

1036 Wass, Hannelore, ed. *Dying: Facing the Facts*. New York: McGraw-Hill Book Co., 1979.

As a basic college text on death and dying, this volume includes an overview of the changing attitudes toward death in the last half of the twentieth century, the essential facts on physiology, sociology, and psychology in relation to dying, the environmental aspects of dying in an institution, and dying with hospice care, the developmental issues of elderly and children, the funeral as part of the social system of death, the theological, pastoral, and philosophical aspects of grief, issues of law, the problem of euthanasia, a critique of the funeral industry and the importance of death education. Each chapter contains periodical and other references. There is a brief annotated bibliography and an index at the close of the volume. Comprehensive and full of references to relevant studies.

1037 Wass, Hannelore, Felix M. Berardo and Robert A. Neimeyer, eds. *Dying: Facing the Facts.* 2nd ed. Washington, D.C.: Hemisphere Pub. Corp., 1988.

Theological and philosophical aspects of death are given less attention in the revised edition of this college text and more emphasis is given to sociology and clinical psychology than in the 1979 text. The revised edition contains new chapters on suicide, the experience of dying, death anxiety, problems in studying death, life preservation and global survival. Chapters deleted from the 1979 volume: the funeral industry, the elderly, death education, physiology of dying. Extensive discussion of death related attitudes and behaviors in society have been compressed into a shorter introduction.

1038 Wilcox, Sandra G., and Marilyn Sutton, eds. *Understanding Death and Dying.* Miltonview, Calif.: Mayfield Pub. Co., 1985.

Various authors with clinical experience have developed a text that combines cognitive learning with affective learning. Self examination and reappraisal is stimulated through an encounter section in each chapter with issues or questions that have been presented in the first part of the chapter.

1.2 HISTORY AND CHANGE
For pre-literate societies, see ANTHROPOLOGY/CULTURE RELIGION (1.4)

1039 Aries, Philippe. *Western Attitudes toward Death: From the Middle Ages to the Present.* Trans. by Patricia M. Ramum. Baltimore: John Hopkins University Press, 1974.

A French historian presents the basic outline of his social history of Western death from the Middle Ages to the twentieth century. Halfway between passive resignation and mystical trust, the medieval "pained" death exhibited confidence and prompt acceptance of what was considered to be one's destiny. All classes performed certain ceremonies when they knew they would die, which were distinguished from later funeral and mourning ceremonies. By the twelfth century there was a shift towards more personal meanings of death in the portrayal of the last judgment, preoccupation with the precise moment of death, macabre themes of physical decomposition, a return to classical emphasis upon funeral inscriptions and personal messages of tombs. By the seventeenth century the emphasis shifted toward the death of other persons with such neurotic themes as the dance of death, rupture of daily relationships which plunged a person into an irrational, violent and beautiful world. Tombs became a place of cultivated memories. But by the end of the nineteenth century death had become shameful and forbidden. Through a revolution that began in the United States and spread to England and then to Europe death was displaced from the home to the hospital without ceremony. Little notice was taken of the fact that death in funerals and sorrow were considered to be morbid. Death replaced sex as a principle forbidden subject. See also Huizinga (1091).

1040 Aries, Philippe. *The Hour of Our Death*. New York: Alfred A. Knopf, 1980.

A French historian surveys changing attitudes toward death from earliest Christian times through the mid-twentieth century in Western Europe and the United States. The strongest presentations are of funerary art and customs from the middle ages to the eighteenth century in France. With erudition and precision the author encompasses history, folklore, literature, religion, public health documents, tombstones and other cultural reminders of overlapping stages of evolution in civilization's pre-occupation with death. The following themes are developed: (1) tame death is the baseline and existed from primordial times up through the early Middle Ages; (2) the high Middle Ages were preoccupied with death of the self in the "Ars Moriendi" and the art of the macabre; (3) death was "remote and imminent" in the seventeenth—early eighteenth centuries, in France, where distance and nothingness became themes; (4) "the other" sentiment which expressed the grief of survivors characterized the nineteenth century "cult of the dead" and graves among both Protestants and Catholics; (5) "invisible death" hung over the twentieth century in which Christianity's doctrines and "scientific" knowledge adapted to these cultural, unconscious shifts. This authoritative analysis of culture is often cited in later works. For a commentary on "invisible death," see Gorer (1131, 1012), May (1159), Jackson (1133).

1041 Choron, Jacques. *Death and Western Thought*. New York: Collier Books, 1963.

A philosopher surveys philosophical attitudes toward death, from antiquity through Old and New Testament, Renaissance, modern philosophy and contemporary answers. Philosophy was often related to death under three aspects: (1) the impetus behind philosophy which aimed at the mastering of death, as in Schopenhauer; (2) the most suitable way to understand Being and of revealing its true nature as penetrated by non-being, as in Heidegger (2019); (3) the condition of philosophizing, a state in which alone the philosopher's quest of true knowledge can be fulfilled, as in Plato (1055, 1067). Beginning with the Renaissance, independent philosophical thought sometimes denied immortality and gave little attention to death. In the twentieth century, analytical philosophers did not discuss the subject, as Nicolai Hartmann, whereas death is considered a philosophical question of importance in our ultimate destiny by the existential philosophers, such as Heidegger (2019), Sartre (2065), Jaspers (2058), Marcel (2228). Useful as a summary of the writing of philosophers on death, especially the existentialists. Careful notes to chapters. See Dunne (6081), Kaufmann (2054).

1042 Hoffmann, Frederick John. *The Mortal No: Death in the Modern Imagination*. Princeton, N.J.: Princeton University Press, 1964.

See 6001.

1043 Jackson, Charles O., ed. *Passing: The Vision of Death in America.* Contributions in Family Studies, no. 2. Westport, Conn.: Greenwood Press, 1977.

The social dimension of death is the focus for a selection of essays, such as death as an event, social responses to death, the cemetery as a cultural institution. The contributions are arranged in chronological order: colonial era, nineteenth century, twentieth century. Two basic theses unify the presentations: the domestication and beautification of death which took place between the late eighteenth and nineteenth century and the twentieth century withdrawal on the part of the living from communion with and commitment to the dying and the dead. Many insightful vignettes.

1044 McGatch, Milton. *Death: Meaning and Mortality in Christian Thought and Contemporary Culture*. New York: Seabury Press, 1969.

A scholar in medieval English literature surveys attitudes, customs and beliefs concerning death from classical Greek and Old Testament times to New Testament literature, the Early Church, the Middle Ages, the Reformation and modern writings of authors such as Tolstoi (3012). There is an easy flow to the writing, which is principally concerned with a harmony of the biblical concept of resurrection with the hellenistic concept of immortality. Better than Choron (1041) on philosophical theology.

1045 Oden, Thomas C. *Crisis Ministries*. New York: Crossroad Publishing Co., 1986.

A professor of theology and ethics arranges the texts of pastoral writers prior to the eighteenth century under headings that include a chapter on "Care of the Dying." Much attention was given in the pastoral literature of Tertullian and Augustine to preparation for death through a watchful life. The search for the meaning of death by Lactantius and others was inconclusive. Care of the terminally ill included discussion of the awareness of death in Lactantius, Calvin, Baxter. Death and burial in writings of pastoral literature emphasized the vision of fulfillment through resurrection and heavenly existence.

1046 Prioreschi, Plinio. *A History of Human Responses to Death: Mythologies, Rituals, and Ethics*. Lewiston, N. Y.: Edwin Mellon, 1990.

In a literary overview of diverse reactions to the inevitability of death the author presents brief references and many excerpts from the thoughts about death that might be found in different ages and cultures.

Primarily valuable for the wide selection of philosophical and literary quotations.

1047 Saffron, Morris H. "Thanatology: A Historical Sketch." In *Loss and Grief: Psychological Management in Medical Practice*, ed. by Bernard Schoenberg, *et al.*, pp. 313–337. New York: Columbia Universtiy Press, 1970.

A thanatologist uses the philosophical studies of Choron (1041, 2002) to survey the role of religion and philosophy from ancient times until the 1960s.

1.21 EASTERN, GREEK, AND ROMAN PHILOSOPHY

1048 Alexiou, Margaret. *The Ritual Lament in Grief Tradition*. London: Cambridge University Press, 1974.

See 6065.

1049 Alster, Bendt, ed. *Death In Mesopotamia*. Copenhagen Studies in Assyriology. Vol. 8. Copenhagen: Akademisk Vorlag, 1980.

From an international conference, papers are published on the general characteristics of death and the mythology and theology of death in ancient Mesopotamia. Other papers deal with death, divination, funerals, occult practices and the after-world.

1050 Aonians, Richard Broxton. *The Origins of European Thought, the Mind, the Soul, the World, Time, and Fate: New Interpretations of Greek, Roman and Kindred Evidence also of Some Basic Jewish and Christian Beliefs*. 1951. Reprint. Salem, N. H.: Ayer Co. Pub., 1976.

Greek mythology and religious rites are given scholarly attention in an anaysis of many sources, including Plato's *Cosmology*. Much of the emphasis is upon the images and ideas of pre-Socratic philosophy.

1051 Budge, E. A. Wallis. *The Book of the Dead*. New Hyde Park, N.Y.: University Books, 1960.

A study of this ancient Egyptian writing shows continual thought about death along with admonition to enjoy life as long as possible. Death is a ferocious plunderer who is not personified by any one god, but was associated both with Sekhmet (The Lady of the Messengers of Death) and Bastet, a cat goddess. The underlying philosophy is of human nature as a psychophysical organism in which the body is essential and must be preserved for future reanimation through highly elaborate rituals.

1052 Cumont, Franz. *Recherches sur le Symbolisme Funéraire des Romaines* [Investigations of the Funerary Symbolism of the Romans]. 1942. Reprint. Salem, N.H.: Ayer Co. Pub., 1976.

In a thorough study of individual monuments, the author interprets the meaning of their symbols and the attitudes toward death which they reveal.

1053 Esnoul, Anne-Marie. *Le Jugement des Morts*. Paris: Edition du Suseuil, 1961.

French Orientalists review ancient civilizations of Egypt, Assyria, Japan, Babylonia, Iran, Islam, Indochina and Israel to provide answers to the question, "What will come to persons after death?"

1054 Ferm, M. E. *The Latin Consolatio as a Literary Type*. St. Louis, Mo.: St. Louis University Press, 1941.

A scholarly study of letters and speeches of consolation presents Cicero's letter to Titius as the first example of consolation in Latin literature.

1055 Friedlander, Paul. *Plato: An Introduction*, trans. by Hans Meyerhoff. New York: Harper and Row, 1964.

Chapter 9 of this volume presents Plato's notions of reincarnation, immediate judgment after death and the ultimate separability of soul and body. The mythological character of these assertions is considered.

1056 Garland, Robert. *The Greek Way of Death*. Ithaca, N.Y.: Cornell University Press, 1985.

A classic scholar surveys funerary rites and attitudes towards death from the time of Homer to the 4th century B.C. Death for the ordinary Greek of that period was not an event in time, but a process that required strenuous efforts on the part of the living to insure the dead person's successful passage to the next world. Most of the information comes from archaeological and literary sources in Athens. Notes and bibliography.

1057 Griffin, Jasper. *Homer on Life and Death*. London: Oxford University Press, 1983.

See 6015.

1058 Hamilton-Pearson, J. and C. Andrews. *Mummies: Death and Life in Ancient Egypt*. New York: Penguin, 1979.

See 4425.

1059 Hopkins, Keith. *Death and Renewal.* Vol. 2, Sociological Studies in Roman History. New York: Cambridge University Press, 1983.

A Roman historian and sociologist examines the association between death and social renewal among the Roman political elite. This includes a probing of the problem of perception and coping with death as seen by both the rich and the poor. Evidence is drawn from gladitorial shows, the mortality and fertility of the ruling class, burial clubs, tombs, funerals, memorials. Bibliography.

1060 Kassell, Rudolf. *Untersuchung zur Griechischen und Römischen Konsolationsliteratur, Zetemata.* [Research into the Greek and Roman Literature of Consolation, Controversial Issues]. Munich: C. H. Beck'sche Verlagsbuchhandlung, 1958.

A scholarly study of the way in which Greek and Latin authors sought to combat fatalism in the face of death. Grief can be systematically combatted by inspirational letters and speeches.

1061 Kurtz, Donna C. and John Boardman. *Greek Burial Customs.* Ithaca, N. Y.: Cornell University Press, 1971.

See 4409.

1062 *La Mort, Les Morts Dans Les Societes Anciennes.* New York: Cambridge University Press, 1982.

French and Italian scholars present studies which generally demonstrate the relationship of the glory of heroes in the ancient Near East to the funeral ceremonies and burial sites that are known through literature and archaeology. Studies range from the city state of Athens to early civilizations of the Celts, Iranians, Egyptians and Indians.

1063 Meyers, Erich M. *Jewish Ossuaries: Reburial and Rebirth.* Rome: Biblical Institute Press, 1971.

An archaeologist offers a description of chambers for the deposit of bones of the deceased by Jewish communities of the Second Temple period. Their significance is related to tombs of the early Bronze Age through the Roman period. In the Middle East during Iron Age I, the bones of a decarnate corpse were swept into a communal ossuary. Jewish ossuaries were for the bones of an individual and were often designed like a house. While Jews remained in Palestine, the ossuary was a symbol for the unity of personality, body and soul. With the dispersion of the Jews in the first century, the ossuary was kept in the hope that the bones of a loved one might be returned to the Holy Land to atone for sins and partake in the Messianic Age. Extensive bibliography.

1064 Montefiore, C. J. G. *Ancient Jewish and Greek Encouragement.* Bridgeport, Conn.: Hartmore House, 1971.

See 2337.

1065 Moore, Clifford Herschel. *Ancient Beliefs in the Immortality of the Soul.* New York: Cooper Square Publishers, 1963.

In non-technical style, the author presents a brief summary of comparisons and contrasts between Homer, Plato, Aristotle, Stoics, eastern Fathers of the Church, Augustine, Thomas Aquinas, medieval mystics and Enlightenment philosophers. Notes and brief bibliography are included.

1066 Rohde, Erwin. *The Cult of Souls and Belief in Immortality among the Greeks.* London: Rutledge and Kegan Paul, 1925.

Greek literature forms the basis for a scholarly analysis of the cult of souls in the age of heroic poems, the development of a belief in immortality around Dionysos, the contributions of the Orphic mysteries, philosophers, poets and tragedians in the Classic period.

1067 Shorey, Paul. *What Plato Said.* Chicago: The University of Chicago Press, 1933.

Plato taught that the soul stands a better chance of attaining some knowledge of truth when separated from the body. Death is more valuable in many ways for everyone than the period of life. Plato sympathized with Socrates' desire for death to escape the confusion that life in the body brings. However, in the *Laws*, Plato taught that a cowardly suicide should be buried apart and without a headstone.

1068 Spencer, A. J. *Death in Ancient Egypt.* London: Penguin, 1982.

A scholarly account of Egyptian burial customs is related to views of death and religion. Illustrations.

1069 Toynbee, Jocelyn M. *Death and Burial in the Roman World.* Ithaca, N.Y.: Cornell University Press, 1971.

A scholarly study begins with ideas of death and the afterlife, funerary rites and cemeteries of the Etruscans. Early Romans were close to the Etruscans in their deep seated belief in the afterlife and in some of the habits of thought and forms of architecture associated with the cult of the dead. Cremation, sometimes known among the Etruscans, became very popular among Romans. Additional chapters describe Roman funerary rites, cemeteries and funerary gardens and an extensive discussion of selected types of tombs, gravestones and tomb furniture. The burial gardens, popular among second-century residents of Alexandria might contain fruit and vegetable trees, dining rooms, summer lounges and apartments for various uses. Notes. See also Toynbee (4410).

1070 Vermeule, Emily. *Aspects of Death in Early Greek Art and Poetry.* Berkeley, Calif.: University of California Press, 1979.

1071 Vuresch, Carolus. *Consolationum a Graecis Romanisque Scriptorum Historia Ceritica.* Leipzig: J. B. Hirschfeld, 1886.

A scholarly examination of the emergence of consolation literature among the Greeks and Romans.

1072 Zandee, Jan. *Death as an Enemy: According to Ancient Egyptian Conceptions.* Leiden: E. J. Brill, 1960.

From an examination of Pyramid Texts and others the author found many examples of death as the enemy of the good life. Salvation from death is possible in the beyond. Most of the texts describe a favorable fate of the dead, although punishment and torture is mentioned for those who are sinners. Many scholastic references.

1.22 CHURCH FATHERS

1073 Augustine. *The City of God.* Trans. by M. Dods. New York: Random House, 1950.

In books XX and XXI an influential theologian for the Roman Catholic church presents biblical and philosophical conclusions concerning future resurrection, heaven and hell. The context of his writings was the destruction of Rome by barbarians. How could God allow this? Augustine answered with the hope of a heavenly city upon which devout persons would fix their faith in the midst of earthly despair. The foreboding of evil in the fifth century and following elevated his teaching that death was punishment for sin that could be traced back to the fall of Adam from perfection. See also Hick, (2213, 198), Dewart (1075), Pagels (1081).

1074 Beyenka, M. M. *Consolation in Saint Augustine.* Washington, D.C.: Catholic University of America Press, 1950.

The combination of both traditional and explicitly Christian forms of consolation are examined in the writings of Augustine, bishop of Hippo.

1075 Dewart, JoAnne E. MacWilliam. *Death and Resurrection.* Wilmington, Del.: Michael Glazier, 1986.

After a brief review of Old and New Testament views of death and resurrection, the author presents representative selections from Fathers of the Church until the time of St. Augustine. She notes that the earliest writers, the Apostolic Fathers gave a more material understanding to the resurrection than would be found in the New Testament accounts by St. Paul and St. John. This may have been part of a struggle against docetic Christology. The apologists who wrote in the latter half of the second century often considered the resurrection in the context of excitement concerning the immanent return of the risen Christ. Third century orthodox writers wrote of the resurrection as that of a material body in opposition to Gnostic questions that deny the resurrection of the body or at least believe that the body will be immaterial. However, Clement of Alexandria and Origen provided intellectual arguments for eternal happiness that made it difficult for their knowledge of God to account for the presence of a material body in the afterlife. St. Augustine provided adamant assertions that the bodily death of the human person is the result of Adam's sin and that the resurrection of Christ provides purification of the soul for those who believe. He believed that the resurrection of Christ was "in true flesh" and gives extensive treatment to the definition of human resurrection of a "spiritual body" which is not to be understood as equivalent to the corruptible "body" or only as a spiritual thought. See also Augustine (1073).

1076 Favez, Charles. *La Consolation Latine Chrétienne*. Paris: J. Vrin, 1937.

A presentation of consolation literature from Latin church fathers.

1077 *Funeral Orations by St. Gregory Nazianzen and St. Ambrose*. Trans. by Leo P. McCauley, *et al*. New York: Fathers of the Church, 1953.

The Christian funeral oration is one of the most elaborate of Christian literary forms; it was adopted from the Greek tradition of the *encomium* and the treatises on grief and consolation. In an introductory section, the Greek and Roman examples are presented from the fourth century B. C. to the first century A. D. and are followed by a summary of orations by church fathers until about 400 A. D. The funeral orations of St. Gregory Nazianzen and St. Ambrose are eulogies that describe the life of the deceased, comparisons with other great heroes of God, references to relatives, details of death and burial and a prayer. The power and beauty of the language was considered appropriate for the grandeur of the character of the deceased.

1078 Gregg, Robert C. *Consolation Philosophy*. Cambridge, Mass.: Philadelphia Patristic Foundation, 1975.

See 4502.

1079 Gregory, Saint. *Pastoral Care*. Trans. by Henry Davis. Westminster, Md.: Newman Press, 1950.

A commanding and vigorous pope of the sixth century describes the responsibility of pastoral care through the discernment of opposites, such as the whole and the sick. The sick are to be admonished with submission to the "scourge of discipline" and to think of the heavenly country that awaits them. Bodily affliction cleanses the soul of evil. The virtues of illness are repentance and patience. The purpose of these admonitions is the reformation of character under the guidance of a priest who is an astute observer of human nature. Correction was sought through discipline of the soul's diseases rather than through openness that brought life-giving experience.

1080 LeGoff, Jacques. *The Birth of Purgatory*. Chicago: University of Chicago Press, 1984.

A French scholar in medieval studies and historical anthropology traces the obscure origins of a belief in Purgatory through foundations first laid by primitive Christianity and eventually developed into the medieval Church. The substantial modification in the spatial and temporal framework of the Christian imagination during this time is traced within the framework of a western society that was thoroughly permeated with religion. Although the word "purgatory" did not appear until the 12th century, some fathers of the church such as Ambrose, Jerome and Augustine believed that certain sinners might be saved, most probably by being subjected to a trial of some sort. As developed in the Middle Ages, purgatory offered a second chance to attain eternal life, so long as the sins to be purified by fire were "venial" rather than unpardonable. A solidarity of the dead with the living was assumed and supported by popular medieval culture. Scholarly notes.

1081 Pagels, Elane. *Adam, Eve, and the Serpent*. New York: Random House, 1988.

A professor of religion describes in chapter VI the debate between fifth century theologians, Augustine, Bishop of Hippo and Julian, Bishop of Eclanum concerning the mystery of human suffering as moral judgment. Augustine vehemently rejected the views of Pelagius and Julian that death was a natural part of humanity. The emperor Honorius was persuaded by Augustine and other North African bishops to expel Julian from office and reverse the earlier teaching of Justin, Irenaeus, Tertullian, Clement and Chrystostom that Adam's sin did not change the structure of nature. His sin resulted in moral and spiritual, not physical death. Augustine's contrary teaching became dominant in the western church, and included a belief that original sin entered the embryo as a result of sexual intercourse. Also, he taught that nature changed in other ways because of Adam's sin: women must suffer in childbirth because she tempted Adam, and agriculture became laborious for men. The author's conclusions are based upon a final work of Augustine, *Opus Imperfectum*, which had not been translated into English. Reliable, original research.

1082 Pelikan, Jaroslav. *The Shape of Death*. Nashville, Tenn.: Abingdon Press, 1961.

See 2235.

1.23 MEDIEVAL "ARS MORENDI"

1083 Aquinas, Thomas. *Summa Contra Gentiles*. Vol. 4. Trans. by C. J. O'Neil. Garden City, N.J.: Doubleday and Co., 1957.

In a discussion of the consummation of the work of salvation, a thirteen century theologian with a lasting influence on Roman Catholic theology considers the state of the soul after death. Punishment and reward are of the essence of God's justice, so souls who receive the reward of virtue must be entirely purified in purgatory. There is an individual judgment at death and there is a last judgment which ratifies the judgment at the hour of death. The interim existence of the soul after death in purgatory became increasingly important. See also LeGoff (1080).

1084 Boase, T. S. R. *Death in the Middle Ages: Mortality, Judgment and Remembrance*. London: Thames and Hudson, 1972.

A generously illustrated book on medieval death covers the grim reality of battle, execution, plaque and burial with interpretations of the religious significance of the Judgment and a continuing cultural preoccupation with death.

1085 Chiffoleau, Jacques. *La Comptabilité De L'Au-Dela' [The Relevance of the Afterlife]*. Paris: Ecole Française de Rome, 1980.

This scholarly and poetic study of the "autumn of the middle ages" in southern France (Avignon) 1340–1530 A. D., delves the meaning of the phrase "the heart is the reclame of death." This is demonstrated in the evolution of images of death as they are seen in the role of the church, funeral rites and pastoral themes that became almost an obsession with the macabre. This gradually gave way to more earthly concerns in this flamboyant, creative period of French civilization.

1086 Comper, Frances M. M., ed. *The Book of the Craft of Dying and Other Early English Tracts Concerning Death*. 1917. Reprint. New York: Arno Press, 1976.

The Craft of Dying and other guidebooks by popular preachers and others from the fourteenth and fifteenth centuries describe public concern and religious views concerning death.

1087 Eller, Vernard. *A Pearl of Christian Counsel for the Brokenhearted.* Ill. by Rosanna Eller. Lanham, Md.: University Press of America, 1983.

This translation of a fourteenth English poem presents narrative answers to questions such as the way in which we cope with loss and the counsel of the Christian gospel for the brokenhearted. The beautiful calligraphic script of the translation is rendered by the author's daughter, Rosanna Eller.

1088 Faber, M. D. "Shakespeare's Suicides: Some Historic, Dramatic and Psychological Reflections." In *Essays in Self-Destruction*, ed. by Edwin S. Shneidman, 30–58. New York: Science House, 1967.

A professor of English clarifies Renaissance attitudes towards suicide through a study of the moralistic views presented in the writings of Shakespeare.

1089 Gibson, Margaret, ed. *Boethius: His Life, Thought and Influence.* Oxford: Basil Blackwell, 1981.

A series of essays by English classical scholars examine the life of Boethius and his circumstances in the fifth century, his scholastic writings and their influence in the Medieval Quadrivium. Several articles discuss the design and impact of his "Consolation of Philosophy" text upon French, English and Northern European traditions of consolation as the answer to misfortune, disease and death. Index. A philological study. For the content of Boethius' philosophy of "consolation," see Reiss (1097).

1090 Gottfried, Robert S. *The Black Death: Natural and Human Disaster in Medieval Europe.* New York: The Free Press, 1983.

The scourge of an unsanitary civilization is considered in terms of its devastating effects upon Europe in the Middle Ages.

1091 Huizinga, Johan. *The Waning of the Middle Ages.* New York: St. Martin's Press, 1967.

At the close of the Middle Ages a sombre melancholy weighed upon peoples' souls. Pessimism became the ground out of which the aspiration of a life of beauty and serenity would flourish, primarily through remedies for the individual soul. Earthly amelioration came through thoughts of an ideal past and hope for a heavenly future. The present world bore the stain of sin, the search for the sublime life vacillated between tearful piety and frigid cruelty. Emotions were formalized in mourning rites, which included extreme fear of announcing a death and great pomp at the "lieing in" of deceased nobles. See also Aries (1039).

1092 Jankofsky, Klaus P. "From Lion to Lamb: Exemplerary Deaths in Chronicles of the Middle English Period." *Omega* 12 (1981–82): 209–226.

The depiction of death and dying by medieval English chroniclers presents death as a physical event with enormous moral consequences. In particular, an account of the death of King Richard the Lionheart shows both concealment and revelation of collective and individual assessments of death. The king on his deathbed rejected advice that he marry off his three daughters with the retort that the daughters were pride (whom he consigned to the Knights of the Temple), avarice (whom he would have sent to Gray Friars) and luxury (who would eat and drink with the Black Friars who never seemed to be satiated).

1093 Katherine of Genoa, Saint. *Purgation and Purgatory: The Spiritual Dialogue*. Trans. by Serge Hughes. New York: Paulist Press, 1979.

See 2316.

1094 Marius, Richard. *Thomas More: A Biography*. New York: Alfred A. Knopf, 1984.

The Lord Chancellor of Henry VIII, who died a martyr for his Catholic faith, wrote in *Dialogue of Comfort* about his own wrestlings with death: hesitations, terrors, ruminations about his choice, final sense of confusion about the reasons for risking his own existence. These final musings in the Tower of London were preceded by a more agitated treatise on death, *The Four Last Things*. This is a call to resist sensuality in the Christian life through vivid presentation of divine judgment. More maintains a dualism of body and soul and believes that the pursuit of bodily pleasures must be overcome through concern for the fate of the soul and the horrors of dying. The four last things, death, judgment, heaven, hell, call up the human qualities of pity, resignation, longing and consolation.

1095 McGatch, Milton. "Some Theological Reflections on Death from the Early Church through the Reformation." In *Perspectives on Death*, ed. by Liston O. Mills, 99–136. Nashville, Tenn.: Abingdon Press, 1969.

A church historian surveys the attempts of theologians from the Greek Fathers through the Reformation to determine what happened to humans after death. Concern for the plight of the soul after death and fear for its destiny came to dominate these studies. Through the centuries, emphasis upon the resurrection gave way to preoccupation with immortality. Corporate salvation—God's restoration of a people—gradually became a preoccupation with individual salvation. See also McGatch (1044).

1096 O'Connor, Mary Catharine. *The Art of Dying Well: The Development of the Ars Moriendi*. New York: AMS Press, 1966.

The Medieval classic on dying is examined for authorship, literary forerunners in a variety of manuscripts in European and English languages and later Catholic and Reformation works in the same tradition as Sir Thomas More's *Four Last Things*. Extensive scholarly bibliography.

1097 Reiss, Edmund. *Boethius*. Boston, Md.: Twayne Publishers, 1982.

As the "last of the Romans and the first of the Scholastics," the late fifth century writings of the patrician Roman Boethius provided the definitive word for medieval thought about misfortune in this world and human free will in relation to God's foreknowledge. In a blending of verse and prose with allegorical persons (that stamp the character of much Medieval and Renaissance literature), blindness is put aside through philosophical directions for serenity that rise above the good or bad of earthly existence. A free spirit of philosophy will range above passions which only blind and enslave humans who rage against the errors of society. Serenity is a search for true happiness, yet this search recognizes the inadequacies of wealth, fame and pleasure, and moves with the help of God toward the heavenly reason which governs all things. Boethius finds authority for this assertion in Plato's *Apology,* which states that evil cannot befall a good person either in life or death. Boethius presents the work of a disciplined mind in his discussions of the great mysteries of providence, fate, chance, predestination and freedom of the will. See also Gibson (1089).

1098 Rolfes, Helmut. "Ars moriendi—Eine Sterbekunst aus der Sorge um das ewige Heil." [Ars Moriendi—An Art of Dying from Worry to Eternal Salvation.] In *Ars Moriendi. Erwägungen zur Kunst des Sterbens*, ed. by Harald Wagner. Freiburg: Herder, 1989.

The author traces the metamorphosis of the cultural and social acceptability of the process of dying from the Middle Ages to the near-taboo status it has in modern life and argues for the need for a return to the acceptance of death as a part of life and social mores governing treatment of the dying and their families. Sub-topics include "Death and Dying on the Horizon of Worry about Eternal Salvation," "Ars Moriendi in the Later Middle Ages," and "Religious and Ideological Reservations to Ars Moriendi."

1099 Saaz, Johannes von. "Death and the Plowman." Trans. by Jacob Needleman. In Death and Bereavement, ed. by Austin H. Kutscher, 99–128. Springfield, Ill.: Charles C. Thomas, 1969.

A "disputation" between plaintiff (the plowman) and the defendant (Lord Death) concerning the death of the plowman's wife does not lessen the pain of bereavement. The only consolation is submission to the higher purposes of God's judgment that are unknown to either plowman or Death.

1100 Wagner, Harald, ed. *Ars Moriendi, Erwägungen zur Kunst des Sterbens.* Freiburg: Herder, 1989.

German scholars present essays on the meaning of the art of dying from the Middle Ages to the twentieth century: Barth (1101); Ebeling (1145); Mansor (2032); Rolfes (1098); Wagner (2127, 6092); Zielinski (3372).

1.24 REFORMATION

1101 Barth, Hans-Martin. "Leben und sterben können. Brechungen der spätmittelalterlichen "ars moriendi" in der Theologie Martin Luthers." [The Ability to Live and Die: Modifications of the Later Medieval Ars Moriendi in the Theology of Martin Luther]. In *Ars Moriendi. Erwägungen zur Kunst des Sterbens,* ed. by Harald Wagner. Freiburg: Herder, 1989.

Although Luther never used the expression "Art of Dying," he wrote often of the reality of death and man's preparation for it. Barth analyzes Luther's writings concerning the place of sacraments and the Word; the assistance of angels, the saints, and all creatures; flight from death and from life; the doctrine of Death and Resurrection; and the art of dying given back to life.

1102 Calvin, Jean. *Institutes of the Christian Religion.* Trans. by John Allen. Vol. I. Philadelphia: Presbyterian Board of Christian Education, 1936.

The father of the Reformed wing of Protestantism agrees with Augustine that the "fall and defection" of Adam is the cause of the curse inflicted on all mankind, which is the death of the soul. Calvin developed a doctrine of double predestination, in which some persons are destined by God to eternal salvation and others to eternal damnation.

1103 Calvin, John. *Letters of John Calvin.* Comp. by Jules Bonnet. Trans. by David Constable. 2 vols. Edinburgh: T. Constable, 1855–1857.

The correspondence of John Calvin presents letters of consolation in bereavement and loss as in those dated August 20, 1538, April 15, 1541, November 1546. Calvin accepts the ancient consolation philosophy that disapproves of irrational mourning. Yet the letters provide a warm personal feeling in which there is room for natural grief. There are exhortations to piety and assurance of the goodness and providence of God.

1104 Jacobi, Jolande, ed. *Paracelsus: Selected Writings*. Trans. by Robert Guterman. Bollingen Series 28. Princeton, N. J.: Princeton University Press, 1951.

The writings of a humane and observant Renaissance physician include his thoughts about death. It is a reminder that upon an appointed day the spirit that has been imprisoned in an earthly body will arise to a judgment of God who alone has given life to the infertile and worthless earthly body.

1105 Langston, A. D. B. "Tudor Books of Consolation." Unpublished doctoral dissertation, University of North Carolina, 1940.

1106 Luther, Martin. *Luther: Letters of Spiritual Counsel*. Ed. and trans. by Theodore G. Tappert. Philadelphia: Westminster Press, 1955.

Letters of consolation, instruction, admonition and encouragement were written by Christian leaders throughout the history of the western church and later given wide circulation. In this tradition, the letters of Martin Luther include many on comfort for the dying and consolation for the bereaved. They might be to prominent citizens such as the Elector Frederick of Saxony, or to Luther's parents or relatives. They speak of good cheer through Christ who has overcome the sufferings of this world and faith in the Christian's participation in Christ's victory over death. Selections also include "Table Talk" in which Luther is described by a friend as one who becomes very close to dying persons so that they would feel reassured by his presence. He inquires concerning the relation of the dying person toward God, the way in which one endured with patience. He commends those who are steadfast in faith and promises to pray for them.

1107 Luther, Martin. *What Luther Says: An Anthology*. Vol. 1. Comp. by Ewald M. Plas. St. Louis, Mo.: Concordia Publishing House, 1959.

Excerpts from various works of a founder of the Reformation include his assertions that death is decidedly unnatural, preparation for death should be made throughout life, death is caused by sin in Paradise, feeling of guilt causes the agony of death and perfect love will cast out that fear. Consolation comes through knowledge that Christians will live forever with Christ and that there is no need to agonize about the time of death, since it has already been determined by God. There is no purgatory.

1108 Pestalozzi, Carl. *Heinrich Bullinger, Leben und ausgewählte Schriften*. Elberfeld, 1858.

This biography of the successor to Zwingli as pastor of Zurich includes references to *Bericht der kranken* (1638), Bullinger's consolations for the dying and bereaved during the plague in Zurich. The emphasis is evangelical and pietistic and includes ministry to prisoners and those condemned to die.

1109 Quistorp, Heinrich. *Calvin's Doctrine of the Last Things*. Trans. by Harold Knight. London: Lutterworth Press, 1955.

Eschatology is treated in book III of the *Institutes* under the heading of salvation. Thoughts about death are not to be satisfied through a doctrine of purgatory or a system of indulgences. The only hope is in acceptance of the sacrificial work of Christ by whose merit the elect are redeemed. All confidence is to be in the immortality to come. This life is to be despised and renounced. The souls of the pious enter into an immediate blessed rest while they await the final resurrection and judgment.

1.25 ENLIGHTENMENT

1110 Bacon, Francis. *The History of Life and Death with Observations Naturall and Experimentall for the Prolonging of Life*. 1638. Reprint. New York: Arno Press, 1976.

In a radical break from the traditions of a Roman medical authority, Galen, and the Greek philosopher Aristotle, a seventeenth-century English physician writes on death, prolongation of life, euthanasia, transfusion and transplantation.

1111 McManners, John. *Death and the Enlightenment*. New York: Oxford University Press, 1981.

Regius Professor of Ecclesiastical History in University of Oxford examines changing attitudes to death among Christians and unbelievers in eighteenth-century France. The study is a detailed and readable reminder of ever present death in previous generations and the attention paid to the rites of death and the cult of melancholy. Based on primary sources in the eighteenth century, the study is an example of French historiography of the history of ideas.

1112 Taylor, Jeremy. *Holy Living and Holy Dying*. Ed. by Marvin D. Hinton. Wheaton, Ill.: Tyndale House Pub., 1986.

In the 1650s, this slender volume (originally published as *Holy Living*, 1650 and *Holy Dying*, 1651) extended the Medieval concentration upon ministry at the death-bed to the modern concern for the whole course of life as a school for dying well. Admonitions are provided concerning the need for vigorous living and moral improvement as the bishop reflects with a sad beauty upon the brevity of life. There must be a daily scrutiny of our actions and ample confession of sins. He has little faith in death-bed confessions and counsels priests to visit the terminally ill before "their reason is useless."

1113 Vovelle, M. *Pieté Baroque et Dechristianisation en Provence au XVIIIᵉ Siecle* (Baroque Piety and Dechristianisation in Provence in the Eighteenth Century). Paris: Plon, 1973.

Through an example of the wills ("spiritual testaments") developed after the Counter-Reformation in 18th century Provence of southern France, the author found that the spiritual element continued in certain formulas of the will, but that those who were dying seemed to be less and less confident of their passage to the other world and more concerned with the physical aspects of death. These changes in the century after the Enlightenment were linked with changing position of women and with changing attitudes within the family.

1.26 PURITAN AND COLONIAL AMERICA

1114 Geddes, Gordon. *Welcome Joy: Death In Puritan New England*. Ann Arbor, Mich.: UMI Research Press, 1981.

Medieval fascination with death and decay lingered on into 17th century New England. There was physical terror and theological anxiety about a state of separation from God. The only hope of perfection, fullness and completion lay in the heavenly realm. Death was God's judgment on sin at which time Satan acted as God's executioner.

1115 Slater, Peter Gregg. *Children in the New England Mind*. Hamden, Conn.: Archon Books, 1976.

Through careful historical research, the author reviews seventeenth-nineteenth century doctrines of children and death in New England. Infant damnation was detailed in Michael Wigglesworth's *The Day of Doom* (1118). This narrative poem of the Judgment Day, heaven and hell was second only to the Bible in popularity. The menace of infant death and doctrines of damnation led parents to many petitions for the salvation of loved children, even though a quiet resignation before God's judgment was recommended from the pulpit. By the 1750s, liberals renounced infant damnation and Calvinists gradually drifted toward individual rather than inherited guilt, but debates between the two parties were spirited until the 1850s influence of Horace Bushnell and Timothy Dwight. Theological tension then shifted toward the parental love of innocent children and the authority of parents in Christian nurture. Activism replaced the fatalism of the an older Calvinism.

1116 Stannard, David E. "Death and the Puritan Child." In *Death in America*, ed. by David E. Stannard. Philadelphia: University of Pennsylvania Press, 1975.

See 3165.

1117 Stannard, David E. *The Puritan Way of Death*. New York: Oxford University Press, 1977.

A professor of history presents the search for death-with-dignity as a window through which various professions can obtain a new perspective on present issues such as the connection between death ritual and the evolution of community purpose and cultural perception. The author centers upon the seventeenth century in America, where ambivalence toward death as punishment and reward caused Puritan children to be terrified by the prospect of death and led to such contradictions as the elaboration of funerals and the necessity of legislation to guarantee that graves would receive minimal care. A scholarly study with voluminous footnotes.

1118 Wigglesworth, Michael. "The Day of Doom or a Poetical Description of the Great and Last Judgment." In *The Puritans,* 585–611. Rev. ed. Ed. by Perry Miller and Thomas H. Johnson, II. New York: Harper and Row, 1963.

See Slater 1115.

1.27 NINETEENTH-CENTURY ROMANTICISM

1119 Darby, Elizabeth and Nicola Smith. *The Cult of the Prince Consort.* New Haven, Conn.: Yale University Press, 1983.

The extravagant decade of grief by Queen Victoria for the loss of Prince Albert is studied in the mass of memorials and styles of clothing that typified her neurotic response for years following his death. Changing social conventions for dealing with death and mourning in the Victorian Age are analyzed.

1120 Farrell, James J. *Inventing the American Way of Death, 1830–1920.* Philadelphia: Temple University Press, 1980.

Rejecting the absurdity and harshness of the Puritan way of death, middle class Victorians and their imitators in America sought to make death appear natural, painless, predictable, beautiful and ultimately inconspicuous. Scientific naturalism was a crucial catalyst of this process. The specialization and prestige of science created a culture of professionalism that was necessary for the development of the funeral industry. Science also supported a belief that death was to be conquered not through assurances of immortality but through the evolution of competent vision of order and security. Death was to be denied, controlled, managed. The changes are documented from study of cemetery and funeral services in Vermilion County, Ill. Chapters include the cosmological contents of death, scientific naturalism, religious liberalism and the development of the modern cemetery and funeral service. Many primary sources are cited along with scholarly studies. Easily read, and with confidence.

1121 Houlbrooke, Ralph, ed. *Death, Ritual and Bereavement.* London: Rutledge, 1989.

On behalf of the Social History Society of the United Kingdom, historians review the relationship of church and family in England between the late 15th and 19th centuries. Chapters consider the meaning of the good death, godly grief, medical responsibilities, burial practices, and the prominence of death in the thinking of Victorian Britain.

1122 Murray, Henry A. "Dead to the World: The Passions of Herman Melville." *In Essays in Self-Destruction*, ed. by Edwin S. Shneidman. New York: Science House, 1967.

See 6028.

1123 Saum, Lewis O. "Death In the Popular Mind of Pre-Civil War America." In *Death in America*, ed. by David E. Stannard, 30–48. Philadelphia: University of Pennsylvania Press, 1975.

The journals and diaries of pre-Civil War Americans not only contained many musings about death but also much on the way that people died and the spiritual impact of the experience, which usually was resignation. Resignation was also expressed as tentativeness about longevity and speeches about inward grace as friends and family gathered about a dying person. The ideal was to "expire mild-eyed," a "triumphant" death which was the final episode of holy living.

1124 Stannard, David E., ed. *Death In America.* Philadelphia: University of Pennsylvania Press, 1975.

A symposium by historians, anthropologists, literary scholars and art historians who survey death in America from Puritan times until 1880. For chapters by contributors, see Stannard (3165); Saum (1123); Douglas (4500); French (4407); Kelly (1305); Meyers (2226); Aries (1001); Goody (1248).

1125 Wells, Ronald V. "Dignity and Integrity in Dying: Insights from Early 19th Protestantism." *Journal of Pastoral Care* 26 (June 1972): 1–27.

An examination of letters written between 1826–1842 demonstrates the ability of many persons to accept death with dignity and courage because of the way in which Christian faith supported them and their loved ones.

1.28   TWENTIETH–CENTURY DENIALS

1126   Aldwinckle, Russell. *Death In the Secular City.* Grand Rapids, Mich.: Wm. B. Eerdmans Publishing Co., 1972.

The dichotomy between death and life in recent American culture may be attributed to the post-Enlightenment denial of individual immortality by atheistic and sceptical eighteenth century philosophers and scientists, with a turn toward naturalism, positivism and Marxism. Bertrand Russell is singled out as the person who contributed to a philosophy of despair and ultimate distrust of human emotions, such as the fear of death. All that is left for persons is to live courageously before total extinction.

1127   Caillois, Roger. *Quatre Essais D'Sociologie Contemporaine (Four Essays on Contemporary Sociology).* Paris, France: Perrin, 1951.

A French sociologist presents a discerning sociological analysis of American attitudes toward death before the days of American sociological and psychological studies of the subject in depth. His conclusion: Americans believe death is not to be feared because of any moral obligation but because there is no reason to dread it—it must absolutely not be thought about, much less spoken about.

1128   Eliot, Thomes D. "Of the Shadow of Death." *Annals of the American Academy of Political and Social Science* 229 (1943): 87–99.

A sociologist with an abiding interest in death research compares attitudes toward death during World War I and World War II.

1129   Eliot, Thomas D. "The Adjustive Behavior of Bereaved Families: A New Field for Research." *Social Forces* 8 (1930): 543–549.

A pioneer in the study of the relationship of society to death is convinced that taboos about death are similar to former taboos about sex which can be overcome. See also Gorer (1012).

1130   Fulton, Robert and Robert Bendickson, eds. *Death and Identity.* Rev. ed. Bowie, Md.: Charles Press, 1976.

See 1146.

1131 Gorer, Geoffrey. "The Pornography of Death." In *Modern Writing*, ed. by W. Phillips and P. Rahv, 56–62. New York: Berkeley Press, 1956.

An anthropologist affirms that death, rather than sex is the pornographic theme of the twentieth century. It must be hidden from public view. See also Gorer (1012), Eliot (1129).

1132 Hick, John. *Death and Eternal Life*. San Francisco: Harper and Row, 1976.

See 2213.

1133 Jackson, Charles O. "Death Shall Have No Dominion: The Passing of the World of the Dead in America." *Omega* 8 (1977): 195–203.

In the present century, the dead have largely lost their social importance, visibility and impact in American society. But for the seventeenth through the nineteenth centuries, the dead world occupied a significant and readily recognizable place in the world of the living, and grew rapidly through most of the nineteenth century. The author examines causes for the twentieth century reversal in relationship between the two worlds: mobility, diminished emotional investment in the family; the elderly rather than the children are doing most of the dying; a temporal and secular outlook maintained no certainty of the afterlife and therefore could not stand the horror of physical decomposition in death—it must be hidden. On the social repression of death, see also Aries (1040), Gorer (1012).

1134 Lerner, Jeffrey C. "Changes In Attitudes Toward Death: The Widow In Great Britain In The Early Twentieth Century." In *Bereavement: Its Psycho-Social Aspects*, ed. by Bernard Schoenberg, *et al.*, 91–118. New York: Columbia University Press, 1975.

From a study of literary resources, the author concludes that the pre-World War I widow was more likely to be better off emotionally than the post-War widow, but more likely to be worse off financially. Pensions for widows improved the financial situation after World War I, but the absence of established customs and resources during bereavement led to despair and isolation.

1135 Park, Roswell. "Thanatology" *Journal of the American Medical Assocciation* 58 (1912): 1243–1246.

A professor of surgery proposes that "thanatology" concentrate on biomedical issues. His article sought to stimulate interest in various questions about death as "biochemical fact." He realized that questions about death would also include the issue of "soul" but felt that theology was so "utterly impotent" that it had almost nothing to do with thanatology as he defined the term. In contrast to Park, European "thanatology" included relevant philosophical theories, as in the 1910 English translation of Metchnikoff (1326) on the relationship between the new biomedical sciences and human optimism in the relief of suffering.

1.29 LATE TWENTIETH–CENTURY REALISM

1136 Blum-Feshbach, Jonathan and Sally Blum-Feshbach and associates. *The Psychology of Separation and Loss.* San Francisco: Jossey-Bass Pub., 1987.

As an example of studies in the 1980s this text relates experiences of separation and loss to human development over the life-span. The loss may include divorce, daily parental absences, moves to a new neighborhood or school, leaving a job, terminating psychotherapy, coping with death. Theories of separation and attachment are related by the sixteen authors to the treatment of such conditions as depression, personality change, schizophrenia, eating disorders, borderline personality pathology, and others. Bibliographies for each chapter. Emphasis on attachment theory provides a modified separation-individuation model in which the theories of Freud are the starting point for later theories of passages through life transitions, as in the writings of Erik Erikson (1338).

1137 Evely, Louis. *In the Face of Death.* Greenwich, Conn.: Seabury Press, 1979.

The Christian philosopy of life is used to evaluate the way in which modern Americans face aging and dying.

1138 Goodman, Lisa M. *Death and the Creative Life.* New York: Springer, 1981.

As part of the ideology of authentic expression in dying that was presented in the 1970s and 80s the author argues that what we fear is not death as such, but rather the incompleteness of our lives at the moment of death. A defense against this fear is to complete our lives through creative activity. From interviews with artists and scientists she suggests that those who are constantly creative have a feeling of immortality. Full knowledge is being fully alive, since life seems most precious when we are about to lose it.

1139 Gutmann, David. "Dying to Power: Death and the Search for Self-Esteem." In *New Meanings of Death*, ed. by Herman Feifel, 335–350. New York: McGraw-Hill Book Co., 1977.

A psychologist relates an upturn in interest in death to late 20th century concern for power: the power of an acceptance of death to bring rebirth, the power of the aged in folk societies, murder as the route to bad power. The author concludes that a "vitalistic" view of death as a precondition for renewal and expansion is no longer confined to religion, but is now appearing in the secular consciousness as well.

1140 Johnston, Ralph C., Jr. *Confronting Death: Psychoreligious Responses.* Ann Arbor, Mich.: U. M. I. Research Press, 1988.

A specialist in religion and medicine evaluates the attitudes and values of the thanatology movement and reviews twentieth century psychologies of consciousness and death. Transpersonal psychologies, sacred tradition, commitment and community are related to the mystery of death. A competent review of modern American philosophies, psychologies and theologies of death, although some authors are missing: Gerkin, Moltmann, Tillich.

1141 Parsons, Talcott. "Death in American Society—A Brief Working Paper." *American Behavioral Scientist* 6 (1963): 61–65.

An eminent sociologist argues that vast changes will occur in the meaning of death among Americans as the causes of premature death continue to be eliminated along with the suffering that has usually been associated with death. To assess these changes, he suggests study of changes in acceptance of death as inevitable, awareness of death, achievements before death, dependence upon God. Will the central symbolic definition of the problem of death be the crucifixion of the mortal Jesus?

1142 Scott, Nathan A. *The Modern Vision of Death.* Richmond, Va.: John Knox Press, 1967.

Death is discussed from the viewpoint of literature, philosophy and science by such authors as Amos N. Wilder, J. Glenn Gray, Hans J. Morganthau, Joseph Haroutunian, Paul Tillich. There is a fascinating account by Joseph W. Mathews of "The Time My Father Died."

1143 Vaux, Kenneth. *This Mortal Coil.* New York: Harper and Row, 1978.

A professor of medical ethics and philosophy describes a cultural evolution of thoughts towards health and disease from (1) traditional through (2) experimental to (3) a time of renovation. "Experimental" came with the rise of scientific hopes for conquest and a strictly organic interpretation of disease. "Renovation" is the integration of the best of "traditional" emphases and spiritual dimensions of existence with gains accomplished through the experimental phase of the nineteenth and early twentieth centuries.

1.3   MODERN WESTERN ATTITUDES

1144   Aries, Philippe. *Western Attitudes Toward Death.* Trans. by Patricia
       M. Ramum. Baltimore: Johns Hopkins University Press, 1974.

       See 1039.

1145   Ebeling, Hans. "Die Strategic Defense Initiative und die Kunst des
       Sterbens. Über Bedingungen der Abschiedlichkeit der Philosophie
       und des Menschen." [The Strategic Defense Initiative and the Art of
       Dying. Concerning the Conditions of Separableness of Philosophy
       and Man]. In *Ars Moriendi. Erwägungen zur Kunst des Sterbens,* ed.
       by Harald Wagner. Freiburg: Herder, 1989.

       The author discusses the inability, or unwillingness, of a modern
technological society to deal with the concept of death, which can be
neither measured nor, to a large extent, controlled. The essay's three sections deal with philosophy and the individual art of of dying, the collective
inability of life, and the general art of dying.

1146   Fulton, Robert and Robert Bendickson, eds. *Death and Identity.* Rev.
       ed. Bowie, Md.: Charles Press, 1976.

       Pertinent research by psychiatrists, psychologists, socialists and
medical personnel is arranged by a sociologist, along with his editorial
comments. The general theme is the shift in the relationship of identity to
death. Questions about this relation were formerly centered in the area of
sacred teaching, but in a modern secular society, the emphasis is upon disaster and disease, which have become private, unspoken problems.

1147   Hoffman, Frederick J. *The Mortal No: Death in the Modern Imagi-
       nation.* Princeton, N.J.: Princeton University Press, 1964.

       See 6001.

1148   Langone, John. *Vital Signs: The Way We Die in America.* Boston:
       Little, Brown and Co., 1974.

       A medical journalist offers a readable and factual interpretation of
the American view of death as it is seen through interviews and excerpts
from printed material. This is a direct look at what happens to the dying
and those who care for them.

1149   Lifton, Robert J. and Eric Olson. *Living and Dying.* New York:
       Bantam Books, 1975.

       Serious themes such as the holocaust and symbolic immortality are
presented for young readers in simple prose with appropriate pictures.

Topics include the place of death in the life cycle, the impact of the nuclear era, the threat of meaninglessness, the possibility of immortality. The themes are treated more extensively in other works by Lifton (1157, 1221).

1150 Mitford, Jessica. *The American Way of Death*. New York: Simon and Schuster, 1963.

The commercialization of death is exposed in this somewhat sensational revelation of pressures and maneuvers of the funeral industry in the immediate post-World War II era. Although the study was superficial in part, some consideration is given to methodological problems in death attitude research and the sociological subjects are wide ranging. A competent list of references are included. Since the author came to the United States from Britain, it is possible that her distaste for American burial customs such as a display of the corpse may have been influenced by her own culture in which such a display is culturally reprehensible.

1151 Wagner, August H., ed. *What Happens When You Die?* London: Abelard Schuman, 1968.

Over a period of thirty years, the editor compiled letters from "the greatest thinkers of the 20th century" on the meaning of death. These range from political leaders such as David ben Gurion to philosophical theologians such as C. E. M. Joad. Content ranges from brief thoughts of Arnold Toynbee on the improbability of personal immortality to copious references to biblical texts by clergy and Upton Sinclair's discussion of the meaning of God in his life.

1152 Woodward, Kenneth L. "How America Lives with Death." *Newsweek*, April 6, 1970, 81–88.

A historian summarized the views of Lifton, Dunne, Kastenbaum and LeShan to show the denial and dilemma of death in a society dominated by expectations of salvation from death through medical and other technologies. He gives special attention to Lifton's "symbolic immortatlity" as a rising force among young adults who find themes of death and rebirth as answers to despair and denial. The author is sympathetic to this return to "the Easter idea of resurrection."

1.31 AWARENESS/DENIAL See also Upon the Dying Person (3.11)

1153 Dumont, Richard G. and Dennis C. Foss. *The American View of Death: Acceptance or Denial?* Cambridge, Mass.: Schenkman Pub. Co., 1972.

From an examination of published sources in sociology, psychology, anthropology and religion, the authors suggests that the culture of the United States and individuals both accept and deny death simultaneously. They conclude that on a conscious, intellectual level the individual accepts death, while on a generally unconscious emotional plane there is denial. Precise study of literature on attitudes toward death, with a comprehensive bibliography. See also Dumont (7007).

1154 Glaser, Barney G., and Anselm L. Strauss. *Time for Dying*. Chicago: Aldine Pub. Co., 1968.

See 3366.

1155 Glaser, Barney G., and Anselm L. Strauss. *Awareness of Dying*. Chicago: Aldine Pub. Co., 1965.

As part of a study on the way that nursing and medical personnel care for terminal patients in the San Francisco metropolitan area, sociologists center upon the characteristic modes of interaction between patients and hospital personnel. Research is directed toward the context of awareness in these interactions: closed awareness, suspected awareness, mutual pretense awareness, open awareness. Awareness of death is acute because the approach of death is bad news, bad news to the patient and a sign of failure to the staff. An individual patient seems alone against a group of professional persons. The patients may not be able to read the signs of approaching death or to understand their meaning. Problems of awareness are presented for patient and staff: direct disclosure of terminality, the unaware and the aware family, the problem of no recovery and comfort, the need for a composure by nurses in the face of death. A closing section discusses sociological aspects of a theory of awareness, methods of data collection and analysis. Index. See also Glaser (3366).

1156 Kavanaugh, Robert. *Facing Death*. Baltimore: Penguin Books, 1974.

In a text on death, the author includes a section on personal emotional responses towards death. We do not fear dying or the dead as much as the unknown and untested feelings that are aroused, and we mask these feelings. Only when these are unmasked can we be effective in ministering to those who are dying and bereaved. This process begins with the reassurance that it is O.K. to feel uneasy or afraid. Remember early, possibly unpleasant attitudes toward death. Listen as others recount their fears, for our own may be the same. See also Grollman (1013).

1157 Lifton, Robert J. *Death in Life: Survivors of Hiroshima*. New York: Random House, 1968.

Seventeen years after the bombing of Hiroshima, survivors were interviewed by an American psychiatrist who found that the major defense of survivors against death anxiety and death guilt is a cessation of feeling.

Psychic numbing came to characterize the entire lifestyle of survivors. This has an adaptive function in which survivors undergo a reversible form of symbolic death in order to avoid a permanent physical or psychic death. Rage is also suppressed. Some made efforts to break out of this psychic numbing years after the actual death immersion. A fighting spirit was developed toward life, which might reassert vitality or release destructive courses. Survivors were characterized by feelings of special need combined with great sensitivity to any reminder of weakness that would create severe conflicts over their developing autonomy. They often cut themselves off from potentially enriching relationships which were perceived to be counterfeit. In some cases this became paranoia of the victim. A great impediment to the relationship to others was fear of contagiousness—which they might transmit to others or receive from those who were dead. The author relates these findings to similar ones from victims of the Holocaust or racial and religious segregation. The author notes that the emphasis upon a process of psychic numbing departs from the traditional psychoanalytic preoccupation with instinct, repression and defense in studies of death. Psychic numbing is the cessation of the formative process, an impairment of symbol-formation. Survivors of any catastrophe must struggle to connect violent loss with inner psychic existence in order that life may be continued. The viable form of this connection must be some sense of symbolic immortality. See also Lifton (1308).

1158 May, Rollo. "The Existential Approach." In *The American Handbook of Psychiatry*. Ed. by S. Arietti, 1348–1361. New York: Basic Books, 1959.

A psychologist whose primary concern was with the resolution of anxiety, considers it necessary for clients to become aware of the threat of non-being so that their sense of existence may be real and released from unconscious fears. Since the primary fear is of death, acceptance of this particular anxiety is the central task of healthy personality development. All other fears and anxieties stem from the primary fear of death.

1159 May, William. "The Sacral Power of Death in Contemporary Experience." In *Perspectives on Death*, ed. by Liston O. Mills, 168–196. Nashville, Tenn.: Abingdon Press, 1969.

A professor of religion sees the conspiracy of silence around death as evidence of a very sacred event that we cannot avoid. Silence before this event came through the loss of a sense of transcendence in relation to death. The transcendence can be recovered, shorn of its otherworldly speculations, when we openly face the threat of death to our human existence and are willing to serve others.

1160 McClay, Marjorie. *To Die With Style!* Nashville, Tenn.: Abingdon Press, 1974.

In a popular affirmation of the "growth" attitude toward death, the author views death as an action to be anticipated and prepared for rather than as a thing to be suffered. It is an achievement, a final creative task for the dying person, family and friends. For a different view, see Cullmann (2200).

1161 Mills, Liston O., ed. *Perspectives on Death.* Nashville, Tenn.: Abingdon Press, 1969.

In the introduction to philosophical and theological articles on death, the editor attributes the denial of death in early twentieth century culture to the Enlightenment. Humans have become glorified and the issues of life and death have been separated. No theological understanding is sought because death is regarded as the result of an accident or of negligence or of disease. The neglect of death has led to a superficial view of health as the absence of pain and conflict. As a pastoral theologian, the author offers suggestions for ministry to the dying and bereaved which he considers to be a neglected work of the church. See also articles by contributors: May (1159); Silberman (2092); Keck (2099); McGatch (1095).

1162 Ruby, J. "Portraying the Dead." *Omega* 19 (1988–89): 1–20.

See 6062.

1163 Watts, Alan. *The Book: On the Taboo Against Knowing Who You Are.* New York: Vintage Books, 1972.

See 2386.

1164 Weisman, Avery D. "On the Value of Denying Death." *Pastoral Psychology* 23 (June 1972): 24–32.

A professor of psychiatry considers denial of death as refusal to accept the fact of a diagnosis, to negate the implications of the diagnosis or to repudiate the very idea of death itself. Any of these strategies should be recognized by helpers as an effort by the patient to maintain a significant self-image and may be necessary for a short period of time. Families and physicians can lead the patient to alternatives through acceptance and safe conduct. This reduces the need of a frightened person to deny or feel alone. See also Weisman (1165, 3622).

1165 Weisman, Avery D. *On Dying and Denying. A Psychiatric Study of Terminality.* New York: Behavioral Pub., 1972.

With rich clinical experience and intellectual acumen the author describes the manifold patterns of denial and offers instruction in the diagnosis of denial through a concern for the patient's perception of the world. His emphasis is upon dying as "psycho-social role as well as a physiological event." The meaning of death is to be found in the way that we systematize our sufferings. The movement from sickness toward "sickness unto death" is a regressive compromise with responsible aims both in the patient and in many physicians. Patients are facing the primary paradox that Freud described in 1915 (4060): the unconscious sense of immortality versus spectator knowledge of death around us. In the final chapter, the author notes that Freud wrote about the non-clinical applications of psychoanalysis in the fifteen years between his first operation for cancer of the mouth and his death. It was during this time that he produced *The Future of an Illusion* in which he asserted that religion was a futile search for an all-protective Father. The search is futile because we all die. See also Weisman (3622).

1.32 FEAR/ANXIETY See also UPON THE DYING PERSON (3.11)

1166 Ansbacher, H. L., and R. Ansbacher. *The Individual Psychology of Alfred Adler.* New York: Basic Books, 1956.

A psychoanalyst investigated the drive for power as a corollary thesis that fear of death originates in fear of loss of prestige.

1167 Bowlby, John. "Grief and Mourning in Infancy and Early Childhood." *Psychoanalytic Study of the Child* 15 (1961): 9–52.

From observations of healthy children (age 2–3) who had been separated from their mothers for a limited period of time to stay in a residential nursury or hospital ward, a psychiatrist noticed a first phase of separation with tears and anger. After several days of protest the children became quiet and seemed to be in despair, with some alternation between despair and hope. Finally the memory of mother seemed to fade and children even failed to show signs of recognition when reunited. If there had been separation for weeks or months the children were often unresponsive to the mother for hours or days when reunited. Then there was an intense show of clinging to the mother followed by rage and anxiety whenever the mother was briefly absent. For an alternative theory, see Corter (1174).

1168 Bowlby, John. *Attachment.* Vol. 1, *Attachment and Loss.* New York: Basic Books, 1969.

A pioneering psychiatrist in the study of widows provided data and theory for many later works. As a result of 20 years of clinical study, the author revised an early trauma theory of Freud (4312) and showed how normal and pathological instincts can be explained in terms of the history of attachment between parent and child. The loss experience relates to a child's formation of a perceptual world. As a child gains autonomy in spite of various anxieties of life, some separation anxiety occurs with the loss of cherished objects or loved ones. Very young children separated from their mothers were observed by the author to show separation anxiety through protests, despair and pre-occupation, loss of interest and emotional detachment. The same process is repeated in a widow who begins mourning with a craving for the deceased, angry efforts at recovery of the lost one, appeals for help, followed by apathy and disorganization and ending with more or less stable reorganization. The individual rebuilds life by attaching to other objects. These findings continue to be developed in three volumes (1168, 1169, 1172). The theoretical structure of volume 1 is object relations theory of inner representation. When a person dies, we have to change the inner representation, though the representation will continue to play a role in our psychic life. A co-worker, Colin Parkes, developed many similar conclusions, but extended his conclusions into the social support and threats to support in grief (Parkes 4244). For another explanation of infants' responses, see Corter (1174). See also Garanzini (1182).

1169 Bowlby, John. *Separation: Anxiety and Anger*. Vol. 2, *Attachment and Loss*. New York: Basic Books, 1973.

In addition to detailed studies of anxiety and anger in the loss of attachment to a loved one, vol. 2 advances beyond classical psychoanalysis in the presentation of several working models which may be present in each self. Significant persons, living or dead, may be attached to each of the working models, but the models will not be equally dominant in the self nor will the self be equally aware of all of them.

1170 Bowlby, John. "Attachment and Loss: Retrospect and Prospect." *American Journal of Orthopsychiatry* 52 (1982): 664–678.

This is excellent autobiographical introduction and overview to the three volume series by the author on attachment and loss.

1171 Bowlby, John. *The Making and Breaking of Affectional Bonds*. London: Tavistock, 1979.

After years of studying reactions to loss among children and adults, the author concludes that there are instinctual responses to the loss of a loved one as an inherited reminder of the necessary closeness of a family group in times of danger. Urges to recover and scold the lost ones are automatic responses that soothe the fear of survival in the wild. The two conditions which activate this attachment behavior are separation and threat. It is especially severe when a person does not have confidence that the loved one is accessible and responsive in a time of need. This confidence usually develops between five months and six years of age. When confidence is not established during this time, distorted forms of attachment to the parents will appear: anxious attachment, compulsive self-reliance, compulsive care-giving. These results of pathogenic parenting will have a pervasive influence upon the way the individual reacts to the loss of a parental figure.

1172 Bowlby, John. *Loss: Sadness and Depression.* Vol. 3, *Attachment and Loss.* New York: Basic Books, 1980.

As a part of an investigation of sadness and separation in the process of adjustment to significant loss, the author replaces multiple working models of the self, developed in vol. 2, with a computer analogy. The organism is considered to be an information processing system and the process of grief seeks to reestablish equilibrium by reorganizing new relationships of the self to the enviroment. A continued internalization of the lost person is now considered to be pathological. These theories are related to those of Parkes (4244), and Worden (4358). They are criticized by Klass (4207). Contents include: trauma of loss, place of loss and mourning in psychopathology, attachment theory, information-processing approach to defenses, adult mourning and mourning of children. See Bowlby (4002).

1173 Chris, P. E. "Attitudes Towards Death Among a Group of Acute Geriatric Psychiatric Patients." *Journal of Gerontology* 16 (1961): 56–59.

From interviews with 62 acute geriatric and psychiatric patients, the author concluded that those with better physical health were less afraid of death than those with poorer health.

1174 Corter, C. M. "The Nature of the Mother's Absence and the Infant's Response to Brief Separations." *Developmental Psychology* 12 (1976): 428–434.

A complication to the findings of Bowlby (1167, 1171) on "separation anxiety" is introduced in the study of infants' response to brief separations from mothers. The author asserts that distress is not inevitable. Exploratory responses by the infant should be given as much importance as the dramatic instances of crying, clinging and displaying other attachment responses that have been prominent in other investigations.

1175 Durlak, J. A. "Relationships Between Attitudes Toward Life and Death Among Elderly Women." *Developmental Psychology* 8 (1973): 146.

In a study of female residents of several retirement homes and nursing homes the author found a significant negative correlation between a fear of death and purpose in life scores.

1176 Erikson, Erik H. *Childhood and Society.* New York: W. W. Norton Co., 1963.

The psychoanalytically oriented psychiatrist who developed psychological-moral stages from birth to death has hypothesized the lack of basic trust as the cause of despair that is also rooted in a fear of death. Contra wise, he argues that individuals do not fear death if they have adopted an integrated lifestyle which is based on trust, order and meaning.

1177 Fenichal, Otto. "A Critique of the Death Instinct." In *Collected Papers of Otto Fenichal: First Series*, 363–72. New York: Norton, 1953.

A psychoanalyst in the Freudian tradition provides an overview of theories and observations concerning the death instinct. See Freud (1181).

1178 Frankl, Victor E. *The Doctor and the Soul*. Trans. by Richard and Clara Winston. New York: Alfred A. Knopf, 1955.

The psychiatrist who found that meaning in life preserved his sanity and inner security in a Nazi concentration camp is personally convicted that acceptance of death is a central task of personality development, especially since other fears and anxieties seem to be rooted in a primary fear of death. Human responsibility in life is based upon its irreversibility and temporality. It is life with risk at the edge of death. See also Frankl (2155).

1179 Freud, Anna. "Discussion of Dr. John Bowlby's Paper." In *Psychoanalytic Study of the Child*. Vol. 15. New York: International Universities Press, 1960.

In the analytic theory of mourning, the bereaved must accept a change in the external world, which is the loss of the cathected object and a change in the inner world. There is a withdrawal of libido from the lost object.

1180 Freud, Sigmund. "Thoughts for the Times on War and Death." 1915. In *Sigmund Freud, Collected Papers*. Vol. 4, 288–317. London: Hogarth Press, 1925.

The father of psychoanalysis affirms our need to consider our own death (inacceptable to the unconscious), the death of loved ones (met with ambivalence) and the death of enemies (which joins the issue of dea and hostility). This early concept dealt with the philosophical issue of imagining our death. Freud considered this to be impossible for we are only present as spectators in viewing the death of others. Freud believed that in the unconscious everyone of us is convinced of our immortality. See also Meyer (1192), Eissler (3456, 22–29). Freud's consideration of his own dying is described by his physician, Schur (3031).

1181 Freud, Sigmund. *Beyond the Pleasure Principle*. 1920. New York: Basic Books, 1975.

In this final revision of his theory of instincts, death is a force which dominates life. Freud postulated that life developed from an inorganic state and the drive for return to that state is the death instinct, an unconscious struggle that continues through life between this desire for return to the original state of the organism and an instinct for the continual creation of love and new life. The death instinct appears clinically in aggression, hostility, destructiveness. (This theory moves beyond earlier formulations in which such phenomenon was viewed as a form of sexuality, sadism). A primary purpose of psychoanalysis is to divert the death instinct from its primary aim of self destruction, but how can this be done without danger to others, since the instinct seeks nothing more than the opportunity of destroying? Therapy involves the study of the fusion and diffusion of these powerful unconscious forces and creates the opportunity for cooperation or at least some neutralization. Eissler (3456) accepts the death instinct, but it has been a subject of debate by other psychoanalysts (Feigenberg 3103, 221) and questioned by his former colleague, Jung (3203). See also Brown (1219), Banks (3100).

1182 Garanzini, Michael J. The Attachment Cycle: An Object Relations Approach to the Healing Ministries. New York: Paulist Press, 1988.

A Catholic professor of theology and psychology relates the attachment theory of Bowlby (1167) to the object relations theories of Freud, Sullivan, Kline, Mahler, Winncott, Fairbairn. The purpose is to show how attachment, separation, loss and reattachment are dynamic processes by which individuals grow throughout life. Through separation and loss we are challenged to accept other persons as truly others and not simply as an object for the self. Case studies are used to show how an understanding of the attachment cycle can assist pastoral counselors in facilitating the process of healing. Bibliography.

1183 Hall, G. Stanley. "A Study of Fears." *American Journal of Psychology* 8 (1897): 147–249.

In a study of 6,500 reported fears by a pioneering American psychologist, death was mentioned fourth most frequently.

1184 Hall, G. Stanley. "Thanatophobia and Immortality." *American Journal of Psychology* 26 (1915): 550–613.

From responses to almost 300 questionnaires, an early American leader in psychology develops a theory of the fear of death and hope of immortality.

1185 Jeffers, F. C., C. R. Nichols, and C. Eisdorfer. "Attitudes of Older Persons towards Death." *Journal of Gerontology* 16 (1961): 53–56.

From a study of projective tests administered to volunteers who are over sixty years of age, it was concluded that the volunteers who reported little or no fear of death and few feelings of rejection and depression had higher signs of mental health.

1186 Kaufmann, Walter. *Existentialism, Religion and Death: Thirteen Essays*. New York: New American Library, 1976.

In chapter 12, the author questions the assertion of Kübler-Ross that there is a universal fear of death. See Kaufmann (2055).

1187 Koestenbaum, Peter. *The Vitality of Death*. Westport, Conn.: Greenwood Press, 1971.

An existential philosopher develops an "image of man" from themes of death, anxiety, freedom and inwardness. One contribution to mature selfhood is the admission that we will die and need no longer act out of fear. With courage we can discard the fraudulent promise of symbolic immortality, which is a self-deception. Those who look realistically upon death will distinguish between the death of another (bodily death without any conclusions about the death of self) and the death of self (the extinction of the observing ego and the annihilation of all being). Existential, phenomenological philosophy and psychotherapy can combine to reveal and neutralize the fear of death which is basically neurotic. The manifestation of this neurosis is anxiety about death as the end of selfhood. The remedy is a vision of life and the world that extends beyond the death of a person. Mere personal concerns can be caught up in the totality of existence through affirmation of a transcendental ego. This is the intellectual love of God, Substance or Nature. The transcendental ego can be part of a religious solution to the fear of death through a mysticism that substitutes beatific vision for the anticipation of death.

1188 Lepp, Ignace. *Death and Its Mysteries*. Trans. by Bernard Murchland. New York: Macmillan Pub. Co., 1968.

A Roman Catholic priest and psychotherapist analyzes the human fear of death and the emotional disturbances associated with this fear. The meaning of death is related to its function in life through questions about the courage to face death and hope for a life beyond physical death. The life instinct is given primacy by the author over death instinct. But life and death must always be related to some greater purpose. The suicide of a resistance fighter under torture is not condemned.

1189 McCarthy, James B. *Death Anxiety: The Loss of Self*. New York: Gardner Press, 1980.

A psychoanalyst investigates attitudes about death as they unfold throughout life in physically healthy people. The author finds an inherent relationship between depression, death anxiety and adjustment problems in separation-individuation. The "fear of death" is investigated in interconnections between death anxiety and neurotic problems in living among children and adults. Death fears are investigated in religion, existential psychology and everyday solutions to fear of death.

1190 Means, M. H. "Fears of 1,000 College Women." *Journal of Abnormal and Social Psychology* 31 (1936): 291–311.

The intensity of fear stimuli for 1000 women indicated that cancer and bereavement were the most fear-provoking.

1191 Menninger, Karl. *Man Against Himself.* New York: Harcourt, Brace and World, 1938.

A noted psychiatrist surveys the psychic relationship between eros and thanatos as seen in fear of death, urges to suicide, symbolic suicides such as asceticism, martyrdom, the neurotic invalid, alcoholism and asocial behavior and psychosis. The study ranges from the possibilities of purposive accidents to sexual impotence.

1192 Meyer, Joachim E. *Death and Neurosis.* Trans. by Margarete Nunberg. New York: International Universities Press, 1975.

A German psychiatrist recognizes that the fear of death is a determining influence in the genesis of many neurosis, but the appearance of a neurosis in old age may be traced primarily to the realization of impending death. Fear of death is not a derivative of separation anxiety, castration fear, or guilt. It is a basic process of accepting mortality. And it does not exist in the unconscious. This is considered to be a departure from the teaching of Freud and is supported by clinical observations, sociological and psychological studies, references to philosophy and theology. The author recommends more emphasis upon the social context of dying and the development of rites of passage for the dying, especially in modern medicine. The references include many German works, English and American. See Becker (2194) and Lifton (1221).

1193 Neale, Robert E. *The Art of Dying.* New York: Harper and Row, 1973.

A professor of psychiatry and religion advocates an open awareness of the certainty of death without assuming knowledge of the time or mode of dying. A variety of exercises are recommended to increase this basic awareness and dispel fear of death and affirmation of life. Fear of death is considered by the author to be unhealthy because it arises from a belief that a person will lose control over life, be incomplete, a failure. We dread the thought of being taken away from those we love. Such fears are really based on neurotic fears in life, a sense of never finishing anything or failing in whatever is attempted. The fruit of courage to openly face unhealthy fears will be a sense of peace as an adventurer into a world of freedom beyond the confines of anxiety about worldly accomplishments. Life will become a time of wonder. The author's theories of death are based upon psychoanalytic assumptions of death fears as a form of neurosis. Classical Christian themes of judgment and eternal life are missing. From the viewpoint of philosophical theology he is criticized for reducing the dread of death to "the flawed products of individual psychic histories" (Johnston 1140, 57). See also Switzer (4016).

1194 Pollak, J. M. "Correlates of Death Anxiety: A Review of Empirical Studies." *Omega* 10 (1979): 97–121.

One hundred and seven references are included in this discussion of research studies on death anxiety.

1195 Rank, Otto. *The Trauma of Birth*. New York: Robert Brunner, 1957.

A psychotherapist who wrote extensively in the first part of the twentieth century presents an examination of separation anxiety that centered upon "birth trauma." Birth is considered by the author to be an overwhelming experience of shock and fear that has significance over the entire span of a person's life. Childhood awareness of anxiety and doubt are prompted by real or anticipated separation from loved ones.Hopefully, individuals learn to manage separations and incorporate the resultant anxiety into their existance. But these times of anxiety quicken an awareness of the primitive fear, "infantile anxiety" of being left alone, abandoned, yearning for comfort and security.

1196 Rochlin, G. *Griefs and Discontents: The Forces of Change*. Boston: Little, Brown and Co., 1965.

The author hypothesizes the dread of abandonment and the "loss complex" as prime motivators of human behavior. Whether the loss is of someone we love or of our self esteem, the results will often be despair. Religion and creativity are the forces that have evolved to repair the damage of this universal loss complex. The very process of identification with others derives from the frustrations and losses that are incurred during early childhood. With age comes a shift of experience from (1) loss followed by restitution to (2) loss followed by impoverishment.

1197 Templer, D. I. "Death-Anxiety as Related to Depression and Health of Retired Persons." *Journal of Gerontology*, 26 (1971): 521–522.

In a study of 75 late middle-age and elderly subjects the author found significant, positive relationships between those with a high fear of death and a high score on tests that measure depression and somatic concerns.

1198 Templer, D. I. and C. F. Ruff. "Death-Anxiety Scale Means, Standard Deviations and Embedding." *Psychological Reports* 29, 1 (1971): 173–174.

Templer's Death-Anxiety scale within a major mental health measure was administered to 3600 adults and adolescents. Those with higher scores on the Death-Anxiety scale were more psychiatrically disturbed than those with lower scores.

1199 Tillich, Paul. *The Courage to Be.* New Haven, Conn.: Yale University Press, 1952.

An influential existential theologian distinguishes three types of anxiety. The anxiety about fate and death was strongest at the end of ancient civilizations. Anxiety about guilt and condemnation peaked at the end of the Middle Ages. Anxiety about emptiness and meaninglessness is the central problem of the modern period. The existential answer to the modern problem is the courage to face life without any literal guarantees of a future in heaven or any of the other forms of theological or psychological security that were offered in the past. See also Heidegger (2019).

1200 Zilboorg, G. "Fear of Death." *Psychoanalytic Quarterly* 12 (1943): 465–75.

From his clinical experience and interest in anthropology, a psychiatrist argues that fear of death is constantly being repressed by psychic mechanisms that prevent the human organism from being overwhelmed. He also observes that the fear of death functions as a healthy instinct for self preservation. See also Eissler (3456).

1.321 COMMITTED AND CONSENSUAL RELIGION

1201 Alexander, Irving E. and Arthur M. Adlerstein. "Death and Religion." In *The Meaning of Death,* ed. by Herman Feifel, 271–283. New York: McGraw-Hill Book Co., 1959.

Two groups of undergraduate males, one religious and one non-religious completed objective tests, background questionnaire information and an interview on dominant life values. Both groups reveal similar patterns in most of the aspects of behavior concerning death. Non-religious subjects were less likely to have, recognize, or report feelings connected with death or burial. Religious subjects were "tender-minded." The religious subjects reported awareness of death before the age of six, whereas less than 30% of the non-religious had similar experiences. The religious subjects were much more likely to keep the problem of death a conscious matter.

1202 Allan, Russell O., and Bernard Spilka. "Committed and Consensual Religion: A Specification of Religion-Prejudice Relationships." *Journal for the Scientific Study of Religion* 6 (1967): 191–206.

Beginning with a sample of 497 subjects, a multiple criteria of religiosity was applied to attain an identified religious group of 210 subjects. Utilizing a factorially stable measure of prejudice, extreme religious prejudice and religious unprejudice groups were formed. Committed and consensual religious orientations were then hypothesized on the basis of five cognitive perspectives which were operationally derived from interviews. Strong correspondence was demonstrated between prejudice and "consensual" religion and an absence of prejudice and "committed" faith. The classifications sought to avoid a subtle emphasis of the earlier work by Allport (1203) in which extrinsic religion was associated with pathology. In the committed/consensual scales, those holding a committed religion evidenced a certainty about religion which was individually authentic, personalized and applied to daily activities and daily practices more than those in the consensual group. The consensual group expressed ideas reflecting a lack of personal worth or meaningfulness and did not consider the world a safe and dependable place in which to live. They verbally conformed to traditional values and ideals in a vague and selective way. In contrast those with a committed religiosity had a well-formed and clear sense of meaning in their religious formulations and this was consistent with their daily activities. They were open and flexible in choosing means to serve the ultimate ends of their faith.

1203 Allport, Gordon W., and M. J. Ross. "Personal Religious Orientation and Prejudice." *Journal of Personality and Social Psychology* 5 (1967): 432–443.

A professor of psychology at Harvard University and an associate developed a questionnaire that discriminated between those who viewed religion as social convenience and those who viewed religion as commitment to God, worship, sacrifice, and ethical standards above social convenience. Final scores showed that believers with an intrinsic religious faith were significantly less prejudiced than those with extrinsic religious belief. The extrinsic/intrinsic variables were used in studies of death by Minton and Spilka (1211). A third religious category was also identified, the indiscriminately pro-religious. These subjects responded positively to most items irregardless of the type of motivation that the scale item was to demonstrate. See also Allan and Spilka (1202).

1204 Berman, A. L. "Belief in Afterlife, Religion, Religiosity and Life-Threatening Experiences." *Omega* 5 (1974): 127–135.

Individuals between ages of 13 and 30 completed a structured questionnaire on the afterlife. 198 persons reported as least one life-threatening experience. These were matched with a control group selected from the original pool of subjects. Both religiously active and religiously inactive subjects responded with anxiety, panic or fear to life-threatening experiences. There was no significant correlation with belief in afterlife.

1205 Dee, Martin and L. S. Wrightsman. "The Relationship Between Religious Behavior and the Concern About Death." *Journal of Social Psychology* 65 (1965): 317–323.

A high degree of religious participation closely correlated with a low fear of death in a selected group of adult church members. Measures included an attitude scale (Likert-Tyson) and a sentence completion technique.

1206 Feifel, Herman. "Attitudes Towards Death in Some Normal and Mentally Ill Populations." In Herman Feifel, ed. *Meanings of Death*, 114–132. New York: McGraw-Hill Book Co., 1959.

See 7011.

1207 Feifel, Herman. "Religious Conviction and the Fear of Death Among the Healthy and the Terminally Ill." *Journal for the Scientific Study of Religion* 13 (1974): 353–360.

From interviews with religious and non-religious subjects, the author concluded the religious were more afraid of death. Religious subjects were defined as those who believe in a divine purpose in the operation of the universe, held a belief in a life after death and accepted the Bible as revealing God's truth. Religious persons not only worried about discontinuance of life upon earth but also fear of hell. Those who believed that they were ready for heaven did not appear to have a reduced fear of death (see also Feifel 7011). In this study of physically healthy persons and a group of terminally ill patients, the author found that religious subjects whether healthy or terminally ill, who were intrinsic in their religion, did not significantly differ from their non-religious counterparts in fear of death across levels of awareness. No multi-item psychometrically-constructed direct death measure was used by Feifel. Perhaps this accounts for different results from those of Spilka (1215).

1208 Feifel, Herman and A. B. Branscom. "Who's Afraid of Death?" *Journal of Abnormal Psychology* 81 (1973): 282–288.

The fear of death at conscious, latent and unconscious levels of awareness was tested in a group of physically ill, mentally ill and healthy subjects. From questions about conscious attitudes toward death, analysis of a phantasy exercise and administration of a word association and color-word test, the authors conclude that while religious persons consciously expressed a lower fear of death and used more positive imagery about death in the phantasy exercise than non-religious persons, they did not differ in latency times to death related words, only to indirect death measures.

1209 Kahoe, Robert D., and R. F. Dunn. "The Fear of Death and Religious Attitudes and Behavior." *Journal for the Scientific Study of*

Religion, 14 (1975): 379–382.

A study of 70 adult Protestant and Catholic church-goers. Death concern was negatively related to intrinsic religion and self-rated religious concern. See Feifel (7011).

1210 Lester, David. "Religious Behaviors and Attitudes Towards Death." In *Death and Presence: The Psychology of Death and the After-Life*, ed. by Andre Godin, 107–124. Brussels: Lumen Vitae Press, 1972.

From an extensive review of research studies on the relationship between religious behavior and attitudes toward death, the author finds little consistency in the results.

1211 Minton, B. and Bernard Spilka. "Perspectives on Death in Relation to Powerlessness and Form of Personal Religion." *Omega* 7 (1976): 261–267.

Through the use of death perspective scales, of Allan and Spilka (1202) and of Allport and Ross (1203), and a powerlessness scale, religiously active Protestants showed a correlation between a positive perception of death and committed religion. Intrinsic religious faith was not found to be associated with any death perspective, although those with extrinsic religion scored higher on eight negatively-perceived death scales.

1212 Nelson, L. D. and C. H. Cantrell. "Religiosity and Death Anxiety: A Multi-Dimensional Analysis." *Review of Religious Research* 21 (1980): 148–157.

From a state-wide probability sample of 1,279 respondents to a questionnaire curvilinearity was evidenced in the relationships between religiosity and all the dimensions of death anxiety: death avoidance, death fear, death denial, and reluctance to interact with the dying. Religious practice was shown to be a better predictor of death anxiety than religious belief. In a multiple regression analysis, religion was found to explain more of the various death fears and reluctance to interact with the dying than did the combination of income, education, age, occupational status, area reared and residence.

1213 Nelson, L. D. and C. C. Nelson. "A Factor Analytic Inquiry into the Multidimensionality of Death Anxiety." *Omega* 6 (1975): 171–177.

A group of one hundred thirty-five students were tested on the subject of death anxiety. A factor analysis identified death avoidance, death fear, death denial and reluctance to interact with the dying. Relationships between factored scores and unfactored index scores are discussed.

1214 Spilka, Bernard, Robert J. Pellingrini and Kathryn Dailey. "Religion, American Values and Death Perspectives." *Sociological Symposium* 1 (1968): 57–66.

The authors believe that the qualitative and quantitative aspects of religion have of considerable impact upon American cultural values. However, tests of 150 psychology students showed weak to moderate patterns of relationship between death perspectives and qualitative measures of religion. There generally was a low association of achievement-success/equalitarian responsibility measures and religious indices.

1215 Spilka, Bernard, *et al.* "Death and Personal Faith: A Psychometric Investigation." *Journal for the Scientific Study of Religion* 16 (1977): 169–178.

Over 300 young adults completed a set of questionnaires in which attitudes toward death were correlated with tests for "intrinsic-committed" and "extrinsic-consensual" expressions. Intrinsic-committed faith was positively associated with views of death as an afterlife of reward and as courage. It was negatively associated with loneliness-pain, indifference, unknown, forsaking dependence, and natural end. These latter views were more closely correlated with extrinsic-consensual faith.

1216 Templer, D. I. and E. Dotson. "Religious Correlates of Death Anxiety." *Psychological Reports* 26 (1970): 875–897.

College students completed Templer's death-anxiety scale, an 86 item religious questionnaire. Religious variables were not significantly associated with death-anxiety.

1217 Templer, D. I. "Death Anxiety in Religiously Very Involved Persons." *Psychological Reports* 31 (1972): 361–362.

This study differed in conclusions from an earlier study of Templer and Dotson (1216) on the same subject. When a group of highly religiously involved, adult retreat attenders (rather than the college students used in the earlier study) were questioned about their religious activities and views of death, those who had a strong certainty about their religious convictions revealed a lower fear of death than college students in the previous study. But since not all religious persons in the study had a low fear of death, the presence of religious belief and a low fear of death within an individual may be a function of personality characteristics yet to be discovered.

1218 Williams, Robert L. and Spurgeon Cole. "Religiosity, Generalized Anxiety and Apprehension Concerning Death." *The Journal of Social Psychology* 75 (1968): 111–117.

In an examination of psychoanalytic literature, the authors find contradictory findings and theories concerning the dimension of insecurity in persons who seem to be religious. The inconsistencies may be traced to varying definitions of religiosity, insecurity and especially to the fear of death. To seek more precision, students in an introductory psychology class were divided into those who considered themselves to be high, intermediate or low in religiousity. These were compared with scores on anxiety and on insecurity. The high religiousity subjects manifested the least anxiety on all dimensions of apprehension concerning death, the intermediate group yielded the highest scores on general anxiety, and the least religious groups showed the greatest generalized insecurity.

1.33 SURVIVAL IN A NUCLEAR AGE

1219 Brown, Norman O. *Life Against Death*. Middletown, Conn.: Wesleyan University Press, 1950.

In a discussion of the psychoanalytical meaning of history, the author contends that Freud's life and death instincts pointed toward an eventual unification that would overcome the duality that caused neuroses. See Freud (1181), Frankl (2155).

1220 Hardin, Garrett. *Promethean Ethics: Living with Death, Competition, Triage*. Seattle, Wash.: University of Washington Press, 1980.

A distinguished biologist believes that death need not be a personal tragedy, for death will always fulfill an essential role in human society. The social importance of death will become even greater in the foreseeable future.

1221 Lifton, Robert J. *The Broken Connection: On Death and the Continuity of Life*. New York: Simon and Schuster, 1979.

A psychiatrist expands and culminates two decades of pioneering research on the social psychology of death, violence, trauma, and radical dislocation with a comprehensive psychology around the thesis that death-threat and its psychological equivalents of separation, disintegration and stasis pervade human life in all of its individual and collective expressions. This threat exists in dialectical tension with the formative or symbolizing process of the imagination which continually seeks to transcend death through symbols of continuity, integration, and purposiveness. With this thesis the author hopes to reject earlier theories and customs in which the transcendence of death was regarded as illusory and compensatory efforts of fearful persons. The reader will bend his or her mind to the writing of this author with much profit. A humane and unifying presentation of ethical naturalism. For a summary of classical theories of unification in Christianity, see Pelikan (2235); in Eastern religions, see Holck (2381). See also Lifton (1157, 2224). Jungian respect for symbols in relation to death is demonstrated by Herzog (2212).

1222 Marris, Peter. *Loss and Change*. New York: Random House, 1974.

A sociologist considers loss in the context of personal and social change. The conservative impulse to maintain continuity and goals and relationships is described, along with the threats of death, the effects of urban development-redevelopment, the destruction of familiar environments. See also Marris (1277).

1223 Peterson, Jeannie and Don Hinrichsen, eds. *Nuclear War: The Aftermath*. New York: Pergamon Press, 1982.

The effects of nuclear war are assessed by experts who consider the medical consequences of radiation and the devastating effects upon the earth. Illustrated.

1224 Shneidman, Edwin S., ed. *Death and the College Student*. New York: Behavioral Publications, 1972.

Papers on death and related topics by college youth show a resonance with deeper issues and conflicts than the crises that are contained in any one generation of life. These are called "extra-temporal crisis situations"by the editor. Some young adults are far advanced into these crises whereas others are retarded in their development. The sampling was limited to young adults (mostly single) in a class at Harvard University.

1225 Simpson, Michael A. "Bibliography of Books on Nuclear Holocaust and Megadeath." In *Dying, Death and Grief: A Critical Bibliography*, by Michael A. Simpson, 217–225. Pittsburg, Pa.: University of Pittsburg Press, 1987.

1226 Vaux, Kenneth. *Will to Live/Will to Die*. Minneapolis, Minn.: Augsburg Publishing House, 1978.

A professor of ethics and medicine provides a philosophical and ethical reflection upon the personal decisions and public policies that must be faced in society and medical care of the dying. The influence of Christianity upon Western culture has provided both a celebration of life, which abhors death and a disdain of life which welcomes death.

1.34 GUILT AND SIN

1227 Goffman, Erving. *Stigma: Notes on the Management of Spoiled Identity*. Englewood Cliffs, N. J.: Prentice-Hall, 1963.

In a review of clinical studies of individuals who are disqualified by society from full social acceptance the author deals with the way an individual controls information about himself or herself, aligns with a group and develops ego identity. Problems of deviation are also considered. A stigma is considered as physical, moral and/or tribal.

1228 Grotstein, James S. "Forgery of the Soul: Psychogenesis of Evil." In *Evil: Self and Culture*, ed. by Marie Colman Nelson and Michael Eigan, 203–226. Vol. 4, Self-In-Process Series. New York: Human Sciences Press, 1984.

A psychoanalyst warns that the "zeal" with which he and other followers of Freud were seeking to relieve unconscious anxiety and guilt had led to a desecration of the "gossamer membrane of innocence" that represents the pristine estate of the child as moral ambiguity between evil and innocence.

1229 Huizinga, Johan. *The Waning of the Middle Ages*. New York: St. Martin's Press, 1967.

See 1091.

1230 Kasper, August M. "The Doctor and Death." In *The Meaning of Death*, ed. by Herman Feifel, 259–270. New York: McGraw-Hill Book Co., 1979.

A physician traces the change from an open recognition of death in the nineteenth century to a time of great optimism in the early twentieth century when science and reason threw out sin and with it the wages of sin, death. The stress upon "scientific objectivity" led many physicians to assume a god-like stature before patients. But patients who were seriously ill had a sense of the physician's emotions and were especially devasted by the appearance of indifference which was usually a professional defence. Doctors became reluctant to make and reveal serious diagnoses.

1231 Huntsberry, W. E. *The Big Hang-up*. New York: Lothrop, 1970.

This is the fictional account of the grief and guilt felt by teenagers who feel responsible for the car crash that kills one of their friends.

1232 Miller-McLemore, Bonnie. *Death, Sin and the Moral Life*. Atlanta, Ga.: Scholars Press, 1988.

See 2142.

1233 Miller-McLemore, Bonnie. "Doing Wrong, Getting Sick, Dying." *Christian Century* February 24, 1988, 186–190.

If dying persons believe strongly that they have caused their fate, feelings of guilt may be intensified with awareness of approaching death. Persons may change churches (rather than attitudes) in an effort to cope with this anxiety. Naturalistic explanations of dying, which allow physicians to gain compliance from patients may fail with guilt-ridden persons and with others who blame the patient for the illness. Because of this anxiety, the traditional rituals of the church (exhortation, sorrow, pardon, absolution) are replaced by morally neutral descriptions of death as stages of denial, anger, bargaining, depression and acceptance. See also Miller-McLemore (2142).

1234 Murphy, Gardner. "Discussion." In *The Meaning of Death*, ed. by Herman Feifel, 317–340. New York: McGraw-Hill Book Co., 1959.

In reviewing previous chapters in *The Meaning of Death* (which was part of a symposium on the psychology of death and dying at the American Psychological Association Convention, 1956) the Director of Research for the Menninger Foundation delineates seven systems of attitudes toward death. He found that a fear of punishment, either temporary or permanent, underlay much of the material in the other chapters and should be given more extensive study. See also Pagels (1081), Slater (1115), Stannard (1117).

1235 Tillich, Paul. *The Courage to Be*. New Haven, Conn.: Yale University Press, 1952.

See 1199.

1.4   ANTHROPOLOGY/COMPARATIVE RELIGION

1236 Becker, Howard and D. K. Bruner. "Attitudes Toward Death and the Dead, and Some Possible Causes of Ghost Fear." *Mental Hygiene* 15 (1931): 828–837.

See 6080.

1237 Bendann, Effie. *Death Customs: An Analytic Study of Burial Rites*. 1930. Reprint. New York: Gordon Press, 1974.

Detailed and well-documented survey of mortuary practices of preliterate groups of Australia, Melanesia, India, and Northeast Siberia. In two parts: the first analyzes the similarities of the groups' customs; the second describes the origin of death, causes of death, disposal of the dead, spirits, attitudes toward the corpse, mourning, grave huts, purification feasts after death, taboos, the role of women, the destruction of property and cults of the dead. The author finds little relation between the natural condition of sorrow at a death and the elaborate rituals that follow. Notes and bibliography.

1238 Brandon, S. G. F. "The Personification of Death In Some Ancient Religions." In *Bulletin of the John Rylands Library* 43 (1960–1961): 317–335.

A professor of comparative religion considers the burial of the dead to be an essential sign of human activity. Humans can reflect about death. Some of these reflections are briefly considered in ancient Egypt, Mesopotamia, Israel, Greece, early Christianity. The author concludes that death was envisaged as the assault or the snatching away from life of a person by some supernatural being. Scholarly notes.

1239 Durkheim, Emile. *The Elementary Forms of the Religious Life.* 1912. Reprint. Trans. by Joseph Ward Swain. Glencoe, Ill.: Free Press, 1947.

A French sociologist attacks the theories of Spencer (1255) and Tylor (1256) that ancestor worship is the earliest religion. He asserted that ancestor cults are not greatly developed except in advanced societies like those of China, Egypt, Greek or Latin cities. He disregarded evidence available in 1912 for a wider distribution of ancestor worship. Durkheim preferred to believe that religious institutions were ultimately founded upon grieving experiences. He insists upon an analysis of interrelationships rather than upon the elaboration of highly speculative evolutionary schema, which had become popular in the last half of the nineteenth century. For example, he believed that an individual's reaction of grief was developed and intensified by participation in ritual wailing.

1240 Eisenberg, Jule. "Freud, the Death Wish and the Problem of Evil." In *Evil: Self and Culture*, ed. by Marie Colman Nelson and Michael Eigan, 227–238. Vol. 4. Self-In-Process Series. New York: Human Sciences Press, 1984.

In *Totem and Taboo* Freud (1246) began with the assumption that the most ancient example of evil intent is a universal primitive belief that the dead are bent on doing harm to the living. Eisenberg maintains that this assumption was rooted in Freud's reading of Frazer's *The Golden Bough* (1244), even though the final summary of that theory includes "the scapegoat" which did not appear in Frazer's work until a 1913 volume in a 13 volume series, just after the publication in German of *Totem and Taboo* by Freud. Neither Frazer nor Freud considered the possibility that primitives were realistic in their belief that evil thoughts, such as death wishes, might sometimes lead to dire effects in the real world. For examples of "dire effects," see Cannon (3003).

1241 Finucane. *Appearances of the Dead: The Cultural History of Ghosts.* London: Junction Press, 1982.

The history of reports of ghosts includes explanations of their characteristics, function and behavior as effected by religious, science and public opinions about death.

1242 Frazer, James G. *Belief in Immortality and the Worship of the Dead.* 3 Vols. New York: Macmillan Pub. Co., 1913, 1922, 1924.

A cultural anthropologist presents a vast array of studies on the connection between worship of the dead and belief in immortality in the tribes of New Guinea, Melanesia, Polynesia and Micronesia. A classic in "primitive religion" studies, which was considered at the time of his Gifford Lectures to be a form of historical-natural theology.

1243 Frazer, James G. *The Fear of The Dead in Primitive Religion*, 3 vols. London: Macmillan Pub. Co., 1933, 1934, 1936. Reprint. New York: Arno Press, 1976.

From studies of primitive religion throughout the world, as recorded by European and English observers of the late 19th century and early 20th century, a Cambridge (England) scholar considers the "enigma of death" both in terms of human beings and of every other living thing. The author concludes that a belief in the survival of the human spirit after death has been general in both primitive and modern cultures. Primitives considered a deceased relative to be more hostile to his descendents after death than during life. Widespread precautions were taken to prevent the return of the dead to this world and actions were adapted to protect the survivors from the hostility of the departed if they should succeed in their efforts to come back. The greatest danger was felt to lie with those of the bereaved who have been closest to the dead person, especially a dead father.

1244 Frazer, James G. *The Golden Bough: A Study in Magic and Religion.* 13 Vols. 3rd ed. New York: Macmillan Pub. Co., 1935.

Influenced by W. Robertson Smith, a Scottish classicist and anthropologist, pursues through thirteen volumes (begun as two volumes in 1890) the rites of kingship and magic in Greek and other ancient civilizations. He shows particular interest in the decreed death of kings after failure of their powers before the people. Many illustrations are offered from nineteenth-century European reports of practices "primitive" societies. The study was influential in linking primitive concepts and modes of thought to social institutions and customs, and may also have influenced Freud (1246), according to Eisenberg (1240).

1245 Frazer, James G. *The New Golden Bough.* Abridged ed. New York: Criterion Books, 1959.

Because the reports on primitive societies in Frazer's 1935 study (1244) were outmoded and superceded by later studies of anthropologists, an abridgment eliminates obsolete secondary reports of primitive societies and provides a foreward to note the strengths and weaknesses of the original work.

1246 Freud, Sigmund. *Totem and Taboo.* In *The Standard Edition of the Complete Psychological Works of Sigmund Freud.* Trans. by James Strachey, Vol. 13, 1–162. London: Hogarth Press, 1955.

From clinical practice and the reading of anthropologists, the father of psychoanalysis concludes that the "murdering horde" acts out a group Oedipus complex through ritual sacrifices. The sacrifice was originally of the father so that the brothers could possess the wives of the father. The totem animal stands for the father who must now be propitiated through forms of worship. One of these is the Christian eucharist which, to Freud, frees the worshipping members from their collective guilt by subservience to the Father. The symbolic sacrifice of Christ unconsciously reunites the totem—the slaying God-Father—with the community of brothers. The anthropological theories behind Freud's hypotheses were those that sought to solve the fear of death in primitive religion by associating rituals of burial and bereavement with submission to a dead father (Frazer 1243, 1244; Smith 1253). See also Eisenberg (1240).

1247 Gennep, Arnold van. *Rites of Passage.* Trans. by Monika B. Vizedon and Gabrielle L. Caffee. Chicago: University of Chicago Press, 1960.

The author criticizes the "folkloriste" of Frazer (1243, 1244) who isolated single ritual acts from their contents. The seasonal observance of magico-religious practices actually form part of a wider constellation of social acts, "rites de passage." Through these rites an individual is instructed and supported in the various stages of growth from pubescence to death. Funeral ceremonies are the final and most dramatic rite of passage by which there is a public separation from the dead and the beginning of attention to the comfort of the ghost and the bereaved. The ceremonies surrounding any territorial passage may be classified into successive stages: separation rituals, transition rituals, entering rituals or reincorporation (as a return of mourners to normal or new duties.)

1248 Goody, Jack. "Death and the Interpretation of Culture: A Bibliographic Overview." In *Death In America*, ed. by David E. Stannard, 1–8. Philadelphia: University of Pennsylvania Press, 1975.

From studies of primitive cultures, the author notes the importance of religion in both the concept of death and the organization of mourning, burials and other funerary rituals.

1249 Humphreys, S. C. and Helen King, eds. *Mortality and Immortality: The Anthropology and Archaeology of Death*. New York: Academic Press, 1982.

Anthropologists provide general reviews of death and specific studies of varying cultures, mainly in Southeast Asia and Melanesia.

1250 Malinowski, Vronislaw. *Magic, Science and Religion*. 1925. Reprint New York: Doubleday and Co., 1954.

On the basis of his investigations of primitive peoples, the author considers death to be the most upsetting and disorganizing of human calculations and probably the main source of religious belief. Primitive persons had an instinctive fear of the corpse in which there is an intermingling of the memory of the dead person and fear of the actual corpse. Funeral customs and beliefs such as life after death counteract fear and re-establish group morale.

1251 Platt, Larry A. *Death and Dying*. Vol. II: *The Anthropology of Bereavment—A Research Bibliography*. With Richard Persico. Statesboro, Ga.: Georgia Southern College: The Social Gerontology Program, 1986.

See 8037.

1252 Reynolds, Frank E. and Earle H. Waugh, eds. *Religious Encounters With Death: Insights From the History and Anthropology of Religions*. University Park, Pa.: Pennsylvania State University Press, 1977.

This collection of essays reflects awareness among historians of religion and anthropologists of the wealth of original historical and ethnographic materials concerning death. Eleven of the fifteen essays are based on papers presented in the American Academy of Religion 1973. Covers major religious perspectives including rituals and myths on death.

1253 Smith, W. Robertson. *The Religion of the Semites*. 1889. Reprint. 3rd rev. ed. New York: Meridian Books, 1956.

Building upon previous investigations by Frazer (1244) and others, the author emphasizes the place of ritual of ritual sacrifice in Hebrew and other Semitic religions. There is much discussion of the "totem animal," a phrase that reappears in early psychoanalytic writings (Freud 1246).

1254 Somersan, Semra. "Death Symbolism: A Cross-Cultural Study." Columbus, Ohio: Ph. D. Dissertation, Ohio State University, 1981.

Ethnographic data from a pre-industrial world-wide sample of 60 societies is collected and analyzed for patterns of belief pertaining to death. Bibliography for each society and general references.

1255 Spencer, Herbert. *The Principles of Sociology.* 1875. 3d rev. ed. New York: Appleton, 1896.

A founder of sociology depends upon Tylor's *Primitive Culture* (1256) for an evolutionary sequences of belief from worship of ancestors into the worship of deities and the growth of funeral rites into the worship of the dead and eventually into religious worship. These theories of ancestor worship had an appeal to psychoanalytic writers who decided that feelings developed for the parents are projected onto supernatural beings. See Freud (1246).

1256 Tylor, Edward B. *Primitive Culture.* 1871. 6th ed. New York: G. P. Putnam and Sons, 1920.

English and European studies of primitive peoples are organized around two foci: the antiquity of ancestor worship and the friendliness or hostility of the ancestors. The author concludes that dead ancestors were passed into the status of deities who would go on protecting the family and harming enemies. Death was the beginning of time to provide sacrifices and offerings to the ancestors who were now out of the body but very much in the soul of the primitive world. The inhabitation of the primitive world by these ancestor-spirits was "animism." The author's belief that the cult of the clan gave rise to later "higher religious institutions" was attacked by Durkheim (1239).

1.5 CULTURAL ANTHROPOLOGY/SOCIOLOGICAL ANALYSIS
See also FUNERALS AND CUSTOMS OF MOURNING (4.6)

1257 Anderson, B. G. "Bereavement as a Subject of Cross-Cultural Inquiry: an American Sample." *Anthropological Quarterly* (1965): 181–200.

1258 Bloch, Maurice and Jonathan Parry, eds. *Death and the Regeneration of Life.* Cambridge: Cambridge University Press, 1983.

Anthropologists study perspectives on death, specifically exploring the interplay of the themes of rebirth and fertility in funeral rituals in different societies—China, India, Africa, New Guinea, and Latin America.

1259 Cartwright, Ann, Lisbeth Hockey, and John L. Anderson. *Life Before Death.* London: Routledge and Kegan Paul, 1973.

A sociologist relates studies of people in the year before death to general questions of terminal illness such as types of illness, available therapies and the way in which needs are met. The part played by hospitals, health services, family, friends, and neighbors is also considered. A reliable, straight-forward investigation.

1260 Charmaz, Kathy. *The Social Reality of Death: Death in Contemporary America.* Reading, Mass.: Addison-Wesley Pub. Co., 1980.

Through a qualitative description of the ways in which the underlying structure of social life is created and maintained as people with diverse interests interact as they face and handle death, the author addresses direct experience of individuals with death and dying: vignettes, cases, statements, literature, unpublished papers, related studies. The basic issue in dying is like that of many ordinary experiences in life: making sense out of one's life and one's world. Bibliography for each chapter.

1261 Eisenbruch, M. "Cross-Cultural Aspects of Bereavement. II: Ethnic and Cultural Variations in the Development of Bereavement Practices." *Culture, Medicine and Psychiatry* 8 (1984): 315–347.

Bereavement practices vary both across cultures and over the course of the history of Western culture. The nature and extent of such variation within ethnic groups in North America are examined, based on a review of relevant literature on Blacks, Chinese, Southeast Asian refugees, Haitians, Italians, Greeks and Hispanics. The nature of widowhood merits particular attention. The impact of Western societies on bereavement practices among the Gusii of East Africa and the Yolngu of Australia is also examined. Several considerations of interest to medical practitioners are noted. See also (6067).

1262 Eliade, Mircea. *Rites and Symbols of Initiation: The Mysteries of Death and Rebirth.* New York: Harper and Row, 1958.

1263 Fabian, J. "How Others Die—Reflection on the Anthropology of Death." In *Death in the American Experience*, ed. by Arien Mack, 177–201. New York: Schocken Books, 1973.

The author describes the use to which anthropological findings have been put in other contexts, notably in philosophical, psychological and sociological approaches to death in modern society.

1264 Farberow, Norman L. ed. *Suicide in Different Cultures.* Baltimore: University Park Press, 1975.

See 3532.

1265 Garrity, Thomas F. and James Wiss. "Death, Funeral and Bereavement Practices in Appalachian and non-Appalachian Kentucky." In

Death and Dying: Views From Many Cultures, ed. by Richard A. Kalish, 99–118. Farmingdale, N.Y.: Baywood Publishing Co., 1980.

An historical survey and a questionnaire study of comtemporary death practices in Kentucky suggest a growing similarity between Appalachian and non-Appalachian regions. There is striking evidence that death-denial, avoidance and invisibility are not the norm in Kentucky. The authors' suggest that death-denying tendencies in American society have been overstated.

1266 Godin, Andre, ed. *Death and Presence: The Psychology of Death and the After-Life.* Brussels: Lumen Vitae, 1972.

Continental and English professors of sociology and psychology present research studies on religious behavior and attitudes toward death. Primary sociological field studies. For annotation of specific articles see Godin (7013); Delooz (2201); Maitre and Martins (7016); Lester (1210).

1267 Habenstein, Robert W., and William M. Lamers. *Funeral Customs the World Over.* Milwaukee, Wis.: Bulfin Printers, 1960.

Richly illustrated and detailed description of funeral and burial practices of many nations and cultures, primitive, folk, urban and rural. The total process in each culture is described, the meaning of death, immediate care of the body, funeralization, mourning, burial, memorialization, and post-funeral rites and practices. The basic culture of a people is reflected in its funeral practices according to Habenstein, a sociologist, and Lamers, an historian-educator. The last chapter draws universal conclusions on death, care of the dead and readjustment of those left behind: funerals and burial rites satisfy basic needs of all people to see meaning in death and to lessen its horror.

1268 Jackson, Maurice. "The Black Experience With Death" In *Death and Dying: Views From Many Cultures,* ed. by Richard A. Kalish, 92-98. Farmingdale, N.Y.: Baywood Publishing Co., 1980.

From spirituals, poetry and contemporary black literature, the author concludes that the norm governing experience of death is more secular than sacred. It presents the practicality that is a value-orientation among many activities of black people and is associated with "immediate gratification."

1269 Kalish, Richard A., and David K. Reynolds. *Death and Ethnicity: A Psychocultural Study.* Los Angeles: University of Southern California Press, 1976.

Attitudes toward death are compared among contemporary Americans, Black, Japanese, Mexican, Anglo-American. The planning and execution of the community interview survey is discussed in irenic style.

1270 Kalish, Richard A., ed. *Death and Dying: Views From Many Cultures. Perspectives on Death and Dying.* Vol. 1. Farmingdale, N.Y.: Baywood Publishing Co., 1980.

Anthropologists and sociologists present their studies on death in isolated communities that still adhere to modifications of old values. North America studies have an emphasis upon ethnic groups. Articles on war and disaster are included. Several historical studies.

1271 Kearl, Michael C. *Endings: A Sociology of Death and Dying.* New York: Oxford University Press, 1989.

In a very readable text that includes brief vignettes, a few charts and pictures, the author organizes many aspects of death under the theme of death as a mirror of life. The facets of the "mirror" include cross-cultural and historical perspectives; impact of death on society; social stratification; religion; secular perspectives, philosopy, social science and biology; work, power and the political order; military experience; the mass media, arts, popular culture; medical systems, life-span perspectives, grief, bereavement and widowhood; existential concerns in death, out of the body experiences and glimpses of the hereafter. The author concludes that modern society has a continuing need for ritual as a means of coping with the feeling states of death. They should provide an individual with some sense of closure and completeness when the end of death is near. The survivors should have been taught how to prepare a loved one for "good" death. Judicious bibliographies at the end of each chapter. Thorough index.

1272 Kirwen, Michael C. *African Widows.* Maryknoll, N. Y.: Orbis Books, 1979.

See 4238.

1273 Krupp, George R. "The Bereavement Reaction: A Special Case of Separation Anxiety-Sociocultural Considerations." *Psychoanalytic Study of Society* 2 (1962): 42–74.

This article centers on adult bereavement in contemporary America, its symptomatology, pathology, and significance. The individual's reaction is conditioned by early infantile neurosis and by biological adaptive mechanisms as well as by the cultural milieu. The intimate nuclear family, the long dependence of children, emphasis on youth and vitality, and the urbanization characteristic of American culture are factors which may account for extreme bereavement crisis.

1274 Krupp, George R., and Bernard Kligfeld. "Bereavement Reaction: A Cross-cultural Evaluation." *Journal of Religion and Health* 1 (1962): 222–246.

From a survey of reactions to the loss of loved one in different regions of the world and different times, the authors conclude that in almost all cases there is present an attempt to regain the lost loved object, and/or a belief in afterlife where one can rejoin the loved one. Bereavement pathology is less common in pre-literate than in civilized societies.

1275 Lunceford, Ron, and Judy Lunceford. *Attitudes on Death and Dying: a Cross-Cultural View.* Los Alamitos, Calif.: Hwong Publising Co., 1976.

A sociological research study on the attitudes of persons with different ethnic, racial and religious backgrounds towards death and dying: considers the implications of religion, age, the change in years, the male and the female, the views of a client-centered psychologist, Carl Rogers.

1276 Mack, A., ed. *Death in American Experience.* New York: Schocken Books, 1973.

Sociologists and anthropologists present aspects of the cultural dimensions of death: the Judaeo-Christian tradition, existential philosophy, and medical technology in relation to attitudes and practices regarding death.

1277 Marris, Peter. *Loss and Change.* New York: Random House, 1974.

An anthropologist applies symbolic interaction analysis to sudden and radical disruption of familiar patterns of relationships such as slum clearance. In contrast to the devastations of such sudden change, he offers the example of tribal associations in Nigeria, where conservatism is a central part of any innovation. In this process, the mourning and projection of ambivalence found in sudden and radical change can be mitigated. Symbolic interaction theory teaches the importance of stable definitions of a situation and the way in which grief is signal of instability. Definitions of the self are lost when a loved one dies and there are changes in the interactions that were related to the self as defined by that other person. Daily contacts provide a sense of self and situation that are crucial in making a person aware of loss in relation to others and in providing help or harm in the restoration of stable definitions of the self. Redefinitions of the self are facilitated or inhibited by the organization of memory and the way in which a person recalls and recognizes evidence of loss. See also Marris (1222).

1278 Mathison, Jean. "A Cross-Cultural View of Widowhood." *Omega* 1, 2 (1970): 201–218.

Examines widowhood in terms of bereavement, role loss and remarriage from the perspective of various cultural contexts, that is, India, China, New Guinea, Trobriand Islands and the United States.

1279 Parsons, Talcott. "Death in American Society—A Brief Working Paper." *The American Behavioral Scientist* 6 (1963): 61–65.

A noted sociologist examines attitudes toward death in American society as indicators of influential, cultural rootage.

1280 Rosenblatt, Paul C., R. Patricia Walsh, and Douglas A. Jackson. *Grief and Mourning in Cross-Cultural Perspective.* Washington, D.C.: HRAF Press, 1976.

Seventy-eight societies are rated on eighty-seven variables concerning mourning practices. The relation of grief to ritual was seen, for example in crying after a loss. This was the most frequent response and was seen in all but the Balinese culture in which it seemed that those who felt a loss were fearful that they would cry if they did not force the opposite expression, such as laughing. The authors related this reaction to religious beliefs which encouraged calmness. In 32 societies the frequency of crying was similar for males and females. In 28 societies, adult females had a greater crying frequency than men.

1281 Stephenson, Peter H., ed. "Dying in Cross-Cultural Perspective." *Omega* 14 (1984): 101–199.

Reviews research and presents case studies discussing aspects of suicide, death, and grief among the people of New Guinea, Vanuatu (a Canadian Hutterite colony), rural Tennessee, Ireland and among American Indians. Rituals, myths, and legends are described in the eight articles of this special issue of *Omega.*

1282 Zborowski, M. *People in Pain.* San Francisco, Calif.: Jossey-Bass, 1969.

See 3236.

1.51 VARIABLES IN VARIOUS CULTURES

1283 Ablon, J. "Bereavement in a Samoan Community." *British Journal of Medical Psychology* 44 (1971): 327–329.

Five years after a disasterous fire, an anthropologist interviewed Samoans who had lost a loved one in that sudden catastrophe. It appeared that they had recovered rapidly and comparatively painlessly from the loss, at least in comparison with Lindeman's reports of survivors from the Coconut Grove fire in the U. S. (Lindemann 4044). When asked about the reactions reported in Lindemann, the Samoans told the anthropologist that they "do not have these things" and that there was no widespread depression among bereaved persons. This may be due to the importance of reciprocity in their culture.

1284 Aguilar, I. and V. Wood. "Therapy through a Death Ritual." *Social Work* 21 (1976): 49–54.

See 4374.

1285 Ahern, Emily. *The Cult of the Dead in a Chinese Village*. Stanford, Calif.: Stanford University Press, 1973.

As a participant-observer the author analyzes the care and management of the dead in Chi'inan, a four-lineage northern Tawainese village. The basis for their ancestor worship is a belief in the reciprocal obligations between the dead and the living. Shrines contain wooden tablets inscribed with the names of the dead who are honored on a regular basis.

1286 Branson, Helen K. "Burial Customs Modified by Cultural Background in Hawaii." *Mortuary Management* 58, 1 (1971): 20–25.

Members of the Family Services Division of the Hawaii Memorial Park discuss Hawaiian funeral customs, the present trend toward cremation, cultural reasons for the practice of cremation and historical background for Hawaiian burial practices.

1287 Buruma, Ian. *A Japanese Mirror: Heroes and Villians of Japanese Culture*. London: Jonathan Cape, 1984.

Japanese films, plays, books and comics, music and customs are explored to reveal the violent and morbid aspects of a collective imagination. Ambivalence toward women is described.

1288 Carstairs, G. M. "Attitudes to Death and Suicide in an Indian Cultural Setting." *International Journal of Social Psychiatry* 1 (1955): 33–41.

Discusses attitudes toward life and suicide in a village of Northwestern India. "For the villagers, death is . . . but one incident in a long series of existences."

1289 Counts, Dorothy Ayers and David R. Counts. "The Cultural Construction of Aging and Dying in a Melanesian Community." *International Journal of Aging and Human Development* 20, 3 (1985): 229–240.

Considers whether modern technology has introduced profound changes into processes of aging and dying. Anthropological literature and author research in New Guinea suggest that aging and dying are cultural constructs, as likely to be complex phenomena in simple societies as in modern ones.

1290 Covarrubias, Miguel. *Island of Bali*. New York: Alfred A. Knopf, 1937.

Chapter 11, "Death and Cremation," has references on Balinese funeral customs.

1291 Craven, M. *I Heard the Owl Call My Name*. New York: Doubleday, 1973.

When a young priest becomes terminally ill, his bishop does not tell him of the physician's diagnosis and sends him to a remote Indian village on the coast of British Columbia. The "wise woman" of the Indian tribe understands that he is dying and the priest finally realizes that he has "heard the owl call his name."

1292 Danforth, Loring M. *The Death Rituals of Rural Greece*. Princeton, N.J.: Princeton University Press, 1982.

See 4364.

1293 De Vos, George and Hiroshi Wagatsuma. "Psycho-Cultural Significance of Concern over Death and Illness among Rural Japanese." *International Journal of Social Psychiatry* 5 (Summer 1959): 5–19.

Illness is interpreted among rural Japanese as a punishment of the self for unacceptable behavior. Or the illness may be an unacceptable hostility towards others which cannot be expressed.

1294 Douglass, William A. *Death in Murelaga: Funerary Ritual in a Spanish Basque Village*. Seattle, Wash.: University of Washington Press, 1969.

Memorials of the dead may be some object associated with the deceased or a sculpture in a prominent place or a photograph. Among the Basque the memory of specific individuals is enshrined in dining room furnished with the household's finest furniture and reserved for banquets. Photographs of present and former household members cover the walls.

1295 Ebersole, Gary L. *Ritual Poetry and the Politics of Death in Early Japan*. Princeton, N.J.: Princeton University Press, 1989.

The practice of double-burial (of the body immediately after death and of the skeletal remains at a later date) is investigated and explained from Japanese texts in mythology, history and poetry of the sixth and seventh century.

1296 Erskine, William H. *Japanese Customs*. Tokyo: Kyo Bun Kwan, 1925.

Description of traditional death customs of urban Japanese are found in Chapters 7, 8, 9, 10.

1297 Goody, Jack. *Death, Property and the Ancestors.* Stanford, Calif.: Stanford University Press, 1962.

A sociologist relates previous studies of primitive religion to his own study of the mortuary customs of the Lodaga of West Africa. The investigation reveals complex relationships between kinships and the ceremonial and financial aspects of burial and mourning.

1298 Green, Judith S. *Laughing Souls: The Days of the Dead in Oaxaca Mexico.* San Diego, Calif.: San Diego Museum, 1969.

The warm family celebrations that surround an anniversary of the dead are described for children and adults in a North American culture.

1299 Headley, Lea A., ed. *Suicide in Asia and the Near East.* Berkeley, Calif.: University of California Press, 1984.

See 3544.

1300 Howard, A. and R. A. Scott. "Cultural Values and Attitudes Towards Death." *Journal of Existentialism* 6 (1965–1966): 161–174.

Discusses the various cultural values that affects American attitudes toward death. American patterns are contrasted with those of Polynesians.

1301 Huber, P. B. "Death and Society Among the Anggor of New Guinea." *Omega* 3 (1973): 233–243.

Deals with the relationship between Anggor representations of the natural phenomenon of death and representations of the autonomous village.

1302 Hsu, Francis L. K. *Under the Ancestors' Shadow: Chinese Culture and Personality.* New York: Columbia University Press, 1948.

In the context of a small town in Southwest China, details, symbols and behavior are explained, including those relating to death and ancestor worship. The culture and personality of the people is put forth in Western ideas.

1303 Kalish, Richard A. and David K. Reynolds. *Death and Ethnicity: A Psychocultural Study.* Los Angeles: University of Southern California Press, 1976.

See 1269.

1304 Keesing, Roger M. *Kwaio Religion: The Living and the Dead in a Solomon Island Society.* New York: Columbia University Press, 1984.

An anthropological study of a community in which one's peer group includes the living and the dead, and where conversation with the spirits and signs of their active presence are routine.

1305 Kelly, Patricia F. "Death in Mexican Folk Literature." In *Death in America*, ed. by David E. Stannard, 42–111. Philadelphia: University of Pennsylvania Press, 1975.

Graves of the Middle Pre-Classical period (1300–800 B. C.) contain finely polished jewelery, side by side by with other graves characterized by great simplicity. In the Classic period (200 B. C.–800 A. D.) Maya and Aztec burial structures showed a concern with death as an important component of the universe organized around war as a supreme activity of men. In the modern period, attitudes toward death are typified by celebrations at All-Soul's, the Day of the Dead. Funerary rituals may be somber, but death is often regarded with humor by the people.

1306 Kirwen, Michael C. *African Widows*. Maryknoll, N.Y.: Orbis Books, 1979.

See 4238.

1307 Lewis, Oscar. *A Death in the Sánchez Family*. New York: Random House, 1969.

See 4182.

1308 Lifton, Robert J., Suichi Kato, and Michael R. Reich. *Six Lives: Six Deaths*. New Haven, Conn.: Yale University Press, 1978.

Modern Japanese attitudes toward death are examined throught the stories of six Japanese intellectuals who describe their feelings about dying and death itself.

1309 Mandelbaum, David G. "Social Uses of Funeral Rites." In *Meanings of Death*, ed. by Herman Feifel, 189–217. New York: McGraw-Hill Book Co., 1959.

See 4396.

1310 Mayes, Christopher L. and Richard A. Kalish. "Cultures in Transition: the Case of the Hmong." Paper presented at the 31st Annual Meeting of the Western Gerontological Society, Denver 1985.

This article reviews the death-related experiences and concerns of Hmong refugees from Laos. Attention is given to describing traditional funerary and burial practices of the Hmong and the barriers to maintaining these practices in the United States. To understand the losses suffered by the Hmong, parallels are drawn between their experiences and those of

Holocaust victims. Due to their immense losses, many older Hmong are experiencing severe mental health problems.

1311 Metcalf, Peter. *A Borneo Journey into Death: Berawan Eschatology from its Rituals.* Philadelphia: University of Pennsylvania Press, 1982.

A study of death rituals and beliefs among the (now ex-) headhunters of central Borneo. A contribution to transcultural thanatology, anthropology and eschatology.

1312 Miller, S. I. and L. Schonfield. "Grief in the Navaho: Psychodynamics and Culture." *International Journal of Social Psychiatry* 19 (1973): 187–191.

In contrast to the yearning and pining for the deceased that may not subside for a year or more in Western cultures, the Navaho express grief for a period of four days after a death. An excessive show of emotion during this time is judged to be inappropriate. After four days, the bereaved are expected to return to their normal activities and give up grief or any discussion of their loss. This is supported by a fear of the power of the spirit of the dead person who would harm a living being who continued to grieve. The authors believe that these prohibitions may lead to depression as a sign of pathological grief reactions.

1313 Moore, Joan. "The Death Culture of Mexico and Mexican-Americans." In *Death and Dying: Views From Many Cultures,* ed. by Richard A. Kalish. Farmingdale, N.Y.: Baywood Publishing Co., 1980.

The culture of Mexico is characterized by an interest in death and by a pervasive anxiety about human capacity to dominate and control environment. Yet, there is a neglect of death in literature on Mexican-Americans. In the United States, Mexican-Americans commonly retain the conservatism of Mexican death rituals, which include the wake, funeral mass, burial, period of mourning and visitation of the grave. All members of the bereaved family are included along with the community. The author includes a research project which reports the relationships and aspects of personality, culture and orientation toward death. Among the factors examined are: role, age, sex, education and religiousness, and ethnicity (Black Americans, Japanese Americans, Mexican Americans). Statistics presented.

1314 Moser, Michael J. "Death in Chinese: A Two-Dimensional Analysis," *Journal of Thanatology* 3 (1985): 169–185.

Seen from the perspective of traditional Chinese behavior toward the dead within the context of social relations, the loss of a member is not construed as a total severance from the world of the living, but as a starting point for a series of continuing social interaction which cut across the boundary between life and death.

1315 Oppenheim, Roger S. *Maori Death Customs*. Wellington: Reed, 1973.

Based on author's thesis, University of Auckland. Includes materials on the management of terminal illness, death, burial and the attendant ceremonies, Fangihanga, the ideology of death, myths, and political effects.

1316 Parkes, Colin M. "Effects of Bereavement on Physical and Mental Health—A Study of the Case Records of Widows." *British Medical Journal*, 1964, Vol. 2: 274–279.

See 1373.

1317 Radcliffe-Brown, A. R. *The Andaman Highlanders*. 1922. Reprint ed. New York: Free Press, 1964.

The author develops a theory of social integration which is based upon the ritual expression of sentiments. Mourning is one example given among the Andamese. It is a time of communal weeping indulged in by friends of mourners who have not themselves experienced a loss.

1318 Skansie, Julie Ellen. *Death is for All: Death and Death-Related Beliefs of Rural Spanish-Americans*. New York: A. M. S. Press, 1985.

An anthropologist examines the continuation of Spanish-American traditions of death in the culture of New Mexico. Two related questions are considered: the perception of one's own death and the obligations or responses imposed by the death of another. Death is viewed both as a universal fact of human existence and a belief in a life beyond that of physical existence. Many specific field observations are recorded. Bibliography.

1319 Steele, R. L. "Dying, Death, and Bereavement among the Maya Indians of Meso-america: A Study of Anthropological Psychology." *American Psychologist* 32 (1977): 1060–1068.

After a few days of mourning, the community encourages bereaved persons to turn away from thoughts of the deceased in order that the spirit of the deceased may be provided with a safe separation from the earth and speed toward the other world. Speedy separation also removes the unfriendliness of death from the bereaved.

1320 Van Arsdale, Peter W. and Carol L. Radetsky. "Life and Death in New Guinea." *Omega* 23 (1984): 155–169.

Using a combination of comparative/historical and ethnographic approaches, the concepts of the "life-death continuum" and the cosmic "life force" are examined for the Asmat tribe of New Guinea. The roles of magic and sorcery are examined in the content of death causation, as is the notion of societal equilibrium/disequilibrium. The symbolism of the skull is covered briefly, being tied to tribal beliefs concerning the attributes of humanness. Of importance are the concepts of probabilism and determinism, introduced to aid the understanding of life-death processes in Melanesian and Western societies respectively. In conclusion, positive adjustments associated with the free expression of grief are examined cross-culturally.

1321 Whyte, Florence. *The Dance of Death in Spain and Catalonia*. 1931. Reprint. New York: Arno Press, 1976.

This study of national character shows the link between Spanish culture and extreme attitudes toward death. The social position of mourners and personal feelings about death are discussed.

1322 Yamamoto, J., K. Okongi, T. Iyiwsaki and S. Yoshimura. "Mourning in Japan." *American Journal of Psychiatry* 125 (1969): 1660–1665.

Reports the results of 20 Japanese widows interviewed during the acute grief stage of mourning. A relatively easy acceptance of loss was found among the Japanese widows in comparison with those in Western cultures. The authors attribute this to Japanese belief in an afterlife for the deceased and to cultivation of the sense of their presence as ancestors. The Western studies for comparison were Parkes (4315) and Marris (4242).

1.52 POLITICAL THANATOLOGY See PUBLIC POLICY (3.8)

1.6 BIOMEDICAL ISSUES

1323 Bichat, Xavier. *Physiological Researches on Life and Death*. Trans. by F. Gold. 1827. Reprint. Salem, N.H.: Ayer Co. Pub., 1976.

A young French physician proclaimed that life is the sum of all those functions which resist death and gave special attention to the functions which could be studied by the scientific method that was strengthened by enlightened rationalism in the 1800s. Moving away from traditional interpretations of death, Bichat studied two levels of death, the natural death that comes gradually from aging, work and poverty and accidental death which brings sudden and deadly trauma to heart, brain and lungs.

1324 Blake, John B. *Public Health in the Town of Boston, 1630–1822*. Cambridge, Mass.: Harvard University Press, 1959.

Disease was more dangerous than Indians to early settlers in America. The trials of public health in the relatively healthy city of Boston are traced: medicine, inoculation, smallpox, yellow fever, sanitation, politics. Population and death rates for 1701–1774 and mortality for 1812–1821 are given in appendices. Notes on sources.

1325 Carrington, Hereward. *Death: Its Causes and Phenomena with Special Reference to Immortality.* 1921. Reprint. Salem, N.H.: Ayer Co. Pub., 1976.

Research and theory on cellular aging and death were blended with traditional British views of death in a comprehensive study of causes and signs of death, the relationship of death to sleep and trance, means of preserving and disposing of the body, biomedical theories about death and aging, philosophical and theological views of death and immortality, psychical research.

1326 Metchnikoff, Elie. *The Nature of Man: Studies in Optimistic Philosophy.* Trans. by P. Chalmers Mitchell. New York: G. P. Putnam and Sons, 1903. Reprint. Salem, N. H.: Ayer Co. Pub., 1977.

The author introduces in this volume two terms that became widely known within a few years: "thanatology" and "gerontology." However, when Park's article on "thanatology" was published in 1912, he made no mention of Metchnikoff (Park, 1135). The two terms are used by Metchnikoff to describe the scientific study of aging and death with a concentration of efforts to ameliorate suffering. He felt optimistic about human nature, despite the philosophical pessimism of Tolstoy because he was bringing to thanatology and gerontology the newer discoveries of biomedicine. See also Metchnikoff (1347).

1327 National Center for Health Statistics. *Facts of Life and Death. DHEW Publication No. 79–1222.* Washington, D. C.: U. S. Government Printing Office, 1976.

This representative compilation of statistics by the National Center for Health Statistics answers questions frequently asked about vital and health statistics for the United States: births, deaths, marriages, divorces, life-expectancy, health characteristics and resources, mortality and leading causes of death. The data is gathered primarily from professional associations and the compilations are published periodically.

1328 National Center for Health Statistics. *Advance Report of Final Mortality Statistics, 1987.* Monthly vital statistics report; vol. 38, 5 supp. Hyattsville, Md.: Public Health Service, 1989.

Summary tabulations from yearly mortality statistics are presented along with specific discussion of death rates, expectation of life at birth and at specified ages, causes of death, HIV infection, Hispanic deaths, drug-related deaths, infant and maternal mortality. More detailed tabulations for each year are published in the *Vital Statistics of the United States. Vol. II— Mortality* which is also available from the National Center for Health Statistics.

1329 Park, Robert. "Thanatology." *Journal of the American Medical Association* 58 (1912): 1243–1246.

See 1135.

1330 Schienfeld, A. "The Mortality of Men and Women." *Scientific American* 198 (1958): 22–27.

One clue to the prevention and treatment of disease may be the continuing finding of studies in other countries that women tend to live longer than men.

1331 Stephens, Charles Asbury. *Natural Salvation: The Message of Science, Outlining the First Principles of Immortal Life on the Earth.* 1905. Reprint. Salem, N.H.: Ayer Co. Pub., 1976.

See 1352.

1.61 LIFE SPAN AND LIFE STYLE

1332 Aton, J. W. "The Art of Aging and Dying." *Gerontologist* 4 (1964): 94–100.

On the basis of his search among the Hutterite religious sect, the author discusses six universal problems of aging as they are dealt with in this strict community: economic insecurity, the inactivity of retirement, prestige loss, social isolation, loss of health and death. Old age adjustment begins when members of the sect are young.

1333 Blum-Feshbach, Jonathan and Sally Blum-Feshbach and associates. *The Psychology of Separation and Loss.* San Francisco: Jossey-Bass Pub., 1987.

See 1136.

1334 Callahan, Daniel. *Setting Limits: Medical Goals in an Aging Society.* New York: Simon and Schuster, 1989.

See 3638.

1335 Capps, Donald. *Life-Cycle Theory and Pastoral Care.* Philadelphia: Fortress Press, 1983.

A professor of pastoral counseling considers the contribution of social scientists to the understanding of seasons of life and the importance of theology and ethics in satisfaction with life in a knowledge that death is approaching.

1336 Carter, Elizabeth A. and Monica McGoldrick, eds. *The Family Life Cycle: A Framework for Family Therapy*. Forward by Murray Bowen. New York: Gardner Press, 1980.

Contributors to this volume discuss the family in later life, the impact of death in serious illness on the family life cycle, systems and ceremonies, rites and passages as viewed by the family.

1337 Crenshaw, David. *Bereavement: Counseling the Bereaved through the Life Cycle*. New York: Continuum Pub. Co, 1990.

A clinical psychologist draws upon a lifetime of work with children during trauma and loss to develop seven task of mourning which appear in various ways throughout the life cycle. Theoretical components of grieving are built upon the studies by Bowlby and the Harvard Bereavement Project. Practical in orientation, the book offers specific advice for greiving of preschool children, school-age children, adolescents, young adults, adults in midlife, and the elderly. Appendix of helping resources and notes.

1338 Erikson, Erik H. *Insight and Responsibiliity: Lectures on the Ethical Implications of Psychoanalytic Insight*. New York: W. W. Norton Co., 1964.

In an overview of the cycle of generations, the author defines wisdom as "detached concern with life itself, in the face of death itself" (p. 133).

1339 Feinberg, M. R., G. Feinberg, and J. J. Tarrant. *Leavetaking: When and How to Say Goodbye*. New York: Simon and Schuster, 1978.

As bibliotherapy for persons experiencing loss, this volume for lay and professional persons presents developmental events in life that lead to anticipatory loss, grief, or actual loss: anguish of the empty nest, loss of parents who have grown old, decline of health, loss of attachment through separation or divorce, re-establishment of roots in a new community, unplanned and unwelcome retirement, perceptions of loss of power and vigor, the final leavetaking which is death. Useful discussion of object loss-role loss.

1340 Fried, Charles. *An Anatomy of Values: Problems of Personal and Social Choice*. Cambridge, Mass.: Harvard University Press, 1970.

The author provides evidence that each person has a life-plan that consists of aims, ends and values. The plan also includes a risk budget, the health and survival needs that may be expended to realize desirable ends in life. People do not sacrifice resources merely to survive or to be healthy. The risk of death and of ill health is for success, friendship and religious convictions. These risks are considered to be personal and voluntary aspects of lifestyle which are beyond political or legal control, but there may be conditions under which individual choices are overridden by larger social goals such as protection of the financial resources of the community, public health, protection of the environment and a conviction that the interference will provide a net balance of good over evil.

1341 Fuchs, Victor R. *Who Shall Live? Health, Economics and Social Choice*. New York: Basic Books, 1974.

See 3642.

1342 Ge, Ellen. "Causes of Death." In *Encyclopedia of Death*, ed. by Robert Kastenbaum and Beatrice Kastenbaum, 38–41. Phoenix, Ariz.: The Orxy Press, 1989.

Some cautions concerning classifications and comparability studies of death causes are summarized by the author. The statistics of any deaths because of communicable diseases among the young has now shifted in the United States to many degenerative diseases of older persons.

1343 Goulet, L. R., and Paul B. Baltes, eds. *Life Span Developmental Psychology: Research and Theory*. New York: Academic Press, 1970.

Human life span developmental psychology is concerned with the description and explication of age related behavioral change from birth to death. Although several thanatologists such as Robert Kastenbaum (1346) have made use of these theories, the contributors to the present volume do not include discussions on dying and death.

1344 Gustafson, E. "Dying: The Career of the Nursing Home Patient." *Journal of Health and Social Behavior* 13 (1972): 226–235.

The passage of time and events for aged nursing home patients are studied in units that are phases of the "career."

1345 Kastenbaum, Robert J. "Death and Development Through the Lifespan." In *New Meanings of Death*, ed. by Herman Feifel, 17–46. New York: McGraw-Hill Book Co., 1977.

Death is viewed from the perspective of children, young adults, midlife and old age.

1346 Kastenbaum, Robert J. *Humans Developing: A Life-Span Perspective*. Boston: Allyn and Bacon, 1979.

This textbook includes death related issues along with other issues in each stage of development. Death is not treated as the last chapter in the book.

1347 Metchnikoff, Elie. *The Prolongation of Life: Optimistic Studies.* Trans. by P. Chalmers Mitchell. 1908. Reprint. Salem, N. H.: Ayer Co. Pub., 1977.

Although this biomedical researcher shared the 1908 Nobel Prize in medicine with Paul Ehrlich, he was primarily concerned with cultural and spiritual questions throughout his life. This volume focuses attention on the possibility and the ideal pattern of stages in human development. See also Metchnikoff (1326).

1348 Pearl, Raymond. *The Biology of Death: Being a Series of Lectures Delivered at the Lowell Institute in Boston in December 1920.* 1922. Reprint. Salem, N. H.: Ayer Co. Pub., 1976.

A prominent American biologist and geneticist turned in mid-career to questions of human demography. This volume considers questions and evidence that helped to form the emerging field of demographic studies concerning death, disease, health.

1349 Raphael, Beverley. *The Anatomy of Bereavement.* New York: Basic Books, 1983.

See 1029.

1350 Sauer, Herbert I. *Geographic Patterns in the Risk of Dying and Associated Factors, Ages 35–74 Years, United States, 1968–72.* Hyattsville, Md.: U. S. Dept. of Health and Human Services, 1980.

Death rates for adults are presented for each state and for over 500 economic areas according to differences associated with mining, elevation, population density, some indexes of patient care resources and especially "enigma of the Southeast." These differences are compared according to sex, race and selected causes of death.

1351 Shneidman, Edwin S., ed. *Death: Current Perspectives.* 3rd ed. Palo Alto, Calif.: Mayfield Pub. Co., 1984.

See 1033.

1352 Stephens, Charles Asbury. *Natural Salvation: The Message of Science, Outlining the First Principles of Immortal Life on the Earth.* 1905. Reprint. Salem, N.H.: Ayer Co. Pub., 1976.

A pioneer in American gerontology advances a theme of the Enlightenment that the Christian promise of salvation from death might be accomplished in secular form by the progress of scientific enterprise. Both theological and medical themes are used in his organization of scattered data in the late nineteenth and early twentieth century to develop a realistic and optimistic view of genetics that would counter the deterministic theories of Weismann. This volume also contains two biographical articles on Stephens.

1353 Weenolson, Patricia. *Transcendence of Loss over the Lifespan.* Washington, D.C.: Hemisphere Pub. Co., 1988.

Based on life-histories of women aged 25 to 67. Psychological, medical and sociological studies are related to an over-arching construct of transcendence and loss. This enables the author to reveal patterns of loss and transcendence that affect our capacity for self-creation. As the author reviews individual life-cycles she distinguishes a few key losses from minor ones and develops a classification based on the ramifications of loss that are often neglected as people strive to bring coherence out of loss that seems to have no meaning. Family, generations and cultures are related. Although philosophical, theological and anthropological aspects of transcendence are not included in the study, the author does consider immortality as one way to transfer emotional attachments from one stage of life to another or from one generation to another. Appendices include questions used in the study, interrater reliability, stressful life events schedule, references, index.

1354 Weismann, Avery D. *The Realization of Death.* New York: Jason Aronson, 1974.

A pioneer physician in thanatology presents a method for reconstructing and synthesizing the events that surround the terminal phase of life. This is done through chapters that outline the questions to be raised in a psychological "autopsy," and extensive case illustrations. The "autopsy" inquiry distinguishes survival and significant survival, death and appropriate death, sickness and responsibility. The patient's dynamic philosophy of life is related to reactions to the terminal phase of life.

1355 Weisman, Avery D. and J. William Worden. "Psycho-Social Analysis of Cancer Deaths." *Omega* 6 (1975): 61–75.

See 1394.

1356 Whiter, Walter. *Dissertation on the Disorder of Death: Or, that State of the Frame under the Signs of Death Called Suspended Animation.* 1819. Reprint. Salem, N. H.: Ayer Co. Pub., 1976.

The Reverend Walter Whiter moved from historical anecdote through clinical observations of the early nineteenth century to present a case for remedying the disorder of death. He describes cases in which those who seemed to be dead had been brought back to life after being struck by lightning or drowned. He urges the public to look in a new and compassionate way upon possibilities that should be tested for a prolongation of life.

1357 Williams, Richard Hays. *Living through the Years: Styles of Life and Successful Aging.* New York: Atherton Press, 1965.

Two officials in the National Institute of Mental Health present disengagement as a central feature of the aging process and its social aspects, with concern for timing, distinctions among the modes of involvement from which disengagement takes place, the possible range of attitudes which different people take and the styles of management they adopt in the disengagement process. Chapters include the world of work, family, living alone or as a couple, minimal involvement throughout life, living fully, success and style, statistical analysis and conclusions. Case studies are presented from interviews and observations of 168 elderly men and women in Kansas City.

1358 Wolff, K. "Personality Type and Reaction Toward Aging and Death: A Clinical Study." *Geriatrics* 21 (1966): 189–192.

Ninety patients in nine psychopathological groups showed an accentuation of life-long personality defenses as they faced the problems of aging and death.

1.62 MORBIDITY AND MORTALITY AMONG THE BEREAVED

1359 Almy, T. P. "Experimental Studies of the Irritable Colon." *American Journal of Medicine* 10 (1951): 60–67.

Irritable-colon sufferers often reported emotional conflicts when they focused on lonely, helpless or generally maladjusted life periods following the death of significant persons.

1360 Bartrop, R. W., E. Luckhurst, L. Lazarus, L. G. Kiloh and R. Penny. "Depressed Lymphocyte Function after Bereavement." *Lancet* 97 (1977): 834–836.

Twenty-six widows were compared at two weeks and six weeks after bereavement with non-bereaved hospital staff members as controls. The widowed showed no difference in number of lymphocytes, antibodies, typical mean serum concentrations and growth hormone. Response of the lymphocytes to mitogens was significantly depressed in the widowed group at six weeks after bereavement. Since response to mitogens is used to assess cellular immunity, this may indicate that by six weeks after bereavement there is some loss of immunity due to the stress.

1361 Berardo, F. "Widowhood Status in the United States: Perspective on a Neglected Aspect of the Family Life Cycle." *The Family Coordinator*, 17 (1968) 191–203.

The number of widows relative to widowers has increased to a 5:1 ratio because mortality among women is lower than among men, wives are typically younger than their husbands, remarriage rates are considerably lower for women than for men.

1362 Clayton, Paula J. "Mortality and Morbidity in the First Year of Widowhood." *Archives of General Psychiatry* 30 (1974): 747–750.

A group of randomly selected widows and widowers (average age 61) and a control group of the same sex and average age were studied for one year. Through interviews with psychiatrically trained personnel 109 of the subjects were seen shortly after bereavement; 90 were seen again after a year. The control group was interviewed after one year. No difference was seen between the two groups in mortality rates after one year. The bereaved experienced significantly more psychological and physical depressive symptoms than their non-bereaved counterparts. There were no differences in the two groups in the number of physician visits, hospitalizations and use of tranquilizers. There was a small but significant increase in use of hypnotics by the bereaved. The authors review literature on the subject which indicates that there is an increased psychological morbidity in the younger widow, but not in the older widowed. References.

1363 Committee for the Study of Health Consequences of the Stress of Bereavement. *Bereavement: Reactions, Consequences and Care.* Washington, D. C.: National Academy Press, 1984.

This study was conducted by the Institute of Medicine at the request of the Office of Prevention of the National Institute of Mental Health. The health consequences of bereavement are discussed in an effort to learn what preventative interventions can be undertaken. Eight intervention programs in various parts of the country were studied and recommendations for clinical practice and for promising research appear in the report.

1364 Ferraro, K. F. "The Effect of Widowhood on the Health Status of Older Persons." *International Journal of Aging and Human Development* 21 (1985): 9–25.

Widows report that they feel less healthy after a loss, but believe that the long physical consequences of their loss are minimal.

1365 Glick, Ira O., Robert S. Weiss, and Colin M. Parkes. *The First Year of Bereavement.* New York: John Wiley and Sons, 1974.

Forty-nine widows and nineteen widowers in the Boston area were interviewed by social workers from the Harvard Laboratory of Community Psychiatry. Most of them were again interviewed after four years. Less than a fourth of the widows lost their husband suddenly and without warning. When a multidisciplinary team examined tape recordings of the interviews, there were several conclusions: most widows continue the psychological work of mourning for their dead husbands for the rest of their lives, with the greatest turmoil and struggle during the first one to three years of grief. Many strange individual reactions, such as consulting the dead spouse are usually benign and should be accepted as individual variations in the mourning process. Mental illness may be precipitated by personal factors, idiosyncratic stress and lack of support in the social milieu. Stress, for 40% of the widows was manifested in the first eight weeks of grief through headaches, dizziness, sleeplessness and loss of appetite which was severe enough to prompt consultation with physicians. Those widows who did not anticipate their husband's death did not move toward remarriage. In a nontechnical style, the book describes the impact of death, early emotional and physical reactions, availability and use of help, ceremonies of leave taking, grieving, continued ties to the husband, acting as mother and provider, changing relationships with family and friends, the recovery process and its patterns, and a summary chapter on dealing with loss. See also Glick (4040, 4227); Parkes (4339); and Young (1382).

1366 Hyman, Herbert Hyrum. *Of Time and Widowhood: Nationwide Studies of Enduring Effects.* Durham, N.C.: Duke University Press, 1983.

General social surveys conducted by the National Opinion Research Center, University of Chicago (1972–1978) were used to trace the effects of widowhood upon an area-probability sampling of non-institutionalized, English speaking adult white women. Findings were checked against those for married, divorced and separated women from the same samples. Widows are less likely than other women to describe their lives as very happy and exciting. Younger divorced women were most likely to develop a "lasting sour outlook on life and society" (p. 35), and are less likely to attend church than widows. In general, divorce or separation had a more negative effect upon social involvement than bereavement for women. Older widows seemed resigned to a loss of financial support than younger widows. Young divorcees are thoroughly dissatisfied with their financial situation, even though it is no worse objectively than that of the widowed. The younger divorcee and widows report their health to be fair or poor in relation to those women who are married. (For comparative conclusions on divorcees after 10 years, see Wallerstein 4125). Older widows rate themselves in good or excellent health just as frequently as do the married. These conclusions were compared with two longitudinal surveys by the Survey Research Center, University of Michigan, with the same form of area-probability sampling. The longitudinal studies (1971 and 1975) show the old widowed to be progressively, more seriously deprived of financial support. Over a period of years, bitterness becomes less prevalent among the recently widowed. Compared with white widowers in the NORC annual national surveys (1972–78), widowers in the Survey Research Center report not only having a less happy and exciting life than their married counterparts, but also are twice as likely to report general dissatisfaction with life as widows. The widowers seldom report satisfaction with friendship. Old, divorced or separated men are the most negative in their outlook on life and society. Old widowers feel desperate about their financial situation and consistently report poor health. Older widowers suffer higher mortality than their married counterparts, but widows do not.

1367 Kraus, Arthur S., and Abraham M. Lilienfield. "Some Epidemiological Aspects of the High Mortality Rate in the Young Widowed Group." *Journal of Chronic Diseases* 10 (1959): 207–217.

A review of statistics published by the National Office of Vital Statistics 1949–1951 showed a lower death rate in the married group than in the single, widowed, divorced at every age. There was a high rate of mortality among those who were widowed under age 35.

1368 Lindemann, Erich. "Modifications in the Course of Ulcerative Colitis in Relationship to Changes in Life Situations and Reaction Patterns." In *Life, Stress and Bodily Disease* ed. by H. G. Wolf, 706–723. Baltimore, Md.: Williams and Wilkins, 1950. Reprinted in Erich Lindemann, *Beyond Grief: Studies in Crisis Intervention.* New York: Jason Aronson, 1979.

A physician reports evidence that disruptions of close emotional relationships play an important part in the etiology of ulcerative colitis. Death was one of the disruptions that might be important. Certainly the relationship between death, physical and emotional disturbance was demonstrated by the author's follow-up of grieving relatives after the Coconut Grove fire (4044). See also Lindemann (4332).

1369 Lynch, James J. *The Broken Heart: The Medical Consequences of Loneliness.* New York: Basic Books, 1979.

From laboratory investigations and clinical work the author provides health professionals and others with the broader personal and social implications of loneliness and loss upon patients, especially those with cardiovascular difficulties. The place of love, companionship and health are examined in relation to the loneliness that can break the human heart.

1370 Maddison, David and A. Viola. "The Health of Widows in the Year Following Bereavement." *Journal of Psychosomatic Research* 12 (1968): 297–306.

From a fifty per cent reply to a mail survey of 375 widows in

Boston and Sydney, matched to 199 married controls, the widows showed more somatic symptoms which are commonly associated with recent bereavement: headaches, dizziness, fainting spells, skin rashes, excessive sweating, indigestion, difficulty in swallowing, and chest pain. Widows visited psychiatrists for treatment of depression more often than the control group.

1371 Maddison, David. "The Consequences of Conjugal Bereavement." *Nursing Times* 65 (1969): 50–52.

A study of health status thirteen months after bereavement showed deterioration in 21% of the bereaved in Boston, Mass. and 32% in Sydney, Australia. A control group showed 7% deterioration in Boston and 2% in Sydney.

1372 Parkes, Colin M. "Effects of Bereavement on Physical and Mental Health—A Study of the Case Records of Widows." *British Medical Journal*, 1964, Vol. 2: 274–279.

As part of a study of widows, the author found that within a six month period following the death of their husbands, widows under age 65 had tripled the number of times they had consulted psychiatrists; prescriptions for sedation had increased seven times. See Glick, (1365); Kraus, A. S., (1367); Parkes (4244); Young, (1382).

1373 Parkes, Colin M., B. Benjamin, and R. G. Fitzgerald. "Broken Heart: A Statistical Study of Increased Mortality Among Widowers." *British Medical Journal* (1969), Vol. 1: 740–743.

Four thousand four-hundred and eighty-six widowers of fifty-five years of age and older were followed up for nine years since the death of their wives in 1957. Of these two hundred and thirteen died during the first six months of bereavement, forty per cent above the expected rate for married men of the same age. The greatest increase in mortality during this period was found in widowers dying from coronary thrombosis and other arteriosclerotic and degenerative heart disease. Twenty-two to twenty-five per cent of the deaths were in the same diagnostic group as the wife's death. After six months, the widowers' mortality rate fell gradually to that of married men of the same age and remained at about the same level. For results of the same study after five years, see Young (1381).

1374 Parkes, Colin M., and R. J. Brown. "Health after Bereavement: A Controlled Study of Young Boston Widows and Widowers." *Psychosomatic Medicine* 34 (1972): 449–461.

Widows and widowers were compared thirteen months after the death of a spouse with a control group who had suffered no bereavement. Widows reported 50% more symptoms of the autonomic nervous symptom than women in the control group and widowers displayed four times as many symptoms as married men in the control group. In comparison with the control group, there was over 25% increase in smoking, alcohol consumption and tranquilizers among the bereaved. The authors found evidence that strong identification with the deceased can be considered an early indicator of pathological development.

1375 Parkes, Colin M. "Determinants of Outcome Following Bereavement." *Omega* 6 (1975): 303–323.

The most serious of life-changes carrying a health-risk is the death of a spouse. The author identifies factors that can alert us to the possibility of poor progress for survival.

1376 Rees, W. D., and S. G. Lutlinds. "Mortality of Bereavement." *British Medical Journal*, (1967), Vol 4: 13–16.

During the first year of bereavement, the death rate among widowed persons was 12.2% versus 1.2% in a control group of the same age, sex and stress factors.

1377 Rush, Benjamin. Medical Inquiries and Observations upon the Diseases of the Mind. Philadelphia: Grigg and Elliott, 1835.

Although the prophet Isaiah spoke about "binding up the broken hearted," the phrase was given medical significance by the observations of a Philadelphia physician who was a signatory of the Declaration of Independence.

1378 Stroebe, Margaret S. and Wolfgang Stroebe. "Social Support and the Alleviation of Loss." In *Social Support: Theory, Research, and Applications*, ed. by I. G. Sarason and B. R. Sarason. Dordrecht: Martinus Nijhoff, 1985.

When differences in depression between married and widowed groups are controlled, there is no significance in self-reported physical health between the two groups.

1379 Stroebe, Margaret S. and Wolfgang Stroebe. "Who Suffers More? Sex Differences in Health Risk of the Widowed." *Psychological Bulletin* 93 (1983): 279–301.

In a review of literature the authors find near unanimous agreement that bereavement can be a contributing cause to mental illness, with depression being the most common disorder. Widowhood is associated with higher mortality for men and the younger widowed. The peak in mortality risk is during the first six months after the death of a spouse for widowers, whereas the highest peak for widows is during the second year of bereavement.

1380 Stroebe, Wolfgang, and Margaret S. Stroebe. *Bereavement and Health.* New York: Cambridge University Press, 1987.

Research professors of psychology, University of Tübingen, provide a rich research review of the impact of bereavement on surviving partners, drawn from the work of psychologists, sociologists, empidemiologists, and psychiatrists. A theoretical perspective of loss is presented with an emphasis upon social contacts and the interpersonal nature of grief. The health consequences of marital bereavement are presented along with specific risk factors and recommendations for reducing the risk of poor bereavement outcome. Comprehensive bibliography of clinical research.

1381 Thompson, L. W., *et. al.* "Effect of Bereavement on Self-Perceptions of Physical Health in Elderly Widows and Widowers." *Journal of Gerontology* 39 (1984): 309–314.

Widows and widowers who were interviewed two months after the loss of a spouse reported more instances of new illnesses or the deterioration of existing ones than the control group. They also reported increased or new medication.

1382 Young, Michael, Bernard Benjamin and Chris Wallis. "The Mortality of Widowers." *Lancet* 2 (1963): 454–456.

A cohort of 4486 widowers, 55 years of age and over were followed for five years after the death of wives in 1957. There was an increase of about 40% mortality in the first six months above that which would be expected in the general population of the same age. After the first six months there was a gradual decrease in mortality toward generally expected levels. For results of the same study after nine years, see Parkes (1373).

1.63 LOSS, DISEASE, AND PREMATURE DEATH

1383 Carr, A. C. and Bernard Schoenberg. "Object-Loss and Somatic Symptom Formation." In *Loss and Grief,* ed. by Bernard Schoenberg, et al., 36–50. New York: Columbia University Press, 1970.

In a review of the empirical literature, the authors conclude that although cause and effect relationship cannot be established between loss and psychological/physical symptoms, there is strong correlational evidence that significant object-loss may precipitate physical illness or deterioration of the sick person.

1384 Engel, George L. "Is Grief a Disease?" *Psychosomatic Medicine* 23 (1961): 18–22.

Comparisons were drawn by a physician between persistent reports of infection and neoplasm after significant losses, especially bereavement. The author hopes for more investigations by medical students of these relationships.

1385 Engel, George L. "The Need for a New Medical Model: A Challenge for Biomedicine." *Science* 196 (1977): 129–136.

A pioneer in studies between grieving and the disease process argues against the outdated disease model of "one germ, one disease, one therapy." He stresses the interaction between psychological and biological factors which is shown in studies of infections which show that an infectious agent is a necessary but not a sufficient cause for a person to show symptoms of disease. Why do some persons show greater resistance than others?

1386 Hinton, John M. "The Influence of Previous Personality on Reactions to Having Terminal Cancer." *Omega* 6 (1975): 95–111.

See 3023.

1387 LeShan, Lawrence and R. E. Worthington. "Some Recurrent Life-history Patterns Observed in Patients with Malignant Disease." *Journal of Nervous and Mental Disorders* 124 (1956): 460–465.

The possibility of a fatal illness out of a life that has become empty is illustrated in the medical history of one patient who described his youth as a time of isolation and despair. In adulthood there was an intense relationship with a child, but when the relationship was lost no deep personal attachment was established with another person. The authors believe that there was some connection between this despairing isolation and the premature death of the person with a malignant disease.

1388 Lipowski, Z. J. "Psychosomatic Medicine in the Seventies: An Overview." *American Journal of Psychiatry* 134 (1977): 233–244.

The relationship of illness to psychosocial stress and personality is included in this review of Psychosomatic medicine in the 1970s.

1389 Marshall, Victor W. "The Last Strand: Remnants of Engagement in the Later Years." In *Death, Dying, Transcending*, ed. by Richard A. Kalish. Farmingdale, N.Y.: Baywood Pub. Co., 1980.

See 3028.

1390 Pattison, E. Mansell. "Psychosocial Predictors of Death Prognosis." *Omega* 5 (1974): 145–160.

See 3239.

1391 Perrin, G. M. and I. R. Pierce. "Psychosomatic Aspects of Cancer." *Psychosomatic Medicine* 21 (1959): 397–421.

In an early study on psychosomatic aspects of cancer, authors present some case studies in which either the loss of a very significant person or an important goal in life leads to a depression that may predispose a person to the development of a malignancy.

1392 Seligman, Martin. *Helplessness: On Depression, Development, and Death*. San Francisco: W. H. Freeman, 1975.

See 3032.

1393 Siegel, Bernie. *Love, Medicine and Miracles*. New York: Harper and Row, 1986.

This is a book by a physician about surviving, about survivor's characteristics, about healing medical insights, and about taking control in order to heal oneself. Siegel's views are integrative. He sees the human being as unitary and recognizes that spiritual health is of equal importance with and inseparable from physical health.

1394 Weisman, Avery D. and J. William Worden. "Psycho-Social Analysis of Cancer Deaths." *Omega* 6 (1975): 61–75.

Terminal and pre-terminal cancer patients were studied by a clinical team to compare the actual survival of individual persons with the expected survival (as measured by the Expected Survival Score). Longevity was significantly correlated with active and mutually responsive relationships. Shorter survival was found among cancer patients who reflected long-standing alienation, deprivation, depression and destructive relationships, which extended into the terminal stage of life. These attitudes of patients found expression in the despondency, desire to die, thoughts of suicide, inordinate complaints, all of which increased their sense of self-defeat and isolation.

Chapter 2

PHILOSOPHICAL THEOLOGY

2.1   THE JOURNEY OF THE SOUL

2001   Boros, Ladislaus. *The Mystery of Death.* New York: Herder and Herder, 1965.

See 2046.

2002   Choron, Jacques. *Modern Man and Mortality.* New York: Macmillan Pub. Co., 1964.

A philosopher examines the modern dilemma of how to cope with an awareness of mortality. After surveying philosophies of death and various evaluations of the "death instinct," the author notes that psychotherapy has sought to help these persons gain a positive attitude toward death through philosophic and psychotherapeutic reconstruction of a person's view of life in which dying becomes a renewal of creative impulses. The author believes that these answers are incomplete because many psychotherapists did not have a philosophy of death and any philosophy of death should be more than a reconciliation with the inevitable. Various attitudes of death are surveyed and evaluated. Although the author has no final answers to questions about mortality, he seems to admire Hume's serene and philosophical skepticism. The work is a penetrating and scholarly study of mortality, with special reference to individual attitudes. Bibliography of 400 titles. For a general survey of philosophy and death, see Choron (1041). For Hume's view of suicide, see Hume (3551).

2003 Choron, Jacques. *Death and Modern Man.* New York: Macmillan Pub. Co., 1972.

A paperback edition of the author's *Modern Man and Mortality* (2002).

2004 Gray, J. Glenn. "The Problem of Death in Modern Philosophy." In *The Modern Vision of Death*, ed. by Nathan H. Scott, Jr., 45–68. Richmond, Va.: John Knox Press, 1967.

The philosophies of Kierkegaard, Jaspers and Heidegger consider the metaphysical origins of the concept of dread or anguish. It is a form of spiritual exposure that is welcomed by Kierkegaard as an incentive to the leap of faith toward God's eternal love. For Jaspers it is an opportunity to see the truth of the world. Nothingness belongs to being. Each person must increase being through an isolated, unsharable quest for meaning. For Heidegger this quest was always to be considered in the present moment. The future is now. The author asks if these theories of existential moments can give life meaning when there is always the possibility of untimely death. Useful summary of paradoxes in existential philosophy. See Kierkegaard (2021), Heidegger (2019), Kunz (2058).

2005 Henderson, Joseph L. and Maud Oakes. *The Journey of the Soul. The Wisdom of the Serpent.* New York: George Braziller, 1963.

A Jungian analyst and a painter review mythology, art and modern psychoanalysis to show how death is an essential condition for growth and for life. Death is seen as a symbol of universal experience of initiation into the cycle of death and rebirth throughout human existence. An extensive selection of myths and illustrations is described by Henderson and illustrated by Oakes.

2006 Holck, Frederick H., ed. *Death and Eastern Thought: Understanding Death in Eastern Religions and Philosophies.* Nashville, Tenn.: Abingdon Press, 1974.

See 2381.

2007 Kierkegaard, Søren. *Concluding Unscientific Postscript to the "Philosophical Fragments."* Trans. by David F. Swenson; completed and ed. by Walter Lowrie. Princeton, N.J.: Princeton University Press, 1941.

A nineteenth century Christian philosopher in Denmark comes to three conclusions about death: We ought to give an ethical expression to the significance of death, a religious expression for victory over death, a resolving word to explain its mystery and a binding word by which we may defend ourselves. Søren Kierkegaard's emphasis upon "existence" was influential in the later philosophical writings about death of Heidegger (*Das Sein*), Jaspers (*Existenz*) and Sartre (*pour-soi*). The concern of Søren Kierkegaard was with the concrete individuality, the anguish, the despair and the loneliness of the individual soul. See also Choron (1041), Kaufmann (2055).

2008 Koestenbaum, Peter. *Is There An Answer to Death?* Englewood Cliffs, N.J.: Prentice-Hall, 1976.

Death reveals to a philosopher our participation in two worlds: the universal and the particular. These can be combined in an existential personality theory that gives hope for growth in a total plan for life that will combine sorrow and joy. Various philosophical exercises are suggested to strengthen the ego through confrontations with death that bring transcendence. These relate consciousness to the self, the world, the brain, time, creation, and immortality. The work is an example of existential phenomenology that seeks to unite body-world relationships. The unity comes through human thought/feeling and is a source of much popular writing on death as a unique opportunity for "growth." A precise philosophical example would be found in Becker (2194); and an imprecise example would be in Kübler-Ross (1021).

2009 Watts, Alan. *The Book: On the Taboo Against Knowing Who You Are*. New York: Vintage Books, 1972.

See 2386.

2.11 TIME AND DEATH

2010 Baillie, John. *And the Life Everlasting*. New York: Charles Scribner's Sons, 1933.

A philosophical theologian maintains the balance between the timeless (abstract truth) and the eternal (God's work in our present existence). Questions of time are important in Christian theology to keep our secular existence relative rather than absolute. This is accomplished when we see all things from the prospect of God's eternal harmony.

See also Baillie 2193.

2011 Barr, James. *Biblical Words for Time*. London: SCM Press, 1962.

Hebrew and Greek words for time in the Old and New Testaments are considered in terms of biblical and philosophical theology, and vocabulary.

2012 Brandon, S. G. F. *History, Time and Deity*. New York: Barnes and Noble, 1965.

A professor of comparative religion describes the chief religious reactions of humans to the problem of time. He discerns a common pattern, one in which time links the problem of the meaning of history with that of deity. A scholarly review based upon anthropology, philosophy and theology. Precise footnotes and extensive bibliography.

2013 Carbine, Michael E. "Concepts of Time in the Psychologies of Freud, Erikson and Rogers." *Soundings* 62 (1979): 9–23.

The historical determinism and retrospective, temporal orientation of Deuteronomic eschatology is seen as an organizing principle for Freud's psychology. The early Christian emphasis upon time as radical transcendence of the this world is seen in the psychoanalytic writings of Erik Erikson. The modern secular meaning of time as a non-dimensional concentration upon the present-immediate is considered to be implicit in the psychological work of Carl Rogers.

2014 Carse, James P. *Death And Existence: A Conceptual History of Human Mortality*. New York: John Wiley and Sons, 1980.

This advanced college text presents views toward death of eastern and western religions and of psychologists and scientists. The purpose is to integrate these varying views into our own self-understanding, with an awareness that a complete knowledge of death is always beyond our comprehension. This is the pursuit of wisdom, especially when conceived of existentially as in Kierkegaard. The discontinuity that comes through death is not an enemy that robs life of its meaning but the existential question which makes life's meaningfulness possible. This theme is related to a careful and perceptive exposition of Heidegger's views on death.

2015 Cullmann, Oscar. *Christ and Time*. Trans. by Floyd Filson. Rev. ed. Philadelphia: Westminster Press, 1964.

In opposition to existential theologians such as Bultmann (2106, 2260) a German Protestant theologian insists: "eschatology is an absolutely chronological concept." Jesus and the church accepted the Jewish concept of "linear time," which is time moving forward from before creation to the second coming of Christ and beyond. This "timeliness" is punctuated by particular redemptive "moments" (*kairoi*) but unlike his Jewish contemporaries, Jesus regarded God's decisive redemptive activity as already taking place in his own ministry, death and resurrection. The church considered this to be "the end-time" until his return. There will be a real parousia of Christ and a transformed creation. The basic theme is of "salvation-history" which is linked to Gerhard Von Rad, Alan Richardson, G. Ernest

Wright, who believe that God's saving purpose is progressively revealed through his action in history which the Bible relates and interprets.

2016 Dodd, Charles H. *The Parables of the Kingdom*. New York: Charles Scribner and Sons, 1936.

A biblical scholar develops a "realized eschatology" in which the time of God's future coming through His Kingdom (*kairos*) is condensed into the present time of human experience (*kronos*). Any thought of a theological future is to be concentrated into present experiences.

2017 Dunne, John S. *Time and Myth: A Meditation on Storytelling as an Exploration of Life and Death*. Garden City, N.Y.: Doubleday and Co., 1973.

A Catholic professor of theology analyzes the human confrontation with the inevitability of death in cultural, personal and religious spheres and views each as a particular kind of myth that takes its form from the impact of time upon the myth. The plain and straightforward style is enriched by literary and psychological references.

2018 Hartshorne, Charles. *The Logic of Perfection and Other Essays in Neoclassical Metaphysics*. LaSalle, Ill.: Open Court Pub. Co., 1962.

A philosopher of much influence upon process theology examines temporal finitude in a chapter on "Time, Death and Everlasting Life." The end of time is not the end of being, for death as an object of reference contains much that exists throughout life. As soon as the possibility of death arises in our understanding of life, both become rich and real, for reality is both continuing, retained and open to further actualization through social immortality. The power for social immortality is the omniscience of God who writes through death "the end" upon the last page of our book of life without any last judgment. The "resurrection" is the synthesis of one's life in God. This is the completion of our individuation.

2019 Heidegger, Martin. *Being and Time*. Trans. by John Macquarrie and Edward Robinson. New York: Harper and Row, 1962.

When the primordial phenomenon of "Being-in-the-world" has been shattered, an isolated subject is all that remains to solve the problem of Reality through "Being-as-present-at-hand." This present state of being is continually restless in the search for potential wholeness. But this search for totality may be diverted by a substitute concern for the death of others, since the observation of such a death is objective. The deeper challenge is to see beyond the corporeal ending of a Thing to the coming change in ourselves from a kind of being to a state of nonbeing. Awareness of the death of another may precipitate awareness that there is a tentative, "not yet" quality to our preoccupation with life as a cumulative piecing together of experiences. The hoped for existential conclusion will be an acceptance of ourselves as a "being-toward-the-end." Death is a way to be. This state of being becomes significant and purposeful when we define ourselves as beings who encounter others with care. This existential purpose of life in the face of death takes precedence over biological and psychological studies which are often limited to the factual phenomenon of "demise"—a concentration upon the end itself. Factual death creates anxiety because we are "in the face of" a potentiality-for-Being that can never be completely realized. This often leads to an everyday and constant tranquilization about death. Courage is required for a thrust toward the uttermost possibility of existence with full knowledge that death will cut short our potential. For a precise exposition of Heidegger, see Carse (2014). For the significance of Heidegger for twentieth-century thought on death, see Choron (1041), Hetzler and Kutscher (2042). See also Kaufmann (2054); Lepp (1188); Tillich (1199); Wahl (2068); Wyschogrod (4073).

2020 Kastenbaum, Robert J. "As the Clock Runs Out." *Mental Hygiene* 50 (1966): 332–336.

Time is less fascinating and precious and death less formidable and devastating among aged institutional people than for younger people.

2021 Kierkegaard, Søren. *The Concept of Dread*. Trans. by Walter Lowrie. Princeton, N.J.: Princeton University Press, 1946.

The 19th century Danish Christian philosopher who was influential upon 20th century existentialists wrote voluminously about inner knowledge, principally from the point of view of one who suffered from a "sickness unto death." In early life, the philosopher began to follow the Socratic maxim: "know thyself." What he knew was dread, an alien power which lays hold of an individual and from which one cannot tear oneself. We dread what we desire, and therefore become impotent, lacking in accountability. To know oneself to the utmost is to experience dread to the utmost, to the point of death and annihilation. Dread molds the individual by destroying all our finitudes. It educates persons in an infinite manner. It is in dread that we demand the presence of God. We are purified by the presence of God, but then we are gripped by a dread of the Absolute from which we cannot turn away. Several generations later, the existentialist philosopher Heidegger sought "a phenomenon that can unlock Being for us." The key is a special feeling that can reveal to us the essence of things (befindlichkeit), the feeling of dread that sharpens our individuality and unifies our most original tendencies. For Heidegger, the dread of Kierkegaard is more than impotence—it is an experience of nothingness that reveals to us the world as a whole (grundbefindlichkeit). For the influence of Kierkegaard upon twentieth-century reflections upon death, see Hetzller and Kutscher (2042). See also Heidegger (2019), Wahl (2068), Gray (2004).

2022 Tillich, Paul. *The Eternal Now*. New York: Charles Scribner's Sons, 1963.

Among sermons delivered in university and college chapels is "The Eternal Now" which summarizes the theology of Tillich concerning the end of life. He warns against speaking "loosely" about life after death because the world of nature will definitely come to an end and we cannot speak about timelessness or endless time. We can only speak in images taken from time. There is no time after time. There is eternity above time. Our present challenge is to turn the curse of the past into a blessing through a belief that the power of God's eternal power is present in us as forgiveness. This gives meaning to our present life that delivers us from menaces from the past.

2.12 HOLY LIVING AND HOLY DYING

2023 Erikson, Erik H. *Childhood and Society*. New York: W. W. Norton Co., 1963.

See 1176.

2024 Frankl, Victor E. *The Doctor and the Soul*. Trans. by Richard and Clara Winston. New York: Alfred A. Knopf, 1955.

See 1178.

2025 Gandhi, Mohatma K. *Why Fear or Mourn Death?* New Dehli: Gandhi Peace Foundation, 1971.

Death is an art as life is an art. It is only a true friend. Only our ignorance causes us grief. Death comes when we cut ourselves off from the source of our being, not when the soul leaves the body. If we affirm this belief in immortality, we can dedicate ourselves to a life of service to the poor and suffering because we do not cling to life and fear death.

2026 Häring, Bernard. *Christian Maturity*. Trans. by Arlene Swidler. New York: Herder and Herder, 1967.

"Maturity" is the twentieth century theological equivalent of medieval and reformation exhortations to live a life of perfect love in the face of approaching death. The modern emphasis is upon appreciation of our own status in the eyes of God which comes through the dignity and freedom of participation in His kingdom. The trials of life, such as serious or terminal illness are to be faced by a confession that sin and neurosis are probably the cause and that theological virtues of faith, hope and love will sustain us.

2027 Haroutunian, Joseph. "Life and Death Among Fellow Men." In *The Modern Vision of Death*, ed. by Nathan H. Scott, Jr., 79–96. Richmond, Va.: John Knox Press, 1967.

When modern individuals become so preoccupied with the "ultimate concern" of their own deaths apart from obligation and appreciation of others, they enter a distorted state of "I–Obsession, Thou–Rejection." Preoccupied with a search for freedom from anxiety about death they unwittingly produce an anxiety about emptiness and meaninglessness. The remedy is a shift from preoccupation with self consciousness to the basic source of anxiety about death which is separation from fellow human beings. A concern for human transactions will raise awareness of death beyond the existential acceptance of anxiety as a natural response to fate. Concern for death should enhance love as a basic quality of life. Christian faith turns anxiety about death into greater work of love through the presence of Christ and others who will share humanity with us.

2028 Kierkegaard, Søren. *The Sickness Unto Death*. Trans. by Walter Lowrie. Princeton, N.J.: Princeton University Press, 1946.

The Danish Christian philosopher who influenced existential philosophy analyzes the torment of despair as an inability to die. The last hope, death, is not available and one despairs about being a self. This "sickness unto death" is resolved by accepting the gift from God of the self as the sign of our humanity, by relating the conscious self to a deeper sense of existence and by open commitment to God as the ground upon which we stand as human beings. See also Kierkegaard (2021).

2029 Landsberg, Paul Ludwig. *The Experience of Death/The Moral Problem of Suicide*. Trans. by Cynthia Rowland. New York: Arno Press, 1977.

A professor of philosophy who was killed by the Nazis considers the nature of personal uniqueness to death in terms of questions about body-soul, body-spirit, body-mind. This concern is for internal integrity, interpersonal sensitivity and the physical factors that influence our life and death. In a discussion of suicide this philosopher who considered himself a "Catholic without being one" advises those who suffer the moral tortures of imminent suicide to consider the sufferings of Christ and the martyrs. This will provide strength and hope for an inner-meaning of life through purification. We can be steadfast in life despite the injustice that continues to come upon us.

2030 Lepp, Ignace. *Death and Its Mysteries*. Trans. by Bernard Murchland. New York: Macmillan Pub. Co., 1968.

A Roman Catholic psychologist stresses the fact that only as we find meaning in life can we find it in death. He presents a view of the afterlife that is drawn from the philosophy of Teilhard de Chardin. See also Lepp (1188).

2031 Lepp, Ignace. *The Challenges of Life.* New York: Alba House, 1969.

A Roman Catholic psychologist draws upon Augustine, Pascal, Kierkegaard and existential philosophers to affirm courage for full humanity, growth and liberation. Life is an adventure that must meet the challenges of sin, fear, unrest and anxiety. Death is mentioned in the final chapter as a bewildering subject to philosophers such as Heidegger because it is associated with absurdity and hopelessness. But for the existential Christian, death is the best possible means of freeing the mind from every-day banalities and of giving life heightened intensity.

2032 Mansor, Josef. "Wer mich zum Freunde hat, dem kann's nicht fehlen." Versuch einer spirituellen Theologie zur Ars moriendi heute." ["He who has me as a friend, can lack nothing": Search for a Spiritual Theology to the Ars Moriendi Today.] In *Ars Moriendi. Erwägungen zur Kunst des Sterbens.* ed. by Harald Wagner. Freiburg, Germany: Herder, 1989.

Manser advocates making a friend of death, since it is a life-long companion and need not be catastrophic. Sub-topics include, "New Search for a Complete View of Life," "Point of Departure for a Modern Ars Moriendi," "Ars Moriendi as a Concrete Discussion with Death." In a well-organized philosophical treatise, Manser discusses eight common problems and attitudes towards death, based on Max Frisch's twenty-five questions concerning death listed in his diary 1966–71.

2033 Marty, Martin. *A Cry of Absence.* San Francisco: Harper and Row, 1983.

In response to "summer" smiling assurances of charismatic religion, a theological professor offers the balance of "winter" religion that has a place for loss, dying, death. The spiritual enterprise is a movement between complementary aspects of faith. It is an image from Karl Rahner. Beginning with a study of the Psalms, half of which have winter images, Marty affirms the presence of God through a journey of hope, trust and affirmation.

2034 Miller, Randolph Krump. *Live Until You Die.* Philadelphia: Pilgrim Press, 1973.

See 1026.

2035 Oppenheimer, Helen. *The Hope of Heaven: What Happens When We Die.* Cambridge: Cowley Pub., 1988.

Questions concerning the nature and destiny of humans are approached with imagination and care in reflections upon death and the meaning of life, the presence of God and the resurrection. The meditations are intellectually alive and pastorally effective. Each chapter closes with brief references to other printed resources.

2036 Shneidman, Edwin S. "Malignancy: Dialogue With Life-Threatening Illnesses." In *Voices of Death*, ed. by Edwin S. Shneidman, 104–139. San Francisco: Harper and Row, 1980.

A noted thanatologist combines clinical practice, the testimony of the dying, and the personality theory of H. A. Murray to conclude that each individual tends to die as he or she has lived, especially in reaction of episodes of threat, stress, failure and challenge throughout life. The goals of therapy with the dying would include: an increase in psychological comfort, respect for the autonomy of the individual, the development of a positive transference toward loving authority figures, the affirmation of limited goals in a life cut short by death.

2037 Steinfels, Peter and Robert M. Veatch, eds. *Death Inside Out.* New York: Harper and Row Publishers, 1975.

See 2066.

2038 Taylor, Jeremy. *Holy Living and Holy Dying.* Ed. by Marvin D. Hinton. Wheaton, Ill.: Tyndale House Pub., 1986.

See 1112.

2039 Vaux, Kenneth L. *Will to Live/Will to Die.* Minneapolis, Minn.: Augsburg Pub. House, 1978.

A professor of ethics and medicine considers the moral question of intended death in the light of Scripture, Christian tradition, and ethical wisdom. The dual forces of life and death must be considered in the development of a reflective self. In medicine, reflection leads to some solution of the paradox of human initiatives against ultimately yielding to the wise ebb and flow of nature. Cultural influences in current debates about euthanasia are summarized. The characteristics of natural and timely death are presented. The Biblical tradition of death is an unfolding of divine revelation on the way in which we ought to live and how we are to die. Notes and bibliography.

2040 Weatherhead, Leslie. *Prescription for Anxiety.* New York: Abingdon Press, 1956.

Written for Christians in the "age of anxiety," this popular book by a pastor is filled with assurance that insight is the answer to generalized worry and psychosomatic symptoms.

2041 Weisman, Avery D. *On Dying and Denying. A Psychiatric Study of Terminality*. New York: Behavioral Pub., 1972.

A purposeful death would be a time for recognizing and resolving long-standing conflicts and for a sense of satisfaction with some harmony between our present conditions and our ideals. We should be able to relax under physical conditions of relative freedom from pain. With confidence we would rely upon others to reduce the emotional and social impoverishment of dying and the continuation of purposes that have been important in our life. The author's view as a pioneering thanaologist is more realistic than the romanticized growth-through-death of Kübler-Ross (1020), Boros (2044), Levine (2059) and others.

2.13 PHILOSOPHICAL DEFINITION OF DEATH

2042 Baird, Robert M. "Existentialism, Death and Caring." *Journal of Religion and Health* 15 (1976): 108–115.

A professor of philosophy shows how effective caring can be reinforced by an existential analysis of death in the writings of Heidegger, Sartre, Tillich, Tolstoy. His conclusion from their writings is the primacy of openness to an individual in order that a dying person may speak responsibly about death through the encouragement of a caring relationship.

2043 Bardis, Panos D. *History of Thanatology*. New York: University Press of America, 1981.

A professor of sociology provides a brief review of major concepts of death in various cultures and times. Since he could find no satisfactory definition of death or proof of the immortality of the soul in any of these sources, he concludes that it is safer and nobler to live for knowledge, love and self-sacrifice.

2044 Boros, Ladislaus. *The Moment of Truth*. London: Burns and Oates, 1962.

A Roman Catholic theologian proposes the thesis that death gives humans the opportunity of a completely personal act. It is a moment above all others for the wakening of consciousness, for freedom, for an encounter with God, for the final decision about eternal destiny. The author combines elements of existential philosophy under methods of theological research recommended by First Vatican Council. A number of dogmas often treated in quite dissimilar ways are brought together in a glorified release from finitude that neglects the painful and frightening aspects of death. For a more paradoxical and realistic view by another Roman Catholic theologian, see Rahner (2317).

2045 Boros, Ladislaus. *The Mystery of Death.* New York: Herder and Herder, 1965.

The starting point for the author's metaphysical discussion of death is a distinction between dying, which we can experience, and death which is not a direct experience. The author is more concerned for the former state which allows us to think about what will happen to us in preparation for the moment of death, rather than upon an evaluation of the state of the soul after death. Following Heidegger (2019), the picture of death is sought now in the inner structure of our human existence. This inner structure compels us toward more and more freedom, but this can only be obtained through an encounter with God who makes us conscious of our eternal destiny. From the viewpoint of theology in the First Vatican Council the author considers the finality of death, the salvation that comes through Christ, the universality of redemption, original sin, purification, the decision of Christ to save us through His death. Scholarly footnotes.

2046 Carse, James P. Death and Existence: A Conceptual History of Human Mortality. New York: John Wiley and Sons, 1980.

See 2014.

2047 Donnelly, John, ed. *Language, Metaphysics, and Death.* New York: Fordham University Press, 1978.

The meaning of death and immortality is debated with erudition by existentially oriented philosophers and theologians. The contributors assume extensive knowledge of philosophy and metaphysics for those that like to stir the mind without really settling upon anything. See especially the chapter of Donnelly on death and Ivan Ilych.

2048 Dunne, John S. *The City of the Gods: A Study in Myth and Mortality.* New York: Macmillan Pub. Co., 1965.

See 6081.

2049 Eckstein, Jerome. *The Death Day of Socrates: Living, Dying and Immortality—The Theater of Ideas in Plato's "Phaedo."* Frenchtown, N.J.: Columbia Pub. Co., 1981.

The famous dialogue of Socrates is presented as Plato's attempt to discredit the idea of heroic suicide. This is a challenge to the usual interpretation of Socrates death as a noble suicide.

2050 Feuerbach, Ludwig. *Thoughts on Death and Immortality*. Trans. by J. A. Massey. Berkeley, Calif.: University of California Press, 1981.

A nineteenth century German philosopher, who was initially influenced by Hegel, examines the metaphysical, psychological and physical reasons, cause and origin of death. In his later works he concludes that the only immortality open to us is a full, active and creative life.

2051 Freud, Sigmund. *Beyond the Pleasure Principle*. New York: Basic Books, 1975.

See 1181.

2052 Hetzler, Florence M. and Austin H. Kutscher, eds. *Philosophical Aspects of Thanatology*. 2 vols. New York: MSS Information Corp., 1978.

Love, theology, philosophy, psychiatry, technology, mystery of thanatology are all parts of a multi-faceted approach to the meaning of death in its emptiness and in its fullness. This is the scope of a collection of short but penetrating articles by philosophers from many American and European universities. Articles range from specific issues in the writing of one philosopher to overviews of death in modern technical society.

2053 Kastenbaum, Robert J. "Psychological Death." In *Death and Dying*, ed. by Leonard Pearson, 1–27. Cleveland, Ohio: The Press of Case Western Reserve University, 1969.

Death may be viewed as a continuum throughout life toward a non-reversible state that may not be defined until the Judgment Day. The author offers some intriguing questions about the impact of thoughts concerning death upon our present life and then presents various images that might be present in a psychological perception of death: a false impression that a person is biologically dead, the feeling that a partner in some personal relation may in some sense be alive but appears to us as less than a "living soul," contacts with persons who go through stereotyped and routine motions as though all inner experience were dead, and the image of those who are so far above merely existing and carrying out the routine of life that we feel ourselves to be only partly alive. For a theological justification of "a non-reversable state" see Cullmann (2015).

2054 Kaufmann, Walter. "Existentialism and Death." In Herman Feifel, ed., *The Meaning of Death*, 39–63. New York: McGraw-Hill Book Co., 1959.

A philosopher evaluates the treatment of death in the writings of Kierkegaard, Jaspers, Heidegger and Camus. See also Wahl (2068), Choron (1041).

2055 Kaufmann, Walter. *Existentialism, Religion and Death: Thirteen Essays.* New York: New American Library, 1976.

A philosopher traces the theme of death in existential writers such as Kierkegaard, Tolstoi, Dostoevsky, Buber, Camus, Sartre, Heidegger, Marcuse. A lucid presentation of complex thinkers.

2056 Koestenbaum, Peter. *Death and Eternal Life.* San Francisco: Harper and Row, 1962.

A philosopher suggests that the current interest in death began with the existential philosophers and has now been taken over by the existential psychologists. He considers death to be an event which defines the individual as both concrete and universal. It gives necessary existential meaning to life. Labeled as "phenomenological existential philosophy" by Johnston (1140).

2057 Kreeft, Peter J. *Love Is Stronger Than Death.* San Francisco: Harper and Row, 1979.

A philosopher discusses three interrelated issues: death, life, God. Out of these strands of meaning, he develops a philosophy of death which organizes around our growing awareness of death as enemy, stranger, friend, mother and lover. The personal sensitivity of his writing is deepened by a final chapter in which he describes his feelings about death as his five year old daughter was in surgery for a brain tumor.

2058 Kunz, Hans. "Critique of Jasper's Concept of Transcendence." Trans. by Mary Feagins. In *The Philosophy of Karl Jaspers*, ed. by Paul Arthur Schilpp, 499–522. La Salle, Ill.: Open Court Pub. Co., 1957.

The author maintains that Jaspers' idea of transcendence rested on the nature of a person's ontological constitution – the knowledge of potential death is the origin of thought that precedes factual death. The imminence of death is closely connected to the potential character of human nature and leads to the transformation from mere being to Existenz; that is, the person moves from unilluminated suspension to an assertion of freedom to enhance and substantiate a reliable way of life. A person is existentially a self only in the act of apprehending. Transcendence can be thought of only in relation to the specific death of a specific individual. The future event can only be known to the individual who apprehends it as the "ultimate situation" of life. This is a subjective, unprovable affirmation. The objective thought of death belonging to life is incomprehensible. Consciousness of our transcendence is a suspension between being-in and being-out-of-the-world. It is not psychologically describable. It is an act of freedom arising from absolute consciousness.

2059 Levine, Stephen. *Who Dies? An Investigation of Conscious Living and Conscious Dying.* Garden City, N.Y.: Doubleday and Co., 1982.

A poet and long-time practitioner of Buddhist meditation combines his experience with Kübler-Ross and the teachings of Sri Nisargadatta to provide philosophy and techniques of meditation that has the goal of calm, simple and compassionate understanding in the face of the frightful power called death. The positive, transcendent approach leaves many uncomfortable questions unanswered.

2060 Macquarrie, John. *Existentialism.* Philadelphia: Westminster Press, 1972.

An existentialist theologian considers a theme that has been prominent in the writing of existentialists, death. Heidegger is considered to be the philosopher who has given the most detailed study to the existential meaning of death and incorporated it into his philosophy of existence. For Heidegger, death is connected with the grasping of human existence as a continually going out into the new. Death abolishes existence rather than completing it. Because death is inwardly appropriated, empirical studies have little relevance. Such studies see death only from the outside, such as determining the time when physical death takes place. Inwardly, death gives us an awareness of existence as a whole, but this is only possible when we think of ourselves as being-toward death. This creates a mode of anxiety in which we are aware of living in the face of the end. To care for ourselves in the midst of this anxiety about vanishing into nothing, we must face the tension between the forward thrust of possibility into the future and the factual limitation of the existence into which we are already thrown. This limitation requires an understanding of the way in which we are "continually falling into the world" and relating to "they." Death is a very unusual possibility because it is the end of all other possibilities. We can either accept death as qualifying all of one's possibilities or we can exclude it from consideration as long as possible. The latter choice is illustrated by Tolstoy in *The Death of Ivan Ilych.* When we become aware of death we accept mortality and the boundaries of existence. To be aware of boundaries is to think of existence as finite whole. This is possible for those who live in the face of an end, but not for those who systematically exclude the thought of death. The continual danger is of "falling"—absorption into the impersonal collectivism of an instrumental world of "they." This danger is accentuated by the vast cultural illusion created to deny death. See also Heidegger (2019).

2061 Maeterlinck, Maurice. *Death.* 1911. Reprint. New York: Arno Press, 1976.

The first publication of this work in France presented the possibilities of annihilation, survival with individual consciousness, or without consciousness, or perhaps integration into a universal consciousness. The book was at first forbidden by the Roman Catholic church and the ban was later removed.

2062 Marcuse, Herbert. "The Ideology of Death," In *The Meaning of Death*, ed. by Herman Feifel, 64–78. New York: McGraw-Hill Book Co., 1959.

A philosopher contrasts the normal attitude toward death as painful, horrible, violent and unwelcome with the Platonic and Romantic view of death as resurrection of the spirit. In Plato, true life demands liberation from the untrue life of our common existence. This will come through self-denial and renunciation. Such denial is the basis of orderly human society.

2063 Metzger, Arnold. *Freedom and Death,* Trans. by Ralph Manheim. London: Human Context Books, 1973.

A professor of philosophy believes that the post-World War II generation is caught between the crumbling myth of the transcendent and the crumbling myth of facts absolute. In an analysis of death, being and freedom he seeks an answer through inner transcendence that will carry the possibilities of life into action. Inner transcendence grows out of our analysis of time, which is a dialectical weaving together of death and resurrection. Death is an integral part of life from the beginning of our existence. The argument proceeds through an analysis perception as will to endure (Husserl), the maintenance of identity throughout divorced happenings (Plato), the various possibilities of human experience (Kant), the rootage of existence (happening) in nothing (Hume), the possibility of boundless impossibility (Heidegger), the instinctual basis of drives toward life and death (Freud). The author concludes that a system of timeless truth can be re-grasped by moderns as a force for transcendence and freedom over death. Careful and complex reasoning with adequate summaries of major philosophical systems that take death seriously.

2064 Needleman, Jacob. "The Moment of Grief." In *Death and Bereavement,* ed. by Austin H. Kutscher, 129–138. Springfield, Ill.: Charles C. Thomas, 1969.

In thoughts about death we enter the emotion of wonder when we realize that death is conceptually linked to time, identity, consciousness, life, matter, change, birth.

2065 Sartre, Jean Paul. *Being and Nothingness.* Trans. by Hazel E. Barnes. New York: Philosophical Library, 1956.

Sartre objects to Heidegger's central emphasis upon "being toward death." Preparation for death is mistaken, because people either think that they will die sooner or later than they expect it. Death does not give meaning, it contributes to the absurdity of life. In a way, Sartre explains the absurdity by positing "nothingness" as an indigenous human tendency. Since death is act of life, it does not have the importance for freedom that is assigned to it by Heidegger. We are not free for dying, since we cannot die at will. Instead, we are free to begin an action, such as a choice to die. Suicide is one means of asserting our liberty. Heidegger's sense of openness to an absolute as part of the resolve of a being toward death is rejected by Sartre. God is dead.

2066 Steinfels, Peter and Robert M. Veatch, eds. *Death Inside Out.* Hastings Center Report. San Francisco: Harper and Row, 1975.

The report is principally concerned with philosophical, ethical and historical issues rather than practical and personal problems. Includes Ariès' "Death Inside Out," and Ivan Illich on the political uses of natural death, Eric Cassell on dying in a technological society, William May, Robert Morson, Paul Ramsey on the indignity of "death with dignity," David Smith on letting some babies die, and other works by Leon Kass and Tristram Engelhardt.

2067 Toynbee, Arnold, *et. al. Man's Concern with Death.* New York: McGraw-Hill Book Co., 1969.

In several articles, Toynbee traces religious attitudes towards death and the inhibition of the concept in the United States. A professor of religious studies, Ninian Smart, categorizes beliefs concerning death in various religions and notes the shift in modern theology from literal to mythic and personal views of death and resurrection. A professor of forensic medicine, Keith Mant, reviews the medical definitions of death in Europe and England from the eighteenth century until the 1960's and concludes that the criteria have not radically changed except for the modern concept of cerebral or brain death. In an epilogue, Toynbee shares his personal feelings about the possibility of imminent death.

2068 Wahl, Jean. *Philosophies of Existence.* Trans. by F. M. Lory. London: Routledge and Kegan Paul, 1959.

This introduction to the basic thought of Kierkegaard, Heidegger, Jaspers, Marcel and Sartre presents philosophies of existence that start from subjective impressions that give meanings to life and death. The first "existentialist" was Kierkegaard in the mid-nineteenth century. Although the author does not discuss death, except in relation to the concept of dread, the volume provides a context for understanding philosophical definitions of death in modern philosophy, psychology and theology.

2069 Watts, Alan. *Death.* Millbrae, Calif.: Celestial Arts, 1975.

A philosopher with a cheerful attitude toward death can find acceptance of his earthly end through a combination of Eastern and Western meditation on the meaning of life and death.

2070 Walton, Douglas B. *On Defining Death: An Analytic Study of the Concept of Death in Philosophy and Medical Ethics.* Montreal: McGill-Queens University Press, 1979.

The epistemology of death as an empirical experience defies resolution. There is no way to verify death or life after death. Some philosophers such as John Hick have made the "enormous evasion" of seeing logic in the eschatological verification of an experience of resurrection—which we have not experienced. The concept of immortality cannot be verified as a logically consistent hypothesis.

2071 Wittgenstein, Ludwig. "On Heidegger On Being and Dread." In *Heidegger and Modern Philosophy: Critical Essays,* ed. by Michael Murray, 80–84. New Haven, Conn.: Yale University Press, 1978.

An existential philosopher relates the concepts of Being and Dread in Heidegger to the concepts of Kierkegaard. It is a running up against the limits of language, the Dread that he will talk nonsense. Whatever one might offer as a definition of the Good, it is always simply a misunderstanding to think that this corresponds in the present to the authentic matter one actually means to convey. We really cannot describe Dread in the face of Being-in-the-World. It is a fundamentally ontological mood in which the Nothing that veils Being is revealed. The haunting question of Heidegger is always "Why is there something, rather than nothing."

2072 Wyschogrod, Edith. *Spirit in Ashes: Hegel, Heidegger, and Man-Made Mass Death.* New Haven, Conn.: Yale University Press, 1985.

See 4073.

2.2 BIBLICAL STUDIES

2073 Bailey, Lloyd R., Sr. *Biblical Perspectives on Death.* Philadelphia: Fortress Press, 1979.

In a comprehensive and competent survey of biblical literature, the author first examines the perspectives on death that are known from Egyptian and Babylonian sources. This is followed by a survey of Old Testament literature on demons, cult of the dead, folk explanations, manifestations of death and reactions to death as presented in Old Testament literature. The transition toward apocalyptic eschatology in the intertestamental literature is presented. The New Testament is reviewed with heavy attention to the writings of Paul. Concluding reflections are on evaluation of literature surveyed, possible implications for bioethics, religion and the fear of death, the deathwardness of the world, liturgical responses to death, biological, psychological and theological maturity. Interesting Old Testament analysis of "bad" and "good" death (48–52).

2074 Brueggemann, Walter. "Death, Theology of." In *Interpreter's Dictionary of the Bible: An Illustrated Encyclopedia, Supplementary Volume*, 219–222. Nashville, Tenn.: Abingdon Press, 1976.

The Biblical understanding of death involves four assumptions about life: personality or soul (*nephes*) is the wholistic center of being and death is the breakup of that center; human life is membership in a community and this is lost through death; membership in a community is based upon a covenant with God; death is inability to participate in the decision-demanding relationships of life.

2075 Charles, R. H. *Eschatology: The Doctrine of a Future Life in Israel, Judaism and Christianity*. 1899. Reprint. New York: Schocken Books, 1963.

This standard work on the Old Testament, the Interbiblical period, and the New Testament, prophetic and apocalyptic views include: life after death, Gehenna, the Messianic Kingdom, the Son of Man, and resurrection from the dead. The author was one of the first to place canonical and non-canonical eschatological writings in the historical, political, ideological and intellectual backgrounds of their times.

2076 Curran, Charles A. "Death and Dying." *Journal of Religion and Health* 14 (1975): 254–263.

A Roman Catholic professor who is skilled in both psychology and moral theology has provided a positive tradition for questions about death. Fear is to be overcome through a faith that allows us to believe in God's love even when we are in a state of helplessness before physical death.

2077 Eichrodt, Walter. *Theology of the Old Testament*. Vol. 2. Trans. by J. A. Baker. 496–529. Philadelphia: Westminster Press, 1967.

A noted Old Testament scholar surveys the development of belief in providence, the underworld, the enslavement of all life to hostile powers of death, the indestructibility of a relationship with God (immortality) and the affirmation of God's wisdom in the face of approaching death.

2078 Jungel, Eberhard. *Death: The Riddle and the Mystery*. Trans. by Ian and Ute Nicol. Philadelphia: Westminster Press, 1974.

A continental theologian affirms that the death which is to be feared according to the Apostle Paul is a break in relationship with God. The curse of this death is a meaningless life. Christ conquers the meaningless of life through his power over sin. This establishes a relationship between God and the believer which is not broken by physical death. The death and resurrection of Christ is a sign of God's participation in the misery of human death and the triumph of his power over that death. Life is the source of information about death. It is life with temporal limitations which maintains our human individuality. Without these limitations, the hope of the resurrection would infinitize the temporal self out of existence in this world. The author strenuously objects to the creation of anxiety about death only in order to witness to Jesus Christ as Savior from death.

2079 Kaiser, Otto and Eduard Lohse. *Death and Life*. Nashville, Tenn.: Abingdon Press, 1981.

Biblical scholars present a scholarly discussion of death, future life, resurrection and the Christian life as part of preparation for life after death. A carefully constructed study.

2080 Pacholski, Richard A. "Thanatology Topics in Literature." In *Death Education II*, ed. by Hannelore Wass, *et al.*, pp. 301–312. Washington, D.C.: Hemisphere Pub. Corp., 1985.

See 8032.

2.21 OLD TESTAMENT AND WISDOM LITERATURE

2081 Brueggemann, Walter. "From Hurt to Joy, From Death to Life." *Interpretation* 28 (1974): 3–19.

The lament literature found in the Old Testament offers an important correction to unrealistic, euphoric notions of faith and the fatalistic view that a tragic reversal is the normal pattern of human experience.

2082 Brueggemann, Walter. "The Formfulness of Grief." *Interpretation* 31 (1977): 263–275.

An Old Testament professor compares and contrasts the lament forms in the Psalter with the stages of grief presented by Kübler-Ross.

2083 Brueggemann, Walter. *The Message of the Psalms: A Theological Commentary*. Minneapolis, Minn.: Augsburg Pub. House, 1984.

An Old Testament scholar believes that a biblical approach to theodicy arises not out of an experience of suffering in general, but against the background of Israel's faith in God who had covenanted with her for a glorious destiny. When Israel lost control over her political destiny, a whole literature, including the book of Job was developed to ask questions about God's justice, system of reward and punishment, of access and benefit. Theodicy concerns the character of God as known through the social system of values. The historical gap between promised glory and present suffering led to many expressions of pain in Israel, especially in the lament psalms, such as Psalm 13. The author refers to these as Psalms of disorientation because they challenge the assumption that our life is ordered and that some equilibrium has been established. Something has gone wrong in the way that people see the results of their belief to be the chosen people of God (Psalm 35 and 86). The author also notes that our present world is increasingly experienced as disoriented and yet churches use only psalms of orientation and reassurance. This is a self-deceptive optimism which ignore the songs of lament, protest and complaint that Israel felt about the incoherence of this world. To grasp these "psalms of darkness" is to act boldly in faith. Our realistic recognition of disorder is proper subject for discourse with God and from him find names for the silences that surround us in our suffering. Faith embraces the darkness of life that a successful and affluent culture would hide.

2084 Crenshaw, James L., ed. *Studies in Ancient Israelite Wisdom.* New York: KTAV Pub. House, 1976.

Old Testament scholars provide a variety of learned answers to a central question in the face of approaching death and present catastrophe, "how does wisdom give purpose to life?"

2085 Cullmann, Oscar. *Christ and Time.* Philadelphia: Westminster Press, 1950.

See 2015.

2086 Davidson, A. B. *Theology of the Old Testament.* Edinburgh: T. and T. Clark, 1984.

The Old Testament solution to death was found in faith rather than in hope. To die was to become separated from God, to be dead was to continue in the state a separation. This world with God or without God was the only distinction. The dead are not souls in the proper sense, for God has deprived them of life.

2087 Johnson, Aubery R. *The Vitality of the Individual in the Thought of Ancient Israel.* Cardiff: University of Wales, 1949.

A professor of Semitic languages examines the synthetic psychology of Hebrew religion in which there is no final extinction of a person. Death destroys the center of vital power in humans so that the individual becomes in Sheol a faint shadow of the unified person in life.

2088 Pedersen, Johannes. *Israel: Its Life and Culture.* 2 vols. London: Oxford University Press, 1926.

In a comprehensive study of Hebrew psychology and anthropology, a professor of Semitic studies finds many references to death in the Old Testament: the departing of the soul, the problem of illness, punishment, violence, unfriendliness, cultish practices, and divinity of the dead. A stimulating, somewhat speculative study.

2089 Robinson, H. Wheeler. *The Religious Ideas of the Old Testament.* London: Gerald G. Duckworth, 1913.

The Hebrew understanding of death is a shadow side of the community of the living. This is consistent with the Hebrew idea of the corporate personality as the essential unit of life. So long as the family of Israel lives, the shadow of life is cast even in the form of the dead, although the existence is so lifeless that no praise of God was possible. The individual would perish when one's life was spilled out on the ground through blood, but existence would continue in the corporate identity of the tribe and clan.

2090 Russell, David Syme. *The Method and Message of Jewish Apocalyptic.* London: SCM Press, 1964.

Doctrines of the resurrection of the dead, the future lot of the wicked and the righteous, the return of the Messiah, the woes of the last days are traced through the formative period of Jewish thought on this subject 200 B.C.–100 A.D.

2091 Scott, R. B. Y. *The Way of Wisdom in the Old Testament.* New York: Macmillan Pub. Co., 1971.

In a popular study that centers upon Job and other wisdom literature such as Proverbs, an Old Testament scholar provides a readable approach to the problem of death in relation to life affirmation.

2092 Silberman, Lou H. "Death in the Hebrew Bible and the Apocalyptic Literature." In *Perspectives on Death*, ed. by Liston O. Mills, 13–32. Nashville, Tenn.: Abingdon Press, 1969.

A professor of Jewish literature suggests that the Hebrew view of death was undergirded by confidence in Yahweh as the creator and sustainer of life and in his purpose for Israel. Oppression and suffering were the context for developing ideas on death and the afterlife. The writings reflect the question of how a good Creator could permit his people to suffer and his purpose to be thwarted. Toward the end of this period of writing, the concept of resurrection (not immortality) and judgment became evident.

2093 Sutcliffe, Edmund Felix. *The Old Testament and the Future Life.* London: Burns, Oates, and Washburne, 1946.

A Jesuit theologian examines Egyptian, Babylonian, Hebrew, Jewish concept of the future life, the situation of Sheol, rewards and punishments after death, purgatory, and resurrection of the body.

2094 Weber, Otto. *Foundations of Dogmatics*, Vol 1. Trans. by Darrell Guder. Grand Rapids, Mich.: Wm. B. Eerdmans Pub. Co., 1981.

A conservative theologian maintains that the Old Testament does not know of an independent power of death, presented as the opponent of God. The actual power of death is the fear of God in His concealment. It is not death we are to fear but God who is the Lord of death even as He is the Lord of life. The promise of immortality is vague and related to the promise of having sons as a guarantee of future posterity. The concept of resurrection is not always connected to immortality and is dimly perceived. See also Weber (2128).

2095 Westermann, Claus. *Praise and Lament in the Psalms*. Atlanta, Ga.: John Knox Press, 1981.

A theologian examines the structure and historical development of the Old Testament praise and lament forms and notes theological variations.

2096 Wolff, Hans Walter. *Anthropology of the Old Testament*. Trans. by Margaret Kohl. Philadelphia: Fortress Press, 1974.

A professor of Old Testament presents various Old Testament phrases that identify the nature of a person and a comprehensive section on the Old Testament concept of time, creation and birth, life and death. This is an authoritative account of Israelite conceptions of the grave, definitions of death, stages of dying, the death of the one and the death of the many.

2097 Zimmerli, Walter. "Concerning the Structure of Old Testament Wisdom." In *Studies in Ancient Israelite Wisdom,* 175–207. Ed. by James L. Crenshaw. New York: KTAV Pub. House, 1976.

An authority in Old Testament studies investigates the central question of wisdom, which is the ordering of life around goodness in the presence of a persistent question: "How do I keep myself from misfortune, especially from premature death?" (p. 193).

2.22 NEW TESTAMENT TEACHING

2098 Grayston, Kenneth. *Dying, We Live: A New Inquiry into the Death of Christ in the New Testament*. New York: Oxford University Press, 1990.

The books of the New Testament are surveyed with reference to the death and resurrection of Christ by a biblical scholar who maintains that talk and thought about the death of Christ can relate theological belief to contemporary human problems of death and life.

2099 Keck, Leander. "New Testament Views of Death." In *Perspectives on Death*, ed. by Liston O. Mills, 33–98. Nashville, Tenn.: Abingdon Press, 1969.

A professor of New Testament argues that there is no New Testament doctrine of death. Jesus assumed death as a physical reality. He accepted contemporary Rabbinic categories of death drawn from apocalyptic thought of the interbiblical period such as judgment, resurrection, reward and punishment. He had no interest in disclosing the mysteries of death and what lies beyond. Death was not the central problem to be resolved: the central problem was openness to the kingdom of God, from whence came the true blessings of life. The early Christian tradition stood within the apocalyptic tradition and considered the resurrection to be part of the whole drama of the end times, which included the final judgment, the defeat of Satan, the vindication of God's pledge to Israel, punishment and reward. Emphasis was not upon a doctrine of immortality and the resurrection of individual persons, but upon a new age that had begun to dawn for all people and a new way of looking at the present. The apostle Paul stresses the resurrection of individuals to eternal life as a consequence of the resurrection of Christ. In times of persecution, the universal fact of death had no power upon Christians because of their faith in a living God. It is his character that presents the central theological issue in our concern about death. He will make good the life that He has called us to live.

2100 Leon-Dufour, Xavier. *Life and Death in the New Testament*. Trans. by Terrence Prendergast. San Francisco: Harper and Row, 1986.

A French biblical scholar develops a comprehensive study of the theology of life and death in the New Testament which is based upon the way in which Jesus and Paul approach the fact of their own deaths and the death of others. One section considers Jesus' teaching on the death of the body, heaven, hell, judgement, the Last Supper, agony in the garden, words from the cross. A second section considers Paul's view of the saving nature of Jesus' death, the meaning of death for individual Christians, a biblical look at what happens after death. A sensitive and clearly written book that is based upon sound scholarship.

2101 Robinson, John A. T. *The Body: A Study in Pauline Theology*. Chicago: Henry Regnery Co., 1952.

An English Protestant scholar develops the Pauline concept of the body (*soma*) as akin to the psychosocial functions of the self. *Soma* provides a sense of unity within the person and with others that is brought to fruition in the resurrection. Since *soma* is made by God for solidarity with others, Pauline thought is different from that of classic Greeks who opposed form and matter, the one and the many, the body and the soul. But there is an attitude "of the flesh" which is rebellion against mortality and obedience to God. From this attitude came the unnatural state which we call physical death. We are redeemed from the powers of death by Christ who assumed "flesh" (*sarx*). The church is the "body of Christ," the concrete reality of his resurrection from the dead. Our resurrection as a spiritual body starts at baptism and is completed on the day of the parousia. Straightforward, fundamental scholarship.

2102 Sullender, R. Scott. "Saint Paul's Approach to Grief: Clarifying the Ambiguity." *Journal of Religion and Health* 20 (1981): 63–74.

A pastoral counselor shows how two traditional approaches to grief–lamentation and consolation are synthesized in the writings of St. Paul.

2.3 TWENTIETH CENTURY THEOLOGY

2103 Anderson, Ray S. *Theology, Death and Dying*. New York: Basil Blackwell, 1986.

A theologian examines death from within the circle of faith in Jesus Christ as the Lord of life who has overcome death. His theological concerns are: the death of human persons is the death of a relationship between persons and God; physical death was a part of the original human nature of Adam; sin caused a separation between the human person and the life-sustaining promise and gift of immortality which issues from God alone; humans are dependent upon God for the gift of immortal life through resurrection from the dead. These themes are arranged under the topics of the contemporary mind, a theology of human death, divine judgment and life after death, Christ's victory over death, Christian hope and perspectives, the connection between biological function and environment. There are numerous references to contemporary and classic theologians under each topic. A comprehensive survey.

2104 Barth, Karl. *Church Dogmatics*. Vol. 3. Trans. by Harold Knight, *et al*. Edinburgh: T and T Clark, 1960.

A major continental theologian asserts that God is the Lord of life. Death can never be a consolation in and of itself, nor can death be considered to have meaning even when considered as a judgment of God. God desires life and not death. The relation between death and human nature depends upon the distinction between dying and death. Dying is intrinsic to our created human nature only in the sense that it gives us a sense of time, finitude and mortality. We are not driven by some inner principle toward death. Dying is intrinsic to human nature as originally created by God before sin. Physical death is not in itself the judgment but only a fact of our finite existence. Our relation to destiny is not determined by death to sin but through faith in Jesus Christ. The judgment of God upon sin is seen through the event of Christ's death. The link between death and sin is broken and all persons are related to the living God in a way that forbids any speculation about the status of those who die outside of knowledge and faith in Christ. Questions about retribution after death can only be discussed in relation to the way Christ has taken all retribution upon himself. In His death and resurrection, Jesus overcame death, not by avoiding or transcending it, but by extending human time and history through death. See also Bush (2107).

2105 Bartsch, Hans Werner, ed. *Kerygma and Myth: A Theological Debate*. Trans. by Reginald H. Fuller. London: S. P. C. K., 1953.

This symposium begins with a reprinting of a 1931 manifesto of a New Testament professor, Rudolph Bultmann. Bultmann, an intuitive scholar of the New Testament, is strongly influenced by the existential philosopher Heidegger (2019). He considers the New Testament view of the world as a three-storied structure to be a myth, along with specific ideas of heaven as the abode of God and his angels and the underworld of hell as a place of torment under the control of Satan. It is "senseless and impossible" for modern persons to accept the mythological elements of the New Testament, which include ideas about the Spirit in sacraments, death as a punishment of sin, and the doctrine of the Atonement. But myth does have an existential value to give people transcendent power with which to control themselves and the world. Bultmann offers a reinterpretation of the New Testament: human existence will provide courage for redemption in the face of corruption and death. Julius Schniewind replies that Bultmann is right in holding that the resurrection cannot be a miraculous proof. It is an object of faith. The world-view and language of the Bible must be translated into our own but Bultmann tends to confuse eschatology with timelessness. He does not do justice to the concept of history in biblical faith. Ernest Lohmeyer notes that Bultmann follows the error of the Enlightenment by restricting myth to a concern for human existence. He does not give enough place to myth as an understanding of God. Bultmann seems to use existentialist philosophy to destroy both the content of revelation and the human interpretation of the revelation. Helmut Theileicke agrees with Bultmann that the message of the Bible is not just straight-forward history. There is an intermediate layer of myth but since myth is the way that humans think in terms of time and space, it should be affirmed rather than rejected in the understanding of spiritual truth. Bultmann has been so negative about myth that he has interpreted the New Testament only in terms of a secular philosophy which he developed from Heidegger. Friedrich K. Schumann believes with Bultmann in an existential understanding of the Gospel message as a Christian interpretation of human life. Finally, Bultmann offers a brief reply to his critics and reaffirms the value of a faith that will subject sanctified truth to judgment. Austin Farrar offers a concluding word of appreciation for the "beautiful precision" of Bultmann's presentation. Bibliography, primarily German. See Bultmann (2262).

2106 Beardslee, William A., et al. *Biblical Preaching on the Death of Jesus*. Nashville, Tenn.: Abingdon Press, 1989.

Process theologians seek to hold contrasting insights in tension so that each may be creatively transformed. Biblical texts are related to an emphasis upon preaching as narrative. Symbols and myth are significant in the narrative and interpretation of the text. The authors have prepared this book for academic use by pastors without any thought of the actual needs of people in a time of suffering or any references to studies of grief and dying.

2107 Busch, Eberhard. *Karl Barth: His Life From Letters and Autobiographical Text*. Philadelphia: Fortress Press, 1976.

Barth, Thurneysen, and Gogarten developed a "dialectal" theology after World War I. We do not look or wait for a second coming of Christ; instead we emphasize the continual paradox of living in the present moment with an awareness of God's movement toward us as the "wholly other." The emphasis on the coming of God is concrete, personal, a divine force from outside time that is uncontaminated by our cultural and philosophical assumptions. The impact upon persons will be a force for freedom, radical newness and otherness in this world. See Barth (2104).

2108 Cousins, Ewert H., ed. *Hope and the Future of Man*. Philadelphia: Fortress Press, 1972.

Theologians and philosophers discuss the contention of Whitehead, Hartshorne, Teilhard de Chardin, and Bultmann that the meaning of openness to God's future is to be found immediately in each moment. The position is supported in papers by John B. Cobb, Jr., Philip Hefner and Carl E. Braaten. Jürgen Moltmann confesses that he is no longer gripped by liberal theology, but he does believe that liberation theology is vital to the Christian understanding of hope because it stresses the suffering of God with us to overcome evil in the world. Wolfhart Pannenberg objects to the secularization of the future by those who develop models in the present to account for future trends. He notes that theology confronts and often runs counter to the present world. The incarnation of God in Christ and the doctrine of reconciliation is more basic to Christian hope than any assumption concerning a continuous social progress. Daniel Day Williams objects to the Neo-Platonist assumption of Pannenberg that the essence of things is identical with the transcendent One. Jürgen Moltmann and Schubert Ogden debate the relation of biological man to nature.

2109 Dodd, Charles H. *The Parables of the Kingdom*. New York: Scribner and Sons, 1936.

An English Protestant scholar of the New Testament presents "realized eschatology" to explain the parables of Jesus that refer to the Final Judgment. Dodd believed that Jesus presented the Kingdom of God as a present reality in his ministry rather than a coming event as taught by his followers. The Gospel of John is considered another example of Jesus' emphasis upon ministry in the present which may be expressed symbolically in apocalyptic language.

2110 Doss, Richard. "Towards a Theology of Death." *Pastoral Psychology* 23 (June 1972): 15–23.

A professor of preaching notes three theological traditions concerning death: theological absolutism which follows Greek philosophy in the separation of soul from body; theological reductionism in which transcendent categories are reduced into finite experience (Heidegger, Tillich); theological realism which affirms the interdependence of humans in relation to a God of love (Bonhoeffer). An adequate theology of death will deal with: the meaning of life; the significance of the death-event; the meaning of life after death. The author concentrates upon the death-event as presented by Berkhof, Thielicke, Rahner, Heidegger.

2111 Doss, Richard. *The Last Enemy*. New York: Harper and Row, 1974.

If we really want to listen and respond to basic problems of human existence, we must develop a theology of death. This theology must provide adequate response to questions about a possible life after death and a final fulfillment of the goals and values experienced in this life.

2112 Kaufman, Gordon D. *Systematic Theology: A Historicist's Perspective*. New York: Scribner, 1969.

An American process theologian believes the consciousness of individuals is bound up with their bodily existence and therefore "we have no reason to suppose that their life continues beyond the grave." Jesus resurrection appearances were hallucinations which convinced the disciples that God's purpose in history would be continued despite the crucifixion. The purpose of theology is to show how God's ongoing purpose is fulfilled within history rather than beyond it.

2113 Lohse, Bernhard and Hans P. Schmidt, eds. *Leben angesichts des Todes* (Life in the Face of Death). Tübingen: J. C. B. Mohr, 1968.

This *Festschrift* celebrating Helmut Thielicke's 60th birthday contains sixteen articles on death from biblical, theological, and historical perspectives. The contents cover, among other things, death in the Old Testament, medieval sermons on death, the death of Jesus and the pain of God, as well as articles on death in non-Judaeo-Christian cultures. See also Thielicke (2146, 2147)

2114 Macquarrie, John. *In Search of Humanity.* New York: Crossroad Pub., 1983.

An existential theologian considers life without end as an intolerable experience. Death places life within a definite framework of time. We are able to measure the events of life with utmost seriousness because of this and redeem whatever is mediocre or unworthy. This can be done without any appeal to the possibility of life beyond death. The theme is similar to that of other existentialists who believe that "being" is like a pole with which we can vault over "non-being."

2115 McGill, Arthur C. *Death and Life: An American Theology.* Ed. by Charles A. Wilson and P. M. Anderson. Philadelphia: Fortress Press, 1987.

A Harvard professor of divinity criticizes the emphasis upon death as a terminal event in the early writings of Kübler-Ross (1020) and presents theological and philosophical justification for a second interpretation of death as the gradual and recurrent experiences where life is known to be failing. The American worship of death is an example of the first definition, for which people make no preparation. The second is the classical Christian definition in which death becomes a part of life as a transformation of the self in the Spirit of Christ. A stimulating monograph.

2116 Mills, Liston O., ed. *Perspectives on Death.* Nashville, Tenn.: Abingdon Press, 1969.

See 1161.

2117 Murphy, Marie. *New Images of the Last Things: Karl Rahner on Death and Life After Death.* New York: Paulist Press, 1988.

The provocative questions of a Roman Catholic theologian about the official teachings of the church concerning life after death are summarized from his writings for a general audience.

2118 Neibuhr, Reinhold. *The Nature and Destiny of Man.* New York: Charles Scribner's Sons, 1953.

A Protestant theologian who was influential in discussing the relationship between Christ and culture presents the paradoxes of "last things" as a threat to the meaning of human life because they introduce the peril of meaninglessness. He distinguishes between (1) chronological time as the end of a past or a life without meaning and (2) the end of meaning which is fulfillment, a consummation of life and work. The latter type of ending has already begun to work in us through the Kingdom of God revealed in Jesus, but the tension between two kinds of ending continue in the Christian symbols of the return of Christ, the last judgment and the resurrection. These symbols are not to be taken literally, for then the dialectical conception of time and eternity would be falsified and the ultimate vindication of God over history would be reduced to a point of history.

2119 Newport, John P. *Life's Ultimate Questions. A Contemporary Philosophy of Religion*. Dallas, Tex.: Word Pub., 1989.

A conservative evangelical scholar provides an overview and analysis of questions in philosophy of religion, which include a discussion of natural and cosmic evil in relation to personal suffering, questions about death, immortality, eternal life and resurrection.

2120 Rahner, Karl. "Death." In *Sacramentum Mundi*. Vol. 2. New York: Herder and Herder, 1968.

All people are original sinners and subject to the law of death. In death the human soul enters into the ground of unity of the universe. The soul is no longer bound to an individual bodily structure. It is the beginning of eternity, an interior act of personal self-fulfillment because it is the maturing self-realization of what a person has become during life. The death of Christ makes his spiritual reality open to the whole world. See also Rahner (2316).

2121 Rahner, Karl. *Foundations of Christian Faith*. Trans. by William V. Dych. New York: Seabury Press, 1978.

A Roman Catholic theologian considers eschatology to be a doctrine of freedom and hope for those who have received grace in Christ. The assertions of Scripture and tradition should be viewed from two viewpoints, the conceptual mode and the real content. Also, eschatological assertions must be interpreted on the basis of present experience of salvation. This does not mean that eschatology is confined to the present alone. There also must be a concern for the future and ultimate fulfillment in God.

2122 Rahner, Karl. *On the Theology of Death*. New York: Seabury Press, 1973.

See 2316.

2123 Thielicke, Helmut. *Living With Death*. Trans. by Geoffrey W. Bromiley. Grand Rapids, Mich.: Wm. B. Eerdmans Pub. Co., 1983.

See 2147

2124   Tillich, Paul. *Systematic Theology*. Vol. 3. Chicago: University of Chicago Press, 1963.

An influential existential theologian considers heaven and hell to be relative terms that cannot be "absolute." All Christian symbols for the "end-time" are provisional answers to the meaning of contradictions in our political, social personal life. Supernaturalistic interpretations of future hope (heaven, eternal life) are denied because they are "relative terms and cannot be absolute." The answer for Tillich is a merging of individual destiny into the destiny of the universe. Christian hope is no more than a symbol which is useful in the service of the ego that takes courage in the midst of the knowledge that human life will end.

2125   Toynbee, Arnold, *et. al. Man's Concern with Death*. New York: McGraw-Hill Book Co., 1969.

See 2067.

2126   Wagner, Harald. "Einleitung. Von einer Theologie des Todes zur Theologie des Sterbens." [Introduction. From a Theology of Death to a Theology of Dying]. In *Ars Moriendi. Erwägungen zur Kunst des Sterbens*. Ed. by Harald Wagner. Freiburg, Germany: Herder, 1989.

Wagner argues for the development of a Christian theology of dying integrated with other disciplines, such as medicine and psychology, citing Karl Rahner's distinction between death and dying.

2127   Wagner, Harald, ed. *Ars Moriendi. Erwägungen zur Kunst des Sterbens*. Freiburg, Germany: Herder, 1989.

The contributions of various German academicians span the arc of historical-theological foundation and systematic elaboration (H. Rolfes, H.-M. Barth) concerning the development of modern spirituality (J. Manser) and the new orientation of medical-therapeutic institutions (T. Kruse, H. R. Zielinski), as well as the demands and possibilities of the Liturgy and Religious Pedagogy (Th. Mass-Ewerd, H. Wagner) to the contribution of philosophy (H. Ebeling) and the literature of our day (W. Falk).

2128   Weber, Otto. *Foundations of Dogmatics*. Vol. 1. Trans. by Darrell Guder. Grand Rapids, Mich.: Wm. B. Eerdmans, Pub. Co. 1981.

Viewed from the biological structure of a human being, an immortal being is unimaginable. This does not preclude the possibility that the human person possesses an immortal soul or self, but such a belief runs contrary to Hebrew anthropology. There is no concept of an immortal soul in the Old Testament. The New Testament does mention the word immortal on three occasions, in which the immortality is related to the risen Christ and the embodied person in the new age. See also Weber (2094).

2129 Wohlgschaft, Hermann. *Hoffnung angesichts des Todes* [Hope in the Face of Death]. Wien: Verlag Ferdinand Schöningh, 1977.

In this reworking of a doctoral dissertation, the author examines the idea of death in the thought of Karl Barth, reviewing German Protestant reactions to Barth and reflecting on Barth's thought primarily in light of Karl Rahner's work.

2130 Wolff, Richard. *The Last Enemy*. Washington, D.C.: Canon Press, 1974.

This is a conservative Christian summary of attitudes toward death in Greek and Roman thought, Hindu and Chinese sages, followed by biblical perspectives on death as the wages of sin and the gift of eternal life through Christ.

2.4 THE MEANING OF DEATH

2131 Brandon, S. G. F. *The Judgment of the Dead: The Idea of Life After Death in the Major Religions*. New York: Charles Scribner's Sons, 1967.

The vindication of moral values in the judgment of the dead is traced from ancient Egypt and Mesopotamia to Greek and Roman culture, Hebrew and Christian, Islam, Iran, Hinduism and Buddhism, China and Japan. Bibliography. Comprehensive scholarship.

2132 Clerk, N. W. (Pseudonym). *A Grief Observed*. New York: Seabury Press, 1961.

See Lewis 2139.

2133 Erickson, Millard. *Christian Theology*. Vol. 2. Grand Rapids, Mich.: Baker Book House, 1983.

A theologian who believes in the historical origin of humanity as presented in Genesis, speaks cautiously of a pre-fallen human nature which is entirely mortal. Previous to this transgression, Adam could die, and as a consequence of his sin he would die. Human nature as originally created was in a state of conditional immortality. Under the right conditions, Adam could have lived forever.

2134 Feifel, Herman, ed. *The Meaning of Death*. New York: McGraw-Hill Book Co., 1959.

See 1008.

2135 Feifel, Herman, ed. *New Meanings of Death.* New York: McGraw-Hill Book Co., 1977.

See 1009.

2136 Freud, Sigmund. *Beyond the Pleasure Principle.* New York: Basic Books, 1975.

See 1181.

2137 Gruman, Gerald, Gordon Geddes, and Michael A. Simpson, eds. *Death as a Speculative Theme in Religious, Scientific and Social Thought.* New York: Arno Press, 1976.

Papers by various authors are reprinted in one volume: Henry George, W. W.Reade, N. Berdayev.

2138 Kierkegaard, Søren. *The Gospel of Our Sufferings.* Trans. by A. S. Aldworth and W. S. Furris. Grand Rapids, Mich.: William B. Eerdmans Pub. Co., 1964.

Kinds of suffering are necessary as a way to show the joy that comes through suffering. Kierkegaard will not ask about what of the world remains behind us, but what of the treasure that we see upon earth and have already stored up in heaven. He is at his best in describing the difficulty of denying oneself in lesser things.

2139 Lewis, C. S. (N. W. Clerk). *A Grief Observed.* New York: Seabury Press, 1961.

An Oxford don and writer of popular Christian works is autobiographical about grief for his wife. Begun, without plans for publication, as a means of self-therapy, it was written informally during his first weeks alone. See also Lewis (2160).

2140 Lundeen, Lyman T. "Faith and the Problem of Death." In *The Church and Pastoral Care,* ed. by Leroy and J. Harold Ellens. Grand Rapids, Mich.: Baker Book House, 1988.

See 4452.

2141 McGatch, Milton. *Death: Meaning and Mortality in Christian Thought and Contemporary Culture.* New York: Seabury Press, 1969.

See 1044.

2142 Miller-McLemore, Bonnie. *Death, Sin and the Moral Life.* Atlanta, Ga.: Scholars Press, 1988.

In a critique of Kübler-Ross and contemporary "death awareness" the author relies on the theology of Don Browning, John Calvin and Paul Tillich to present a link between sin and death that provides moral guidance for a Christian approach to death. Paul Ramsey (3614) is cited as one who oversimplified the moral dimension by concentrating upon "death as enemy."

2143 Neale, Robert E. *The Art of Dying*. New York: Harper and Row, 1971.

In the life-cycle model for dying, a theologian emphasizes death as a natural event that can be made tolerable by openly and courageously seizing life on its own terms. Various exercises are proposed to tell our story about death as initiation into an anticipation of new life. The terrors of death are treated as misperceptions that betray our personal resentments of the nature of life. Although the author is a Protestant minister, the theories of death are based upon psychoanalytic assumptions of death fears as a form of neurosis. Classical Christian themes of judgment and eternal life are missing.

2144 Rahner, Karl. *On the Theology of Death*. New York: Herder and Herder, 1967.

See 2318.

2145 Schillebeeckx, Edward, and Boniface Willems. *Thanatology. The Problem of Eschatology. Concilium* vol. 41. New York: Paulist Press, 1969.

In volume 41 of *Concilium*, continental theologians discuss the "end time" (eschatology) in terms of the judgment of God, biblical and post-biblical thoughts concerning the judgments of God, the resurrection, eternal life.

2146 Thielicke, Helmut. *Death and Life*. Trans. by Edward Schroeder. Philadelphia: Fortress Press, 1970.

A noted German theologian considers two options concerning death, as (1) a connection with nothingness or (2) as a way to understand life, the world and humans as beings who move toward death as a meaningful enterprise. The latter option is embraced by the author as being close to the biblical doctrine of humanity. His focus is upon sin and redemption, death and resurrection. The study is both psychologically and theologically insightful. See also Thielicke (2147).

2147 Thielicke, Helmut. *Living With Death*. Trans. by Geoffrey W. Bromiley. Grand Rapids, Mich.: Wm. B. Eerdmans Pub. Co., 1983.

Death raises questions about our uniqueness as persons. How do we continue to personally experience ourselves and be aware of death? A noted

German theologian considers this question in the thinking of modern poets and philosophers such as Goethe, Hegel, Nietzsche, Marx. Their consideration of death as an absurdity is an attempt to repress the anxiety that nevertheless persists about death. Death is more than a natural process. It is also a personal event that can only be understood in the light of transcendent purposes for persons. Old and New Testament themes of overcoming death are then presented. *Zoe* refers in the New Testament to human life lived as history with God, both in our biological life and in the life of obedience and love that survives physical death. See also Thielicke (2146), Lohse (2113).

2148 Tillich, Paul. *Systematic Theology.* Vol. 2. Chicago: University of Chicago Press, 1957.

An existential theologian argues that man is naturally mortal. Sin does not produce death, but gives death power which is conquered only in participation with the Eternal. The idea of any cellular or psychological structural change in a person because of the Fall is absurd and unbiblical. The death spoken of in the Genesis account of the Creation and the Fall is not the introduction of mortality into the human race. A theological distinction is possible between physical death as natural and spiritual death as unnatural, caused by sin. For a more biblical exegesis of the connections and distinctions between natural and spiritual death, see Moody (2277).

2149 Wohlgschaft, Hermann. *Hoffnung angesichts des Todes* [Hope in the Face of Death]. Wien: Verlag Ferdinand Schöningh, 1977.

See 2129.

2.41 PAIN AND SUFFERING

2150 Buttrick, George. *God, Pain and Evil.* Nashville, Tenn.: Abingdon Press, 1966.

A noted Methodist pastor and writer provides human understanding and sympathy for pain and evil along with assurances of God's continuing presence and suffering with us.

2151 Claypool, John. *Tracks of a Fellow Struggler.* Dallas, Tex.: Word Pub., 1974.

See 4472.

2152 Cooper, Burton Z. *Why, God?* Atlanta, Ga.: John Knox Press, 1988.

A Presbyterian professor of philosophical theology presents the vulnerable suffering of God with us in the face of tragedy, suffering and evil. He considers such issues as the nature of God in God's power and purpose, the meaning and place of suffering in human life, and how we can go forward in the face of problems that have concerned church theologians and modern Christian writers like himself.

2153 Dougherty, Flavian, ed. *The Meaning of Human Suffering*. New York: Human Sciences Press, 1982.

Essays from the Congress on the Meaning of Human Suffering held at Notre Dame are ecumenical and international. Roman Catholic and Protestant theologians join with sociologists and philosophers to speak about social evil, personal suffering and grief. The essays are uneven in quality but illuminating in the range of topics and circumstances.

2154 Fichter, Joseph H. *Religion and Pain*. New York: Crossroad Pub. Co., 1981.

See 3225.

2155 Frankl, Victor E. *The Doctor and the Soul*. Trans. by Richard and Clara Winston. New York: Alfred A. Knopf, 1955.

Amid the horrors of a Nazi concentration camp, a Jewish psychiatrist faces the possibility that death will take away all meaning in life. He developed an existential theory of logotherapy in which the meaning of human is based upon its irreversible character. We are temporal and singular and must make the most of the time given to us. Death is properly a part of life as an incentive to life with meaning in the face of temporal limitations. One quality of mature life is responsibility both to self and to the community. The author rejects the Freudian assumption that people are dominated by instincts, since the instincts only make proposals and the ego decides what to do about these proposals. Mature decision-making is a sign of spiritual freedom from fatalism and a paralyzing fear of death. Even the deforming existence of the concentration camps hide the thought that there are purposes in life which can yet be fulfilled even though suffering will be a part of this process.

2156 Gerstenberg, E. W. and W. Schrage. *Suffering*. Trans. by John E. Steely. Nashville, Tenn.: Abingdon Press, 1977.

A specialist in the Old and New Testaments counters widely-held views that the Bible teaches acceptance of suffering. The faith of the Israelites prompted them to struggle against the causes of suffering. In the New Testament, victory over affliction is proclaimed as possible through faith in Jesus. However, suffering is expected as a result of public witness and confession of faith. Prayers of faith are seen in the New Testament as affirmations of unconditional trust in the midst of fear and pain, rather than assurances that physical illness will always be reversed. A precise study that shatters many ancient and modern stereotypes.

2157 Hans, Daniel T. *God on the Witness Stand: Questions Christians Ask in Personal Tragedy.* Grand Rapids, Mich.: Baker Book House, 1987.

With intimacy and authenticity a pastor describes his feelings about the terminal illness of his young daughter in a series of sermons. Each sermon relates a biblical text to his confession that tragedy can "grind up innocent victims," that he has asked God for answers and still is uncertain, but in some way he has retained hope for the future. See also Claypool (4470).

2158 Hauerwas, Stanley. *Naming the Silences.* Grand Rapids, Mich.: Wm. B. Eerdmans, 1990.

A theological ethicist uses stories of suffering by children to show why we seek a deliverer from disease and mortality. As a modern deliverer, medicine has often hidden the silences that surround suffering by children. Our pain can find a voice when we are in a community capable of absorbing our grief. This is a function of Christian worship.

2159 Israel, Martin. *The Pain That Heals.* London: Mowbray, 1981.

A physician who is also an Anglican priest asserts the creative potentiality of suffering for those who have perseverance and courage. In a series of meditative essays, he examines the ravages of pain, psychic despair and physical disintegration that is a human approximation to the dark depths into which Christ entered to demonstrate God's involvement in human suffering. Physical pain, anguish for others, torments in relationships are all considered to be part of the growth of character into the redemptive work of Christ. Many psychological and theological insights are provided to realistically encounter fear and despair in a way that will lead to a constructive life through prudence and providence.

2160 Lewis, C. S. *The Problem of Pain.* London: Geoffrey Bles, 1940.

An Oxford don considers the paradox of human experience of pain beside a good assurance that ultimate reality is righteous and loving. Answers are considered in terms of (1) divine omnipotence: God has created a free natural order in which laws of nature seem good to some and bad to others; (2) divine goodness: pain may come because God is altering those who can become fully lovable; (3) the painful alteration of a person may be necessary because human love has missed the mark; (4) the first missing of the mark was self-will that resulted in the Fall: God has assumed a suffering nature which the evil of the Fall has produced; (5) most pain comes because of the way people treat each other. Animal pain comes from Satan. See also Lewis (2139).

2161 Moulyn, Adrian C. *The Meaning of Suffering.* Westport, Conn.: Greenwood Press, 1982.

A physician seeks a philosophical link between the intrinsic value of suffering and the way that human beings live in time. His solution is a heroic mode of existence which is realistic about imperfections and factors in human existence, but also optimistic in the way that suffering creates wholeness in human beings, unifies reality with ideals and fills life with meaning. Numerous philosophical and theological sources are cited.

2162 Oates, Wayne E. *The Revelation of God in Human Suffering*. Philadelphia: Westminster Press, 1959.

With devotion and insight, a pastoral psychologist examines the impact of the suffering of Christ upon varied aspects of human suffering: purpose, fellowship, maturity, self-defense, aloneness, blindness, purity of heart, anger, grief and responsibility.

2163 Payne, Barbara. "Pain Denial and Ministry to the Elderly." *Theology Today* 38 (1981): 30–36.

The role of religion in responding to pain and to dying is a directed area of research by the author who serves as a professor of gerontology. Research might help to clarify confusion about reasons why the elderly, when dying are assumed to be more religious. It may be that they are afraid of death and are suffering from chronic pain. A more effective ministry will come when pastors are more aware of the work done in pain centers, hospices and nursing homes.

2164 Richmond, Kent D. *Preaching to Sufferers*. Nashville, Tenn.: Abingdon Press, 1988.

See 4481.

2165 Schilling, S. Paul. *God and Human Anguish*. Nashville, Tenn.: Abingdon Press, 1980.

A theologian analyzes secular and religious theories of human suffering and seeks to reconcile the agonizing reality of evil and suffering in the world with faith in the power and goodness of God.

2166 Simundson, Daniel J. *Faith Under Fire*. Minneapolis, Minn.: Augsburg Pub. House, 1980.

A Lutheran pastor and chaplain presents a traditional biblical view of suffering in relation to pessimism as found in sections of the Old Testament, the meaning of suffering for others as found in Isaiah 40–55, the types of advice given in the book of Job, eschatology and the apocalyptic among Old Testament prophets, the new meaning of hope in specific life situations through Christ. A readable survey without reference to critical scholarly questions.

2167 Soelle, Dorothee. *Suffering*. Trans. by Everett R. Kalin. Philadelphia: Fortress Press, 1975.

The emphasis of this theologian is upon personal misery, which may be eliminated only by those who themselves are exposed to senseless, unnecessary suffering. The theme is commended by Surin (2189). For a more precise biblical exegesis of suffering, see Gerstenberg (2156).

2168 Sutcliffe, Edmund Felix. *Providence and Suffering in the Old and New Testament*. London: Thomas Nelson and Sons, 1983.

An Old Testament professor considers Old Testament beliefs concerning sin and its consequences, the necessity of corporate solidarity combined with individual responsibility, vicarious suffering and the bewilderment of the Psalmist and of Job. The New Testament ideas of suffering are traced in terms of future life and the example of Christ. A careful and judicious exegetical study.

2169 Tournier, Paul. *Creative Suffering*. San Francisco: Harper and Row, 1982.

A Swiss psychiatrist and philosopher reviews the lives of many persons who attained success in life after the stimulus of suffering in younger years.

2170 Weatherhead, Leslie. *Salute to a Sufferer*. London: Epworth Press, 1962.

Through a series of questions and answers a popular pastor and author offers the "plain man" a Christian philosophy of suffering. For example, God allows what He does not will, such as sin. Chance is an event which God did not intend and which humans could not foresee. The sense of suffering is a deeper knowledge of God's care. Disease is with us because God has not yet finished making His universe.

2.42 THEODICY: EVIL AND THE WILL OF GOD
See also GUILT/SIN (1.34), CRISIS INTERVENTION (3.252).

2171 Basinger, David. *Divine Power in Process Theism: A Philosophical Critique*. Albany, N.Y.: State University of New York Press, 1988.

A philosopher examines a basic assumption of process theology: God alone unifies the processes of life as the most influential individual that humans can experience, but only by persuasion. The God of process theology has no coercive power to unilaterally control anything. The impact of this assumption is examined. Some of the conclusions are: much evil is unnecessary and God cannot in any direct sense be held responsible for it; the ultimate evil is our "perpetual perishing" over which God is victorious, but not so victorious over injustice, physical or mental anguish and death; petitionary prayer does generate "efficacious conscious thoughts" without any hope that God would actually unilaterally intervene in the world; communion with God is primarily through subconscious spiritual growth.

2172 Becker, Ernest. *Escape from Evil.* New York: Free Press, 1975.

Human evil arises from a natural and inevitable urge to deny mortality and achieve a heroic self-image. Various philosophers, a psychologist and a sociologist are used to illustrate his thesis, which is primarily drawn from the works of Otto Rank. The author died of cancer in 1974 and the publication is posthumous. See Becker (2194).

2173 Cairns, D. S. *The Riddle of the World.* London: SCM Press, 1937.

How can humans know that they are higher beings and yet be entangled and eventually destroyed by nature? Cairns believes in a spiritual foundation of the world that can give people confidence in the presence of destruction and death. God comes to us as a source of power in the midst of our choices as one who suffers with us. A judicious philosophical and theological study.

2174 Cooper, Berton Z. *Why, God?* Atlanta, Ga.: John Knox Press, 1988.

Out of his own grief at the death of a son and a daughter, a Presbyterian professor of philosophical theology explains suffering and evil in terms of Barth and Whitehead. Barth accepts the logical contradiction of affirming both the all-controlling nature of divine and the concept of Nothingness, the evil that arises in the wake of God's positive creation. Whitehead affirms a limitation in God's eternal power because he must always be related to a changing, limited world. He must be continually redeeming that which he has created. The well-developed theological arguments are presented in the context of very human examples about anxiety, suffering and despair.

2175 Cowburn, John. *Shadows and the Dark.* London: SCM Press, 1979.

A Jesuit writer rejects the view that God planned everything in advance and the view that there is no purpose in the world. He argues for evolution as a necessary feature of material existence in which evil is considered to be inexcusable, unjustifiable and inexplicable. The strength of the book is in individual decision making and weakest in discussion of social and cosmic evil.

2176 Davis, Stephen T., ed. *Encountering Evil.* Atlanta, Ga.: John Knox Press, 1981.

Five scholars from Clairmont School of Theology present varying views concerning evil, with a summary of traditional theism by the editor.

Authors include references to the thought of Alfred North Whitehead and Charles Hartshorne, existentialism, analytic philosophy.

2177 Forsyth, P. T. *The Justification of God*. London: Independent Press, 1957.

Instead of rational optimism that promises progress, the author affirms redemption of the world through the sacrificial death of Christ. The reality of massive evil is faced in the judgment of God upon the world, but it is a saving judgment in which God suffers with us as his Son triumphs over evil through the cross. The work was provoked by World War I. The themes are sometimes complicated, as in the chapter on metaphysics and redemption. But it spoke to a despairing generation in the same manner as Karl Barth and Reinhold Niebuhr.

2178 Griffin, David Ray. *God, Power and Evil: A Process Theodicy*. Philadelphia: Westminster Press, 1976.

If there is a providential God who is perfect in both power and moral goodness, why is there evil in the world? The issue is discussed from the perspective of process theology (Whitehead and Hartshorne). Traditional and historical answers are presented from the Bible, Plato, Aristotle, Plotinus, Augustine, Aquinas, Spinoza, Luther, Calvin, Leibniz, Barth, Hick, Ross, Fackenheim, Brunner, Berkeley. In various ways these revere God as controller of the universe. The author alters this view through process philosophy in which the power of God is considered to be imperfect. This is a "non-traditional" theodicy in which God not only *does* not but also in principle *could* not completely control events in the world but is still worthy of worship because He exemplifies perfect moral goodness as we really understand that term. We can hope for a better future without belief in an afterlife.

2179 Hall, Douglass John. *God and Human Suffering: An Exercise of the Theology of the Cross*. Minneapolis, Minn.: Augsburg Pub. House, 1986.

The author rejects theoretical explanations of evil in favor of participation in suffering where the drama of evil leads to self-revelation. Any answers to the problem of evil can only be answered in terms of historical circumstances: who is asking a question about evil today and why?

2180 Hartshorne, Charles. *The Logic of Perfection*. La Salle, Ill.: Open Court Pub., 1962.

In Chapter Ten a process philosopher presents an alternative to the understandings of death found in classical theists. His hypothesis of a "limitation" in God's power to do good in the world became the philosophical position for a best-seller by Rabbi Kushner (2183).

2181 Hick, John. *Evil and the God of Love*, 2nd ed. New York: Harper and Row, 1978.

A philosopher-theologian surveys the problem of evil as discussed by (1) Augustine, who insisted upon a historical fall from perfection and inherited guilt, and (2) Irenaeus, who maintained that the fall did not eradicate God-consciousness and that consciousness can pull humans toward perfection. The critical nature of Hick's questions are the greatest value of the book, which concludes with a suggestion of pain and suffering as necessary features in a world in process of soul-making. See also Hick (2213).

2182 Joshua, Jean-Pierre. *Discours Chretiens Et Scandale Du Mal*. Chalet, 1979.

A member of the Dominican Order who is also an M.D. discusses the many difficulties of evil as explained by atheists, agnostics and Christians such as Augustine. The author feels that a solution will come through studies that go beyond natural philosophy to the compassion of God for his people in suffering.

2183 Kushner, Harold S. *When Bad Things Happen to Good People*. New York: Varkolen-Schocken Books, 1981.

The book that became a bestseller was written after the death of the author's son at age fourteen. In personal suffering Rabbi Kushner decided he could worship a God who hates suffering but cannot eliminate it. There is wisdom and compassion in many practical suggestions in this readable book. "God helps those who stop hurting themselves." Hall (2179) notes that one of the elements missing from Kushner is any account of God's love. Consequently, the sufferer must derive whatever meaning can be found from personal experience without any divine resources such as grace. See also Hartshorne (2180), Claypool (4472).

2184 Maritain, Jacques. *God and the Permission of Evil*. Trans by Joseph W. Evans. Milwaukee, Wis.: Bruce Pub. Co., 1966.

With precise logic, a Roman Catholic philosopher depends upon Aquinas for a belief that all which we do comes from God and all we do which is evil comes from ourselves because God has the first initiative in the line of being and because we have the first initiative in the line of non-being. God has given us the free will to shatter our being.

2185 McGill, Arthur C. *Suffering: A Test of Theological Method*. Forward by Paul Ramsey and William F. May. Philadelphia: Westminster Press, 1982.

A theologian approaches the problem of evil by examining the concept of power: demonic power that is violent, destructive, and dominative versus the power of God as creative, totally open, self giving and expansive. Service characterizes God's relationship to the world rather than domination. Suggestions are given for the development of a theological method that will follow from our reception of a serving and suffering God.

2186 Means, James E. *A Tearful Celebration*. Portland, Oreg.: Multnomah Press, 1985.

After many years of pastoral experience, a professor in a conservative Protestant theological seminary is faced with difficult questions after the death of his wife by cancer. He steadfastly and sensitively seeks to reconcile his belief in an all-powerful God who "has considered it necessary to make us all subject to disease, suffering, accident and death," and at the same time believe in the compassion of God as a comforter of all his children.

2187 Nelson, Marie Colman, and Michael Eigan. *Evil: Self and Culture*. Vol. 4, Self-In-Process Series. New York: Human Sciences Press, 1984.

Various authorities range from a study of witchcraft in the Middle Ages to modern psychoanalytic concepts of evil. Psychologists discuss evil in dreams, the death wish and instinct. Innocence and experience is explored theologically by Walter James Lowe.

2188 Peterson, Michael L. *Evil and the Christian God*. Grand Rapids, Mich.: Baker Book House, 1982.

An evangelical Protestant seeks to remove apparent incompatibility between God and evil and to show that the character of evil in the world supports a theistic conception of reality. The author seeks to bring together thought, feeling and volition in considering the problem of evil.

2189 Sanford, John A. *Evil: The Shadow Side of Reality*. New York: Crossroad Pub. Co., 1981.

Jungian analyst and Episcopal priest, Sanford explores common ground between psychology and Christianity on the question of evil. Evil and good are in the depth of the psyche. Individuality requires the transcendence of limited-ego views of evil and the achievement of an inclusive perspective of the Self. Sanford views the Old Testament as a totality of opposites in which evil has the role of curing us of our wrong directions in life. Jesus stood for the coexistence of good and evil, while Paul presented an unhealthy understanding of spirit versus flesh. While the book is psychologically sophisticated, the exegesis is faulty, especially in comparison with Cullmann's (2200, 25–39) careful exegetical study of Paul as a unifier of body and soul, rather than a dualist.

2190 Surin, Kenneth. *Theology and the Problem of Evil.* Oxford: Basil Blackwell, 1986.

A philosophical theologian considers two perspectives on the presence of evil and suffering in a world created by an omnipotent and morally perfect God. The philosophical theism of the Enlightenment created a "problematic deity" that has lead to much contemporary confusion. The author seeks to clarify the issues by labeling (1) a "theoretical approach" typified by Plantinga, Swinburne, Hick and other process theologians; and (2) a "practical approach" illustrated by Soelle, Moltmann, Forsyth. Two characters of Dostoevsky are used to evaluate these two approaches. The practical approach wins, with emphasis upon an "incarnate salvation" in which concerned persons identify solidly with those who are afflicted. A lucid summary of elusive opinions.

2191 Taylor, Michael J., ed. *The Mystery of Suffering and Death.* Staten Island, N.Y.: Alba House, 1973.

The relationship between the doctrine of God and the presence of suffering in human life is explored by philosophical theologians: Ladislaus Boros, Roger Troysfontines, Jürgen Moltmann, John Hick, Albert Outler.

2.5 TRANSCENDING DEATH

2192 Badham, Paul. *Immortality or Extinction?* Totowa, N. J.: Barnes and Noble Books, 1982.

A professor of theology and philosophy of religion collaborates with his wife who has a particular concern for exploring non-reductionistic, monistic materialism. They agree that the language of Christian hope has reference to some future state and is not primarily concerned with the context of present earthly life. Support for the future life can no longer rely on the traditional framework of Christian belief. Paranormal claims for immortality are then considered. Living communion with God, attested by human experience is the only basis for a trust for a life after death.

2193 Baillie, John. *And the Life Everlasting.* New York: Charles Scribner's Sons, 1933.

An Edinburgh professor of divinity investigates anthropology, philosophy, theology and poetic literature for answers concerning skepticism of traditional Christian teaching about eternal life. In the course of inquiry, two options are rejected for the present time: tribalism with its purely corporate ethic and immortality and brahminism with a thorough-going denial of the claims of individuality and a contended reabsorption of all finite spirits into one general fund of spiritual life. Two alternatives remain: a radical pessimism and hope in everlasting life with God. To support the Christian hope of eternal life, the author examines various theological views and the philosophical questions of secular/sacred/time/eternity strangers/pilgrims. See also Baillie (2010).

2194 Becker, Ernest. *The Denial of Death*. New York: Free Press, 1973.

In a synthesis of philosophy, anthropology and sociology, Becker draws upon Otto Rank's psychology to combat the terror of insignificance through death that motivates (a) an unnecessary life-long struggle for heroic self-esteem and (b) a necessary, narrowed perception of the world that represses all terror. The author believes that the fear of death is intrinsic to our nature as persons and that all sickness of the soul is rooted in the denial and repression of this reality. The author's viewpoint is described as "existential-phenomenological" by Johnston (1140). The work needs the unity and vitality of symbolization in a discussion of death and the meaning of life (Lifton 1221, 51–52). See also Meyer (1025), Neale (1193), Becker (2172).

2195 Becque, Maurice, and Louis Becque. *Life After Death*. Vol.28, *20th Century Encyclopedia of Catholicism*. Trans. by P. J. Hepburn-Scott. New York: Hawthorne Books, 1960.

The authors review the future life in contemporary literature and philosophy. This is followed by chapters on the idea of death in various ancient religions, Islam, Protestantism. Remaining chapters provide explicit Roman Catholic teaching concerning heaven, hell, purgatory and the resurrection.

2196 Brunner, Emil. *Eternal Hope*. Trans. by Harold Knight. Philadelphia: Westminster Press, 1954.

An influential Swiss Protestant theologian does not consider death to be an original element in the divine order in creation. It has arisen from disorder. In systematic fashion the author reviews related Christian doctrines of time and eternity, the negative promise (AntiChrist) and the progressive hope (utopian millenium), present history and future advent of Christ, death as the transition to eternal life, mythological elements in the New Testament message of the end of history, the last judgment and the problem of universal redemption.

2197 Charles, R. H. *A Critical History of the Doctrine of a Future Life: In Israel, in Judaism, and in Christianity*. London: Adam and Charles Black, 1899.

An influential professor of biblical Greek provides an authoritative and exhaustive study of the synthesis of individual and national beliefs in individual immortality and messianic kingdom in the Old Testament, followed by the study of the expansion of these doctrines in the apocryphal and apocalyptic literature, 200 B. C.–100 A. D., and concluding with separate studies of eschatology in various sections of the New Testament. The author maintains a four stage development of eschatology in the writings of Paul. Divine inspiration is assumed for the Old Testament and the New Testament, but as a progressive revelation that moved, for example, toward a doctrine of hell as a place of spiritual rather than corporeal punishment.

2198 Chidester, David. *Patterns of Transcendence: Religion, Death and Dying*. Belmont, Calif.: Wadsworth Pub. Co., 1990.

This comprehensive and judicious survey of transcendence considers the following patterns that recur in the history of religions: the affirmation of kinship bonds that are unbroken by death, ecstasy in this life as a rehearsal for death, cultural rituals and commemoratives of the dead and mythic transcendence that prepare the living for the afterlife. After looking at the traditional religions of Australia, Africa and North America, Eastern and Western theories and practices are considered with special reference to the *Tibetan Book of the Dead* and to the *Divine Comedy* of Dante. Patterns of transcendence in America are carefully reviewed. Excellent choice of references at the end of each chapter. Extensive index.

2199 Clarkson, George E. *Grounds For Belief In Life After Death*. Lewiston, N.Y.: E. Mellon Press, n. d.

A summary of the thoughts of Nicholas Berdyaev, Gabriel Marcel and Paul Tillich on eternal life. Includes the Ingersoll Lecture on the immortality of man, 1962 "Symbols of Eternal Life" by Paul Tillich. Bibliography.

2200 Cullmann, Oscar. *Immortality of the Soul or Resurrection of the Dead?: The Witness of the New Testament*. London: Epworth Press, 1958.

A continental theologian distinguishes Christian teaching concerning the resurrection from Greek belief concerning immortality. The serenity of Socrates is contrasted with the troubled soul of Jesus as he faces death. A provocative thesis that provoked much controversy among theologians.

2201 Delooz, Pierre. "Who Believes in the Hereafter?" In *Death and Presence: The Psychology of Death and the After-Life*, ed. by Andre Godin, 17–38. Brussels: Lumen Vitae Press, 1972.

A poll taken in ten European countries (1968) shows that belief in the hereafter is generally less widespread than belief in God. The same conclusion is reached by a comparison with polls in the United States.

2202 Dewart, JoAnne E. MacWilliam. *Death and Resurrection*. Wilmington, Del.: Michael Glazier, 1986.

See 1075.

2203 DeWolf, L. Harold. *Eternal Life: Why We Believe*. Philadelphia: Westminster Press, 1980.

A Methodist professor of theology surveys non-Christian beliefs concerning the afterlife, some modern questions of doubt, biblical affirmations concerning personal life after death and some evidences from near-death experiences. The traditional doctrine of eternal punishment is rejected. Notes and brief bibliography. Readable without reflection upon critical problems.

2204 Eliade, Mircea. *Death, Afterlife and Eschatology*. San Francisco: Harper and Row, 1974.

This anthology of religious texts for use in college teaching by a distinguished French philosopher is composed of short sections from primitive religion, ancient Near East, Islam, late Buddhism, Zen. See also Carse (2014), Kramer (2328).

2205 Fechner, Gustav Theodor. *The Little Book of Life after Death*. Trans. by Mary C. Wadsworth. Introduction by William James. 1904. Reprint. New York: Arno Press, 1976.

The relationship of human identity, self-fulfillment and death are considered from a study of both Western and Eastern philosophies of religion.

2206 Frazer, James G. *Belief in Immortality and the Worship of the Dead*. 3 Vols. New York: Macmillan Pub. Co., 1913, 1922, 1924.

See 1242.

2207 Graham, Billy. *Facing Death and the Life After*. Waco, Tx.: Word Books, 1987.

A noted evangelist uses many illustrations to combine healthy realism with confident hope in a discussion of the certainty of death, changing attitudes, the death of children, dealing with grief, the question of euthanasia, life as preparation for death and the hope of eternal life. Trust in Christ for salvation is presented as the ultimate strength against natural terror of death.

2208 Grof, Stanislav and Christina Grof. *Beyond Death: The Gates of Consciousness*. New York: Thames and Hudson, 1980.

This illustrated text finds support from ancient religion and modern parapsychology for biological death as the beginning of an adventure in consciousness. From a variety of ancient and modern sources, the authors develop "maps" of the stages of the afterlife.

2209 Griffin, Nathaniel Edward and Lawrence Hunt, eds. *The Farther Shore: An Anthology of World Opinion On the Immortality of the Soul.* Boston: Houghton Mifflin Co., 1934.

After a brief preface to each selection, the editors provide excerpts on immortality from philosophers, theologians, poets and public figures from 216 B. C. to 1918.

2210 Hartshorne, Charles. *The Logic of Perfection.* La Salle, Ill.: Open Court Pub. Co., 1962.

An essay in this book on the meaning of continued significance after death into "the memory of God" is a treatment of the meaning of life after death by a process theologian.

2211 Heim, Karl. *Die Gemeinde Des Auferstandenen.* [The Community of the Resurrected One]. Munich: Neubau-Verlag, 1949.

A German philosophical theologian affirms that God who raised Christ from the dead has the power to bring the dead back to life. Without the exercise of this power there is no life after death and we pass into nothingness. The Christian, however passes into the hands of God. It is only when we are annihilated that we can be truly resurrected. Men, beasts, even plants are alike in death. Our only concern about death is the continuation of our faith in God. No spiritualism or hypothesis of any kind is necessary.

2212 Herzog, Edgar. *Psyche and Death.* Trans. by David Cox and Eugene Rolfe. New York: G. P. Putnam and Sons, 1966.

A Jungian analyst traces the evolution of images onto which we project the concept of death: dog, wolf, snake, bird, horse. As humankind matures, these primitive images reappear in death legends and in dreams, a number of which are discussed as an expression of psychic development. The experience of encountering death is an opportunity for the religious growth of the soul for it increases our awareness that we exist in the past and in the future. This is a specifically human awareness. The author resists Freudian attempts to reduce images of the psyche which protect the ego from reality. He finds that these images nourish the inner and cultural life of an individual in the midst of a literal and material Western world that has neglected the spiritual aspects of life and death, which is ruled over by the archetype of divinity. Respect for symbols is also found in Lifton (1221, 2224). See also Jung (2218, 3206).

2213 Hick, John. *Death and Eternal Life.* San Francisco: Harper and Row, 1976.

A process theologian surveys contemporary views of death in sociology, psychology and parapsychology, followed by a review of Christian, Hindu and Buddhist views. In the Christian views, the author finds two fundamentally different types of theology which are traced to variant cultural images. One strain, influenced by the Greeks and Stoics, speaks of death as the event where the loving Lord of life receives back the life that was loaned to humans. Believers go to "live with Christ" and fully experience that which they have foretasted under the conditions of existence as eternal life. The other strain is traced to Judaism and introduced into Christian thought by the Apostle Paul. Death is punishment for sin. This view became dominant in the Christian world through Augustine in the fifth century and Anselm in the eleventh century. See also Hick (2254).

2214 Hocking, William E. *The Meaning of Immortality in Human Existence.* New York: Harper, 1957.

A Harvard professor of philosophy is devoted to classical idealism in his discussion of some of the needless obstacles to a just judgment of what one would think about death, immortality and a total sense of human life. The author challenges every reader to become a new knower of old things with grace and beauty.

2215 Howells, William Dean, *et al. In After Days: Thoughts on the Future Life.* 1910. Reprint. Salem, N. H.: Ayer Co. Pub., 1976.

Nine influential authors in the later half of the nineteenth century present the themes of religious faith and sacred duty in relation to death. Of much influential was Henry James' article "Is There a Life after Death?"

2216 Hügel, Friedrich Von. *Eternal Life: A Study of Its Implications and Applications.* Edinburgh: T. and T. Clark, 1913.

A German scholar finds a full eschatological element in the life and teaching of Christ alongside of a prophetic and ethical element. These elements are reviewed and compared in Oriental religions, Judaism, Hellenism, primitive Christianity, the Middle Ages, Kant, and those who followed him such as Schleiermacher. The impact of Darwin is considered along with some study of present social problems and institutional religion. Although this "Catholic modernism" was condemned by Pope Pius X, it became a well-balanced classic in this field.

2217 Johnson, Christopher Jay and Marsha G. McGee, eds. *Encounters With Eternity: Religious Views of Death and Life After Death.* New York: Philosophical Library, 1986.

Summaries of official teachings on death and the afterlife are presented along with a short introduction to each faith group: Assemblies of God, Bahai's, Baptist, Buddhism, Churches of Christ, Church of Jesus Christ of Latter Day Saints, Hinduism, Islam, Judaism, Lutherans, Presbyterianism, Roman Catholicism, Seven-Day Adventist Church, Unitarian-Universalism, United Methodist Church. The appendix contains brief questions and answers of each group concerning heaven, salvation, hell, the Last Judgment, resurrection, the fate of those who have another belief, purgatory, recognition of persons after death, cremation, suicide, reincarnation. A useful compendium.

2218 Jung, Carl G. "On Life After Death." In *Memories, Dreams, Reflections*. New York: Pantheon, 1963, 299–326. London: Routledge and Collins, 1963.

Questions of immortality can be answered by hints from the unconscious, for example in dreams. The author uses his own dreams as illustrations which are linked to later incidents which reveal the meaning of the dream. Some dreams show a desire to obtain in death that which was denied in life. The question behind the dream is: am I related to something infinite or not? See also Herzog (2212), Jung (3203).

2219 Kelsey, Morton T. *Afterlife: The Other Side of Dying*. New York: Crossroad Pub. Co., 1985.

A Christian mystic, pastor and professor who bases many of his theories upon the teachings of Jung, affirms a Christian hope of an afterlife and seeks to show how the present denial of belief comes from an inadequate view of the world and a pre-modern view of science. Evidence for eternal life is presented from testimonies of those who survive near death experiences, extra-sensory experiences of the living with the dead, spiritualism, parapsychology, dreams, reincarnation and the poetic imagination. Those who are aware of the complexity of the unconscious will be prepared for a ministry to the dying that has room for some kind of existence beyond this life. This may include reincarnation, but there is no room for a permanent literal hell. Hell is a refusal in this life to believe in a heaven of grace or love in the life to come. God will seek out and restore to himself those who have rejected him. Bibliography for a class working with the dying. Notes and general bibliography.

2220 Küng, Hans. *Eternal Life?: Life After Death as a Medical, Philosophical and Theological Problem*. Trans. by Edward Quinn. Garden City, N. Y.: Doubleday and Co., 1984.

A prominent Roman Catholic theologian discusses medical, philosophical, and theological problems concerning life after death in a range from Raymond Moody's account of near death experiences to philosophical discussions of Feuerbach and existentialists. The author considers questions concerning the resurrection as containing affirmations concerning "today and now" along with "tomorrow and then." Eternal life is reasonable in all that God has intended for us through Jesus of Nazareth. In contrast, the search for immortality through parapsychology and spiritualism is based on the materialistic philosophy of evidence. For examples see Kelsey (2219), Moody (3348). There are closing questions about the meaning of a venture of faith by those who trust in God and those who do not. Notes and index. For kindred theological reflections from a Roman Catholic viewpoint, see Rahner (2318) and for a more conservative opinion see Schmaus (2287). Varying Catholic, Protestant and Jewish opinions are collected in Muckenhirn (2280).

2221 Lamont, Corliss. *The Illusion of Immortality*. New York: Philosophical Library, 1950.

A student of John Dewey abandons his earlier convictions concerning immortality and presents evidence against immortality from a study of science, philosophy, sociology, religion and history. The most important problem is a tendency of historic religions to make immortality more important than the existence of God.

2222 Leuba, James H. *The Belief in God and Immortality*. Boston: Sherman, French and Co., 1916.

A professor of psychology who pioneered in the combination of primitive religion with contemporary psychological questions considers the meaning of personal immortality, the ghost-soul in primitive societies and the "modern conception of immortality." Through literary sources and through questionnaires to college students. The author shows an erosion of belief during later adolescence in a personal God and in personal immortality.

2223 Lewis, Hywel D. *Persons and Life After Death*. New York: Barnes and Noble, 1978.

As a sequel to his earlier *The Self and Immortality* (1973) the author argues for the ultimacy of the self on the basis of intuitive self knowledge. This intuitive awareness could be rationally supported by available religious evidence, rather than by studies of paranormal phenomenon. Resurrection of the body is rejected because it places emphasis on corporeality. For the contrary see Grant (2253).

2224 Lifton, Robert J. "The Sense of Immortality: On Death and the Continuity of Life." In *New Meanings of Death*, ed. by Herman Feifel, 273–290. New York: McGraw-Hill Book Co., 1977.

A pioneer in the study of historical situations that involved violence and massive deaths, such as the bombing of Hiroshima developed a central paradigm for humanity: the understanding of death in relation to the continuity of life. This involves an awareness of the various modes of symbolic immortality, accounting for the sense of mortality that develops over the course of a lifetime through some death imagery, and providing some workable means of correcting pathological responses to death anxiety. On the subconscious level we are neither convinced of our immortality nor sure that we shall die, so we adopt a middle position that formulates images of a symbolic continuation of life. See Lifton (1221).

2225 Lifton, Robert J. *The Broken Connection: On Death and the Continuity of Life*. New York: Simon and Schuster, 1979.

See 1221.

2226 Meyers, Mary Ann. "Gates Ajar: Death in Mormon Thought and Practice." In *Death In America*, ed. by David E. Stannard, 112–133. Philadelphia: University of Pennsylvania Press, 1975.

Saints conceived of the universe as an ongoing process which sustained them in the darkest hours of their 1846 trek to Zion. Adam and Eve did not corrupt the human race, but they did set in motion a process by which waiting spirits might become "personages of tabernacle." Christ released souls from the bondage of death and made eternal progression possible. This was the vision of Joseph Smith. Much joy was expressed concerning the longed for return of Christ, which would be followed after a thousand years by a time of judgment. The test of Mormons after death was to restore the gospel to multitudes who had died before they had an opportunity to hear it. Visions of the dead were common. Funerals were as austere as those of New England ancestors.

2227 Macquarrie, John. *Christian Hope*. New York: Seabury Press, 1978.

A Protestant existential theologian presents "ongoing participation in the life of God" as an alternative to some of the "speculation" which promised too much in Judaism and was only partially answered in the New Testament. Theologians have sought to complete the New Testament through two types of eschatology: (a) individual, this-worldly, revolutionary, realized; (b) social, cosmic, other-worldly, revolutionary, future. Bultmann is more representative of (a), while Moltmann and Pannenberg are more representative of (b). The author tries to incorporate some of the strengths and weaknesses of the different positions

2228 Marcel, Gabriel. *Presence and Immortality*. Pittsburgh, Pa.: Duquesne University Press, 1967.

An existential philosopher considers the distinction between egocentric desire and hope as a prophetic assurance that we will be eternally loved. This is possible through a "trans-subjective presence" which is real in our existence. This is the mystery of being because of the non-objective character of presence. See also Wahl (2068).

2229 McGregor, Geddes, ed. *Immortality and Human Destiny*. New York: Paragon House Publishers, 1985.

A professor of philosophy has gathered papers from the 1984 conference of the New Ecumenical Research Association. These range widely from humanistic evaluations of after-death experiences to studies of the Mormon millennium, the teachings of the Unification Church, African perspectives, and theological opinions of Tillich and Stendahl. A Presbyterian pastor, David Read, contrasts the rise of secular apocalyptic beliefs with the silence of traditional Protestant churches concerning Last Things.

2230 Moltmann, Jürgen. *The Future of Creation*. Philadelphia: Fortress Press, 1979.

From previous writings: *The Theology of Hope, The Crucified God, The Church and the Power of the Spirit*, a noted continental theologian has brought together his specific views on creation as the beginning of life and the promise of a new creation (eschatology). A variety of topics are covered: eschatology, hope, creation, theology of the cross, biomedical ethics.

2231 Montagu, Ashley. *Immortality, Religion and Morals*. New York: Hawthorn Books, 1971.

A cultural anthropologist focuses on his lifetime preoccupation with the need of humans for spiritual life as it is known through biology, philosophy, morals, religion. The function of immortality as an incentive to meaningful existence is considered along with the reasons why this motivation has kept the view of immortality alive. The author considers the kind of immortality in which moderns can believe and the various ways in which it is used to meet important problems of our day.

2232 Morey, Robert A. *Death and the Afterlife*. Minneapolis, Minn.: Bethany House Pub., 1984.

A conservative Protestant defines biblical terms: spirit, soul, body, Sheol, grave, Gehena, eternal punishment. Then he presents an apologetic for the traditional biblical teaching of death, which is contrasted with universalism, annihilation, or the occult.

2233 Osler, William. *Science and Immortality*. Boston: Houghton Mifflin and Co., 1904. Reprint. Salem, N. H.: Ayer Co. Pub., 1976.

A distinguished professor of medicine presents the Ingersoll lectures on immortality 1904. He examines three modern solutions: the Laodiceans are so occupied with getting and spending that they are practically uninfluenced by any ideas of immortality; the Gallionians who care nothing about immortality because they have reached the intellectual conviction there is no hope in the grave, or that like Darwin, the question is left open while they pursue natural interests; the Teresians, who follow the faith exemplified by St. Teresa in a sentiment of immortality that combines idealism and realism, head and heart. He asked in this lecture if humans had ever been anything but materialistic and secular in daily life. He notes the seeming irrelevance of "last things" amid the bustling activity of the clinic and the hospital, but he is careful to note deathbed behavior of five hundred patients. After surveying the four ways in which the science of his generation seemed to have shattered the very foundations of traditional belief, he offers his own confession of faith.

2234 Pannenberg, Wolfhart. *Theology and the Kingdom of God.* Ed. by Richard John Neuhaus. Philadelphia: Westminster Press, 1969.

Christian hope in the future must not be connected so much to certitude as to venturing risk on the basis of reasonable possibilities. The uncertainties of human life can be unified through new courage in a genuine and radical possibility of a future in God. The Kingdom of God is an overarching reality that continually instructs our existence. The emphasis is always upon questions concerning our being rather than upon what we do. Love promises fulfillment to us both in the past and in the present. We must recognize that human anxieties erect structures of hostility to the future which appear to bring security. The only strength for our future is trust in a Father who cares and loves. Those who dare to act in full awareness of the partiality of human sight are those who fulfill the highest quality of discipleship which is rationality.

2235 Pelikan, Jaroslav. *The Shape of Death.* Nashville, Tenn.: Abingdon Press, 1961.

A Protestant theologian examines some of the forms of pessimism about life and optimism about God that developed in the Christian community in the second and third centuries: Tatian, Clement of Alexandria, Cyprian, Origen, and Irenaeus. Five geometric figures are used to summarize the "shape of death" that characterized these Patristic theologians. The basic themes clarify diverse viewpoints to be found in the early church.

2236 Pieper, Josef. *Death and Immortality.* New York: Herder and Herder, 1969.

A Roman Catholic moral theologian argues for the persistence of individuality in being beyond death through a popular discussion of the meaning of separation of body and soul, the relation of sin to death, the meaning of death, freedom and eternity.

2237 Pittenger, Norman. *After Death—Life and God.* New York: Cross-road/Seabury Press, 1980.

A philosophical theologian writes out of his conviction that God is self disclosing in the total event of Jesus of Nazareth as pure and unbounded love, but he also writes as an existentialist who examines the biblical presuppositions that precede an interpretation of God's love in our present life. Following Bultmann he sees the world in process with both subjective and objective experience to be considered in any convictions concerning the future. Whitehead and Hartshorne are important in his "demythologizing" of traditional teaching concerning any literal "rising" from the dead of the physical body of Jesus or of the resurrection of any human being to a literal heaven or hell.

2238 Reichenbach, Bruce R. *Is Man the Phoenix?: A Study of Immortality.* Washington, D.C.: Christian College Consortium, 1978.

A philosopher considers the philosophical arguments for immortality in Plato, Augustine and Kant, and evaluates the theological argument of Paul. He concludes that acceptance of immortality depends on acceptance of divine revelation. The philosophical meaning of immortality and the problems of dualism and monism are considered in relation to immortality.

2239 Robinson, John A. T. *In the End God.* New York: Harper and Row, 1968.

A scholarly and provocative Anglican bishop seeks to revive interest in the "four last things": death, judgement, heaven, hell. These are myths in which modern persons have no interest, but they can be revitalized by an empirical discipline of theology that is based upon Christian existence in today's history. Human existence can be seen as more than a time sequence that ends in final death. It can be reinterpreted as fulfillment of purpose that is related to time as ultimate destiny in God. God's *kairos* has power over temporal *kronos*. His power is manifested in the present reality of purposeful living. The Bible opposes doctrines of survival and immortality of the soul and upholds the resurrection of the body. Resurrection is a doctrine of the present time for building up the whole person within the body of Christ. The power of God's love will triumph over death and hell to bring all people into eternal fellowship with him.

2240 Robinson, John A. T. *Jesus and His Coming.* London: SCM Press, 1957.

A scholarly Anglican bishop believes that the hope of a return of Christ was not a part of Jesus' original teachings. It was an invention of the early church sometime between A. D. 30 and 50. Jesus did share the contemporary Jewish expectation of a final vindication of God and his saints and the end of present world order, judgment and resurrection. These were used by Jesus in expectation of immediate vindication following his sufferings. This was fulfilled in his resurrection and going to God. The "visitation" that resulted was the Fall of Jerusalem in A. D. 70. In distinction from C. H. Dodd, (2265) the author describes his interpretations as "inaugurated eschatology."

2241 Royce, Josiah. *The Conception of Immortality.* 1900. Reprint. New York: Greenwood Press, 1968.

In the Ingersoll Lectures on Immortality, 1899, a Harvard professor of philosophy considers the mystery of humanity to be the mystery of individual nature, that is, the uniqueness of an individual. The philosophical solution to this mystery lies in conceiving every person as so related to the world and to the very life of God, that in order to be an individual at all a person has to be very much nearer to the Eternal than in our present life we are accustomed to observe. This nearness provides a purpose in life by which our conscious awareness of incompleteness is given rationality, wholeness and finality.

2242 Shebbeare, C. J. *The Problem of the Future Life.* Oxford, England: Basil Blackwell, 1939.

Any book written by "Chaplain to His Majesty the King and Master of the Wear Valley Beagles" deserves some mention. The author is also a pastor and professor of pastoral theology who uses conventional moderation and philosophic idealism to give assurance of heaven and to reduce the logical possibility of eternal punishment.

2243 Simpson, Michael. *Death and Eternal Life.* Notre Dame: Fides, 1971.

In this slender volume a Roman Catholic philosopher of religion notes the way in which traditional Christian concepts of "last things" are mixed with mythology. He reinterprets traditional concepts of Christian hope, death, and resurrection with continual emphasis upon the personal responsibility of the individual and the mystery of eternal destiny.

2244 Stendahl, Krister, ed. Immortality and Resurrection—Death in the Western World: Two Conflicting Currents of Thought. New York: Macmillan Pub. Co., 1965.

Theologians discuss linguistic symbols of immortality: Greek, biblical, church fathers. These are their Ingersoll lectures on immortality, given annually at Harvard University. Oscar Cullmann provides a controversial interpretation of the New Testament view of resurrection and Henry J. Cadbury presents Jesus' interpretation of immortality. The view of the Greeks and of the Church Fathers on immortality are interpreted by Harry A. Wolfson and Werner Jaeger.

2245 Stendahl, Krister. "Immortality is Too Much and Too Little." In *Immortality and Human Destiny*. New York: Paragon House Publishers, 1985.

A former bishop of Stockholm and later Dean of the Divinity School, Harvard University declares on the basis of his biblical study that neither the Old Testament nor the New Testament are interested in the immortality of the soul. The New Testament emphasis is upon the resurrection which answers the question of theodicy: how does God make this a moral universe? See Stendahl (2244).

2246 Streeter, B. H., et.al. *Immortality: An Essay in Discovery*. New York: Macmillan Pub. Co., 1917.

Biblical scholars, philosophers and physicians present essays that argue for the belief in personal immortality. They consider the impact of modern thought upon traditional doctrines of resurrection, judgment, heaven and hell, with some modifications such as eventual redemption from hell of the "incurably selfish" and a view of heaven that rejects literal pictures and emphasizes goodness, truth and beauty. Spiritualism is studies as a reaction to traditional Protestant teaching about heaven and hell. A seance derives its power from psychological communications from the inner mind of the medium or agent. Many difficulties are found with reincarnation. Karma is considered to be a false theory of justice. Theosophy is presented as a state of the believers own mentality that cannot be accepted as a source of accurate information about the unseen world.

2247 Thielicke, Helmut. *Death and Life*. Trans. by Edward Schroeder. Philadelphia: Fortress Press, 1970.

See 2146.

2248 Tillich, Paul. "The Eternal Now." In *The Meaning of Death*, ed. by Herman Feifel, 30–38. New York: McGraw-Hill Book Co., 1959.

A theologian presents the Christian message of death as time running toward an end. The end is an eternity that empowers a believer to live with courage now. This gives a person incentive to "repent," to discard elements of being into the past so that they will no longer have power in the present. The sign of this deliverance from the power of time is forgiveness and a sense of rest.

2249 Torrance, T. F. *Space, Time and Resurrection*. Grand Rapids, Mich.: Wm. B. Eerdmans Pub. Co., 1976.

A theologian argues that the resurrection of Jesus is a radical transformation of existing concepts of the resurrection. There is no precedent for resurrection within time and history. But this argument is contrary to that of Pannenberg (2283 who believed that the resurrection of Jesus was consistent with ideas of resurrection in later Judaism. Torrance believes the resurrection of Christ raises humans to a new level of reality that is fully human. The threat of nothingness is cast down. Human kind is now taken up into God. See also Pannenberg (2234).

2.51 RESURRECTION OF THE BODY

2250 Badham, Paul. *Christian Beliefs About Life After Death*. New York: Macmillan, 1976.

An English Protestant theologian believes that mind or soul can be correlated with brain but that there is no complete union The concept of soul is required to ensure personal continuity beyond this life, but any thought of physical resurrection is to be rethought as a "re-embodiment in heaven." The empty tomb of Jesus was a hallucination. After death Jesus continued telepathic communication into the minds of his disciples.

2251 Barth, Karl. *The Resurrection of the Dead*. Trans. by H. J. Stenning. New York: Fleming H. Revell Co., 1933.

A major Continental theologian concludes from an exegetical study of 1 Corinthians 15 that the resurrection of Christ is the foundation of the church, central to the meaning of faith, truth and reality for Christians. Without this focus in 1 Corinthians, the letters of Paul to the Romans, the Philippians and the Colossians cannot be understood.

2252 Cavallin, Hans C. C. *Life After Death*. Lund, Sweden: C. W. K. Gleerup, 1974.

From his doctoral thesis at Uppsala University, the author provides an exegetical study of the Pauline argument for the resurrection of the dead in 1 Cor. 15 and its background in Judaism, the Hellenistic culture, the gospel tradition and the teachings of the church. Extensive footnoting and bibliography.

2253 Grant, Robert M. "The Resurrection of the Body." *Journal of Religion*. 28.2 (April 1948): 120–130; 28.3 (July 1948): 180–208.

The religious development of the doctrine of the resurrection of the body is traced in Jewish and Christian Scriptures in article one. Article two presents a philosophical apologetic for the resurrection of the body among the Church Fathers. Scholarly New Testament study.

2254 Hick, John. *Faith and Knowledge*. Ithaca, N.Y.: Cornell University Press, 1966.

A philosopher argues that the resurrection of the body is verifiable in the sense that the concept of continued personal identity under these circumstances does not violate logical consistency of thought.

2255 Ladd, George E. *I Believe in the Resurrection of Jesus*. Grand Rapids, Mich.: Wm. B. Eerdmans Pub. Co., 1975.

A conservative biblical theologian surveys all of the New Testament ideas of resurrection, discusses various interpretations and affirms the historicity of the resurrection.

2256 Martin-Acherd, Robert. *From Death to Life*. Trans. by John Penney Smith. Edinburgh: Oliver and Boyd, 1960.

A professor of Old Testament language and theology illustrates the emergence of the doctrine of the resurrection in ancient Israel and early Judaism. The complexity of the development of these ideas in the Old Testament is presented with scholarly acumen and penetrating diagnosis of each passage of Scripture.

2257 Richards, H. J. *Death and After: What Will Really Happen?* Mystic, Conn.: Twenty-Third Publications, 1987.

The troublesome topics of resurrection of the body, heaven, eternal life, judgment, hell, the coming of Christ are presented for a general audience by a religious educator who is familiar with scholarly skepticism concerning literal interpretations of the New Testament, and yet holds to the reality of traditional theological doctrines.

2258 Schep, J. A. *The Nature of the Resurrection Body*. Grand Rapids, Mich.: William. B. Eerdmans Pub. Co., 1964.

A professor of New Testament presents a conservative theological interpretation of flesh and body in the Old and New Testament as a background for a discussion of the resurrection body of Jesus and the nature of the believer's resurrection body. This will be a body of "glorified flesh."

2.52 ESCHATOLOGY/APOCALYPTIC

2259 *Apocalyptic Spirituality*. Trans. by Bernard McGinn. New York: Paulist Press, 1979.

Present trial, imminent judgment and future salvation characterize the works of selected fathers of the church and medieval writers: Lactantius, Adso of Montier-en-Der, Joachim of Fiore, the Franciscan Spirituals, Savanorola. There is a universal view of history as a divinely ordered structure, a profound pessimism about the present and an optimism about the vindication of the just and judgment of the wicked. With these hopes death will be transcended. There is a scholarly introduction to each writer.

2260 Barth, Karl. *Church Dogmatics*. Vol. 4/3, 1. Edinburgh: T. & T. Clark, 1961.

An influential Protestant "dialectical" theologian affirms and discusses the resurrection of Jesus Christ, which has already occurred and which is the basis of all other manifestations of Christ, the outpouring of the Holy Spirit at Pentecost, and the parousia by which Christ reveals and confirms to the whole of creation what has already been accomplished for the salvation of the world.

2261 Bultmann, Rudolf. "History and Eschatology in the New Testament." *New Testament Studies* 1 (1954–1955): 5–16.

A German Protestant Theologian presents the Israelite view of history as a glorious future which is conditional upon the obedience of the people, and a view of history that will end at a time determined by God. The latter view is apocalyptic and prevails in the New Testament. The teachings of Jesus concentrate on the day of judgment. In Paul, history is swallowed up in eschatology, for the decisive history is not of the world or of Israel but of what a person experiences in the self. See also Bartsch (2105).

2262 Caird, G. B., *et al. The Christian Hope*. London: SPCK, 1970.

A collection of papers by Protestant theologians at the annual conference of the Society for the Study of Theology, University of Birmingham, England: G. B. Caird argues that the disciples of Jesus found evidence for the resurrection because of some quality that they had observed in the human conduct and experience of Jesus. Evidence for the resurrection of the body, a new heaven and earth are given from the New Testament. Wolfhart Pannenberg believes that Christianity cannot do without an eschatology that is historical because this is the basis for the reconciliation of the world in Christ. I. T. Ramsey traces philosophical and theological distinctions between eternal as everlasting time and our consciousness of something eternal in us. He combined these in a model of "cosmic disclosure," an awareness of transcendence in our present human existence. James Klugman, editor of *Marxism Today* explains hope and motivation as the making of our own history, predicting and shaping the future, changing human nature, without any sense of predetermination by God. Ninian Smart supports the worship of the immortal God in a way that will allow us to affirm values in the face of death without recourse to the reassuring myths of human immortality. W. A. Whitehouse surveys varying philosophical (Kant, Heidegger) and theological (E. L. Mascall) terms that express our awareness of a physical universe in relation to God as the Creator of heaven and earth.

2263 Charles, R. H. *Eschatology: The Doctrine of a Future Life in Israel, Judaism and Christianity.* 1899. New York: Schocken Books, 1963.

See 2075.

2264 Cullmann, Oscar. *Christ and Time.* Rev. ed. Philadelphia: Westminster Press, 1964.

See 2015.

2265 Dodd, Charles H. *The Parables of the Kingdom.* New York: Scribner and Sons, 1936.

An English theologian developed a formula of "realized eschatology" in which the person and mission of Jesus has already begun on earth both as judgment and as salvation. Any references to a future hope of his return would be interpreted symbolically. The theology is similar to that of Bultmann in which the content of the Christian hope is not drawn from any future event but from a personal decision at any given time to accept new life from God. See also Robinson (2240).

2266 Grässer, Eric. *Die Naherwartung Jesu (Jesus' Understanding of the End Time).* Stuttgart, Germany: K. B. W. Verlag, 1973.

A German professor of New Testament studies reviews questions presented by scholars since the nineteenth century concerning the preaching of Jesus about the end-time. He first considers the possibility that Jesus may have had a wrong idea about the near end of the world, or his language may have content which we can no longer recover. The author also considers the perspective of Jesus concerning the future kingdom of God and the implications of his understanding of the world for Christian responsibility today.

2267 Guardini, Romano. *The Last Things.* Trans. by Charlotte D. Forsyth and Grace B. Branham. New York: Pantheon Books, 1954.

A Roman Catholic scholar presents a readable account of teaching on death as a result of sin, suffering as purification, resurrection of the body, redemptive aspects of the last judgement (hell is not mentioned) and eternal life in Christ.

2268 Guy, Harold A. *The New Testament Doctrine of the "Last Things."* London: Oxford University Press, 1948.

A theologian examines eschatology both in terms of the faith of an individual and the cosmic events that will effect the universe as a whole. The study is prepared for a general audience through a survey of various books of the Old and New Testament. This leads to a general conclusion that the early church expected a Second Coming of Jesus to earth during their life-time, an upsurge of evil before this event and a final judgment by God. There is assurance of eternal life with God for some, but the author has no certainty whether the New Testament teaches punishment or annihilation for those who reject the truth now or who are rejected at the Judgment.

2269 Hendrikson, William. *The Bible On the Life Hereafter*. Grand Rapids, Mich.: Baker Book House, 1959.

From a conservative biblical viewpoint, the author discusses individual and general eschatology in terms of immortality, the intermediate state, signs of the return of Christ, the last judgment, the final state of the wicked and the righteous.

2270 Herzog, Frederick, ed. *The Future of Hope*. New York: Herder and Herder, 1970.

The author believes that history is an element of the future and that history for Christians is primarily eschatological. Other theologians are considered: Harvey Cox, Langdon Gilkey, Van Harvey, John Macquarrie.

2271 Kantonen, T. A. *The Christian Hope*. Philadelphia: Muhlenberg Press, 1954.

Biblical and theological references from a Lutheran perspective are used to combine traditional and contemporary aspects of eschatology, such as realized and futuristic hope. A useful review of traditional doctrines, including disputed questions about the "intermediate state" between the time of death and the final resurrection.

2272 Ladd, George E. *The Last Things: An Eschatology For Laymen*. Grand Rapids, Mich.: Wm. B. Eerdmans Pub. Co., 1978.

A conservative Protestant scholar considers prophecies concerning the "end times" from two points of view: (1) separate programs of fulfillment for Israel and the Christian church; (2) progressive revelation with a strand of unity from the Old through the New Testament. The author supports the second interpretation of "last things" and notes numerous errors in the former interpretation, which is commonly called "dispensationalism."

2273 Mathews, Shailer. *The Social Teaching of Jesus*. New York: Macmillan Pub. Co., 1897.

Doctrines of "last things" or Christian hope in the coming kingdom of God are to be redefined as an ideal social order that will progressively bring people close to God and to each other. The author is a representative of the "liberal" school of Protestant theology of the late 19th and early 20th century which followed the teaching of Hegel, Schleiermacher, Ritschl, and Harnack.

2274 Metz, Johannes B. *Theology of the World.* Trans. by William Glen-Doepel. New York: Herder & Herder, 1971.

A Catholic theologian places the future hope of the church for "emerging" and "arising" in the present. This will offer a "creative and militant eschatology" which will overthrow oppressive power structures in society. The "heavenly city" does not lie ahead of us as a distant and hidden goal. We must verbalize the political potential of faith and hope for the present.

2275 Miranda, Jose Porfino. *Being and the Messiah: The Message of St. John.* Trans. by John Eaglesom. Maryknoll, N. Y.: Orbis Books, 1977.

A Roman Catholic "liberation" theologian fears that an eschatology oriented to an ultimate future will betray work for radical change in the present. He develops a form of "realized" eschatology. We must look and work for liberation and justice in the present.

2276 Moltmann, Jürgen. *Theology of Hope.* New York: Harper and Row, 1967.

A Protestant theologian reinterprets the doctrine of "last things" as a doctrine of hope, the starting point for a new understanding of God in history, of Christ and salvation, of the church and her mission. This is a reinterpretation of traditional eschatology which focused upon the end of time rather than upon present reality. Counteracting the despair of some existentialist philosophers, the author believes that a theology of hope is possible in this life as a force for social change and cultural transformation. It begins a revolutionary change that includes a radical shift in attention toward justice and compassion for those who suffer. This is based the hope of God coming toward us in this life, rather than the expectation of life after death. See also Gerkin (3320).

2277 Moody, Dale. *The Hope of Glory.* Grand Rapids, Mich.: Wm. B. Eerdmans Pub. Co., 1964.

A conservative Protestant scholar provides a detailed account of eschatological topics: earthly and eternal life, death as destruction and departure, the resurrection of life and of judgment, the immediacy and inheritance of the Kingdom, the "filling up" of God's time in Israel and the Gentiles, the Antichrist, the Day of the Lord (*parousia*), the new creation and the holy city. Scriptural index. An excellent resource for biblical passages on each topic and some theological references.

2278 Moody, Dale. *The Word of Truth: A Summary of Christian Doctrine Based on Biblical Revelation.* Grand Rapids, Mich.: William. B. Eerdmans Pub. Co., 1981.

A conservative Protestant scholar traces biblical teaching concerning sin and salvation, personal eschatology and the future kingdom of God. From a study of Pauline theology, the author notes two teachings about death. In the first, death is referred to as a spiritual state that became a part of human life through the Fall. In the second, death is referred to as a physical end of life which may have been part of God's original plan for creation. Eschatological interpretations preserve the progressive unity of Old and New Testament and demonstrate errors in dispensationalism (which gave great emphasis to a return of Jews to Palestine before the end of the world).

2279 Moule, C. F. D. *The Meaning of Hope.* Philadelphia: Fortress Press, 1963.

There is an urgency of decision in the Christian message, but this does not include threats of hell, for what God did in Christ cannot be ultimately defeated and all loved ones will be accepted by God.

2280 Muckenhirn, Maryellen, ed. *The Future As the Presence of Shared Hope.* New York: Sheed and Ward, 1968.

Participants at the John XXIII Institute Theology Symposium concentrate upon the existential thrust of the future in relation to the present awareness of reality by each human being. The viewpoint is one of hope that is lived out and shared with others. Various interpretations of this future orientation are presented, with an awareness of departure from traditional scholastic theology in which eschatology refers to death, judgment, hell and heaven. The traditional approach is considered to be unreal and highly imaginative. The Protestant, Roman Catholic and Jewish theologians are: Moltmann, Gilkey, Rylaarsdam, Borowitz, Schaldenbrend, Burrell and Crossan.

2281 Otto, Rudolph. *The Kingdom of God and the Son of Man.* London: Lutterworth Press, 1938.

A theologian affirms a paradox about the teaching of last things in the Gospels. Jesus expected the future coming of the Kingdom in the future with power and urgency, and yet at the same time preached that the Kingdom had already come. He lived and taught as if the world would continue beyond his lifetime.

2282 Pache, René. *The Future Life.* Trans. by Helen I. Needham. Chicago: Moody Press, 1962.

A voluminous and literalistic biblical survey of death and the dead, the world of spirits, the resurrection, eternal perdition and heaven.

2283 Pannenberg, Wolfhart. *Jesus, God and Man.* 2nd ed. Trans. by Lewis L. Wilkins and Duane A. Priebe. Philadelphia: Westminster Press, 1977.

A Protestant theologian who claims to be more interested in history than Barth or Bultmann, writes of the resurrection of Jesus as a foretaste or anticipation of the end of history. To the author, resurrection can be historically verified. In opposition to "demythology," he asserts a dimension of future fulfillment beyond this world and his history which is expressed in apocalyptic thought: final judgment, resurrection of the body. These are seen as rational historical events as they were modified by Jesus from earlier Jewish expectations.

2284 Papin, Joseph, ed. *The Eschaton: A Community of Love.* Villanova, Pa.: Villanova University Press, 1971.

Eschatology, a term which does not appear in England before the 19th century is addressed by Roman Catholic and Protestant theologians: Krister Stendahl, Avery Dulles, Frederick E. Crowe, Eulalio Baltazar, Edward Gannon, Walter J. Burghardt. Scholarly papers that assume competence in theology and philosophy. Notes after each chapter.

2285 Petry, Ray C. *Christian Eschatology and Social Thought.* New York: Abingdon Press, 1956.

A Protestant professor of church history seeks to correct an exclusive emphasis of the mid-twentieth century upon the present social scene as the ultimate, heavenly community. His study traces the interconnection of eternal and temporal concerns in historical Christian thought. Last things, the resurrection, the last judgment, the end of history are traced in the writings of church fathers and medieval theologians. Extensive bibliography.

2286 Rahner, Karl. *Foundations of Christian Faith: An Introduction to the Idea of Christianity.* New York: Seabury Press, 1978.

An encyclopedic Roman Catholic theologian concludes his summary of theology with a section on eschatology as both individual and collective. That is, the purposes of God will be fulfilled both in the uniqueness of individuals and in the world as a stage for the drama of salvation. Christian doctrine concerning last things are interpreted from a "hermeneutical" principle that makes a distinction between the formulation of a dogma and the transmission of a psychological image into the experience of individuals. The author's emphasis is upon the conception of images rather than upon content. An example would be the interpretation of hell as a feeling that human freedom will end in eternal loss, but that the world and all in it will "in fact" enter into eternal life with God.

2287 Schmaus, Michael. *Justification and the Last Things.* New York: Sheed and Ward, 1977.

The author presents the official picture of Catholic eschatology in the light of changes inaugurated by Second Vatican Council (1962–1965). Christian hope is for a transformed world beyond the end of history. The Church is the mediator of this absolute future. The second coming of Christ should not cause speculation about chronology but act as a reminder that historical time will end and that there will be a resurrection of the dead. The unbaptized live within the effective sphere of the risen Lord and this relationship calls for a final maturing. The resurrection of an individual may take place immediately upon death, although there will always be an interval before the final gathering of all the redeemed into the glorified body of Christ. There will be no further opportunities for repentance and growth beyond the grave, but the majority of those who have turned to God will require a process of purification.

2288 Schnackenburg, Rudolph. *Christ, Present and Coming.* Trans. by Edward Quinn. Philadelphia: Fortress Press, 1978.

A Roman Catholic professor of New Testament presents the present power and coming hope of God's kingdom as reassurance for the present and future. The signs of the Kingdom of God calls for repentance, being open to what is new, continuing steadfast in faith, courage for righteous action. Endurance is presented by the apostle Paul as power to hope in the midst of affliction, including sentence of death. The transitoriness of earthly things is contrasted with the grandeur of eternity with God and redemption of the creation. The gospel of John describes our inner penetration of the present world that proclaims present fellowship with Jesus rather than a longing for the return of Christ which is characteristic of Paul.

2289 Schweitzer, Albert. *The Quest for the Historical Jesus.* 2nd ed. New York: Macmillan Pub. Co., 1948.

A German theologian, medical missionary and interpreter of Bach aroused much controversy in his claim that the central motive in the mission of Jesus was a belief that the end of the world would occur during his generation. Jesus came as the herald of a new kingdom which was to appear suddenly and miraculously and supplant the existing world order. He had no long range program, founded no church, did not prepare his disciples to carry on his work and taught only an "interim ethics" expedient for the brief interval before the kingdom. When Jesus found that the kingdom did not come during his ministry, he began voluntarily to seek his own death as the necessary birth pangs of the new age.

2290 Sullivan, Clayton. *Rethinking Realized Eschatology*. Macon, Ga.: Mercer University Press, 1988.

A Southern Baptist scholar centers upon the "realized eschatology" of C. H. Dodd to illustrate a deficiency of many modern theories concerning eschatology. They neglect the evidence in the Synoptic Gospels (Matthew, Mark, Luke) that the kingdom of God is a future hope, not a present reality. The author suggests a more "Christological" version of realized eschatology in which the emphasis is upon person rather than event. What is the ultimate religious significance of the coming Kingdom of God for the individual believer? Appendix includes all listings of references to Kingdom in the Synoptic Gospels. Relevant bibliography.

2291 Toon, Peter. *Puritans, the Millennium and the Future of Israel*. Cambridge: James Clark and Co., 1970.

The first Reformers of the sixteenth century adopted the traditional Augustinian eschatology in which the thousand years described in Revelation chapter 20 was the period of church history from the time of Christ to the end of the world. Most Protestant writers followed this interpretation of Revelation and described its symbolic vision as prophecies concerning the downfall of the Turks, the destruction of the city of Rome, the demise of the Papacy and the ultimate triumph of Protestant biblical religion. In the sixteenth and seventeenth century the influence of Theodore de Beza's Notes on the New Testament led to an interpretation of Romans 11:25ff as a belief that a large number of Jews would be converted before the end of the world and the last judgment. These are concepts of "millenarianism."

2292 Travis, Stephan H. *Christian Hope and the Future*. Downers Grove, Ill.: InterVarsity Press, 1980.

A conservative British theologian surveys Protestant theological opinion in the 20th century and concludes that the most popular emphasis has been upon the future of humans in this world. The present volume seeks to address a neglected area of Christian teaching which is the ultimate purpose of God for humans. This is the basic Christian hope. Systematic theological issues are considered: the second coming of Christ, the resurrection of the dead, immortality and the intermediate state, the last judgement, purgatory, resurrection, eternal punishment. A useful summary of theological opinion concerning "last things." Unfortunately, no index or bibliography.

2.521 LAST JUDGMENT

2293 Barth, Karl. *Church Dogmatics*. Vol 3/2. Edinburgh: T & T Clark, 1960.

In this section of his systematic theology, a renowned Continental theologian asserts that all humans have been positively elected to salvation with reprobation placed solely upon Jesus as the Son of God who vicariously bears this judgment for all. This has been made possible through the incarnation, life, death and resurrection of Jesus Christ. All persons will face final judgment in light of what God has done for them in Christ. God remains free, through this decision for all humanity through Jesus Christ, to determine the final destiny of all persons as He desires.

2294 Ladd, George E. *The Blessed Hope*. Grand Rapids, Mich.: Wm. B. Eerdmans Pub. Co., 1956.

A conservative Protestant professor develops a biblical theology of the second advent of Christ in which the salvation of the body is completed. The book of Revelation is interpreted as "futurism," in which there will be a final incarnation of evil upon the earth, the martyrdom of many Jews who profess faith in Christ as the Messiah, a triumphal return of Christ to establish a millennial (1000 year) kingdom upon the earth. There is no "rapture of the saints" before the time of tribulation and the establishment of the millennial kingdom. The book was influential in questioning the "pre-tribulation" beliefs of many late 19th century conservative Protestant leaders which found wide popularity through the Scofield Reference Bible.

2295 Martin, James Perry. *The Last Judgment in Protestant Theology from Orthodoxy to Ritschl*. Grand Rapids, Mich.: Wm. B. Eerdmans Pub. Co., 1963.

A Protestant theologian provides an authoritative history of eschatology and of the Last Judgment in particular in the course of Protestant theological development from the 17th to the 19th century and finds that many of the attitudes and anxieties of the twentieth century derive from those of the last three centuries. The Protestant orthodoxy of the seventeenth century was eroded by philosophical and other forces of idealism, rationalism, and modern anthropological studies, especially by Ritschl.

2296 Morris, Leon. *The Biblical Doctrine of Judgement*. London: Tyndale House Pub., 1960.

This scholarly monograph presents Old and New Testament teachings concerning the profound dissatisfaction with the present world that was felt by Old and New Testament writers who looked to God for some final satisfaction in a future judgment, which in some cases might begin in this life. Judicious quotations from eminent theologians fill the footnotes.

2297 Stuart, Moses. *Exegetical Essays on Several Words Relating to Future Punishment*. Boston: Codman Press, 1830.

A professor of sacred literature examines biblical words associated with future punishment of humans and concludes that the writers intended a literal sense to their warnings about a place of punishment after death.

2.522 HEAVEN AND HELL

2298 Berdyaev, Nicolas. *The Destiny of Man*. New York: Charles Scribner's Sons, 1937.

A Christian existential theologian includes sections on death and immortality, hell and paradise in a comprehensive study of ethical knowledge and anthropology. Hell is considered in existential terms as a subjective aspect of human experience. This is an illusory realm of non-being from which all humans will be liberated by Christ as Savior. Any thought of paradise in the future will involve us in insoluble contradictions, so we can only think of paradise in terms of eternity. Eternity is a present thought through which we escape from time. It is the beginning of creativity and ecstasy.

2299 Bouckham, Richard J. "Universalism: A Historical Survey." *Familios* 4, 2 (January 1979): 48–54.

The issues of hell and universalism are traced from the early Fathers of the Church to such modern universalists as J. A. T. Robertson and John Hick.

2300 Brandon, S. G. F. *The Judgment of the Dead: The Idea of Life after Death in Major Religions*. New York: Charles Scribner's Sons, 1967.

Many cultures portray death as an evil which results from the defilement of life. Torment and judgment follow death in the literature of ancient Egypt, Iran, India, China, Japan, the Christian New Testament. In all of these the sufferings of the damned are depicted with brutal realism.

2301 Dearmer, Percy. *The Legend of Hell*. London: Cassell and Co., 1929.

Spurred by the World War I questions of soldiers: "How can a just God send people to everlasting torment?", a King's College, London professor provides a popular survey of various views of hell through the ages and some of the psychological, social and theological reasons for the idea of everlasting punishment. Upon examination of New Testament passages, the author concludes that there have been additions and changes to the New Testament, plus mistranslations that maintained a belief in everlasting punishment. However, the author concludes that the teachings of Jesus were so far in advance of his age and ours that his followers found it difficult to understand that goodness is a principle that prevails by its own light and does not depend upon punishment. Jesus spoke about "punishment" only as a parallelism between sin and disease that is "completely vindicated by

modern science: pain is prophylactic and educative." We are to avoid thinking about vengeance because God does not think about vengeance. He forgives all and will lead all to a moral conception of his love.

2302 Himmelfarb, Martha. *Tours of Hell: An Apocalyptic Form in Jewish
and Christian Literature*. Philadelphia: University of Pennsylvania
Press, 1983.

Ranging from ancient books of the dead through Dante's *Divine
Comedy*, the author focuses upon Jewish and Christian descriptions of hell:
Hebrew, Greek, Latin, Ethiopian and Coptic. A discussion of Muslim and
other texts is included.

2303 Marty, Martin, Stewart E. Rosenberg, and Andrew M. Greeley.
What Do We Believe? The Stance of Religion in America. New
York: Meredith Press, 1968.

In a survey of Gallup Polls, 1952 and 1965, Protestant, Jewish and
Catholic scholars comment on the findings. After their essays the tabulations of questions include those on heaven (belief in afterlife is 80% for
Catholic, 71% for Protestant, 6% Jewish, 26% other and none) and hell
(affirmed by 70% Catholic, 54% Protestant, 3% Jewish, 20% other and
none).

2304 Mew, James. *Traditional Aspects of Hell (Ancient and Modern)*.
1903. Reprint. Ann Arbor, Mich.: Gryphon Books, 1971.

Similarities and discrepancies are noted in a popular treatment of
various hells: Egyptian, Brahmin, Buddhist, Zoroastrian, classic, Scandi-
navian, Hebrew, Christian, Muslim, barbarian.

2305 Morey, Robert A. *Death and the Afterlife*. Minneapolis, Minn.:
Bethany House, 1984.

Sin caused separation from God and spiritual death for all persons.
Physical death separates persons into those awaiting judgment and damnation or resurrection to eternal life and fellowship with God. Those who
have not placed their faith in Christ in this world will exist as conscious,
personal beings in a state of perpetual torment. God does not pass over sins
and remain the God of the Scriptures at the same time. This is true for both
Old and New Testament teachings about God. Physical death seals the fate
of those who are already spiritually dead.

2306 Paternoster, Michael. *Thou Art There Also: God, Death, and Hell*.
London: SPCK, 1967.

An Anglican chaplain at Cambridge believes that God's purpose to
save all humans will come to pass in His time. Two views of the afterlife

are contrasted, with representative examples of each: (1) death is an evil to be avoided and any life that follows it is greatly inferior to this life; (2) death is a gate for a more abundant life and is much better than our present existence. The latter view contains two variations. In one, the "soul" is immortal and detachable from the body at death. In the other, (considered to be the biblical view by the author) human existence is a unity of body and soul with no guarantee of continuing existence unless God raises the human person from the dead.

2307 Rahner, Karl. "Hell." In *Sacramentum Mundi*. Vol. 3, 7–9. New York: Herder and Herder, 1969.

A Roman Catholic theologian explains hell as the cosmic, objective aspect of loss which is outside human consciousness. Literal biblical references to "fire" are to be interpreted as metaphors. Hell is an eternity for those who maintain inner obduracy toward grace.

2308 Ramsey, Ian. *Talk of God*. New York: St. Martin's Press, 1969.

A theologian presents a series of arguments against the traditional Christian teaching that God subjects certain people to everlasting punishment. God is forgiveness and reconciliation. Through His Son He has shown His eternal Love, not eternal Wrath. The very character of God speaks against everlasting retribution.

2309 Rowell, Geoffrey. *Hell and the Victorians*. Oxford: Clarendon Press, 1974.

Notable theological controversies are described. A competent biblical scholar, F. D. Maurice was dismissed from King's College, London in 1853 for denying eternal punishment and refusing to believe that death brought an end to hope. "Universalist" doctrines were advocated by Andrew Jukes, *The Second Death and Restitution of All Things* (1867) and by Samuel Cox, *Salvator Mundi* (1877) and continued to gain support into the 20th century.

2310 Simon, Ulrich. *Heaven in the Christian Tradition*. New York: Harper and Brothers, 1958.

Relying heavily upon an Old Testament scholar, R. H. Charles' study of the Apocrypha and Pseudepigrapha, the author begins his survey with ancient beliefs toward heaven and the almost total eclipse of such belief in the 19th and 20th century. This is followed by discussion of Hebrew and Christian views of the "God of heaven." Chapters describe the society of heaven, its life, the heavenly warfare between Satan and Christ, the place of heaven in Christian worship. The author stays close to the biblical texts and seeks to avoid literal fanaticism or liberal vagueness.

2311 Smith, Wilbur M. *The Biblical Doctrine of Heaven*. Chicago: Moody Press, 1968.

A popular text on various aspects of biblical references to heaven by a conservative Protestant scholar.

2312 Tillich, Paul. *Systematic Theology*. Vol. 2. Chicago: University of Chicago Press, 1957.

An existential theologian interprets biblical statements of punishment after death as symbols of despair and meaninglessness. God alone is eternal, so a human being cannot understand or be a part of eternal condemnation. Both eternal life and eternal death are actually a way of speaking about the existential reality of the present.

2313 Walker, D. P. *The Decline of Hell: Seventeenth-Century Discussions of Eternal Torment*. Chicago: University of Chicago Press, 1964.

From primary sources of English philosophers and theologians of the seventeenth century, the author traces the tension between belief in everlasting hell and God's love. The result of debates on this subject led to less public preaching on hell and fewer arguments for vindictive justice by God. The author stays close to his quoted sources and does not consider the sociological and psychological forces which may also have contributed to the demise of an unpopular doctrine.

2.523 PURGATORY

2314 Aquinas, Thomas. *Summa Contra Gentiles*. Vol. 4. Trans. by C. J. O'Neil. Garden City, N.Y.: Doubleday and Co., 1957.

See 1083.

2315 Harley, Marta Powell. *A Revelation of Purgatory by An Unknown Fifteenth–Century Woman Visionary*. Lewiston, N.Y.: E. Mellen Press, 1985.

After introducing the teaching of the church concerning purgatory and the popularity of visions concerning the after life, the author provides a translation of a typical 15th-century vision of three stages of purgatory, with notes and editorial comments. The three stages are hell, purgatory, earthly paradise. Then the soul enters heaven.

2316 Catherine of Genoa, Saint. *Purgation and Purgatory: The Spiritual Dialogue*. Trans. by Serge Hughes. New York: Paulist Press, 1979.

A 15th-century mystic describes transformation of the self to the love of God. First there is a narration of the voyage of the soul and the body, with self-love as arbitrator. This voyage includes purgatory, which is endurable because guilty persons are willing to suffer for their sins and because this suffering will bring them closer to God. The second part of the book describes the final illness of the saint. A disciple recounts her struggles of human frailty (body, self-love) against the spirit (soul). During a terminal illness of four months there was painful internal bleeding, visions of a divine face that made her laugh, out of the body experiences. Introduction to the life of the mystic and notes on the translation.

2317 LeGoff, Jacques. *The Birth of Purgatory.* Chicago: University of Chicago Press, 1984.

See 1080.

2318 Rahner, Karl. *On the Theology of Death.* Trans. by Charles H. Henkey. New York: Seabury Press, 1973.

The survival of the soul after death takes place in the form of a pan-cosmic event. The soul does not escape the cosmos, but the cosmos becomes the new body of the soul. The being of the self becomes open to the entire cosmic reality. Purgatory is a process by which the soul is freed progressively from the disharmony which it experienced while in the temporal body in order to achieve maturity and total openness to its harmony with the entire cosmos. Overall, the doctrine of the resurrection is viewed as a pan-cosmic corporeality. In contrast to Boros (2045) Rahner confronts the destructiveness and horror of death. There is also tension between external fate and personal meaning. See also Rahner (2120).

2.53 PARANORMAL/SPIRIT WORLD/REINCARNATION (SEE ALSO 3.4)

2319 de Silva, Lynn A. *Reincarnation in Buddhist and Christian Thought.* Colombo, Sri Lanka: Christian Literature Society of Ceylon, 1968.

In an attempt to encourage dialogue between Buddhists and Christians the author presents the following arguments for reincarnation: the memory of some people about a previous life; immortality of the soul; the moral law which guides our destiny. Buddhist and Christian responses to these arguments are given, with special attention to the problem of suffering. The author points to the higher or lower forces present in every person which fight with each other in the fulfillment of individual destiny. Reincarnation takes place during life and not when we enter into physical death.

2320 Leary, T., R. Metazner, and R. Alpert. *The Psychedelic Experience: A Manual Based on the Tibetan Book of the Dead.* New Hyde Park, N.Y.: University Books, 1964.

Psychedelic experience is modeled after three phases described in The Tibetan Book of the Dead: non-game ecstasy, hallucinations, re-entry. Technical comments on drugs and instructions for use in a series of visions are given.

2321 Morey, Robert A. *Death and the Afterlife*. Minneapolis, Minn.: Bethany House, 1984.

David Hume regarded concepts of human life as impossible apart from a structure of sensory experience. This led to a decline of belief in the afterlife and a preoccupation with rich experiences of human feeling. The emphasis was more akin to occult practices and beliefs of the Middle Ages than to the traditional view of life after death. The occult became a fashionable part of British society.

2322 Myers, F. W. H. *Human Personality and Its Survival of Bodily Death*. London: Longmans, Green and Co., 1919.

The author presents trances, hypnotism, hysteria and other states which give evidence, as he sees it for life after death. A surviving "subliminal self" exists in all living human beings and explains the psychic abilities of the living. He opposes this theory to the classical spiritualist position that such phenomenon were produced by departed spirits. Extensive appendices contain detailed case material. The text is introduced by an influential psychologist, Gardiner Murphy.

2323 Stevenson, Ian. *Twenty Cases Suggestive of Reincarnation*. 2d ed. Charlottesville, Va.: University Press of Virginia, 1974.

From personal investigations a Professor of Psychiatry and Director of the Division of Parapsychology of the University of Virginia presents 20 cases of people who have claimed that they remember an earlier life upon earth. The claims are usually made by a young child, whose memories of earlier life fade after several years. Cases occurred in India, Sri Lanka, Brazil, Lebanon, Tlingit Alaskan Indians. 18 of the cases are a follow-up after 8 years from the original interview.

2324 Stevenson, Ian. *Cases of the Reincarnation Type*. Charlottesville, Va.: University Press of Virginia, 1975.

Near and Far East cases of reincarnation presented from a scientific viewpoint suggest the possibility of reincarnation.

2325 Toynbee, Arnold *et al. Life After Death*. New York: McGraw-Hill Book Co., 1976.

Various philosophers, theologians, social scientists, psychics and historians present evidence for their belief in extrasensory communication with the dead and personal consciousness that survives the physical death of the body. Few references to professional literature. Extensive index.

2326 Walker, E. D. *Reincarnation*. Point Loma, Calif.: Aryan Theosophistical Press, 1923.

A teacher of Theosophy examines the transmigration of souls through Western literature, ancient writings, the Bible and early Christianity, the modern Far East. Questions are answered about the transmigration through animals and the possibility of death, heaven and hell. The final answer is Karma, the companion truth of reincarnation. Bibliography.

2.6 DEATH IN WORLD RELIGIONS (SEE ALSO 3.3).

2327 Klein, S. *The Final Mystery*. New York: Doubleday, 1974.

See 6120.

2328 Kramer, Kenneth Paul. *The Sacred Art of Dying*. New York: Paulist Press, 1988.

Eastern and Western viewpoints on death are presented through the creation stories of Hindu, Buddhist, Zen, Tibetan, Chinese, Mesopotamian, Egyptian, Greek, Hebraic, Christian, Islamic, and American Indian creation stories. Primary source materials are presented along with a discussion of a common factor in each tradition, the self in relation to the death-rebirth experience. From this common theme emerges the teaching that dying is a sacred art. Each tradition affirms that one must discover how to outlive the end of the world while yet alive. Recommended journal exercises and questions for experiencing death in life. Recommended bibliography. The author tries to stay close to the sources in each tradition and with religious rather than psychological issues. See also Carse (2014), Kramer (2327).

2329 Prickett, John. *Death*. London: Lutterworth Educational Press, 1980.

From an interfaith dialogue in education, the meaning of death and awareness of God is presented by authorities in varying religious traditions: Baha'i Faith, Buddhism, Catholic, Protestant, Eastern Orthodox Christian, Hinduism, Humanism, Islam, Judaism, Sikhism.

2330 Reynolds, Frank E. and Earle H. Waugh. *Religious Encounters With Death: Insights From the History and Anthropology of Religions*. University Park, Pa.: Pennsylvania State University Press, 1977.

Historians of religion, anthropologists, and religious leaders present historical and ethnographic essays prepared originally for the American Academy of Religion, 1973. Comparative studies of death are introduced by Mircea Eliade's essay on mythic formulas. Victor Turner connects pilgrimage with death and salvation. Other essays are from the perspective of Meso-America and Africa, the traditions of India, Japanese Buddhism, Ancient Israel, Hassidic thought, Islam, American Christian traditions.

2.61 JEWISH

2331 Brayer, Menachem M. "The Psychology of the Halakh of Bereavement." In *A Psychology—Judaism Reader*, ed. by Reuvent Bulka and Moshe Ha Levi Spero, 184–210. Springfield, Ill.: Charles C. Thomas, 1982.

Jewish customs of mourning are related to the phase theories constructed by Freud, Bowlby, Parkes, and others.

2332 Bulka, Reuven P. "Death in Life—Talmudic and Logo-Therapeutic Affirmations." *Humanitas* 10 (1974): 33–42.

A rabbi who is impressed with Frankl presents the Talmudic dialogue with death as a mortification of the self, an investigation of the past to improve the future, and investment of life energies in this pursuit. Both the Talmud and the theories of Frankl take an affirmative attitude toward death. Talmud: faith in God who can make life positive; Frankl: secular affirmation of the natural order and a belief that attitudes can be both positive and realistic.

2333 Cohn, Heim. "Suicide in Jewish Legal and Religious Tradition." *Mental Health and Society* 3 (1976): 129–136.

See 3520.

2334 Gerson, Gary D. "The Psychology of Grief and Mourning in Judaism." *Journal of Religion and Health* 16 (October 1977): 261–275.

The mourning practices of Judaism take account of the following reactions to grief: denial of death, distance from others, guilt feelings, mental distress which is often identified as sorrow. Coping with death is divided into the periods of immediate mourning, seven days after burial, thirty days after burial. Parents continue the custom of mourning for the following eleven months.

2335 Frankl, Victor E. *The Doctor and the Soul*. Trans. by Richard and Clara Winston. New York: Alfred A. Knopf, 1955.

See 2155.

2336 Lamm, Maurice. *The Jewish Way in Death and Mourning*. New York: Jonathan David Publishers, 1969.

A rabbi interprets the ancient tradition of Judaism through issues that are relevant to contemporary readers: from the moment of death to the funeral service, the funeral service and the internment, a brief and year-long mourning observance, post-mourning practices and beliefs concerning the world beyond the grave. Scholarship of an Orthodox rabbi is combined with knowledge of the behavioral sciences to provide an authoritative text.

2337 Montefiore, C. J. G. *Ancient Jewish and Greek Encouragement*. Bridgeport, Conn.: Hartmore House, 1971.

A liberal Jewish philosopher prepared during World War I his thoughts on the comparison and contrast of Jewish and Greek solutions to the problem of physical and moral suffering. In both there is comfort in the rationality of the universe, especially the idea of righteousness. The world is good and governed by goodness. Humans are good and find comfort in communion with the ultimate good. The differences are that Judaism speaks to all, whereas Stoicism speaks to the few. Jews speak for goodness and Stoics of reason; one worships the divine love and the other adores the divine intelligence. There is more human warmth and "progress" in Judaism than in Stoicism. In surveying these two approaches to consolation in the face of moral and physical evil, the author is critical of the rabbinic emphasis upon suffering as a result of sin and emphasizes the later Jewish "redemption through the inner presence of God in this world and future heavenly rest." The Greek view is more heroic in this life, with more thought placed on serenity in the face of approaching death than in hope of a life beyond death.

2338 Pollock, George H. "On Mourning and Anniversaries: The Relationship of Culturally Constituted Defense Systems to Intra-Psychic Adaptive Processes." *Israel Annals of Psychiatry* 10 (1972): 9–40.

The author summarizes research on difficult personal adjustment to loss, which may be manifest in self-infliction among various cultures and suggests that Jewish rituals provide stages of mourning that enhance healthy grieving. In Jewish culture the bereaved are assisted both by the family and the community to face loss. The role of the comforter is praised in the Torah. Family unity is enhanced by seven days of mourning in one dwelling, "The House of Sheva."

2339 Riemer, Jack, ed. *Jewish Reflections on Death*. New York: Schocken Books, 1974.

Essays are presented on the Jewish experience of death, suffering, and solace, traditional and modern rabbinical and psychological. Subjects include the problems of medical technology and modern society, the way in which the Jewish tradition functions, a personal confrontations with death or bereavement, the religious and psychological meanings of Jewish law in relation to death and mourning.

2340 Riemer, Jack and Nathaniel Ial Stampfer. *Ethical Wills: The Jewish Tradition.* New York: Schocken Books, 1983.

The authors present a series of traditional writings by parents to their children on the meaning of life and the wishes of parents for their children.

2341 Silberman, Lou H. "Death in the Hebrew Bible and the Apocalyptic Literature." In *Perspectives on Death*, ed. by Liston O. Mills, 13–32. Nashville, Tenn.: Abingdon Press, 1969.

See 2092.

2342 Spiro, J. D. "The Jewish Way of Death." *American Judaism* 27 (1964): 16–19.

Status seeking in the selection of funeral services and coffins has become a social pressure upon Jews. It should be resisted in favor of simplicity in death rituals.

2.62 CATHOLIC

2343 *Apocalyptic Spirituality.* Trans. by Bernard McGinn. New York: Scholars Press, 1979.

See 2259.

2344 Aquinas, Thomas. *Summa Contra Gentiles.* Vol. 4. Trans. by C. J. O'Neil. Garden City, N.Y.: Doubleday and Co., 1957.

See 1083.

2345 Becque, Maurice, and Louis Becque. *Life After Death. 20th Century Encyclopedia of Catholicism.* Vol.28. Trans. by P. J. Hepburn-Scott. New York: Hawthorne Books, 1960.

See 2195.

2346 Boros, Ladislaus. *The Moment of Truth.* London: Burns and Oates, 1962.

See 2045.

2347 Boros, Ladislaus. *The Mystery of Death.* New York: Herder and Herder, 1965.

See 2046.

2348 Curran, Charles A. "Death and Dying." *Journal of Religion and Health.* Vol. 14 (1975): 254–263.

See 2076.

2349 Fargues, Marie. *The Child and the Mystery of Death.* Glenrock, N.J.: Dews Books, 1966.

See 3051.

2350 Fichter, Joseph H. *Religion and Pain.* New York: Crossroad Pub. Co., 1981.

See 3225.

2351 Flynn, Eileen P. *AIDS: The Catholic Call for Compassion.* Kansas City: Sheed and Ward, 1985.

See 3277.

2352 Guardini, Romano. *The Last Things.* Trans. by Charlotte D. Forsyth and Grace B. Branham. New York: Pantheon Books, 1954.

See 2267.

2353 Harley, Marta Powell. *A Revelation of Purgatory by An Unknown 15th—Century Woman Visionary.* Lewiston, N.Y.: E. Mellen Press, 1985.

See 2315.

2354 Hellwig, Monika K. *What Are They Saying About Death and Christian Hope?* New York: Paulist Press, 1978.

A writer for the Missionary Society of St. Paul the Apostle presents the official teachings of the Catholic church concerning the state of the soul after death in succinct and non-technical prose.

2355 Joshua, Jean-Pierre. *Discours Chretiens Et Scandale Du Mal.* Chalet, 1979.

See 2182.

2356 Katherine of Genoa, Saint. *Purgation and Purgatory: The Spiritual Dialogue.* Trans. by Serge Hughes. New York: Paulist Press, 1979.

See 2316.

2357 Kelly, Nathan F. *The Emergence of Roman Catholic Medical Ethics: An Historical-Methodological-Bibliographical Study*. New York: E. Mellen Press, 1979.

See 3435.

2358 Knauber, Adolf. *Pastoral Theology of the Anointing of the Sick: Rite of Anointing and Pastoral Care of the Sick*. Collegeville, Minn.: The Liturgical Press, 1975.

See 3337.

2359 Küng, Hans. *Eternal Life?: Life After Death as a Medical, Philosophical and Theological Problem*. Trans. by Edward Quinn. Garden City, N. Y.: Doubleday and Co., 1984.

See 2220.

2360 LeGoff, Jacques. *The Birth of Purgatory*. Chicago: University of Chicago Press, 1984.

See 1080.

2361 Lepp, Ignace. *Death and Its Mysteries*. Trans. by Bernard Murchland. New York: Macmillan Pub. Co., 1968.

See 2030.

2362 Lepp, Ignace. *The Challenges of Life*. New York: Alba House, 1969.

See 2031.

2363 Maeterlinck, Maurice. *Death*. 1911. Reprint. New York: Arno Press, 1976.

See 2061.

2364 Maritain, Jacques. *God and the Permission of Evil*. Trans by Joseph W. Evans. Milwaukee, Wis.: Bruce Pub. Co., 1966.

See 2184.

2365 Miranda, Jose Porfino. *Being and the Messiah: The Message of St. John*.Trans. by John Eaglesom. Maryknoll, N. Y.: Orbis Books, 1977.

See 2275.

2366 Niklas, Gerald R. and Charlotte Stephanics. *Ministry to the Hospitalized*. New York: Paulist Press, 1975.

This text is for Roman Catholic priests who serve as voluntary general hospital chaplains. Empathetic care is presented in medical psychology and thanatology. Selected bibliography for each chapter on types of religious care and ministry to persons with varying types of illness.

2367 Nowell, Robert. *What a Modern Catholic Believes About Death.* Chicago: Thomas More Press, 1972.

This is a brief and popular presentation of Catholic beliefs concerning feelings about death, assurance of resurrection, the meaning of the last judgement, purgatory, honesty in facing death. Notes.

2368 Pieper, Josef. *Death and Immortality.* New York: Herder and Herder, 1969.

See 2236.

2369 Rahner, Karl. "Death." In *Sacramentum Mundi.* Vol. 2. New York: Herder and Herder, 1968.

See 2120.

2370 Rahner, Karl. "Hell." In *Sacramentum Mundi.* Vol. 3, 7–9. New York: Herder and Herder, 1969.

See 2307.

2371 Rahner, Karl. *On the Theology of Death.* New York: Seabury Press, 1973.

See 2318.

2372 Rahner, Karl. *Foundations of Christian Faith.* Trans. by William V. Dych. New York: Seabury Press, 1978.

See 2121.

2373 Schillebeeckx, Edward, and Boniface Willems. *Thanatology. The Problem of Eschatology. Concilium* vol. 41. New York: Paulist Press, 1969.

See 2145.

2374 Schmaus, Michael. *Dogmas 6: Justification and the Last Things.* New York: Sheed and Ward, 1977.

See 2287.

2375 Schnackenburg, Rudolph. *Christ-Present and Coming.* Trans. by Edward Quinn. Philadelphia: Fortress Press, 1978.

See 2288.

2376 Simpson, Michael. *Death and Eternal Life.* Notre Dame: Fides, 1971.

See 2243.

2.63 PROTESTANT
See TWENTIETH CENTURY THEOLOGY (2.3) and TRANSCENDING DEATH (2.5).

2.64 EASTERN

2377 Al-Najjar, Sheikh Yusuf. "Suicide and Islamic Law." *Mental Health and Society* 3 (1976): 137–141.

See 3507.

2378 de Silva, Lynn A. *Reincarnation in Buddhist and Christian Thought.* Colombo, Sri Lanka: Christian Literature Society of Ceylon, 1968.

See 2319.

2379 Evans-Wentz, W. E. *The Tibetan Book of the Dead.* London: Oxford University Press, 1957.

This ancient work provides instruction on the meeting of death and an introduction to experiences after death.

2380 Kapleau, Philip, ed. *The Wheel of Death: A Collection of Writings From Zen Buddist and Other Sources on Death-Rebirth-Dying.* New York: Harper and Row, 1971.

Sacred texts and selections from Zen masters are presented to help a dying person achieve a calm and deliberate death, facilitate a satisfactory rebirth and provide some liberation from painful bondage to birth and death. Survivors can be heartened by the realization that both they and a loved one see death and life as transitory.

2381 Holck, Frederick H., ed. *Death and Eastern Thought: Understanding Death in Eastern Religions and Philosophies.* Nashville, Tenn.: Abingdon Press, 1974.

From the Vedic through contemporary philosophers such as Gandhi and Tagore, specialists trace the history and development of Eastern thought and tradition about death. Most of the emphasis is upon Indian sources with some reference to Chinese and Japanese. Authors assert that Westerners know how to live and Easterners know how to die, which means that the former know how to plan a decent and comfortable life in terms of worldly value, while the latter know how to plan for death under the guidance of spiritual values without anxiety, fear and grief.

2382 Lee, Young. *Death and Beyond in the Eastern Perspective*. New York: Science Publishers, 1974.

The Eastern perspective of Ying-Yang is presented in terms of dying, death and reincarnation. Differences in Eastern and Western perceptions are explained as "either-or" and "both-and."

2383 Lee, Jung Young. *Death Overcome: Towards a Convergence of Eastern and Western Views*. New York: University Press of America, 1983.

The dialogue between a terminally ill college student and his tutor on Eastern religion and philosophy is edited so as to emphasize the intellectual rather than the rawer emotional content.

2384 Mehdi, Syed Muslim. *Death and Death Ceremonies*. Karachi: Peermahomed Ebrahim Trust, 1972.

Islamic funeral rites and customs, pertaining to the Shiite religious practices.

2385 Smith, Jane Idleman and Yvonne Yazbeck Haddad. *Islamic Understanding of Death and Resurrection*. New York: State University of New York Press, 1983.

A study of concepts of life after death in Islam, based on both classical and contemporary works and field research.

2386 Watts, Alan. *The Book: On the Taboo Against Knowing Who You Are*. New York: Vintage Books, 1972.

A philosopher confronts the delusion of the lonely separate ego alienated from the universe, with skillful understanding of Eastern and Western religions and philosophies.

Chapter 3

COUNSELING
THE TERMINALLY ILL

3.1 EMOTIONAL IMPACT OF DYING

3001 Barber, T. X. "Death By Suggestion: A Critical Note." *Psychosomatic Medicine* 23 (1961): 153–155.

The author believes that poison, starvation and organic disease are the usual causes of "voodoo death" rather than any biochemical response to fear.

3002 Beauvoir, Simone de. *A Very Easy Death.* Trans. by P. O'Brien. New York: G. P. Putnam and Sons, 1966.

A proud mother's clinical humiliation is sensitively described alongside the conflicting love and hostility her daughter experienced in confronting the death. The mother was not told that she was dying. The early relationship of the daughter to the mother will be found in the three volumes of Simone de Beauvoir's memoirs. The death of Simone de Beauvoir is described in Marks (3008).

3003 Cannon, Walter B. "Voodoo Death." *Psychosomatic Medicine* 19 (1957): 182–190.

A physician presents his evidence for the thesis that biochemical responses to socially induced fear may lead to death.

3004 Cousins, Norman. *Anatomy of an Illness as Perceived by the Patient: Reflections on Healing and Regeneration.* New York: W. W. Norton Co., 1979.

A writer who suffered from an elusive illness took a creative role in the therapeutic process by describing his attempts to be active and objective in the patient-physician interplay. He found a renewal of health through laughter and cultivation of the will to live. The persuasive generalizations of this unusual patient should be checked through the medical and other references that he includes in a bibliography.

3005 Kalish, Richard A. *Death, Dying, Transcending.* Perspectives on Death and Dying Series, no. 3. Farmingdale, N.Y.: Baywood Pub. Co., 1979.

Articles by clinicians and researchers are reprinted from *Omega* on the dying process, psychological and social aspects of death by cancer, and the effects of circumstances upon bereavement: suicide, accident, old age. See especially Kalish on the onset of the dying process and Weismann and Worden on psychology and sociology of cancer deaths.

3006 Kastenbaum, Robert J. and Ruth Aisenburg. *The Psychology of Death.* New York: Springer Pub. Co., 1972.

See 1018.

3007 Kübler-Ross, Elisabeth. *Questions and Answers on Death and Dying.* New York: Macmillan Pub. Co., 1974.

Brief answers are given by the author to the questions most commonly brought to her in workshops for helping professionals. See Kübler-Ross (1020).

3008 Marks, Elaine. *Simone de Beauvoir: Encounters with Death.* New Brunswick, N.J.: Rutgers University Press, 1973.

Through a series of quotations from the writings of Simone de Beauvoir, the author traces an obsession central to modern sensibility, the awareness of mortality. This awareness may be seen in the "death of God," death during the occupation of France, the death of de Beauvoir's mother and other members of her family plus the description of some near-death encounters of her own and of Sartre. See also de Beauvoir (3002).

3009 Noyes, Russell, Jr. and Roy Kletti. "The Experience of Dying from Falls." *Omega* 3 (1972): 45–52.

From interviews with near-fatal victims, the author posits phases of resistance, life review and transcendence. In the transcendent phase one seems to be traveling to a previously unknown realm, and also feel oneness or unity with other human beings and the universe. Victims who pass into the transcendent phase emerge in a state of "good health." See also Noyes (3352).

3010 Royse, David. "The Near-Death Experience: A Survey of Clergy's Attitude and Knowledge." *Journal of Pastoral Care* 39, 1 (1985): 31–42.

A questionnaire survey of 174 clergy reveals a number of near-death accounts being made to clergy. The reports are seldom "hellish" and tend instead to make a person more religious and have less fear of death. Responses of the clergy to these narrations were mixed, with a high degree of caution.

3011 Smith, Jo Ann Kelly. *Free Fall*. Valley Forge, Va.: Judson Press, 1975.

With the undergirding of Christian faith, the author wrote an account of her feelings about death during the last months of her life. The title of the book comes from her sense of exhilaration in a "leap of faith" that increasingly separates her from those whom she loves, but also gives her freedom.

3012 Tolstoi, Lev Nikolaevich. *The Death of Ivan Ilych*. Trans. by Louise and Aylmer Maude. New York: Health Sciences Pub. Corp., 1973.

Feelings of defectiveness, sadness, shame and anger are graphically described by the Russian nineteenth century novelist, Tolstoy. The sense of loneliness and isolation experienced by the dying Ivan Ilych is compounded by his enforced dependency and regression. The fluctuations and inconsistencies of the dying process are described. Fighting gives way to resignation, then denial takes over until the reality of dying again intrudes. Hope, confusion and despair appear almost simultaneously before the final acceptance of pain and death. Then there is no more fear, no more darkness, only light and then the last breath. Three months of struggle have ended.

3013 Troup, Stanley B., and William A. Greene. *The Patient, Death and the Family*. New York: Charles Scribner's Sons, 1974.

An interdisciplinary panel presents a personal and readable account of their answer to the question, why are we dissatisfied with how we die today? Philosophical, historical, medical and personal viewpoints on death and dying are presented with a pleasing mixture of professional insight and informed humanism. Notes and illustrations.

3.11 UPON THE DYING PERSON

3014 Alsop, Stewart. *Stay of Execution: A Sort of Memoir*. Philadelphia: J. B. Lippencott, 1973.

A well-known columnist describes with clarity and humor his process of "adjustment" to his own terminal illness.

3015 Bowlby, John Loss: *Sadness and Depression*. Vol. 3, *Attachment and Loss*. New York: Basic Books, 1980.

See 1172.

3016 Carey, Raymond G. "Living Until Death." *Hospital Progress*, February 1974.

Eighty-four terminal patients were interviewed by Protestant hospital chaplains to investigate emotional adjustment in the face of death. Conversations with the patients showed the following concerns: level of anticipated and actual discomfort, previous close contact with a dying individual, religious orientation, amount of interest and concern exhibited by the patient's nearest of kin and local clergymen, and amount of education.

3017 Diggory, James. *Self-Evaluation: Concepts and Studies*. New York: John Wiley and Sons, 1966.

The author summarizes the relation of self-concept to death with a statement that death is feared because it eliminates opportunity to pursue goals that are important to self-esteem. The conclusion is reached without dividing subjects by age groupings. No elderly are included.

3018 Fairbanks, Rollin J. "Ministering to the Dying." *Journal of Pastoral Care* 2 (Fall 1948): 6–14.

A pastoral counselor suggests that ministers will usually find the mood of a dying person to be either: (1) resigned (2) impatient or (3) fearful.

3019 Feldman, M. J. and M. Hersen. "Attitudes Toward Death in Nightmare Subjects." *Journal of Abnormal Psychology* 72 (1967): 421–425.

On a ten item Death Scale a marked relationship was found between scores on the scale and nightmare frequency of subjects. The more frequent nightmare subjects had a history of deaths of relatives and close friends, especially when the subjects were under ten years of age.

3020 Franz, Marie-Louise Von. *On Dreams and Death*. Boston: Shambhala, 1986.

An analyst who was closely associated with Carl Jung provides insights and examples of the way that dreams reveal unconscious responses to and revelations of death. Symbols in the dream may represent the responses to a variety of losses in our daily life or may be a reminder that we are all moving forward to physical death. The author applies Jungian psychology to the second half of life when more and more messages come to us from the unconscious, including the darkness to which we must accommodate. The symbols of ancient Egypt and medieval alchemy are presented as illustrations of death symbols and signs that some harmony has been achieved in death and rebirth (resurrection). Philosophy, theology and parapsychology provide explanations for some of these symbols. See also Freud (3021), Herzog (2212), Jung (2218), and Wheelwright (3034).

3021 Freud, Sigmund. "Dreams of the Death of Persons of Whom the Dreamer Is Fond." In *Complete Psychological Works of Sigmund Freud*. Vol. 4., 248–271. London: Hogarth, 1953.

Children during the Oedipal phase have dreams of the death of those of whom they are fond. Adults also have such dreams, which represent death wishes toward the loved object. For an alternative description and explanation of dreams, see Franz (3020), Herzog (2212), Jung (2218), Wheelwright (3034).

3022 Hersen, M. "Personality Characteristics of Nightmare Sufferers." *Journal of Nervous and Mental Disease* 153, 1 (1971): 27–31.

From tests with a group of institutionalized patients in a state mental hospital, the author concluded that those who suffered from frequent nightmares showed more anxiety and lower ego strength than other patients and reported a heightened concern about death.

3023 Hinton, John M. "The Influence of Previous Personality on Reactions to Having Terminal Cancer." *Omega* 6 (1975): 95–111.

From a study of sixty married patients who were terminally ill of cancer, the author tried to correlate various features of their pre-morbid personality with their behavior during the disease. Interviews were conducted with the spouse of the patient and an attending nurse. He concluded that the way a patient lives will influence the manner of a person's dying. The degree of depression or anxiety when dying did not differ between persons who were previously stable and those who were previously neurotic. Difficulty in adapting to situations during life were associated with more rejection and reserve while dying and lead to loneliness and isolation. Adjustment in earlier life also gave a stronger tendency to depression and anxiety during hospitalization. Active persons with an ability to reach decisions displayed a greater awareness that they were dying and more appreciation of the care that they received. There was a strong correlation between their adaptation to dying and their general feeling of satisfaction with life such as the experience of a happy marriage. The strength of religious belief had no affects on reaction in the face of death.

3024 Hutschnecker, A. A. "Personality Factors in Dying." In *The Meaning of Death*, ed by Herman Fiefel, 237–250. New York: McGraw-Hill Book Co., 1959.

Personality changes among the terminally ill are not extensive, although there is often an initial feeling of depression.

3025 Klein, R. "A Crisis to Grow On." *Cancer* 28 (1971): 1660–1665.

A social worker describes the psychological task that a breast cancer patient must perform and specifies the crisis intervention techniques by which staff members will help her through the crisis period.

3026 Kübler-Ross, Elisabeth. *To Live Until We Say Good-bye.* Englewood Cliffs, N.J.: Prentice-Hall, 1978.

The uniqueness of dying is expressed with compassion and hope by a popular pioneer writer on dying. See Kübler-Ross (1020)

3027 Lieberman, Morton A. "Psychological Correlates of Impending Death: Some Preliminary Observations." *Journal of Gerontology* 20 (1965): 181–190.

A clinician finds that even before physicians find medical evidence that a person is dying, there will be observable changes: decreased energy, emotional withdrawal, simplified perceptions, difficulty in coping with complex problems.

3028 Marshall, Victor W. "The Last Strand: Remnants of Engagement in the Later Years." In *Death, Dying, Transcending*, ed. by Richard A. Kalish. Farmingdale, N.Y.: Baywood Pub. Co., 1980.

A sociologist examines reasons for continuing living among the elderly in a retirement village. Most residents suggested in interviews that death frequently comes too late. Yet, they continue to hold on to life because of a desire to live for and with other people. If this "last strand" is broken through the death of a husband for instance, then the will to live is diminished.

3029 Nungesser, Lon G. and William D. Bullock. *Notes on Living Until We Say Goodbye: A Personal Guide.* New York: St. Martin's Press, 1988.

A worker with the terminally ill emphasizes the advantage of having an open awareness of one's mortality and an active involvement in promoting health. Non-technical advice is given on empowerment when a terminal diagnosis is presented, the stigma of others people's reaction to illness, coping with daily living that effects health and morale, the development of hope and realism, working through events and relationships while caring for the self, managing medical, social and economic needs. Annotated bibliography.

3030 Osis, Karlis, and Erlandur Haraldsson. *At the Hour of Death*. New York: Avon Books, 1977.

Over 190 doctors and nurses were interviewed for reports of deathbed visions, patients' reports of apparitions, a sense of peace and serenity during pain, visions of another world. The book contains brief references from the reports of medical personnel, data from other clinical or questionnaire studies and a variety of hypotheses concerning the meaning of death and the messages that surround it.

3031 Schur, Max. *Freud: Living and Dying*. New York: International Universities Press, 1972.

The physician of Sigmund Freud until his death describes the relationship between Freud's courageous facing of the fear of death and his last works on the same subject. A personal and reflective account of steadfast friendship.

3032 Seligman, Martin. *Helplessness: On Depression, Development, and Death*. San Francisco: Scribner, 1975.

Helplessness and hopelessness are seen as contributors to anxiety, depression, sudden death and fatal illnesses. The author considers these to be learned behaviors that can be counteracted through various forms of therapy.

3033 Weingarten, Violet. *Intimations of Mortality*. New York: Alfred A. Knopf, 1978.

A novelist begins a personal journal after her first operation for cancer and continues it through her last two years. Her accounts include a negative evaluation of much that she found in literature on death.

3034 Wheelwright, Jane H. *Death of a Woman*. New York: St. Martin's Press, 1981.

A Jungian analyst describes therapy with a woman who is dying. Her dreams form many of her thoughts about death for presentation to the analyst and their mutual interpretation. A saga of insight and courage.

3.12 UPON FAMILY AND FRIENDS

3035 Agee, James. *A Death in the Family*. New York: Bantam, 1969.

A psychologically oriented novel describes the impact of the sudden death of a young father upon a loving family. The protective irrationality of various family members is vividly portrayed. There are insightful scenes of the way in which children often misunderstand and are misunderstood by the adults around them in the time of death.

3036 Alther, Lisa. *Kinflicks*. New York: Alfred A. Knopf, 1975.

A very human, lively novel of varying responses to death.

3037 Beauvoir, Simone de. *A Very Easy Death*. New York: G. P. Putnam and Sons, 1966.

See 3002.

3038 Bowlby, John. *The Making and Breaking of Affectional Bonds*. London: Tavistock Publications, 1979.

Articles by the author on the general theme of separation anxiety are included in this collection of his works: "Childhood Mourning and its Implications for Psychiatry (1961)", "Separation and Loss within the Family (1968–1970)", "The Making and Breaking of Affectional Bonds (1976–1977)." A comprehensive reference section includes many articles and books by the author on separation anxiety and mourning.

3039 Gordon, Norman B., and Bernard Kutner. "Long Term and Fatal Illness and the Family." *Journal of Health and Human Behavior*, 6(1965): 190–196.

Parental behaviors and attitudes toward fatal and long-term illnesses of children are discussed in terms of inner attitudes, types of adjustments and relationships within the family. Some suggestions are given concerning the duty of the physician during the initial trauma and long-term understanding of illness by parents.

3040 Grollman, Earl A. *When Your Loved One Is Dying*. Boston: Beacon Press, 1980.

A well-known religious counselor and thanatologist discusses the emotional turmoil that results from the approaching death of a loved one. Emotional reassurance and guidance towards courage and dignity are combined with practical advice on hospices, hospitals, home-care, will, taxes, insurance and the funeral.

3041 Kalish, Richard A. "Dying and Preparing for Death: A View of Families." In *New Meanings of Death*, ed. by Herman Feifel, 215–232. New York: McGraw-Hill Book Co., 1977.

A leading thanatologist describes dying at different stages of life, planning for death, the dying process, and broken attachments as aspects of the impact of dying and death upon a family. References to research studies in the chapter and a list of references.

3042 Maddison, David and Beverley Raphael. "The Family of the Dying Patient." In *Psychological Aspects of Terminal Care*, ed. by Bernard Schoenberg, *et al.*, 185–200. New York: Columbia University Press, 1972.

Responses to a dying family member are examined in terms of responses by individuals, the family as a group and the family in relation to society. Key issues are conflict mobilization, defensive operations, role changes. Professional interventions are discussed.

3043 Wahl, C. W. "Helping the Dying Patient and His Family." *Journal of Pastoral Care* 26 (1972): 93–98.

A psychiatrist suggests that a challenge to the erroneous beliefs that terminally ill persons and their families have about dying may be one of the most valuable contributions made by the staff.

3.121 A CHILD'S SENSE OF IMPENDING LOSS

3044 Anthony, Sylvia. *The Discovery of Death in Childhood and After.* New York: Basic Books, 1972.

See 6096.

3045 Archibald, Herbert C., D. Bell, C. Miller and R. D. Tuddenham. "Bereavement in Childhood and Adult Psychiatric Disturbance." *Psychosomatic Medicine* 24 (1962): 343–351.

See 3062.

3046 Bernstein, Joanne E. *Books to Help Children Cope with Separation and Loss*, 2nd ed. New York: R. R. Bowker, 1983.

See 8005.

3047 Bluebond-Langer, Myra. *The Private Worlds of Dying Children.* Princeton, N.J.: Princeton University Press, 1978.

From her study of children aged 3 to 9 who were hospitalized for leukemia, an anthropologist emphasizes the children's role in initiating and maintaining the social order in which they are patients. There is a review of literature on the awareness and communication process of terminally ill children, a play that dramatizes a child's journey into a pediatric ward, the reasons why dying children choose to conceal their awareness from adults. Bibliography. A luminous entry into the mind of children who are protective as well as protected.

3048 Bowlby, John. "Childhood Mourning and Its Implications for Psychiatry." *American Journal of Psychiatry* 118 (1961): 481–498.

After a review of literature and four clinical studies of adult psychiatric patients the author concludes that the loss of a mother is most significant before age five and that between age five and fourteen the loss of either mother or father is of equal significance as a contributing factor to mental illness or delinquency.

3049 Brenner, Avis. *Helping Children Cope with Stress.* Lexington, Mass.: D. C. Heath and Co., 1984.

In discussing the specific stress of coping with death, the author advises brief discussion which would be continued again when the child is ready for more. Stages of awareness and acceptance by the child are described in terms of protest, grief and acceptance. Helpful adult responses are suggested for each of these stages.

3050 Cook, Sarah Sheets, ed. *Children and Dying: An Exploration and Selected Bibliographies.* Rev. ed. New York: Health Sciences Publishing Corp., 1974.

See 4188.

3051 Fargues, Marie. *The Child and the Mystery of Death.* Glenrock, N.J.: Dews Books, 1966.

Modern and Catholic education are blended in a lucid presentation of a child's understanding of the mystery of death. Discussion questions for teachers and clergy are included.

3052 Fassler, J. *Helping Children Cope.* Ill. by W. B. Hogan. New York: Free Press, 1978.

A student of children's literature presents a brief discussion of professional viewpoints and an analysis of selected books, primarily for four to eight year olds on such topics as separation experiences, hospitalization and illness, lifestyle changes, stress events or situations. Strong and weak points of some thirty books are discussed.

3053 Furman, Erna. *A Child's Parent Dies: Studies in Childhood Bereavement.* New Haven, Conn.: Yale University Press, 1974.

From clinical study of bereaved children and from a review of psychoanalytic literature, the author offers many useful summaries of a child's ability to cope with loss, such as a mental ability to deal with loss, the role that a dead person played in the life of a child, the circumstances that surround the loss and the grieving process that follows. A sixty-four page review of literature relates this work to other studies. Lengthy case examples by individual therapists appear throughout the text.

3054 Grollman, Earl A., ed. *Explaining Death to Children*. Boston: Beacon Press, 1967.

See Grollman 6112.

3055 Jewett, Claudia L. *Helping Children Cope with Separation and Loss*. Boston, Mass.: Harper Common Press, 1982.

Detailed suggestions are offered for responses by adults that will be compassionate and realistic for young children as they move from a stage of protest concerning news of a death to a time of sadness, temporary regression, attempts to find a dead person, some guilt and anger and finally an acceptance of the loss and closer bonds with surviving relatives.

3056 Jewett, Claudia. *Helping Children Cope with Separation and Loss*. Rev. ed. Washington D.C.: Hemisphere Pub. Corp., 1984.

The principle issues for adults who wish to help children in a time of loss are outlined along with suggestions on communication.

3057 Lester, Andrew D., ed. *When Children Suffer: A Sourcebook for Ministry with Children in Crisis*. Philadelphia: Westminster Press, 1987.

A professor of pastoral counseling found that few pastors gave any systematic attention to pastoral relationships with children, even at a time of crisis. To meet this need he assembled chapters by academically and clinically competent leaders in medicine, psychology and theology to highlight the particular crises of school-age children: divorce, bereavement, hospitalization, terminal and chronic illness, abuse, disability, stress and anxiety. Characteristic resources to meet these needs are described in terms of an abiding physical presence as a caring adult, listening, representing God, serving as advocate for the children with social, legal, emotional and spiritual resources.

3058 Lonetto, Richard. *Children's Conceptions of Death*. New York: Springer Pub. Co., 1980.

With a general background of childhood development theory and research on death related concepts, the author presents extensive interviews with Canadian children as reflected in the reproduction of many of their comments and drawings. Three stages of a child's concept of death may be identified from ages 3 through 12.

3059 Nagy, Maria H. "The Child's View of Death." *Journal of Genetic Psychology* 73 (1948): 3–27. Reprinted in *The Meaning of Death*, ed. by Herman Feifel, 79–98. New York: McGraw-Hill Book Co., 1959.

Children in Budapest, Hungary, ages 6–10 made drawings about death and some made written responses to the general question of "what comes to your mind about death" The sample was almost equally divided between boys and girls. In discussion, the author first offered some observations about children under 5 years of age. They think either of death as a departure in sleep or a departure that is gradual or temporary. Between the ages of 5 and 9 death is considered as a person that children try to keep distant from themselves. Children aged 9 and 10 recognize death as a process which takes place in all of us and leads to the dissolution of bodily life. It is inevitable. The author stated that there were sampling limitations and that the conclusions would be tentative. Later investigators modified these tentative conclusions. Bluebond-Langer (3047) found children to be aware of the meaning of death at a much earlier age than Nagy had found, possibly because Bluebond-Langer based her research on work with terminally ill children. A replication of Nagy's study by Stillion and Wass (3060) did not demonstrate the personification of death in stage two of Nagy's study.

3060 Stillion, Judith M. and Hannelore Wass. "Children and Death." In *Dying: Facing the Facts,* ed. by Hannelore Wass, ed. Washington, D. C.: Hemisphere Pub. Co., 1979.

Studies are reviewed concerning the views of healthy and terminally ill children toward death, with helpful guidelines for caregivers and the family of the terminally ill child and a plea for open discussions of death with healthy children. References and brief annotated bibliography.

3061 Young, Elizabeth F. "Preparatory Understanding of Death: The Young Child." In *Children and Dying: An Exploration and Selected Bibliographies.* Rev. ed. by Sarah Sheets Cook, 81–96. New York: Health Sciences Pub. Corp., 1974.

A teacher of pre-schoolers observes ways in which children handle loss and separation and suggests strategies by which parents can help children prepare for both pleasant and unpleasant solitude. Annotated bibliography of books for adults about death and discussion of death in books for children.

3.1211 FUTURE MENTAL HEALTH
See also MORBID GRIEF AND GUILT/PATHOLOGY (4.53)

3062 Archibald, Herbert C., D. Bell, C. Miller and R. D. Tuddenham. "Bereavement in Childhood and Adult Psychiatric Disturbance."

Psychosomatic Medicine, 24 (1962): 343–351.

One thousand patients in a Veterans Administration mental hygiene mental outpatient clinic were compared with a control group and with results of other investigations of childhood bereavement. The V. A. patients showed an appreciably greater frequency of bereavement in childhood than did the general population study. The authors believe that loss of a parent in childhood constitutes a non-specific trauma that results in psychiatric vulnerability.

3063 Arthur, Bettie and Mary L. Kamme. "Bereavement in Childhood." *Journal of Child Psychology and Psychiatry* 5 (1964): 37–49.

A case study of the families of eighty-three disturbed children who had experienced the death of a parent reveal a high incidence of both intellectual and emotional problems either directly or indirectly related to the loss.

3064 Barry, Herbert Jr., Herbert Barry III, and Erich Lindemann. "Dependency in Adult Patients Following Early Maternal Bereavement." *Journal of Nervous and Mental Disease* 140 (1965): 196–206.

Characteristics of adult psychiatric patients who suffered a bereavement before age 4 were compared to other psychiatric patients who suffered a bereavement between ages 11–17. Dependency was a prominent characteristic of the first group.

3065 Beck, A. T., B. B. Sethi and R. W. Tuthil. "Childhood Bereavement and Adult Depression." *Archives of General Psychiatry* 9 (1963): 295–302.

There was a significantly greater incidence of parent loss in childhood among those who were highly depressed as compared with non-depressed patients in a psychiatric ward or clinic.

3066 Berlinsky, Ellen B. and Henry B. Biller. *Parental Death and Psychological Development*. Lexington, Mass.: Lexington Books, 1982.

From an examination of empirical studies on personality variables and parent death during childhood, two psychologists concur with the general findings that changes in the nature and course of a child's behavior may result from variables involved in parental bereavement. Many researchers have oversimplified the situation and many variables need additional investigation, such as the possible link between a child's incentive to achieve and the early loss of a parent. A judicious and provocative study.

3067 Deutsch, Helene. "Absence of Grief." *Psychoanalytic Quarterly* 6 (1937): 12–22.

From cases in which the reaction to the loss of a beloved object is a complete absence of the manifestations of mourning, the author concludes that death of a beloved person must produce reactive expression of feeling in the normal course of events, omission of such reactive responses is to be considered just as much a variation from the normal as excess in time or intensity, unmanifested grief will be found expressed to the full in some way or other.

3068 Hill, O. W. and J. S. Price. "Childhood Bereavement and Adult Depression." *British Journal of Psychiatry* 113 (1967): 743–751.

A significantly higher number of depressed subjects had lost their fathers by age 15 than had a control group. But the loss of mothers did not differ. The relative age of the father may have been significant.

3069 Langmeier, Josef and Z. Matejcek. *Psychological Deprivation in Childhood.* Ed. by G. L. Mangam. New York: John Wiley and Sons, 1975.

Two clinical psychologists in Prague consider the impact of social forces after World War II in Eastern Europe upon the care of children: the social orphan, the child of uninterested or divorced parents, the "collectivized" child. Models of child depravation in the past are contrasted with those of contemporary society. In addition to their sociological and psychological analysis, the authors present case studies and some drawings by some the deprived children. Extensive bibliography drawn from American, English and European sources.

3070 Markusen, Eric and Robert Fulton. "Childhood Bereavement and Behavior Disorders: A Critical Review." *Omega* 2 (1971): 107–117.

The authors find that most studies of the bereavement–later behavior disorder hypothesis harbor methodological problems which have generated discrepant findings. This is especially true of retrospective studies. The author's anteriospective study of over 11,000 ninth grade students in Minnesota, 1954 with extensive follow-up in 1956, 1960, 1966 tentatively indicates that early parental bereavement may significantly affect adult behavior, specifically with respect to offenses against the law.

3071 Moriarity, David M., ed. *The Loss of Loved Ones.* St. Louis, Mo.: Warren H. Green, 1983.

On the basis of his clinical experience with adult patients, a psychiatrist discusses the effects of early loss of a parent upon the development of the personality—usually leading to depression because of unconscious identification with the lost one. The second section of the book presents theoretical and clinical discussion by a psychoanalytically oriented psychiatrist, a judge, a Protestant minister, a Roman Catholic priest, and children's drawings about death.

3072 Munro, Alistair. "Childhood Parent Loss in a Psychiatrically Normal Population." *British Journal of Preventive and Social Medicine* 19 (1965): 69–70.

In a study of children who had lost a parent with no subsequent history of serious psychiatric disorder, the author concludes that childhood grief for a parent is of questionable value as an indicator of later mental illness.

3073 Munro, Alistair. "Parental deprivation in depressive patients." *British Journal of Psychiatry* 112 (1966): 443–457.

In comparison of a group of depressed in-patients with a group of psychiatrically normal persons, the author finds no justification for the loss of a parent as a factor in depressive illness. From a review of literature, he finds that the samples were usually depressed, institutionalized children and that the loss of the father was seldom explicated.

3.122 IMPACT OF DEATH UPON ADOLESCENTS

3074 Arundel, H. *The Blanket Word*. Nashville, Tenn.: Nelson, 1973.

This novel describes the feelings of a nineteen year old girl as she faces the painful death of her mother. The idealism and self-doubts of young people are sensitively presented with honesty about the meaning of love in the face of death.

3075 Bermann, Eric. *Scapegoat*. Ann Arbor, Mich.: University of Michigan Press, 1973.

A therapist began to visit the family of a troubled eight year old and discovered the family secret: the father has a heart condition that creates chronic fear of impending death. To maintain the pretense that all was well despite the eroding anxiety of unmentionable fears, psychological pressure was continually exerted upon the eight year old as an expendable scapegoat. This was done unconsciously and was never admitted by the family in six years of conversations by the therapist with them about the deteriorating behavior of their child. The narration of the case includes professional discussion of other studies and theories concerning family interaction and responses to death. Extensive bibliography.

3076 Bernstein, Joanne E. *Loss and How to Cope with It*. New York: Seabury Press, 1977.

This guidebook for youth explores the nature of loss, the impact of death and the personal responses that may be expected. Additional assistance is suggested concerning books, films and organizations.

3077 Colman, Hila. *Sometimes I Don't Love My Mother*. New York: Morrow, 1977.

This novel describes the resentment, anger and guilt of a seventeen year old girl who is faced with decisions about help for her mother and alternate plans for college after the sudden death of her father.

3078 Huntsberry, W. E. *The Big Hang-up*. New York: Lothrop, 1970.

See 1231.

3079 Kastenbaum, Robert J. "Time and Death in Adolescence." In *The Meaning of Death*, ed. by Herman Feifel, 99–113. New York: McGraw-Hill Book Co., 1959.

Two hundred and sixty adolescents, male and female, made a set of judgments in an experiment that show an intense preoccupation with the present, little explicit structuring of the remote future, more explicit structuring of the past.

3080 Shoor, M., and M. H. Speed. "Death, Delinquency, and the Mourning Process." In *Death and Identity*, ed. by Robert Fulton. New York, John Wiley and Sons, 1965.

Several studies of bereaved young people, age 14–17 showed disengagement from regular behavior patterns. They had previously conformed to social expectations, but now presented such disturbances as burglary, running away from home, sexual misbehavior, depression and underachievement.

3081 Wersba, Barbara. *Run Softly, Go Fast*. New York: Atheneum, 1970.

This fictional account of the impact of his father's funeral upon a nineteen year old boy is a realistic account of the difficulties that adolescents have in accepting parents as human beings with faults. Some of these faults come to the young man's mind as he begins to discover more about his father and his feelings for his father in the months that follow the funeral. In time a new perspective comes to the young man. The writing of a journal helps him to resolve anger and facilitate his grieving.

3.123 ADULTS AND CARE OF CHILDREN

3082 Adams, David W. *The Psychosocial Care of the Child and His Family in Childhood Cancer: An Annotated Bibliography.* Ontario, Canada: Dept. of Social Work Services, McMaster University Medical Center, 1979.

See 8003.

3083 Adams, David W. and E. J. Deveau. *Coping With Childhood Cancer: Where Do We Go From Here?* Reston, Va.: Reston Pub. Co., 1984.

A social worker and a nurse in pediatric oncology prepare a guide for parents and family members that describes the impact of cancer upon the child, the family and friends. The emphasis is upon honesty and realism in communication and care.

3084 Buckingham, Robert W. *A Special Kind of Love: Care of the Dying Child.* New York: Continuum, 1983.

The writer uses various accounts to describe the impending loss of a child from the viewpoint of friends, teachers, counselors, health-care professionals. List of helping organizations, hospice program for children, bibliography.

3085 Cohen, M. and L. M. Lipton. "Spontaneous Remission of Schizophrenic Psychoses Following Maternal Death." *Psychiatric Quarterly* 24 (1950): 716–725.

The authors discuss case histories in which the death of a patient's mother appeared to relate to spontaneous remission of psychotic symptoms.

3086 Corr, Charles A. "Books for Adults: An Annotated Bibliography." In *Helping Children Cope with Death: Guidelines and Resources,* ed. by Hannelove Wass and Charles. A. Corr. Washington, D.C.: Hemisphere Pub. Co., 1982.

See 8007.

3087 Dobihal, Edward F., and Charles W. Stewart. *When a Friend Is Dying: A Guide to Caring for the Terminally Ill and Bereaved.* Nashville, Tenn.: Abingdon Press, 1984.

In this straightforward and practical book for a general audience a chaplain and a professor of pastoral theology draw upon their years of experience to provide perspective and practical helps for those who minister to the dying and bereaved as friends. Religious resources and references to the work of the church and clergy are additional assets of this volume.

3088 Evans, Jocelyn. *Living with a Man Who Is Dying.* New York: Taplinger Pub. Co., 1971.

The death of a husband at age 33 of abdominal cancer is badly handled by well-meaning doctors. Husband and wife are still able to achieve a relatively dignified and peaceful death at home.

3089 Grollman, Earl A. *Talking About Death: A Dialogue Between Parent and Child.* Rev. ed. Boston: Beacon Press, 1976.

An explicit and observant guide to parents on feelings of parent and child as they are expressed in discussion about death. Includes a read-along for children, with illustrations. A parent's guide for explaining death is divided into age categories and is followed by specific statements of children about death and advice on communication to parents. There is additional specific guidance on such topics as the child's loss of a brother or sister. A listing of resources include organizations, cassettes, films, books.

3090 Gunther, John. *Death Be Not Proud.* New York: Harper and Row, 1949.

See 4204.

3091 Corr, Charles A., and Donna M. Corr, eds. *Hospice Approaches to Pediatric Care.* New York: Springer Pub. Co., 1985.

Concerns for the dying child, family and care-givers are combined in a multidisciplinary approach: physical, psychological, social, spiritual. Emphasis of articles is upon assessment of needs, utilization of both personal and professional skills, development of more initiation, coordination of care, after-care of grieving children and parents. Written for both professionals and volunteers who care for children at home or in a hospital. Plain writing with many examples and relevant references to research and clinical studies.

3092 Hamovitch, Maurice B. *The Parent and the Fatally Ill Child.* Duarte, Calif.: City of Hope Medical Center, 1964.

The parent participation program in the pediatrics department of the City of Hope Medical Center is evaluated. The program was not successful in reversing marked problems in adjustment in a fifth of the sample, but for most families the program was an effective means of dealing with fatal illness. Some of the variables; (1) a fourth of the families have serious difficulty in coping with life-tasks and this increased their difficulties in dealing with a terminal illness; (2) divorce, separated or previously married parents showed a significantly greater number of problems in relation to a dying child; (3) children with non-operable sarcomas placed special anxieties over a longer period of time with parents; (4) children beyond the age of ten displayed more problems with parents than with the younger aged groups. Perhaps this was because older children talked more about death. Staff and parents were uncomfortable with this and had more guilt. Younger children were more tranquil and quickly overcame separation anxiety; (5) nurses especially welcomed the presence of parents; (6) parents went almost immediately into a pattern of pre-occupation with their loss and personal tragedy for themselves after hearing the diagnosis; (7) the most difficult time for shock and self-pity for families was during the first three months after they heard the diagnosis. Relatives and friends often avoided the family during this time; (8) fathers seemed to suffer more than mothers after the death of the child, perhaps because mothers were more likely at the end to be looking forward to the child's release from suffering; (9) parents were very appreciative of the living accommodations and free meals provided for them during the time of their care for child. Short bibliography and a sample case.

3093 Hickman, Martha Whitmore. *Last Week My Brother Anthony Died.* Ill. by Randie Julian. Nashville, Tenn.: Abingdon Press, 1984.

See 6115.

3094 Hempe, S. O. "Needs of Grieving Spouse in a Hospital Setting." *Nursing Research* 24 (1975): 113–120.

Nursing intervention techniques and attitudes are described for the care of both a dying patient and family members.

3095 Jury, Dan and Mark Jury. *Gramp.* New York: Grossman Pub., 1976.

A direct account of the grueling dying of Frank Tugend, as recorded in photographs and words, by a family who made his death an act of love. When, at age eighty-one, he removed his false teeth and announced that he was no longer going to eat or drink because of his physical deterioration, his family respected his wishes and did not hospitalize him. Three weeks later, he died at home. "Superb" (Simpson 8039, 66).

3096 Kübler-Ross, Elisabeth. *On Children and Death.* New York: Macmillan Pub. Co., 1983.

A popular physician and writer on thanatology assembles cases, letters, advice, spiritual thoughts. The author warns against denial and bargaining because of her observations that children know when they are dying. Suggestions are given on how to mourn and support groups are recommended such as Compassionate Friends. Extensive bibliography on children, stress, dying, death.

3097 Levy, Erin Linn. *Children are not Paper Dolls: A Visit with a Bereaved Sibling*. Freeley, Colo.: Counseling Consultants, 1982.

Six bereaved children present their feelings about deceased siblings through direct quotations in a discussion group, drawings, poems and their photos.

3098 Sanders, Catherine M. *Grief: The Mourning After: Dealing with Adult Bereavement*. New York: John Wiley and Sons, 1989.

This book for caregivers provides a theoretical framework for understanding the process of bereavement and for stimulating further research. After summarizing some pioneer studies on grief work, the author describes phases of bereavement (shock, awareness, conservation, healing, renewal) and then considers such variables as complicated grief, personality differences, social and situational variables. The family constellation, the death of a child, a spouse and a parent are given separate treatment. Practical applications for intervention with the bereaved are given. References.

3.13 UPON PROFESSIONAL AND OTHER HELPERS
See also CARETAKING PROFESSIONS (5.0)

3099 Adams, David W. *Childhood Malignancy: The Psychosocial Care of the Child and His Family*. Springfield, Ill.: Charles C. Thomas, 1979.

In a text for professionals, a medical social worker addresses the full range of psychosocial issues that have to do with children and cancer, stressing the value of honesty and realism. An emphasis upon interdisciplinary care and on team roles and functions.

3100 Banks, Sam A. "Dialogue on Death: Freudian and Christian Views." *Pastoral Psychology* 14 (June 1963): 41–49.

A general hospital chaplain examines the strength and weakness of Freudian views of death vis-à-vis Christian theology. He concludes that the work of Freud serves as a corrective for some of the oversimplifications and biases concerning motives and needs of the dying.

3101 Crane, Diana. *The Sanctity of Social Life: Physicians' Treatment of Critically Ill Patients*. New York: Russell Sage Foundation, 1975.

A valuable study based on extensive interviews, observations, hospital record audit, and detailed questionnaires. While withdrawal of treatment is widespread in some types of cases, positive euthanasia is rare. Both adults and children seem to be regarded as "treatable" while they retain the potential for interacting in some meaningful way with others.

3102 Eissler, K. R. *The Psychiatrist and the Dying Patient.* New York: International Universities Press, 1955.

See 3456.

3103 Feigenberg, Loma. *Terminal Care: Friendship Contracts With Dying Cancer Patients.* Trans. by Patrick Hort. New York: Brunner/Mazel, 1980.

A Swedish oncologist details the practical ways in which he has tried to live out this objective: the primary task for the therapist is to allow the dying patient to live until he dies. In an intimate narrative style the author presents five case histories that illustrate the contact of a dying person with hospital staff. This is followed by an analysis of the demands for knowledge, empathy and self-awareness that are made upon the staff in a patient-centered approach to the terminally ill. There is an extensive annotation of selected literature in thanatology. See also Feigenberg (3200).

3104 Freihofoeher, P., *et al.* "Nursing Behaviors in Bereavement: An Exploratory Study." *Nursing Research* 25 (1976): 332–337.

Through a study of care for 25 pairs of terminally ill patients and their loved ones, the authors seek to determine nursing behaviors that will offer support, comfort and ease of suffering.

3105 Fuller, Thomas and Allan Reed. "More Alive Than I." *Pastoral Psychology* 23 (June 1972): 33–40.

A pastor and a chaplain consider a case in which nursing and other personnel put physical distance themselves and a dying person as a shield against anxiety. Psychological and physical closeness were restored when nurses and chaplains recognized that the patient needed to reflect upon a terrifying experience, appreciate group support, and find some explanations. She was assured that staff would remain with her as a dying person.

3106 Garfield, Charles A. "Impact of Death on the Health-Care Professional." In *New Meanings of Death*, ed. by Herman Feifel, 143–152. New York: McGraw-Hill Book Co., 1977.

From his personal responses to Larry, a terminally ill cancer patient, a psychologist describes the way in which he confronted fears about his own death, the need to be more of a friend than a healer, the closing of the communication gap with family, learning from the patient about pain and death, and saying good-bye.

3107 Klagsbrun, S. C. "Cancer, Emotions and Nurses." *American Journal of Psychiatry* 126 (1970): 1237–1244.

See 3132.

3108 Kleinman, Arthur. *The Illness Narratives: Suffering, Healing and the Human Condition.* New York: Basic Books, 1988.

A physician argues that suffering is more devastating than it needs to be because doctors are often unaware of what the patient experiences as illness. The world of the patient can be opened to medical personnel through "illness narratives" in which patients and their families reveal the way in which psychic states, cultural values and social relationships define what it means for them to be ill. Absorbing examples are given of the way in which patients and family experience suffering, disability, loss and the threat of death. Methods are suggested for the care of the chronically ill and for a meaning-centered model of medical education and practice.

3109 La Grand, L. E. "Reducing Burnout in the Hospice and the Death Education Movement." *Death Education* 4 (1980): 61–75.

Suggestions for the control of burnout are cognitive modification, exercise outlets, relaxation techniques, stimulus control.

3110 Lester, David, *et al.* "Attitudes of Nursing Students and Nursing Faculty Toward Death." *Nursing Research* 23 (1974): 50–53.

Attitudes towards death and dying are studied among undergraduate, graduate nursing students and nursing faculty.

3111 Osis, Karlis. *Deathbed Observations by Physicians and Nurses.* New York: Parapsychology Foundation, 1961.

See 3355.

3112 Peretz, David, *et. al.* "A Survey of Physicians' Attitudes toward Death and Bereavement: Comparison of Psychiatrists and Non-psychiatrists." *Journal of Thanatology* 1 (1971): 91–100.

Psychiatrists, in contrast to non-psychiatric colleagues, expected guilt to occur between a dying person and the "the bereaved-to-be." A majority of psychiatrists and non-psychiatrists agree that it was always or frequently important that the bereaved be advised of approaching death. Expression rather than repression of feelings was favored by both professional groups. Signs and symptoms of bereavement were noted more often by psychiatrists than by other physicians, although there was general agreement concerning these signs and symptoms of bereavement. Conclusions were based upon a 14.6% response to a questionnaire.

3113 Reippere, Vicky and Ruth Williams, eds. *Wounded Healers.* New York: John Wiley and Sons, 1985.

A variety of mental health workers describe a wide range of depressive symptoms which they have experienced in their own life, some brief and self-limiting episodes and others severely disabling, chronic or recurrent. No typical pattern of depression emerged in the study of mental health workers. The circumstances under which depression occurred were quite varied and might and might not have obvious precipitating factors. Precipitating events were in the individual's private life: a birth of a baby, death or loss of a loved one, changes of country, adjustment to personally unsatisfying feminine stereotypes. The "wear and tear" of their work did not seem to be a contributing factor.

3114 Saul, L. J. "Reactions of a Man to Natural Death." *Psychoanalytic Quarterley* 28 (1959): 383–386.

Six months in the life of a physician with carcinoma of the stomach reveal his delusional views of reality at the same time that he had sound attitude and judgment. The will to live produced the wish-fulfilling delusions.

3115 Speck, Peter. *Loss and Grief in Medicine.* London: Baillierie Tyndall, 1978.

A general hospital chaplain describes the awareness of medical personnel to the responses of patients to a wide variety of losses that may be experienced in obstetrics and gynecology, surgery and medicine. The attending grief is a struggle to remain human. Professional personnel who are inattentive to the grief of patients may leave them abandoned in anger and frustration. The book is filled with clear combinations of theory and practice and contains a number of relevant case studies. The influence of religion and culture are included to enhance understanding of grief and provide courage to face handicaps.

3116 Weisenhütter, Eckart. *Blicknachdrüben: Selbsterfahrungen im Sterben.* [View into the Beyond: Self-Experiences in Dying]. 3rd ed. Gütersloh: Gütersloher Verlag, 1976.

See 3361.

3.2 TERMINAL CARE

3.21 CARING RELATIONSHIPS/COMMUNICATION/THERAPY

3117 Anderson, Herbert. "After the Diagnosis: An Operational Theology for the Terminally Ill." *Journal of Pastoral Care* 53 (1989): 141–151.

A professor of pastoral care presents excerpts from patients with life-threatening illness to show how theology may assist them to wait actively, remember gratefully, hope realistically and trust courageously. Patients develop images that make sense out of their experience. They are drawn as much from personal views of theology as they are from official religious teaching.

3118 Balint, Michael. *The Doctor, His Patient and the Illness*. New York: International Universities Press, 1957.

The author served as consultant to fourteen general practitioners in research seminars at the Tavistock Clinic that began with a discussion on drugs and quickly moved toward a general theme in medical practice, the character of the physician as context and contributing factor in healing. The book summarizes discussions on diagnosis that considers both the personality of the patient and the illness, the development of a listening mode in helping patients manage themselves in illness and conclusions about the "apostolic function" of physician. This latter phrase describes (1) the tendency of some patients to invest the physician with parental powers to support or reject and (2) the need of the physician to notice how much regression is occurring in the patient and how much maturity should be demanded from the patient. These are vital aspects of a patient's attitude toward illness, and consequently of recovery. Although the book is not specifically related to death and dying, the research summaries are as vulnerable and insightful as any others on the subject of caring relationships that include professional responsibilities.

3119 Berrigan, Daniel. *We Die Before We Live: Talking With the Very Ill*. New York: Seabury Press, 1980.

See 3388.

3120 Brody, Howard. *Stories of Sickness*. New Haven: Yale University Press, 1987.

The author contends that suffering is produced and alleviated by the meaning that a person attaches to experience. This is done through the telling of stories which relate individual experiences to the explanatory constructs of the society and culture and place experiences within the context of an individual's history. Medicine is constantly engaged in this kind of placement of experience by providing a patient with descriptions that turn the illness experience into a positive direction: acceptable to the patient's existing belief system and worldview, in a setting where the patient believes there are caring individuals, with communication of mastery or control over the illness experience, i.e. either the patient or the medical personnel. Physicians contribute to the positive explanation of experience through reassuring narratives, solicitous attitudes and reassuring rituals that promise control of events.

3121 Carey, Raymond. "Counseling the Terminally Ill." *Personnel and Guidance Journal* (November 1976): 124–126.

As part of the "Living Until Death Program," the research chaplain at Lutheran General Hospital, Chicago discusses anxieties connected with terminal illness and an approach to counsel that includes awareness of the patient's point of view, sensitivity to changing moods, discovery of secular and religious resources for the patient, the maintenance of familiar emotional and social surroundings, the discovery of meaning and value in the midst of unchanging and deteriorating conditions.

3122 Davidson, Glen W. *Living With Dying.* Minneapolis, Minn.: Augsburg Pub. House, 1975.

Based upon his clinical study of dying persons, a professor of thanatology described the meaning of dying in terms of loss, change, conflict, suffering and triumph. Christian emphasis. Readable and reliable.

3123 Feigenberg, Loma. *Terminal Care: Friendship Contracts With Dying Cancer Patients.* Trans. by Patrick Hort. New York: Brunner/Mazel, 1980.

See 3103.

3124 Found, K. I. "Dealing with Death and Dying Through Family Centered Care." *Nursing Clinics of North America* 7 (1972): 53–64.

For the benefit of children and parents who are handling the stress of death and dying, the author describes the meaning of loss, coping with crisis, prevalent attitudes toward death, recognition of the grieving process and appropriate intervention.

3125 Freeman, L. "Care of the Dying Patient." *Journal of Family Practice* 3 (1976): 547–555.

Family practice grand rounds provide an opportunity for physicians and other staff members to discuss their experiences with the dying. Some review of statistical data.

3126 Garfield, Charles A. ed. *Psychosocial Care of the Dying Patient.* New York: McGraw-Hill Book Co., 1978.

See 3378.

3127 Greene, William A. "The Physician and His Dying Patient." In *The Patient, Death and the Family*, ed. by Stanley B. Troup and William A. Greene, 85–96. New York: Charles Scribner's Sons, 1974.

A physician discusses the growth of interest in dying and attributes much to the increase of teamwork among physicians with other professionals. The author recommends that physicians should offer care in cooperation with family, nurses, and specially trained personnel.

3128 Grollman, Earl A. *In Sickness and In Health*. Boston: Beacon Press, 1987.

A rabbi who has written extensively about death provides help for family members who want to move from helplessness to helpfulness, to cope with their own emotional upheaval and to better understand the needs of a loved one who is very ill. This is done through poetic meditations of several pages on varying topics.

3129 Harker, B. L. "Cancer and Communication Problems: A Personal Experience." *Psychiatry and Medicine* 3 (1972): 163–171.

A mental health professional offers suggestions to patients, family and friends, helpers and professionals concerning the special problems of communication about cancer.

3130 Heulsinkveld, K. B. "Cues to Communication with a Terminal Cancer Patient." *Nursing Forum* 11 (1972): 105–113.

Examples are given of the way in which nurses can assist patients and families to communicate about the transition from life to death.

3131 Hinton, John M. "Talking with People About to Die." *British Medical Journal*, (1974), Vol. 2: 25–27.

Sixty patients who are receiving care for terminal cancer offer their comments on communication with the professional staff.

3132 Klagsbrun, S. C. "Cancer, Emotions and Nurses." *American Journal of Psychiatry* 126 (1970): 1237–1244.

A cancer research unit in which patient and family were encouraged to work together became a popular place for nurses to work. Mutual functioning of the family on an adult level decreased anxiety, depression and the patient's feeling of being a burden.

3133 Kalish, Richard A. *Caring Relationships: The Dying and the Bereaved*. Vol 2, Perspectives on Death and Dying Series. Farmingdale, N. Y.: Baywood Pub. Co., 1979.

Clinicians present their experience on relationships with the dying, the bereaved, and their roles as nurses and physicians.

3134 Kikuchi, J. "How the Leukamic Child Chooses His Confident." *Canadian Nurse* 71 (1975): 22–23.

A child with a life-threatening illness will confide in those persons who are sensitive enough to pick up indirect cues that are given by the child to test reactions.

3135 Kleinman, Arthur. *The Illness Narratives: Suffering, Healing and the Human Condition.* New York: Basic Books, 1988.

See 3108.

3136 Kopp, Ruth Lewshenia. *When Someone You Love Is Dying: A Handbook for Counselors and Those Who Care.* Grand Rapids, Mich.: Zondervan Pub. House, 1980.

There is much clinical wisdom in the advice of this physician on the problem of a patient's denial of diagnosis, difficulty in hearing prognosis and handling such unacceptable feelings as anger and frustration. Practical advice is offered for family members. The role of faith and the importance of a realistic view of faith healing are included as part of a Christian perspective on death.

3137 Maes, John L. *Suffering: A Caregiver's Guide.* Nashville, Tenn.: Abingdon Press, 1990.

From personal experience with patients and a knowledge of literature on suffering the author focuses on the response of specific persons to suffering. Those who suffer are urged to "name" the experience as one way to gain some control over pain and anxiety. Many other suggestions are given in readable fashion for those who suffer and those who care.

3138 Marshall, Victor W. "The Last Strand: Remnants of Engagement in the Later Years." In *Death, Dying, Transcending*, ed. by Richard A. Kalish. Farmingdale, N.Y.: Baywood Pub. Co., 1980.

See 3028.

3139 Naylor, Harriet H., et al., eds. *The Role of the Volunteer Director in the Care of the Terminal Patient and the Family.* New York: Arno Press, 1981.

The identity of the volunteer is the focus of numerous and brief articles by thanatologists who work with volunteers in the care of the dying. Volunteers are discussed in relation to organizations with which they serve, relations with patients and families, management of personal reactions to service as a volunteer, and some discussion of the philosophy for volunteer work. An appendix includes brief annotations of recommended readings, listing of national centers for voluntary action.

3140 Nighswonger, Carl A. "The Vectors and Vital Signs in Grief Synchronization." In *Anticipatory Grief*, ed. by Bernard Schoenberg, *et al.*, 267–276. New York: Columbia Press, 1974.

A chaplain describes practical ways in which a dying patient and family may "mesh their grief gears." This is most possible when both patient and family depend upon a common community support system. It is inhibited by cultural attitudes and social practices that avoid the reality of death. The most important sign of family progress through grief is a common sense of hope, first for a cure, then for less pain in the patient, then an ability to survive as a family.

3141 Norton, Janice. "Treatment of a Dying Patient." In *The Interpretation of Death*, ed. by Hendrik Marinus Ruitenbeek, 19–38. New York: Jason Aronson, 1973.

A psychiatrist provides a detailed case study that illuminates the psychodynamic complexities of one women's struggle illness.

3142 Ruitenbeek, Hendrik Marinus, ed. *The Interpretation of Death*. New York: Jason Aronson, 1973.

Various psychoanalysts provide a range of discussions concerning death and dying that moves beyond traditional psychoanalytic concerns and makes death and its implications understood in the multi-professional world of thanatology and in the world of artists and writers.

3143 Parsell, S. and E. M. Tagliarenia. "Cancer Patients Help Each Other." *American Journal of Nursing* 74 (1974): 650–651.

A self-help group for cancer patients which was initiated by a medical center provides a supportive climate and an opportunity to discuss consistent themes such as helplessness, life and death, the problems of everyday living.

3144 Peck, Rosalie, and Stefanics Charlotte. *Learning to Say Good-Bye: Dealing With Death and Dying*. Muncie, Ind.: Accelerated Development Inc., 1987.

This warm and insightful recounting of day to day advocacy of the dying is not only an incentive for caring attitudes; it is also a guidebook for the changing of medical programs toward mutual responsibility of patient and staff as they face the ultimate aloneness of dying. Helpful details and directions are given for implementing a thanatology program.

3145 Purves, Andrew. *The Search for Compassion: Spirituality in Ministry*. Louisville, Ky.: Westminster/John Knox Press, 1989.

A professor of pastoral theology and spirituality presents the theological meaning of compassion as a ministry that grows out of the life of God and God's care for the world.

3146 Richards, Larry O., and Paul Johnson. *Death and the Caring Community*. Portland, Oreg.: Multnomah Press, 1980.

An authority in Christian education and a physician describe in popular terms the needs of the terminally ill and the response of the caring community. A basic course in caring is outlined and a variety of resources are recommended. The emphasis is conservative Protestantism.

3147 Saunders, Cicely. *Care of the Dying*. Nursing Times reprint. London: Macmillan Pub. Co., 1959.

This graceful and practical book presents "hospice" as a facility to provide good terminal care for dying persons (St. Christopher's Hospice in the south of London.) It served as a model for many others. A special concern of the facility was medication and nursing. Patients were well cared for with a conscious aim of relieving all the discomforts and symptoms associated with the dying. No steps were taken to prolong life, but many steps were taken to relieve the discomfort of pain, nausea, disability in breathing, insomnia, agitation. The Christian view of dying was emphasized through the fittings and decorations of the hospital as well as a number of clergypersons who were in attendance upon those who were dying. Colin M. Parkes served as psychiatric consultant to the hospital on a weekly basis.

3148 Scarry, Elaine. *The Body of Pain: The Making and Unmaking of the World*. New York: Oxford University Press, 1985.

See 3233.

3149 Schiff, Harriet Sarnoff. *Living Through Mourning*. New York: Penguin Books, 1986.

On the basis of her work with support groups for grieving parents, spouses, children, siblings and friends, the author who had lost her ten year old son, discusses the road to healing through sorrow, denial, anger, guilt, depression, powerlessness, faith and acceptance. A third of the book is devoted to the guidelines for a support group.

3150 Schoenberg, Bernard, *et al.*, eds. *Loss and Grief: Psychological Management in Medical Practice*. New York: Columbia University Press, 1970.

In a symposium prepared primarily by psychiatrists, a wide range of loss-reactions are discussed: bodily organs, sexual dysfunction, chronic illness, aging. Chapters also include child and family reactions to the death of a child or the death of another family member. Staff, family and patient management of dying in adulthood is discussed. Grief is discussed in terms of professional feelings, history and theology of thanatology, treatment of the subject in literature. Annotated bibliography by Richard Kalish.

3151 Shepard, Martin. *Someone You Love Is Dying*. New York: Harmony, 1975.

A physician prepares a guide for helping and coping for both the healthy and the ill who must communicate about death: recognizing and accepting the confusion and the range of our emotional reactions; giving honest information and diagnosis to a person who is dying; evaluating alternatives to standard medical treatment; eliminating pain; finding ways to comfort those we love; considering the advantages of dying at home; appreciating the problems of a family before and after a death; making prudent financial arrangements; how to overcome the fear of death. Readable, relaxed, with one or two incidental references to religion and afterlife.

3152 Shneidman, Edwin. *Voices of Death*. New York: Harper and Row, 1980.

A pioneering thanatologist assists individuals to a better understanding and interaction with loved ones who may be dying through many personal documents: letters, diaries, journals, confessions, reminiscences, tape-recorded interviews and statements. The author adds a commentary based upon various research studies, his own experience and case histories. An impressive challenge to self-evaluation: how do we choose to think about the way in which we die?

3153 Simonton, C. O., and S. S. Simonton. "Belief Systems and Management of the Emotional Aspects of Malignancy." *Journal of Transpersonal Psychology* 7 (1975): 29–47.

A physician who combines imaging, relaxation and psychotherapy presents three "extremely important factors" in the relationship between emotions and cancer treatment: the belief systems of the patient, the family, the physician. The belief system of the patient is usually negative, but occasionally a patient will visualize wellness or healing by God and there will be a spontaneous remission. Extensive bibliography. Both theory and methodology are called into question by other studies (Kalish 1017, 287–289).

3154 Sourkes, Barbara M. *The Deepening Shade: Psychological Aspects of Life-Threatening Illness*. Contemporary Community Health Series. Pittsburgh, Pa.: University of Pittsburgh Press, 1982.

A psychologist presents a synthesis of the critical issues which confront the dying patient, the family and caregiver with special emphasis upon the impact of living with a life threatening illness. A straightforward and sensitive presentation of psychotherapy is presented in the opening chapters for all members of a healing team. This is followed by chapters on life-cycle issues, and loss which show the common struggle of all individuals. The process of life-threatening illness as it unfolds through time is presented in chapters on diagnosis, neutral time, anticipatory grief and terminal issues. Of special value to medical personnel is the final chapter in which a nineteen year old woman describes her struggle with cancer and insensitive medical personnel. A psychiatrist annotates the interview with marginal notes. An excellent general text for all professional persons who are willing to work together in humane care of the terminally ill, the family and each other.

3155 Vanauken, Sheldon. *A Severe Mercy*. San Francisco: Harper and Row Pub., 1977.

A young and sophisticated couple face the wife's decline toward death through a mysterious illness. Faith and sorrow are mixed in the husband's story of their relationship and the special consolation and guidance that came in correspondence with his spiritual mentor, C. S. Lewis. Among the eighteen letters of Lewis to the author are some written while Lewis' wife was dying. When Donna, my wife, read the first portion of the book on the loving life of Sheldon and Jean, she wrote on the flyleaf: "magic moment bathed in bliss, passion poised on tenderness."

3156 Verwoerdt, Adrian. *Communication with the Fatally Ill*. Springfield, Ill.: C. C. Thomas, 1966.

A practical guide of the process of informing the patient and the family of terminal illness includes principles and techniques of communication, nature and management of defense mechanisms and emotional reactions.

3157 Whitman, H. H. and S. J. Lukes. "Behavior Modification for Terminally Ill Patients." *American Journal of Nursing* 75 (1975): 98–101.

Various behavior modification techniques are suggested when the behavior of a terminally ill patient becomes a problem to self, family and nurses.

3158 Worcester, Alfred. *The Care of the Aging, the Dying and the Dead*. 1935. Reprint. New York: Arno Press, 1976.

After his retirement from the Hygiene Department of the Medical School of Harvard University, the author prepared this brief and thoughtful text on the attitudes of medical students that would enhance "devotion to the patient rather than to his disease." He gave special emphasis to an area of the art of medicine that he felt was neglected, caring for the dying. This is to be accomplished through constant attendance to the patient and steady comfort to the stricken family. He also urges physicians to advise mourners concerning "the proper disposal of their dead." This would also include medical supervision of preparation of the burial of the body, the suggestion of post-mortem examination to the family, specific recommendations for funeral expenses that will show respect for the dead without leading to "ridiculous extravagance." The superiority of cremation should be discussed with the family. This pioneering essay is remarkable for defining the responsibilities of the physician in terms of compassion and awareness of the needs of patient and family rather than a restriction of interest to biomedical concerns in a hospital.

3159 Yalom, I. D. and C. Greaves. "Group Therapy for the Terminally Ill." *American Journal of Psychiatry* 134 (1977): 396–400.

In a four year experience with therapy groups for patients with metastatic carcinoma, the authors found that members of the group helped each other by moving out of morbid self-absorption and by finding that they had much value to share and to teach each other.

3.22 LIFE STAGES OF THE DYING PERSON

3160 Kalish, Richard A. "The Effect of Death Upon the Family." In *Death and Dying*, ed. by Leonard Pearson. Cleveland, Ohio: The Press of Case Western Reserve University, 1969.

A pioneer in thanatology summarizes contemporary American views of death, including loss of belief in an after-life and then distinguishes the impact of death upon the family when the dying person is older, middle-aged or a child.

3161 Pattison, E. Mansell. *The Experience of Dying*. Englewood Cliffs, N.J.: Prentice-Hall, 1977.

The process of dying is viewed developmentally by a psychiatrist as "the living-dying intervals." His chapters and several by other medical clinicians demonstrate compassion for patients and staff, familiarity with professional literature and ability to discuss cases from both the patient and staff point of view. An authoritative text for health professionals that is written without professional jargon. Topical bibliography.

3.221 CHILDREN

3162 Aries, Philippe. *Centuries of Childhood: A Social History of Family Life*. New York: Alfred A. Knopf, 1962.

In medieval society, a child belonged to the world of adulthood as soon as he could live without the constant attention of his mother. It was not until the sixteenth and seventeenth centuries, and then only among the upper classes that the modern idea of childhood as a distinct phase of life began to emerge in areas such as art, literature, games and dress.. See also Stannard (3165), Aries (1039).

3163 Deford, Frank. *Alex: The Life of a Child.* New York: Viking, 1983.

See 3211.

3164 Natterson, J. M. and A. G. Knudson, Jr. "Observations Concerning Fear of Death in Fatally Ill Children and Their Mothers." *Psychosomatic Medicine* 22 (1960): 456–465.

Over a two year period of time thirty-three children developed growing fears of separation, mutilation and then death. Mothers reacted to the death threat with initial denial and later came to a calm acceptance, with improved integration and sublimation. The hospital staff were less well integrated during the terminal phase of the child's illness.

3165 Stannard, David E. "Death and the Puritan Child." In *Death in America*, ed. by David E. Stannard, 9–29. Philadelphia: University of Pennsylvania Press, 1975.

Puritan journals, autobiographies and histories are filled with specific references to the differences between children and adults, with special attention to the conversion of the children who are considered to be depraved because of the sin of Adam. Much attention was given to the stability and healthiness of the family, yet 1 in 10 infants died and usually 3 out of 9 children born to the average family would die before reaching age 21. Pastors such as Increase Mather added additional terror to parents and children in a world of Indian attacks from without and inner attacks of witches and demons.

3.222 ADOLESCENTS

3166 Corr, Charles A. and Joan N. McNeil, eds. *Adolescence and Death.* New York: Springer Pub. Co., 1986.

In a search for what is distinctive in adolescent encounters with death, various authors consider the limits of adolescent resources, their values and concerns in coping with death. Topics include death themes in adolescent music, responses to the threat of nuclear warfare, the special issues of terminating an adolescent pregnancy, responses to suicide, talking about death with parents and peers, counseling and death education. Annotated bibliography on books for adolescents and adults, audio-visual resources. Organizational resources are listed. Pertinent references at the end of each chapter.

3167 Hughes, Ann. *Hunter in the Dark*. Toronto: Clark, Irwin and Co., 1982.

See 6019.

3.223 THE AGED

3168 Bengston, Vern L. and Kay Warner Schaie, eds. *The Course of Later Life: Research and Reflections*. New York: Springer Pub. Co., 1989.

Through multidisciplinary research an overview is presented of current issues and perspectives that reflect scientific analysis of the course of later life, with special appreciation for the pioneering of James E. Dirren. Emphasis is placed upon demographic studies and neurobiology. References for each chapter.

3169 Butler, Robert N. *Why Survive? Being Old in America*. New York: Harper and Row, 1975.

This Pulitzer prize book deals with attitudes towards aging, specific problems, organizations and government programs. Bibliography.

3170 Callahan, Daniel. *Setting Limits: Medical Goals in an Aging Society*. New York: Simon and Schuster, 1987.

See 3638.

3171 Cummings, E., and William W. M. Henry. *Growing Old, the Process of Disengagement*. New York: Basic Books 1961.

A benefit of disengagement in relation to death of the elderly is seen in lessened anxiety over fulfilled plans and projects. The web of interaction with others has been unraveled. This differs from the death of the young and middle-aged, who feel torn from life as death approaches.

3172 Fecher, Vincent John. *Religion and Aging: An Annotated Bibliography*. San Antonio, Tex.: Trinity University Press, 1982.

See 8014.

3173 Haber, Carole. *Beyond Sixty-Five: The Dilemma of Old Age in America's Past*. New York: Cambridge University Press, 1982.

A professor of history notes the beginning of models of old age and superannuation in the colonial era which still has some influence in the twentieth century. She traces the erosion of power among the elderly in the nineteenth century as cities grew and industrialization replaced agricultural pursuits. In the last part of the nineteenth century, old age pensions became an essential part of paternalistic plans for eliminating the old from the work force. Footnotes and bibliography.

3174 Hendricks, Jon. *Institutionalization and Alternative Futures*. Farmingdale, N. Y.: Baywood Pub. Co., 1979.

See 3367.

3175 Jackson, Jacquelyne Johnson. *Minorities and Aging*. Belmont, Wadsworth Pub. Co., 1980.

Research is presented from social, behavioral, and medical scientists on nine primary minority groups in America with an aging population. In addition to chapters on demographics, physiology, psychology and sociology, the author evaluates for older minority populations. Extensive bibliography and index.

3176 Johnson, Elizabeth S. and John B. Williamson. *Growing Old: The Social Problems of Aging*. New York: Holt, Rinehart and Winston, 1980.

Injustices experienced by the aged are presented in four categories: victimization, exploitation, discrimination and oppression. To what extent are these injustices found in American society, in which sub-groups, and with what resources for coping? Retirement for example is dealt with in terms of preference or accommodation.

3177 Jury, Dan and Mark Jury. *Gramp*. New York: Grossman Publishers, 1976.

See 3095.

3178 Kalish, Richard A. *The Latter Years: Social Applications of Gerontology*. Monterey, Calif.: Brooks/Cole Pub. Co., 1977.

Persons in the speciality of gerontology in a variety of fields present articles on applied social gerontology: the provision of direct services, initiating and developing programs, planning and developing policy for the aged. Articles include statistical studies, psychological, economic, retirement, health and illness, politics and the law, social institutions, housing and transportation, social and health services, institutional living. References and list of organizations.

3179 Kalish, Richard A. "The Aged and the Dying Process: The Inevitable Decisions." *Journal of Social Issues* 21 (1965): 87–96.

The decisions of the aged and caregivers involve minicommunication and relationship issues.

3180 Kastenbaum, Robert J. and B. L. Mishara. "Premature Death and Self-Injurious in Old Age." *Geriatrics* 26 (1971): 71–81.

In a study of elderly residents in mental hospitals, the authors found men were more vulnerable to self-injurious behavior than women. The behaviors included refusal to eat, refusal of medications, eating foreign objects, self-mutilations.

3181 Kastenbaum, Robert J. "Death and Bereavement in Later Life." In *Death and Bereavement,* ed. by Austin H. Kutscher, 28–54. Springfield, Ill: Charles C. Thomas, 1969.

On the basis of a mental health research project, the author found that elders are often forced into a reduced style of life because they are considered less important than younger people. They are not preoccupied with fear of death or oblivious to their fate. Readiness for death varies from person to person. There is often a succession of bereavements, an overload that leads to adverse changes that are mistakenly attributed to "growing old."

3182 Kra, Siegfried. *Aging Myths: Reversible Causes of Mind and Memory Loss.* New York: McGraw-Hill Book Co., 1986.

A physician marshals a variety of studies to show that senility is not a part of the natural aging process. When it does occur, the condition is reversible. Alzheimer's disease is also discussed.

3183 Miller, Marv. *Suicide After Sixty: The Final Alternative.* New York: Springer Pub. Co., 1979.

In a comprehensive review of geriatric suicide, the author presents the reactions of the elderly to severe physical illness, mental illness, institutionalization, death of a spouse, retirement, alcohol and drug abuse. Personal issues are also discussed. The role of the physician is presented. There is a chapter on the cooperation of some wives in their husband's suicides. Suggestions are given to decrease the number of suicides. The appendix includes a review of research and a bibliography.

3184 Munnichs, Joep M. A. *Old Age and Finitude.* Basel: S. Karger, 1966.

A careful study of the elderly in Holland revealed that most respondents had positive attitudes towards dying and death. Some of the differences between these persons and those who used evasive strategies are discussed. Attitudinal changes occurred as persons moved from a "young-old" attitude of actively thinking about death to an "old-old" attitude in which people did not give much thought to death.

3185 Nelson, F. L. and N. L. Farberow. "Indirect Self-Destructive Behavior in the Elderly Nursing Home Patient." *Journal of Gerontology* 35 (1980): 949–957.

Among 99 male patients in nursing homes who engaged in indirect self-destructive behavior, researchers found that failure to eat and drink appropriately, and non-compliance with medical regimes were the most common methods used by patients. The indirect methods served as an alternative form of suicide for many of the patients.

3186 Osgood, Nancy J., Barbara A. Bryant, and Aaron A. Lipman. "Patterns of Suicidal Behavior in Long-term Care Facilities: A Preliminary Report on an Ongoing Study." *Omega* 19 (1988–89): 69–78.

See 3574.

3187 Pruyser, Paul W. "The Ambiguities of Religion and Pain Control." *Theology Today* 38 (1981): 5–15.

Religion allots pain and pleasure, and assumes the authority to dispose either. This ambiguous must be appreciated in any attempts to bring the most pervasive religious modality of pain relief which is the giving of hope. The author is a clinical psychologist with special interest in psychology of religion.

3188 Shurt, S. D. "Attitudes Toward Old Age and Death." In *Death and Identity,* ed. by Robert Fulton, 161–169. New York: John Wiley and Sons, 1965.

In a comparison of two groups of white, elderly unmarried females, the author found through the administration of a Thematic Apperception Test that the apartment dwellers were significantly lower in the fear of death than the institutionalized patients. Physicians rated the apartment dwellers as healthier even though the institutionalized women rated themselves as healthier than the apartment dwellers rated themselves.

3189 Sinick, Daniel. *Counseling Older Persons: Careers, Retirement, Dying.* New York: Human Sciences Press, 1977.

See 4173.

3190 Stephens, Charles Asbury. *Natural Salvation: The Message of Science, Outlining the First Principles of Immortal Life on the Earth.* 1905. Reprint. Salem, N. H.: Ayer Co. Pub., 1976.

See 1352.

3191 Sullender, R. Scott. *Losses in Later Life: A New Way of Walking with God.* Mahwah, N. J.: Paulist Press, 1989.

A pastoral counselor provides a survey of the major losses in the later years of life: youth, family, parents, work, spouse, health, identity. The style is informative and affirming, with an emphasis upon willingness to accept the value of being the age we are without making idols of the past. See also Sullender (4519).

3192 Williams, Richard Hays. *Living through the Years: Styles of Life and Successful Aging.* New York: Atherton Press, 1965.

See 1357.

3193 Zarit, Steven H. *Readings in Aging and Death: Contemporary Perspectives.* 2nd ed. New York: Harper and Row, 1982.

Various popular and research articles are presented on aging, longevity and biological aspects of aging, psychological, sociological and social aspects, death, dying and mourning.

3.23 LIVING–DYING INTERVALS

3194 Garfield, Charles A., ed. *Stress and Survival: The Emotional Realities of Life-Threatening Illness.* St. Louis, Mo.: C. V. Mosby Co., 1979.

The capacity of humans to endure life under protracted crisis and injury is considered by clinicians in psychology, psychiatry, nursing and medical specialties. Insights are given for emotional support for patients and family. This is distinguished list of contributors who concentrate on bio-medical and psychological aspects of stress.

3195 Glaser, Barney G. and Anselm L. Strauss. *Awareness of Dying.* Chicago: Aldine Pub. Co., 1965.

See 1155.

3196 Pattison, E. Mansell. "The Living-Dying Process." In *Psychosocial Care of the Dying Patient,* ed. by Charles A. Garfield, 133–168.

A psychiatrist describes the personal dimensions of the living-dying experience, which include the subjective viewpoint of the dying person, objective observations by professionals of psychological and social coping mechanisms used by the dying person. The author reviews literature on attitudes toward death and then reviews questions concerning stages, phases or trajectories. Various phases or intervals are delineated from clinical studies. Definitions of death are reviewed. Suggestions are given for helping the dying. References.

3197 Pattison, E. Mansell. *The Experience of Dying.* Englewood Cliffs, N. J.: Prentice-Hall, 1977.

See 3161.

3198 Whitzel, L. "Behavior of the Dying Patient." *British Medical Journal* (1975) Vol. 2: 81–82.

One hundred and ten dying patients were studied twenty-four hours before death and two hundred and fifty patients during the weeks before death. Results show that sixty per cent were well oriented as to time and space twenty-four hours before death and twenty-six per cent were well oriented 15 minutes before death.

3.231 "STAGES" OF DYING

3199 Churchill, Larry R. "The Human Experience of Dying: The Moral Primacy of Stories over Stages." *Soundings* 62 (1979): 24–37.

In evaluating the "stages" of dying as presented by Kübler-Ross (1020) the author considers "stage" to be an unfortunate concept because of the linear and progressive implications. This tendency to categorize and control can be reduced by questions to patients about varying sensations as death approaches. This is an opportunity for them to narrate a part of their life story as they would organize the sequence without attempting to be consistent or rational. Each patient teaches us the unique significance of a final chapter in life, but not "by the book."

3200 Feigenberg, Loma. *Terminal Care: Friendship Contracts With Dying Cancer Patients.* Trans. by Patrick Hort. New York: Brunner/Mazel, 1980.

As part of his clinical observations (Feigenberg 3103) a Swedish thanatologist warns that the division of dying into stages by Kübler-Ross (1020) is based upon impressions that have not been verified. Perhaps the use of this regular sequence has given many people a sense of security and confidence. It certainly should not be used by clinicians as a checklist for the process of dying. There is no right or wrong way to die, so far as psychological sequence is concerned. See Feigenberg (3103).

3201 Garfield, Charles A. "Consciousness Alteration and Fear of Death." *Journal of Transpersonal Psychology* 7 (1975): 147–175.

When theological students completed a self-report instrument, their fear of death scores were low. When they were monitored for heart rate and galvanic skin response there was a high arousal to death related stimuli. In discussing these contrary responses the author found from interviews that theological students lacked many answers to questions about death, even though they adhered to Christian faith. In similar tests, the author found that they scored high on sensitivity death stimuli, whereas psychedelic drug users, Zen meditators, and Tibetan Buddhists were less influenced. The author describes this lack of influence through statements in interviews with the Zen and Tibetan groups that death has no place in their model of time, so they think of death as an illusion. Contemplating death would be a waste of time.

3202 Jeffers, F. C., C. R. Nichols and C. Isdorf. "Attitudes of Older Persons Towards Death." *Journal of Gerontology* 16 (1961): 53–56.

In a study of elderly subjects, the researchers found that those who used religious terminology to talk about death and immortality were less afraid of death than those who avoided the use of religious terminology.

3203 Jung, Carl G. "The Soul and Death." In *The Meaning of Death*, ed. by Herman Feifel, 3–15. New York: McGraw-Hill Book Co., 1959.

As an analytic therapist, Jung was astonished to see how little ado the unconscious psyche makes of death. Perhaps this is because death and life are one process in which young adults have panic-fear of life which is gradually displaced by the middle of life with a sense of vitality among those who are ready to die with life. Religion provides some of the symbols by which this unconscious psychic activity can become a source of realistic comfort to persons as they approach death. The emphasis upon religion and the lack of emphasis upon death is in marked contrast to the theories of his former teacher, Sigmund Freud, who gave much attention to pathological death symptoms (Freud 4312) and postulated a death instinct in unconscious struggle with a life instinct (Freud 1181). See also Jung (2218), Herzog (2270).

3204 Kastenbaum, Robert J. "Is Death a Life Crisis? On the Confrontation with Death in Theory and Practice." In *Life-Span Developmental Psychology: Normative Life Crises*, ed. by N. Daton and L. H. Ginsberg, 19–50. New York: Academic Press, 1975.

A clinician and researcher on death and dying does not believe that the stage theory of dying (Kübler-Ross) provides sufficient attention to the nature of various diseases, sex and age differences, ethnicity and other subcultural backgrounds, personality or cognitive styles, or the sociopsychical milieu. Research studies do not find evidence of five predictable stages of psychological adaptation among the dying.

3205 Kübler-Ross, Elisabeth. *On Death and Dying*. New York: Macmillan Pub. Co., 1968.

An influential work in which a pioneer in thanatology advances her model of the "five stages" in the progress of the dying patient: denial, anger, bargaining, depression, acceptance. See Kübler-Ross (1020) and Ross (7021).

3206 Kuykendall, George. "Care for the Dying: A Kübler-Ross Critique." *Theology Today* 38 (1981): 37–48.

A pastor criticizes the five stages of psychological preparation for death in the writings of Kübler-Ross as an easy movement toward acceptance of death that is unrealistic and isolating for the dying. A movement from denial to anger may well be a slide toward deeper depression as patients feel deserted by the world and low in self-esteem. Also, the stage of bargaining may not be as childish as Kübler-Ross concludes, and may be an effort to maintain some real contact with the world. Also, the final stage of acceptance is often observed in the dying to be more like exhaustion and depletion than any peaceful resolution of life's termination. Kübler-Ross seems to have developed a prescription for a liberation of innocent humanity that does not fit empirical descriptions of how people actually die. There seems to be a pre-occupation with out-of-the-body experiences that add additional justification to the philosophical assumption that death is the final stage of growth. These assumptions are contrasted with the biblical view of death as a terrible ill to be met by confidence in God who testified through his Son that the fear of death can be overcome, despite the darkness and the suffering of the cross.

3207 Ross, Elisabeth [Kübler-Ross]. "The Dying Patient as Teacher." Chicago Theological *Seminary Register* 57, 3 (December 1966): 1–14.

See 7021.

3208 Schulz, Richard and David Aderman. "Clinical Research and the Stages of Dying." In *Death, Dying, Transcending*, ed. by Richard A. Kalish, 30–36. Farmingdale, N.Y.: Baywood Pub. Co., 1980.

Beginning with an assessment of the highly subjective categories of Kübler-Ross (1020) the authors review clinical research on the stages of the dying process and conclude that very little is really known.

3.232 CHRONIC ILLNESS/LONG TERM CARE

3209 Cousins, Norman. *Anatomy of an Illness as Perceived by the Patient: Reflections on Healing and Regeneration*. New York: W. W. Norton Co., 1979.

See 3004.

3210 Davidson, Glen W. "The Waiting Vulture Syndrome." In *Bereavement: Its Psychosocial Aspects*, ed. by Bernard Schoenberg, *et al.* New York: Columbia University Press, 1975.

Families may reject a dying patient for not "expiring" at an expected time. In a case history and discussion the author makes recommendation to the staff for helping patient and family to overcome this alienation.

3211 Deford, Frank. *Alex: The Life of a Child.* New York: Viking, 1983.

The battle of a child against cystic fibrosis is described in terms of the bravery of a child that knew her disease was incurable, the ordeal of physical therapy and the grief of the surviving family.

3212 Hinton, John M. *Dying.* 2nd ed. Baltimore: Penguin Books, 1972.

See 1016.

3213 Kleinman, Arthur. *The Illness Narratives: Suffering, Healing and the Human Condition.* New York: Basic Books, 1988.

One of the four tasks in effective clinical care of the chronically ill is to affirm the patient's experience of illness through concepts that the laity would accept as a therapeutic approach. Also, the life story of the patient should become the center of a clinical biography that interprets illness through those myths that are unique to the individual.

3214 Malcolm, Andrew H. *This Far and No More.* New York: Times Books, 1987.

Through the diary of Emily Bauer the author describes slow, anguished decisions by which Emily gave up her battle with ALS (Lou Gehrig's disease) and terminated use of her life-support system at age 40.

3215 Roach, Marion. *Another Name for Madness.* Boston: Houghton-Mifflin Co., 1985.

The author describes the decline of her mother who suffers from Alzheimer's disease. The quality of the mother's life before institutionalization is described, along with insights into the disease, the struggles of the family and the possibility of aid and support.

3216 Solzhenitsyn. A. *Cancer Ward.* New York: Bantam, 1969.

The author is a participant observer in a Russian cancer hospital of people diverse political persuasions and different lifestyles who are united in similar emotions as they face a life-threatening disease.

3217 Strauss, Anselm L. and Barney G. Glaser. *Chronic Illness and the Quality of Life*. St. Louis, Mo.: C. V. Mosby, 1975.

Sociologists concentrate upon psychosocial rather than medical aspects of of living with chronic illness: management of crisis and treatment programs, control of symptoms and strategies of to maintain normal life. Specific diseases are considered in final chapters by clinicians.

3218 Strong, Maggie. *Mainstay: For the Well Spouse of the Chronically Ill*. Boston: Little, Brown and Co., 1988.

Out of her ten year experience with a beloved husband who developed multiple sclerosis, a mother of two children describes the deterioration of his health, the loss of his job, her increasing responsibility as parent, breadwinner, manager, negotiator and "mainstay" for her husband and family. Much practical advice is given on personal feelings, therapy and support groups, relationships with children. Specific advice for medical and legal issues. The book is filled with honest portrayals of the depression, impotence, fatigue, downward mobility, isolation, anxiety and loneliness that accompanies chronic illness in a nuclear family. Brief bibliography.

3219 Trumbo, Dalton. *Johnny Got His Gun*. New York: Bantam Books, 1970.

An antiwar novel in which a nineteen-year-old World War I veteran has been left after multiple injuries, blind, speechless, and limbless. He beats out messages on his pillow with his head, begging to be taken out of his hospital room, to show the world a survivor of Every War.

3220 Wright, H. T. *The Matthew Tree*. New York: Pantheon Books, 1975.

A daughter writes of the last seven years of her father's life as he faced multiple strokes.

3.24 PHYSIOLOGY AND MEDICINE

3221 Hinton, John M. "The Physical and Mental Distress of the Dying." *Quarterly Journal of Medicine*. New Series 32 (1963): 1–21.

This study is considered by Feigenberg to be "the first serious attempt by anyone to analyze and systematize the physical and psychological symptomatology of dying persons." (Feigenberg 3103, 241). Hinton reports the number of persons who were distressed, in what way, and how different kinds of distress relate to the disease or personal life, and finally the distress changes as the patient approaches death. There were 102 patients represented in the study matched with a control group of patients suffering from serious but not fatal illnesses. Forty-five percent of the dying patients suffered from depression and thirty-seven per cent from anxiety. Percentages for the control group were less.

3.241 MEDICAL DETERMINATION OF DEATH.
See DEFINING DEATH (4.81)

3.242 PAIN: CONTROL AND COMMUNICATION

3222 Barber, Joseph and Cheri Adrian. *Psychological Approaches to the Management of Pain*. New York: Brunner/Mazell, 1982.

Various medical psychologists present a wholistic view of pain derived from or linked to behavioral science by which pain can better be understood and described through non-medically/surgically based interventions to reduce suffering. The articles describe relief of pain for the back, during childbirth, during cancer and in cases of shingles. But there is no discussion of intractable pain in the care of the terminally ill or references to hospice work in the examples cited.

3223 Copp, Laurel Archer, ed. *Perspectives on Pain*. New York: Churchill-Livingstone, 1985.

Clinicians describe ways for patients to cope with pain, the meaning of pain in culture and in the hospital, the specific issues faced by children and women. Also: architecture, nurse education, policy, ethics, music, exercise.

3224 Epstein, G., L. Weitz, H. Roback and E. McKee. "Research on Bereavement: A Selective and Critical Review." *Comprehensive Psychiatry* 16 (1975): 537–546.

Some of the conclusions abstracted from a review of literature were: at every age, widowed males/females experienced a higher risk of dying than married persons of corresponding age and sex; excess in risk is greater for widowers than widows; for each sex the excess in risk is greater at the younger ages; death in the family produces an increased mortality rate among close relatives, especially surviving spouses; the highest death rates occur in the first six months of bereavement; replicated studies in both England and the United States show that the risk of dying is at least twice as great for widows and widowers at all age levels for a great variety of diseases than in the general population.

3225 Fichter, Joseph H. *Religion and Pain*. New York: Crossroad Pub. Co., 1981.

From written questionnaires returned by 692 health-care professionals in Catholic general hospitals and from personal interviews and observations, the author discusses the importance of religion as a source of meaning during suffering in a secular society. However, his research shows that physicians are the least likely of all the health professionals to concern themselves about spiritual matters. Nurses are more concerned than either physicians or social workers. The growth of pastoral care departments in Catholic hospitals is noted, but marginal to the central medical concerns of the hospitals.

3226 Flesch, Regina. "A Guide to Interviewing the Bereaved." *Journal of Thanatology* 3 (1975): 93–103.

Bereaved persons were interviewed in eight areas: immediate emotional reaction to a death, hostility, religion, sense of time, preoccupation with memories, continuing attachment to the deceased, altered role in the world, changed picture of self, possibility of resumption of old associations and the formation of new ones. All this occurred in one interview. Respondents recommended a series of shorter talks on these subjects.

3227 Fordyce, Wilbert E. *Behavioral Methods for Chronic Pain and Illness.* St Louis, Mo.: C. V. Mosby, 1976.

Clinicians provide a review of pain as a clinical problem with specific remedies through the theories of operant conditioning and techniques of behavioral analysis and change, treatment goals and biofeedback, assessment, selection of patient and treatment methods, orientation for patient and family, patient management of pain medications. Extensive bibliography.

3228 Hunt, J. M., *et al.* "Patients with Protracted Pain: A Survey Conducted at the London Hospital." *Journal of Medical Ethics* 3 (1977): 61–73.

Thirteen patients with protracted pain and twenty nurses who cared for them were interviewed. Patients had low expectations of recovery, physicians did not utilize the individual character of analgesic doses, nurses were over-ready to accept unrelieved pain, non-verbal forms of communication with the staff were often ignored, teaching about pain and its relieve was inadequate.

3229 Melzack, Ronald, J. G. Ofiesh, and Balfour Mount. "The Brompton Mixture: Effects on Pain in Cancer Patients." *Canadian Medical Association Journal* 115 (1976): 125–129.

The report of a study at the Montreal Palliative Care Service offers two conclusions, that patients treated with the Brompton mixture and aphenothiazine were those who had more pain relief than those treated in other ways, and that those who received the Brompton mixture in the Palliative

Care Unit reported better results than those who received the same treatment in other wards or private rooms of the hospital.

3230 Melzack, Ronald and Patrick D. Wall. *The Challenge of Pain.* Rev. ed. New York: Basic Books, 1982.

Research, theories and principles of pain are considered in terms of its nature and management. References are included to hospice and to palliative care.

3231 Oates, Wayne E. and Charles E. Oates. *People In Pain: Guidelines for Pastoral Care.* Philadelphia: Westminster Press, 1985.

A father who is a pastoral counselor and a son who is a psychiatrist have chapters on the medical aspects of pain, and religious and psychological ways of comfort.

3232 Saunders, Cicely. "The Treatment of Intractable Pain in Terminal Cancer." *Proceedings of the Royal Society of Medicine.* 56 (1961): 195.

3233 Scarry, Elaine. *The Body of Pain: The Making and Unmaking of the World.* New York: Oxford University Press, 1985.

Pain is unshareable and able to destroy community because we cannot feel the pain of another. Thus the world of an individual is destroyed by individual pain. Language and communication are also destroyed. However, medicine brings pain into public discourse, especially as a skilled physician hears the fragmentary language of an individual's pain and coaxes it into clarity with interpretations. Unfortunately, many patients feel that physicians do not trust or hear the voice of the patient because the physicians seem to be preoccupied with the physical events related to pain.

3234 Twycross, Robert G. and Sylvia A. Lack. *Symptom Control in Far Advanced Cancer: Pain Relief.* Baltimore, Md.: Urban and Schwarzenberger, 1983.

Two hospice-trained physicians use their own work and experience to provide physicians and pharmacists with a comprehensive account of the management of pain in far advanced cancer. This practical and detailed account of the drugs, techniques used in palliative pain control is considered to be "absolutely outstanding" by Simpson (8039, 159).

3235 Wall, Patrick D. and Ronald Melzack, eds. *Textbook of Pain.* New York: Churchill-Livingston, 1984.

Medical clinicians describe every aspect of the nature of pain, the full range of clinical pain syndromes and pain treatments.

3236 Zborowski, M. *People in Pain*. San Francisco, Calif.: Jossey-Bass, 1970.

The author finds that pain is expressed by patients in languages "that are both anthropological and cultural." His investigations show that old Americans and Irish Americans inhibit pain expression, the former because they "take it in stride" and the latter because they fear to be seen "like babies." Italian-Americans and Jewish-Americans encourage pain expressions, the former to rally support from peers and expect satisfaction with pain relief, the latter because of a belief in catharsis and a call for attention to underlying causes rather than to symptom removal. These differences among groups in attitude towards pain can influence pain tolerance.

3.243 PROGNOSIS

3237 Kay, D. W. K., V. Morris and F. Post. "Prognosis in Psychiatric Disorders of the Elderly: An Attempt to Define Indicators of Early Death and Early Recovery." *Journal of Mental Science* 102 (1956): 129–140.

Elderly persons were able to predict the death, or discharge from care of 75% of a group of patients admitted for observation to a mental health unit.

3238 Noltenius, Harald W. *Human Oncology*. Vol. 1: *Pathology and Clinical Characteristics*. Rev. ed. Baltimore, Md.: Urban and Schwarzenberg, 1988.

This first volume of a revised and expanded edition of the former *Manual of Oncology* is an atlas of basic tumor pathology and clinical characteristics. Tumors are listed with their morphological appearance, clinical symptoms, biological behavior, principles of treatment, prognosis, new research directions. The major emphasis is upon site-specific review, which is done in a basic outline form with topographical cross-referencing. There are references to current literature at the end of each chapter.

3239 Pattison, E. Mansell. "Psychosocial Predictors of Death Prognosis." *Omega* 5 (1974): 145–160.

A psychiatrist followed twelve men with a 50% short-term mortality risk over a period of 18 months. Neither initial basic physiologic status or basic psychological measures were predictive. However, measures of functional social abilities were predictive. The importance of having something or someone to live for is significant.

3240 Weisman, Avery D. and Robert J. Kastenbaum. "The Psychological Autopsy: A Study of the Terminal Phase of Life." *Community Mental Health Journal* Monograph No. 4 (1968): 43–58.

After reviewing eighty cases over a five year period, the authors classified two basic responses to impending death. One was by patients who were aware and accepting of impending death, and who withdrew from daily activities and remained inactive until the end. The other group was also aware, but choose to vigorously engage in daily life activities and even to initiate new activities and interpersonal relationships. Fear of dying was observed rarely and then only in patients who were grossly impaired.

3.244 COPING WITH CANCER/SURGERY

3241 Abrams, Harry S. "Adaptation to Open-Heart Surgery: A Psychiatric Study of Response to the Threat of Death." *American Journal of Psychiatry* 122 (1965): 659–667.

In a study of twenty-three patients who were undergoing open-heart surgery it was found that the operation presents a symbolic and realistic threat to life. Anxiety and the use of denial are described.

3242 Abrams, Ruth D. "The Patient with Cancer—His Changing Pattern of Communication." *New England Medical Journal* 274 (1966): 317–322.

When cancer is considered irreversible, there may be a decrease in communication and an increase of depression among patients because of fears concerning death, dying and abandonment. Communication with cancer patients is described in terms of stages of the disease: initial, advancing and terminal. Case studies.

3243 Adsett, C. A. "Emotional Reactions to Disfigurement from Cancer Therapy." *Canadian Medical Association Journal* 89 (1963): 385–391.

Emotional reactions to disfigurement and loss from cancer therapy are discussed, with case illustrations. The losses may occasion intense stress and strain, evoke irrational fears from childhood of lessened self-esteem and personal attraction. There may be specific reactions related to the meaning of a bodily organ, especially in the loss of a breast, ovaries, or facial disfigurement.

3244 Ahmed, Paul, ed. *Living and Dying with Cancer*. New York: Elsevier, 1981.

Clinicians consider various psychosocial aspects of living with cancer in a way that provides realistic and hopeful support for patients and family.

3245 Ashbrook, James B. "Living with Cancer as Fantasy and Fact: First Encounter." *Pastoral Psychology* (Winter 1988): 75–84.

A pastoral counselor and theological professor describes his personal reactions to the diagnosis of cancer and the way in which he adapted to life with cancer in both fantasy and fact. He relies upon spiritual, medical, psychological resources to maintain well-being in the face of life-threatening illness.

3246 Cassileth, Barrie R. and Peter A. Cassileth. *Clinical Care of the Terminal Cancer Patient.* Philadelphia: Lea and Febinger, 1982.

Tumor biology is reviewed in terms of medical complications, family therapy, psychosocial problems, home care, hospice and symptom control.

3247 Cullen, J. W., B. H. Fox, and R. N. Isom, eds. *Cancer: The Behavioral Dimensions.* New York: Raven Press, 1976.

Psychosocial issues in cancer prevention, detection, diagnosis, treatment, rehabilitation and long-term care are considered by experts in medicine and behavioral sciences. Topics range from the effectiveness of anti-smoking programs to physician attitudes. There is an emphasis upon decision-making by the terminally ill and an awareness of coping behavior that will provide emotional stability for the patient.

3248 Flynn, E. D. "What It Means to Battle Cancer." *American Journal of Nursing* 77 (1977): 261–262.

A nurse describes for other nurses the experience of metastatic cancer as a new world of confusion and uncertainty.

3249 Germain, Carol. *The Cancer Unit: an Ethnography.* Wakefield, Mass.: Nursing Resources, 1979.

Interactions between physicians, patients and nurses in cancer unit are studied. Illustrative quotations and conversations show both the strength and weaknesses of staff relationships.

3250 Goldberg, Richard, and Robert M. Tull. *The Psychosocial Dimensions of Cancer: A Practical Guide for Healthcare Providers.* New York: The Free Press, 1983.

A psychiatrist and a psychologist describe the techniques and values of their treatment program to make patients and their families working allies of the health professional. Intended for professionals in all disciplines and students who work with cancer patients, the book provides extensive discussion of research findings and brief clinical illustrations concerning children, adolescents, and adults. Medical disorders masquerading as psychiatric symptoms are distinguished from psychiatric aspects of medication. Specific attention is given to the management of pain, the personal challenge of working with cancer patients, information disclosures, and treatment refusals. Semi-structured interviews for the patient are outlined.

3251 Jensen, Mark. "Some Implications of Narrative Theology for Ministry to Cancer Patients." *Journal of Pastoral Care* 38 (1984): 216–225.

See 3315.

3252 Koocher, Gerald P. *The Damocles Syndrome: Consequences of Surviving Childhood Cancer.* New York: McGraw-Hill Book Co., 1981.

Relevant psychosocial literature and statistics are presented along with psychiatric interviews of persons who survive childhood cancer.

3253 Morra, Marion and Eve Potts. *Choices: Realistic Alternatives in Cancer Treatment.* New York: Avon, 1980.

Through a question and answer organization the authors provide clear and practical answers to a multitude of enquiries from patients and families about cancer treatment.

3254 Parkes, Colin M. "The Emotional Impact of Cancer on Patients and Their Families." *Journal of Laryngology and Otology* 89 (1975): 1271–1279.

The psychosocial transitions and phases inherent in living with cancer and grieving over impeding loss are described both with a view to the patient and the family.

3255 Rosenbaum, Ernest H. *Living with Cancer.* New York: Praeger, 1975.

See 3370.

3256 Rosenbaum, Ernest H. and Isadora R. Rosenbaum. *A Comprehensive Guide for Cancer Patients and Their Families.* Palo Alto, Calif.: Bull Pub. Co., 1980.

A comprehensive guide for patients and families explains the nature of cancer and therapy. Advice is given on maintaining motivation for life, dealing with stress, exercise, eating, sexuality. Various supportive organizations are listed.

3257 Sutherland, A. M. and C. E. Orbach. "Psychological Impact of Cancer and Cancer Surgery: Depressive Reactions Associated With Surgery for Cancer." *Cancer* 6 (1953): 958–962.

Patients with emotional problems involving self-destructiveness may be very vulnerable to acute pre-operative anxiety about death or mutilation in surgery.

3258 Spinetta, J. J. and Patricia Deasy-Spinetta, eds. *Living with Child-hood Cancer*. St. Louis, Mo.: C. V. Mosby, 1981.

With the possibility of long-term survival of children with cancer, the editors review past work in the field and introduce such topics as changing patterns in pediatric oncology, stress, denial, ethical and religious issues, the kinetic Family Drawing, non-medical cost, siblings, hypnosis, schooling, long-term decisions, bad physical impairment, marriage, employment and insurance.

3259 Turnage, M. N. and A. S. Turnage. *More Than You Dare to Ask: The First Year of Living with Cancer*. Atlanta, Ga.: John Knox Press, 1976.

Ann and her minister husband provide a personal narrative of their questioning of the meaning of illness and death and the guidance provided to them by a strong and practical faith.

3260 Ulrich, Betty Garton. *Rooted in the Sky: A Faith to Cope with Cancer*. Valley Forge, Pa.: Judson Press, 1989.

A pastor's wife describes her personal and spiritual difficulties in living through diagnosis and treatment for cancer. Peace and confidence came to her through the encouragement of Christian friends, prayer and the competence and concern of physicians and nurses.

3261 Waxenberg, S. D. "The Importance of the Communication of Feelings About Cancer." *Annals of the New York Academy of Science* 125 (1966): 1000–1005.

See 3462.

3262 Weisman, Avery D. and T. P. Hackett. "Predilection to Death: Death and Dying as a Psychiatric Problem." *Psychosomatic Medicine* 23 (1961): 233–256.

The cases of five surgical patients are presented. All expressed some inclination to die during surgery and this happened to all of them.

3263 Weisman, Avery D. *Coping with Cancer*. New York.: McGraw-Hill Book Co., 1979.

A noted clinician provides a readable and reliable discussion of hope and coping, quality of survival, safe-conduct, informed uncertainty, truth-telling and denial in response to the impact of cancer upon the emotional and physical life of a person. Major concerns of cancer patients are reviewed along with a study of anticipatory grief. Highly recommended by Simpson (8039).

3.245 PSYCHOPHARMACOLOGY/DRUG THERAPY

3264 Lipman, A. G. "Drug Therapy in Terminally Patients." *American Journal of Hospital Pharmacy* 32 (1975): 270–276.

The use of various drugs are discussed in relation to the discomforting symptoms of degenerative diseases: pain, anxiety, nausea, vomiting and depression.

3265 McCaffrey, M. and L. L. Hart. "Undertreatment of Acute Pain with Narcotics." *American Journal of Nursing* 76 (1976): 1586–1591.

Effective and safe use of narcotics for the relief of pain is shown through a study of pharmacological information to be above the common practice of underuse by physicians.

3266 Melzack, Ronald, *et al.* "The Brompton Mixture: Effects on Pain in Cancer Patients." *Canadian Medical Association Journal* 115 (1976): 125–129.

See 3229.

3267 Mount, Balfour, *et al.* "Use of the Brompton Mixture in Treating the Chronic Pain of Malignant Disease." *Canadian Medical Association Journal* 115 (1976): 122–124.

Experience in pain control in hospices has developed a method of treatment that emphasizes prevention of pain. Patients are delivered from fear of acute pain by ability to have some control over medication after training in discerning the time when chronic pain should be alleviated.

3268 Twycross, Robert G. and Sylvia A. Lack. *Symptom Control in Far Advanced Cancer: Pain Relief.* Baltimore, Md.: Urban and Schwarzenberger, 1983.

See 3234.

3.246 LIFE EXTENDING TECHNOLOGIES/RESUSCITATION

3269 Cohen, Cynthia B. *Casebook on the Termination of Life-Sustaining Treatment and the Care of the Dying.* Bloomington, Ind.: Indiana University Press, Hastings Center, 1988.

A variety of cases are presented as they impact upon the patient and family, physicians and nurses, lawyers and administrators. Ethical issues and possible courses of action are suggested. See also Hastings Center (3271).

3270 Gruman, Gerald J. *The History of Ideas about the Prolongation of Life: The Evolution of Prolongevity Hypotheses to 1800. 1966.* Reprint. New York: Arno Press, 1976.

The author examines the scientific and cultural expressions, from ancient times to 1800, that life could be extended and also considers references to the opposing position that life cannot or should not be prolonged by human agency.

3271 Hastings Center. *Guidelines on the Determination of Life-Sustaining Treatment and the Care of the Dying: a Report.* Bloomington, Ind.: Indiana University Press, 1987.

The ethics of patient autonomy are related to a wide range of medical treatments and varying conditions of patients. Traditional distinctions between "ordinary" and "extraordinary" resources are rejected. Instead, the initiative of the patient and the integrity of the professional helper are basic to mutual decision making about continuation of treatment, palliative care, or termination of treatment (which does not include euthanasia). Guidance is provided on the negations of treatment directives ("living will") by patient and staff, medical guidelines on the declaration of death, policies for ethics committees, administrative issues in the transfer of patients from one facility to another, economics. Classified bibliography, a list of selected legal authorities, index.

3272 Murray, Thomas H. and Arthur L. Caplan, ed. *Which Babies Shall Live? Humanistic Dimensions of the Care of Imperiled Newborns.* Clifton, N.J.: Humana Press, 1985.

Authors consider the historical, religious, legal and medical aspects of decisions to treat or refuse care for imperiled infants.

3273 Shelp, Earl E. *Born to Die? Deciding the Fate of Critically Ill Newborns.* New York: The Free Press, 1986.

A medical ethicist presents changing ideas of personhood that impact decisions by parents, the hospital and the state concerning life-sustaining measures for critically ill infants.

3274 Whiter, Walter. *Dissertation on the Disorder of Death Or, that State of the Frame under the Signs of Death Called Suspended Animation.* 1819. Reprint. New York: Arno Press, 1976.

Instances of resuscitation are described. The author urges a more vigilant attempt to revive those who are thought to be dead. Written in a time when the fears of premature burial were occasionally realistic.

3.25 SPECIAL CIRCUMSTANCES
See also CIRCUMSTANCES/STRESS (4.2)

3.251 AIDS

3275 Amos, William E., Jr. *When AIDS Comes to Church*. Philadelphia: Westminster Press, 1988.

A solid, conservative introduction to AIDS ministry by a Baptist pastor and congregation to a person with AIDS and family members.

3276 Douglas, Paul Harding and Laura Pinsky. *The Essential AIDS Fact Book*. Rev. ed. New York: Pocket Books, 1991.

Prepared under the auspices of Columbia University Health Service as an update of an AIDS pamphlet. Includes a national resource listing.

3277 Flynn, Eileen P. *AIDS: The Catholic Call for Compassion*. Kansas City: Sheed and Ward, 1985.

A Roman Catholic professor of medical ethics seeks to increase the sense of reason and compassion of medical personnel and other members of society who deal with AIDS-related issues. She reviews traditional Catholic moral teaching and concludes that a more permissive stance would encourage monogamous unions among homosexuals and lessen the incidents of HTLV-3 which occurs following casual sex.

3278 Fortunato, John. *AIDS: The Spiritual Dilemma*. San Francisco: Harper and Row, 1987.

The author, a lay theologian who is also a psychotherapist emphasizes the importance of embodiment and of the Christian hope of resurrection as we struggle with God's reality in the face of AIDS.

3279 Giraldo, G. and E. Beth, eds. *Epidemic of Acquired Immune Deficiency Syndrome (AIDS) and Kaposi's Sarcoma*. New York: Karger, 1984.

Covers interrelationships between viruses, immunologic responses, genetics and oncogenesis, classic and endemic forms of Kaposi's sarcoma, epidemiology of AIDS, clinical features of AIDS and Kaposi's sarcoma, and other topics.

3280 Hoffman, Wendell W. and Stanley G. Grenz. *AIDS Ministry in the Midst of an Epidemic*. Grand Rapids, Mich.: Baker Book House, 1990.

A clinical professor of medicine and a professor of systematic theology develop a conservative Christian response to AIDS that will address many practical forms of care-giving. After discussing barriers to care from conservative Christians, medical perspectives on AIDS are presented in six chapters. The next six chapters consider barriers that must be overcome through compassion, general guidelines for appropriate interpersonal and religious attitudes in care-giving, social advocacy of care for persons with AIDS and those who care for them. The ethics of intervention are stressed. Appendices include epidemiology of AIDS, medical classifications, references to relevant medical articles and some in theology. Glossary. No case studies or examples of "hands-on" ministry.

3281 Hughes, A.; J. Martain and P. Franks. *AIDS Home Care and Hospice Manual*. San Francisco: Visiting Nurse Association of San Francisco, 1987.

A useful "how to" book for procedures in daily care of home-bound persons with AIDS.

3282 Institute of Medicine and the National Academy of Sciences. *Confronting AIDS: Directions for Public Health, Health Care, and Research*. Washington, D. C.: National Academy Press, 1986.

Delves into the complex medical, social, ethical, financial and research problems arising from AIDS. Available from 2101 Constitution Ave., Washington, DC 20418

3283 Kübler-Ross, Elisabeth. *AIDS: The Ultimate Challenge*. New York: Macmillan Pub. Co., 1987.

A popular author on death and dying describes in detail the clash of money, politics and ego in caring for AIDS patients. She describes her attempts to develop a care center for babies with AIDS on or near her farm in Monterey, Virginia.

3284 Martelli, Leonard J, with Fran D. Peltz and William Messina. *When Someone You Know Has AIDS: A Practical Guide*. New York: Crown Pub., 1987.

With warm and compassionate narratives and first-person accounts, the authors provide a factual précis on dealing with the tragedy of AIDS. It is not so much a work on how to die as it is one on how to be human.

3285 Miller, David. *Living with AIDS and HIV*. New York: Macmillan Pub. Co. 1987.

Practical advice on the myriad physical and mental problems of AIDS patients.

3286 Moffatt, M. A., *et al.*, eds. *AIDS: A Self Care Manual*. Santa Monica, Calif.: IBS Press, 1987.

A comprehensive book, with an accent on the spiritual and religious dimensions of AIDS. The book includes plainly written sections on the socio-psychological perspectives on AIDS, a medical overview and information, treatment alternatives, recommendations for prevention, self-care, taking care of business, legal and social services, spiritual and healing resources. There is a glossary of terms and a listing of AIDS-related organizations, resource material, self-care forms and charts. Authoritative and humane.

3287 Monette, Paul. *Borrowed Time: An AIDS Memoir*. San Diego, Calif.: Harcourt Brace Jovanovich, 1988.

This story of two men, one who dies, the other whose immune system is compromised, is a poignant study of denial, which is perhaps the most significant psychological feature of the AIDS crisis.

3288 Nungesser, Lon G. *Epidemic of Courage*. New York: St. Martin's Press, 1987.

How to handle the psychological and sociological impact of AIDS.

3289 Kadzielski, Mark A. *AIDS: Legal Implications for Health Care Providers*. St. Louis: The Catholic Health Association of the United States, 1987.

Focuses on confidentiality, personnel issues, discrimination, tort liability to patients and employers and combatting health care employees' fears. Available from 4455 Woodson Road, St. Louis, MO 63134.

3290 Slaff, James I., and John K. Brubaker. *The AIDS Epidemic*. New York: Warner Books, 1985.

Presents the known facts about AIDS as of 1985. Focuses also on how you can protect yourself and family.

3291 Shelp, Earl E. and Ronald H. Sunderland. *AIDS and the Church*. Philadelphia: Westminster Press, 1987.

An introduction to AIDS ministry issues for churches.The author discuss medical, social class, ethical and pastoral aspects of ministry to persons with AIDS. Notes and selected references.

3292 Shilts, Randy. *And the Band Played On: Politics, People and the AIDS Epidemic*. New York: St. Martin's Press, 1987.

This is an exhaustive chronological account of the AIDS epidemic as related to American social and political culture and public policy.

3293 Smith, Walter J. *AIDS: Living and Dying with Hope*. New York: Paulist Press, 1988.

A professor of psychology who is trained in theology offers information on the AIDS syndrome and disease, medical and pastoral care. The pastoral advice is to recognize the dangers of rejection, denial in the Christian community and the need to accept the anger that is in many AIDS patients. Brief excerpts from pastoral ministry to AIDS patients are included throughout the book. There is a plea for the church to avoid homophobia and be tolerant of persons whose sexual practices do not conform to church tradition. Psychological needs of AIDS patients are described and there is a lengthy letter from a neurologist with Kaposi's sarcoma to his priest. This is part of a chapter on making peace with the past during terminal illness. The need of black and Hispanic persons with AIDS is discussed. The final chapters discuss ministering to families during a person's terminal illness and the process of grief and bereavement.

3294 Snow, John. *Mortal Fear: Meditations on Death and Aids*. Cambridge, Mass.: Cowley Pub., 1987.

An Episcopal professor of pastoral theology used his own time of waiting for the diagnosis of a cancerous growth in his own body to write meditations on death with specific reference to those who knew that they were dying of AIDS.

3295 Tilleraas, Perry. *The Color of Light*. Hazelton Meditation Series. San Francisco: Harper and Row, 1989.

Love and confidence characterize the brief meditations offered by a free-lance writer for each day of the year. After a brief thought from some source, the author advises self-love, self-acceptance and forgiveness as alternatives to guilt and shame. Each meditation closes with some positive thought including a blessing for anger, grief, rage. The "total acceptance" of the affirmations include such statements as "I am the soul of world."

3296 Tyckoson, David A., ed. *AIDS*. 2nd. ed. Phoenix: Oryx Press, 1986.

Lists and summarizes important books, articles, and other publications covering all aspects of the disease.

3.252 DISASTERS/TRAUMA/CATASTROPHIC ILLNESS
See also THEODICY: EVIL AND THE WILL OF GOD (2.42) and
ACCIDENTS/CATASTROPHES (4.21)

3297 Figley, Charles R., ed. *Trauma and Its Wake*. Vol. 2, *Traumatic Stress Theory, Research, and Intervention*. New York: Brunner/ Mazel Pub., 1986.

This resource for professionals who work with severely traumatized individuals, families and communities provides articles on the latest thinking on trauma from a psychological perspective. The general organization is theory, research and intervention.

3298 Katz, Jay and Alexander Morgan Capron. *Catastrophic Diseases: Who Decides What? A Psychosocial and Legal Analysis of the Problems Posed by Hemodialysis and Organ Transplantation.* New York: Russell Sage Foundation, 1975.

An exploration of the nature and effects of catastrophic illness: preservation of life, reduction of suffering, personal integrity and dignity, pursuit of knowledge, economy and public interest. Professional issues are considered, such as development of technical procedures, authority and capacity of the physician-investigators and patient-subjects, the functions of informed consent, limitations of consent. The stages of decision making are reviewed, the activities of professional and public institutions involved, proposals for the formulation of policy regarding the allocation of resources and selection of donors, the administration of such major medical interventions at local and national levels, with a review of decisions and consequences.

3299 Parad, Howard J., Harvey L. P. Resnik, and Libbie G. Parad, eds. *Emergency and Disaster Management: A Mental Health Sourcebook.* Bowie, Md.: Charles Press, 1976.

The authors describe mobile psychiatric emergency teams, home treatment of the suicidal person, maintenance programs and crisis hostels. Various modes of crisis intervention are discussed. Specific studies are included on various physical disasters. Preventive programs are recommended. Bibliography.

3300 Resnik, Harvey L. P. and Harvey L. Reuben, eds. *Emergency Psychiatric Care: The Management of Mental Health Crises.* Bowie, Md.: Charles Press, 1975.

General concepts and principles of crisis intervention and specific emergencies related to alcohol, drug abuse, family crisis and environmental disasters are presented by various authors. See also Switzer (3325).

3301 Trimble, Michael R. *Post-Traumatic Neurosis.* New York: John Wiley and Sons, 1981.

An English psychiatrist reviews the diagnosis and treatment of lingering psychological effects of neurological injuries from a 1766 account of melancholia after a neck injury in a carriage, to current debates about compensation for "whiplash." Medical references.

3.3 RELIGIOUS RESOURCES FOR THE DYING

3302 Ainsworth-Smith, Ian and Peter Speck. *Letting Go: Caring for the Dying and the Bereaved.* Tiptree, England: Anchor Press, 1982.

English hospital chaplains present their experience: the death of a baby, an adolescent, an elderly person, sudden death by accident, spouse, reactions of people facing their own imminent death. Ties and customs concerning death and dying are examined along with recommendations for the work of the clergy. Some facilities for cancer patients are listed.

3303 Albers, Gregg R. *Counseling the Sick and Terminally Ill.* Dallas, Tx.: Word Pub., 1989.

Christian counselors are advised by a physician concerning a wide variety of situations in which care can be offered to the critically, chronically and terminally ill. Special medical situations are described and spiritual resources are recommended. Practical advice in simple prose. Bibliography.

3304 Autton, Norman. *The Pastoral Care of the Dying.* London: S. P. C. K., 1966.

In the classic tradition of pastoral care, an English chaplain discusses the history of the art of dying, the fear of death and the need to tell the truth to patients who want to know. Pastoral care of the dying is discussed in terms of the ministry of various hospital professions, the family and the priest. All of these must understand their own reactions to dying and death along with the needs of the patients for security and presence. The priest is to lead the patients to penitence, to set their worldly affairs in order, and to have faith that God suffers with them in this time of distress. The sacraments of penance, holy communion and holy unction are discussed. A variety of litanies, prayers and hymns are included.

3305 Bane, J. Donald, *et. al.*, eds. *Death and Ministry: Pastoral Care of the Dying and the Bereaved.* New York: Seabury Press, 1975.

Physicians, nurses, chaplains, parish clergy, psychiatrists and others contribute short articles on psychological needs of a dying person, the emotional process of grief, the facilitation of communication between the dying person and the family, importance of "presence," listening, and warnings against imposition of a priest's, religious commitments on others, the integration of religious tradition with death, personal experience, ethical and legal questions, work with other professionals.

3306 Bowers, Margaretta K., Edgar N. Jackson, James A. Knight, Lawrence LeShan. *Counseling the Dying*. New York: Jason Aronson, 1964.

Psychiatrists and pastors develop a personal approach to the dying through the creation of a mental attitude that will move a person toward the final event of life with calmness and dignity. The major resource is a religious faith that gives a person completeness in relationship within the self and with others. Impersonal withdrawal by helpers can be reduced by honest admission of the normal fear of dying and the defense of impersonal, professional attitudes. Disgust, despair, resentment, and dependency must be faced in the therapeutic relationship through honest discussions about dying and the problems of relationships. In such encounters, pastors may escape through verbalization and ritual, or they may embody the meaning of life that comes through identification with the self-hood of God in Jesus. To the authors, this means self awareness and spiritual realizations that death is not defeat but a final expression of faith. The book was a pioneering effort to bring dynamic psychology into the tradition of ministering to the sick, with little attention to the content of theology and belief in the supernatural that characterized earlier Christian traditions.

3307 Branson, Roy. "Is Acceptance a Denial of Death? Another Look at Kübler-Ross." *Christian Century* 92 (May 7, 1975): 464–468.

The author links the theories of Kübler-Ross (1020) to ethical naturalism and prefers the theology of Oscar Cullman (2200) who believes in a link between death and sin through Christian faith.

3308 Cabot, Richard and Russell Dicks. *The Art of Ministering to the Sick*. New York: Macmillan Pub. Co., 1936.

This classic in the field of pastoral counsel was written by Richard Cabot, a distinguished physician in Boston, and Russell Dicks, the first chaplain with clinical training at the Massachusetts General Hospital. Separate chapters present the viewpoints of medicine and pastoral care concerning the needs of patients, their complaints and circumstances, suggestions for bedside ministry. Religious resources such as prayer are discussed with authenticity and appropriateness. The theological position is that of liberal Protestantism. But the work rises above any theological or philosophical categories in the realism and mystery with which case histories are used to show the need for sensitive awareness in the process of illness and/or dying.

3309 Calhoun, Gerald J. *Pastoral Companionship: Ministry with Seriously-Ill Persons and Their Families*. Mahwah, N. J.: Paulist Press, 1986.

A Roman Catholic pastoral counselor combines human compassion with religious resources in care of the seriously ill and their families. The emphasis is on relationship rather than on doctrine. Compassion, honesty, trust and confrontation are suggested as the means by which prayer may be a resource. Chapters also include advice on decision-making, sacramental ministry to the dying, seeking justice for the ill who are aged or handicapped, training lay ministers, and supervising ministerial students.

3310 Carey, Raymond G. "Emotional Adjustment in Terminal Patients: A Quantitative Approach." *Journal of Counseling Psychology* 21 (1974): 433–439.

Eighty-four patients in a Lutheran general hospital received pastoral counseling and responded to a detailed questionnaire. Results indicated that emotional adjustment to awareness of a limited life expectancy was not related principally to religious orientation, although this was an important factor. Instead, emotional adjustment was influenced more by a patient's physical condition (level of discomfort), previous experiences with dying persons, interpersonal relationships. The most important aspect of the religious variable was the quality of the religious orientation rather than religious affiliation or verbal acceptance of religious beliefs.

3311 Dicks, Russell L. *My Faith Looks Up.* Philadelphia: Westminster Press, 1949.

A pastoral counselor provides practical suggestions for relaxation, Scripture passages and sensitive prayers for those who seek divine aid through adoration, faith, forgiveness, rest, reassurance, courage, confidence, praise. The writing is rich in understanding and warm in compassion.

3312 Dobihal, Edward F. and Charles W. Stewart. *When a Friend Is Dying: A Guide to Caring for the Terminally Ill and Bereaved.* Nashville, Tenn.: Abingdon Press, 1984.

See 3087.

3313 Gerkin, Charles. *Crisis Experience in Modern Life: Theory and Theology for Pastoral Care.* Nashville, Tenn. Abingdon Press, 1979.

Crises are discussed with Eriksonian framework: includes death, bereavement, generation conflict, identity crisis. The author begins with an analysis of contemporary culture and its loss of belief in divine providence to sustain individuals through crisis. He proposes the theology of hope, of God's future-oriented action, as in the writings of Jürgen Moltmann. He also opts for an "incarnational" model of pastoral care, meaning (1) the pastor incarnates Christ for the individual in crisis and (2) the goal is for the individual to discern signs of God's current and future-directed activity in the midst of crisis. In discussion of dying, Gerkin explicitly rejects

234 Death and Dying

"heroic humanism" and focuses upon the pain and abandonment of Christ on the cross. See also Moltmann (2276).

3314 Hubbard, David Allan. *Why Do I Have to Die?* Glendale, Calif.: Regal Books, 1978.

The president of an evangelical theological seminary presents meditations on various questions about death from a biblical perspective.

3315 Jensen, Mark. "Some Implications of Narrative Theology for Ministry to Cancer Patients." *Journal of Pastoral Care* 38 (1984): 216–225.

A chaplain describes the way in which a caregiver elicits and listens to stories. The pastor or chaplain can serve as an artist who encourages persons to integrate sacred stories into their particular lives and communities.

3316 Kinast, Robert L. *When a Person Dies: Pastoral Theology in Death Experiences*. New York: Crossroad, 1984.

A Roman Catholic priest combines case studies with theological reflections on care for the dying.

3317 Linn, Mary Jane, Dennis Linn and Matthew Linn. *Healing the Dying: Releasing People to Die*. New York: Paulist Press, 1979.

A Catholic family who had been prominent in faith healing offer a series of meditations for the dying that are built around the traditional seven last words of Jesus on the cross. The organization is a meditation, a prayer, reflection questions and space for comments by the readers. The emphasis is upon inner visualization of the presence of Jesus. The special poignancy of the book is found in the preface, which describes the attitudes of Mary Jane Linn on the day that she was killed in an auto accident. This was four months after finishing the manuscript on *Healing the Dying* and illustrates a theme of the book that a person can complete his or her unfinished business in life and then—at least in the opinion of her brothers—choose to die.

3318 Nouwen, Henri J. M. *The Wounded Healer*. Garden City, N.Y.: Doubleday, 1972.

A Catholic priest who also holds a Ph.D. in clinical psychology centers upon the minister's role as that of a wounded healer. Pain and hurt are the source for the love, care and hope that a pastor provides in a world of loneliness, alienation and grief. Evil is real and radical and yet, potentially, meaningful. The section on dying contains the devastating case of a farmer who failed to communicate with a student chaplain and who died during an operation while he was filled with hopelessness and despair.

3319 Oden, Thomas C. *Crisis Ministries.* New York: Crossroad Pub. Co., 1986.

See 1045.

3320 Platt, Larry A. and Roger G. Branch. *Resources for Ministry in Death and Dying.* Nashville, Tenn.: Broadman Press, 1988.

Sociologists with an emphasis upon social change and moral values, and authorities in other fields present well-written summaries: death in American society, the life-cycle, care of the dying patient, the funeral, the meaning of grief and bereavement, resources for death-related ministry. Helping organizations are listed, along with audio-visual sources and a brief bibliography.

3321 Reeves, Robert B., Jr., Robert E. Neale and Austin H. Kutscher. *Pastoral Care of the Dying and the Bereaved: Selected Readings.* New York: Health Sciences Pub. Co., 1973.

Reprints of professional articles by chaplains, pastoral counselors, physicians and psychologists include studies on the needs of the dying and their treatment by pastors and chaplains, the religious views of caregivers and the conspiracy of silence, medical and pastoral understanding of grief, the work of the church and pastors in counseling of the grieving and participation in funeral customs, Judaism and bereavement, the right to die.

3322 Saunders, Cicely. *Beyond All Pain: A Companion for the Suffering and Bereaved.* London: SPCK, 1983.

Poems and readings are provided to assist those who are facing death and bereavement to find comfort and strength through prayer and meditation. Selections include those from psychiatrists such as Frankl or theologians such as Sayers.

3323 Soulen, Richard N., ed. *Care for the Dying.* Atlanta, Ga.: John Knox Press, 1975.

Various Protestant authorities discuss dying from the viewpoint of ethics, pastoral and systematic theology, Scripture, and philosophy. Case studies, personal experience and research studies are included in a general overview of depression, suicide and both internal and social influences upon the terminally ill.

3324 Sullender, R. Scott. Grief and Growth: Pastoral Resources for Emotional and Spiritual Growth. New York: Paulist Press, 1985.

See 4519.

3325 Switzer, David K. *The Minister as Crisis Counselor*. Nashville, Tenn.: Abingdon Press, 1974.

After a general discussion of crisis theory and counseling, the author centers upon unresolved grief as a central motivating force in many emotional and behavioral disorders. The dynamics and stages of grief are discussed, along with the needs of the grieving person and the psychological requirements of clergy and others who provide ministry.

3326 Thompson, Melvin. *Cancer and the God of Love*. London: SCM Press, 1976.

An Anglican priest describes the care of a cancer patient not only in terms of an understanding of the effects of cancer upon personality, but also with sensitive concern to the symbols by which patient and chaplain can probe deeply into the place of suffering in relation to a loving God. Emphasis is placed upon the way that persons experience doctrines rather than upon a defense of any particular doctrine. The theological viewpoint is similar to that of John Hick (2181).

3327 Watson, David. *Fear No Evil*. Wheaton, Ill.: Harold Shaw Publishers, 1984.

A charismatic Anglican priest describes his questions and convictions during an 11 month struggle with terminal cancer. Personal courage, faith, support from family, friends, a congregation and faith healers sustained him in a conviction that he would be healed. He died at age 50, a month after completing the final chapter of the book during continuous attacks of asthma.

3328 Wise, Robert L. *When There Is No Miracle*.Glendale, Calif.: Regal Books, 1977.

A pastor uses Scripture, theology, and examples from his ministry to show how the presence of God can be felt even in the midst of pain that has not disappeared because of prayer.

3.31 SACRAMENTS/RITUALS/PRAYER
See also DEATH IN WORLD RELIGIONS (2.61)

3329 Autton, Norman. *The Pastoral Care of the Dying*. London: S. P. C. K., 1966.

A book written from the sacramental wing of the Anglican Church. The author reviews medieval and early modern "art of dying" literature, then discusses the contemporary hospital. Emphasis is on survival of death as intrinsic to Christian faith, and on sacramental action of a priest. A traditional approach is taken to liturgies for use with the sick, dying and for the dead.

3330 DelBene, Ron, Mary Montgomery and Herb Montgomery. *Into the Light.* Nashville, Tenn.: Upper Room, 1988.

An Episcopal missionary for spiritual development encourages the dying patient and loved ones to develop a short "breath prayer" to bring effortless calm in the midst of fear and anxiety. The prayer is one part of a listening of ministry touch and compassion which is described through examples which are intimate and realistic.

3331 Didier, Jean-Charles. *Death and the Christian.* Trans. by P. J. Hepburn Scott. New York: Hawthorn Books, 1961.

The biblical, theological and historical background is given for the "Church's medicine" during sickness, followed by explanations concerning the administration of holy oil, the modern liturgy and discipline for the anointing of the sick, and the effects of the sacrament on bodily health, the forgiveness of sin and spiritual strengthening. The sacramental anointing is to be available to the sick whether they are in danger of immediate death or not and whether or not there is any prospect of miraculous intervention on God's part. The function is related to the Eucharist and to the right of commendation for a departing soul.

3332 Dulany, Joseph P. *We Can Minister With Dying Persons.* Nashville, Tenn.: Discipleship Resources, 1986.

Techniques of relaxation and direct meditation are adapted to the use of those who care for the dying. The author describes the personal requirements for this task and the processes through which a dying person is led through psychological and religious phases of relaxation.

3333 Droege, Thomas A. *Guided Grief Imagery: A Resource for Grief Ministry and Death Education.* New York: Paulist Press, 1987.

A Protestant theological professor explores the images of faith which Christians have used throughout the centuries in their encounters with death, including those in the New Testament and in the liturgy of the church in various historical periods. Then he presents exercises in guided imagery for use by Christians both privately and in groups. The purpose is to use the imagination as a way to incorporate the experiences of death and dying into the wholeness and fulness of life. Exercises are detailed from a reading of selected psalms or passages in the New Testament.

3334 Gusmer, Charles W. *And You Visited Me: Sacramental Ministry to the Sick and Dying.* New York: Pueblo Pub. Co., 1984.

This is a detailed exposition of the history and meanings of the Roman Catholic liturgies of anointing and viaticum, with a focus on the changed post-Vatican II rites. The author emphasizes the pastoral context, and the personal and spiritual needs of the sick and dying in relation to the rites. The historical survey shows how anointing came to be mixed with penance in "extreme unction."

3335 Higgins, John J. *Merton's Theology of Prayer*. Spencer, Mass.: Cistercian Publications, 1971.

The published work of a noted member of a Roman Catholic order that stressed silence and contemplation is presented with the theme that mediation is not futile introspection or preoccupation with self-understanding. It is knowledge of God that will penetrate us with His love. Themes include union with God, transformation of consciousness, asceticism and contemplative prayer and a critical evaluation. Although preparation for death is not a specific subject in the evaluation, the book contains many themes such as self-denial which are characteristic of the Ars Moriendi tradition. Bibliography.

3336 Kerney, LeRoy G. "Pastoral Use of 'The Seven Last Words' in Terminal Care." In *Psychosocial Aspects of Terminal Care*, ed. by Bernard Schoenberg, et.al., 333–342. New York: Columbia University Press, 1972.

The senior chaplain for the National Institutes of Health provides meditations on the relationship of the words of Jesus upon the cross with the feelings of the terminally ill and those who minister to them.

3337 Knauber, Adolf. *Pastoral Theology of the Anointing of the Sick: Rite of Anointing and Pastoral Care of the Sick*. Collegeville, Minn.: The Liturgical Press, 1975.

The liturgy of sacramental administration is explained. Ritual responses, Scripture readings and prayers are provided along with suggestions for supplementary reading. An officially approved commentary that includes the Revised Roman ritual of the Second Vatican Ecumenical Council. The author emphasizes the Vatican II decision for a "continuous rite" that provides a faithful ministry to the sick and dying. This is considered a more pastoral form of spirituality than the emphasis of earlier centuries upon one final "last rite" with a preoccupation upon "preparation for glory."

3338 Nolan, T. "Ritual and Therapy." In *Anticipatory Grief*, ed. by Bernard Schoenberg, *et al.*, 358–364. New York: Columbia University Press, 1974.

A pastor who is also a registered nurse believes that religious ritual has a therapeutic effect on cancer patients and their families in coping with anticipatory grief.

3339 *Pastoral Care of the Sick: Introduction and Pastoral Notes.* Liturgy Documentary Series 3. Washington, D. C.: United States Catholic Conference, 1983.

Sacramental rites of the church are described both as a comfort to sick in time of anxiety and restoration of health and as comfort and strength for Christians in the passage from this life. Specific instructions are given for anointing of the sick and for care of the dying. The work is an outgrowth of the Second Vatican Council in which translations of the Roman Ritual into English and other languages were encouraged and the sacraments administered according to the varying conditions of the sick. This would provide a "continuous rite" of care throughout illness, including terminal illness.

3340 Snow, John. *Mortal Fear: Meditations on Death and Aids.* Cambridge, Mass.: Cowley Pub., 1987.

See 3294.

3.4 NEAR DEATH EXPERIENCES

3341 Gallup, George Jr. *Adventures in Immortality.* New York: McGraw-Hill Book Co., 1982.

Over 1500 adults in over 300 selected localities were interviewed in a random sample of the general population regarding near-death experiences. 15% gave reports of a "close call" with death. One-third of this 15% reported some sort of mystical encounter, such as an overwhelming sense of peace and painlessness, review of the individual's past in a rapid and compressed fashion, special sensation of being in another world, out-of-body sensation, visualization of something going around them, feeling the presence of other beings, audible sounds of human voices, encounter with bright lights, presence of a tunnel, premonition about future events. The reports contain a mixture of those who felt the psychological threat of death, such as victims of a crime and 22 others who were critically ill.

3342 Greyson, Bruce and Charles P. Flynn, eds. *The Near-Death Experience: Problems, Prospects, Perspectives.* Springfield, Ill.: Charles C. Thomas, 1984.

Medical researchers, some sociologists, psychologists and theologians find the near-death experience to bring an increase in desire to serve others, a loss in the fear of death, a belief in afterlife, belief in the presence of God, a belief that life has meaning. This is often a shift from previous value-systems of the subject.

3343 Greyson, Bruce. "The Near-Death Experience Scale: Construction, Reliability and Validity." *Journal of Nervous and Mental Disease* 171 (1983): 369–375.

As a self-scoring questionnaire or as an interviewer rated instrument, the Near-Death Experience Scale of sixteen items contains four components: cognitive, affective, paranormal, transcendental.

3344 Grof, Stanislav and Joan Halifax. *The Human Encounter with Death.* New York: E. P. Dutton, 1977.

The experience of dying is investigated as part of the use, application and understanding of psychedelic drugs. The book contains studies of psychedelic therapy with individuals dying of cancer, mythological interpretations from Joseph Campbell, discussions at the Esalen Institute of the Inner Journey of the Soul.

3345 Heaney, John J. "Recent Studies of Near-Death Experiences." *Journal of Religion and Health* 22 (1983): 116–130.

Through a survey of research and reflections upon near-death experiences, the author concludes that the experiences are deep stirrings of the individual and collective psyche, combined with some ESP phenomena.

3346 Kalish, Richard A. "Experiences of Persons Reprieved from Death." In *Death and Bereavement,* ed. by Austin H. Kutscher, 84–98. Springfield, Ill: Charles C. Thomas, 1969.

3347 McLaughlin, Steven A. "Near-Death experiences and personal religion: A further investigation." 1983 Ph.D. diss., Graduate School of Psychology, Fuller Theological Seminary, Pasadena, Calif.

The relationship between religion and near-death experiences was examined by interviewing 40 near-death experiencers who in addition were given a series of tests to measure religious orientation and religious change. No relationship was found between religious orientation prior to the near-death experience and the depth of the experience. A significant correlation was found between the depth of the near-death experience and a subsequent increase in both the importance of religion and religious activity.

3348 Basford, Terry K. *Near-Death Experiences: an Annotated Bibliography.* New York: Garland Publishing, 1990.

3349 Moody, Raymond A., Jr. *Reflections on Life After Life.* New York: Bantam, 1977.

3350 Moody, Raymond A., Jr. *Life After Life*. Harrisburg, PA: Stackpole Books, 1976.

A physician who is also a Ph.D. in philosophy provides an analysis of selected case histories in which he finds basic components of near-death experience ranging from the "black tunnel" to "my life flashing by," with some references to an intense light radiating love and security.

3351 Moss, David M., III. "Near-Fatal Experience, Crisis Intervention and the Anniversary Reaction." *Pastoral Psychology* 28 (1979): 75–95.

A pastoral counselor reviews literature on near-fatal experience with an emphasis upon repercussions associated with passive assaults to the self. Recommendations for counseling. References.

3352 Noyes, Russell, Jr. and Roy Kletti. "Depersonalization in the Face of Life-Threatening Danger: A Description." *Psychiatry* 39 (1976): 19–27.

Calm and mystical states in near-fatal incidents are often preceded by marked resistance and life review.

3353 Noyes, Russell, Jr., *et al*. "Depersonalization in Accident Victims and Psychiatric Patients." *Journal of Nervous and Mental Disease* 164 (1977): 401–407.

In a factor analysis of near-death experiences the authors found: (1) a depersonalization factor of a strange or unreal self, objects small and far away, detachment from the body and a wall between the self and emotions; (2) hyper-alertness factor: vivid, sharp and speeded thoughts, altered sense of the passage of time; (3) mental clouding and revival of memories.

3354 Noyes, Russell, Jr. and Roy Kletti. "The Experience of Dying from Falls." *Omega* 3 (1972): 45–52. Reprinted in *Death, Dying, Transcending*, ed. by Richard A Kalish, 129–136. Farmingdale, N. Y.: Baywood Pub. Co., 1980.

Persons falling from mountains describe a sense of unreality and lack of feeling which may pass in a few days. The study includes translation of a report by Albert Heim (1892) of near fatal accidents. In examining these reports over a period of twenty-five years Heim found a common pattern: sense of calm and acceptance, greatly increased mental alertness, rapid and objective thought processes. The passage of time seemed greatly slowed and some individuals experienced a rapid review of memories.

3355 Osis, Karlis. and Erlander Haraldsson. "Deathbed Observations by Physicians and Nurses: A Cross-Cultural Survey." In *A Collection of*

Near-Death Research Readings. Ed. by Craig R. Lundahl. Chicago: Nelson-Hall, 1982.

This cross-cultural study of death-bed visions of patients who were dying or near death was obtained by interviews with physicians and nurses in the United States and India. From an almost equal number of cases in the two countries, similar dying experiences emerged, such as apparitions of human figures, visions of heavenly abodes, landscapes, gardens, elevation of mood with feelings of serenity, peace and elation. Americans saw deceased human figures while Indian patients usually saw religious figures.

3356 Ring, Kenneth. *Life at Death: A Scientific Investigation of the Near-Death Experience.* New York: Coward, McCann and Geoghegan, 1980.

In structured interviews with 102 persons who came primarily by referral from doctors and hospital personnel, subjects were interviewed within two years of their near-death episode. Tape-recorded interviews were judged by the author and two graduate students in clinical psychology, who used a weighed Core Experience Index. Of the elements to be rated, 72.8% were scored in agreement by all three judges for a given subject. The near-death experiences consisted of five stages with progressively fewer subjects reaching the later stages: strong feelings of peace and contentment, sense of detachment, entering a dark region or tunnel, a light which was often described as brilliant gold and of indescribable beauty, entrance into the realm of light where the subject met deceased relatives or spiritual beings such as Jesus or God and talked with them. For women a higher percentage of near-death experiences occurred as a result of illness. For men the experience was more often during accidents or suicide attempts. Illness victims had a higher percentage of experiences than accident or suicide victims. There was only a modest relationship between the severity of a subject's physical condition and the depth of the experience.

3357 Royse, David. "The Near-Death Experience: A Survey of Clergy Attitudes and Knowledge." *Journal of Pastoral Care* 39 (1985): 31–42.

From the reports of a questionnaire answered by 174 clergy, the author concludes that it is not rare for near-death accounts to be reported to clergy and that such reports were hardly ever "hellish" in tone. Near-death experiencers tend to become more religious and their fear of dying is lessened.

3358 Sabom, Michael B. *Recollections of Death: A Medical Investigation.* New York: Harper and Row, 1982.

A cardiologist reports the experiences of 116 persons who had come near to dying, usually as a result of cardiac arrest. 55% were interviewed within one year of the near-death event. 43% of the patients reported a near-death experience when they were close to physical death. Six patients gave such detailed accounts of medical procedures, in agreement with hospital records, that the author concluded that these were actual out-of-body experiences in which the mind separates from the unconscious physical body.

3359 Sabom, W. Stephen. "Near-Death Experiences: A Review from Pastoral Psychology." *Journal of Religion and Health* 19 (1980): 130–140.

From a review of published interpretation of near-death experiences, a pastoral counselor provides suggestions for sensitive inquiries with subjects of the experience.

3360 Springer, Rebecca Ruter. *IntraMuros*. Forest Grove, Oreg.: Booksearchers, n. d.

See 6038.

3361 Weisenhütter, Eckart. *Blicknachdrüben: Selbsterfahrungen im Sterben* [View into the Beyond: Self-Experiences in Dying]. 3rd ed. Gütersloh: Gütersloher Verlag, 1976.

After a close encounter with death, a psychiatrist explores similar experiences in others and finds a peak experience of blissfulness in the near-death state of conscious collaboration. The experience changed his relationships with patients.

3362 Zaleski, Carol. *Otherworld Journeys: Accounts of Near-Death Experience in Medieval and Modern Times*. New York: Oxford University Press, 1987.

In a cultural symbolism level of analysis, Zaleski sees religious imagination working in narratives of near death experiences. A serious work of scholarship.

3.5 INSTITUTIONAL/HOME CARE

3363 Baulch, Evelyn M. *Home Care: A Practical Alternative to Extended Hospitalization*. Millbrae, Calif.: Celestial Arts, 1980.

Advice is offered on many facets of home care for persons recuperating from traumatic injury, facing a life-threatening illness, or chronically ill. The process of care begins with preparation of the home, choice of nurse or physical therapist, the emotional problems of patient and caregiver in the home, special needs of children, elderly, handicapped,

AIDS patient. The emphasis is upon holistic healing and suggestions are made to provide a sense of hope and dignity for patient and family. The informal writing covers a wide range of specific issues from bladder and bowel care to psychic healing. Bibliography and index.

3364 Brim, Orville G., Jr., Howard E. Freeman, Sol Levine, and Norman A. Scotch, eds. *The Dying Patient*. New York: Russell Sage Foundation, 1970.

The relationship between dying and medical conduct is considered from the perspective of sociology, economics, medicine and the law by fourteen contributors. The editors sense a reawakened interest in and concern for cultural beliefs about death, the low quality of care of the dying, heroic acts, surgical innovations, the ability of a professional to empathize with the dying, the unfilled promises of public health policy, the effect of value changes such as a decline of belief in an afterlife, the need for more systematic social research on prolongation and termination of life. Annotated bibliography by Richard Kalish.

3365 Kopp, Ruth Lewshenia. *Encounter With Terminal Illness*. Grand Rapids, Mich.: Zondervan Pub. House, 1980.

A physician who has been active in the hospice movement presents in narrative form the problems of denial, the doctor-patient relationship, the impact of terminal illness upon the family, personal responses to dying and the way to prepare for death. The book is an updating of the traditional Christian approaches with modern medical and psychiatric understanding of the role of anger and acceptance in the care of the dying.

3366 Glaser, Barney G. and Anselm L. Strauss. *Time for Dying*. Chicago: Aldine Pub. Co., 1968.

From observations and interviews of six San Francisco hospitals and hospitals in Italy, Greece and Scotland, sociologists trace the reciprocal effects that patients, family, staff and institutional structures have upon one another in the context of the hospital as a work institution during terminal situations. The movement of the patient is traced through successive stages that bring him or her to death, the way in which these movements are integrated with the structure of the hospital and the ability of the hospital to adapt to the changing needs of the patient. The organizational structure of different wards in hospitals on the behavior of staff members is observed along with practical suggestions for the handling of dying patients. The theoretical model is that of a trajectory which has duration and shape. See also Glaser (1155).

3367 Hendricks, Jon. *Institutionalization and Alternative Futures*. Farmingdale, N. Y.: Baywood Pub. Co., 1979.

With special reference to persons 75 years of age and older various authorities consider their maintenance in the community, the quality of institutional life, and the dilemmas of homes for the aged and retirement villages. References.

3368 Parkes, Colin M. "Home or Hospital? Terminal Care as Seen by Surviving Spouses." *Journal of the Royal College of General Practioners* 28 (1978): 19–30.

Terminally ill patients under age 65 were interviewed: 65 home-centered patients and 100 hospital centered patients. No hospice patients were included. Pain in the hospital-centered patients was not significantly reduced during the terminal period, while home-centered patients were more likely to remain mobile and in clear consciousness. However, home-centered patients experienced an increase in unrelieved pain. Suggestions were offered for the improvement of home-care programs.

3369 Pearson, Leonard, ed. *Death and Dying: Current Issues in the Treatment of the Dying Person.* Cleveland, Ohio.: The Press of Case Western Reserve University, 1969.

Thanatologists examine images of death, psychotherapy, hospice care, the family and awareness of dying. Extensive annotated bibliography. For annotations of chapters see Kastenbaum (2053), LeShan (3399), Saunders (3403), Kalish (3160), Strauss (5029), Pearson (8035).

3370 Rosenbaum, Ernest H. *Living with Cancer.* New York: Praeger, 1975.

A positive and humane description of living with terminal illness, based on eleven case histories of very different people with cancer.

3371 Sudnow, David. *Passing On: The Social Organization of Dying.* Englewood Cliffs, N. J.: Prentice-Hall, Inc., 1967.

A sociological study of death in a county hospital and its management by the staff; including counting of deaths and their visibility, social death, preparing and moving bodies, how we announce death and bad news, uses of a corpse.

3372 Zielinski, Helmut. "Religion und Sterbebegleitung auf der Station für Palliative Therapie in Köln." [Religion and the Attendants of the Dying at the Station for Palliative Therapy in Cologne.] In *Ars Moriendi. Erwägungen zur Kunst des Sterbens*, ed. by Harald Wagner. Freiburg, Germany: Herder, 1989.

Because of the prevalence in medicine of treating the hospital as an "organic repair shop," rather than as a place where people can die in dignity, the caretaker of the soul must work with the commission of spreading his own beliefs and experience of the Good News. Zielinski also discusses the differences between caring for the sick at home and in the hospital, the goals of the hospice movement, the Station for Palliative Therapy in Cologne, the influence of Elisabeth Kübler-Ross, and recognizing the needs of the soul. Further topics are the hope that faith gives, dismission of dying patients from the hospital, helping the dying to die (euthanasia), and mourning.

3.51 MEDICAL/NURSING SERVICES

3373 Adams, David W. *Childhood Malignancy: The Psychosocial Care of the Child and His Family.* Springfield, Ill.: C. C. Thomas, 1979.

A social worker combines a review of literature and clinical experience to demonstrate multidisciplinary care for dying children and family.

3374 Ajemian, Ina and Balfour Mount, eds. *The R. V. H. on Palliative/ Hospice Care: A Resource Book.* New York: Arno Press, 1980.

The realistic and relevant work of the Royal Vic Hospital, Montreal is described in its comprehensive in-patient, home-care and consultation services. Selections include bereavement follow-up, staff selection, stress and burn-out, volunteer selection, training. Considered by Simpson to be the best and most comprehensive resource (8039).

3375 Charles-Edwards, Allison. *The Nursing Care of the Dying Patient.* Beaconsfield, U. K.: Beaconsfield Pub., 1983.

Practical advice on general nursing care of the dying describes necessary skills and the use of equipment. The personal needs of the nursing staff are considered.

3376 Cotter, Z. M., Sr. "Institutional Care of the Terminally Ill." *Hospital Progress* 52 (1971): 42–48.

Institutional care of the dying can be strengthened by charismatic leadership and caring community.

3377 Doyle, D., ed. *Palliative Care: The Management of Far-Advanced Illness.* Beckenham, U. K.: Croom Helm, 1983.

Various medical and psychological specialists present techniques of pain and symptom control, therapy for specific diseases, ethical issues, palliative care. Topics include a variety of diseases other than cancer that are life-threatening.

3378 Garfield, Charles A. *Psychosocial Care of the Dying Patient.* New York: McGraw-Hill Book Co., 1978.

This introductory text for nursing and medical students is comprehensive, with brief articles by noted authorities who write with authenticity. The recurring theme is emotional accessibility as a major resource of professional personnel in the care of those who are suffering from life-threatening illness. To enhance this, the following issues are surveyed: general guidelines, the feelings of patients and family, the relationship of the doctor to the patient, the living-dying process, counsel for the family, ethical and medical issues, new programs such as hospice and cooperation of patients with physicians in administration of drugs such as the Brompton mixture, a proposed course on death and dying for medical students. Some bibliography for each chapter.

3379 Germain, Carol. *The Cancer Unit: an Ethnography.* Wakefield, Mass.: Nursing Resources, 1979.

See 3249.

3380 Gonda, Thomas and John Ruark. *Dying Dignified: The Health Professional's Guide to Care.* Reading, Mass.: Addison-Wesley, 1984.

See 3624.

3381 Benoliel, Jeannie Quint. *The Nurse and the Dying Patient.* New York: Macmillan Pub. Co. 1967.

Based on data from unstructured interviews with students and teachers in nursing schools, the author concludes that nurses soon learn that they cannot afford to lose their composure, not so much because of the effect it might have on the patient but because it would disrupt the nursing function. Avoidance and aloofness compensate for a lack of training in handling emotions concerning the dying. The author suggests an approach to the dying that would include meaningful death and the possibility of recovery, better communications between doctor and nurse, more specific teaching on communication and coordination of assignments so that no one caregiver is overwhelmed. See also Glaser and Strauss (1155, 3366).

3382 Robbins, Joy, ed. *Caring for the Dying Patient and the Family.* Lippencott Nursing Series. New York: Harper and Row, 1983.

The staff of St. Joseph's Hospital provide practical advice on assessment, symptom removal, physical care, communications, home care, special problems, religious beliefs and practices, staff needs, the "last offices." A reliable model of clinical care.

3383 Saunders, Cicely, ed. *The Management of Terminal Disease.* Chicago, Ill.: Yearbook Medical Publishers, 1978.

The management of cancer in a British hospice is the setting for these studies of the general philosophy of treatment, psychological aspects, pain relief, in-patient, out-patient and domiciliary management.

3384 Shneidman, Edwin. "Some Aspects of Psychotherapy with Dying Persons." In *Psychosocial Care of the Dying Patient*, ed. by Charles A. Garfield, 201–218. New York: McGraw-Hill Book Co., 1978.

The primary task of helping a dying person is to focus on the person. The author presents this theme in psychotherapy with dying persons as (1) the philosophical (moral-ethical-epistemological) aspects of the dying process; (2) the sociological (situational) aspects; and (3) the psychological (characterological) aspects. Nuances of special tasks with dying are listed.

3385 Simon, Nathan M., ed. *The Psychological Aspects of Intensive Care Nursing*. Bowie, Md.: Robert J. Bradie Co., 1980.

Nurses are advised on the assessment of patients in an intensive care unit, common syndromes and defenses that are observed, strategies for dealing with staff stress and specific treatment issues.

3386 Weisman, Avery D. "Misgivings and Misconceptions in the Psychiatric Care of Terminal Patients." In *Psychosocial Care of the Dying Patient,* ed. by Charles A. Garfield, 185–200. New York: McGraw-Hill Book Co., 1978.

A psychiatrist describes attitudes about death which may be held by experienced professionals, notes the presence of professional and personal despair of physicians in treating the dying, and illustrates misconceptions with a case study.

3.511 HOSPICE

3387 Abbott, John W., ed. *Hospice Resource Manual for Local Churches*. New York: Pilgrim Press, 1988.

Various professionals in the hospice movement provide a resource manual for study by church and community groups. The history and development of hospice care is detailed, with special attention to the role of the church. A biblical and theological basis for hospice is presented, along with a discussion of spiritual pain and strength, strategies for coping with loss and bereavement. Four models of hospice care are described: independent, hospital based, home health agency, community/coalition approach. Hospice quality and standards are presented from a consumer perspective. Reimbursement by the insurance companies and corporations is discussed, along with suggestions for the funding of a hospice. Annotated bibliography.

3388 Berrigan, Daniel. *We Die Before We Live: Talking With the Very Ill*. New York: Seabury Press, 1980.

The emotional impact of caregiving for the terminally ill is forcefully presented by a priest who is also a poet and a protester. Awareness of his own feelings and those of the persons to whom he ministered in a hospice setting will evoke compassion for and concern about the conditions under which people die.

3389 Corr, Charles A. and Donna M. Corr. "Situations Involving Children: A Challenge for the Hospice Movement." *Hospice Journal* 1 (1985): 63–77.

When a child is dying in a hospice, or when children are grieving for someone who is dying, the issues to be considered are: care, networking, interdisciplinary teamwork, coordination.

3390 Craven, J. and F. S. Wald. "Hospice Care of Dying Patients. *American Journal of Nursing* 75 (1975): 1816–1822.

A hospice centers upon the needs of the dying for relief from distressing symptoms, the security of a caring environment, sustained expert care and the assurance that they and their family will not be abandoned.

3391 Davidson, Glen W., ed. *The Hospice: Development and Administration*. Washington, D. C.: Hemisphere Pub. Co., 1978.

The development of hospital and home care aspects of the hospice movement are traced in articles by administrators in the United States and Canada: motivation and stress in staff, team training, evaluation research, spiritual support in hospice care as a continuing search for wholeness and dignity among patients, legal issues. Annotated bibliography, description of media resources.

3392 Du Bolay, Shirley. *Ciceley Saunders*. London: Hodder and Stoughton, 1984.

Dame Ciceley Saunders is presented in this popular biography not only as a pioneer in the development of the hospice movement, but also as a person who matured through both pain and romance to become a person of strong soul and professional strength.

3393 Franco, Vincent W. "Reverence for the Humanity of the Dying: The Hospice Prescription." *Journal of Pastoral Care* 36 (1982): 46–55.

A rationale is presented for hospice programs as an attempt to help dying patients in the spiritual quest for wholeness and dignity. The historic origins of the hospice movement are reviewed along with its philosophy and its adoption in North America.

3394 Hamilton, Michael P. and Helen F. Reid, eds. *A Hospice Handbook: A New Way to Care for the Dying*. Grand Rapids, Mich.: Wm. B. Eerdmans Pub. Co., 1980.

In a popular presentation that stresses the role of religion in care of the dying, hospice practitioners describe the needs of the dying, the practical aspects of hospice organization and the delivery of care during the terminal illness.

3395 International Work Group in Death, Dying and Bereavement. "Assumptions and Principles Underlying Standards for Terminal Care." *American Journal of Nursing*. 79 (1979): 296–297.

This influential report presented assumptions and principles for terminal care in general and for patient, family and staff-oriented practice.

3396 Irion, Paul E. *Hospice and Ministry*. Nashville, Tenn.: Abingdon Press, 1988.

From his work with sixty pastors who had ministered to parishioners as hospice patients, a professor of pastoral theology and pastoral care coordinator of a hospice discusses the way in which the church and the hospice work together to enhance care for the dying. Topics include the role of the pastor, working with the hospital/hospice staff, the relationship of pastoral theology to hospice philosophy, ministry to dying persons, the patients family, children and AIDS patients.

3397 Kübler-Ross, Elisabeth, and Josefino B. Mango. *Hospice: A Handbook for Families and Others Facing Terminal Illness*. Santa Fe, N.Mex.: Bear and Co., 1982.

The narration of patients' stories and the impressions of family and staff provide useful information on care of the dying and emphasize the resource of unconditional love. A final section answers questions on the establishment of a hospice.

3398 Kutscher, Austin H., *et al.*, eds. *Hospice U.S.A.* New York: Columbia University Press, 1983.

In short articles 34 thanatologists recommend a sense of dignity among the dying that is based upon the image of the self as spiritual and intellectually confident. This can provide motivation for caregivers as they assist people to maintain wholeness and control of the self in midst of pain and despair. Although these are lofty ideals, the editor and others show increasing realism in evaluating the exalted philosophy and great promises of early hospice experience and experimentation. A growing maturity of the hospice movement is reflected in the first articles on the past and present, followed by reflection on ethical and human issues in terminal care, relationships to the dying, the approaches of specific professions, specific illnesses. The "socialization" of the movement may also be seen in articles on alternatives to in-hospice care and medical education.

3399 LeShan, Lawrence. "Psychotherapy and the Dying Patient." In *Death and Dying*, ed. by Leonard Pearson, 28–48. Cleveland, Ohio: The Press of Case Western Reserve University, 1969.

Drawing upon 12 years experience with a wide variety of cancer patients, and much work as a psychotherapist, the author is concerned with the will to live in physically ill patients. A therapist must first come to terms with the philosophical issues of life and death, so that therapy will enrich life rather than block death due to inhibitions in the therapist. Acceptance of life means exploration of the inner nature of the self and its potential. Patients fight for life more because they wish to live than because they are afraid of death. This may require some discussion of faith as it is used by Paul Tillich as a state of being ultimately concerned about inner development. Basic to this arousal of faith is deep emotional contact between therapist and patients which emphasizes honesty rather than kindness. Patients can examine their own fear of death when the therapist is open to internal questions without fear. Look at the continuing process of inner expansion rather than the external accomplishments with which people usually reassure themselves. Then self-rejection is reduced and patients are more comfortable with feelings. References include a full listing of clinical articles by the author on the topic.

3400 Munley, Anne. *The Hospice Alternative.* New York: Basic Books, 1983.

The director of Apostolic Planning for the Congregation of the Immaculate Heart of Mary, describes her participation as a sociologist in the daily life of a hospice. From this experience she goes beyond the discrete stages of dying advocated by Kübler-Ross and unfolds a complex process of dying that is filled with contradictions and conflicting tensions. She also considers a hospice in the larger social context of community planning, economic and political future. Her discussion of spiritual support is insightful. A listing of hospice organizations, bibliography, notes.

3401 Paige, R. L. and J. F. Looney. "Hospice Care for the Adult." *American Journal of Nursing* 77 (1977): 1812–1815.

Clinical specialists for the hospice project of St. Luke's Hospital Center, New York City, describe the integration of a hospice team within a hospital medical center.

3402 Saunders, Cicely. *Care of the Dying*. Nursing Times reprint. London: Macmillan Pub. Co., 1959.

See 3147.

3403 Saunders, Cicely. "The Moment of Truth: Care of the Dying Person." In *Death and Dying*, ed. by Leonard Pearson, 49–78. Cleveland, Ohio: The Press of Case Western Reserve University, 1969.

The medical director of the influential St. Christopher's Hospice, London, describes her early work at St. Joseph's Hospice as centering upon how the patient is, rather than upon how doctors' thought the treatment is working. The emphasis upon "being" rather than "doing" led to a treatment distinction between the prolonging of living and the usually medical emphasis upon the prolonging of dying. The family was encouraged to fill the vacuum that often surround the patient in a medical facility. More than half of the patients not only knew that they were dying but talked about it with the physicians. An attempt is made to balance clarity in a patient's thought with a reduction of pain. Religion in this religiously oriented hospital is visualized as reaching out trustfully between patient and staff. We learn the care of the dying from the dying themselves.

3404 Saunders, Cicely. "Dying They Live: St. Christopher's Hospice." In *New Meanings of Death*, ed. by Herman Feifel. New York: McGraw-Hill Book Co., 1977.

St. Christopher's Hospice was founded in 1948 with a legacy of 500 pounds given by a man who, having escaped from the Warsaw ghetto, died of cancer in a busy surgical ward in London at the age of 40. The original motto was "I'll be a window in your home." The founding physician describes the growth of the facility, the meaning of hospitality, the expansion into homecare programs, the control of chronic pain through doctor-patient cooperation, the teaching program, the Christian philosophy of the hospice.

3405 Saunders, Cicely. "The Hospice: Its Meaning to Patients and their Physicians." *Hospital Practice* (June 1981): 93–108.

A pioneer in the hospice movement describes the role of the physician in the quality of the patient's remaining life rather than it's prolongation. The example of St. Christopher' Hospice in London is described.

3406 Stoddard, Sandol. *The Hospice Movement: A Better Way of Caring for the Dying*. New York: Random House, 1978.

One of the first comprehensive accounts of the hospice movement describes the history of the medieval hospice and the eventual merger with many functions into the modern hospital. The book is representative of issues faced in the emergence of varying types of hospices in the United States.

3407 Scott, S. "On the Spot Death Education Counseling." In *New Directions in Death Education and Counseling,* ed. by R. A. Pacholski and C. A. Carr., 6–13, Arlington, Va: Forum for Death Education and Counseling, 1981.

A hospice nurse describes the recognition of her limitations and the way she became more competent and confident through reading, listening to experts and most all from observations and discussions with patients and family.

3408 Walborn, Karen Ann. "A Nursing Model for the Hospice: Primary and Self-Care Nursing." *Nursing Clinics of North America* 15 (1980): 205–217.

Specific instructions are provided for nurses to enhance the ability of the patient to maintain control over life until death. Special characteristics of the nurse include an acceptance of the patient-family concept, effective functioning as a member of a multi-disciplinary team and recognizing others needs as separate from one's own.

3409 Zimmerman, Jack M. *Hospice: Complete Care for the Terminally Ill.* Baltimore: Urban and Schwarzenberg, 1981.

A text for a multi-disciplinary team that will develop a hospital-based hospice program. Emphasis is placed upon practical management of the terminally ill with illustrations from the Church Hospital Hospice Care Program, followed by questions of symptom control, emotional and psycho-social needs of the patients, management of the hospital team, organization, financing and staffing. Commonly asked questions about hospice care are then answered.

3410 Zorza, Victor, and Rosemary Zorza. *A Way to Die.* New York: Alfred A. Knopf, 1980.

Two competent writers narrate the last days of their 25 year old daughter in a hospice that brought them competence, hope and humanity. The horror and panic of operations, chemotherapy, radiation and medical misunderstanding were overcome in the quiet and competent atmosphere of Oxford University's hospice.

3.52 HOME CARE

3411 Abrams, Ruth D., Gertrude Jameson, Mary Pohlman and Sylvia Snyder. "Terminal Care in Cancer." *New England Medical Journal* 232 (1945): 719–724.

In a discussion of providing adequate terminal care, physicians consider family ability to care for the patient at home and the patient's wishes with respect to care at home.

3412 Blewett, L. J. "To Die at Home." *American Journal of Nursing* 70 (1970): 2602–2604.

Four inactive nurses assist a terminally ill patient to remain at home and spend her last few months with her family.

3413 Callari, Elizabeth S. *A Gentle Death: Personal Caregiving to the Terminally Ill.* Greensboro, N. C.: Tudor Pub., 1986.

Written from a nurse's perspective, the book is a personal testimony of practical strategies. Personal confrontation with death is combined with professional service.

3414 Dobihal, Edward F., Jr. "Talk or Terminal?" *Connecticut Medicine* 38 (1974): 364–369.

A chaplain who was instrumental in the development of hospice programs describes the planning and coordination of a patient-family unit care for the terminally ill.

3415 Evans, Jocelyn. *Living with a Man Who Is Dying.* New York: Taplinger Pub. Co., 1971.

See 3088.

3416 French, J. and D. R. Schwartz. "Terminal Care at Home in Two Cultures." *American Journal of Nursing* 73 (1973): 502–505.

The home care of a Navajo Indian and of a white woman are compared and contrasted.

3417 Lamerton, Richard. *Care of the Dying.* Westport, Conn.: Technomic Pub. Co., 1976.

An English medical officer has prepared a practical guide for the care of dying persons at home. Dignity and comfort are stressed. Many examples of care are given. Bibliography.

3418 Little, Deborah Whiting. *Home Care for the Dying*. Garden City, N. Y.: Dial Press, 1985.

On the basis of professional advice that the author received while caring for her dying grandmother, the author began preparation of a practical book for the non-professional on care of patients at home. A how-to-do-it book on hard choices to be made with love and understanding.

3419 Malkin, S. "Care of the Terminally Ill at Home." *Canadian Medical Association Journal* 115 (1976): 129–130.

Physical, emotional and psychological care of forty-seven terminally ill patients at home is described.

3420 Martinson, I. M., *et al.* "Home Care for the Child." *American Journal of Nursing* 77 (1977): 1815–1817.

The care at home of terminally ill children is discussed on the basis of work with 29 children.

3421 Rosenbaum, Ernest H., and Isadora R., eds. *Going Home: A Home-Care Program*. Palo Alto, Calif.: Bull Pub. Co., 1980.

A manual for the home-care of the cancer patient includes planning for the move home, impact on the family, activities and aids for daily living, precise care for bodily functions. Supplemented by video tapes.

3.6 MORAL AND PROFESSIONAL ISSUES

3422 Abrams, Natalie and Michael D. Buckner, eds. *Medical Ethics: A Clinical Textbook for the Healthcare Professions*. Cambridge, Mass.: MIT Press, 1983.

This collection of concepts and clinical practice includes sections on abortion, allocation of scarce resources, euthanasia, professional codes, and key legal cases.

3423 Ashley, Benedict M., Kevin D. O'Rourke. *Ethics of Healthcare*. St. Louis, Mo.: Catholic Health Association of the United States, 1986.

As a textbook for courses in medical ethics and for the general reader, the authors present a comprehensive study of spiritual ministry and health care which is based on the assumption that total health requires the balance and effective functioning of all human potentialities. The specific issues of death and dying are treated in chapters on human research and triage, sexuality and reproduction, suffering and death. Study questions and brief cases are provided for each chapter. Selected and annotated bibliography. Index. A readable overview of post-Vatican II teachings of the Roman Catholic church.

3424 Ashley, Benedict M. and Kevin D. O'Rourke. *Healthcare Ethics: A Theological Analysis.* 3rd ed. St. Louis, Mo.: Catholic Health Association of the United States, 1989.

Guided by statements of the U. S. Catholic Conference, two specialists in moral theology and ethics include an extensive section on suffering and death in their text. The response of healthcare professionals to suffering and death is reviewed and the phenomenon of the fear of death is considered from the viewpoint of Christian spirituality. Specific ethical decisions are discussed such as suicide, euthanasia and allowing to die. Extensive bibliography and index.

3425 Beauchamp, Tom L., and Seymour Berlin, eds. *Ethical Issues in Death and Dying.* Englewood Cliffs, N.J.: Prentice-Hall, 1978.

As professors in the Center for Bioethics, Georgetown University, the editors stress the importance of ethical judgments in treatment of the dying. Contributors to the book show the importance of critical analysis and ethical theory in the treatment of largely unresolved controversies on the definition and determination of death, suicide, rights of the dying patient, euthanasia and natural death, the significance of life and death. The reprinted articles range through medicine, law, morality, theology and literature. Textbook format with brief introduction to each issue, selected bibliography, general bibliographies and the *Encyclopedia of BioEthics* articles.

3426 Brodie, Howard. *Ethical Decisions in Medicine.* 2nd ed. Boston: Little, Brown and Co., 1981.

Key issues in ethics are discussed: including informed consent, determination of the quality of life, abortion, ethical participation in decisions by patient and staff, allocation of scarce resources, euthanasia—active and passive, terminal care. Organized for self-instruction.

3427 Childress, James F. *Who Should Decide? Paternalism in Health Care.* New York: Oxford University Press, 1982.

A professor of religious studies and medical education examines the metaphor of father as applied to health care professionals. Under what conditions should a paternalistic professional determine what a patient needs when this is not what the patient wants or is capable of judging? Theory and cases are combined in relation to telling the truth and disclosing information, suicide and suicide prevention, refusal of life-saving medical treatment, active euthanasia, prevention of early death. Notes at the end of each chapter.

3428 Dunstan, G. R. and E. A. Shinebourne, eds. *Doctors' Decisions: Ethical Conflicts in Medical Practice.* New York: Oxford University Press, 1989.

Practitioners in a wide variety of specialties describe the process of making ethical decisions in clinical practice. A moral philosopher, a Christian theologian and rabbinic scholar evaluate their practice.

3429 Fletcher, Joseph. *Morals and Medicine.* Boston: Beacon Press, 1954.

A professor of Christian ethics presents freedom of choice and knowledge of the things from which to choose as basic to human rights in life, health and death. Specific issues include: the right to know the truth, controlled parenthood, artificial insemination, sterilization, euthanasia. The book is written to assist physicians in medical decisions in the context of their professional expertness and concern for the unique quality of individuals in a particular social context. The writing is vivid and direct.

3430 Fox, Renee C. *Experiment Perilous: Physicians and Patients Facing the Unknown.* Philadelphia: University of Pennsylvania Press, 1974.

This contribution to medical sociology considers patients and doctors in a high-risk medical research ward who must face problems and stress together, and jointly confront death.

3431 Goldstein, D. M., and L. Walters, eds. *Bioethics: A Guide to Information Sources.* Detroit: Gale Research Co., 1982.

See 8018.

3432 Gruman, Gerald J. "Ethics of Death and Dying: Historical Perspective." *Omega* 9 (1978–79): 203–237.

3433 Haring, Bernard. *Medical Ethics.* Notre Dame, Ind.: Fides Pub., 1973.

A Roman Catholic moral theologian examines medical questions of life, death, health and disease as part of the sacredness of nature and wholeness of human personality in a social context. The writing is guided not only by official pronouncements of the Roman Catholic church but also by many references to scientific and ethical studies.

3434 Jakobovits, Immanuel. *Jewish Medical Ethics.* New York: Philosophical Library, 1959.

From ancient and modern Jewish sources, a rabbi quotes sources on the duty to save life, laws of mourning, attitudes to pain in humans and animals, the pain of death, informing patients on their deathbed, euthanasia, the dead and their treatment. Some references to Roman Catholic sources. Extensive bibliography.

3435 Kelly, Nathan F. *The Emergence of Roman Catholic Medical Ethics in North America: An Historical-Methodological-Bibliographical Study.* New York: E. Mellen Press, 1979.

The tradition of moral theology in Roman Catholicism is traced from before the twelfth century to the twentieth century. This is followed of the development of pastoral medicine, a specific instance of moral theology upon medical issues. The twentieth century designation of "medical ethics" as the successor to pastoral medicine is reviewed through works from the late 19th to the mid 20th century that guide the ethics of Roman Catholic medical personnel. Later chapters describe the theological methodology used in ethical decisions: double effect physicalism, ecclesiastical positivism. Extensive bibliography.

3436 Kluge, Eike-Henner W. *The Practice of Death.* New Haven, Conn.: Yale University Press, 1975.

A professor of philosophy opposes the new morality of indifference to moral judgments with a reasoned conviction that principles of absolute and intrinsic value are in the universe and our awareness. Traditional, psychological and ethical positions are presented in relation to abortion, suicide, euthanasia, infanticide, senicide. Although the author does not seek complete closure on these complex questions, he consistently upholds moral traditions above ethical relativism or utilitarianism.

3437 McCormick, Richard A. *Notes on Moral Theology, 1981–1984.* Lanham, Md.: University Press of America, 1985.

A Jesuit priest and professor of Christian ethics, Kennedy Institute for Bio-ethics at Georgetown University, addresses many current issues including divorce, preservation of life, sterilization and abortion. The annual is composed of articles from *Theological Studies*, and previous *Notes on Moral Theology* that were published for 1965–1980.

3438 Nelson, James Bruce. *Human Medicine: Ethical Perspectives on New Medical Issues.* Minneapolis, Minn.: Augsburg Pub. House, 1973.

A Protestant theological professor presents secular, Protestant and Roman Catholic views on abortion, artificial insemination, human experimentation, genetics, euthanasia and organ transplants. A reliable summary of varying viewpoints with documentation.

3439 O'Rourke, Kevin D. and Dennis Brodeur. *Medical Ethics: Common Ground for Understanding.* St. Louis, Mo.: Catholic Health Association of the United States, 1986.

Professors of canon law and moral theology provide essays for students and professors in courses on healthcare ethics. Written by Roman Catholics for a pluralistic community, the essays explore the functions that human persons have in common and the goals of medicine that are evident in the physician-patient relationship. They are organized into three sections: the physician as an ethicist in a pluralistic society, principles of medical ethics in relation to specific issues and prominent cases that have ethical questions.

3440 O'Rourke Kevin D. and Dennis Brodeur. *Medical Ethics: Common Ground for Understanding*. Vol. II. St. Louis, Mo.: Catholic Health Association of the United States, 1989.

In an attempt to serve a wide audience of healthcare professionals and interested persons from every occupation across the United States, professors of canon law and moral theology present and apply ethical principles to contemporary problems and issues arising from scientific research, medical practice, and health care delivery. Although their basic commitment is to the official teaching of the Roman Catholic church, the authors seek a logical and reasoned approach to ethical problems. A special emphasis of the volume is upon the equality of persons in the physician-patient relationship that will uphold the dignity and worth of each person. The more equalitarian and broadly based viewpoints of the authors in this 1989 volume are shown by the inclusion of a first chapter on "Medicine: Not an Exact Science," and later chapters on varieties of ethical systems and a presentation of two ethical approaches on human beings. These chapters were not in the 1986 edition, O'Rourke and Brodeur (3439).

3441 O'Rourke, Kevin D. and Philip Boyle. *Medical Ethics: Sources of Catholic Teachings*. St. Louis, Mo.: Catholic Health Association of the United States, 1989.

Professors of canon law and moral theology provide reasons for the official teaching of the Roman Catholic church for ethical problems which concern Catholic healthcare professionals. The discussions combine a judgment of conscience enlightened by faith with concern for the medical condition of patients. After presenting general teachings of the church about human persons in relation to issues of medical ethics, the authors discuss decisions of conscience from the viewpoint of particular actions which involve decisions by medical personnel. Most of the book presents excerpts from official statements by the Second Vatican Council or the Papal Magisterium on such specific issues as proxy consent, pain relief, organ donation, ordinary and extraordinary means to prolong life, withholding life support.

3442 Purtilo, R. B., and C. K. Cassel. *Ethical Dimensions in the Health Professions*. Philadelphia: W. B. Saunders, 1981.

A physical therapist and a physician provide an introductory text for nurses and other healthcare workers on moral aspects of professional duties. Major ethical issues are presented with an emphasis upon actions taken by varying professions and the existential quality of patient relationships. The book goes beyond the rather limited concerns of physicians which were represented by other texts. See Abrams and Buckner (3422), Brody (3120).

3443 Ramsey, Paul. *The Patient as Person: Explorations in Medical Ethics.* New Haven, Conn.: Yale University Press, 1970.

A professor of religion with special interest in medical ethics has provided insight into the quandary of physicians concerning such dilemmas as the meaning of consent in human experimentation, improving procedures for determining when a person has died, the limits upon caring for the dying, tissue and organ donation, choosing among patients to receive scarce and vital treatment. There are many references to legal decisions.

3444 Ramsey, Paul. *Ethics at the Edges of Life: Medical and Legal Intersections.* New Haven, Conn.: Yale University Press, 1978.

See 3613.

3445 Reich, Warren T., *et al.*, eds. *Encyclopedia of Bioethics.* 4 vols. New York: Free Press, 1978.

Contributors and advisors to the Kennedy Institute for Bioethics, Georgetown University, present philosophical and clinical studies on a wide range of controversial topics such as abortion, quality of life, suicide and truth-telling.

3446 Shotter, Edward, ed. *Matters Of Life And Death.* London: Darton, Longman and Todd, 1970.

With the support of the Bishop of Durham the London Medical Group developed interdisciplinary discussion of medico-moral questions: moral differences in medical decisions concerning inevitable vs. unexpected threat of death (Francis Camps); the nature and management of terminal pain (Cicley Saunders); the promotion of an identity among the dying of a personality that will have the equanimity of Christ before death (J. Dominian); the factors which influence reactions to loss among widows (C. Murray Parkes); the moral imperative for organ transplant donors (R.Y. Calme, W. J. Dempster). Support for the discussions of these physicians in the area of morality and religion are provided in a final essay by a professor of Moral and Social Theology (G. R. Dunstan).

3447 Simmons, Paul D. *Birth and Death: Bioethical Decision-Making.* Philadelphia: Westminster Press, 1983.

A professor of Christian ethics draws upon historical and contemporary resources in religion, philosophy, law and ethics to discuss abortion, euthanasia, biotechnical parenting and genetics. Many references to biblical and theological sources. Especially valuable for those who are willing to see how religious resources, including the Bible are used by disputants on both sides of complex medical and ethical issues of modern life. For example, the biblical perspective on the meaning of personhood focuses on concrete instances of people rather than abstractions like conception or substances that may be infused at conception or during gestation. There is no biological definition of personhood in the Bible. "The Bible holds open the possibility, therefore, that abortion may be consistent with the will of God" (95).

3448 Steinfels, Peter and Robert M. Veatch, eds. *Death Inside Out.* Hastings Center Report. New York: Harper and Row, 1975.

See 2066.

3449 Thompson, Ian, ed. *Dilemmas of Dying: A Study in the Ethics of Terminal Care.* Edinburg: Edinburg University Press, 1979.

After two years of discussion, a working group of health care professionals provides a practical statement of issues on professional involvement with the dying and the bereaved. Case studies consider: intervention, patients' rights, including the right to die, conscience and professional duty, inter-professional decision-making, where to draw the limits in the personal and professional drain of caring for the bereaved, recommendations for death education and professional training in the caring of the dying and bereaved. Suggested readings for each topic and a selected bibliography.

3450 Veatch, Robert M. *Death, Dying and the Biological Revolution: Our Last Quest for Responsibility.* New Haven, Conn.: Yale University Press, 1976.

A director of the Death and Dying Group of the Kennedy Institute of Society, Ethics and the Life-Sciences was stimulated by the Karen Quinlan case to begin philosophical and theological reflections upon the maze of technical, medical and legal facts that have surfaced around the following issues: Is death moral?; Is the concept of death rooted in a philosophical analysis of the nature of persons and the locus of death located in the anatomy and physiology of the human body?; How do we choose not to prolong dying?; If competent persons may refuse medical treatment, what are the conditions under which guardians may refuse treatment for the incompetent?; What about public policy?; What do surveys show that patients want to know about the truth?; Is there a responsible treatment of mortal remains or organ transplants?; What distinctions need to be made for public policy concerning natural death? Bibliography. See also Veatch (3501).

3451 Weir, Robert F. *Ethical Issues in Death and Dying.* New York: Columbia University Press, 1977.

Practitioners in the life-sciences, law, medicine, philosophy and religion intend to reduce the fear and fascination of many professionals in the discussion of death and dying and to increase the interface of medicine, law and ethics. Reprints of varying quality are organized under the headings of truth-telling, determining death, allowing to die, euthanasia and suicide.

3452 Williams, Robert H. "Our Role in the Generation, Modification and Termination of Life." *Archives of Internal Medicine* 124 (1969): 215–236.

A physician discusses medical-ethical questions concerning the amount and type of life that should be generated, the extent to which life should be modified, and the extent of efforts in prolonging life. Results of a questionnaire to physicians on some of these issues are included.

3.61 TELLING THE TRUTH

3453 Aitken-Swan, Jean and E. C. Easson. "Reactions of Cancer Patients on Being Told their Diagnosis." *British Medical Journal* 1 (1959): 779–783.

When 231 selected cancer were told of their diagnosis, only 7% of the patients disapproved of being told.

3454 Carey, Raymond G. and Emil J. Posavac. "Attitudes of Physicians on Disclosing Information to and Maintaining Life for Terminal Patients." *Omega,* 9 (1978–79): 67–76.

Four parallel surveys compared physicians with nurses and hospital chaplains and a non-hospital sample of college students on attitudes toward informing terminal patients of their condition and toward active and passive euthanasia. The hypothesis was confirmed that apparent contradiction on recent reports on the attitudes of physicians may be due to shift toward more openness with terminal patients on the part of physicians over the last decade. 87% of physicians in the survey felt that patients "have an unqualified right to know the truth if they request the information." With respect to sustaining life in terminal patients, there was almost unanimous support for passive euthanasia among all four groups of respondents. However, active euthanasia received majority approval only from student nurses and college students.

3455 Christ, A. E. "Attitudes Toward Death Among of Acute Geriatric Psychiatric Patients." *Journal of Gerontology* 16 (1961): 56–59.

Although patients are often fearful of death, they are usually willing and relieved to discuss it. A physician should broach the topic of death with a terminal patient.

3456 Eissler, K. R. *The Psychiatrist and the Dying Patient.* New York: International Universities Press, 1955.

A psychoanalyst is in general agreement with Freud's concepts of the death instinct and the repetition compulsion. Freud believed that death in the form of a death instinct becomes a force which dominates life and the goal of all life is discovered in death. This was the thesis of *Beyond the Pleasure Principle* (1181). In the author's psychoanalytic practice, a fear of death was seen as a force for self-preservation that wards off ego destruction. One purpose of psychoanalysis is to aid a patient to recognize the reality of death as a natural event. This is the process of "ortho-thanatasia". To do this, the illusion of eternal life must be destroyed. The author's theory is in marked conflict with the third of his extensive case studies in which a widow proved to be "a woman of good judgment" in business matters and also courageous in facing and recovering from serious surgery. A malignancy discovered during surgery was not reported to her. When she asked the author for the truth about her condition, he concealed the true nature of her disease upon the assumption that she would have become psychotic if the truth were revealed. The author wished to maintain the "illusion of her recovery" despite knowledge that she postponed financial aid to relatives because she thought that she would live longer. Fear of death functions for human self preservation and is a derivative of other fears such as those of bodily and ego annihilation. Ego destruction is a function of a human ability to sense futurity. See also Zilboorg (1200).

3457 Hinton, John M. "Problems in the Care of the Dying." *Journal of Chronic Disease* 17 (1964): 201–205.

The author summarizes studies in which an encouragement of awareness between physician and dying patient was more effective than alternative approaches to communication during dying.

3458 Kelly, W. D. and S. R. Freisen. "Do Cancer Patients Want to Be Told." *Surgery* 27 (1950): 822–26.

The great majority of one hundred patients with known cancer and one hundred patients without known cancer told physicians that they wanted to be told about the presence of cancer.

3459 Reeves, Robert B., Jr. "To Tell or Not to Tell the Patient." In *Death and Bereavement,* ed. by Austin H. Kutscher, 5–9. Springfield, Ill: Charles C. Thomas, 1969.

A Protestant chaplain is less concerned about the problem of telling the truth when a patient does not want to hear and more concerned about those who withhold the truth when the patient is ready to hear it. His assumption is that most patients know that they are dying, so emphasis should be placed upon the removal of anxiety that blocks communication in staff or family.

3460 Ullman, Marcia A. "Determination: The Final Developmental Task." *Clinical-Gerontolist.* 4, 4 (1986): 50–53.

A therapist can assist the final discussion of feelings about death between a parent who is dying and a child by encouraging reminiscences and passing on the family history, experiencing anticipatory grief and talking about the child's accomplishments.

3461 Veatch, Robert M. *Case Studies in Medical Ethics.* Cambridge, Mass.: Harvard University Press, 1977.

A professor of medical ethics at the Kennedy Institute of Society, Ethics and Life Sciences, Georgetown University, provides guidelines that will identify ethical issues in medicine and emphasize the most important element which is the person who is responsible for a decision. Case studies are used to illustrate these principles as they apply to current problem areas in ethics and medicine. In a chapter on "Truth-Telling" the author affirms a positive response by medical personnel to a request for information from a patient. Difficulties are discussed in relation to specific cases. There are no specific references to theology or philosophy in the discussion of these cases. See also Veatch (3501).

3462 Waxenberg, S. D. "The Importance of the Communication of Feelings About Cancer." *Annals of the New York Academy of Science* 125 (1966): 1000–1005.

Although professionals differ among themselves concerning what the terminally cancer patient should be told, it appears from samplings that the large majority of physicians do not tell their patients, while the large majority of the cancer patients and their families wish to be told.

3.62 EUTHANASIA

3463 Behnke, John A., and Sissela Bok, eds. *The Dilemmas of Euthanasia.* Garden City, N.Y.: Doubleday, 1975.

Editors of the journal *BioScience* bring together the articles of physicians, lawyers and sociologists who seek to arrive at a common definition of euthanasia and to present historical and contemporary professional opinions that will aid in problem-solving in medical practice and legal determinations. The definition of irreversible coma by the Ad Hoc

Committee of the Harvard Medical School to Examine the Definition of Brain-Death (4486) is included.

3464 Church of England. Board of Social Responsibility. *On Dying Well.* London: Church Information Office, 1975.

The medical director of St. Christopher's hospice, other physicians, moral and pastoral theologians, a lawyer and the chairperson of the Institute on Religion and Medicine conclude that when adequate medical care is not available, mercy killing may be morally justified. The Working Party did not believe that this could be made into law, for this would produce greater evils than it would remove. Statistics on use of diamorphine to relieve pain in terminal illness. Brief bibliography.

3465 Downing, A. B., ed. *Euthanasia and the Right to Die.* New York: Humanities Press, 1969.

The case for voluntary euthanasia is presented as the right of an individual to choose a merciful release through death. The symposium was stimulated by a bill introduced into the House of Lords for the legalization of voluntary euthanasia. Contributions include chapters by chairpersons of the Euthanasia Society of Britain, lawyers, ethicists (Joseph Fletcher), philosophers (Anthony Flew), physicians and the Dean of St. Paul's, London.

3466 Eliot, Thomas D. "Attitudes Toward Euthanasia." *Research Studies, State College of Washington* 15 (1947): 131–134.

In a study of attempts to legalize euthanasia in 1947, 46.1% of a small sample expressed willingness to permit a physician to hasten death, 45% were unwilling. 68.3% said they would not aggressively object to legalize euthanasia. 31.1% would object.

3467 Fletcher, Joseph. *Morals and Medicine.* Boston: Beacon Press, 1954.

A theological professor challenges the idea that physiological life is sacred and is to be preserved at all costs. Consciousness of self and personal qualities of freedom are to be preserved during dying in order that a person may continue a human existence. The termination of life support systems for the terminally ill may be a good and moral choice in many instances.

3468 Group for the Advancement of Psychiatry. *The Right to Die: Decision and Decision-Makers.* New York: Jason Aronson, 1974.

Contributions to a better psychological understanding of death and death-related behavior are made by various contributors with different viewpoints. For example, Jack Weinberg argues that the imposition of life upon an individual who does not wish it is possible only when we assume a commitment to improve the quality of that individual's life. Montague Ullman notes the inconsistency of states that make exceptions to the sanctity of life principle in war, capital punishment and abortion but not in relation to the end of rational existence.

3469 Gruman, Gerald J. "An Historical Introduction to Ideas About Voluntary Euthanasia: With a Bibliographic Survey and Guide Survey for Interdisciplinary Studies." *Omega* 4 (1973): 87–138.

Voluntary euthanasia is defined in relation to "transcendent values and a concept of self-death." Attitudes and beliefs are traced from the Renaissance to the 20th century. Notes and guide for interdisciplinary studies. Bibliography.

3470 Gula, Richard M. *What Are They Saying About Euthanasia?* Mahwah, N. J.: Paulist Press, 1986.

A professor of moral theology considers various viewpoints on euthanasia in chapters on the determination of death, the moral issues and positions of Catholics and Protestants on euthanasia, caring for the dying, and the moral art of terminal care. Includes the declaration on euthanasia by the Vatican Congregation for the Doctrine of the Faith, June 26, 1980. Notes and selected readings.

3471 Heifetz, Milton and Charles Mangel. *The Right to Die*. New York: G. P. Putnam and Sons, 1975.

With many case studies, a physician concludes that "appropriate medication" could be supplied by physicians to patients who wish to die after long and painful illness. No law should be passed to legalize euthanasia. The Living Will and the rights of patients to determine style and time of death are vigorously presented.

3472 Hendin, David. *Death as Fact of Life*. New York: W. W. Norton Co., 1973.

In a comprehensive view of death the author provides arguments for and against the legalization of euthanasia. The criteria by which death is ascertained is expanded beyond legal definitions to encompass unique circumstances. The author discusses the role of the dying patient, the manner in which doctors deal with terminal patients and their reasons for withholding or disclosing knowledge of patients' conditions.

3473 Horan, Dennis J., and David Mall, eds. *Death, Dying and Euthanasia*. Washington, D. C.: University Publications of America, 1977.

In this voluminous approach to the value judgments that should be formed about death in relation to modern medical practice, physicians, theologians, ethicists, sociologists, lawyers consider the following issues: when does death occur and how do we define it?; what about involuntary euthanasia of the defective newborn?; ethical, religious and moral aspects of euthanasia including Paul Ramsey's indignant article on the indignity of death with dignity (3629); the legal aspects of "mercy killing," humane medicine and a concerned society in treatment of the dying; legal aspects of euthanasia; suicide and the patient's right to reject medical treatment. Some chapters are full of footnotes and others are full of practical advice.

3474 Humphrey, Derek and Ann Wickett. *The Right to Die: Understanding Euthanasia*. New York: Harper and Row, 1986.

Co-founders of the Hemlock Society in Los Angeles explore the historical, cultural and legal background of "mercy killing" and discuss such specifics as the handicapped, the right-to-life viewpoint, hospice, technology, health cost, constitutional rights and religion. Appendices on films and organizations dealing with death. Notes and bibliography.

3475 Humphrey, Derek and Ann Wickett. *Jean's Way: A Love Story*. New York: Quartet Books, 1978.

A founder of the Hemlock Society and his second wife narrate the progressive physical deterioration of his first wife, the willingness of the husband to administer a fatal drug upon the request of the wife, and his reactions to her death. The book was published to tell a very human story and also demonstrate a moral obligation that transcended existing laws against euthanasia. The bereavement and recovery of the husband is retold as the chapter on "Derek" in Campbell and Silverman (4200)

3476 Jorgenson, David E. and Ron C. Neubecker. "Euthanasia: A National Survey of Attitudes toward Voluntary Termination of Life." *Omega* 11 (1980–81): 281–292.

From the 1977 National Opinion Research Center General Survey, the authors found that favorable attitudes toward suicide correlated with favorable attitudes toward euthanasia. Religiosity and other religious indicators were negatively associated with pro-euthanasia attitudes. Whites and males were more favorable toward euthanasia than Blacks and females.

3477 Kohl, Marvin. *The Morality of Killing: Sanctity of Life, Abortion and Euthanasia*. New York: Humanities Press, 1974.

A theory of moral killing is developed with the tools of abstract logic and linguistic analysis. The principle of self-defense is related to the sanctity of life principle. It is possible for euthanasia to be a kind act and therefore to be moral.

3478 Kohl, Marvin, ed. *Beneficent Euthanasia.* Buffalo, N.Y.: Prometheus Books, 1975.

As a foundation for debates about the legalization of beneficent euthanasia, philosophers, psychiatrists, physicians, Roman Catholic, Protestant and Jewish clergy discuss such basic issues as the nature of the prohibition against killing, the requirements of human dignity, the problems of consent and the extent of obligation. Bibliography or notes with each chapter and annotated bibliography.

3479 Koop, C. Everett. *The Right to Live, the Right to Die.* Wheaton, Ill.: Tyndale House Pub., 1976.

A physician and well-known speaker in conservative Christian colleges (and later Surgeon-General of the United States) writes out of his experience in the surgical care of children and as an evangelical Christian against any liberalization of abortion laws. This is the "right to live." The "right to die" is illustrated in the case of Karen Quinlan. He concludes as a Christian that medical experience with the dying would never allow him to take deliberate action with the motive of terminating a patient's life, but he might withhold treatment that could be considered extraordinary or heroic because the quality of the life in the patient would not be enhanced by such measures.

3480 Ladd, John, ed. *Ethical Issues Relating to Life and Death.* New York: Oxford University Press, 1979.

Professors of philosophy and one physician present papers on euthanasia including the article of James Rachaels which appeared in the *New England Journal of Medicine* (9 January 1975, 78–80). Notes at the end of each chapter.

3481 Larue, Gerald A. *Euthanasia and Religion: Survey of the Attitudes of World Religions to the Right to Die.* Los Angeles: The Hemlock Society, 1985.

A professor of biblical history who is also a therapist for those who suffer loss summarizes the opinions of almost 30 religious groups on euthanasia for the terminally ill. Based on answers to a questionnaire. Bibliography.

3482 Lynn, Joanne, ed. *By No Extraordinary Means: The Choice to Forego Life-Sustaining Food and Water.* Bloomington, Ind.: Indiana University Press, 1989.

A distinguished assembly of jurists, physicians, ethicists were assembled on the President's Commission for the Study of Ethical Problems in Medicine and Biomedical and Behavioral Research. Four problems were addressed in the papers which they presented as a foundation for this volume: Is it murder assisting suicide to withhold nutrition and hydration from a terminal patient? What empirical data is there about the effects on patients of not using artificial feeding techniques? How are guidelines applied by the average decision-maker? Will a decision not to feed patients lead to decay in our moral life? Papers considered the issues, the formulation of a moral response, perspectives on the law, the considerations of particular populations and a case study (of Claire C. Conroy). Notes to each chapter and selected bibliography.

3483 Malcolm, Andrew H. *This Far and No More.* New York: Penguin, 1989.

See 3214.

3484 Maguire, Daniel C. *Death By Choice.* Garden City, N. Y.: Doubleday and Co., 1974.

A Marquette University professor of moral theology presents arguments in defense of the morality of abortion and mercy death under certain circumstances. The Spanish translation of this book received an *Imprimatur* from the Roman Catholic church. The author gives special attention to the unique experience of a pregnant woman who is considering abortion and some of the male-related socio-economic causes of unwanted pregnancies. The plain presentation of wisdom by the author is a challenge for liberal Catholic colleagues to recognize the moral revolution in health-care and to establish questions that the "right wing of the church should answer."

3485 Melton, J. Gordon. *The Churches Speak On: Abortion.* Detroit, Mich.: Gale Research, 1989.

After a brief historical essay on the abortion debate, official pronouncements of North American religious bodies and ecumenical organizations are documented. Index to religious organizations.

3486 Munk, William. *Euthanasia or Medical Treatment in Aid of an Easy Death.* London: Longmans, Green, and Co., 1887. Reprint. New York: Arno Press, 1977.

A nineteenth century physician reflects upon his clinical management of dying persons with remarks upon the phenomena of death, the symptoms and modes of dying and the medical management of the dying, including the "trustworthy remedy in opium and nutrition." Emphasis is upon the usual peacefulness of death. No reference to active euthanasia as it is known in the twentieth century.

3487 Nagi, Mostafa H., Neil G. Lazerine and Meredith D. Pugh. "Attitudes of Catholics and Protestant Clergy toward Euthanasia." *Omega*

8 (1977–1978): 153–163. *Journal of Religion and Health* 20 (1981): 186–200.

A sociologist conducted a random sample of Cleveland clergy and found that Protestant clergy more than Catholic clergy were substantially in favor of disclosure of terminal illness, allowing an easy death for the terminal patient upon request and facilitating the role of the physicians in cases of terminal illness. Fundamentalist Protestant were less approving than liberal Protestants.

3488 Oden, Thomas C. *Should Treatment Be Terminated?* New York: Harper and Row, 1976.

A theologian with much interest in pastoral work and psychotherapy has summarized the best of arguments for and against termination of treatment and has rejected the excess of both. Useful guidelines are provided with an emphasis upon the application of theology and ethics to the needs of an individual and family. The author believes that "mercy killing" robs a suffering person of "profound learning possibilities".

3489 Pohier, Jacquer, and Detmar Mieth. *Suicide and the Right to Die.* Consilium #179. Edinburg: T. and T. Clark, 1985.

Physicians, philosophers, ethicists, theologians and sociologists present papers on suicide, problems raised by the medical and hospital context of death in Western countries, the right of the terminally ill to die with dignity. The viewpoint is primarily that of Roman Catholic moral theology.

3490 Portwood, Doris. *Common-sense Suicide.* New York: Dodd-Mead and Co., 1978.

Rational suicide for the elderly and ailing is proposed along with an urging toward legislation for active euthanasia.

3491 Preston, Caroline and John Horton. "Attitudes among Clergy and Lawyers toward Euthanasia." *Journal of Pastoral Care* 26 (1972): 108–115.

Questionnaires returned in Seattle by 100 ministers and 104 lawyers provided 9 to 1 support for negative euthanasia and for decisions made by patients about pain medication regime and decisions concerning autopsy/ transplant procedures after death. Lawyers were evenly divided concerning positive euthanasia whereas fewer ministers supported positive euthanasia.

3492 Rachles, James. *The End of Life: Euthanasia and Morality.* New York: Oxford University Press, 1986.

A professor of philosophy examines arguments for and against euthanasia, and offers an alternative to traditional views. He defends the belief that there is a profound difference having a life and merely being alive.

3493 *Report on Euthanasia, with Guiding Principles.* St. Louis, Mo.: The Lutheran Church–Missouri Synod, 1979.

A Commission on Theology and Church Relations of the Lutheran Church–Missouri Synod presents the thinking of theologians, ethicists and medical experts. Euthanasia is condemned as a deliberate acceleration of death contrary to God's gift of life to humanity, but extraordinary means need not be used to prolong the existence of the dying.

3494 Russell, O. Ruth. *Freedom to Die: Moral and Legal Aspects of Euthanasia.* Rev. ed. New York: Human Sciences Press, 1977.

A professor of pediatrics at John Hopkins Hospital reviews the increased attention to and sympathy with freedom to die as demonstrated in professional interdisciplinary conferences and public opinion polls. A thorough historical review is given to thought and action on euthanasia from before 1930 through 1974 including the celebrated cases of Quinlan, van Dusen and Haemmerli. Arguments and proposals for the legalization of euthanasia are discussed. Appendices include legislative proposals, extensive bibliography, cases in court. Euthanasia societies are described. Bibliography.

3495 Schwartzenberg, L. and P. Viansson-Ponte. *Changer la Mort.* Paris: Albin-Michel, 1977.

A professor of oncology and a journalist review French views of euthanasia and report some cases of active euthanasia.

3496 Spring, Beth and Ed Larson. *Euthanasia: Spiritual, Medical and Legal Issues in Terminal Health Care.* Portland, Oreg.: Multnomah Press, 1988.

Short case studies present the difficult care decisions that one faces at the end of life. This if followed by a review of the euthanasia debate with special emphasis upon Christian perspectives. A conservative response to the euthanasia debate.

3497 Sullivan, Joseph V. *The Morality of Mercy Killing.* Westminster, Md.: Newman Press, 1950.

The author gives definitions of natural, moral, therapeutic and merciful euthanasia and a history of the subject. The Roman Catholic position on euthanasia is presented—God's law is absolute and euthanasia is forbidden. The work concludes with a discussion of the Roman Catholic philosophy of suffering and it's relation to painful death.

3498 Thielicke, Helmut. *Living With Death.* Trans. by Geoffrey Bromiley. Grand Rapids, Mich.: Wm. B. Eerdmans Pub. Co., 1983.

As part of his discussion of death (Thielicke 2146), a German theologian argues that the right to die is a function of the dignity of life which God has given to us. He suggests the term "orthothanatasia," right-dying. Human dignity is located in the human personality rather than in biology.

3499 Tooley, Michael. *Abortion and Infanticide.* London: Oxford University Press, 1983.

This interdisciplinary survey encompasses historical, philosophical, moral and anthropological approaches to abortion and infanticide.

3500 Trowell, Hugh. *The Unfinished Debate on Euthanasia.* London: SCM Press, 1973.

A special panel of the British Medical Association held meetings for a year to discuss various aspects of euthanasia and presented a report which is an appendix to this volume. The report rejected euthanasia as a part of medical practice. An additional appendix, written by the Voluntary Euthanasia Society, challenges this opinion. The Voluntary Euthanasia Bill, presented to Parliament in 1969 is another appendix. The book also includes a summary of materials used by the committee such as the history of suicide and euthanasia, legal, ethical, medical, psychological aspects of euthanasia, followed by principles of voluntary euthanasia, which is defined as a request to the patient's doctor for suicidal facilities, possibly including lethal tablets or injections supplied by the physician. This is rejected by the author who is an Anglican priest.

3501 Veatch, Robert M. *A Theory of Medical Ethics.* New York: Basic Books, 1981.

In a general text on medical ethics that draws on the traditions of religion and philosophy, a professor at the Kennedy Institute, Georgetown University favors a social contract among equals. Historic principles of doctor-patient relations are assessed. Specific moral problems are considered: warning a potential murder victim, breaking confidentiality, high-risk health planning, homosexual husband, research on human placentas, active killing with parental consent, justice versus efficiency, medical means to execute prisoners. The author consistently upholds the sacredness of human life and rejects "merciful killing." See also Veatch (3450).

3502 Walton, Douglas N. *Ethics of Withdrawal of Life-Support Systems.* Westport, Conn.: Greenwood Press, 1983.

From the viewpoint of an intensive care unit in a modern hospital, the author offers a plain summary of dialectical reasoning as the theory of choice in a pluralistic society. Recent cases of withdrawal treatment in an intensive care unit are then reviewed. The next chapters review cases and principles where moral decisions are made to stop heroic treatments. This is followed by an analysis of the decision-making process. Written for a reflective person who has no medical or philosophical background. Bibliography.

3503 Wennberg, Robert N. *Terminal Choices: Euthanasia, Suicide and the Right to Die.* Grand Rapids, Mich.: Wm. B. Eerdmans Pub. Co., 1989.

A professor of philosophy relates medical questions to theological issues such as the providence of God in decisions about dying and the conscience of a Christian in contemplation of suicide. Greco-Roman attitudes, the Bible, Jewish traditions and Christian theologians such as Augustine and Aquinas are reviewed. The emphasis is pro-active: what should the *patient* do or have done. Written from the "evangelical Protestant" tradition.

3504 Wertenbaker, Lael T. *Death of a Man.* Boston: Beacon Press, 1974.

A wife describes the last sixty days of her husband as honest, realistic and sharing. There was competent professional assistance. The husband sought to commit suicide three times during these sixty days. Strong sedatives brought no more than temporary slumber. When he is finally able to slash his wrists and bleed to death, his wife holds him upright and gives him additional morphine to insure a painless death.

3505 Wilson, Jerry B. *Death By Decision.* Philadelphia: Westminster Press, 1975.

A professor of philosophy examines medical, moral and legal dilemmas of euthanasia. Principle arguments of Catholic and Protestant theologians are summarized and five principles are offered to support the practice of euthanasia.

3.63 SUICIDE

3506 Al-Najjar, Sheikh Yusuf. "Suicide and Islamic Law." *Mental Health and Society* 3 (1976): 137–141.

Suicide is a criminal act whenever a person willfully injures self in order to avoid the problems and dangers of life. The individual is guilty of wrecking an edifice constructed by God. It is not criminal to die before an enemy can extract secrets from a prisoner or as a martyr. For those in a hopeless impasse, suicide is forgiven and eternal fire is averted.

3507 Alvarez, Alfred. *The Savage God: A Study of Suicide.* New York: Random House, 1972.

A poet and critic tried suicide and found no justification for death or synoptic vision of life. Instead, the result was years of psychological darkness. Then he studied the memoir of Sylvia Plath, a gifted writer who was a suicide. He then examines literary presentations of suicide and finds them to be fallacies that try to devalue an act that cannot be denied or reversed. There are detailed discussion of Dante in the Middle Ages, John Donne in the Renaissance, William Cowper, Thomas Chatterton in the Age of Reason, the agonies of the Romantics and the bleak tomorrow of Dostoevsky. The modern period reveals so many deaths of artists by suicide that the author considers it to be the savage god of a chaotic age. He concludes that suicide is neither a disease nor a mortal sin. It is a terrible but utterly natural reaction to strain, narrow, unnatural necessities we sometimes create for ourselves. It is no longer an option for him. He must live. Notes.

3508 Aquinas, Thomas. *St. Thomas Aquinas' Summa Theologica*. Vol. 2. New York: Benzinger Brothers, 1947.

An influential medieval theologian affirmed the earlier teaching of Augustine (3509) and offered three arguments against suicide: suicide is contrary to the inclination of nature and is therefore a mortal sin, voluntary death will injure the community of which a person is a part, killing of the self usurps the prerogative of God to announce sentence of death and life. All suicide is morally dangerous since no time is left to expiate it by repentance. No repentance means no pardon. A modern philosopher Jacques Choron argues that this severe judgment is mitigated by the Roman Catholic doctrine of purgatory which gives the suicide some chance of entering heaven after much punishment. See also Choron (3517).

3509 Augustine. *The City of God*. Trans. by M. Dods. New York: Random House, 1950

An early Christian theologian who was influential upon medieval theologians presented suicide as murder, "for those who die by their hand have no better life after death." His advice that life is a better choice was widely accepted in the medieval church and reaffirmed by the most comprehensive philosopher-theologian of the medieval period, Thomas Aquinas (3508)

3510 Baechler, Jean. *Suicides*. New York: Basic Books, 1979.

In an attempt to find answers to the reasons for suicide, the author proposes answers that are more individual than social: escapist, aggressive, oblative (sacrifice), ludic (a dangerous game). A reflective exploration of the way in which we perceive ourselves and death.

3511 Battin, M. P. and R. W. Maris, eds. *Suicide and Ethics*. New York: Human Sciences Press, 1983.

Philosophers review the views of others on suicide, present their own theories and evaluate the contemporary philosophical literature on suicide.

3512 Bayet, Albert. *Le Suicide et la Morale*. 1922. Reprint. Salem, N.H.: Ayer Co. Pub., 1976.

French attitudes toward suicide are studied by a sociologist in the tradition of Durkheim (3527).

3513 Beck, Robert N. and John B. Orr. *Ethical Choice, A Case Study Approach*. New York: The Free Press, 1970.

In a section of the book on studies in individual ethics, the authors present a brief discussion of suicide and then present excerpts from the thoughts of Seneca, William James, Albert Camus.

3514 Bonhoeffer, Dietrich. *Ethics*. New York: Macmillan Pub. Co., 1955.

A German theologian who was martyred by the Nazi's evaluates the traditional doctrine of suicide as an unforgivable sin. Suicide is a specifically human act because it issues out of the freedom which human beings possess. Although suicide is wrong, it is not decided in terms of human morality but only in terms of faith in God. From this perspective, suicide is the freedom of a human person to act in self-justification over and against God. Despair becomes the occasion for this act of self-justification to take place. This is sin, but it does not condemn us to hell for many Christians have died without repenting of their sins. To single out suicide for special condemnation is to grant too much importance to the last moment of life.

3515 Cain, Albert C., ed. *Survivors of Suicide*. Springfield, Ill: Charles C. Thomas, 1972.

Family considerations for those who survive suicide are considered by a variety of clinicians under the categories of early recognition of potential suicide because of history of suicide in families, studies of the disturbed reactions of children to the suicide of a parent, various procedures who must survive the impact of suicide, and several case studies.

3516 Camus, Albert. *The Myth of Sisyphus and Other Essays*. New York: Vintage Books, 1955.

A French philosopher who was often impressed with the absurdity of life considers suicide to be a pivotal philosophical issue for it confronts us with the worth of life.

3517 Choron, Jacques. *Suicide*. New York: Charles Scribner's Sons, 1972.

A philosopher-consultant to the Los Angeles Suicide Prevention Center considers the psychological and philosophical problems of suicide, including a few references to the concept of suicide as a moral problem or a mental illness. Various philosophers are discussed. Reference notes. See also Choron (1041, 2002).

3518 Choron, Jacques. "Suicide and Notions of Death." In *Proceeding of the Fourth International Conference For Suicide Prevention*, ed. by Norman L. Farberow. Los Angeles: Del Mar, 1968.

Both consciously and unconsciously held convictions concerning death are to be explored in a suicidal person. Consciously held convictions are not necessarily identical with the fantasies exhibited by a person who becomes suicidal. Notions of death may be classified as either potentially suicide—promoting or suicide inhibiting. The notion of death as a kind of sleep is itself suicide-promoting. Theological and philosophical convictions, such as the notion of eternal punishment may be suicide-promoting for one person, and a suicide-inhibitor for another. Inquiry into a patient's notions and attitudes towards death will not only have diagnostic value, it will also be of therapeutic value when attempts are made to discredit suicide—promoting notions. See also Choron (3516).

3519 Clemons, James T., ed. *Sermons on Suicide*. Louisville, Ky.: Westminster/John Knox Press, 1989.

See 4473.

3520 Cohn, Heim. "Suicide in Jewish Legal and Religious Tradition." *Mental Health and Society* 3 (1976): 129–136.

Suicide may be excused in cases such as those of Saul, where death was imminent. Hanna killed herself during torture so that she would not forsake God's law. The historian Josephus states that those who threw themselves from a precipice at Masada were following the laws of God in the face of ignominious death. A person is not condemned if the act of suicide is taken as a symptom of insanity.

3521 Curran, David K. *Adolescent Suicidal Behavior*. Washington, D.C.: Hemisphere Pub. Corp., 1987.

Sublethal acts or suicidal attempts, rather than committed suicides are the focus of this summary of research on adolescent suicidal behavior. The injurious impact of modern society on adolescents is first discussed, followed by a statistical study of the scope of attempted and committed suicides by adolescents. A chapter on the meaning and reasons for suicidal behavior investigates the long-standing emotional disturbances that are exacerbated by adolescence. Those who attempt suicide are often attempting to solve a problem of living rather than hasten their death. Their desperate acts provoke neglect and hostility from adults. Closing chapters consider assessment, treatment, education and prevention. Both research and the author's clinical experience support presentations in each chapter. References and index.

3522 Donne, John. *Biothanatos*. 1646. Reprint. New York: Arno Press, 1976.

The paradox of self-suicide is presented by an influential philosopher of the seventeenth century who rejected medieval prohibitions of suicide in favor of compassion by the community for anyone who was driven by the universal human longing for death. As a preacher and poet, Donne sowed the seeds for respect of individual decisions that characterize twentieth-century discussions of suicide. The work is edited for modern readers, with introduction, in (3523).

3523 Donne, John. *Suicide*. Ed. by William A. Clebsch. Chico, Calif.: Scholars Press, 1983.

In the mid-17th century, the English poet and preacher, John Donne rejected the teaching of Augustine and Aquinas that suicide is unforgivable because no suicide could repent of his or her act. Donne believes that the wholesale condemnation of suicide sprang from a lack of charity toward the neighbor. It presumes more than it could know in declaring that suicidal could not repent. God's grace was ignored. Also, the universal human yearning for death was not considered. Instead, people had accepted the teaching of Aquinas that self-preservation was a universal law of nature. His arguments represent a transition from the dialectical disputation of medieval moral theology to Renaissance freedom in which the mind and emotions were the master shapers of doctrine. Concise introduction by the editor. Useful glossary of names. A reprint with Latin title is in (3522).

3524 Douglas, Jack D. *The Social Meanings of Suicide*. Princeton, N.J.: Princeton University Press, 1967.

A professor of sociology evaluates the historical context for Durkheim's classic study, *Suicide*, with the assertion that the official statistics on suicide in late 19th century France were highly unreliable and that Durkheim's explanation of suicide rates in terms of abstract social meanings was a projection of his own theory. The author also argues that suicidal actions are better studied by an examination of the way the individuals construct for themselves the meaning of their action. See also Durkheim (3527).

3525 Dublin, Louis I. *Suicide*. New York: Ronald Press Co., 1963.

The Vice-President for the Metropolitan Life Insurance Company uses his training as an epidemiologist to examine the relationship between individual emotional conflict and the pressures that are brought by mores, approved patterns of life, age, sex, race, urban-rural, war and religion. A useful survey of the history of suicide begins with primitive peoples and continues through Jewish, Greek, Roman, medieval and modern times. A final section reviews various attempts to prevent suicide and closes with an emphasis upon sound mental health.

3526 Dunne, Edward J., John L. MacIntosh and Karen Dunne-Maxim, eds. *Suicide and Its Aftermath.* New York: W. W. Norton Co., 1987.

A variety of clinicians and researchers consider the needs of families in which there has been a suicide. Many of the contributors were themselves survivors of another family member's death. Issues considered are: social context, aftermath in family and professional relationships, first responders as caregivers, therapeutic approaches, research and educational needs. A listing of suicide survivor groups, reading list, suggestions for survivors. Bibliography and index.

3527 Durkheim, Emile. *Suicide: A Study in Sociology.* 1897. Trans. by John A. Spaulding and George Simpson. New York: The Free Press, 1966.

A pioneering sociologist realigned available statistics in France and other European countries around race, heredity, social class, and different types of suicide. Suicide, which had appeared as a highly individual and personal phenomenon was now seen to have implications in social structure and the functioning of an individual in that structure. The social forces of a collective conscience could be seen in the development of three classes of suicide: egoistic, which results from lack of integration of the individual in society; altruistic, characteristic of individuals who are rigorously governed by custom and habit and who kill themselves because of higher commandments concerning religious sacrifice or political allegiance; anomic, the dull resignation and despair that follows the chronic tyranny of modern economy over individual needs. This type of suicide may even occur when sudden wealth comes to a person as greater opportunity than the individual can manage. See Douglas (3524), Ginsberg (3538), Morselli (3569),Taylor (3599).

3528 Eckstein, Jerome. *The Death Day of Socrates: Living, Dying and Immortality—The Theater of Ideas in Plato's Phaedo.* Frenchtown, N. J.: Columbia Pub. Co., 1981.

See 2050.

3529 Evans, Glen and Norman L. Farberow. *Encyclopedia of Suicide.* New York: Facts on File, 1988.

After an excellent history of suicide by Farberow, the text provides short summaries on subjects of suicide (A–Z), from psychological concerns to political and legal factors, socio-economic, educational, religious. Tabulations on suicide rates are given by age groups and methods of suicide. There are listings of suicide prevention and crisis centers. Recommended journals and a bibliography on suicide.

3530 Farber, Maurice L. *Theory of Suicide*. 1968. Reprint. Salem, N.H.: Ayer Co. Pub., 1976.

A social scientist in the tradition of his teacher Kurt Lewin illuminates the inner experiences and behaviors of people who face despair in many settings. The relationship between hope and suffering in prisoners is documented as part of a general theory of suicide. The personality characteristics of those who are especially vulnerable to self-destruction are identified along with the stresses of society that impelled the vulnerable person.

3531 Farberow, Norman L. and Edwin S. Shneidman, eds. *The Cry For Help*. New York: McGraw-Hill Book Co., 1961.

After years of listening to cries for help and searching for new ways to provide help, an interdisciplinary team of therapists who have been associated with Suicide Prevention Center in Los Angeles discuss suicide from two viewpoints: the procedures and operations of a community center and the theoretical approaches of private practitioners (psychoanalytic, analytic psychology, Adler, Sullivan, Horney, non-directive). Extensive bibliography, 1897–1957.

3532 Farberow, Norman L., ed. *Suicide in Different Cultures*. Baltimore: University Park Press, 1975.

Experts on the relationship between culture and suicide examine suicide in various cultures: European, American, Far East. Variables for discussion are history, culture, religion, geography, attitudes toward suicide, literature, mourning practices. Authoritative cross-cultural symposium.

3533 Farberow, Norman L., ed. *The Many Faces of Suicide: Indirect Self-Destructive Behavior*. New York: McGraw-Hill Book Co., 1980.

The author acknowledges his debt and those of others to Menninger (3567) who developed Freud's concept of the death instinct and described its manifestation in indirect self-destructive behavior. He organizes the contributions of many authors under theory and concepts, physical illness used against self, drug abuse, alcohol abuse, hyper-obesity, cigarette smoking, self-mutilation, auto accidents, gambling, criminal activity and deviance, stress-seeking and high risk sports. Written mainly by psychiatrists and clinical psychologists, several of the authors raise social as well as psychological issues: what is the influence of society upon the compulsive addictions of individuals?

3534 Fedden, Henry Romilly. *Suicide: A Social and Historical Study.* 1938. Reprint. Salem, N.H.: Arno Press, 1980.

Suicide as a horror is traced through tribal custom, the ancient world's concept of the individual liberty to die, the teaching of the early Christian church, the Renaissance and the Enlightenment. Illustrations.

3535 Beck, Aaron T, Harvey L. P. Resnik, and Dan J. Lettieri. *The Prediction of Suicide.* Philadelphia: Charles Press, 1986.

Psychiatrists and psychologists present historical and philosophical perspectives on classification, modern schemes and scales of classification, research issues in prevention, clinical issues in prediction, application of death prediction scales, risk-rescue ratings, medical toxicology.

3536 Finch, Stuart M., and Elva Poznanski. *Adolescent Suicide.* Springfield, Ill: Charles C. Thomas, 1971.

Psychiatrists describe suicidal attempts and threats in unstable adolescents overcome by external events repugnant to their sensitive nature. Although some suicidal attempts are manifestations of a serious psychotic or neurotic disorder, as a rule they are a genuine appeal to others as reality is precociously and painfully experienced. Personality profile, family pattern, home situation, sociological, ecological, and psychiatric factors should be investigated. Clinical references at the end of each chapter.

3537 Getz, William L., David B. Allan, R. K. Myers and K. C. Linder. *Grief Counseling with Suicidal Persons.* Lexington, Mass.: Lexington Books, 1983.

Pragmatic advice with clinical examples are provided for non-professional counselors who work under supervision during crisis intervention with suicidal persons.

3538 Ginsberg, Ralph B. *Anomie and Aspirations: A Reinterpretation of Durkheim's Theory.* New York: Arno Press, 1980.

Durkheim's (3527) explanations of suicide are contrasted and compared with contemporary studies of greed, panic and aspiration.

3539 Giovacchini, Peter. *The Urge to Die: Why Young People Commit Suicide.* New York: Macmillan Pub. Co., 1981.

The adolescent questions of personal identity and purpose are related to the urge toward suicide through illuminating examples from the work of a psychoanalyst.

3540 Grollman, Earl A. *Suicide: Prevention, Intervention, Postvention.* Boston: Beacon Press, 1971.

A rabbi presents pastoral and psychological views of suicide through history, representative theorists, social context, prevention, intervention, and postvention. There is a summons for community action. Written for a general audience. Brief bibliography.

3541 Halbwachs, Maurice. *Le Cause du Suicide.* 1929. Reprint. New York: Arno Press, 1975.

A disciple of Durkheim presents a balanced assessment of social and individual determinants of suicide. He considers social and psychopathological explanations to be complementary. Rural societies have lower suicide rates than urban societies because, according to the author, suicide rates are related to the degree of complexity of a society. Extensive analysis of official suicide statistics.

3542 Hatton, Corrine Loing, Sharon McBride Valente, and Alice Rink, eds. *Suicide: Assessment and Intervention.* New York: Appleton-Century-Crofts, 1977.

Members of the Los Angeles Suicide Prevention Center describe practical issues in suicide prevention. Very helpful for the training of those who must face sudden emergencies.

3543 Hatton, Corrine Loing, Sharon McBride Valente, and Alice Rink, eds. *Suicide: Assessment and Intervention.* 2nd ed. Norwalk, Conn.: Appleton-Century-Cross, 1984.

This handbook for the assessment of suicidal risk and for effective intervention is a desk reference for professional helpers. Separate sections deal with suicide in childhood, young adolescence, late adolescence, young adulthood.

3544 Headley, Lea A., ed. *Suicide in Asia and the Near East.* Berkeley, Calif.: University of California Press, 1983.

Clinical and statistical data is presented by various authorities on suicide for Eastern cultures from Japan to Egypt. These include religious cultures that condemn suicide. The study includes occurrence of suicide, methods, religious teachings, historical and social aspects.

3545 Heim, André. *Adolescent Suicide.* Trans. by A. M. Sheridan Smith. New York: International University Press, 1970.

A French authority on mental health provides theoretical and practical opinions on both suicide and adolescence. An exploratory study that questions accepted opinions. The author believes that adolescents possess peculiarities that make them more liable than others to suicide, with an emphasis upon the early absence of the father and tendency to resort to action in the absence of integration into any group. Suicide is not a psychosis because it is the inability of an adolescent to build up defensive barriers.

3546 Hendin, Herbert. *Suicide in America.* New York: W. W. Norton Co., 1982.

In a psychosocial approach to suicide, a professor of psychiatry examines the psychodynamics of suicide in differing social groups and shows how cultural social conditions and institutions influence individual values and aspirations. Special attention is given to clinical and social correlates to suicide within American society: violence, alcohol abuse, homosexuality.

3547 Hendin, Herbert. *Suicide and Scandinavia.* New York: Grune and Stratton, 1964.

A psychoanalyst interviewed patients in Denmark, Sweden and Norway who had made suicide attempts. The suicide rates are higher in Sweden and Denmark than in Norway, but for different reasons. A "performance" is seen in suicide with strong self-hatred for failure. The "dependency loss" in Denmark becomes a technique for arousing guilt in those who seem to have abandoned a sensitive and passive patient. Norway exhibited a "moral" form that was influenced by the puritanical setting of their culture.

3548 Henry, Andrew F. and James F. Short, Jr. *Suicide and Homicide.* New York: Free Press, 1954.

See 4063.

3549 Hewett, John H. *After Suicide.* Philadelphia: Westminster Press, 1980.

From his pastoral experience, theological training and references to standard works in thanatology, the author provides a readable guidebook for coping with acute grief, problems in the family (especially children), the relation of suicide to Jewish and Christian traditions, coping with rejection by some and finding understanding with others. Anniversary memorial services. Recommended reading.

3550 Hillman, James. *Suicide and the Soul.* New York: Harper and Row, 1964.

Influenced by Carl Jung and experience with the Suicide Prevention Center in Los Angeles, the author warns that whenever treatment is directly hastening to reduce or overcome experience, something is being done against the soul. The reality of the psyche must be taken as seriously as the reality of the body. A study of philosophical positions shows that suicide is one of the human possibilities—death can be chosen. The last section of the book presents the challenge of hoping and growing without overdependence upon medical status or psychological invulnerability.

3551 Hume, David. "On Suicide." In *Essays, Moral, Political and Literary*, by David Hume. New ed. New York: Oxford University Press, 1963.

"The best-reasoned statement in English, and perhaps in any language of the Enlightenment's position on the subject" (Choron 3517, 127). The traditional view is that suicide is a crime. Hume can find no reason why the general and immutable laws of God and nature have been encroached on by the death of a person who is overcome by the cruelty of pain and misery in this world. He dismisses the traditional objection that human life has special value with the assertion "the life of a man is of no greater importance to the universe than that of an oyster" (p. 590). Having demolished to his satisfaction arguments against suicide as a crime against the self, Hume then turns to the traditional objection that suicide harms society. Since a man tired of life is often a burden to society, how can he hinder society if he dies? Since no one throws away a life so long as he thinks it is worth keeping, a service to society is rendered by the example of a man who has the prudence and courage to remove himself as a burden from this world.

3552 Jacobs, Jerry. *Adolescent Suicide*. New York: John Wiley and Sons, 1971.

On the basis of interviews with adolescents who have attempted suicide and their parents, usually within forty-eight hours of the attempt, the author considers personal factors, behavioral problems, broken homes, disciplinary techniques and their implications for suicide prevention. Traditional theories of suicide are evaluated and new perspectives are suggested.

3553 James, William. "Is Life Worth Living?" In *Ethical Choice*, ed. by Robert M. Beck and James B. Orr., pp. 82–88. New York: Free Press, 1970.

For religious persons, belief in the reality of an invisible world provides assurance that life is worth living. Such faith is valuable when we believe what is in line with our own needs. James concludes: "Believe that life *is worth living, and your belief will help create the fact.*" (p. 88).

3554 Kastenbaum, Robert J. and B. L. Mishara. "Premature Death and Self-Injurious in Old Age." *Geriatrics* 26 (1971): 71–81.

See 3180.

3555 Kastenbaum, Robert J. *Death, Society and Human Experience.* 2d. ed. St. Louis, Mo.: C. V. Mosby, 1981.

In his discussion of the relationship of society to the human experience of death, the author notes that suicide is a rational alternative to life in some cultures but is regarded in American society as sinful, criminal, weakness or madness. These cultural interpretations will affect mourning, along with awareness of the purpose of suicide for an individual as reunion, refuge, retribution, penalty, failure, or an unintentional mistake. A readable and comprehensive survey.

3556 Cain, Albert C., ed. *Survivors of Suicide.* Springfield, Ill: Charles C. Thomas, 1972.

After historical articles on suicide, such as Benjamin Rush on "Suicide in Families," mental health clinicians consider the emotional responses of children to a suicide by parents, the impact on other family members of suicide by a child, spouse, or friend and several individual case studies on reconstruction after a traumatic loss.

3557 Klagsbrun, Francine. *Too Young to Die: Youth and Suicide.* Boston: Houghton Mifflin Co., 1976.

In one of first books on suicide written for discussion with adolescents with adults, the realities of suicide among young people are surveyed and suggestions are given for help in a crisis situation or in the aftermath of a suicide. A youth suicide is then discussed in the larger context of cultural and social situations. A sensitive presentation for a general audience.

3558 Kobler, Arthur L. and Ezra Stodland. *The End of Hope.* New York: The Free Press of Glencoe, 1964.

A clinician and a social psychologist present suicide as the outcome of a process of social interaction. Data is drawn from research literature and an intense study of suicides in a small psychiatric hospital. Several extensive case studies are presented to show that those who intend suicide will communicate this in some way verbally so that an attempt might be thwarted. The patient is devastated if those around him respond to his suicide attempt with fear, hopelessness or indifference. The authors show the way in which confidence was presented by psychiatric staff with patients for several years. Later, when the staff was demoralized, four patients committed suicide in half a year.

3559 Landsberg, Paul Ludwig. *The Experience of Death/The Moral Problem of Suicide.* Trans. by Cynthia Rowland. New York: Arno Press, 1977.

See 2029.

3560 Lester, David. *Why People Kill Themselves: A 1980's Summary of Research Findings on Suicidal Behavior*. 2nd ed. Springfield, Ill: Charles C. Thomas, 1983.

From the 2000 articles and books on suicide published in a decade before 1980 in English, the author focuses on research and theory in psychology, sociology, anthropology, psychiatry, nursing, toxicology and others. Prominence is given to studies that focus on why people kill themselves rather than on the problem of preventing suicide, the effects of suicide on the environment, the consequences of the act upon others. For references before 1970, readers are referred to the first edition. Under topical headings a paragraph is given to each study. References at the end of each chapter. No index.

3561 Lester, Gene and David Lester. *Suicide: The Gamble with Death*. Englewood Cliffs, N.J.: Prentice Hall, 1971.

A summary is presented of relevant research on the meaning of suicide: classifying death states, heredity and environment, childhood experience, personality differences, aggressiveness, communication and thought processes. Sociological concerns and theories are presented along with resources for preventing suicide.

3562 Litman, Robert E. "Sigmund Freud on Suicide." In *Essays in Self-Destruction*, ed. by Edwin S. Shneidman, 324–244. New York: Science House, 1967.

After 1911, Freud revised his theory of the instincts in order to provide appropriate recognition of the importance of self-destructiveness. He supplemented rather than replaced libido theory, as in "Mourning and Melancholia" (4312) in which he postulated the identification of the ego with the abandoned object. The shadow of the object falls upon the ego and makes the ego appear psychologically to be the forsaken object. The resulting "shadow" object is not fully integrated into the total personality and this is the "fault line" along which ego splitting occurs. Narcissistic persons are especially vulnerable to this splitting which will result in disorganization and regression. The regression becomes dangerous when a stage of sadism is reached in the primitive unconscious and the "shadow" ego is identified as the lost object that must be killed. Narcissistic persons get rid of the objectionable and forsaken object through suicide. In Freud's theory-building and case analysis no attention is paid to the role of others in a suicide (spectator, participants, rescuer or betrayer). The author feels that experience has confirmed Freud's statement that each suicide is multiply determined. The complex psychoanalytic explanations are arranged by him in terms of general features, specific suicide mechanisms, specific predisposing conditions. References. See Freud (4312).

3563 Lukas, Christopher and Henry M. Seiden. *Silent Grief: Living in the Wake of Suicide*. New York: Charles Scribner's Sons, 1987.

A survivor and a psychologist describe what it is like to be left behind in a way that will offer help to others in moving on with life. Both information and comfort are in the personal narration of family responses to suicide, the many bargains that loved ones make with themselves, the memory of the deceased and society. A final section describes ways to respond to suicide both by giving and getting help in listening and talking. Self-help groups are listed. Short bibliography and notes.

3564 Lum, Doman. *Responding to Suicidal Crisis: for Church and Community*. Grand Rapids, Mich.: Wm. B. Eerdmans Pub. Co., 1974.

A pastoral counselor presents a practical resource for clergy and lay persons in which philosophical and theological thoughts on suicide are summarized. Suicide prevention is then discussed in the context of crisis intervention. Recommendations are given for involving the church in suicide prevention. The results of a questionnaire are given on suicide counseling and theology of Los Angeles Protestant clergypersons. Topically organized bibliography.

3565 MacIntosh, John L. *Suicide among Children, Adolescents, and Students: A Comprehensive Bibliography*. Monticello, Ill.: Vance Bibliographies, 1981.

See 8027.

3566 MacIntosh, John L. *Research on Suicide: A Bibliography*. Bibliographies and Indexes in Psychology No. 2. Westport, Conn.: Greenwood Press, 1985.

See 8028.

3567 Menninger, Karl. *Man Against Himself*. New York: Harcourt, Brace and World, 1938.

A psychiatrist believes that people kill themselves in selected ways, fast or slow, soon or late. These suicides are classified as chronic (such as addictions), focal (self-mutilations, accidents, frigidity), organic (the choice of suicide as a lesser evil in cases of intractable pain). The theories begun by Ferenczi, Groddack, Jellife, White, Alexander, and others are used to show how various forms of sickness may be seen as variants of self-destructiveness.

3568 Miller, Marv. *Suicide After Sixty: The Final Alternative*. New York: Springer Pub. Co., 1979.

The deadly seriousness of older Americans who wish to kill themselves is demonstrated through threats to the self-esteem of the elderly: severe physical illness, mental illness, dependency and institutionalization, death of a spouse, retirement, alcoholism and drug abuse, pathological personal relations. Annotated review of research. Bibliography.

3569 Morselli, Henry. *Suicide: An Essay on Comparative Moral Statistics.* 1882. Reprint in English. Salem, N.H.: Ayer Co. Pub., 1976.

The work of this Italian statistician was basic for Durkheim's later studies of suicide (3527). Morselli considered the morals of a society to be the most important cause of suicide rates.

3570 Nietzsche, Friedrich Wilhelm. *Human, All Too Human.* 1881. Stuttgart: Kroner Verlag, 1953.

"Prevention of Suicide: There is a justice according to which we take a man's life, but there is none whatsoever when we deprive him of dying: this is only cruelty" (aphorism 88).

3571 Moss, L. M. and D. M. Hamilton. "The Psychotherapy of the Suicidal Patient." *American Journal of Psychiatry* 112 (1956): 814–820.

The authors believe that bereavement was the precipitating factor in suicide attempts by many persons in psychotherapy.

3572 Nelson, F. L. and N. L. Farberow. "Indirect Self-Destructive Behavior in the Elderly Nursing Home Patient." *Journal of Gerontology* 35 (1980): 949–957.

See 3185.

3573 Novak, David. *Suicide and Morality.* New York: Scholars Studies Press, 1975.

Specific prohibitions of suicide by Plato, Aquinas, and Kant are examined for general ethical principles that precede rational judgments concerning particular situations. These philosophers regarded suicide as an option open to rational choice. This is in contrast to modern empirical and therapeutic emphases upon suicide as the symptom of unconscious conflicts. A philosopher such as Plato emphasized the importance of social ties in obtaining a high level of existence and making rational choices. To Plato, suicide was anti-social and should be recognized by isolation and unmarked graves. Plato and Aquinas prohibited suicide on the basis of a real relationship with God, which is ignored in contemporary suicidology. The opinion of the author is expressed within the framework of a revelational theology, which was not the primary concern of Plato, Aquinas and Kant in discussing suicide. Their concern was with the human attempt to transcend finitude, which they believe one cannot overcome. Only God is transcendent.

3574 Osgood, Nancy J., Barbara A. Bryant, and Aaron A. Lipman. "Patterns of Suicidal Behavior in Long-term Care Facilities: A Preliminary Report on an Ongoing Study." *Omega* 19 (1988–89): 69–78.

Four-hundred and sixty three long-term care facilities answered a questionnaire of suicidal behavior. One per cent of the total sample of residents engaged in some type of suicidal behavior, usually "indirect life-threatening behavior." A much smaller percentage engaged in overt suicidal acts from which 80% survived. The old-old are most at risk of death from participation in suicidal behavior in long-term facilities.

3575 Patros, Philip G., and Antonia K. Samoo. *Depression and Suicide in Children and Adolescents: Prevention, Intervention and Postvention.* Boston: Allen and Bacon, 1989.

For the benefit of teachers and counselors who are in contact with students who want to know more about suicide, the authors provide an overview of child and adolescent suicide studies: family patterns, the view of death among children and adolescents, depression. Another section of the book aids school personnel recognize signals of depression and suicidal behavior, sift out misinformation and be sensitive to sources of student stress. Intervention are then discussed along with suggestions for prevention and follow-up. Brief case studies. Listing of specific problems and solutions to aid in learning. Professional references.

3576 Peck, Michael L., Norman L. Farberow and Robert E. Litman, eds. *Youth Suicide.* Springer Series on Death and Suicide. New York: Springer Pub. Co., 1985.

Senior staff members of the Los Angeles Suicide Prevention Center address the psychodynamics of suicide-prone youth, the impact of social change, the role of the family, types of intervention strategies. Brief clinical references and longer case studies are found throughout the book. References at the end of each chapter.

3577 Perlin, Seymour, ed. *A Handbook for the Study of Suicide.* New York: Oxford University Press, 1975.

3578 Plath, Sylvia. *The Bell Jar.* New York: Bantam. 1971.

A novel, autobiographical in some respects, about a nineteen-year-old girl who attempted suicide when she found life difficult to bear.

3579 Prentice, Ann E. *Suicide: A Selective Bibliography of Over 2,200 Items.* Metuchen, N.J.: Scarecrow Press, 1974.

See 8038.

3580 Pretzel, Paul W. *Understanding and Counseling the Suicidal Person.* Nashville, Tenn.: Abingdon Press, 1972.

From the viewpoint of his training in theology and psychology, a clinical psychologist explores motives, recognition, prevention of suicide and the personal feelings of a counselor. A chapter deals with the grief reactions of a surviving spouse, child, or parent and the support and interpretation that can be given by a pastor or psychotherapist. Specific advice is offered to clergypersons.

3581 Reynolds, David K. and Norman L. Farberow. *Suicide: Inside and Out.* Berkeley, Calif.: University of California Press, 1976.

From participant observation in a psychiatric hospital and from a review of research studies, the authors describe staff-patient interactions, assessment, problem-solving by the staff, the difficulties of suicide prevention.

3582 Richman, Joseph. *Family Therapy for Suicidal People.* New York: Springer Pub. Co., 1986.

From a family systems perspective, an experienced psychologist discusses assessment of suicidal risk, effective forms of problem solving, tension reduction and conflict resolution within the family. Many clinical illustrations. Extensive bibliography.

3583 Rudestam, K. E. and D. Imbroll. "Societal Reactions to a Child's Death by Suicide." *Journal of Consulting and Clinical Psychology* 51(1983) 461–462.

The damning of parents and a general lack of support for survivors is illustrated in the reaction of people to four different newspaper accounts of the death of a ten year old girl, either through disease, overdose, or hanging. The greatest sense of shame was projected upon parents in the account of death by hanging.

3584 Schuyler, D. "Counseling Suicide Survivors: Issues and Answers." *Omega,* 4 (1973): 313–321.

In addition to the usual measures of counsel for the bereaved, particular attention must be paid to the lack of social and emotional support for the survivors of a suicide of a loved one. There is also a sense of desertion by the person who committed suicide. Guilt among survivors may be intense, along with anger toward the deceased.

3585 Seward, Jack. *Hara-Kiri: Japanese Ritual Suicide.* Rutland, Vt.: Charles E. Tuttle Co., 1968.

The historical and sociological background of a unique Japanese method of self-destruction (suppuku) is described as the integral part of the discipline of the warrior class, a form of suicide often awarded to an offender as a form of honorable but necessary punishment. The aggressive views of Shintoism and the negative views of Buddhism are assessed.

3586 Shneidman, Edwin S. and Norman L. Farberow, eds. *Clues to Suicide*. New York: McGraw-Hill Book Co., 1957.

Psychiatrists, psychologists and sociologists present their clinical impressions, sometimes supported by psychological tests and sociological data: theoretical and experimentals considerations, the clinical problems in psychotherapy and prevention, the thoughts of a suicidal person as present in genuine and simulated suicide notes. The most significant single result was a finding that the psychodynamics of suicide were different for age groupings: egoistic suicide in which there was a disputation within the mind; dyadic suicides that are related to deep unfulfilled needs and wishes pertaining to a significant partner; ageneratic suicides that follow from the individual's sense of failing in the inexorable march of generations.

3587 Shneidman, Edwin S., ed. *Essays in Self-Destruction*. New York: Science House, 1967.

Psychiatrists, psychologists, sociologists and historians present selected frontiers of thought related to self-destruction: literary and philosophic, sociological and ethnographical, psychological and psychiatric, taxonomic and forensic.

3588 Shneidman, Edwin S., ed. *On the Nature of Suicide*. San Francisco: Jossey-Bass, 1969.

The editor details the growing interest in suicide by comparing the 1910 psychoanalytic meetings on suicide in Vienna with the 1968 conference of the American Association of Suicidology. Papers reprinted from the 1968 conference are by Jacques Choron, Louis Dublin, Paul Friedman, Robert Havighurst, Karl Menninger, Erwin Stengel, Lawrence Kubie, Leslie Farber, Jack Douglas, David Bakan, Sidney Jourard. The papers present varieties of perspectives from psychiatry, psychology, sociology.

3589 Shneidman, Edwin S., Norman L. Farberow and Robert E. Litman, eds. *The Psychology of Suicide*. New York: Science House, 1970.

Three pioneers of the Los Angeles Suicide Prevention Center provide a collection of readings from their publications, 1955–1966, under the headings of Theory and Taxonomy, Administration and Organization, Statistics and Demography, Diagnosis and Evaluation, Therapy and Treatment, Forensic and Professional Issues, Biography and Literature and Book Reviews. Bibliography.

3590 Shneidman, Edwin S., ed. *Death and the College Student*. New York: Behavioral Publications, 1972.

See 1224.

3591 Shneidman, Edwin S., ed. *Suicidology: Contemporary Developments*. New York: Grune and Stratton, 1976.

In a text that became a standard, the author provides a classic balance of early studies such as David Hume with twentieth century topics such as trends in U.S. rate of suicide, validity scales for assessment of suicide risk, the inner thoughts of those at risk, clinical, philosophical and legal issues.

3592 Shneidman, Edwin S. and Norman L. Farberow. "Suicide and Death." In *The Meaning of Death*, ed. by Herman Feifel, 284–301. New York: McGraw-Hill Book Co., 1979.

From clinical and research records on persons who had committed suicide versus those who had attempted or threatened suicide, or were non-suicidal, the authors conclude that confused suicidal logic is primarily a problem of identification. The suicidal person accepts erroneous premises and invalid conclusions which lead to suicide because of a fallacious identification between the self as experienced by the self and the self as it feels itself experienced by others.

3593 Shneidman, Edwin S. *Suicide Thoughts and Reflections, 1960–1980*. New York: Human Sciences Press, 1981.

Collected articles of the author on suicide contain "some of his best and some of his less-known work. Representatively dazzling." (8039, p. 156.)

3594 Shneidman, Edwin S. *Definition of Suicide*. New York: John Wiley and Sons, 1985.

A noted thanatologist believes that effective remediation depends upon accurate assessment, which in turn depends on meaningful definition. Definitions are drawn from both clinical and statistical studies with much inspiration from Melville's *Moby Dick*. The common psychodynamic theme in definitions of suicide would be psychological pain. See also Murray (6028).

3595 Shorey, Paul. *What Plato Said*. Chicago: The University of Chicago Press, 1933.

See 1067.

3596 Sprott, S. E. *The English Debate on Suicide*. La Salle, Ill: Open Court Pub. Co., 1961.

In *Biothanatos* (3522), poet John Donne in 1647 questioned the philosophical and theological abhorrence of suicide. It appeared at a time when Puritans were known for the pious contemplation and depressive temperament that were considered pre-dispositions to suicide. With the rise of rationalism in the eighteenth century, the philosopher Hume entered a storm center of debate at a time when suicide rates were rising. His essay "On Suicide" argued that individuals are competent and lawful judges of their pain and they commit suicide without disturbing the laws of providence. The debate was of long standing. Anglicans and Puritans theoretically gave little or no chance for the salvation of suicide, but on the practical side they taught only God knew the fate of the suicide. Anglicans also quoted the condemnation of suicide by Augustine and Aquinas. One bishop, Cranmer, taught that suicide is sure damnation.

3597 Stengel, Erwin, and Nancy G. Cook. *Attempted Suicide*. Westport, Conn.: Greenwood Press, 1982.

Suicide is considered in the light of its effects on the human environment. Five groups of persons who have made suicidal attempts were interviewed. Instead of a concentration upon the self destructive aspects of suicide, the authors demonstrate the impact of a suicidal attempt on the life situation of patients, such as the effects of suicide threats upon other members of a family. A pioneering and painstakingly assembled monograph.

3598 Stone, Howard W. *Suicide and Grief*. Philadelphia: Fortress Press, 1972.

A pastoral counselor considers the grief reaction that occurs after a suicide in the family. Specific directions are offered for pastors who seek to understand the connection between grief and suicide, the relation of grief to age, sex, education, religion, responsibilities of the bereaved. Pastoral care is described from the time of the funeral to the months that follow, including the problem of unadaptive grief. Recommendations are based upon research in Los Angeles County with questionnaires and interviews among 30 males and 30 females who had experienced a suicide in their family within the last two years. Statistical results are included. Annotated bibliography.

3599 Taylor, Steve. *Durkheim and the Study of Suicide*. London: Macmillan Co., 1982.

After reviewing some modern insights and inadequacies in the interpretation of Durkheim (3527), the author examines existing sociological work on suicide rates and details the work of coroners and others in determining the causes of death. He suggests four basic meanings of suicide: thanatation, submission, appeal and sacrifice—all elements of risk-taking.

3600 Wallace, Samuel E. *After Suicide.* New York: John Wiley and Sons, 1973.

A sociologist explores the experience of twelve women who survived their husband's suicide. In interviews throughout the first year after suicide, the author traces the wife's growing need to meet increasing emotional demands. In more than half the cases, an emotionally overloaded marriage had broken down finally just before the suicide occurred and in all the remaining cases the husband's physical or mental disorders had gravely interfered with the marital relationship. The case study method of the author collects excerpts from interviews with various respondents under various categories, such as the socially dying, the physically dying and the strangers to death. Bibliography.

3601 Wolman, D. J., ed. *Between Survival and Suicide.* New York: Gardner Press, 1976.

The social and philosophical challenge of suicide is considered by various authors as an existential problem, of flight into death or from death, the issue of continuing life, personal and ethical considerations.

3602 Zilboorg, G. "Suicide Among Civilized and Primitive Races." *American Journal of Psychiatry* 92 (1936): 1347–1369.

A psychiatrist with an interest in history concludes that suicide is probably as old as murder and may be almost as old as natural death.

3603 Zosman, Jack, and David L. Davidson, eds. *Organizing the Community to Prevent Suicide.* Springfield, Ill: Charles C. Thomas, 1971.

At a multidisciplinary workshop of the Center for Studies On Suicide Prevention of The National Institute of Mental Health, suicidologists consider the development of a prevention program: finding and training nonprofessional and professional workers, organizing, planning, and administering a suicide prevention center.

3.64 ABORTION/INFANTICIDE

3604 Carmen, Arlene and Howard Moody. *Abortion Counseling and Social Change: From Illegal Act to Medical Practice.* Valley Forge, Pa.: Judson Press, 1973.

This book describes the work of a Clergy Consultation Service on Abortion, a safe clinic that included both physicians and nurses and clergy counselors. Authors describe the difficulties of keeping up with demand for services when abortion laws in New York state were liberalized.

3605 Gorman, Michael J. *Abortion and the Early Church.* Downers Grove, Ill.: InterVarsity Press, 1982.

The author traces attitudes and regulations concerning abortion in the ancient world, among Jews and Christians of the first century, and in the established Christian world of the fourth and fifth century. Although Christians, Jews and pagans condemned abortion, Christians were distinctive in their concern for the well-being of the fetus as God's creation. There were early Christian denunciations of abortion as murder before opposition developed to contraception.

3606 Harrison, Beverley Wildung. *Our Right to Choose: Toward a New Ethic of Abortion.* Boston: Beacon Press, 1983.

An ethicist challenges many assumptions about the moral dilemma of abortion with carefully considered and forthright presentation of women's right to make procreative choices. They must be confined to the narrower option of elective abortion. Theologies behind the moral debate are examined, a liberating theological perspective is advanced, the history of Christian teaching on abortion is reconceived from a feminist perspective. Comprehensive notes.

3607 Jung, Patricia Beattie, and Thomas A. Shannon, eds. *Abortion and Catholicism: The American Debate.* New York: Crossroad, 1988.

Numerous articles articulate the various perspectives on abortion from a Roman Catholic perspective: liberal and traditional Catholic viewpoints, feminist approaches, morality in public policy, moral consistency within the church and problem of public dissent from official teaching.

3608 Kohl, Marvin, ed. *Infanticide and the Value of Life.* Buffalo, N.Y.: Prometheus Books, 1978.

A professor of philosophy reviews religious considerations that forbid killing of infants that were born with little expectancy of life or a meaningless existence. A symposium of theologians and philosophers consider many questions: religious, ethical, anthropological, psychological, medical, legal, ideological and philosophical.

3609 Muldoon, M. *Abortion: An Annotated Indexed Bibliography.* New York: E. Mellen, 1980.

See 8029.

3610 Nicholson, Susan Teft. *Abortion and the Roman Catholic Church.* J. R. E. Studies in Religious Ethics/II. Knoxville, Tenn.: Religious Ethics, 1978.

Through an examination of Roman Catholic law and teaching and case illustrations, the author presents various arguments and implications of Roman Catholic condemnation of abortion, with special treatment of the principle of "double-effect." Various inconsistencies are noted within Roman Catholic doctrine especially when related to the principle of double-effect and to therapeutic abortion.

3611 Piers, Maria W. *Infanticide.* New York: W. W. Norton Co., 1978.

The author explores the history of the deliberate killing of infants. By the 20th century, the fantasy of infanticide in an individual's unconscious had been largely prohibited, but neglect, cruelty and violence arose out of conditions in which children were abused or neglected. The author calls for greater social responsibility for the conditions under which children could reach their potential. Special emphasis is placed upon conditions that would allow women to reach their maternal potential. A helpful study of our need to confront inner urges to destructiveness. Adequate bibliography.

3612 *Preserving the Right to Choose.* New York: American Civil Liberties Union, 1986.

See 3647.

3613 Ramsey, Paul. *Ethics at the Edges of Life: Medical and Legal Intersections.* New Haven: Yale University Press, 1978.

A Protestant ethicist with special interest in medical issues states his conclusions concerning abortion and "dying well enough" as opposite extremes of life to be considered in light of Scripture, theology, culture and legal issues. The author fears that boundless freedom for abortion will precipitate submission to "people selection." In relation to the end of life, the author discards the usual classification of ordinary-extraordinary and wishes to present the test for extending or withholding aid to be a patient's potentiality for significant personal life, for some relationship to God, and for interrelationships with other human beings.

3614 Speckhard, Anne. *Psycho-Social Stress Following Abortion.* Kansas City: Sheed and Ward, 1987.

A family therapist presents findings from her research interviews with thirty women who were identified as having chronic and long term high stress reactions to their abortion experience. There were delays in the grief process because of various inhibitions, such as reluctance to disclose the pregnancy to families-of-origin. Out-of-wedlock sexual behaviors were kept secret. Denial and repression were used to cope with stress. Many of the subjects found relief from their guilt by turning to religion and a concept of God as one who forgives. Many of the indicators of stress following abortion did not appear until months or years after the abortion had taken place. The author is to be commended for including the introductory letter to prospective subjects, the interview schedule and graphic tabulations of results.

3615 Vaux, Kenneth. *Birth Ethics: Religious and Cultural Values in the Genesis of Life.* New York: Crossroad, 1989.

A professor of ethics in medicine considers such specific ethical issues as abortion, human sexuality, AIDS, eugenics, in-vitro fertilization, neo-natal care and child abuse. Specific interpretations are given in terms of Christian doctrines of suffering, death and transfiguration. The discussion is well-documented and there is an excellent index.

3616 Wennberg, Robert N. *Life in the Balance: Exploring the Abortion Controversy.* Grand Rapids, Mich.: Wm. B. Eerdmans Pub. Co., 1985.

A professor of philosophy presents a systematic moral evaluation that examines varying positions (professional, social, personal), the meaning of persons made in the image of God, the particular time when an embryo has a full-fledged right to life and the opposing principles of actuality and potentiality. Relevant considerations are given for making a decision and examining the law. The author offers a "reasonable conclusion" that an individual's moral standing begins at conception.

3.65 NATURAL VS. ARTIFICIAL DEATH
See also LIFE EXTENDING TECHNOLOGIES/RESUSCITATION (3.246)

3617 Battin, Marguerite Pabst. *Ethical Issues in Suicide.* Englewood Cliffs, N.J.: Prentice-Hall, 1982.

A philosopher presents varying viewpoints on the question of suicide as a morally permissible or completely proscribed choice of death. Judicious summaries are provided of authorities who argue from a religious, social, philosophical or moral viewpoint, with special emphasis upon contemporary issues such as the concept of rational suicide, paternalism, human rights. The author concludes that suicide is more potentially rational and dignity-promoting than we now recognize. At the same time, she applauds workers and researchers who seek to prevent irrational or pathological choices of death. Footnotes and index.

3618 Callahan, Daniel. "Natural Death and Public Policy." In *Life Span*, ed. by Robert M. Veatch. New York: Harper and Row, 1978.

A "natural" death is one that occurs when (1) one's life-work has been accomplished (2) one's moral obligations have been met (3) death won't cause others to despair and (4) won't include unbearable pain.

3619 Degner, Lesley. "The Relationship between Beliefs Held by Physicians and Their Life-Prolonging Decisions." *Omega* 5 (1974): 223–232.

A majority (79.4%) of 92 physicians in a sample favored the withdrawing of treatment from the terminally ill in at least 2 out of three imaginary situations. A comparison of these decisions with the physicians' belief in God and afterlife yielded no significant differences. Physicians who favored withdrawal of treatment from the terminally ill knew death as a negative rather than as a neutral or positive phenomenon.

3620 Thielicke, Helmut. *The Doctor as Judge of Who Shall Live and Who Shall Die.* Philadelphia: Fortress Press, 1976.

The theological substance of the Houston Conference on Ethics in Medicine and Technology was provided by the author, with responses from other members of the conference. The lectures of Thielicke dealt with the ambiguity of medical progress, the problems of organ transplants, the prolongation of life. What are the consequences of prolonging life?

3621 Weir, Robert F. *Abating Treatment with Critically Ill Patients: Ethical and Legal Limits to the Medical Prolongation of Life.* New York: Oxford University Press, 1989.

An expert on the interface of medicine, law and ethics seeks to determine what is relevant for rational decision-making about the prolongation of life. Abating treatment does not mean the end of all palliative care and treatment, nor is it the equivalent of euthanasia. In addition to a discussion of actual cases, the author includes such specifics as the writing of a living will, durable power of attorney, a five-step approach to prospective planning.

3622 Weisman, Avery D. *On Dying and Denying: A Psychiatric Study of Terminality.* New York: Behavioral Pub., 1972.

As part of his discussion of dying, based upon years of clinical experience, the author suggests that death may be viewed as appropriate in certain cases. It is acceptable because it is the auspicious moment that leads to a decisive change. This is the Greek concept of time as *kairos*. It permits a purposeful end to physical life which include an optimum reduction of pain and suffering and the willingness to yield control to others in whom we have confidence. This is not likely to occur for most people. See Weisman (1165).

3.66 DYING WITH DIGNITY

3623 Crane, Diana. *The Sanctity of Social Life: Physician's Treatment of Critically Ill Patients.* New York: Russell Sage Foundation, 1975.

See 3101.

3624 Gonda, Thomas and John Ruark. *Dying Dignified: The Health Professional's Guide to Care.* Reading, Mass.: Addison-Wesley, 1984.

From their experience in caring for terminally ill persons, two physicians discuss terminal care, chronic disease, children, suicide and mourning with some attention to cultural factors and demographic trends. Continuity in the text is provided through the use of recurring clinical examples.

3625 Kobrzycki, P. "Dying with Dignity at Home." *American Journal of Nursing* 75 (1975): 1312–1313.

The author describes the way in which teaching and coordination enabled a young man to live and die at home even though he needed complex care.

3626 Krant, Melvin J. *Death and Dignity: The Meaning and Control of a Personal Death.* Springfield, Ill.: C. C. Thomas, 1974.

An oncologist presents meaningful ways toward self-control of dying that can be supported by the family, community and staff.

3627 Kübler-Ross, Elisabeth. *Living With Death and Dying.* New York: Macmillan Pub. Co., 1981.

Through a variety of case illustrations and personal advice, help is provided in understanding the different languages by which terminally ill adults and children try to convey their inner knowledge and needs. These include personal conversations during house calls and hospital calls, the use of drawings made at significant times in one's life, and understanding of the parent's need to care and the issue of sudden death.

3628 Kübler-Ross, Elisabeth. *Working It Through.* Photographs by Mal Warshaw. New York: Macmillan Pub. Co., 1982.

A popular thanatologist describes the five-day workshops in which she helped both the terminally ill and caregivers to describe their experiences to each other and to learn how to vent their feelings of fear, anger, and love. The themes of life, death, and transition were expanded in later workshops to include other types of loss.

3629 Ramsey, Paul. "The Indignity of 'Death with Dignity.'" In *On Moral Medicine: Theological Perspectives in Medical Ethics*, ed. by Stephen E. Lammers and Allen Verhey, 185–196. Grand Rapids, Mich.: Wm. B. Eerdmans Pub. Co., 1987.

A Protestant ethicist examines the roots of the "death with dignity" philosophers and finds that they deny the dread of death as oblivion. The author considers the awareness to be an indignity that can be faced with freedom to encompass death with dignity as in the Hebrew wisdom literature. Miller-McLemore (2142) criticizes the article as oversimplified morality. See also Horan (3473).

3630 Vanderpool, Harold Y. "The Ethics of Terminal Care." *Journal of the American Medical Association* 239 (1978): 850–852.

Modern society places few premiums on suffering and death. It is not valued as a dignified and uplifting time and can hardly serve as a moral basis for the care of most terminally ill persons. It is more realistic to draw on shared values of worth that are important throughout life, such as truthful information about decisions and procedures, acceptance of anger and denial, the preservation of autonomy and self-control.

3.7 LEGAL ISSUES

3631 *A Legal Guide to the Living Will: Selected Case Law and Commentary on Medical Treatment/Non-Treatment of the Terminally Ill.* New York: Concern for the Dying, 1979.

Brief statements are made in this pamphlet concerning the living will, medical decision-making and the law.

3632 Back, Kurt W. and Hans W. Baade. "The Social Meaning of Death and the Law." In *Aging and Social Policy*, ed. by John C. McKinney and Frank T. de Vyver, eds., 302–329. New York: Appleton-Century-Crofts, 1966.

While modern society tends to isolate the dying and the dead, American law permits the dying and the dead more power through such devices as wills and trusts.

3633 Dacey, Norman F. *How to Avoid Probate.* New York: Crown Pub., 1965.

The difficulties and expenses of probate and settling estates are presented along with specific discussions of trust and donations that will reduce expenses. Forms of necessary legal instruments are included.

3634 Dondera, A. Edward and J. Douglas Peters, eds. *Legal and Ethical Aspects of Treating Critically and Terminally Ill Patients.* Ann Arbor, Mich.: AUPHA Press, 1982.

Proceedings of the American Society of Law and Medicine cover ethical, medical and legal aspects of dying. Ethical and medical guidelines are suggested and right to die laws are compared across states.

3635 McHugh, James T. *Death, Dying and the Law.* Huntington, Ind.: Our Sunday Visitor, 1976.

With the support of the Roman Catholic Bishops' Committee for Pro-Life Activities, members of the committee, a psychiatrist and a professor of theology assemble scientific and legal information to enhance loving human relationships and moral decisions that surround death, including questions about brain-death, death laws, euthanasia, prolongation of life. Bibliography.

3636 Robertson, John A. *The Rights of the Critically Ill.* New York: Bantam Books, 1983.

In conversational style a legal authority considers legal resources and rights during a variety of decisions for the terminally ill and includes appendices on organizations, state laws, and living wills.

3637 Schaffer, Thomas L. and Robert E. Rodes, Jr. "Law for Those Who Are to Die." In *New Meanings of Death*, ed. by Herman Feifel. New York: McGraw-Hill Book Co., 1977.

Two professors of law at Notre Dame University use case studies to show the impact of legal issues upon death through attempts at philanthropy, trust, transfers of ownership, divorce, publishing of information. Each of these cases present a fundamental tension between the living and the dying and the principal of law with which each view is settled. References.

3.8 PUBLIC POLICY

3638 Callahan, Daniel. *Setting Limits: Medical Goals in an Aging Society.* New York: Simon and Schuster, 1987.

Established social conceptions of the meaning "old," "aging," "premature death" have been redefined as functions of the state-of-the-art of medicine at any given moment. The resultant rise in expectations of care for the elderly has led to a huge percentage of the total healthcare dollar being spent for the elderly and equally large percentage of that consumed in the last year of life. The author argues for some kind of rationing our resources in care for the elderly. No new technologies should be developed or applied to the old that are likely to produce only chronic illness and a short life, increase the present burden of chronic illness, or to extend the lives of the elderly with no significant improvement in their quality of life. Government support for these decisions through medicare reimbursement would discourage the development of marginally beneficial items. Such decisions will come when society regains a sense of a "natural span of life" which he would expect to be in the late 70's or 80's. A "tolerable" death would not be determined solely on the basis of medical maintenance but also on the basis of satisfactory accomplishment of life possibilities, the satisfactory completion of moral obligations, without giving offense to sensibility or cause despair or rage at the finitude of human existence.

3639　Callahan, Daniel. *What Kind of Life: The Limits of Medical Progress.* New York: Simon and Schuster, 1990.

The co-founder and director of the Hastings Center seeks to answer difficult but increasingly urgent questions of national policy and resource allocation for health care. This volume broadens the scope of inquiry begun in an earlier book, *Setting Limits,* which focused on the crisis in health care for the elderly. He asks for public policy that will focus on prevention of disease and disability and pursue effective long term solutions to basic health needs. We should ease the frantic struggle to postpone death. Goals of health should be explicitly articulated and culturally accepted definitions of health and an equitable system of resource distribution should be developed. Caring attitudes in the medical system should replace fascination with technology. A balance should be found between curing and caring.

3640　Childress, James F. "Priorities in the Allocation of Healthcare Resources." *Soundings* 62 (1979): 256–275.

Issues of biomedical ethics and public policy are concentrated in this article upon three questions "What scarce resources should be put into health care? with how much for prevention and how much for crisis medicine? and who has priority to receive the resources?"

3641　Feigenberg, Loma and Robert Fulton. "Care of the Dying: A Swedish Perspective." *Omega* 8 (1977): 215–228.

The authors urge a consideration of public policy that would alleviate the pain, apprehension, torment and loneliness of dying with a sure knowledge that terminal care is available in both human and medical terms. The lack of rules/norms is exposed in current public service and standards of care for the terminally ill are presented in a manner appropriate to Swedish medical concepts and conditions.

3642 Fuchs, Victor R. *Who Shall Live? Health, Economics and Social Choice.* New York: Basic Books, 1974.

A medical economist uses economics to discuss the distribution of scarce medical resources in relation to the needs of the sick and the dying. This includes strategies for alternatives uses of resources and for awareness of varying needs of populations for care. Economics enter the health scene primarily through the physician who makes most of the decisions concerning what we pay for medical care. The necessity for choice is urged upon medical care personnel, health insurance companies, public regulatory authorities, medical schools and drug companies.

3643 Hauerwas, Stanley. *Suffering Presence.* Notre Dame, Ind.: University of Notre Dame Press, 1986.

A theological ethicist reflects upon his work with the Council for the Retarded, the volunteers and professional workers, the patients and families who responded to illness with care and courage. His summary: "humane medicine is impossible to sustain in a society which lacks the moral capacity to care for the mentally handicapped." Chapters include an emphasis upon medicine as moral art, theological reflections on brain-death, suicide, reasons for living, the ethics of experimentation upon human subjects especially with children, *in vitro* fertilization, the moral challenge of the handicapped and the tyranny of normality. The author combines a knowledge of the literature on medical and social ethics with many clinical examples.

3644 *Health and Health Care: A Pastoral Letter of the American Catholic Bishops.* Washington, D. C.: United States Catholic Conference, 1982.

Catholic bishops urge equitable distribution of health care resources for all persons and approve the medical emphasis more personalized patient care. Medical-moral issues must be discussed. A special emphasis is given to service for the poor that includes prevention as well as a cure.

3645 Kastenbaum, Robert J. "Death Penalty." In *Encyclopedia of Death,* ed. by Robert Kastenbaum and Beatrice Kastenbaum, 85–89. Phoenix, Ariz.: Oryx Press, 1989.

After a brief survey of the death penalty throughout history, capital punishment is reviewed in various Western nations and sections of the United States. Current controversy is described and key references are included.

3646 Letts, Harold C. *Health Care in America: A National Illness.* New York: Lutheran Church in America, 1974.

A series of articles by health practitioners and denominational leaders (Lutheran) describe public policy for care of the sick and dying in Canada and the United States. Issues for public policy include planning and regulation, accessibility of health care, cost of benefits, training and distribution of medical personnel, accountability for quality care, public education for health, the ministry of individual congregations.

3647 *Preserving the Right to Choose.* New York: American Civil Liberties Union, 1986.

This small book offers practical advice for legal and loving coping with violence and disruption at abortion clinics. This includes creating a climate of reasonable understanding with public officials, security measures and relevant constitutional principles and court procedures when "pro-life" advocates use intimidation or violence against abortion clinics.

3648 Russell, O. Ruth. *Freedom to Die: Moral and Legal Aspects of Euthanasia.* Rev. ed. New York: Human Sciences Press, 1977.

See 3494.

3649 Veatch, Robert M. *Death, Dying and the Biological Revolution: Our Last Quest for Responsibility.* New Haven, Conn.: Yale University Press, 1976.

See 3450.

3.9 ECONOMICS

3650 Consumers' Reports, ed. *Funerals: Consumers' Last Rites.* New York: W. W. Norton Co., 1977.

The editors of Consumer Reports present an overview of the high cost of funerals and burials both in terms of money and emotions, alternatives to the conventional funeral, the specifics of financial arrangements for a funeral and burial, the alternatives of cremation and direct burial. The possibility of memorial societies and pre-need plans. Appendices legal and financial information. Notes from a variety of sources.

3651 Lippett, Peter E. *Estate Planning: What Anyone Who Owns Anything Must Know.* Reston, Va.: Reston Pub. Co., 1979.

Various options for estate planning are reviewed along with recommended procedures and an assessment of consequences.

3652 Porter, Sylvia. *Sylvia Porter's New Money Book for the 80's.* Garden City, N.Y.: Doubleday and Co., 1979.

3653 Wiest, Walter E., ed. *Health Care and Its Cost: A Challenge for the Church*. Lanham, Md.: University Press of America, 1988.

Essays in this volume consider the impact of rising costs of health care in the United States and the ethical questions raised by them. After chapters of factual information and specific issues of treatment related to rising costs, there are essays on Christian ethical principles and suggestions for consumer awareness in church and community.

Chapter 4

GRIEF

4.1 THE GRIEVING PROCESS/STAGES

4001 Averill, J. R. "Grief: Its Nature and Significance." *Psychological Bulletin* 70 (1968): 721–748.

"Bereavement behavior" is considered to be a total response pattern to the loss of a loved object. This includes the components of mourning (social expectations) and grief (distress of biological origin following loss). The features of grief include (a) symptoms of withdrawal, fatigue, sleep disturbance, loss of appetite; (b) the symptoms are connected to a well-defined stimulus situation which is a real or imagined loss, which is resolved through new object relations; (c) the phenomenon appears both among human beings and in higher primates; (d) the emotions are extremely stressful both in body and mind and yet behavior during grief is not conducive to the establishment of new relations which would alleviate stress.

4002 Bowlby, John. "Process of Mourning." *International Journal of Psycho-Analysis* 42 (1961): 317–340. Reprinted in *The Meaning of Despair*, ed. by Willard Gaylin, 263–320. New York: Science House, 1968.

From his studies of separation anxiety among widows and children who suffer loss, a psychiatrist suggests a three stage pattern of the grief process: (1) an instinctual urge to recover the loss object, which may be recognized as weeping and anger, (2) despair or disorganization, and (3) reorganization directed toward a new object. In contrast, pathological grief is a persistent desire for union with a permanently lost object. See also Bowlby (1168).

4003 Bowlby, John. *Loss: Sadness and Depression*. Vol. 3. *Attachment and Loss*. New York: Basic Books, 1980.

As part of his clinical study of loss the author finds that the process of grief will characteristically include these processes: (1) a stage of being stunned along with some denial of the loss; (2) an urge to find, recover and reunite with the lost person; (3) despair, disorganization and depression concerning the future; and (4) a final phase of reorganization and the return of interests and appetites. See also Bowlby (1170, 1172).

4004 Brewster, Henry H. "Grief: A Disrupted Human Relationship." *Human Organization*, 9(1950): 19–22.

A case history provides clear demonstration of the interactional problems to be found in a grieving person, including interdependence of two partners in a human relationship and how behavior and subjective state of the survivor changes when relationship has been broken by death, and the need for bereaved to release emotional ties to the deceased, subsequent to replacement of the type of interaction lost. If there is an inability to tolerate attending emotional distress, morbid grief reaction develops, in which distress of grief is hidden by a protracted state of emotional preoccupation and impairment of mental functioning. Thus a neurosis results, requiring psychiatric help.

4005 Glick, Ira O., Robert S. Weiss, and C. Murray Parkes. *The First Year of Bereavement*. New York: John Wiley and Sons, 1974.

See 1365.

4006 Gorer, Geoffrey. *Death, Grief, and Mourning*. Garden City, N.Y.: Doubleday, 1965.

See 1012.

4007 Lewis, C. S. *A Grief Observed*. New York: Seabury Press, 1961.

See 2139.

4008 Parkes, Colin M. "Seeking and Finding A Lost Object: Evidence From Recent Studies of the Reaction to Bereavement." *Social Science and Medicine* 4 (1970): 187–201.

During the "angry" phase of grief, mourners have an urge to recover the lost object (see Bowlby 1169). For a time the permanence of the loss is disregarded, but since the act of searching is unrewarded, the loss becomes more real. Symptoms of the "searching" are restlessness, physical searching for the deceased, preoccupation with thoughts of the lost one, the fixing of attention upon stimuli that suggest the continual presence of the deceased. Then comes disorganization and despair followed by a final phase of reorganization.

4009 Parkes, Colin M. *Bereavement: Studies of Grief in Adult Life.* New York: International Universities Press, 1972.

See 4244.

4010 Pollock, George H. "The Mourning Process." *Chicago Theological Seminary* 57, 3 (December 1966): 15–23.

The Director of Research for the Chicago Institute for Psycho-analysis describes the process of mourning as a "series of operations and stages whose appearance seems to follow a sequential pattern": a first response of shock, a second response of inadequacy and despair that contains many physical signs of pain, a third phase in which the separation is accepted. Persons "with earlier unresolved conflicts in this sphere" take longer and have an intense reaction, whereas persons with "healthy object relationship" of total assimilation or identification with the lost one will have a "comparatively short-lived" mourning process that comes "to a spontaneous end." The article is contained in the same issue of the *Register* which has a description by Elisabeth Ross (later known as Kübler-Ross) on her "experiment and experience" with theological students as they sought together to understand dying patients. I do not know if Dr. Ross had read the original publication of Dr. Pollock's article in volume 42 of the *International Journal of Psycho-Analysis*, 1961.

4011 Schoenberg, Bernard, *et al.,* eds. *Loss and Grief: Psychological Management In Medical Practice.* New York: Columbia University Press, 1970.

As part of a general study of the medical aspects of loss management, the clinical practice of a psychiatrist in relation to loss and grief is presented as adaptive or maladaptive responses to loss: a child's reaction to death in the family and the reaction of family and medical personnel to the fatal illness of a child, reaction to loss and management of organs or functions of the body, reactions to patient by family and staff, grief in literature, hospital chaplaincy. Annotated bibliography in addition to references for each chapter. See Schoenberg (3150).

4012 Schoenberg, Bernard, *et al.,* eds. *Bereavement: Its Psychosocial Aspects.* New York: Columbia University Press, 1975.

In cooperation with the Foundation of Thanatology, clinicians in health services and sociologists present brief reviews of the bereavement process, the family, the health profession and therapeutic intervention.

4013 Silverman, Phyllis R. "Services to the Widowed: First Steps in a Program of Preventive Intervention." *Community Mental Health Journal* 3 (1967): 37–44.

From her experience in counseling widows, the author describes an initial phase of impact (shock, numbness, denial), a longer phase of anger, depression, search for meaning, coping with loneliness, painful memories and continuing attachment to the deceased, fluctuations between denial and acceptance. A third phase involves acceptance of the loses and its consequences. There is an acknowledged change in the self image of the survivor and a capacity for reinvestment in sources of satisfaction.

4014 Simos, Bertha G. *A Time to Grieve: Loss as a Universal Human Experience*. New York: Family Service Association of America, 1979.

A social worker presents a comprehensive study of fear of loss, duration of mourning, initial responses, denial, somatic distress and other personal reactions. There is hope in the interpretation of loss as an agent of change. The work appeared before the stage model of grief was widely questioned.

4015 Spiegel, Yorick. *The Grief Process: Analysis and Counseling*. Trans. by Elsbeth Duke. Nashville, Tenn.: Abingdon Press, 1977.

A German pastoral theologian combines a psychoanalytic point of view with sociological knowledge in a review of literature on theory and symptomatology of grief and the process of bereavement. The social aspects of grief are considered as status transitions and the role of various care-giving agents in the transaction is presented. Psychoanalytic topics of coping are then examined in detail: narcissistic, aggressive, libidinal. Theoretical relationships to theology and the church are discussed. Bibliography.

4016 Switzer, David K. *The Dynamics of Grief: Its Source, Pain and Healing*. New York: Abingdon Press, 1970.

A pastoral counselor notices that an acute grief reaction is remarkably similar to a classic anxiety attack. Protective devices avoid and diminish the severity of pain through denial, repression, regression, idealization, identification. Through these defences a person reduces the fear of the loss of the self through separation. See also Bowlby (1171); Neale (1193); Zilboorg (1200).

4017 Tatelbaum, Judy. *The Courage to Grieve: Creative Living, Recovery and Growth Through Grief*. New York: Harper and Row, 1980.

In a very readable style the author provides personal advice on an understanding of the stages of grief for lay readers. Hope is given that life can be creative for those who have the courage to work through stages of grief to recovery. This positive approach to grief is based on principles of gestalt therapy. See also Di Giulio (4226).

4018 Weizman, Sabine Gross and Phyllis Kamm. *About Mourning: Support and Guidance for the Bereaved.* New York: Human Sciences Press, 1985.

A psychiatrist and a free-lance writer describe the process of mourning in terms of family loss, the loss of various relationships and the significance of the family as a support system. The style is friendly and many examples are given to help individuals confront death throughout life. See also Lopata (4241), Pincus (4229).

4019 White, Robert B. and Leroy T. Gathman. "The Syndrome of Ordinary Grief." In *American Family Physician* 8 (1973): 97–104.

From their experience in family practice, two physicians describe definable stages of grief: (1) shock, numbness, disbelief; (2) painful longing and preoccupation with memories and mental images; (3) resolution and resumption of ordinary life activities.

4.11 ANTICIPATORY GRIEF

4020 Fulton, Robert and J. Fulton. "Psychological Aspects of Terminal Care: Anticipatory Grief." *Omega* 2 (1971): 91–99. Reprinted in *Caring Relationships: The Dying and the Bereaved*, ed. by R. A. Kalish. 87–96. Farmingdale, N.Y.: Baywood Pub. Co., 1980.

Families of the terminally ill usually go through a phase of grief before the physical death of a loved one. This will include depression experienced by various members of the family, an increased concern for the terminally ill person, various ruminations about the approaching death and some attempts to adjust to the consequences of loss. Preconditioning absorbs the reality of the loss over a period of time, encourages the resolving of past conflicts and expressions of feelings, initiates changes about life and identity and starts plans for the future without a feeling that the loved one is being betrayed.

4021 Futterman, E. H. and M. Sabshin. "Parental Anticipatory Mourning." In *Psychosocial Aspects of Terminal Care*, ed. by B. Schoenberg, *et al.*, 243–274. New York: Columbia University Press, 1972.

The mellowing process of grief is strengthened by the anticipatory sorrow of parents who become progressively convinced that a child's death is inevitable, experience physical, psychological and interpersonal turmoil associated with the coming loss, a sense of confidence in both the worth of

the child and of life in general, the withdrawal of some emotional investment from the child and a fixed image of the child that will endure beyond
death. The parents' detachment is not so much from the child who is dying
as it is from their existential image of the child as a growing being. See
also references in THE LOSS OF A CHILD (4.42) and Rando (4025).

4022 Knight, James A. and Frederic Herter. "Anticipatory Grief." In
     Death and Bereavement, ed. by Austin H. Kutscher. Springfield, Ill:
     Charles C. Thomas, 1969.

A psychiatrist and a surgeon present the special problems of grief
that follows long anticipated death. The death is anti-climatic, without
drama. A transient resurgence of grief may come, but dulled by months of
anticipation. The end is often marked by a sense of release from protracted
anguish and suffering. The suppressed relief may bring on confusion and
guilt.

4023 Janis, I. L. *Psychological Stress.* New York: John Wiley and Sons,
     1958.

Anticipatory grief was noted as a benefit to surgery patients who did
the "work of worry" prior to surgery. Thus less anesthesia was necessary
and post-operative pain was born as a consequence that had been predicted.
Pre-operative patients benefited from conversations with amputees.

4024 Pattison, E. Mansell. "Help in the Dying Process." In *American
     Handbook of Psychiatry,* ed. by S. Iretia. Vol. I, 685–700. New
     York: Basic Books, 1974.

A psychiatrist defines the fears of patients and their families in
coping with anticipatory grief and offers positive suggestions for help in
the process of dying.

4025 Rando, Therese A. "An Investigation of Grief and Adaptation in
     Parents Whose Children Had Died From Cancer." *Journal of
     Pediatric Psychology* 8 (1983): 3–20.

One factor in the adjustment of parents to the death of children is the
length of time in which death is anticipated. When this was less then six
months or longer than eighteen months, parental adjustment was difficult.
A long illness increased anger. See also Futterman and Sabshin (4021).

4026 Rando, Therese A., ed. *Loss and Anticipatory Grief.* Lexington,
     Mass.: Lexington Books, 1986.

Through interdisciplinary contributions, this book provides a fore-
warning of loss in a positive and creative way. Authorities from various
disciplines demonstrate the dangers of premature detachment from the

dying person, poor communication, lack of appropriate acts and failure to close the relationship. Examples are provided of the way in which therapeutic intervention can aid both the dying person and those who mourn to experience anticipatory grief and receive realistic guidance and support for the work of grief that goes on through death, mourning and resolution of loss. Specific questions are provided on such issues as personal, social and spiritual experience that conditioned attitudes towards death among the aging. Other sections are more for professionals on the specific psychological issues that are to be faced in caring for the dying and grieving family members. Practical and precise wisdom offered in a spirit of equalitarian understanding.

4027 Schoenberg, Bernard, *et al.*, eds. *Anticipatory Grief.* New York: Columbia University Press, 1974.

All possible fields that could contribute to the management of anticipatory grief seem to be represented in brief chapters organized around introductory concepts, clinical aspects, childhood illness, the health professions, the management of anticipatory grief and pastoral work. Some references to research and much to the experience of individual professionals.

4.2   CIRCUMSTANCES/STRESS
See also SPECIAL CIRCUMSTANCES (3.25)

4028 Gersten, J. C., *et al.* "Child Behavior and Life Events: Undesirable Change or Change per se?" In *Stressful Life Events*, ed. by Barbara Snell Dohrenwend and Bruce P. Dohrenwend, 159–170. New York: John Wiley and Sons, 1974.

In the study of a large sample of children, the authors conclude that a balance of desirable and undesirable events is a better predictor of crippling stress than a cumulative total of all changes measured.

4029 Hoff, B. Lee Ann. *People in Crisis: Understanding and Helping.* 3rd ed. Menlo Park, Calif.: Addison-Wesley Pub. Co., 1989.

The personal and cultural context of crises are presented for frontline crisis workers and others. The text reviews crisis theory and practice, violence as an organ of and response to crisis, situational and transitional states such as change during life passages, and a crisis update on AIDS. Selected bibliography.

4030 Hulmes, T. H. and R. H. Rahe. "The Social Readjustment Rating Scale." *Journal of Psychosomatic Research* 11 (1967): 213–218.

An objective self-report measure was developed to assess forty-three critical life events, of which death was number one (100) and divorce was number 2 (73). Numbers on this Social Readjustment Rating Scale (100, 73, etc.) weighed the magnitude that each event would require. Later researches concluded that the desirability of change should be given heightened significance along with measures of the amount of life change (Gersten 4028).

4031 Lindemann, Erich. "Psychological Factors as Stressor Agents." In *Stress and Psychiatric Disorder: Mental Health Research Fund Proceedings*, ed. by J. M. Tanner. Oxford: Blackwell Scientific Publications, 1960.

Bereavement is considered to be a response to social stress brought on by the loss of interaction with a loved one. The response will be healthy if the individual can reorganize the social system in a rewarding way.

4032 Mitchell, Kenneth R., and Herbert Anderson. *All Our Losses, All* · *Our Griefs: Resources for Pastoral Care.* Philadelphia: Westminister Press, 1983.

Two pastoral counselors consider the uniqueness of grieving responses to loss with an evaluation of that which is helpful and unhelpful. Instead of a repetition of stages of grief, the authors state that no two occasions are ever exactly the same. In part this is due to the variety of contexts of grief, which are presented. Caring responses to bereavement involve the theological proclamation that we have been made responsible by God to care for one another in any of the six major types of loss: material, relationship, intra-psychic, functional, role, systemic. A grief is often a combination of several types of loss. Whatever the loss, grief must be encouraged with an open expression of the personal responses of an individual. At times it is difficult to follow the theological assumptions of the authors, since some of the theological reflections come out of psychological discussions and seem to be more implicit than explicit.

4033 Oates, Wayne E. *Your Particular Grief.* Philadelphia: Westminster Press, 1981.

A pastoral psychologist identifies five distinct types of grief, stages of grief, psychological and spiritual resources for recovery. A sensitive study for those who are ready to review grief in their lives and others.

4034 Selye, Hans. *The Stress of Life.* 2nd ed. New York: McGraw-Hill Book Co., 1976.

In a readable presentation of the physiological ability of the body to cope with stress, a physician identified a set of reactions as the General Adaptation Syndrome. It appears in the stages of alarm reaction, resistance, exhaustion. When the power of adaptation is exceeded by the stress, diseases of adaptation may result, such as ulcers. The findings were similar to those of Lindemann, who related them first to crises in human relationships (4332) and later to a sudden loss (4044).

4035 Sheskin, Arlene and Samuel E. Wallace. "Differing Bereavements: Suicide, Natural, and Accidental Death." In *Death, Dying, Transcending*, ed. by Richard A. Kalish. Farmingdale, N.Y.: Baywood Publishing Co., 1980.

Data is compared from two studies of widows and offer the following observations about circumstances: time to anticipate the death of a spouse is important in the widow's ability to accept relief as an appropriate bereavement reaction; the most severe reactions were to unanticipated death, for the world had suddenly lost its meaning; emotional distress is accentuated when the widow blames herself, especially in the search for explanations after suicide; bereavement is a lonely and isolating experience regardless of cause of death and there are few good listeners available to bereaved persons (clergy were seen only in their ceremonial role by widows); recovery is facilitated over the period of a year by both imagined as well as real-life independence in identity, role and relationships.

4.21 ACCIDENTS/CATASTROPHES

4036 Bush, John C. *Disaster Response: A Handbook for Church Action*. Scottsdale, Pa.: Herald Press, 1979.

An executive of the Kentucky Council of Churches discusses long-range planning for disaster readiness, how people react to disasters and models for disaster ministries, some theological considerations of catastrophe. The book includes comprehensive listings of governmental, denominational and private resources.

4037 Des Pres, Terrence. *The Survivor: An Anatomy of Life in the Death Camps*. New York: Pocket Books, 1976.

From personal accounts and other studies, the Holocaust survivor is seen as the new hero of the twentieth century, for this person endures under prolonged crises and the threat of death.

4038 Erikson, Kai T. *Everything in Its Path: Destruction of Community in the Buffalo Creek Flood*. New York: Simon and Schuster, 1976.

After presenting the sociological background of the Appalachian mountain ethos, the author discusses his findings concerning the individual trauma of shock among those who were bereaved and the collective trauma of all in losing a sense of community. Two years after the disaster, survivors reported that they had lost interest in keeping an intact household. They had been crowded into trailer homes with no concern for their former neighborhoods and were at the dead end of a long history of deprivation in mining towns.

4039 Gleser, Goldin C., Bonnie L. Green, and Carolyn Winget. *Prolonged Psychosocial Effects of Disaster*. New York: Academic Press, 1981.

Members of the University of Cincinnati Department of Psychiatry reviewed the documents of survivor-plaintiffs after the collapse of a slag dam at Buffalo Creek, West Virginia in 1972. There were follow-up studies of some plaintiffs from a questionnaire on sleep. It was clear that disturbances in this area were the most striking evidence of the disaster for more than two years following. The authors also found that victims that suffered the traumatic loss of family members were more severely disturbed than those who had only lost material possessions. In households where the family atmosphere was supportive, children showed less psychopathology than other children. Children of school age suffered more difficulties than those of pre-school age. The scattering of families into trailer camps attributed to a sense of victimization among survivors.

4040 Glick, Ira O., Robert S. Weiss, and Colin M. Parkes. *The First Year of Bereavement*. New York: John Wiley and Sons, 1974.

Among findings concerning widows was a disinclination to remarry among widows who had no time of anticipatory grief. The depth of grief was similar between those who had time and those who did not, but those who had experienced a sudden loss would not risk the possibility of another loss for themselves or their children. The ability to cope with stress was questioned in their own minds. See Glick (1365).

4041 Harvey, Carol D. H. and Howard B. Bahr. *The Sunshine Widows: Adapting to Sudden Bereavement*. Lexington, Mass.: Lexington Books, 1980.

Two surveys 1972, 1977 of the wives of miners killed in the Sunshine Mine disaster were used to review the events of the disaster, characteristics of the women and the families before the fire. Then there is the recounting of the blame, scapegoating, community reactions and tensions that lead to adjustments in the community network. Personal reactions at the time of the fire and five years later are recounted.

4042 Hershiser, Marvin R. and E. L. Quarantelli. "The Handling of the Dead in a Disaster." In *Death and Dying: Views From Many Cultures*, ed. by Richard A. Kalish, 132–144. Farmingdale, N.Y.: Baywood Pub. Co., 1980.

In a study of reports from grief after the death of 237 people in Rapid City, South Dakota during a 1972 flood, much respect for the dead was shown by those who were involved in rescue operations, with a high priority given to the "proper" completion of the task.

4043 Lifton, Robert J. *Death in Life: Survivors of Hiroshima*. New York: Random House, 1968.

During a study of the impact of atomic destruction the author notes reasons why Americans have difficulty dealing with death after World War II: representation, exclusion of the aged and dying, movement toward the nuclear family, secularization away from religion, faith in the advances of medical technology, a blotting of sensitivity to individual death in the face of mass death and destruction. See also Lifton (1157, 1308).

4044 Lindemann, Erich. "Symptomatology and Management of Acute Grief." *American Journal of Psychiatry*, 101(1944): 141–148.

After the death of many persons in the "Coconut Grove" nightclub fire, psychiatric interviews were conducted with bereaved disaster victims. Additional observations were made of psycho-neurotic patients who lost a relative during the course of treatment, relatives of patients who died in the hospital and relatives of members of the Armed Forces. The total sample was 101 patients. An analysis of the interviews led to the following conclusions: (1) Acute grief is a definite syndrome with psychological and somatic symptomatology; (2) this syndrome may appear immediately after a crisis, or it may be delayed or it may be exaggerated or apparently absent; (3) in place of the typical syndrome there may appear distorted pictures, each of which represent one special aspect of the grief syndrome; (4) by appropriate psychological techniques these distorted pictures can be successfully transformed into a normal grief reaction with resolution. The symptomatology of normal grief is described as: somatic sensations occurring in waves lasting from 20 minutes to an hour at a time, a feeling of tightness in the throat, choking with shortness of breath, need for sighing, an empty feeling in the abdomen, a lack of muscular power and an intense subjective distress described as tension or mental pain. In the acute phase of grief there is also a sense of unreality, emotional distance from other people, feelings of guilt and some tendency to respond with irritability and anger. Each of these points may become severe and signal possible pathology. A possibility of pathology is heightened by attempts to avoid the intense distress connected with the grief experience and to avoid the expression of emotion necessary for it. If this continues for some time, the following morbid grief reactions may appear: a postponement of any emotional response, alteration of conduct such as overactivity without a sense of loss, acquisitions of symptoms belonging to the last illness of the deceased, the development of a recognized medical disease (ulcerative colitis, rheumatoid arthritis, and asthma), difficulties in relationships with friends and relatives, furious hostility against specific persons, a sense of "going through the motions of living" that sound schizophrenic, a lasting loss of patterns of social interaction, "stupid axiom" that signal self-punitive behavior within, and agitated depression. Brief examples from patients or relatives are given. The essential task of managing normal or pathological grief is to share in the grief work so that the grieving person can be extracted from bondage to the deceased and find new patterns of rewarding interaction. Special attention should be given to any under-reaction of the bereaved. Religious agencies are considered to be the leader in dealing with bereaved under normal conditions, and psychiatric treatment may be indicated if there is unusual and sustained hostility. The study and conclusions were foundational for many other studies and have been cited in many texts on thanatology. For example, Stroebe considers this to be "the first systematic-empirical study of morbid grief reactions." (1379, 17). Lindemann's conclusion that "grief work" is necessary to overcome a loss became axiomatic in grief therapy and introduced a term that is constantly repeated. See Lindemann, (4332), Selye (4034).

4045 Pennebaker, J. W. and R. C. O'Heeron. "Confiding in Others and Illness Rate among Spouses of Suicide and Accidental Death Victims." *Journal of Abnormal Psychology* 93 (1984): 473–476.

In a survey of survivors whose spouses had either died in an accident or by suicide, the authors found evidence that bereaved individuals benefit from talking about this loss to friends. They also found a positive correlation between the increase in illness rates (from before to after the death) and the bereaved person's ruminating about the spouse's death.

4046 Pine, Vanderlyn R., ed. *Responding to Disaster*. Milwaukee, Minn.: Bulfin, 1974.

With support from the Emergency Preparedness and Disaster Committee of the National Funeral Directors Association a sociologist gathered articles on disaster: legal and medical, federal government, funeral director, emergency plans. The most commonly discussed disasters were air crashes, mine fires and flash floods. Bibliography.

4047 Pine, Vanderlyn R. "Grief Work and Dirty Work: The Aftermath of an Air Crash." In *Death and Dying: Views From Many Cultures*, ed. by Richard A. Kalish, 126–131. Farmingdale, N.Y.: Baywood Pub. Co., 1980.

From participant observation of rescue operations after thirty-two persons were killed during a plane crash in New England, a sociologist found that rescue experts concentrated upon their technical task rather than offering solace and sympathy to relatives who would have distracted them. Although volunteers and experts worked together in the initial handling of corpses, the sheer number of gruesome remains led most "willing workers" to disappear and identification experts and funeral directors were left with upsetting work that went on for days.

4048 Hodgkinson, Peter E., and Michael Stewart. *Coping with Catastrophe*. London: Routledge, 1991.

Skilled therapists describes immediate and long-term attempts of people to cope with catastrophe.

4049 Wolfstein, Martha. *Disaster: A Psychological Essay*. 1957. Reprint. New York: Arno Press, 1977.

A psychologist gives special attention to the inner, psychic dynamics of the experience of a disaster. These dynamics include an upsurge of loving feelings toward others just after a disaster and the sense of humility expressed by survivors as an attempt to avoid being punished by The Powers That Be for feeling superior to those who have perished. She also considers the question of why some people ignore clear warnings and others take precautions for safety. The material is organized into sections on threat, impact and aftermath.

4050 Winslow, Gerald R. *Triage and Justice*. Berkeley, Calif.: University of California Press, 1982.

A professor of religion considers the ethics of rationing life-saving medical resources during disasters such as earthquakes. Rawls' theory of justice as fairness is used to judge the ethical question: how should medical resources be allocated when there are too few to save the lives of all the who need them? Extensive bibliography.

4.22 VIOLENCE/WAR/HOMICIDE
See also RAPE/BATTERED WOMAN SYNDROME (4.361)

4051 Allen, Nancy H. *Homicide*. New York: Human Sciences Press, 1980.

A public health worker uses case histories from varying police departments and bio-statistics to provide guidelines for homicide prevention.

4052 Bedau, Hugo Adam, ed. *The Death Penalty in America*. 3rd. ed. Oxford: Oxford University Press, 1982.

Empirical investigations, philosophical and legal opinions are presented in a survey of American attitudes toward the penalty, problems of terrorism, deterrence and the death penalty, criminal justice and the capital offender, moral and other arguments for and against the death penalty. Bibliography, table of cases.

4053 Blume, Judy. *Tiger-Eyes*. Scarsdale, N. Y.: Bardbury Press, 1981.

When her father is murdered in his store during a robbery, a young daughter learns to cope with the death and to assist her mother and little brother as well. This is a realistic presentation of consequences to violent death.

4054 Coerr, Eleanor. *Sadako and the Thousand Paper Cranes*. New York: G. P. Putnam and Sons, 1977.

An American recounts the story of a young girl who gradually died because of atomic bomb radiation. She tried to fold one thousand oragami paper cranes because Japanese children believe that if you make a wish with each one, your wish will come true. She died before she had folded a thousand cranes and obtained her wish to get well. Classmates completed a thousand cranes in her memory and this has been repeated in following years by children in other parts of the world.

4055 Denton, Donald D., Jr. "Ethical and Therapeutic Reflections from a Survivor of the Seige at Khe Sanh." *Journal of Pastoral Care* 42 (1988): 309–317.

A pastoral counselor who was also a veteran of the Viet Nam war describes his counsel with a despairing veteran of the same conflict. The author noted the ethical dilemma of survivorship versus suicide in his client and proposed questions from the ethical system of James Gustafson that would mitigate despair through a consideration of reflections such as: "What is God enabling and requiring us to be and to do in these circumstances.?" This therapeutic modality encouraged a latent impulse for life with ethical meaning in spite of the wish for death by the client.

4056 Devine, Philip E. *The Ethics of Homicide*. Ithaca, N.Y.: Cornell University Press, 1978.

A professor of philosophy includes abortion, capital punishment, euthanasia, suicide and war under the classification of homicide. His moral rule against homicide is "primae facie wrong in itself, apart from the bad side effects it is also likely to have." Bibliography.

4057 Eliot, Thomas D. "War Bereavements and Their Recovery." *Marriage and Family Living* 8 (1946): 1–6.

At the close of World War II, a pioneer in research on death and society compares bereavement from wartime killing with the usual causes of bereavement.

4058 Elliot, Gil. *Twentieth Century Book of the Dead*. New York: C. Scribner, 1972.

The millions of deaths in the twentieth century from wars and the technology of violence are described in terms of impact upon society and human nature.

4059 Frank, Anne. *Anne Frank: The Diary of a Young Girl*. Trans. by B. M. Mooyaart-Doubleday. New York: Noble and Noble, 1972.

The diary of a sensitive girl concludes with her death in a Nazi concentration camp but is extended before and afterwards in the story of other events in her family.

4060 Freud, Sigmund. "Thoughts for the Times on War and Death." In Sigmund Freud, *Collected Papers*. Vol. 4, 288–317. London: Hogarth Press, 1925.

The father of psychoanalysis evaluated the early twentieth century Western assumption that death was a mere accident which enlightened humans should control. In such a culture death would not be viewed as fear of divine judgment, but as a fear of infringement on life, liberty, pursuit of happiness. The true nature of death is distorted or suppressed. Unfortunately, Freud did not distinguish between the existential necessity of death and our feelings about the particular cause of death from disease or accident. (For some of these distinctions, see Kastenbaum and Aisenberg, 1018). But he did distinguish between our inability to conceive of our own death, which is a sign of our unconscious sense of immortality and our pleasurable thought about the death of another, especially an enemy. The theme of subconscious sense of immortality is reinterpreted as a primary paradox by Weisman (1165) and as "symbolic immortality" by Lifton (2224). For a study of Freud's personal struggle with death, see Schur (3031).

4061 Friedlander, A. H., ed. *Out of the Whirlwind: A Reader of Holocaust Literature*. New York: Schocken, 1976.

Fiction, drama, poetry, survivor, and eyewitness accounts, philosophical and theological discussion, art and literature are combined in this anthology of the holocaust.

4062 Glatstein, J.; I. Knox; and S. Margoshes, eds. *Anthology of Holocaust Literature*. New York: Athenieum, 1975.

Poems, short-stories, sections of novels, diaries, autobiographies and eyewitness accounts are provided of ghetto and concentration camp life under the Nazi's. A glossary of terms, biographies of authors and introduction are included.

4063 Henry, Andrew F. and James F. Short, Jr. *Suicide and Homicide*. New York: Free Press, 1954.

The authors conclude that suicide varies negatively and homicide positively with the strength of external restraint over behavior. This is based on a discerning analysis of the psychology of aggression, the sociology of culture (especially in Durkheim and Weber) and the statistical studies of trends and cycles. Notes and bibliography.

4064 Simpson, Michael A. *Dying, Death and Grief: A Critical Bibliography*. Pittsburgh, Pa.: University of Pittsburgh Press, 1987

Lists of titles are included in brief chapters on murder, terrorism, nuclear holocaust and megadeath.

4065 Hinton, S. E. *The Outsiders*. New York: Dell, 1967.

In a first person description of adolescence in a Southwestern city that is divided by gangs, the author describes the loyalty of friends and closeness of three brothers who try to form a family in the midst of a violent world that involves a suicide and the death of a friend.

4066 Lifton, Robert J. *Home from the War: Vietnam Veterans—Neither Victims nor Executioners*. New York: Simon and Schuster, 1973.

In a study of Vietnam veterans the author finds that enduring psychic scars continue after immersion in the imagery and situations of death as both victims and executioners in Southeast Asia.

4067 Pasternack, Stefan A., ed. *Violence and Victims*. New York: Spectrum Publications, 1975.

Psychiatrists and social workers recommend evaluation and treatment for dangerous persons, child-abusing parents, rapists, or men who have committed atrocities in the military. Some specialized issues are aggression in adolescence, pseudo-homosexual panic and violence, the treatment of accidental victims, anger and anxiety.

4068 Roskies, David G. *Against the Apocalypse: Responses to Catastrophe in Modern Jewish Culture*. Chicago: University of Chicago Press, 1984.

Jewish responses to a variety of catastrophes, disasters and persecutions are presented as recurrent traumas of history that culminate in the 20th century as the Holocaust.

4069 Santoli, Al. *Everything We Had: An Oral History of the Vietnam War: by Thirty-Three American Soldiers Who Fought It*. New York: Random House, 1981.

4070 Seiden, Richard H. and Raymond P. Freitas. "Shifting Patterns of Deadly Violence." *Suicide and Life-Threatening Behavior* 10 (Winter 1980): 195–209.

Although total suicide rates have been stable (1966–1975), there has been a dramatic shift towards reduction of suicide among the aged and an unprecedented increase of suicide and homicide at younger ages.

4071 Sonnenberg, Stephen M., Arthur S. Blank, Jr., and John A. Talbott, eds. *The Trauma of War: Stress and Recovery in Viet Nam Veterans.* Washington, D.C.: American Psychiatric Press, 1985.

Psychiatrists, psychologists and social workers provide clinical accounts of the psychological ravages of war upon veterans who received various modes of treatment. Special readjustment needs of blacks, Hispanics and women veterans are also addressed. The development of therapy of post-traumatic stress disorder is reviewed.

4072 Wiesel, Elie. *Night.* New York: Avon Books, 1969.

The author's experience of suffering in a Nazi concentration camp is described in the novel of a young boy and his father who must face existential questions of suffering, death, horror.

4073 Wyschogrod, Edith. *Spirit in Ashes: Hegel, Heidegger, and Man-Made Mass Death.* New Haven, Conn.: Yale University Press, 1985.

Building upon the wound of nuclear annihilation and the horrors of Nazi concentration camps, a philosopher offers the following presuppositions: before World War I, death was dominated by the "authenticity paradigm" which was exclusively concerned with the end of a self-contained monad. The philosophic understanding of WWI introduced philosophies such as that of Zeno in which death was seen with a new logic; large numbers of persons could be killed by persons in power who think that there is an infinite reserve of other victims. This philosophy of mass death can be related to Hegel's theory that war is necessary for the sublimation of individual ego on behalf of the state. To Hegel this was a higher form of reason. There was no higher power, for God could be negated in the Hegelian philosophy that considers nothing outside of human intelligibility. Heidegger remained within the domain of a traditional view of death as the end of a self-contained monad and did not grasp the importance of human social relationships for an understanding of death. The author's emphases is upon inner personal relationships expressed in language, thinking, self and society. See Heidegger (2019), Wittgenstein (2071).

4.221 POST TRAUMATIC STRESS DISORDER

4074 Braun, Bennett, ed. *Treatment of Multiple Personality Disorder.* Washington, D.C.: American Psychiatric Press, 1986.

In defense against prolonged childhood trauma, patients develop multiple selves as a necessary defense. Guidelines for the treatment of this devastating type of trauma provide guidelines for help to persons who suffer traumatic stress in adulthood.

4075 Brende, Joel O. and Erwin R. Parson. *Vietnam Veterans: The Road to Recovery.* New York: Plenum Press, 1985.

Solid treatment considerations are provided for those who work with Vietnam veterans who suffer from post-traumatic stress.

4076 Cleland, Max. *Strong at the Broken Places.* Lincoln, Va.: Chosen Books, 1980.

The director of the Veterans Administration under President Carter provides a personal account of the physical and emotional trauma that he suffered as a Vietnam veteran.

4077 Figley, Charles R., ed. *Trauma and Its Wake.* New York: Brunner/ Mazel, 1985.

Both theoretical and treatment considerations are provided in this reliable study of post-traumatic stress disorder.

4078 Sinclair, N. Duncan. *Horrific Trauma: A Pastoral Response.* New York: Hayworth Press, 1991.

A pastoral counselor provides for clergy a study of post-traumatic stress syndrome that is based upon his experiential and clinical background.

4079 Sonnenberg, Stephen M., Arthur S. Blank, Jr., and John A. Talbott, eds. *The Trauma of War: Stress and Recovery in Viet Nam Veterans.* Washington, D. C.: American Psychiatric Press, 1985.

Various authors with experience in the treatment of Vietnam veterans present theory and clinical practice for the treatment of post-traumatic stress.

4080 van der Kolk, Bessel A., ed. *Post-Traumatic Stress Disorder: Psychological and Biological Sequelae.* Washington, D. C.: American Psychiatric Press, 1984.

The lasting imprint of trauma upon the human body is described along with the psychological considerations of reactions to stress.

4.23 LOSS OF PHYSICAL FUNCTION/AMPUTATION

4081 Adsett, C. A. "Emotional Reactions to Disfigurement from Cancer Therapy." *Canadian Medical Association Journal* 89 (1963): 385–391.

Reactions are discussed to mastectomy, colostomy, hysterectomy, amputation of a limb and facial disfigurement. The losses occasion intense stress and strain and may recall irrational fears of childhood that are related to self-esteem and personal attractiveness. Common emotional reactions are: regression with increased dependency needs, anxiety, depression, hostility with occasional paranoid tendencies, hypochondrisis, denial and counterphobic reactions, obsessive-compulsive orientation, and acute psychotic breaks.

4082 Marinelli, Robert P. and Arthur E. Dell Orto, eds. *The Psychological and Social Impacts of Physical Disability*. New York: Springer Pub. Co., 1977.

Various authors consider the psychological and social implications of physical disability in terms of "helping" versus "medical" models, barriers to normality, the child and the family, personal impact of disability, adjustment to the community, stigma and social rehabilitation, sexuality, contributions and rights, varieties of therapies and helping modalities. There are recommendations of books, journals, organizations, structured group experiences in rehabilitations and physical handicap.

4083 Rush, B. F., Jr. "A Surgical Oncologist's Observations." In Bernard Schoenberg, *et al.*, eds., *Anticipatory Grief,* 97–107. New York: Columbia University Press, 1974.

A surgeon describes the way in which the loss of functions and bodily organs impacts upon the self-concept of the patient and requires attention to both emotional and physical aspects of survival by the medical staff as they seek to offer care and compassion.

4084 Schoenberg, Bernard, *et al.*, eds. *Loss and Grief: Psychological Management In Medical Practice*. New York: Columbia University Press, 1970.

See 3150.

4085 Speck, Peter. *Loss and Grief in Medicine*. London: Bailliere Tyndale, 1978.

A general hospital chaplain describes the physical losses which represents a series of deprivations to which a person has to adjust. For the aged this may mean physical, social, mental reduction in significance. For patients in obstetrics, gynecology, general surgery and medicine it may be the sudden loss of a baby or grief over the loss of limb or some vital capacity such as eyesight or hearing. In addition to practical recommendations during the process of grief, the author outlines attitudes to suffering and death among Christians, Jews, Muslims, Hindus, Sikhs, Buddhists, Chinese and humanists. See also Speck (3115).

4.24 SUDDEN/EXPECTED

4086 Agee, James. *A Death in the Family.* New York: Bantam, 1969

See 3035.

4087 Engel, George L. "Sudden and Rapid Death During Psychological Stress: Folklore or Folkwisdom?" *Annals of Internal Medicine* 74 (1971): 771–782.

From newspaper reports of psychological accidents, the author was able to determine the life settings of 99 men and 64 women, such as sudden death during acute grief or on the anniversary of a death. Various studies are cited in which explanations are offered for the relationship of overwhelming excitation to sudden death.

4088 Horowitz, Mardi Jon. *Stress Response Syndromes.* 2nd ed. Northvale, N.J.: Jason Aronson, 1986.

The shock of sudden death is included among stress response syndromes by the author: witnessing a suicide, coping with the death of a parent, suicide of a friend. Bibliography.

4089 Lehrman, S. R. "Reactions to Untimely Death." *Psychiatric Quarterly* 30 (1956): 564–578.

Grief reactions tend to be more normal when death occurs in an aged person and when it has been expected. Pathological reactions to death are more frequent when the death is untimely and sudden. Reactions to untimely death represent a defense against an unbearable, painful affect or a defense against a serious internal ego-threats such as suicide. Five case histories.

4090 Parkes, Colin M., and Robert S. Weiss. *Recovery From Bereavement.* New York: Basic Books, 1983.

See Parkes 4339.

4091 Rheingold, Joseph C. *The Mother, Anxiety and Death: The Catastrophic Death Complex.* Boston: Little, Brown and Co., 1967.

The fear of mutilation and annihilation are considered in relationship to the bonding of mother and child, the meaning of anxiety and the psychology of death. The context is pathology and therapy of the neurosis.

4092 Shneidman, Edwin S. *Voices of Death.* New York: Harper and Row, 1980.

Personal documents present the feelings of persons who know that they will die soon, or thought that they would: survivors of accidents and suicide attempts, those sentenced to execution, aware of a malignant disease, in mourning. Elegant clinical study of a problem that has puzzled philosophers: do we really experience death?

4.3 CATEGORIES OF LOSS

4.31 PETS

4093 Carrick, C. *The Accident.* New York: Seabury Press, 1976.

See 6103.

4094 Coburn, J. B. *Anne and the Sand Dobbies.* New York: Seabury, 1964.

See 6105.

4095 Graeber, C. *Mustard.* New York: Macmillan Pub. Co., 1982.

See 6110.

4096 Mallonie, Bryan and Robert Ingpen. *Lifetimes: The Beautiful Way to Explain Death to Children.* New York: Bantam Books, 1983.

See 6123.

4097 Newman, Nanette. *That Dog!* Ill. by Marilyn Hafner. New York: Thomas Y. Crowell, 1983.

See 6128.

4098 Nieburg, Herbert A. and Arlene Fischer. *Pet Loss: A Thoughtful Guide for Adults and Children.* New York: Harper and Row, 1982.

A journalist and a grief therapist present advice for both parents and children that considers variations in grief and such specific issues as "putting your pet to rest" and getting a new pet.

4099 Sanford, Doris. *It Must Hurt a Lot.* Ill. by Gracie Evans. Portland, Ore.: Multnomah Press, 1985.

With colorful illustrations for the text, the author provides a book to be read to young children as they grieve for the loss of a pet.

4100 Viorst, J. *The Tenth Good Thing about Barney*. Ill. by Eric Blegrad. New York: Atheneum, 1971.

See 6135.

4101 Warburg, Sandol Stoddard. *Growing Time*. Boston: Houghton-Mifflin, 1969.

See 6136.

4102 Zeligs, Rose. "Death Is Part of Life." *California Parent-Teacher* 36 (1959): 7–12.

A child's reaction to the death of a pet is reported in this article. Most parents would like to spare their children reality of death, but that is impossible. A child should be taught that death is a natural part of life for all things. Ideally such learning should be gradual and in the course of daily experience by which ideas and attitudes are absorbed from the adult world.

4.32 DIVORCE

4103 Blume, Judy. *It's Not the End of the World*. Scarsdale, N.Y.: Bradbury Press, 1973.

A twelve year old girl hopes that her parents will become reconciled. Finally she accepts the reality of divorce.

4104 Burns, Bob. *Through the Whirlwind*. Nashville, Tenn.: Oliver-Nelson Pub., 1989.

Divorce is described as a whirlwind of emotions that move through stages of grief and recovery. Emotions similar to those of any other loss will surface: denial, anger, despair and new sources of hope.

4105 Donaldson, Kenneth and Irene Donaldson. *Married Today, Single Tomorrow: Marriage Breakup and the Law*. Garden City, N. Y.: Doubleday, 1969.

Expert financial and legal counsel is available for divided households and for those who are left alone with the care of children. The objective advice is important during the grief stages of numbness and anger in divorce.

4106 Epstein, Joseph. *Divorced in America: Marriage in an Age of Possibility*. New York: E. P. Dutton, 1974.

The emotional impact of a marriage that died is intertwined with social and moral history of divorce by an author who is describing his own pilgrimage of grief and restoration of life.

4107 Gardner, Richard A. *The Boys' and Girls' Book about Divorce, with an Introduction for Parents.* Scranton, Pa.: Science House, 1970.

Teenagers are advised by a child psychiatrist about the emotional problems of a parent's divorce: blame, anger, fear of being alone, getting along with parents who live apart.

4108 Goff, Beth. *Where is Daddy?* Boston: Beacon Press, 1969.

This book for pre-school children is the story of a child who is confused and frightened when her parents became divorced, but is able to make an adjustment.

4109 Goode, William J. *After Divorce.* Glencoe, Ill.: Free Press, 1956.

The losses and partial recovery of divorced women with children is described in this systematic study of urban Detroit.

4110 Grollman, Earl A. *Talking About Divorce and Separation: A Dialogue Between Parent and Child.* Ill. by Alison Cann. Boston: Beacon Press, 1975.

Conversation of parents with children about divorce is facilitated through drawings and texts for children that express their hurt, bewilderment and anger. This is followed by some suggested statements for parents to use in opening up the emotional aspects of their feelings and those of children about divorce. Helping agencies are then listed and books are suggested for children and for adults. Warm and confident advice.

4111 Heatherington, E. M., M. Cox and R. Cox. "Family Interaction and the Social, Emotional, and Cognitive Development of Children following Divorce." Paper presented at the Johnson Conference on the Family, Washington, D. C., 1978.

Findings are based upon measures of social interaction of children after divorce and from longitudinal analyses of individual and family functioning at various periods of time after divorce of parents. The absence of the father because of divorce was associated with a lower level of cognitive and sexual functioning in boys two years after the divorce. Girls at the same age did not appear to be similarly affected. In the absence of the father, the quality of mother-child interactions showed changes in functioning and adjustment for both boys and girls. The authors wonder if similar results would be found when the reason for father absence was due to the death of the father rather than divorce.

4112 Kindard, Wendy. *Lucky Wilma*. New York: Dial Press, 1973.

Some joy comes out of the sadness of divorce when a young girl is able to look forward to each Saturday with her daddy.

4113 Lexau, Joan M. *Me Day*. New York: Dial Press, 1971.

A young black child has fantasies about the return of his absent father and invents a "Me Day."

4114 Lund, Dale A., ed. *Older Bereaved Spouses: Research with Practical Applications*. Washington, D.C.: Hemisphere Pub. Corp., 1989.

See 4264.

4115 Madow, L. and S. E. Hardy. "Incidence and Analysis of the Broken Family in the Background of Neurosis." *American Journal of Orthopsychiatry* 17 (1947): 521–528.

In this post World War II study, a disproportionate number of neurotic soldiers were found to come from broken homes, relative to a normal military population.

4116 Mann, Peggy. *My Dad Lives in a Downtown Hotel*. Garden, N.Y.: Doubleday, 1973.

A grade-school aged boy recounts his feelings about divorce. Finally he realizes that he is not to blame for parents' separation and that he is still loved by them.

4117 Mazer, Harry. *Guy Lenny*. New York: Delacorte Press, 1971.

This book for grade school children describes the problems of a boy who is caught in a custody battle between bitter parents.

4118 Mindey, Carol. *The Divorced Mother: A Guide to Readjustment*. New York: McGraw-Hill, 1969.

An author who went through divorce and later remarried is able to warn others of the emotional problems that will be sustained during the loss of a relationship. Suggestions are given for a more meaningful and constructive life.

4119 Oates, Wayne E. *Pastoral Care and Counseling in Grief and Separation*. Philadelphia: Fortress Press, 1976.

Separation in grief situations include death, mourning and divorce; the emphasis is on creative growth through expression of feelings, support from others who have "made it," and a non-judgmental empathetic pastoral presence. See Oates (4516).

4120 Rice, Joy and David G. Rice. *Living through Divorce: A Developmental Approach to Divorce* Therapy. New York: Guilford Press, 1986.

Therapists are urged by the authors to consider divorce in terms of object and role loss. Treatment of choice will be a model of life trajectory in which divorce is integrated into individual, marital and family life cycles of the divorced person.

4121 Smoke, Jim. *Growing through Divorce.* Eugene, Oreg.: Harvest House Pub., 1985.

In this self-help book, divorce is considered in terms of stages similar to those of grief and the attitudes are described as positive or negative mourning. Practical advice is given for day to day exercises in growth towards reintegration and possible remarriage.

4122 Spilke, Francine. *What About Me?* New York: Crown Pub., 1979.

A book that is written for adults to read to a child addresses common fears and such specifics as legal procedures in the medium of stories that would interest a child.

4123 Stolz, Mary. *Leap before You Look.* New York: Harper and Row, 1972.

This is the story of a young teenager's recognition that her parents are about to divorce and that she is not able to accept it.

4124 Wallerstein, Judith S. and J. B. Kelly. *Surviving the Breakup: How Children and Parents Cope with Divorce.* New York: Basic Books, 1980.

In a five-year follow-up to the response of young children to parental divorce, the authors found that about a third of the children appeared to be doing especially well personally, socially and educationally. They had very positive self-concepts and showed generally high levels of confidence that included coping well with experiences related to the divorce. About a third expressed rather severe adjustment problems which included social difficulties, loneliness, alienation and depression. Less than a third showed ups and downs in coping with their life situation and appear to have an average response to school and social demands. The divorce appeared to have some negative impact upon their self-esteem and overall confidence.

4125 Wallerstein, Judith S., and Sandra Blakeslee. *Second Chances: Men, Women and Children a Decade after Divorce.* New York: Ticknor and Fields, 1989.

From a fifteen year study of sixty divorced families in Marin County, Calif., divorce appears as a never-ending chain of events, relocations and radically shifting relationships strung through time. Half the women and a third of the men were still intensely angry at their former spouses after ten years. The anger poisoned their lives and colored their relationships with their children. A quarter of the women and a fifth of the men remained unable to get their lives back on track. Only half of the men and women describe themselves as happy. Most of the children describe their lives as consumed by their parents' divorces. They felt that their childhood had been lost. Often they were underachieving, self-depreciating and sometimes angry young men and women. Troubles with intimacy appeared in their adult relationships. Unfortunately there is no control group of this study. Is the author measuring the effects of divorce or of the enormous social change of the last ten years among upper-middle class persons in California?

4126 Weiss, Robert S. "The Emotional Impact of Marital Separation." In *Divorce and Separation: Context, Causes and Consequences*, 201–210. Ed. by George Levinger and Oliver C. Moles. New York: Basic Books, 1979.

A professor of sociology considers the disruption of attachment to be a major source of emotional disturbance following separation. The loss of a spouse is also intermeshed with changes of an individual's social role and relationships with children, kin and friends. The presenting syndrome of the loss is "separation distress" which was first described in relation to bereaved persons who had suffered the physical loss of spouse. Notes from fifty respondents, divorced, indicated two adjustments. First is the adjustment to the disillusion of the marriage: legal process, property settlement, custody arrangements, social networking, a variety of emotions triggered by loss. The second adjustment is the development of a new lifestyle: new residence, living on less, getting a job, applying for welfare, relating to new schedules or the absence of children. Sex differences appeared in the area of economics, where only one out of twenty-two men reported major economic problems caused by the divorce while twenty-eight women in the study said that they were substantially worse off in the area of finances. For a comparison of widowhood and divorce, see Hyman (1366).

4127 Wheeler, Michael. *No-Fault Divorce*. Boston: Beacon Press, 1974.

The trauma of divorce may be reduced if truthful and humane legal procedures are followed. Although a mother and father may come to an agreement through informal procedures, the children will receive better protection through legal representation by a court-appointed attorney.

4.33 PLACES/RELOCATION

4128 Aldrich, C. K. "Personality Factors and Mortality in the Relocation of the Aged." *Gerontologist* 4 (1964): 92–93.

Among the aged, psychological patterns of adaptation and specific types of emotional responses to stress situations are significant determinants of survival. This conclusion was reached from a study of relocated residents from a home for the aged which was closed for administrative reasons.

4129 MacRobert–Galezka, Helen G. "Death in the Family." *Journal of Pastoral Care* 36 (1982): 56–65.

A pastor describes reactions of church members to the sudden burning of their village church and the ways in which the pastor responded.

4.34 DECAY OF THE ENVIRONMENT

4130 Anglemyer, Mary, *et al. A Search for Environmental Ethics: An Initial Bibliography.* Washington, D. C.: Smithsonian Institution Press, 1980.

See 8004.

4131 Barnette, Henlee H. *The Church and the Ecological Crisis.* Grand Rapids, Mich.: William B. Erdmans, 1972.

Theological and ethical perspectives on the ecological crisis are discussed. Causative elements such as population growth are presented along with the possibility of various survival strategies. The appendices include a discussion of evil and nature and a sermon by John Claypool on the theology of ecology. Bibliography.

4132 Berry, Wendell. *The Unsettling of America: Culture and Agriculture.* San Francisco: Sierra Club, 1977.

A poet, teacher and farmer traces the historical roots of industrial economics to a "mentality of exploitation" which continues to grow with agribusinesses and the petrochemical industry. At the same time the general population is encouraged to eat adulterated, "efficiency" foods and to waste resources. The author looks with fondness upon the "nurtured" farms of the Amish and others.

4133 Cahn, Robert. *Footprints on the Planet: A Search for an Environmental Ethic.* Foreword by Jacques Cousteau. New York: Universe, 1978.

An investigative reporter provides case studies of varying policies toward the environment which vary from those of large industrial corporations to the Nature-Conservancy and small communities of alternate technologies and simple living. The author finds that environmental concerns which arise in the internal discussions of company executives will rarely influence company policy and that churches have not followed the religious leaders who are strong advocates of an environmental ethic. The role of government is also discussed.

4134 Carson, Rachel L. *Silent Spring*. Boston: Houghton Mifflin, 1962.

One of the first publications to focus world attention on the environmental hazard of pesticides includes a discussion of relationships between humans and the environment in the physical world and in the world of thought relationships between science and humanities. The stress of the author is upon the reverence for the miracle of life that is beyond our comprehension even when there are times when we must struggle against it. Notes and bibliography.

4135 Dorst, Jean. *Before Nature Dies*. Trans. by Constance D. Sherman. Boston: Houghton Mifflin, 1970.

From a French perspective the author reviews the history of mankind as both ravager and defender of nature. The spiritual and physical need for a sound environmental ethic is stressed. Color plates, black and white photographs, drawings, bibliography, index.

4136 Douglas, William O. *The Three Hundred Year War: A Chronicle of Ecological Disaster*. New York: Random House, 1972.

An eminent jurist and conservationist traces the history of the destruction of America's wilderness from the earliest settlers to the culmination of an age of technology. Spiritual awakening must be combined with aggressive and responsible citizen action, for laws alone are inadequate to avoid ecological disaster.

4137 Elder, Frederick. *Crisis in Eden: A Religious Study of Man and Environment*. New York: Abingdon Press, 1970.

Contrasting schools of environmental thought are the "inclusionist" which present a wholistic approach to humans in the natural order and the "exclusionist" which hold humans apart from nature and superior to it. The theological and social differences of these positions are discussed in relation to short and long range decisions regarding the environment. The author suggests a new approach of restraint, reverence for life, dedication to the quality of existence and rediscovering harmony between humans and environment.

4138 Hornblower, Margot. "The Beastly Harvest." *Washington Post Magazine* July 8, 1979: 18–24.

With dramatic illustrations the author explores the illegal traffic in endangered species of both plants and animals and the cruelty in the legal trade of these species. This is attributed to human indifference.

4139 Kellogg, William W. and Margaret Mead, eds. *The Atmosphere: Endangered and Endangering*. Bethesda, Md.: U.S. Department of Health, Education and Welfare, 1977.

Papers from a 1977 conference at the National Institute of Environmental Health Services challenge society to make the decisions that will rescue an endangered planet. Some specifics of the challenge are presented in chapters on human cost and benefits of environmental change and the intriguing question: will mankind behave rationally? Bibliography.

4140 *Man, Society and the Environment*. Trans. by Yuri Shirakov. Moscow: Progress Publishers, 1975.

Researchers from the Institute of Geography of the U.S.S.R. Academy of Sciences present a Marxist interpretation of society and nature in three parts (1) primitive and capitalist societies, (2) the Soviet experience in exploration and development of natural resources and improvement of the environment, (3) practical and cultural issues which include the establishment of wildlife preserves and problems related to international seas, (4) socio-economic issues. Bibliography.

4141 Mark, Leo. *The Machine in the Garden: Technology and the Pastoral Ideal in America*. New York: Oxford University Press, 1964.

The pastoral ideal of a nation of small farmers with a few mechanics and industrialists was developed early in the American experience and found able exponents in such founding fathers as Thomas Jefferson. The author examines the place of myths, fantasies and ideals of pastoralism in selected literary figures and their works. Extensive notes and index.

4142 McKenzie, John L. "God and Nature in the Old Testament" *Catholic Biblical Quarterly* 14 (January 1952): 18–39. 14 (April 1952): 124–145.

Both the early Hebrews and other ancient peoples lived close to nature and developed a view of the deity as Creator. The Hebrews alone viewed this deity as absolute, independent and a unity. In the Old Testament nature is an expression of wisdom, for she exhibits a visible order and regularity beyond human understanding. Yahweh dominates nature and manifests his passion through natural phenomena. Although these ideas changed over time in the development of Hebrew religion, there was always a strong interaction between God, humans and nature. This is contrasted with the relatively modern development of ambitions in science and technology that boast of the "conquest of nature."

4143 Merchant, Carolyn. *The Death of Nature: Women, Ecology and the Scientific Revolution.* San Francisco: Harper and Row, 1980.

A historian of science explores the connection between women's issues and ecology. She concludes that the advancement of science has set back the cause of women because the earth is no longer regarded as a nurturing mother to be cherished. This was the beginning of the death of nature through the acceleration of the exploitation of human and natural in the name of scientific culture and progress. Many illustrations are given of this shift in the thought of Western Europe around the year 1600. The women's movement and the ecology movement seek to re-establish an older worldview based on cooperation between humans and nature.

4144 Nash, Roderick. *The Rights of Nature: The History of Environmental Ethics.* Madison, Wis.: University of Wisconsin Press, 1989.

An environmental activist presents various legal, theological and philosophical arguments for a belief that ethical standing does not begin and end with human beings. The assertion is supported from Greek and Roman philosophers and from contemporary environmental ethics which extends to the environment the natural rights theory of American liberalism.

4145 Passmore, John. *Man's Responsibility for Nature: Ecological Problems and Western Traditions.* New York: Charles Scribners' Sons, 1978.

A professor of philosophy analyzes Western attitudes towards nature and defines the intellectual considerations that must be resolved to develop an adequate ecological policy. He finds that the attitude of the West has not always been a destructive one. Reactions and adaptation to nature have been much more complex. The central question is "*how much* should one conserve?"

4146 Simon, Seymour. *Life and Death in Nature.* New York: McGraw-Hill Book Co., 1976.

This book for grade school children uses experiments with earth-worms to show the balance of nature, the composition, ecology, problems of overpopulation. The continuity of life is explained through the way that nutrients for our daily life may have once been part of a flower or some ancient animal in the past.

4147 Thomas, William L., ed. *Man's Role in Changing the Face of the Earth*. Chicago: University of Chicago Press, 1971.

Background papers by eminent scholars consider various topics for an international symposium held in 1955: historical, economic, geographical, sociological, anthropological, cultural, ethical and philosophical. References, illustrations, index.

4148 *International Union for the Conservation of Nature and Natural Resources. Animals and Plants Threatened with Extinction*. Morges, Switzerland: International Union for the Conservation of Nature and Natural Resources, 1963.

Papers and reports stress the necessity to preserve Africa's flora, fauna, and habitats both as a continuing economic and cultural resource and as to avoid a biological catastrophe. African and European speakers were invited to this conference sponsored by the United Nations.

4.35 PRIMARY/SECONDARY LOSS/LONELINESS

4149 Hartog, J., J. R. Andy, and Y. A. Cohen, eds. *The Anatomy of Loneliness*. New York: International University Press, 1980.

Various aspects of loneliness, with special emphasis upon those that are most at risk, such as widows, are presented in essays by Thoreau, Fromm-Reichman, Buber, Tillich and others.

4150 Jackson, Edgar N. *Understanding Loneliness*. Philadelphia: Fortress Press, 1980.

A pastor who is an authority on grief presents the complexity of feelings that arise from past life experiences, social patterns and obscure environmental factors. The impact of loneliness is traced upon health, group life and personality development. Loneliness is a social epidemic in modern society with much acting out in religion and society. Biblical insights are presented. The concluding chapter describes creative solitude as the ability to be alone without being lonely. Notes.

4151 Lopata, Helena Z. "Loneliness: Forms and Components." In *Loneliness: The Experience of Emotional and Social Isolation*, ed. by R. S. Weiss, 102–115. Cambridge, Mass.: The MIT Press, 1973.

Loneliness is a major problem for widows. It is described by the author along with techniques of coping such as busyness, new roles and relations, focusing on one's social role. Widows prefer to live alone rather than to move into the homes of married children. Independence is desirable. See also Lopata (4241).

4152 Moustakas, Clark E. *The Touch of Loneliness*. Englewood Cliffs, N.J.: Prentice-Hall, 1975.

An author who has written extensively on loneliness presents letters selected from over a thousand that he has received to verify and validate the common situations that modern people experience when they feel alone. Although the letters reveal some sense of terror and emptiness, there is also a sense of opportunity for new awareness and growth that turns loneliness into the satisfactions of solitude.

4153 Peplau, Letitia Anne and Daniel Perlman, eds. *Loneliness: A Sourcebook of Current Theory, Research and Therapy*. New York: John Wiley and Sons, 1982.

Psychologists and sociologists present papers on the nature of loneliness, the causes and consequences, the assessment, the distribution in society, the relationship to life cycle. Basic research findings and theories are presented about loneliness along with possible interventions for helping lonely people. Comprehensive bibliography.

4154 Weiss, Robert S. *Loneliness: The Experience of Emotional and Social Isolation*. Cambridge, Mass.: The MIT Press, 1973.

Building upon research and reflection, a psychiatrist and colleagues in psychiatry and sociology examine a common form of human distress that has received little professional or scientific attention. Two kinds of loneliness are discussed: emotional isolation which results from the loss or lack of a truly intimate tie and social isolation which is the consequence of lacking a network of involvement with peers. John Bowlby discusses attachment theory in relation to the nature and origin of affectional bonds (see Bowlby 1168). From a study of bereaved subjects, C. Murray Parkes presents separation anxiety as an aspect of the search for a lost object (see Parkes 4244).

4.36 DISENFRANCHISED

4155 Carder, Muriel M. "Journey Into Understanding Mentally Retarded People's Experiences Around Death." *Journal of Pastoral Care* 41 (1987): 18–31.

A chaplain who began her ministry among mentally retarded adults who had traditionally avoided any mention of the death of residents, chronicles her seven years of experience with procedural changes, a deepening sense of community, reduction in staff fears and attitude changes toward death among mentally retarded adults. Reactions and responses of the mentally retarded resembled those of normal people.

4156 Strom, Kay Marshall. *Helping Women in Crisis: A Handbook for People Helpers*. Grand Rapids, Mich.: Zondervan Pub. House, 1986.

A handbook for Christian helpers describes crises of women in the late twentieth century: alcohol and drug abuse, child abuse, child molestation, incest, infidelity, rape, suicide, teenage pregnancy, wife abuse, why me? Specific suggestions are offered for help in each category, professional resources and self-help groups are listed and reading is suggested.

4.361 RAPE/BATTERED WOMAN SYNDROME

4157 Burgess, Ann Wolvert and Linda Lytle Holmstrom. *Rape, Crisis and Recovery*. Bowie, Md.: R. J. Brady Co., 1979.

From work with 146 children, adolescents and adults who were victims of sexual trauma in Boston, the authors present a longitudinal study of crisis responses of victims to rape, counseling methods that are useful in working with victims and recovery issues identified by rape victims. It is a perceptive presentation of the victims' point of view and the reactions of those who formed the community reaction: police, medical personnel, criminal system authorities and community programs. Realistic discussion of short and long term issues in counseling.

4158 Clarke, Rita-Lou. *Pastoral Care of Battered Women*. Philadelphia: Westminster Press, 1986.

A pastor reviews the cultural context of patriarchy, sexism and violence that permit and encourage violence towards women. She then explores the psychological dimension of battering, both the inner and the interpersonal dynamics. Theological issues and the role of the pastor are also considered. Bibliography and recommended resources.

4159 Finkelhor, David. *Sexually Victimized Children*. New York: Free Press, 1979.

The similarities between sexual abuse of children and rape are presented. The child is victimized more by age, naiveté and relationship to the older person than by the aggressive intent of an abusive attacker. The author's conclusions are based upon a questionnaire in which young adults recall sexual experiences, usually incest.

4160 Groth, A. Nicholas. *Men Who Rape*. New York: Plenum Press, 1979.

The director of a sex offender program considers the psychology of the rapist. Developmental histories, lifestyles, motivation may predispose a person toward sexual violence. Situational factors are also examined.

4161 Lehan, James. *Pastoral Care for Survivors of Family Abuse*. Louisville, Ky.: Westminster/John Knox Press, 1989.

Drawing upon experience with adults who were children of abuse, the author distinguishes the "victim" who is still suffering from the "survivor" who is seeking help. Chapters include recognition and understanding of abuse, the use of religion to justify family violence, ways by which pastors and others may provide community, spiritual, physical and psychological resources through the church or survivors.

4162 Russell, Diana E. H. *Rape in Marriage*. New York: Macmillan Pub. Co., 1982.

A professor of sociology used funding from the National Institute of Mental Health to conduct a large-scale survey of women residents in San Francisco to determine the prevalence of marital and extra-marital rape and other sexual assaults. The findings were instrumental in the passage of a California law on wife rape. This study reports the prevalence of the practice, characteristics of husbands and wives, the view of women as property, torture and murder of wives, strategies adopted by some wives and wife rape in other countries. Appendices include selected cases of wife rape and state by state information. Notes.

4163 Schwendiger, Julia R. and Herman Schwendiger. *Rape and Inequality*. Beverley Hills, Calif.: Sage Publications, 1983.

Sociologists who are active in the Bay Area Women Against Rape, emphasize socio-economic factors and their relationship to the causes of rape throughout history. In an international context, rape is tied to the development of social inequality. The authors argue that the socio-economic factors that lead to sexual inequality have nothing to do with the instincts for power and aggression that are alleged to be naturally inherent in men. Bibliography.

4164 Walders, Candice. *Invisible Wounds*. Portland, Oreg.: Multnomah Press, 1987.

Five woman who have been rape victims cooperate with a rape crisis counselor in a discussion of the most common questions which are raised by victims. The book is specifically addressed to the Christian community in the hope that church and community will no longer ignore, sensationalize, or scandalize the woman who was raped.

4165 Walker, Lenore E. *The Battered Woman Syndrome*. New York: Springer Publishing Co., 1984.

On the basis of a three year research program (NIMH grant) a psychologist reports on her strategies in the development of a battered women research center at a small private college in Denver. Psychological issues in domestic violence are discussed, literature is reviewed. Applications are suggested for varying professional fields, such as law and clinical psychology.

4166 Warshaw, Robin. *I Never Called It Rape*. New York: Harper and Row, 1988.

On the basis of a nation-wide survey conducted by *Ms.* a journalist explains what "date-rape" is, how it happens and how it has remained so hidden a crime for so long. A program for change is suggested. A psychologist, Mary P. Koss, answers questions about the survey itself which was funded by the National Institute of Mental Health.

4.362 ORPHANS

4167 Simpson, Eileen B. *Orphans: Real and Imaginary*. New York: Weidenfeld and Nicolson, 1987.

The first part of this absorbing book is the autobiographical story of orphanhood by the author who avoided confrontation with her painful past until the death of her husband threw her into a "second orphanhood." The second part is an overview of history and literature which points up the grossly inadequate care provided for orphans.

4.363 INFERTILITY

4168 Houghton, Diane and Peter Houghton. *Coping with Childlessness*. London: George Allen and Unwin, 1984.

The emotional aspects of involuntary childlessness are considered in this readable volume along with recommendations for coping with miscarriage.

4169 Menning, Barbara Eck. *Infertility: A Guide for the Childless Couple*. Englewood Cliffs, N. J.: Prentice-Hall, 1977.

The grieving process is a necessary part of healing for an infertile couple, but it may be hindered or blocked by the lack of any recognized loss, the socially unspeakable nature and uncertainty of the loss, or the absence of a social support system.

4.364 RETIREMENT

4170 Haber, Carole. *Beyond Sixty-Five: The Dilemma of Old Age in America's Past*. Cambridge University Press, 1982.

See 3173.

4171 Johnson, Elizabeth S., and John B. Williamson. *Growing Old: The Social Problems of Aging.* New York: Holt, Rinehart and Winston, 1980.

See 3176.

4172 Palmore, Erdman, *et al.* "Stress and Adaptation in Later Life." *Journal of Gerontology* 34 (1978): 841–851.

Medical events had the most impact on the physical adaptation of 375 participants in a longitudinal study, but medical events had surprisingly little impact on social-psychological adaptation. Retirement had the most negative social-psychological effects, but had little effect on physical adaptation. Several other major life events, often referred to in professional literature as stressors, had less serious long-term outcomes than were expected.

4173 Sinick, Daniel. *Counseling Older Persons: Careers, Retirement, Dying.* New York: Human Sciences Press, 1977.

The special considerations of older clients are considered in terms of retirement counseling, dying from terminal illness, suicide, bereavement. Trends and recommendations from conferences by various agencies are presented. Readings related to older women are listed along with periodicals for older persons and addresses of organizations. References.

4174 Szinobacz, Maximiliana, ed. *Women's Retirement: Policy Implications of Recent Research.* Beverley Hills, Calif.: Sage Pub., 1982.

With a primary orientation upon theory generating rather than theory testing, various authors consider data on the retirement of women in terms of employment status, work history, life-situation, preparation for retirement, adjustment. The service needs of women retirees are considered. Bibliography.

4.4 RELATION TO THE DECEASED (ROLES AND RELATIONSHIPS)

4175 Agee, James. *A Death in the Family.* New York: Bantam, 1969.

See 3035.

4176 Eliot, Thomas D. "The Bereaved Family." *Annals of the American Academy of Political and Social Sciences* 160 (1932): 184–190.

Bereavement is typically a family crisis in which the primary effects are sense of unreality, shock, self-injury, grief. Some secondary, social effects are seen in escape, compensation, inner identification with the loved one. There may be disturbance of family unity which will result in some reshaping of family roles and hopefully family agreement regarding new roles. Grief may increase or decrease family solidarity.

4177 Grollman, Earl A. *What Helped Me When My Loved One Died.* Boston: Beacon Press, 1981.

The survivors of family tragedies describe their feelings and the way they were helped. The emphasis is upon sharing and patient, resolute decisions to live. Friendly, intimate, courageous conversations.

4178 Hollingsworth, Charles E. and Robert O. Pasnau. *The Family In Mourning: A Guide For Health Professionals.* New York: Grune and Stratton, 1977.

Two psychiatrists are joined by psychologists, nurses, other psychiatrists, a social worker and a cardiologist in a discussion of the implications of tragic death upon families. The grieving spouse and the role of psychotherapy receive special treatment. Circumstances are significant: sudden death, terminal illness, loss of children, grief following abortion and stillbirth. Differing belief systems, rituals and practices of religion are presented as important for patient, family and the staff's understanding of these resources. The work of psychiatric consultants is presented in relation to specific kinds of loss such as a tragic birth, a transplant, or the stress of a coronary care unit. The format is the case of a dying patient and family which is then discussed from varying professional viewpoints, along with professional opinions and some references to clinical research studies.

4179 Jensan, G. D. and J. G. Wallace. "Family Mourning Process." *Family Process* 6 (1967): 56–66.

From two family case studies the authors conclude that therapeutic management must observe the relationship of a single surviving child to the interpersonal reactions of the family. In this way the needs blocked by mourning can be opened to family resources.

4180 Kisner, Jeffrey Allan. "A Family Systems Approach to Grief." In *Pastoral Psychology* 28 (1979–1980): 265–276.

The stage theory of grief is blended with family systems literature in this article and is illustrated with case study. Pastoral and theological questions are presented.

4181 Klein, Melanie. "Mourning and Its Relation to Manic-Depressive States." *International Journal of Psycho-Analysis* 21 (1940): 125–153.

In an investigation of Freudian theories concerning mourning as a contributor to manic-depressive states, the author draws attention to the role played by family and friends in promoting recovery from loss. The theme was later explored by Gorer (1012) and Lopata (4240).

4182 Lewis, Oscar. *A Death in the Sánchez Family*. New York: Random House, 1969.

Members of a Mexican family tell their stories about the funeral of their aunt. Her life was impoverished but often heroic. Her death illuminated her life and the culture of poverty in which she lived. The family struggled to provide a decent burial for her.

4183 Lund, Dale A., ed. *Older Bereaved Spouses: Research with Practical Applications*. Washington, D.C.: Hemisphere Pub. Corp., 1989.

See 4264.

4184 Pattison, E. Mansell. "The Fatal Myth of Death in the Family." *American Journal of Psychiatry* 133 (1966): 674–678.

The pathogenic effects on a child of the death of a parent are the result of the family's culture-bound inability to integrate death as a natural part of the process of living. The family tries to deal with death by the avoidance mechanisms of myth and family mystification; it is this process which is pathogenic rather then the experience with death itself. A case study is presented. See Pattison (3161).

4185 Shuchter, Stephen R. "How the Family Physician Can Help Patients Adjust to the Death of a Spouse." *Medical Aspects of Human Sexuality* 18 (1984): 30–32, 36, 41–44, 49, 54.

To assist patients in dealing with the pain of loss without being overwhelmed, an attending physician can note that there often will be an avoidance of any reference to the deceased. Avoidance may appear in distracting work, reading or TV viewing, attempts to fill up the loss with drugs, alcohol or food, preoccupation with the details of the loss, escape into sudden decisions about selling a home or developing a new personal relationship, the flow of feelings through prayer that will allow relief from any guilt and provide a sense of protection and caring, some intellectualization and rationalization, and contact with people who can flow with intense feelings of loss, loneliness and despair.

4.41 EXPLAINING DEATH TO CHILDREN

4186 Bernstein, Joanne E. *Books to Help Children Cope with Separation and Loss*. 2nd ed. New York: R. R. Bowker, 1983.

See 8005.

4187 Best, Pauline. "An Experience in Interpreting Death to Children."
       Journal of Pastoral Care 2 (Spring 1948): 29–34.

In a time when death was a social taboo, a religious educator
describes the death of a child in a way in which the pastor, Sunday School
teachers and others open up conversation about a child's death with other
children and adults.

4188 Cook, Sarah Sheets, ed. *Children and Dying: An Exploration and
       Selected Bibliographies.* Rev. ed. New York: Health Sciences Publish-
       ing Corp., 1974.

Physicians, psychologists, clergy and others present short papers on
the feelings of children about death and the reactions of adults. Papers on
explaining death and helping children to cope with death are included.
Bibliography.

4189 Grollman, Earl A. *Talking About Death: A Dialogue Between Parent
       and Child.* Ill. by Gisela Heau. Rev. ed. Boston: Beacon Press, 1976.

In keeping with a saying quoted from Ralph Waldo Emerson that
sorrow makes us all children again, the author aids grieving parents and
children to talk together about death. The first section contains drawings
and a description of death in the language of children. The next section
guides parents through the difficult questions of children about death. This
is followed by a section on professional help, the loss of a sibling, suicide,
the attitudes of parents, a listing of helping agencies and recommendations
of books, audio-visual materials by age groupings.

4190 Jackson, Edgar N. *Telling a Child About Death.* New York: Channel
       Press, 1965.

In conversational style a sensitive pastor explains when and how
adults can overcome their own fear of death and talk with children about
death in ways that children experience their feelings and fears of loss.
Emphasis is upon "talking it over" by giving information and sharing feelings. The author finds that children show their feelings about grief through
their behavior.

4191 Krementz, Jill. *How It Feels When a Parent Dies.* New York: Alfred
       A. Knopf, 1981.

See 4222.

4192 Langer, Marion. *Learning to Live as a Widow.* New York: J. Mess-
       ner, 1957.

The unique feature of this early book of advice on the mastery of the widow's grief is a call for the happily married woman to think ahead about the impact of widowhood in the future. A resource appendix is provided.

4193 LeShan, Eda. *Learning to Say Good-By: When a Parent Dies.* New York: Macmillan Pub. Co., 1976.

See 4223.

4194 Lonetto, Richard. *Children's Conceptions of Death.* New York: Springer, 1980.

See 3058.

4195 Sargent, Marilyn. *Talking to Children About Death.* Rockville, Md.: Department of Health, Education and Welfare, 1990.

A pamphlet from the National Institute of Mental Health describes the awareness of children about death, barriers to communication, honesty of parents in not having all the answers, recognition of developmental stages and individual differences, learning to listen to the child's concerns, the relation of religion to loss, visits to the dying and funerals.

4196 Sherrill, Helen and Lewis J. Sherrill. "Interpreting Death to Children." *Journal of Religious Education* 46 (October 1951): 4–6.

In a time when religious and other publishers forbade the mention of death in publications for children, two professors of religious education provide theological and psychological insights to encourage and guide parents, pastors and relatives in a discussion of death with young children.

4197 Wass, Hannelore and Charles A. Corr, eds. *Childhood and Death.* Washington, D.C.: Hemisphere Pub. Co., 1984.

Clinical viewpoints are presented on the topics of death-related thoughts and fears, patterns of coping and ways to be of help during the process of dying, bereavement, suicide, death education both at home and in schools. The intention of the authors to provide a volume that examines all facets of death that involve children has been admirably accomplished.

4198 Wass, Hannelore and Charles A. Corr, eds. *Helping Children Cope with Death: Guidelines and Resources.* Rev. ed. Washington, D.C.: Hemisphere Pub. Co., 1984.

Practical treatment is offered for the full range of issues in which children and death are linked: guidelines for parents, counselors and teachers, annotated bibliographies of books for adults and children, audiovisuals. In a lucid text for parents, pastors, teachers and health professionals there are guidelines on the thoughts of children and others about death and the way these thoughts are expressed, the communication of a pastor with a child encountering death, helping with death education, the specifics of teaching children to cope with problems of death. Annotated bibliographies are provided on books for children, books for adults, audio-visual resources, plus a topical and title index to these resources.

4199 Zeligs, Rose. *Children's Experience With Death*. Springfield, Ill: Charles C. Thomas, 1974.

A psychiatrist presents a simple and concrete narration of her experience with children who have been disturbed by experiences about death.

4.42 THE LOSS OF A CHILD

4200 Campbell, Scott and Phyllis R. Silverman. *Widower*. Englewood Cliffs, N.J.: Prentice-Hall, 1987.

The authors present transcribed interviews with twenty widowers ranging in age from thirty to ninety-four: professionals, businessmen, blue-collar workers. Most of the widowers had children and most were satisfied in their marriage. These are retrospective interviews which came anywhere from several weeks to ten years after the death of the spouse. The stories go step-by-step through the history of the marriage and the attempts of each man to develop a new life alone or as a single parent. The authors bring together some common themes at the end of each interview and provide some advice.

4201 Claypool, John. *Tracks of a Fellow Struggler*. Dallas, Tex.: Word Pub., 1974.

See 4472.

4202 Cobb, Beatrix. "Psychological Impact of Long Illness and Death of a Child on the Family Circle." *Journal of Pediatrics* 49 (1956): 746–751.

A social worker describes an early attempt to bring families into the treatment program for terminally ill children. Quotations from parents give the article a sense of immediacy in describing family reactions to remissions and regressions following experimental treatment, the impact of enforced separation of parents and on children, reaction of parents to death and the role of religion in bringing acceptance after a period of rebellion.

4203 Donnelly, Katherine Fair. *Recovering From the Loss of a Child*. New York: Macmillan Pub. Co., 1982.

Parents describe their struggles to live a day at a time with grief and hope that the expression of their innermost thoughts may benefit others. An extensive description is given of organizations that help the bereaved.

4204 Gunther, John. *Death Be Not Proud*. New York: Harper and Brothers, 1949.

In masterful prose an author describes the death of his twelve year old son, the personal reactions of parents, friends and community.

4205 Hans, Daniel T. *God on the Witness Stand: Questions Christians Ask in Personal Tragedy*. Grand Rapids, Mich.: Baker Book House, 1987.

See 2157.

4206 Johnson, Sherry E. *After A Child Dies: Counseling Bereaved Families*. New York: Springer Pub. Co., 1987.

After fifteen years of therapy with hundreds of bereaved parents and families, a grief therapist with a background in nursing writes for practitioners who counsel survivors, particularly families who have experienced the death of child. She covers development of a child's conception of death, family themes in coping with death, grief symptoms, the first, second, and third year of bereavement, therapeutic interventions and professional burnout. References to literature are at the end of each chapter. Extensive bibliography and a selected list of children's books on death and dying. Very readable style.

4207 Klass, Dennis. *Parental Grief: Solace and Resolution*. New York: Springer Pub. Co., 1988.

From personal interviews and newsletters of the Compassionate Friends, a psychologist describes the process and resolution of parental grief, the anatomy of social support through Compassionate Friends, the bridge and resolution of grief among parents of murdered children, and the discovery of an authentic self as the bereaved help those who are dying. There is an extensive discussion of John Bowlby's model of grief. Bibliography.

4208 Koop, C. Everett and Elizabeth Koop. *Sometimes Mountains Move*. Wheaton, Ill: Tyndale House Pub., 1979.

Christian parents describe their shocked disbelief and gradual recovery from the sudden death of a young adult son. Traditional belief in the resurrection and heaven sustain them.

4209 Lang, Gordon. "A Method for Doing Grief-Work with Families Who Have Had a Child Die with Cancer." *Journal of Pastoral Care* 38 (1984): 209–215.

A pastoral counselor describes his work with couples who meet in small groups to discuss their loss of a child through cancer. The theories of

Erich Lindemann were used in the interpretation of the themes: reviewing the life of the child, reflecting on the meanings of the child's life, restructuring relationships, liberating memories of the dead child and recognizing the reality of a form of resurrection.

4210 McClowry, Sandra G., *et al.* "The Empty Space Phenomenon: The Process of Grief in the Bereaved Family." In *Death Studies* 11 (1987): 361–374.

Forty-nine families who experienced a death in the family following childhood cancer were interviewed 7–9 years after the death. Many parents and siblings were still experiencing pain and loss because of an empty space that is created by the death. Responses to the grief were: getting over it, feeling the emptiness, keeping the connection.

4211 Miles, M. S., and E. K. B. Crandalls. "The Search for Meaning and It's Potential for Affecting Growth in Bereaved Parents." *Health Values: Achieving High Level Wellness* 7 (1983): 19–23.

Parents who report growth following the death of a child have a strong faith, are compassionate and caring toward others, are increasingly aware of the preciousness and fragility of life.

4212 Quezada, Adolfo. *Goodbye, My Son, Hello*. St. Meinrad, Ind.: Abbey Press, 1985.

With deep affection for a lost son and with a poetic ability to express his own feelings, a father describes the pain of his journey through grief to a renewed sense of God's presence. Written by a counselor two years after the accidental death of his son, the book is an excellent resource for grieving parents.

4213 Rando, Therese A., ed. *Parental Loss of a Child*. Champaign, Ill.: Research Press, 1986.

The unique issues and difficulties associated with mourning for one's child are explored by a variety of experts who offer both comprehensive analysis of the severity and complexity of parental bereavement and specific guidance for clinical intervention and therapeutic support procedures. Issues considered are: guilt in bereaved parents, sudden infant death syndrome, death of a child by suicide, family therapy after the death of a child, communicating with surviving children, advice from a bereaved parent to physicians, clergy, funeral directors.

4214 Smith, A. A. *Rachel*. New York: Morehouse-Barlow, 1974.

An Episcopal priest describes his reaction to the sudden and unexpected death of a ten year old daughter. The impact of the death upon himself and his family is presented in order that a sense of normalcy might come to others who share the same tragedy in the midst of that which seems so abnormal. Short list of things for surviving parents to do or not to do are given along with encouragement for the entire community to be involved in honest acceptance of painful memories and support as the family tries to resume normal life.

4215 Videka, Sherman, L. "Coping With the Death of a Child: A Study Over Time." *American Journal of Orthopsychiatry* 52 (1982): 688–698.

In a longitudinal study the author found that altruism and investment in a new role or meaningful activity reduced depression among bereaved parents. Others fled into maladaptive coping such as denial of the death, drugs or alcohol, obsessive preoccupation with the deceased child.

4216 Wargotz, Helen. "Widowers With Teenage Children." In *Death and Bereavement,* ed. by Austin H. Kutscher, 257–269. Springfield, Ill: Charles Thomas, 1969.

The director of a program, "guidance for motherless homes" suggests mealtimes and other opportunities for parent and child to discuss their feelings about death and many other interests, concerns and problems. A plan should be made for substitute maternal figures for bereaved children aged 3–6.

4217 Willis, R. Wayne. "Some Concerns of Bereaved Parents." *Journal of Religion and Health* 20 (1981): 133–140.

A chaplain describes his experience in a pediatrics intensive care unit where he developed a support group for bereaved parents. The themes that consistently surfaced were preoccupation with the hour of a child's death, anniversaries, anger, guilt, depression, the reaction of siblings, the restructuring of life, yearning for reunion, the need for support systems, times of outreach and empathy with others.

4218 Wolterstorff, Nicholas. *A Lament for a Son.* Grand Rapids, Mich.: Wm. B. Eerdmans Publishing Co., 1987.

A philosopher who has lost his son in a mountain-climbing accident, visits the grave a year later and writes like Job on the impact of suffering upon a Christian father.

4.43 THE DEATH OF A PARENT

4219 Anderson, Herbert. "The Death of a Parent: Its Impact on Middle Aged Sons and Daughters." In *Pastoral Psychology* 28 (Spring 1980): 151–166.

A pastoral counselor considers finitude as the central task of mid-life which is intensified by the death of a parent in three ways: being without a parent is like being a middle-aged orphan; the death of one or both parents may finally make autonomy possible; when the last parent dies, death seems closer because the buffer is gone.

4220 Becker, D. and F. Margolin. "How Surviving Parents Handle Their Young Children's Adaptation to the Crisis of Loss." *American Journal of Orthopsychiatry* 37 (1967): 753–757.

Nine children under seven years of age who had experienced the death of a parent were observed along with the surviving parent. There is a discussion of communication between parent and child and the possibility of therapeutic intervention.

4221 Buchsbaum, Betty C. "Remembering a Parent Who Has Died: A Developmental Perspective." *Annual of Psychoanalysis* 15 (1987): 99–112.

The intellectual capabilities of adolescence are considered necessary for a stable coherent memory of a deceased parent. The resolution of mourning is characterized by a view of the parent as a self-contained, independent person whose identity is preserved in the mind.

4222 Krementz, Jill. *How It Feels When a Parent Dies*. New York: Knopf, 1981.

Boys and girls between the ages of 8 and 15 were photographed and invited to provide a brief essay on their feelings about the death of one of their parents. The theme is assurance for children that their feelings of grief are normal and that they can cope with the situation.

4223 LeShan, Eda. *Learning to Say Goodbye: When a Parent Dies*. Macmillan Pub. Co., 1978.

This book for young people in grief stresses confidence that coping is not beyond the capabilities of children who are permitted to share feelings in open communication with sympathetic and concerned adults.

4.44 THE LOSS OF A SPOUSE/SEX DIFFERENCES

4224 Butler, Robert N. and Myrna I. Lewis. *Sex After Sixty*. New York: Harper and Row, 1976.

The joys of sex in later years are described, along with chapters on grief work, dating and remarriage.

4225 Bowling, Ann and Ann Cartwright. *Life after a Death: A Study of the Elderly Widowed.* London: Tavistock, 1982.

The experiences and attitudes of 350 elderly widowed men and women, relatives, friends and neighbors are considered in terms of the help received by the widows or not received when they turn to others for support.

4226 Di Giulio, Robert C. *Beyond Widowhood: From Bereavement to Emergence and Hope.* New York: The Free Press, 1989.

A widower writes from his personal experience, structured interviews with 83 widows and varies research studies about four stages of bereavement in widowhood: encounter, respondence, emergence and transformation. He offers encouragement and advice concerning the emergence and transformation of a mourning person that is based upon the reports of many women that there was significant relief and optimistic anticipation in their thoughts of a new life on their own. Women are less shaken in their personal identity by the loss of a spouse than widowers. In contrast, women are more likely to have friendships which provide the intimacy, acceptance and self-validation that are critical to the bereaved's well being. Notes, suggested readings, a list of support organizations.

4227 Glick, Ira O., Robert S. Weiss, and Colin M. Parkes. *The First Year of Bereavement.* New York: John Wiley and Sons, 1974.

As part of a study of widows and widowers, the authors find that men and women appear to be similar in the effective bond they have maintained with their spouse, but men and women organize their lives differently in society. Consequences for grief are: men tend to define what has happened to them as a dismemberment rather than an abandonment; they ended emotional display more quickly than women; there was a greater commitment to realism and less tendency to blame fate or become angry; they often felt guilty for having failed their spouses in some way; there was little rehearsing of the events that led to the death of a spouse, either in inner conversation or with family members and friends. See Glick (1365).

4228 Parkes, Colin M. "Recent Bereavement as a Cause of Mental Illness." *British Journal of Psychiatry* 110 (1964): 198–204.

See 4314.

4229 Pincus, Lily. *Death and the Family.* New York: Vintage Books, 1974.

An experienced therapist from the Tavistock Institute of Human Relations in London describes the death of her husband ten years previously and then gives a number of cases in which the interaction of couples becomes a basis for understanding reactions to grief. Bereavement may be based (1) on projection, in which differences are tolerated and each partner maintains identity; coping is determined by the survivors' individual strength and flexibility rather than by age. Or bereavement may be based (2) upon identification, in which case old age will be very significant because it involves the survivor in dependent and regressive needs that make separation an insurmountable threat. The author also presents the processes of mourning and grief, repressed mourning, the special problems of widows, sons and daughters. Counsel is offered on the way to talk about grief with those who mourn and during days of health. Many relevant illustrations among words of wisdom.

4230 Peterson, James A. *On Being Alone.* Washington, D.C.: American Association of Retired Persons, 1980.

An attractive pamphlet presents living through bereavement with permission to grieve and make adjustments in family, society, finances, legal affairs and employment.

4231 Shuchter, Stephen R. *Dimensions of Grief: Adjusting to the Death of a Spouse.* San Francisco: Jossey-Bass Pub., 1986.

On the basis of a multi-dimensional model of grief, a psychotherapist presents the necessary task of renewal for a bereaved spouse: learning to experience, express and integrate painful affects: adapting to the affects; integrating the continuing relationship with the dead spouse; maintaining health and continuity of social function: adapting to altered relationships: developing and integrating a healthy self-concept and a stable world-view.

4232 Stillion, Judith M. *Death and the Sexes: An Examination of Differential Longevity, Attitudes, Behaviors, and Coping Skills.* Washington, D.C.: Hemisphere Pub. Corp., 1985.

The author investigates differences between the sexes in average life expectancy, death related roles and attitudes, homicide and suicide, bereavement and other topics. The study of these differences by a developmentally oriented psychologist provides an opportunity for all persons to examine their perspective on life and living.

4233 Wertenbaker, Lael T. *Death of a Man.* New York: Random House, 1957.

A husband describes his feelings before his death and his wife completes the account of their mutual search for a rational and ethical death.

4.441 WIDOW

4234 Bowlby, John. *Attachment.* Vol. 1, *Attachment and Loss.* New York: Basic Books, 1969.

As part of an extensive clinical study of widows over a 20 year period, a British psychiatrist identifies the following sequence in the mourning process: a phase of numbing that may last from a few hours to a week and may be interrupted by intense distress and anger; several months and sometimes years of yearning and searching for the lost one; a time of disorganization and despair; a time of more or less social reorganization. See Bowlby (1168).

4235 Caine, Lynn. *Widow*. New York: William Morrow, 1974.

This honest autobiographical account of widowhood includes sections on overcoming loneliness and stress, facing life as a single parent, contemplating new romantic relationships.

4236 Darby, Elisabeth and Nicola Smith. *The Cult of the Prince Consort*. New Haven, Conn.: Yale University Press, 1983.

See 1119.

4237 Hyman, Herbert Hyrum. *Of Time and Widowhood: Nationwide Studies of Enduring Effects*. Durham, N.C.: Duke University Press, 1983.

See 1366.

4238 Kirwen, Michael C. *African Widows*. Maryknoll, N.Y.: Orbis Books, 1979.

A Roman Catholic missionary and anthropologist investigated the complaint of East African Christian leaders that Western emphasis upon the nuclear family showed no understanding of tensions created in African marriage and family customs. The author's contribution to this dilemma is a sociological survey of over a thousand African adults and one hundred and fifteen Catholic church leaders in four traditional Tanzanian societies. Special attention is given to the moral and theological issue of care for a widow by her brother-in-law. As in the Old Testament, so in many African societies there is a group orientation relationship that surrounds marriage.

4239 Kligfeld, Bernard and George R. Krupp. "Sexual Adjustment of Widows." *Sexology* (November 1966): 230–233.

Social attitudes complicate some of the problems of readjustment for widows. Rules for sexual behavior are confusing, frequently unrealistic and contradictory.

4240 Lopata, Helena Z. *Widowhood in an American City*. Cambridge, Mass.: Schenkman, 1972.

Among a heterogeneous sample of 301 widows in the Chicago area, the author found that some adjusted to their new lives with a sense of independence, confidence, activity and freedom above that experienced during life with a husband. But widows are sometimes socially ostracized by other other women whose husbands are still alive. Experiences following death are usually more severe for widows than those of widowers, for many widows face feelings of incompetence, incompleteness and isolation. This is often complicated by loneliness. The author is a specialist in role-modification studies.

4241 Lopata, Helena Z. *Women as Widows: Support Systems*. Westport, Conn.: Greenwood Press, 1979.

A sample of three hundred widows, fifty years of age or older, are sampled in the Chicago area. The concentration of the study is upon support systems of widows in urbanizing centers and reflects the forms of integration available to or forced on widows in an urban American community. The author found an absence of helping professions and groups during the period of the husband's illness, immediately after his death, when the widow was trying to establish a new life and later. Widows reported very restricted lives with lessened support systems. Support came to some widows who could draw upon help from the past in the form of home, finances, children, relatives and friends. An unusual value of the study is a printing of the widow questionnaire in the appendix. Bibliography.

4242 Marris, Peter. *Widows and Their Families*. London: Rutledge and Kegan Paul, 1958.

From interviews with 72 working class widows in London with several dependent children, the author details physical symptoms, loss of contact with reality, inability to comprehend the loss, brooding over memories and clinging to possessions, feeling that the dead man is still present, talking to him as if he were still alive, a tendency to withdraw from everything that recalls the loss, hostility against the doctor, fate and self. Two years after death of the spouse, the widows felt their lives were futile and empty. Marris linked psychological studies of grief with the role played by ritual and by society in assisting the bereaved. See also Lopata (4240), Gorer (1012).

4243 Miller, Jolonda. *You Can Become Whole Again: A Guide to Christians in Grieving*. Atlanta, Ga.: John Knox Press, 1981.

A widow with two young children describes her ability to work through grief and get going with life again. A tough-minded approach to her own conscious and subconscious reactions to accidental death, plus the presence of Christian friends were her major resources. The book is organized as paragraphs on some aspect of grief work. This is followed by several scriptural sentences and an empathetic prayer. An example of sturdy spirituality.

4244 Parkes, Colin M. *Bereavement: Studies of Grief in Adult Life.* New York: International Universities Press, 1972.

On the basis of 12 years of bereavement research, the author concludes that widows seem to be on a restless search for the lost person. Conclusions are based upon an analysis of literature and the author's interviews with 22 London widows, 4 widowers and 17 widows at the Bethlehem Royal Hospital. Findings are presented in terms of the nature of the principle components of the reaction to bereavement, the effects of bereavement upon physical and mental health, the non-specific reaction to stress in general, the highly specific "search" component that characterizes grieving, the ways in which we attempt to avoid or postpone grief and the part played by feelings and anger and self-reproach, followed by the gradual building up of a fresh identity. The "broken heart" phenomenon is discussed (see Parkes, Benjamin, Fitzgerald 1373). Morbid or atypical forms of grief are noted and a final chapter considers bereavement as one among many major transitions that constitute challenge and readjustment to life. Conclusions are similar to those of John Bowlby (1168) in emphasizing grief as a process of realization that a loss has really occurred. But Parkes goes beyond Bowlby in studying the social side of grief, such as deprivation of companionship, income, social status. Status may be reduced because of the stigma society places upon survivors.

4245 Silverman, Phyllis R., *et. al.,* eds. *Helping Each Other in Widowhood.* New York: Health Sciences Pub. Co., 1974.

The development of widow-to-widow programs is described by various authorities who have aided this development.

4246 Silverman, Phyllis R. *Helping Women Cope With Grief.* Beverly Hills, Ca.: Sage 1981.

The founder of a widow-to-widow program offers advice on grief and grieving with specific attention to the problem of maintaining identity as a person, working through the loss of a spouse, the loss of a child as a birth mother, the loss of respect as battered woman. Recommendations are given for linking relationships and mutual help. See also Lopata (4241), Silverman (4348).

4247 Taves, Isabella. *The Widow's Guide.* New York: Schocken Books, 1981.

Practical steps to recovery are offered in relation to dynamics, personal health, family relationships, work and stress.

4248 Temes, Roberta. *Living with an Empty Chair: A Guide Through Grief.* Amherst, Mass.: Mandala, 1977.

A practical approach to grief experienced by children and adults is offered, along with advice on the way to receive help through counseling.

4.442 WIDOWER

4249 Kohn, Jane Burgess, and Willard K. Kohn. *The Widower.* Boston: Beacon Press, 1978.

4250 Lewis, C. S. *A Grief Observed.* New York: Seabury Press, 1961.

See 2139.

4251 Mojtabai, A. G. *Autumn.* Boston: Houghton-Mifflin, 1982.

See 6026.

4252 Schoen, Elin. *Widower: A Daughter's Compelling Account of How a Man Overcame Grief and Loneliness.* New York: William Morrow, 1984.

The daughter of a widowed man writes of her father's experiences following thirty-seven years of marriage, including his hasty attempt to remarry.

4253 Young, Michael, Bernard Benjamin and Chris Wallis. "The Mortality of Widowers." *Lancet* 2 (1963): 454–456.

See 1382.

4.45 SIBLING GRIEF

4254 Leon, Irving G. "The Invisible Loss: The Impact of Perinatal Death on Siblings." *Journal of Psychosomatic Obstetrics and Gynecology.* 5 (1986): 1–14.

Along with a review of literature there is a case example of an 8 year old boy whose behavior and mood improved after mother and child talked about his sister's death six years before. The case is analyzed with suggestions for the way in which parents can help their children deal with perinatal loss.

4255 Moriarity, Irene. "Mourning the Death of an Infant: The Sibling's Story." *Journal of Pastoral Care* 32 (1978): 22–33.

Parents are encouraged to discuss the loss of a sibling. An example is given of a four year old boy who felt some vague guilt about the death of a baby sister. Young children may feel abandoned when parents withdraw into grief or concentrate all attention upon other siblings. There may also be a fear of God arising from parental statements. Books, games, group conversation are recommended along with attendance at wakes and funerals.

4256 Romond, Janice Loomis. *Children Facing Grief.* St. Meinrad, Ind.: Abbey Press, 1989.

After an introductory explanation of communication between siblings, the author presents letters written by children age 8 to 15 as an explanation of the circumstances and their feelings about the death of a sibling.

4257 Rosen, Ellen. "When a Sibling Dies." *International Journal of Family Psychiatry* 7 (1986): 389–396.

The initial impact on the surviving child in a family that experienced loss of a child is discussed and illustrations are given from the author's research.

4258 Zeligs, Rose. "Death Casts Its Shadow on a Child." *Mental Hygiene* 51 (1967): 9–20.

Psychotherapy helped a boy differentiate between sleep and death after the sudden death of his one year old brother. There were guilt feelings resulting from a fear of death wishes, rejection resulting from being shielded from family participation in the funeral and fear of death during sleep. Parental cooperation was elicited to provide reassurance of his individual worth and some understanding of the concept of death.

4.46 THE ADULT FRIEND WHO MOURNS/CO-WORKER

4259 Schoenberg, B. Mark. "When a Friend Is Mourning." In *Bereavement Counseling: A Multi-Disciplinary Handbook,* edited by B. Mark Schoenberg, 239–250. Westport, Conn.: Greenwood Press, 1980.

Bereavement counseling is a kind of crisis intervention that majors on empathetic understanding. Various practical suggestions are given by the author for those who are friends of the bereaved, for those who are closest in the concentric circles of friendship to the ones who have suffered a loss. Assistance is recommended in the movement from the passive numbing of grief to the active flow of feeling in mourning.

4260 Stringfellow, William. *A Simplicity of Faith*. Nashville, Tenn.: Abingdon Press, 1982.

An activist Anglican priest mourns the death of a companion-poet in alternating descriptions of feelings of loss for his friend and resolution of tensions concerning the approach of his own death through diabetes. Incisive personal faith and enduring purpose in life are the religious resources with which the author faces more than a year of intense grief. This is intimate meditative prose with occasional stabs at the insensitivity of hospitals and physicians.

4.47 THE AGED

4261 Broden, Alexander. "Reaction to Loss in the Aged." In *Loss and Grief: Psychological Management in Medical Practice*, ed. by Bernard Schoenberg, A. Carr, D. Peretz, and A. Kutscher, 199–217. New York: Columbia University Press, 1970.

Among the aged who grieve, there may be a preoccupation with bodily organs and functions which serve as substitute for concern for the deceased, or the preoccupation may be an attempt by the bereaved to keep the loved one alive by identification with symptoms.

4262 Kastenbaum, Robert J.. "The Mental Life of Dying Geriatric Patients." *Proceedings of the Seventh International Congress of Gerontology* (1966): 153–159.

A study of geriatric patients revealed more positive than negative references to death. and did not support the common belief that aged persons are in poor mental health or in poor mental contact as they are dying.

4263 Kastenbaum, Robert J. "Death and Bereavement in Later Life." In *Perspectives in Aging*, ed. Francis G. Scott and Ruth N. Brewer, 227–240. Eugene, Oreg.: Oregon Center for Gerontology, 1971.

Many of the negative behavior patterns that are associated by society with old age may be the result of a bereavement overload. Attempts to ease this burden may be thwarted by the cautions of elderly persons toward a reinvestment of feelings, but they will benefit from new friends and partners.

4264 Lund, Dale A., ed. *Older Bereaved Spouses: Research with Practical Applications*. Washington, D.C.: Hemisphere Pub. Corp., 1989.

Current findings on older spouses are presented by investigators from various professional fields. The emphasis is upon research generated information that will be of practical value to a variety of professionals, students, family members. Much of their research is developed from longitudinal designs. Almost 3,000 persons participated in the nine studies that are reviewed in various chapters. Issues considered are: impact and course of bereavement, factors influencing bereavement adjustments, comparisons of widowhood and divorce, interventions and implications for research. See also Hyman (1366), Wallerstein (4124), Lopata (4240), Parkes (4360).

4265 Mojtabai, A. G. *Autumn*. Boston: Houghton-Mifflin, 1982.

See 6026.

4266 Stern, Karl, Gwendolyn M. Williams and Miguel Prados. "Grief Reactions In Later Life." *American Journal of Psychiatry*, 108 (1951): 289–294.

Twenty-five subjects in later life showed tendencies toward somatic illness after the death of a spouse. There was little overt grief or conscious feelings of guilt.

4.48 PERINATAL DEATH

4267 *A Guide to Resources in Perinatal Bereavement*. Washington, D.C.: National Center for Education in Maternal and Child Health, 1988.

See 8001.

4268 Bourne, S. and E. Lewis. "Delayed Psychological Effects of Perinatal Deaths: The Next Pregnancy and the Next Generations." *British Medical Journal* 289 (1984): 146–148.

Problems that may occur during a healthy pregnancy following a stillborn or newborn birth are addressed in terms of: importance of mourning the death of a stillborn child, need for parental support and counseling during a subsequent pregnancy, impact of perinatal death on the medical staff working with the parents.

4269 Case, Ronna. "When Birth Is also a Funeral." *Journal of Pastoral Care* 32 (1978): 6–21.

A chaplain presents her experiences with mothers after stillbirth and includes conversation concerning a request for baptism and offers suggestions for pastoral care.

4270 Davis, M. "Miscarriage: Remnants of a Life." *Marriage and Family Living* (February 1986): 15–17.

Through a diary the author describes her feelings and the events her miscarriages. She included biblical passages that relate to each of the different events and places that remind her of the loss.

4271 Defrain, John. *et al. Stillborn—The Invisible Death.* Lexington, Mass.: Lexington Books, 1986.

From interviews with 350 parents who experienced a stillbirth, this popular work includes findings from the study and a transcript from a support group meeting. Principles for working with parents are presented and a self-study guide for parents and an annotated list of selected readings.

4272 Feeley, Nancy and Laurie Ann Gottlieb. "Parents' Coping and Communication Following their Infant's Death." *Omega* 19 (1988–89): 51–68.

Twenty-seven couples who had experienced a still-birth, neonatal death or Sudden Infant Death completed questionnaires. Mothers used seeking social support, escape-avoidance, and pre-occupation to a significantly greater extent than did fathers. Both mothers' and fathers' coping strategies, six to twenty-seven months post-loss were concordant than discordant.

4273 Friedman, Rochelle and Bonnie Gradstein. *Surviving Pregnancy Loss.* Boston: Little, Brown and Co., 1982

Medical and psychological aspects of spontaneous abortion, stillbirth and ectopic pregnancy are presented from clinical studies and personal accounts. The father's point of view is included. List of support groups and extensive bibliography.

4274 Fritsch, Julie and S. Isles. *The Anguish of Loss.* Longlake, Minn.: Wintergreen Press, 1988.

The grief of a mother following the death of her newborn son is portrayed through photographs of sculpture and short poems.

4275 Ilse, S. *Perinatal and Infant Bereavement: Resource Manual for Funeral Directors.* Milwaukee, Minn.: National Funeral Directors Association, 1986.

Funeral directors can aid in grief resolution by helping parents and family members create memories through funerals and memorialization. A brief history is provided of past practices in caring for mothers, hospital treatment, notification of death, funeral preparation, follow-up process. Resource information for local and national parent support groups is included. Bibliography, audio-visuals.

4276 La Roche, C., *et al.* "Grief Reactions to Perinatal Death A Follow-up Study." Canadian *Journal of Psychiatry* 29 (1984): 14–19.

From a long-term evaluation of 30 women who experienced perinatal death the authors emphasize the importance of identifying abnormal depression. They recommend physical contact between a mother and the baby as one means to reduce the possibility of normal depression.

4277 Lewis, E., and A. Page. "Failure to Mourn a Stillbirth: An Overlooked Catastrophe." *British Journal of Medical Psychology* 51 (1978): 237–241.

Neglect of mourning for a stillborn child may lead to unresolved feelings of guilt and doubt, fantasies and problems in future parenting. The authors suggest that parents be encouraged to look at or hold their dead baby, take an active part in the certification of the stillbirth, name the child and provide it with a memorable funeral. Siblings should be included in this funeral ritual. Isolation is often severe because there is so little to talk about or to share with other parents.

4278 Limbo, R. K. and S. R. Wheeler. "Coping with Unexpected Outcomes." *Nurses Association of the American College of Obstetrics and Gynecology Update Series* 5 (1986): 1–8.

Childbirth educators can help parents cope with unexpected pregnancy outcomes. The article describes possible reactions to pregnancy outcomes, preparation for loss as a part of the childbirth education curricula, the role of the educator in providing information, guidance and support.

4279 Panuthos, C. and C. Romero. *Ended Beginnings: Healing Childbearing Losses.* South Hadley, Mass.: Bergin and Garvey Pub., 1984.

A wide range of losses are discussed: infant death, miscarriage, stillbirth, abortion, infertility. Specific suggestions are given to parents as they help grieving children. Bibliography and list of parent support groups.

4280 Peppers, L. G., and R. J. Knapp. "Maternal Reactions to Involuntary Fetal/Infant Death." *Psychiatry* 43 (1980): 155–159.

Maternal grief is found to be the same for miscarriage, stillborn death or sudden infant death.

4281 Pizer, H. and C. O. Palinski. *Coping with a Miscarriage.* New York: New American Library, 1981.

This book for the public describes the types of medical intervention and treatment services provided during and after a miscarriage, plus chapters about responsibilities of fathers and their reactions.

4282 Rosenblatt, Paul C. and L. H. Burns. "Long-Term Effects of Perinatal Loss." *Journal of Family Issues* 7 (1986): 237–253.

Thirty-four adults who had experienced instances of perinatal loss were interviewed. Individual reactions are reported, the nature of the support provided and ways of dealing with feelings of grief that last for as long as forty-four years.

4283 Verdevelt, Pam W. *Empty Arms*. Portland, Oreg.: Multnomah Press, 1984.

A pastor's wife and professional counselor describes the confusion with which she faced the news that there was no heartbeat from the child in her womb. She describes her own recovery and the process of grief in those with whom she has shared counsel after miscarriage or stillbirth. A final chapter offers hope and comfort from the Bible.

4284 Videcke, Sherman, L. and M. Lieberman. "The Effects of Self-Help and Psychotherapy Intervention on Childloss: The Limits of Recovery." *American Journal of Orthopsychiatry* 55 (1985): 7–82.

A longitudinal study of the effects of bereaved parents participation in a self-help group and in psychotherapy show that active participants experienced unique changes in attitudes about bereavement.

4285 Woods, John R. and Jenifer L. Esposito, eds. *Pregnancy Loss: Medical Therapeutics and Practical Considerations*. Baltimore, Md.: Williams and Wilkins, 1987.

This medical text provides a step-by-step approach for professionals who encounter patients that experience pregnancy loss: issues and events, individual professional roles, perceptions of the patient and her partner. Psychological aspects of patient management form an integral part of medical care-intervention in a multidisciplinary team approach.

4.481 SUDDEN INFANT DEATH SYNDROME

4286 Bergman, Abraham B. *The "Discovery" of Sudden Infant Death Syndrome*. New York: Praeger, 1986.

The recognition of SIDS is described by the author as an issue of medical politics. A disease that was mostly ignored in the 1970's gained recognition mainly through the National SIDS Foundation.

4287 Golding, Jean, Sylvia Limerick and Aidan McFarlane. *Sudden Infant Death: Patterns, Puzzles, and Problems*. Seattle, Wash.: University of Washington Press, 1985.

The results of the Oxford research linkage study and others are used to review epidemiology, causation, family reactions, counseling, prevention, help for families. Excellent.

4288 Knight, Bernard. *Sudden Death in Infancy: The "Cot Death" Syndrome*. London: Faber and Faber, 1983.

A forensic pathologist describes the nature and circumstances of sudden infant death, possible causes and prevention and the problems of coping with the death. List of literature and organizations.

4289 Kotzwinkle, W. *Swimmer in the Secret Sea*. New York: Avon, 1975.

A young couple describe the trauma of sudden complications during the birth process, the unsuccessful attempts of the medical personnel to bring their stillborn son back to life and their decision to build a simple pine box and bury their baby in the woods. The grim realities of this process are openly discussed within the context of a spirit of triumph through love and faith.

4290 Leon, Irving G. "The Invisible Loss: The Impact of Perinatal Death on Siblings." *Journal of Psychosomatic Obstretics and Gynecology*. 5 (1986): 1–14.

See 4254.

4291 Limbo, R. K. and S. R. Wheeler. "Coping with Unexpected Outcomes." *Nurses Association of the American College of Obstetrics and Gynecology Update Series* 5 (1986): 1–8.

Childbirth educators can help parents cope with unexpected pregnancy outcomes. The article describes possible reactions to pregnancy outcomes, preparation for loss as a part of the childbirth education curricula, the role of the educator in providing information, guidance and support.

4292 May, H. J. and F. J. Breme. "SIDS Family Adjustment Scale: A Method of Assessing Family Adjustment to Sudden Infant Death Syndrome." *Omega* 13 (1982–83): 59–74.

This scale identifies critical tasks for adjustment on a continuum from maladaptive to highly adaptive.

4.5 GODLY AND DEADLY SORROW

4293 Becker, Howard. "The Sorrow of Bereavement." *Journal of Abnormal and Social Psychology* 27 (1933): 391–410.

In an exposition of the theories and empirical principles of sorrow (with illustrations drawn from case studies made by the writer), the variety of personal reactions include those who give free vent to loss through violence in outward behavior, those who are tearless and mute, those who sink under the sense of weakness and discouragement, and those who engage in activity approaching frenzy.

4294 Chesser, Barbara Russell. *Because You Care: Practical Ideas for Helping Those Who Grieve.* Waco: Word Books, 1987.

A human relations specialist offers practical suggestions for relatives and friends who attend the bereaved before, during and after funerals and up to a time of return to social life. The author recognizes the devastating emotional loss of death along side of the wisdom that can be expressed over a period of time by those who care. Bibliography, suggested readings, listening of support groups for the bereaved.

4295 Davidson, Glen W. *Understanding Mourning.* Minneapolis, Minn.: Augsburg Publishing House, 1984.

A professor of medical humanities brings together the findings of psychiatrists such as John Bowlby and Colin Murray Parkes with Christian ministry toward those who mourn. Concepts of disease, feelings and faith are utilized to help people tell their story. Mourning is considered in terms of shock and numbness, searching and yearning, disorganization and depression. There is a discussion of mourning that is almost over. Models are presented for helping mourners to see the ways to reorient themselves and to solve problems. The desired orientation to life will be understanding basic survival needs, personal esteem, ability to relate to others, desire to include coping skills and deepen one's understanding of life. A very readable and compassionate study based upon cases and references to professional studies.

4296 Jackson, Edgar N. *The Many Faces of Grief.* Nashville, Tenn.: Abingdon Press, 1977.

A pastoral specialist on the psychodynamics of grief presents a lifetime of experience with the many aspects of personal reactions which may be baffling and often contradictory. An empathetic study that will bring comfort and insight.

4297 Mitchell, Kenneth R. and Herbert Anderson. *All Our Losses, All Our Griefs: Resources for Pastoral Care.* Philadelphia: Westminister Press, 1983.

See 4032.

4.51 SOCIAL AND PSYCHOLOGICAL EXPECTATIONS

4298 Greer, Ina M. "Grief Must Be Faced." *Christian Century* 62 (1945): 269–271.

In an early protest against the growing silence and secularization of grief, the author states that grief should be openly experienced. Otherwise it may emerge in imaginary or psychosomatic symptoms. The church is challenged to continue a ministry by prayers for the dead and days of remembrance and to encourage friends to be understanding and supportive. Medical or psychiatric assistance may be necessary if physical or mental problems emerge.

4299 Manning, Doug. *Comforting Those Who Grieve: A Guide for Helping Others.* San Francisco: Harper and Row, 1985.

An experienced clergyperson provides a brief and readable guide on the way that friends and relatives may meet the expectations of those who wish to comfort the bereaved.

4300 Taylor, S. E. "Adjustment to Threatening Events: A Theory of Cognitive Adaptation." *American Psychologist* 38 (1983): 1161–1173.

Grief work can be an effective coping strategy when it involves a search for meaning in the experience, some attempt to gain mastery over the events of life and an effort to rebuild self esteem. In this way social identity can be restored. This is different from the withdrawal into sadness which characterizes a passive process of ruminating about a loss. Social support from relatives and friends helps to bring a grieving person out of passivity and isolation, but the individual must also be willing to confide in others and seek some inner reorganization of thoughts and feelings.

4301 Volkart, Edmund H. and Stanley T. Michael. "Bereavement and Mental Health." In *Explorations in Social Psychiatry*, ed. by A. H. Leighton, J. A. Clausen and R. N. Wilson, 281–307. New York: Basic Books, 1957.

The authors consider a bereaved person to be in a category which is culturally defined. The emotions of the bereaved person consist of various degrees and intensities of the sense of loss, hostility, guilt. When these are minimal, there is less vulnerability to mental health problems and when they are maximal and complicated there is a high initial vulnerability to mental health problems in bereavement.

4.52 DEPRESSION, REALISTIC AND PATHOLOGICAL

4302 Beck, A. T. *Depression: Clinical, Experimental, and Theoretical Aspects.* New York: Harper and Row, 1967.

The "cognitive triad" of depressed patients includes a negative self-concept, pessimistic view of the world, hopeless view of the future.

4303 Costello, C. G. "Depression: Loss of Reinforcer or Loss of Reinforcer Effectiveness?" *Behavior Therapy* 3 (1972): 240–247.

The bereaved have lost many rewards in life and even the available ones may have lost their reinforcing quality. The loss reinforcement may be due to endogenous biochemical and neurophysical changes that depress appetite and libido. It is also possible that memories of pleasant activities with the deceased will elicit such sadness that all the former joy of such activities is extinguished.

4304 Feighner, J. P., *et al.* "Diagnostic Criteria for Use in Psychiatric Research." *Archives of General Psychiatry* 26 (1972): 56–73.

A diagnosis of "definite depression" would require patients to be in a severely depressed mood for a period of more than one month and to exhibit such symptoms as poor appetite or weight loss, sleep difficulty, loss of energy, loss of interest in usual activities (or decrease in sexual drive), feelings in self-reproach or guilt, diminished ability to concentrate, recurrent thoughts of death or suicide, including thoughts of wishing to be dead.

4305 Freud, Sigmund. "Mourning and Melancholia." In Sigmund Freud, *The Collected Papers.* Ed. by Ernest Jones. Vol. 4, 152–170. New York: Basic Books, 1959.

See 4312.

4306 Gallagher, D. E., et al. "Effects of Bereavement on Indicators of Mental Health in Elderly Widows and Widowers." *Journal of Gerontology* 38 (1983): 565–571.

One hundred and thirteen widows and ninety-eight widowers over the age of 55 were compared with married controls through various health measures. The odds for mild to severe depression after two months of bereavement were 1.5 times higher for the bereaved than for the married controls.

4307 Klerman, G. L. "Affective Disorders." In *The Harvard Guide to Modern Psychiatry*, ed. by A. M. Nicholi, Jr., 252–282. Cambridge, Mass.: Harvard University Press, 1978.

The central symptom of depression is sadness. This is often accompanied by anxiety, fear, intense worry. Severely depressed patients also lack motivation for relationships or events that would give them pleasure.

4308 Wahl, C. W. "The Differential Diagnosis of Normal and Neurotic Grief Following Bereavement." *Archives of the Foundation of Thanatology* 1 (1970): 137–141.

In comparing nine persons with normal grief reactions to nineteen persons with neurotic grief reactions, the author characterized neurotic grief as excessive, filled with irrational despair and helplessness, loss of personal identity, fear of death, inability to cope with ambivalence for the deceased, a sense of the deceased' death as a rejection of survivors, self-reproach for the death, continuing dependency upon the deceased, including some similar physical symptoms, protracted apathy, heightened irritability, aimless hyperactivity without appropriate affect.

4.53 MORBID GRIEF AND GUILT/PATHOLOGY
See also FUTURE MENTAL HEALTH (3.1211)

4309 Deutsch, Helene. "Absence of Grief." *Psychoanalytic Quarterly* 6 (1937): 12–22.

From cases in which the reaction to the childhood loss of a beloved object is a complete absence of the manifestations of mourning, the author looks for a defense mechanism that represses some childhood loss.

4310 Edelson, Stuart R., and Porter H. Warren. "Catatonic Schizophrenia As A Mourning Process." *Diseases of the Nervous System*, 24 (1963): 527–534.

Catatonic schizophrenia is viewed as one process of mourning which begins in protest and then moves to despair and detachment. Bereavement is viewed as a family crisis that moves from the primary sense of unreality, shock, self-injury, grief to behavior patterns that may include escape compensation and inter-identification with loved one.

4311 Fleming, J. and S. Altschul. "Activation of Mourning and Growth by Psychoanalysis." *International Journal of Psycho-Analysis* 44 (1963): 419–431.

In a study of adult patients who had lost a parent by death in childhood and who were now being treated by psychoanalysis it was found that reality-denial, a form of pathological mourning, interfered with maturation. Psychoanalytic treatment was able to help activate the interrupted mourning process.

4312 Freud, Sigmund. "Mourning and Melancholia." In Sigmund Freud, *The Collected Papers*. Ed. by Ernest Jones. Vol. 4, 152–170. New York: Basic Books, 1959.

In a 1917 paper, Freud considers mourning (*Trauern*) as a normal process of grief. A healthy ego works through the grief process. But, a fragile, pre-neurotic self falls into melancholia, a pathological state filled with self reproaches. The mourner has regressed to a state of narcissism in which the loved one is reproached: "Why was I abandoned?" This intolerable question is unconsciously shifted to reproaches against the self and subsequent loss of self-esteem. The mechanism occurs as the unresolved anxieties and insecurity of childhood loss of a mother are recapitulated in an adult loss. Freud outlines four "grave departures" from normal grief: painful deduction, loss of interest in the outside world, loss of capacity to love, and indecision of activity (Bowlby did not find these to be satisfactory criteria 4002, 322). Freud associated grief with clinical depression, which he called melancholia, because both were reactions to loss. But his differentiation between them—no self reproach or low esteem in mourning—was surpassed in later investigations which showed self reproach and low self-esteem as a frequent symptom in healthy grieving. In later studies, object-loss became a term for actual or threatened loss of any significant object (Peretz 4317). See Bowlby (1168), Stroebe (1377), Parkes (4339).

4313 Jackson, Edgar N. "Grief and Religion." In *The Meaning of Death*, ed. by Herman Feifel, 218–233. New York, McGraw-Hill Book Co., 1959.

A pastoral authority on grief presents three psychological processes that must be dealt with as protection against destructive phantasy and illusion: the incorporation of the deceased person as a part of the self, a substitution of loss by the attachment of emotion to someone outside of the mourner, and guilt over the feeling of freedom that comes when a loved one dies.

4314 Parkes, Colin M. "Recent Bereavement as a Cause of Mental Illness." *British Journal of Psychiatry* 110 (1964): 198–204.

In a study of 94 mental patients who had experienced bereavement not more than six months before their present psychiatric difficulties, 78 had lost a parent or a spouse. The author examines incidence of recent bereavement in pre-illness histories of psychiatric clinic patients and relates volume of incidence of bereavement among clinic population to that expected by chance. Loss of spouse was 6 times chance. Loss of a parent was only a fraction above chance. Study of age, sex and diagnostic information concludes the article.

4315 Parkes, Colin M. "Bereavement and Mental Illness." *British Journal of Medical Psychology* 38 (1965): 1–26.

In one of his earliest contributions to the study of bereavement, the author compares the symptomatology of psychiatric patients with that of a randomly selected sample of London widows. The psychiatric problems of the patients had begun during the terminal illness or within six months after the death of a parent, spouse, sibling or child. Parkes concluded that only one out of twenty-one patients had reactions that fell within limits of normal grief. The other twenty suffered distortions or exaggerations of grief which caused them to be regarded as mentally ill. He identified three forms of these distorted or exaggerated reactions to grief: chronic, delayed, inhibited. These categories were revised in a 1983 study, Parkes and Weiss (4339). More attention was given to antecedent factors such as the expectedness of the loss, relationship to the deceased, patterns of communications about the loss.

4316 Paul, Norman L. and George H. Rosser. "Operational Mourning and Its Role in Conjoint Family Therapy." *Community Mental Health Journal* 1 (1965): 339–345.

A defense against further loss and disappointment may be adopted by a grieving relative who will influence other members of the family, especially children. An "operational mourning" technique is designed to bring sharing of feelings between members of the family in order that they may understand reasons for their current relational difficulties and restore some equilibrium to the family.

4317 Peretz, David. "Development Object-Relationships at Loss." In Bernard Schoenberg, *et al*, eds. *Loss and Grief: Psychological Management in Medical Practice*, 3–19. New York: Columbia University Press, 1970.

Loss may appear in several forms: loss of a valued person, loss of some aspect of the self, loss of external objects, developmental loss that is associated with some life change. The extent and type of response to loss depends upon the personality of the individual and the relationship between the bereaved and the lost object and the values of society.

4318 Siggins, L. "Mourning: A Critical Survey of the Literature." *International Journal of Psycho-Analysis* 47 (1966): 418–438.

Grief reactions are classified as normal, pathological, and clinically recognizable psychiatric illnesses precipitated by bereavement. Normal mourning reactions include guilt, anger, relief, and internalization of positive and negative aspects of the relationship to the lost one. Mourning is pathological when there is failure to deal with the reality of death. Bibliography.

4319 Stroebe, Margaret S. and Wolfgang Stroebe. "Who Suffers More? Sex Differences in Health Risk of the Widowed." *Psychological Bulletin* 93 (1983): 279–301.

See 1378.

4320 Volkart, Edmund H. and S. T. Michael. "Bereavement and Mental Health." In *Explorations in Social Psychiatry*, ed. by A. H. Leighton, J. A. Clausen and R. N. Wilson, 281–307. New York: Basic Books, 1957.

The authors' hypothesize that the relationship between bereavement and mental health is a function of both ego strength and of the history of the relationships between the bereaved and the deceased.

4.54 RESOURCES FOR RECOVERY
See also RELIGIOUS RESOURCES (4.7)

4321 Averill, J. R. and P. A. Wisocki. "Some Observations on Behavioral Approaches to the Treatment of Grief Among the Elderly." In *Behavioral Therapy in Terminal Care: A Humanistic Approach*, ed. by H. J. Sobel. Cambridge, Mass.: Ballinger, 1981.

The symptoms of grief rather than intrapsychic aspects of grief are the focus of therapy for the elderly bereaved. Primary issues are the reduction of physiological complaints, increase in physical activity, more adaptive self-concepts and thought patterns, reduction in addictions such as alcohol, improving the quality of social interaction and physical or social support systems.

4322 Bailey, Robert W. *The Minister and Grief.* New York: Hawthorn Books, 1976.

See 6151.

4323 Black, Dora and M. A. Urbanowicz. "Family Intervention With Bereaved Children." *Journal of Child Psychology and Psychiatry and Allied Disciplines* 28, 3 (1987): 467–476.

On the basis of interviews with 45 families in which a parent had died and left a child or children under 16 years of age, a treatment group showed some benefits from the brief intervention that had occurred one or two years before after the initial bereavement. Half of the families were assigned to a control group which did not receive treatment.

4324 Bozarth-Campbell, Alla. *Life is Good-bye, Life is Hello.* Minneapolis, Minn.: CompCare Pub., 1982.

This self-help book considers grief as the loss of a part of one's self. Individuals may find themselves in one of four styles of grieving: the hero, the martyr, the crazy person, the fool. The response is to one of many kinds of loss: death, birth and parenting, changes in place or position, separation, spiritual alienation, sickness, failure of position or self-esteem. The art of grieving requires creativity in the face of reality. The author is an Episcopal priest and therapist who has been through many types of loss in her own life.

4325 Chesser, Barbara Russell. *Because You Care: Practical Ideas for Helping Those Who Grieve*. Waco, Tx.: Word Books, 1987.

A human relations specialist presents many examples of life-enhancing acts by which friends can reach out to the grief-stricken: listening, attending a funeral service, giving a hug, writing a note, extending an invitation. Appendices include support groups for the bereaved and suggested reading.

4326 Grollman, Earl A. *Time Remembered: A Journal for Survivors*. Boston: Beacon Press, 1987.

In a modern transformation of the classical art of consolation literature and a diary of grief, a rabbi expresses a specific mood, pain or search for healing on one page and asks questions which a grieving person may then enter on the next page, which is blank. Appendices include information on support groups, checklist of resource persons, vital personal material, acknowledgement letters.

4327 Hurietes, Edna J., *et al.* "Religion in the POW/MIA family." In *Family Separation and Reunion: Families of Prisoners of War and Servicemen Missing in Action*, ed. by Hamilton I. McCubbin, *et al*, pp. 85–93. Washington, D.C.: Govt Print Off, 1974.

Among 215 wives of POW/MIA servicemen, those who found help in coping with the absence or loss of a husband were older, more active in church affairs, had less tendency to date and had fewer guilt feelings. Wives who did not find religion helpful were those who had moved on toward a reorganization of the family and a closing out of the husband's role, with some feelings of guilt.

4328 James, John W. and Frank Cherry. *The Grief Recovery Handbook*. New York: Harper and Row, 1988.

A step by step program for moving beyond loss is described by the co-founders of the Grief Recovery Institute. Recovery begins with recognition of lack of preparation to deal with loss, the identification of myths and inappropriate responses of others who are ill prepared to deal with loss. Preparing for change comes next, with a choice to recover, finding support for self and a partner, preparing a loss history graph and finding solutions through awareness, responsibility, communications, action and the obtaining of a new perspective.

4329 Jones, David. "The Griefwork Project: The Effects of Group Therapy on Successful Coping with Grief." Ph.D. dissertation, University of Southern California, 1979.

Thirty-six widows and widowers (89% female, 11% male) were divided into treatment and control groups who had suffered the loss of a spouse within one year. Although the treatment subjects did not score significantly higher than control subjects on various measures, those who entered treatment as potentially poor outcome grew significantly over "good outcome" participants. The therapy was most effective for those whose spouses died after short illnesses, or who had poor attitudes, or who felt much guilt or blame at the loss of their spouses.

4330 Kinast, Robert L. *When a Person Dies: Pastoral Theology in Death Experiences*. Riverside, New York: Crossroad, 1984.

A pastoral counselor considers theological questions in relation to a variety of grief experiences such as a grandmother's death, a boy's accidental death, a wife's premature death, a brother's suicide. The death of Jesus and a relational theology of death are explored.

4331 Kreis, Bernadine and Alice T. Battie. *Up from Grief: Patterns of Recovery*. New York: Seabury Press, 1969.

From their own feelings of grief and an analysis of 500 interviews with those who grieve (mostly women) the authors provide a very intimate, realistic and compassionate encouragement for the sharing of grief with others and an awareness of the normal stages of recovery: shock, suffering, recovery of purpose and meaning in life. Specific attention is given to grief, loneliness, sex, the way to help a friend in grief, helping ourselves and receiving help from the clergy.

4332 Lindemann, Erich. *Beyond Grief: Studies in Crisis Intervention*. New York: Jason Aronson, 1979.

The importance of preventative mental health and the value of many friends, neighbors, communities and professional helpers are stressed in seminal papers of the author. These include exploration of the psychological and somatic effects of bereavement, intervention in a variety of acute situations and illness, the coping processes and environmental supports of people under stress, the community context for human function and mental health intervention, the role of the mental health professional and the relationship of professions to social change. The final chapter is his speech to colleagues who cared for him during a lingering terminal illness.

Biographical data and a listing of the published papers of the author include a 1950 report on the relationship between a loss of security and interpersonal relationships and ulcerative colitis. The first report of this study was given to the Massachusetts Psychiatric Society in 1942, nine months before his investigations of grief after the Coconut Grove fire. See also Lindemann (1368).

4333 Lieberman, Morton A., Leonard D. Bowman and Associates. *Self-Help Groups for Coping with Crisis*. San Francisco: Jossey-Bass, 1979.

This resource book explores the way that self-help groups are started and structured, who participates in them, how they work and how their impact may be evaluated. A variety of programs are explained, especially those for widows.

4334 Lund, Dale A., ed. *Older Bereaved Spouses: Research with Practical Applications*. Washington, D.C.: Hemisphere Pub. Corp., 1989.

See 4264.

4335 Madara, Edward J. and Barrie Alan Peterson. "Clergy and Self-help Groups: Practical and Promising Relationships." *Journal of Pastoral Care* 41 (1987): 213–220.

Clergy may be involved in self-help groups through acting as a referral source, as an initiator of groups, as a provider of meeting space, as a supporter of religious organization's self-help efforts and by initiating self-help groups for clergy themselves. A list of self-help clearing houses is included.

4336 Maddison, David and Beverley Raphael. "Conjugal Bereavement in the Social Network." In *Bereavement: Its Psychosocial Aspects*, ed. by Bernard Schoenberg, *et al.*, 26–40. New York: Columbia University Press, 1975.

In contrasting good outcomes with bad outcomes of grief, the authors found that the availability of other people was a crucial variable influencing the resolution of grief. The quality of social networks and contacts were very important. Widows with a bad outcome reported opposition to their free expression of grief and anger. See also Di Giulio (4226), Lopata (4241).

4337 Mawson, D., I. M. Marks, L. Ram, and R. S. Sturn. "Guided Mourning for Morbid Grief: A Controlled Study." *British Journal of Psychiatry* 138 (1981): 184–193.

Individuals with unresolved grief are encouraged in therapy to consider the impact upon imagination and real life of painful memories that had been avoided in relation to the loss of the deceased. Repeated description of these is encouraged along with hope that persons will write notes or visit the cemetery in a way that says good-bye. Instructions are given upon writing and thinking about the deceased in a way that will bring feelings of grief to the surface. There was modest improvement in a group that focused upon the deceased versus a control group that was encouraged to avoid thinking of death and the deceased. In the former group there was less phobic avoidance and depression.

4338 Melges, F. T., and D. R. DeMaso. "Grief-Resolution Therapy: Reliving, Revising and Revisiting." *American Journal of Psychotherapy* 34 (1980): 51–61.

Widows are encouraged to dialog with the deceased in order to acknowledge the finality of the loss, differentiate self from the deceased, express tears and rage, deal with ambivalence and misdirected anger, specify different types of grief reactions, release unspoken bondages, explore secrets and unfinished business, express love and forgiveness, and gain permission from the memory of the deceased to find new relationships and options.

4339 Parkes, Colin M. and Robert S. Weiss. *Recovery From Bereavement.* New York: Basic Books, 1983.

Based on empirical findings from the Harvard Bereavement Study, the authors conclude that normal grief can be facilitated through therapeutic interventions that clarify ambivalent relations to the deceased. Overt expressions of grief are encouraged. In contrast, chronic grief is made worst through encouragement to express feelings, for unnecessary dependance upon the group is heightened. The therapeutic goal for chronic grief would be increased autonomy and a more active role of the grieving person in making decisions. Those who suffer from unanticipated loss are special in that they require many opportunities to talk about the implications of their loss, to make sense out of it and to bring order into their lives at a time that they had been overwhelmed with stress and insecurity. In a revision of Parkes' 1965 classification of pathological grief (4315), Parkes and Weiss describe three syndromes: unexpected-grief, ambivalent-grief, and chronic-grief. See also Parkes (4360).

4340 Paul, Norman L., and George H. Grosser. "Operational Mourning and Its Role in Conjoint Family Therapy. *Community Mental Health Journal* 1 (1965): 339–345.

The operational mourning technique is designed to involve the family in a belated mourning experience with extensive grief reactions resulting in empathy and understanding of the origins of the present relational difficulties. Includes case illustrations.

4341 Peterson, Ronnie. "The Compassionate Friends." *Death Education* 8 (1984): 195–197.

The work of the The Compassionate Friends (founded 1969) is presented as the help which those who have experienced the death of a child can offer to others who are coping with grief and rediscovering their relationships with the living. See also Silverman (4347).

4342 Rando, Therese A. *Grieving: How to Go On Living When Someone You Love Dies.* Lexington, Mass.: Lexington Books, 1988.

In this compassionate and informative book for the general public, a thanatologist brings her skill as a counselor to such topics as learning about grief, recognizing the impact of sudden versus anticipated death, facing family reorganization after the death (spouse, parent, sibling, child), the resolution of grief through inner work and social rituals, some ways to solve practical problems. Advice is given on finding effective professional and self-help group assistance, for which addresses are listed. References and index.

4343 Raphael, Beverley. "A Psychiatric Model for Bereavement Counseling." In *Bereavement Counseling: A Multi-Disciplinary Handbook*, ed. by B. Mark Schoenberg. Westport, Conn.: Greenwood Press, 1980.

The issues to be considered in bereavement counsel would include differences between adults and children, the prediction of high risk bereavement patterns, the development of aims, therapeutic assessment support and the use of both generalizations and probes into reality, support for the mourner. Specific aspects of this time of probing and support are discussed. References.

4344 Rosenblatt, Paul C. *Bitter, Bitter Tears: Nineteenth-Century Diarist and Twentieth-Century Grief Theories.* Minneapolis, Minn.: University of Minnesota Press, 1983.

A psychologist evaluates and amplifies contemporary theories of grief from his reading of nineteenth-century diarists in the United States and Canada. The findings from the diaries match well with those of modern studies of grief such as those of Glick, Weiss, and Parkes (1365). However, psychological theories that associate grief with pathology should be amended in the light of findings from the diaries that healthy persons might grieve for a period of time, discontinue the grief and then continue the grieving process at a later time. A healthy ego needs some time for fresh perspective and restoration of energy. During phases of struggle and gradual surrender to the loss of a loved one, religious beliefs and mourning practices were more prominent in the 19th century than in modern theories. The book is a confident correlation of content analysis with psychological theories of personal reactions to loss. Extensive bibliography.

4345 Schoenberg, B. Mark., ed. *Bereavement Counseling: A Multidisciplinary Handbook.* Westport, Conn.: Greenwood Press, 1980.

In a collection of essays designed for professional and lay readers, authors with experience in many areas of thanatology provide a comprehensive overview of such subjects as separation anxiety and object loss, the fear of death, various counseling models and programs for bereavement training, the role of the nursing profession and the work of the clergy in loss management and counseling, the child's concept of death, bereavement in the elderly and help for a friend who is mourning. Bibliography at the end of each chapter. Index.

4346 Schwab, John J., *et al.* "Studies in Grief: A Preliminary Report." In *Bereavement: Its Psychosocial Aspects*, ed. by Bernard Schoenberg, *et al.*, 78–90. New York: Columbia University Press, 1975.

Widowed persons were interviewed one year after their loss. Their current grief reaction was classified as resolved or unresolved. The resolved group reported that human relationships, especially those in which their feelings were accepted, brought healing. They had someone to talk with over a period of time. The unresolved group found that friends and relatives would talk about the loss for only a few weeks.

4347 Silverman, Phyllis R. "The Widow-to-Widow Program." *Mental Hygiene* 53 (1969): 333–337.

Every newly-widowed woman under the age of sixty in a lower-middle class community of two hundred and fifty thousand was contacted by another widow to provide friendship and help after the death of her husband. Four hundred and thirty women were reached in a period of two and a half years and two-thirds chose to involve themselves in a program of friendship other widows. The mutual friendship, home visits, talks about experiences demonstrated the value of one widow as a friend to another. Both those who are helping and those who are helped attended group meetings with an aide to discuss questions, leisure, work, children. Such discussions could help withdrawn widows to master any sense of shame they felt and venture out into the world.

4348 Silverman, Phyllis R. *Helping Women Cope with Grief.* Beverly Hills, Calif.: Sage, 1981.

From her studies of widows and widowers, the author concludes that the caregivers were often inadequate because they had little understanding of grief and would withdraw with some parting advice about a "a stiff upper lip." The author then developed a Widow to Widow Program for approximately 600 newly widowed women under the age of 65 and found that widows who had achieved a sense of reorganization provided a unique contribution to the care of those women who were more recently bereaved.

4349 Sjoden, P. O., S. Bates, W. S. Dockens, eds. *Trends in Behavior Therapy.* New York: Academic Press, 1979.

Articles include a chapter on behavior therapy for pathological grief reactions and one on the problems of learned helplessness.

4350 Slaikeu, Karl and Steve Lawhead. *The Phoenix Factor: Surviving and Growing Through Personal Crisis.* Boston: Houghton Mifflin, 1985.

Practical ideas are given for friends and others who helped those who are in a crisis of grief and other loss. Compassion and professional insights are given in case histories.

4351 Smith, Elwyn A. *A Spiritual Exercise for the Grieving.* Philadelphia: Fortress Press, 1984.

A Presbyterian minister of pastoral care offers brief reflections and prayers for the first seven days of mourning: meaning, separation, tears, affliction, death, resurrection, the kingdom life.

4352 Tatelbaum, Judy. *The Courage to Grieve: Creative Living, Recovery and Growth Through Grief.* New York: Harper and Row, 1980.

In a readable style, a psychotherapist who has experienced grief in her own life presents self-help topics for breaking through denial of death and a building resolution of grief.

4353 Tatelbaum, Judy. *You Don't Have to Suffer.* New York: Harper and Row, 1989.

A psychotherapist draws upon her experience in workshops and with clients to discuss common areas of suffering: separation from others, grief recovery, relationship with our parents, our bodies and health. The author advises the restoration of health through forgiving and completing relationships with people and events in our lives. A strategy for transformation will include commitments to others and to ourselves, so that life will not be seen as a predicament but as a challenge and a gift. Influenced by Gestalt therapy and EST training.

4354 Volkan, V. "'Re-Grief' Therapy" *Bereavement: It's Psychological Aspects,* ed. by B. Schoenberg, *et al.* 334–350. New York: Columbia University Press, 1975.

Those who have a chronic pathological hope that the deceased will return and who are fixated upon the initial reaction to death may benefit from "re-grief" therapy. There is often ambivalence toward the deceased and a need to participate in funeral rites that were never accepted as final.

4355 Whitaker, Agnes, ed. *All in the End is Harvest: An Anthology for Those Who Grieve*. London: Darton, Longman and Todd, 1984.

Poetry and prose for the bereaved are presented with notes and advice.

4356 Williams, W. Vail and Paul R. Polak. "Follow-Up Research in Primary Prevention: A Model of Adjustment in Acute Grief." *Journal of Clinical Psychology* 35 (1979): 35–45.

Bereaved families who had received preventative intervention service were compared with non-intact families. A preventative interventative service had little or no impact upon the bereaved families and may have been harmful because of a delay or interference with time-honored bereavement processes.

4357 Willis, R. Wayne. "Some Concerns of Bereaved Parents." *Journal of Religion and Health* 20 (1981): 133–140.

See 4217.

4358 Worden, J. William. *Grief Counseling and Grief Therapy: A Handbook for the Mental Health Practitioner*. New York: Springer Publishing Co., 1982.

The focus of treatment should be upon any task that a grieving person is unable to meet. Usually the therapy will concentrate first upon the acceptance of the reality of a loss, or upon the fact that a loved person is dead and that sense of presence must be released. In some way a person must experience the pain of grief, which is more than intellectual acceptance of a loss. This process will also include the expression of both positive and negative emotions in such a way that the grieving person can acknowledge both. Out of this will come some redefinition of the relationship to the deceased. Finally there will be some adjustment to an environment in which the loved one is missing. Problem solving will be a large part of this readjustment toward emotional investment in other relationships. Grief therapy is presented for the resolving of pathological grief. Special types of losses are described along with a description of family systems and the counselor's own grief. Brief sketches are given of 12 responses to grief. For example, guilt in the bereaved may be connected with some specific aspect of the loss of a loved one, whereas guilt in clinical depression is associated with a general sense of culpability. A recommended resource on research/clinical practice.

4.55 INTEGRATION/REMARRIAGE

4359 Kreis, Bernadine. *To Love Again: An Answer to Loneliness.* New York: Seabury Press, 1975.

In a warm and personal discussion of loneliness, a divorcee describes the reorganization of her life in a way that would bring fulfillment. This includes advice on the way to meet and attract others, decisions about sex, recognizing and avoiding the traps of transitional relationships. She found remarriage and illustrates the ways in which many others have come "to love again." See also Kreis (4331).

4360 Parkes, Colin M. and Robert S. Weiss. *Recovery from Bereavement.* New York: Basic Books, 1983.

As part of a study of normal grief, the authors cite three tasks in recovery: the development of an explanation of the loss and some identification of the inevitable cause; an ability to face the loss after repeated confrontations with obsessive review of thoughts, memories and feelings; the development of a new identity that is consistent with the circumstances of a changed state toward the deceased. The discrepancy between the world that is and the world that was has now been accepted. See (4339).

4.6 THE FUNERAL AND CUSTOMS OF MOURNING
See also RITUALS/MORES/HOLIDAYS/ANNIVERSARY REACTIONS (6.13)
CULTURAL/SOCIAL ANALYSIS (1.5)
VARIABLES IN VARIOUS CULTURES (1.51)

4361 Bendann, Effie. *Death Customs: An Analytic Study of Burial Rites.* 1930. Reprint. New York: Gordon Press, 1974.

See 1237.

4362 Bloch, Maurice and Jonathan Parry, eds. *Death and the Regeneration of Life.* Cambridge: Cambridge University Press, 1982.

Funeral rituals in relation to symbols of rebirth and fertility are examined by anthropologists in articles concerning China, India, New Guinea, Latin America and Africa. The relationship between death and rebirth is shown in terms of exchange and transaction, marriage and procreation which become transcendental images that devalue biology and sexuality. The spiritual and control sources of life are elevated. Bibliography for each article.

4363 Brandon, S. G. F. "The Personification of Death In Some Ancient Religions." In *Bulletin of the John Rylands Library* 43 (1960–1961): 317–335.

See 1238.

4364 Danforth, Loring M. *The Death Rituals of Rural Greece.* Princeton, N.J.: Princeton University Press, 1982.

A professor of anthropology uses many photographs and on-site observations to describe the way in which the rituals of rural Greece attempt to mediate the opposition between life and death. Three aspects of this mediating process are: the rites of passage that bring about a transition from life to death; the systems of imagery in the funeral laments; the importance of rituals to continue a relationship between the bereaved and the dead. There is an extensive period of mourning over the body of the deceased, vigils by widows and a digging up of the bones after seven years for placement in the village ossuary.

4365 "Death and the Disposal of the Dead," *Encyclopedia of Religion and Ethics*, ed. by James Hastings, IV (1912): 411–511.

The practice and motivation for funeral customs of all the great religions of the ancient and modern world are presented.

4366 Ford, Josephine Massyngberde. *The Silver Lining: Eleven Personalized Scripturalized Wake Services.* Mystic, Conn.: Twenty-third Publications, 1987.

A professor at the University of Notre Dame, Indiana provides liturgies of prayer, scripture and responses for mourning under varying circumstances. The theoretical link between the mourner and the deceased is a belief in healing sleep. Each liturgy is a "wake" in which the living keep watch and remember those who have "fallen asleep."

4367 Goody, Jack. *Death, Property and the Ancestors.* London: Tavistock Publications, 1962.

See 1297.

4368 Habenstein, Robert W. and William M. Lamers. *Funeral Customs the World Over.* Milwaukee, Minn.: Bulfin Printers, 1960.

See 1267.

4369 Huntington, Richard, and Peter Metcalf. *Celebrations of Death: The Anthropology of Mortuary Rituals.* New York: Cambridge University Press, 1979.

The authors explore the significance of death in various cultures, including Borneo, Madagascar, ancient Egypt, Renaissance France with the focus on the corpse as the central symbol of the meaning of life as well as of death. Van Gennep's (1247) theory of funerals as a final folk rite of passage is used to explain mortuary rituals. These findings are related to American rituals of death. Bibliography.

4370 Morgan, Ernest. *Dealing Creatively With Death: A Manual of Death Education of Simple Burial.* Rev. ed. Burnsville, N.C.: Celo Press, 1984.

This tenth edition of a *Manual of Simple Burial* introduces the importance of death education, living with the dying at home or in hospice, group support in bereavement, the right to die or refuse treatment, simple burial and cremation, memorial societies, death ceremonies, the importance of anatomical gifts such as autopsy and organ banks, bibliography, organizations, suggestions for teachers, living will, descriptions of burial boxes, addresses of memorial societies, sample death ceremonies information about organ donation. Informative volume for sane and inexpensive burial practices and care of the bereaved.

4371 Polson, C. J., R. P. Brittain and T. K. Marshall. *The Disposal of the Dead.* New York: Philosophical Library, 1953.

This comprehensive study of burial and cremation practices, especially in England, includes historical survey, descriptive material and a summary of attitudes toward cremation in several religious groups.

4372 Puckle, Bertram S. *Funeral Customs, Their Origin and Development.* London: T. Werner Laurie, 1926.

A survey of folklore and customs surrounding the physical aspects of death: death warnings, preparation for burial, wakes and wailers, mutes and totemism, bells, feasts, processions, burial places, flowers and body snatching, plagues, state and public funerals, cremation, embalming, memorials and epithets. Quite an assortment of quaint information. A few footnotes. The more lengthy illustrations are English.

4373 Turner, Ann Warren. *Houses for the Dead: Burial Customs through the Ages.* New York: McKay, 1976.

For readers aged 12 and over this history of burial customs includes a description of funeral vehicles, the exposure of bodies, scavengers, the beliefs of various cultural groups.

4.61 THE FUNERAL

4374 Aguilar, I., and V. Wood. "Therapy through a Death Ritual." *Social Work* 21 (1976): 49–54.

In a study of various funeral rites which are traditional in Mexico, the authors find beneficial bereavement outcomes. They criticize the deritualizing impact of North American culture on traditional Mexican patterns.

4375 Bergen, M. Betsie and Robert R. Williams. "Alternative Funerals and Exploratory Study." *Omega* 12 (1981–82): 71–78.

The beliefs and attitudes of members of a small Midwestern urban Protestant congregation were examined through a questionnaire on death, grief and conventional rituals surrounding death and attitudes toward alternative practices and values. An example of alternative funeral preparations would be work by family, close neighbors, friends and pastors to construct a wooden coffin for the deceased and to dig a grave beneath fruit trees for the burial. A bill of $170.00 was paid to a mortician for claiming the body from the hospital and preparing the legal burial papers. A funeral service was held after the body had been buried. Questionnaires showed that the alternative plan more effectively afforded the congregation an opportunity to participate in the funeral. Those who described the memorial service after burial as worship and praise in celebration of life also believed that the alternative funeral offered more support and strength to the bereaved. Burial of the body prior to the funeral service was not considered helpful. In summary, congregational support and involvement of the mourners in the alternative funeral arrangements were considered the most significant part of the alternative funeral.

4376 Biddle, Perry H., Jr. *Abingdon Funeral Manual*. Rev. ed. Nashville, Tenn.: Abingdon Press, 1976.

A Protestant manual for funerals includes advice on planning and conducting the service, the use of music and other resources, elements of a funeral sermon, special issues of suicide and the death of an infant, a church policy on funerals. Liturgies are recommended for Methodists, Presbyterians, United Church of Christ, Baptists, Lutherans. A "free" memorial service is included. Annotated bibliography.

4377 Blackwood, Andrew W. *The Funeral: A Source Book for Ministers*. Philadelphia: The Westminster Press, 1942.

A Presbyterian professor of practical theology describes the role of a pastor, funeral arrangements and public services. Recommendations are given concerning music, scripture reading, prayers, obituaries, poems, sermons. Varieties of funerals are graveside, cremation, military and fraternal. Problems of records, cost, codes and sudden or shameful death are considered. There is a lengthy anthology of poems. A standard Protestant work at mid-century.

4378 Morgan, Ernest, ed. *A Manual of Death Education & Simple Burial*. Burnsville, N.C.: Celo Press, 1980.

This excellent handbook, originally published as *A Manual of Simple Burial* in 1962, has been updated in 1984. See Morgan (4370).

4379 Bowman, Leroy. *The American Funeral*. Westport, Conn.: Greenwood Press, 1973.

Based on five years of research of funeral practices in the United States, this early study in thanatology offers insights on the planning of a sensible funeral.

4380 Chakour, Charles M. *Brief Funeral Meditations for Unusual Situations*. Nashville, Tenn.: Abingdon Press, 1971.

Affirmation and empowering are the themes of these mediations arranged under such areas as sudden death, suicide, no family–few friends, infant death.

4381 Christensen, James L. *Funeral Services*. Westwood, N. J.: Fleming H. Revell, 1959.

A pastor organizes scripture, meditation and prayer under many headings which include victims of accidents, cancer, murder, suicide, mental illness, poor reputation, outstanding Christian, infants, young mothers, the aged. The mediations offer both comfort and instruction to the grieving with an awareness of pain, and occasional references to death as an enemy.

4382 Coburn, J. B. *Anne and the Sand Dobbies*. New York: Seabury, 1964.

See 6105.

4383 Consumers Reports, ed. *Funerals: Consumers' Last Rites*. New York: W. W. Norton Co., 1977.

Suggested alternatives to the conventional funerals of the 1970's are presented in this resource book on the funeral business that is prepared for a general audience.

4384 Corley, E. A. *Tell Me About Death. Tell Me About Funerals*. Ill. by P. Pecoraro. Santa Clara, Calif.: Grammatical Sciences, 1973.

A funeral director writes for persons aged 8–12 about the function of a funeral home. The style is that of a funeral director explaining to a young girl the answers that are often raised by children about death, funerals and the words of comfort that are given by parents.

4385 *Instructions of the Revised Roman Rites*. London: Collins Liturgical Publications, 1979.

In accord with the Second Vatican Council's Constitution on the Liturgy, emphasis is shifted from the causality of the sacraments to an appropriate relationship between human senses and the theological efficacy of the sacramental signs. After this introductory explanation by Christopher Walsh, the rites of the church are described. Funerals may now be celebrated in a variety of places and with a concern for all the people of God: parents, relatives, caretakers, Christian community, clergy. The varying circumstances of the deceased and the family are to be considered in the choice of prayers and biblical selections.

4386 Irion, Paul E. *The Funeral and the Mourners: Pastoral Care of the Bereaved*. Nashville, Tenn.: Abingdon Press, 1954.

This early and successful attempt to combine psychological insights with traditional pastoral services has become a model for ministry at the time of death and after: grief counsel and funeral messages by clergy, the psychodynamics of the grief reaction, the elements of the funeral service and funeral practices. Specific questions are proposed for pastors who wish to be self-critical in this service. The implications of a funeral service for the total ministry of the church are concentrated upon the personal issues of grief. Read this before you conduct a funeral.

4387 Irion, Paul E. "Selecting Resources for the Funeral." *Pastoral Psychology* 8 (November 1957): 33–40.

A chaplain recommends religious resources which are appropriate for those who grieve during a funeral and rejects those resources that are easily misunderstood, repress grief or present God as the cause of death.

4388 Irion, Paul E. *The Funeral: Vestige or Value?* Nashville, Tenn.: Abingdon Press, 1966.

A professor of pastoral theology evaluates American funerals and presents ten criteria for the evaluation: the sharing of loss by the community with the bereaved; the relationship of the living to those who have died; strengthening of relational patterns among the living; the reinforcement of the reality of death; recollections of the deceased and recapitulations of relationships; the finality of death and freedom to develop new relational patterns without violating the integrity of the previous relationships; the release of feelings by mourners; meaningful relationship to religious or philosophical resources for understanding and accepting suffering; perspective on the meanings of life and death; a more complete understanding of the totality of persons as body-mind-spirit. Compassionate and comprehensive.

4389 Irion, Paul E. *A Manual and Guide for Those Who Conduct a Humanist Funeral Service*. Baltimore: Waverly Press, 1971.

A Protestant professor of pastoral theology provides a manual on the funeral for those who are uncommitted to any religious institution. The author provides a brief explanation of the needs most commonly found among the bereaved and some simple guidelines for one who conducts the funeral; a standard pattern for the funeral organized around the requirements of the mourners, representative funeral service designed for general use, a collection of readings and poems.

4390 Irion, Paul E. "The Funeral and the Bereaved." In V. R. Pine, *et al.*, eds. *Acute Grief and the Funeral.* Springfield, Ill: Charles C. Thomas, 1976.

One goal of a funeral is to begin the movement from a relationship of presence that has characterized the status of the loved one with mourners in the past to a relationship of memory that will characterize the relationship in the future. The interlocking fingers of emotional ties must now begin to loosen as emotional energy is withdrawn from the deceased.

4391 Jackson, Edgar N. *The Christian Funeral: Its Meaning, Its Purpose, and Its Modern Practice.* New York: Channel Press, 1966.

A pastor who pioneered in studies of grief presents an analysis of the religious significance of the funeral with special emphasis on funeral meditation.

4392 Lamers, William, Jr. "Funerals are Good for People—M.D.'s Included." *Medical Economics*, 46(June 23, 1969): 104–107.

In discussing the benefits of a funeral, a psychiatrist provides his definition: an organized, purposeful, time limited, flexible, group centered response to death.

4393 Lamm, Maurice, and N. Eskreis. "Viewing the Remains: A New America Custom." *Journal of Religion and Health* 5(1966): 137–143.

See 6069.

4394 Lewis, Oscar. *A Death in the Sánchez Family.* New York: Random House, 1969.

See 4182.

4395 Malinowski, Vronislaw. *Magic, Science and Religion.* New York: Doubleday and Co., 1954.

See 1250.

4396 Mandelbaum, David G. "Social Uses of Funeral Rites." In *Meaning of Death*, ed. by Herman Feifel, 189–217. New York: McGraw-Hill Book Co., 1959.

Social uses of funerals includes disposition of the corpse, reorientation of the bereaved, social adjustment of the community to a loss. These functions are described in the funeral ceremony of the Kota of South India. Ritual weeping occurs at specific times, such as during a "dry funeral" that may be held once each year, or every two years for the benefit of widows and widowers. Similarities and contrasts are given of two American Indian tribes, the Cocopa and the Hopi. The author believes that culture in the United States has become deritualized and leaves bereaved persons helpless in their loss. See also Aguilar (4374).

4397 Mathews, Joseph W. "The Time My Father Died." In *The Modern Vision of Death*, ed. by Nathan H. Scott, Jr. Richmond, Va.: John Knox Press, 1967.

A Presbyterian pastor recounts what he felt and said on the day that his father died and afterwards as he spoke during his funeral.

4398 Morgan, Ernest. *Dealing Creatively with Death. A Manual of Death Education and Simple Burial*. Ninth Edition. Burnsville, N.C.: Celo Press, 1984.

See Morgan 4370.

4399 Nelson, Thomas C. *It's Your Choice: the Practical Guide to Planning a Funeral*. Glenview, Ill.: Scott, Foresman and Co., 1983.

Practical advice is offered on various options for dispositions of a body, the cost of a funeral and basic services, additional services that may be desired, caskets, cemetery plots and other purchases, method of payment for a funeral. The advice is specific, such as a caution that the law does not require the buying of a particular liner or vault that is expensive because it is watertight. Information is given on consumer groups, funeral organizations, organ donation societies, the living will, coping with loss and death benefits. Extensive list of memorial societies in the United States and Canada. Price comparison forms and other helpful forms are provided.

4400 Pine, Vanderlyn R., *et al.*, eds. *Acute Grief and the Funeral*. Springfield, Ill: Charles C. Thomas, 1976.

The psychological and sociological impact of bereavement is described during the period of acute grief by physicians, psychologists, clergy persons, sociologists, nurses, gerontologists, philosophers, educators, attorneys and funeral directors. These are mainly short testimonies from long experience.

4401 Poovey, W. A. *Planning a Christian Funeral: a Minister's Guide*. Minneapolis, Minn.: Augsburg Pub. House, 1978.

With the purpose for offering support for funeral planning and sermon preparation, the book first offers practical suggestions regarding preparation of the funeral; the second section consists of individual and contextual funeral sermons written by twenty different ministers. The intent of the author is to help the pastor who often with little notice faces the task of preaching and officiating in a variety of contexts for those who grieve.

4402 Presbyterian Church (U.S.A.) *The Funeral: A Service of Witness to the Resurrection.* Philadelphia: Westminster Press, 1986.

Liturgical scholars assisted the Office of Worship in the preparation of liturgies for the dying and bereaved that contain prayers, responses, Scripture passages, recommended music. A short bibliographical essay contains a judicious listing of liturgical and theological resources, plus some sociological and historical studies of death. Unfortunately, the liturgical experts do not follow the person-centered approach of Irion (4386, 4388) in open acceptance of the pain and ambiguities of the death experience. Repeated theological assurance leaves an impression in the liturgics that God will immediately make all things good because He is in perfect control of all that has transpired. Since the theological emphasis of the liturgies is upon the joy of Christians as they are reminded of the resurrection, liturgies do not include another New Testament emphasis (highlighted by Cullmann 2200) that death is a great enemy to be faced with pain, tears, uncertainty and anger. The volume is a "trial use" resource before revision as a service book of the Presbyterian Church.

4403 Raether, Howard C. and Robert C. Sleter. "Immediate Postdeath Activities in the United States." In *New Meanings of Death*, ed. by Herman Feifel, 233–250. New York: McGraw-Hill Book Co., 1977.

A Director of the National Funeral Directors Association and a professor in a department of mortuary science provide a useful overview of the funeral: its history, pattern of responses to death, the activities that are a part of burial, questions about the procedures in funerals, prearrangements and future possibilities. The authors conclude that the ancient ceremonies of the dead can be well adapted to our culture if we remain sensitive, perceptive and adaptive to the needs of people.

4404 *Reformed Liturgy and Music* 20 (Fall 1986): 188–237.

The theological background for the development of *The Funeral: A Service of Witness to the Resurrection* (4402) is presented as an appropriate time to praise God who is the source of all life and to proclaim in the assembly of believers the central promises of the Gospel. The task force for the development of a new funeral rite in the Presbyterian church sought a return to early Christian practice of celebrating communion as a part of the memorial service for the dead and choosing hymns which are appropriate for the praise of God, affirmation of life everlasting and concern for the deceased. The needs of the bereaved to mourn are given scant attention in this enthusiastic emphasis upon death as a release to a larger and happier life.

4405 Wallis, Charles L., ed. *The Funeral Encyclopedia*. Grand Rapids, Mich.: Baker Book House, 1973.

The author brings together typical elements of a Protestant funeral service, sermon meditations under a series of classifications and anthology of funeral poems and prayers. Professional duties and role for clergy are described.

4406 Zuck, Lowell H. "The Changing Meaning of the Funeral in Christian History." *Pastoral Psychology* 8 (November 1957): 17–26.

From the earliest times Christian paid respect in funerals to the bodies of the dead as temples of the Spirit of God. Funeral practices are surveyed from early times till the 20th century.

4.611 CEMETERIES

4407 French, Stanley. "The Cemetery as Cultural Institution: The Establishment of Mount Auburn and the 'Rural Cemetery Movement.'" In *Death in America*, ed. by David E. Stannard, 69–91. Philadelphia: University of Pennsylvania Press, 1975.

Mount Auburn cemetery, near Harvard college was constantly shown to foreign visitors to prove that America was not a cultural wasteland, for it was "a pleasure garden instead of a place of graves." But in Philadelphia graveyards were temporarily vacant lots that were soon obliterated by new housing. In the rural South, family burial plots were seldom honored when there was a change in land ownership. Early in the nineteenth century the urge to provide continual care with taste for the dead lead to the fencing of family plots in rural areas and the development of memorial parks in cities. Romanticism became the art form of death.

4408 Humphreys, S. C., and Helen King, eds. *Mortality and Immortality: The Anthropology and Archeology of Death*. New York: Academic Press, 1982.

Various papers from the Research Seminar in Archeology and Related Subjects, London University, describe the medical and anthropological information that can come from grave sites, ancient and modern.

4409 Kurtz, Donna C. and John Boardman. *Greek Burial Customs*. Ithaca, N.Y.: Cornell University Press, 1971.

From archaeological evidence (cemeteries, mounds, gravestones, vases) in Athens and Attica, the authors prepare a detailed account of practices and rites that reflect ancient Greek attitudes toward death and the possibility of an afterlife. The range of study is from the end of the Bronze Age through the Classical period. Illustrations, maps, notes.

4410 Toynbee, Jocelyn M. *Death and Burial in the Roman World*. Ithaca, N.Y.: Cornell University Press, 1971.

See 1069.

4411 Walker, G. A. *Gatherings from Graveyards: Particularly Those of London, with a Concise History of the Modes in Internment among Different Nations, from the Earliest Periods*. 1839. Reprint. New York: Arno Press, 1977.

A nineteenth reformer exposes the dangers of careless burial methods in his general study of burial and funeral techniques.

4412 Williams, Melvin G. *The Last Word*. Boston: Oldstone Enterprises, 1973.

The study of New England graveyards presents their arts and inscriptions along with instructions on the way to make rubbings from stones. Illustrated.

4.612 OBITUARIES/EPITAPHS

4413 Alden, Timothy. *A Collection of American Epitaphs and Inscriptions with Occasional Notes*. 1814. Reprint. New York: Arno Press, 1977.

A collection of American epitaphs is arranged by states, city and persons within each city. Explanatory notes reveal early American attitudes to death.

4414 Jarboe, Betty M. *Obituaries: A Guide to Sources*. 2nd ed. Boston: G. K. Hall, 1989.

Abstracts and indexes of obituaries are catalogued by U.S. states plus brief international references. Indexed.

4415 Lattimore, Richmond. *Themes in Grief and Latin Epitaphs*. Urbana, Ill.: University of Illinois Press, 1962.

The form, style and diction of epitaphs are explored along with their meaning for and understanding of death and immortality.

4.613 MEMORIAL SOCIETIES

4416 *A Multitude of Voices: Funerals and the Clergy.* Washington, D.C.: Continental Association of Funeral and Memorial Societies, 1980.

As a part of the Consumer Funeral Information project, brief and informative essays on various parts of the funeral are presented for use in church bulletins or other publicity. The stress is upon advanced planning, funeral philosophy, reasonable and economic decisions.

4417 Harmer, Ruth Muldey. *The High Cost of Dying.* New York: Collier Books, 1963.

An indignant and informative history and contemporary evaluation of the influence of culture and economics upon burial practices, with a closing section on the rational and humane answer provided through burial societies.

4418 Nelson, Thomas C. *It's Your Choice: A Practical Guide to Planning a Funeral.* Glenview, Ill.: Scott, Foresman and Co., 1983.

See 4399.

4.62 THE MORTUARY INDUSTRY

4419 Foreman, James. "Theory and the Ideal Type of the Professional: The Case of the Funeral Director." *Omega* 4 (1973): 221–228.

From a content analysis of funeral directors' journal articles, 1905, 1939, 1963, a sociologist finds a "sanitizing" in 1905, "naturalizing" in 1939, "sympathizing" in 1963.

4420 Habenstein, Robert W. and William M. Lamers. *The History of American Funeral Directing.* Rev. ed. Milwaukee, Minn.: Bulfin Printers, 1962.

After a brief review of burial practices from early Christian times through the Renaissance, two sociologists center upon the science of embalming and undertaking among English speaking peoples in the sixteenth century and afterwards. The institutional growth of the modern funeral service is described.

4421 Mitford, Jessica. *The American Way of Death.* New York: Simon and Schuster, 1963.

See 1150

4422 Pine, Vanderlyn R. *Caretaker of the Dead: The American Funeral Director*. New York: Irvington Pub, 1975.

See 5034

4423 *Report of the Presiding Officer on Proposed Trade Regulation Rule Concerning Funeral Industry Practices*. Washington, D. C.: Federal Trade Commission, 1977.

Critical statements concerning practices of the funeral industry are summarized from public hearings.

4.63 DECISIONS ABOUT THE BODY

4424 Belgum, David. "Memorial Service as Part of the Deeded Body Program." *Journal of Pastoral Care* 36 (1982): 30–35.

A chaplain and professor in the medical school describes a memorial service for the families of a deceased person whose body has been willed to a medical facility. The service is designed both to show respect for the deceased and to meet the emotional needs of the family.

4425 Hamilton-Pearson, J. and C. Andrews. *Mummies: Death and Life in Ancient Egypt*. New York: Penguin, 1979.

Embalming for members of the royal or upper classes in ancient Egypt are described with some technical details and references to theology.

4.631 CREMATION

4426 Basevi, W.H.F. *The Burial of the Dead*. London: Geoige Routledge and Sons, 1920.

An historical, cross-cultural study of burial and cremation from prehistoric times to the early twentieth century.

4427 Browne, Thomas. *Hydrotaphia, Urne-Buriall*. 1658. Reprint. New York: Arno Press, 1977.

Burial urns of antiquity are considered from a literary, philosophical and anthropological viewpoint with comments both upon the nobility and sacredness of human life and the self-deceptions and defenses against death.

4428 Cobb, John Storer. *A Quarter-Century of Cremation in North America*. Boston: Knight and Millet, 1901.

The moving forces behind the development of cremation societies and crematoriums are presented in this historical sketch.

4429 "Cremation," in *The Catholic Encyclopedia* IV (1908): 481–483.

Roman Catholic views of cremation are summarized from early times to through the canon law prohibiting cremation in the late nineteenth century.

4430 Erichsen, Hugo. *The Cremation of the Dead.* Detroit, Mich.: D. O. Haynes and Co., 1887.

A physician who was the founder of the Cremation Society of America presents the history of cremation.

4431 Fraser, James W. *Cremation: Is It Christian?* Neptune, N.J.: Loizeaux Brothers, 1965.

Biblical literalism and conservative theology are used to repeat arguments against cremation that were used in the 19th century.

4432 Frehof, Solomon B. *Reform Jewish Practice and Its Rabbinic Background.* Cincinnati, Ohio: Hebrew Union College Press, 1944.

In this Scriptural and Talmudic presentation of Reformed Judaism there is a section on cremation as it is viewed from both the Orthodox and Reformed Jewish tradition.

4433 Irion, Paul E. *Cremation.* Philadelphia: Fortress Press, 1968.

After a review of the history of cremation, a pastoral theologian discusses modern cremation. Chapters consider psychological, theological, legal and pastoral concerns. The appendix includes a useful text, self-scored, for or against cremation. Annotated bibliography. An objective and sensitive discussion of a poorly understood subject.

4434 Mendelsohn, Simon. "Cremation." *Ciba Symposia* 11 (8 Spring, 1951): 1318–1348.

A professor of pharmaceutical history presents articles on the evolution of the cremation cult, the development of modern cremation and early examples of cremation in the United States. Bibliography.

4435 Rush, Alfred C. *Death and Burial in Christian Antiquity.* Washington, D. C.: The Catholic University of America Press, 1941.

Early Christian attitudes and funerary customs are surveyed from a Roman Catholic perspective that includes a suppression of cremation.

4436 Wilson, Arnold and Hermann Levy. *Burial Reform and Funeral Cost.* London: Oxford University Press, 1938.

See 4445.

4.64 FINANCIAL COSTS

4437 Arbio, Raymond. *The Cost of Dying and What You Can Do About It.*. San Francisco: Harper and Row, 1974.

From the viewpoint of the Continental Association of Funeral and Memorial Societies, the author presents practical steps to accelerate social change for the creation of the development of consumer-owned facilities for funerals that would decrease dependence upon the established funeral industry.

4438 Berko, Robert L. *Complete Guide to Government Benefits for Veterans, Their Families and Their Survivors.* South Orange, N.J.: Consumer Education Research Center, 1984.

A summary of death benefits is included in this brief manual.

4439 Bowman, Leroy. *The American Funeral: A Study in Guilt, Extravagance, and Sublimity.* Washington, D.C.: Public Affairs Press, 1959.

A social scientist sees the funeral as an anachronism in urban mass society and seeks ways to make it more economical. Cremation, for example, is supported.

4440 Dowd, Quincy L. *Funeral Management and Cost.* Chicago: University of Chicago Press, 1921.

In this early social scientific study of the funeral, the emphasis is upon a more rational and economical approach to death rituals.

4441 Harmer, Ruth Muldey. *The High Cost of Dying.* New York: Collier Books, 1963.

The business methods of the funeral industry are evaluated for the popular market. As the title indicates, the financial costs of dying are highlighted.

4442 *Planning Funerals.* Athens, Ga.: University of Georgia, College of Agriculture, n.d.

Specific information and recommendations are offered concerning the financial aspects of preparation for a funeral. Concise and helpful.

4443 U.S. Federal Trade Commission. Seattle Regional Office. *The Price of Death: A Survey and Consumer Guide for Funerals, Cemeteries and Grave Markers.* Seattle, Wash.: Federal Trade Commission, 1975.

A pamphlet describes a variety of choices available for a funeral, cemetery space and grave marker. Explanations are given concerning the way in which decisions are made about each of these traditional signs of respect for the dead and the reasons for variations in cost are given. A detailed survey is included to check on items of cost from various providers. Read it now. (Federal Trade Commission, 2840 Federal Building, Seattle, WA 98174).

4444 U. S. Federal Trade Commission. "Consumer Guide to the FTC Funeral Rule." *Facts for Consumers*, April 1984.

In a leaflet the Bureau of Consumer Protection, Federal Trade Commission, presents advice and information on federal rules for various economic aspects of burial. Professional agencies for funeral and memorial services are listed with addresses.

4445 Wilson, Arnold and Hermann Levy. *Burial Reform and Funeral Cost*. London: Oxford University Press, 1938.

In seeking a more economic and rational approach to the customs of grief, the authors include historical surveys as well as current analyses and suggestions. Includes the history of cremation in various cultures.

4.7 RELIGIOUS RESOURCES See also PHILOSOPHICAL THEOLOGY (2.0)

4446 Autton, Norman. *The Pastoral Care of the Bereaved*. London: S.P.C.K., 1967.

An English chaplain in the classical tradition of pastoral care discusses the care of the bereaved and the funeral. The book is noteworthy for an historical section on the art of consolation and a judicious selection of spiritual letters of consolation.

4447 *Foi et Vie* 83 (1984): 1–65.

From a French Roman Catholic perspective, articles describe ministry to widows in the early church and throughout the ages of the Catholic church, the mission of widows in the church today, and the place of widows in the "Messianic plan of God."

4448 Grollman, Earl A. *Living When A Loved One Has Died*. 2nd ed. Boston: Beacon Press, 1987.

With insight and tenderness, a rabbi provides brief and poetic thoughts about shock, suffering, recovery and a new life. For those who must manage the emotions of grief and creatively confront death.

4449 Irion, Paul E. "Selecting Resources for the Funeral." *Pastoral Psychology* 8 (November 1957): 33–40.

See 4387.

4450 Jackson, Edgar N. *You and Your Grief.* New York: Hawthorn Books, 1962.

A clergyperson draws on his long experience as a pastor and therapist to offer consolation and guidance for the bereaved in an intimate and simple self-help book.

4451 Kutscher, Austin H. and Lillian G. Kutscher, eds. *Religion and Bereavement.* New York: Health Sciences Pub. Corp., 1972.

Thirty-three clergyman provide brief guidelines in chapters on the practical problems faced by bereaved persons. Selection of topics was from analysis of a multiple-choice survey of widows, widower and clergy. An anthology of music selections is included. The brief studies by Edgar Jackson are especially helpful.

4452 Lundeen, Lyman T. "Faith and the Problem of Death." In *The Church and Pastoral Care*, ed. by Leroy and J. Harold Ellens. Grand Rapids, Mich.: Baker Book House, 1988.

A Lutheran theologian presents the implication of faith for a pastoral approach to death: (1) The complex and mysterious character of death exposes the partial projective of all answers to death and enhances the wonder of human existence. (2) In dealing with death as a part of life, faith offers symbolic resources such as trust and doubt. (3) The specific circumstances of a person are to be taken seriously because the Christian faith affirms the importance of finite history. (4) The incarnate nature of Christian faith alerts us to experiences of grace and hope this side of the grave, which give meaning to life in the face of approaching death. (5) The doctrine of the resurrection alerts us to the possibility that life comes from death in a most surprising manner. The hope of the resurrection provides a symbolic framework for the ultimate importance of our finitude.

4453 Madara, Edward J. and Barrie Alan Peterson. "Clergy and Self-help Groups: Practical and Promising Relationships." *Journal of Pastoral Care* 41 (1987): 213–220.

See 4335.

4454 Mitchell, Kenneth R. and Herbert Anderson. *All Our Losses, All Our Griefs: Resources for Pastoral Care.* Philadelphia: Westminster Press, 1983.

See 4032.

4455 Phipps, William E. *Death: Confronting the Reality.* Atlanta:, Ga.: John Knox, 1987.

See 6155.

4456 Rogers, William F. "The Pastor's Work with Grief." *Pastoral Psychology* 14 (1963): 19–26.

A chaplain uses the findings of Lindemann (4044) and others to demonstrate the needs of mourners to talk about the deceased. Clergy are especially helpful in confronting guilt feelings of the bereaved and encouraging clarification. The key question is: What is the origin of these feelings?

4457 Spilka, Bernard, *et al.* "The Role of Theology in Pastoral Care for the Dying." *Theology Today* 38 (1981): 16–29.

See Spilka 5006.

4458 Westberg, Granger E. *Good Grief.* Philadelphia: Fortress Press, 1971.

A professor of medicine and religion relies primarily upon the research of Lindemann (4332, 4044) as he considers the expression of emotion, acceptance of the shock and distress of grief, guilt, anger, resistance, and gradually return of hope and affirmation of reality.

4459 Wiersbe, Warren W. and David W. Wiersbe. *Comforting the Bereaved.* Chicago: Moody Press, 1985.

Biblical and psychological perspectives of death and grief are presented in terms of various situations such as a child's death, a suicide, multiple deaths, a death at Christmas.

4.71 SACRAMENT AND LITURGY

4460 Anderson, Herbert and Edward Foley. "Liturgy and Pastoral Care: The Parable of Dying and Grieving. *New Theology Review* 1, 4 (November 1988): 15–27.

The dying and grieving process is examined from a pastoral and liturgical perspective. The loneliness of death and grieving is given special attention and the value of narrative is presented as an antidote.

4461 Church of England, Liturgical Commission. *Funeral Services.* Cambridge, England: Cambridge University Press, 1974.

The approved liturgy for the Church of England includes the service in the church and the committal, followed by a presentation of the funeral of a child and committal. Also: a form at the internment of the ashes, a service before a funeral, holy communion, a selection of additional prayers.

4462 Ford, J. Massyngbaerde. *The Silver Lining: Eleven Personalized Scripturalized Wake Services.* Mystic, Conn.: Twenty-third Publications, 1987.

See 4366.

4463 Forrester, Duncan, James I. H. McDonald and Gian Tellini. *Encounter with God.* Edinburg: T. and T. Clark, 1983.

In this review of the history of theology and place of worship in the church, there is a brief and insightful section upon worship and pastoral care including: funerals, theology of death and grief.

4464 Hatchett, Marion J. *Commentary on the American Prayerbook.* New York: Seabury Press, 1980.

An Episcopal professor of liturgics provides a brief review of Episcopal liturgies for the dead, pp. 477–500 in a general liturgical commentary.

4465 Herdahl, Lowell O. *The Lonely House: Strength for Times of Loss.* Lima, Ohio: C.C.S. Pub. Co., 1989.

Daily devotional prose covering a sixteen week period is accompanied by Scripture references, a prayer and a thought for the day. Faith is made real in the face of severe loss.

4466 Maloney, George. *Death Where Is Your Sting?* New York: Alba House, 1984.

A Jesuit priest who has written on Eastern and Western Christian spirituality provides meditations for the bereaved that are built around an understanding of grief, the therapy of love through purgatory, the communion of saints, the union of the living and the departed through the healing power of Christ (this includes aborted infants), the consolation of heaven, Christ's descent into hell and resurrection from the dead.

4467 Maas-Ewerd, Theodor. "Motive für die Ars moriendi in der katholischen Sterbe-und Begräbnisliturgie." (*Motives for the Ars Moriendi in the Catholic Death and Burial Liturgy*). In *Ars Moriendi. Erwägungen zur Kunst des Sterbens*, ed. by Harald Wagner. Freiburg, Germany: Herder, 1989.

In an examination of the Catholic liturgy for Ars Moriendi. Maas-Ewerd points out the essential and helpful nature of the liturgy to the dying and the bereaved.

4.72 LITERATURE AND LETTERS

4468 Hein, Marvin. *Meditation on Death: Like Shock of Wheat*. Scottdale, Pa.: Herald Press, 1981.

Twenty-two meditations used by the author in the parish ministry portray God as a sovereign who upholds creation, governs history and calls us to see all our living and dying in the light of that sovereignty.

4469 Nouwen, Henri J. M. *In Memoriam*. Notre Dame, Ind.: Ave Maria Press, 1980.

A Roman Catholic priest writes a letter to his friends about the death of his mother. It is realistic and insightful, with a fresh interpretation of death from a Christian perspective.

4.73 PREACHING

4470 Beardslee, William A., *et al. Biblical Preaching on the Death of Jesus*. Nashville, Tenn.: Abingdon Press, 1989.

See 2106.

4471 Chiles, John R. *A Treasury of Funeral Messages*. Grand Rapids, Mich.: Baker Book House, 1960.

A pastor with 29 years of service in the same church presents scripture passages that are appropriate for various ages and conditions of the deceased, a short text on a variety of sermons which are based upon traditional Protestant orthodoxy.

4472 Claypool, John. *Tracks of a Fellow Struggler*. Dallas, Tex.: Word Pub., 1974.

A clergyperson responds in four sermons to the crisis points of the terminal illness of his daughter: the shock of the first diagnosis, the unanticipated major relapse, the finality of death in the first year of bereavement and a reflective overview after several years. The existential honesty of the author in dealing with personal and spiritual issues is refreshing. See also Hans (2157).

4473 Clemons, James T., ed. *Sermons on Suicide*. Louisville, Ky.: Westminster/John Knox Press, 1989.

A collection of sermons on suicide offers a variety of biblical texts, interpretations, literary references, medical insights, current statistics, personal illustrations, and practical suggestions. Understanding of suicide and grief are provided for those who may feel guilt or shame about suicide.

4474 *Funeral Orations by Saint Gregory Nazianzen and Saint Ambrose.* Trans. by Leo P. McCauley, *et. al.* New York: Fathers of the Church, 1953.

See 1077.

4475 Hans, Daniel T. *God on the Witness Stand: Questions Christians Ask in Personal Tragedy.* Grand Rapids, Mich.: Baker Book House, 1987.

See 2157.

4476 Hughes, Robert G. *A Trumpet in Darkness: Preaching to Mourners.* Philadelphia: Fortress Press, 1985.

A Lutheran pastor and professor presents a strategy for communicating with mourners that includes the importance of the type of death, the meaning of the cross in the face of death, the objectives of a funeral sermon and the analysis of a specific sermon in the light of these objectives.

4477 Irion, Paul E. *The Funeral and the Mourners: Pastoral Care of the Bereaved.* Nashville, Tenn.: Abingdon Press, 1954.

See 4386.

4478 Irion, Paul E. *The Funeral: Vestige or Value?* Nashville, Tenn.: Abingdon Press, 1966.

See 4388.

4479 Motter, Alton, ed. *Preaching About Death.* Philadelphia: Fortress Press, 1975.

Sermons chosen from Protestant, Eastern Orthodox and Roman Catholic perspectives vary in content from psychological insights about death to affirmations of death as a part of God's will. Meeting death with faith and dignity is the theme of many sermons and nearly all stress the resurrection as ultimate Christian hope.

4480 Rahner, Karl. *Meditations on Hope and Love.* London: Burns and Oates, 1976.

Brief meditations by an eminent Roman Catholic theologian include "Obedient Unto Death," "Lighten Our Darkness," "Faith, Hope and Love."

4481 Richmond, Kent D. *Preaching to Sufferers*. Nashville, Tenn.: Abingdon Press, 1988.

A Methodist pastor who suffered the loss of his young son illustrates
the inadequacies of many approaches to the problem of suffering and feels
that a view of God who stands with us in suffering is the best hope and consolation for those who are in difficult days of pain. The book is valuable as
a summary of theological positions that must be considered in the light of
personal feelings about suffering and in the way that pastoral comfort is
presented.

4482 Tillich, Paul. *The New Being*. New York: Charles Scribner's Sons,
1955.

Sermons delivered in Union Theological Seminary, New York
include "Love is Stronger Than Death." The refugees and exiles of this life
can face the horror of our time through love which creates something new
out of the destruction caused by death. The isolating power of the End is
overcome by participation with others in infinite love.

4483 Steimle, Edmund A. *God the Stranger: Reflections About Resurrection*. Philadelphia: Fortress Press, 1979.

A Protestant professor of homiletics who was widely known for his
radio preaching on "The Protestant Hour" presents thirteen sermons on the
resurrection with occasional references to death.

4484 Wallis, Charles L., ed. *The Funeral Encyclopedia*. Grand Rapids,
Mich.: Baker Book House, 1971.

See 4405.

4485 Winkler, Eberhard. *Die Leichenpredigt im Deutschen Luthertum bis
Spener*. München, Germany: Chr. Kaiser Verlag, 1967.

Funeral sermons in German Lutheranism are considered from the
time of Luther through orthodoxy and pietism to Philip Spener. Selected
sermons are presented along with notes concerning the author, sources, the
form and method of the sermon, the content. The content in the 16th and
17th century might include the significance of the dead person, the
overcoming of death through faith and trust in God, references to hell and
calls to repentance, preparation for death through instruction on the way to
die as a blessed person in Christ, resurrection and eternal life. The author
provides a final summary on the preaching of this period. Notes and
bibliography.

4.8 PROFESSIONAL/MEDICAL CARE

4.81 DEFINING DEATH

4486 Ad Hoc Committee of the Harvard Medical School to Examine the Definition of Brain Death. "A Definition of Irreversible Coma." *Journal of the American Medical Association* 205 (1968): 337–340.

In proposing criteria for brain death, a "flat" electroencephalogram (EEG) was a new assessment added to traditional monitoring operations to determine death. The EEG assessment along with the assessment of no circulation to or within the brain, found widespread application. See President's Commission (44901.

4487 "An Appraisal of the Criteria of Cerebral Death: A Summary Statement." *Journal of the American Medical Association* 237 (1977): 982–986.

Physicians in the National Institute of Neurological Disease and Stroke prepare a summary statement on the criteria of cerebral death based on a collaborative study of 503 comatose and apneic patients.

4488 Carson, Rachel L. *Silent Spring*. Boston: Houghton Mifflin, 1962.

In this well-researched text in a mood of reverence for both human life and the physical world around us, the author advances constant examples and studies of the way in which modern technology has poisoned the environment. She analyzes the world of thought in science and humanities on earth studies and concludes with a conviction that we should reverence the environmental forces that are around us even as we must struggle against some of them. Substantial bibliography.

4489 Gervais, Karen Grandstrand. *Redefining Death*. New Haven, Conn.: Yale University Press, 1986.

A philosopher purposes that patients who are permanently unconscious should be declared dead. Human life involves existence as a person, and this is only possible when the brain has the capability of consciousness. She examines and corrects the Uniform Declaration of Death Act. Public policy should define death as the permanent cessation of consciousness, but allow people to elect a less radical policy for their own treatment. The opinions of other authorities in medicine, philosophy and law are presented.

4490 Hoffman, John C. "Clarifying the Debate on Death." *Soundings* 62 (1979): 430–447.

A professor of religion examines the definitions of death presented by Veatch, Schwager, Ramsey and Kass and concludes that the definition of death depends upon a clarification of views concerning human life.

4491 President's Commission for the Study of Ethical Problems in Medicine and Biomedical and Behavioral Research. *Defining Death: A Report on the Medical, Legal, and Ethical Issues in the Determination of Death.* Washington, D.C.: Government Printing Office, 1981.

The Harvard criteria for brain death (4486) were considered to be adequate for the determination of death, although some flaws were noted. After an extensive review of topics concerning the definition of death and public policy the Commission recommends that death be defined for an individual who has either irreversible cessation of circulatory and respiratory functions, or irreversible cessation of all functions of the entire brain, including the brain stem.

4492 Silverman, Daniel. "Cerebral Death—The History of the Syndrome and Its Identification." *Annals of Internal Medicine* 74 (1971): 1003–1005.

The development of easily manageable mechanical respirators and a means of maintaining circulation has generated a syndrome that appears in the autopsy of patients who have had relatively long periods on the respirator. The original brain lesion will have disappeared and been replaced by widespread death of tissue. The author surveys medical moves toward identification of death, ethical and legal questions.

4493 Smith, Andrew J. K. and J. Kiffin Penry. *Brain Death: A Bibliography with Key-Word and Author Indexes.* Washington, D.C.: DHEW Publication No. (NIH) 73–347, 1972.

4494 Veith, Frank J., *et al.* "Brain Death: I. A Status Report of Medical and Ethical Considerations." *Journal of the American Medical Association* 238 (1977): 1651–1655.

Physicians and lawyers seek to establish the scientific validity of current clinical and laboratory criteria for determining complete destruction of the brain or brain death. Total destruction of the brain constitutes a determinant of death, which is in accord with secular philosophy and the three main Western religions.

4495 Walton, Douglas N. *On Defining Death: An Analytic Study of the Concept of Death in Philosophy and Medical Ethics.* Montreal: McGill-Queen's University Press, 1979.

The author seeks to distinguish between a concept of death and criteria for defining death in a clinical setting. The concept of death is built upon the nature of a person. The criteria of death has been built upon clinical studies that have become increasingly complicated and unsatisfying. Answers to the definition of death must be sought not only through multidisciplinary studies, but also with reference to philosophical concepts. See also Winter (4496).

4496 Winter, Arther, ed. *The Moment of Death*. Springfield, Ill.: Charles C. Thomas, 1969.

Physicians examine the concept of biological death from different viewpoints: neuroscientist, cardiac surgeon, medical examiner. Death is related to the basic qualities of humanity. Topics include mentation, brain death, death as a process, current legal decisions.

4497 Veatch, Robert M. "The Definition of Death: The Problems for Public Policy." In *Dying: Facing the Facts*, 2nd ed., ed. by Hannelore Wass; Felix Verardo and Robert A. Neimar, pp. 29–53. Washington, D.C.: Hemisphere Pub. Corp., 1988.

A professor of medical ethics discusses preliminary issues to the public policy decision about the definition of death, outlines the issues of the debate from the 1960's to the 1980's and presents some remaining issues for consideration. A growing consensus supports some kind of brain-oriented definition of death, but some problems of public policy are far from settled. Review questions and references.

4.9 GRIEF COUNSEL/CONDOLENCE

4498 Becker, Howard. "Some Forms of Sympathy." *Journal of Abnormal and Social Psychology*, 26(1931): 58–68.

Sympathy is a term with a long and varied history. But, instead of gaining in precision and definiteness, it has gradually become one of the vaguest concepts with which the social psychologist has to deal. The author feels that a point has now been reached where it must either be discarded or given a precise, limited meaning. "Sympathy" may include emotional solidarity, imitation, participation, contagion, intuition, identification.

4499 Donnelley, Nina Hermann. *I Never Know What To Say*. New York: Ballantine Books, 1987.

A chaplain who believes that there is a loving God who nevertheless allows ultimate misery to exist, presents her own struggles with this concept as a means to help those who are mourning. Through the use of readable case narratives, she demonstrates the individuality of grief and the need to listen to, talk to, love and touch those who must deal with denial and numbness, hurt and ache, final peace and reconstruction of life. Professional advice offered in the personal way.

4500 Douglas, Ann. "Heaven Our Home: Consolation Literature in the Northern United States, 1830–1888." In *Death in America*, ed. by David E. Stannard, 49–68. Philadelphia: University of Pennsylvania Press, 1975.

Death-bed scenes and celestial communications crowded the bookstalls in the decades before and after the Civil War, with encouragement toward elaborate funerary practices, conspicuous methods of burial and commemoration, and microscopic viewings of a much inflated afterlife. Congregational and Unitarian clergy edited both religious and secular periodicals in which consolation was aimed primarily toward a middle-class, feminine audience. Horace Bushnell was a leader in proposing feeling as a substitute for dogma in the literature. Best sellers such as *Stepping Heavenward* (1869) by Elizabeth Prentiss presented the ideal pastor's wife hastening to the side of those who mourn and joining them in prayers and tears. The loved one was idolized and the mourners were exhorted to find faith in Christ. Consolation was preoccupied with the last scenes of the dying, the earthly resting places of the dead and the celestial destination and doings of the blessed.

4501 Flesch, Regina. "The Condolence Call." In *Death and Bereavement,* ed. by Austin H. Kutscher. Springfield, Ill: Charles Thomas, 1969.

When a condolence call is made by someone who is not a member of the family, the greatest obstacle to communication lies in the sympathizer's unpreparedness for the mourner's anger. In traditional cultures there is little place for the unexpected. For example, a traditional Irish wake funeral has an established pattern for the words and the wailing of all who participate.

4502 Gregg, Robert C. *Consolation Philosophy*. Cambridge, Mass.: Philadelphia Patristic Foundation, 1975.

This doctoral dissertation analyzes the Greek letters of consolation of Basil of Caesaria, and the letters of Gregory of Nyssa and Gregory of Nazianzus. After an analysis of consolatory literature in the Hellenistic period he examines the work of these Cappadocians as a combination of Greek philosophy and Christian theology. Concentrated bibliography.

4503 *Grief Support Training for Clergy and Congregations: Training Manual*. Washington, D.C.: American Association of Retired Persons, 1989.

As the first step in developing long-term grief support systems in the community, three training sessions are described in which clergy and laypersons may recognize and understand the grief process, design programs for individual congregations. Objectives, procedures, content, exercises and some suggestions for lectures are a part of the manual. Bibliographies and notes. Suggestions for organization of the program in church and community. The emphasis upon group participation is important and the detailed instructions are necessary for most clergy who have no training in death education.

4504 Grollman, Earl A. *Living When A Loved One Has Died.* Boston: Beacon Press, 1977.

See 4448.

4505 Grollman, Earl A. *Time Remembered: A Journal for Survivors.* Boston: Beacon Press, 1987.

See 4326.

4506 Harding, Rachael and Mary Dyson. *A Book of Condolences: From the Private Letters of Illustrious People.* New York: Continuum Pub. Co., 1981.

The ancient art of consolation is presented through letters of comfort for the bereaved from illustrious writers, from Pliny and Cicero to Byron and Shaw.

4507 Ingram, Timothy L., E. C. Herley and Mary Tom Riley. "Grief Resolution Therapy in a Pastoral Context." *Journal of Pastoral Care* 39 (1985): 69–75.

In the discussion of the use of grief resolution therapy by pastors, the authors differentiate between a normal and unresolved grief reaction and outline the appropriate treatment procedures for each.

4508 Jackson, Edgar N. *Understanding Grief: Its Roots, Dynamics and Treatment.* Nashville, Tenn.: Abingdon Press, 1957.

A pioneer in the relationship of religion and psychology to grief presents the goal of caregivers as assistance to those who grieve in the releasing of emotional ties despite discomfort and sorrow. This is necessary to replace the feeling of loss. The mourners must be willing to yield to this process to accept the pain of looking realistically at the loss and to participate actively in the work of mourning instead of trying to escape or deny it. They must also realize that grief can be delayed but not postponed indefinitely without morbid consequences. A number of specific strategies are suggested and indicators provided for grief that is normal and grief that is pathological.

4509 Justice, William G., Jr. *When Your Patient Dies.* St. Louis, Mo.: Catholic Health Association of the United States, 1984.

A Protestant chaplain uses his own experience and that of doctors and nurses to develop the communications skills of health professionals who minister to the grief-stricken at the time of death.

4510 Lindemann, Erich. "Grief and Grief Management: Some Reflections." *Journal of Pastoral Care* 30 (1976): 198–207.

The work of a counselor with the bereaved is related to some features of the bereaved state such as the initial time of great perplexity and preoccupation, a time of resurrecting the deceased in the survivor, a sense of loss for a shattered self-image, a time of confrontation concerning the loss and a reaffirmation of activities that benefit self and others. No definite sequence is intended in the author's reflection upon grief.

4511 Manning, Doug. *Don't Take My Grief Away.* San Francisco: Harper and Row, 1984.

A Baptist pastor and family counselor provides meditation on the premise that grief is not an enemy but a friend. Grief is considered a natural part of walking through hurt and growth by which a person will learn to live again. Clear, conversational, convincing.

4512 Mayfield, L. H. *Behind the Clouds—Light: Meditations for the Sick and Distressed.* New York: Abingdon Press, 1965.

A hospital chaplain provides brief meditations of compassion, comfort and hope.

4513 Moylan, David H. "Contemporary Letters of Consolation." *Pastoral Psychology* 8 (November 1957): 41–46.

A Protestant pastor presents letters to the bereaved as one heart speaking to another, with a realistic presentation of death, acceptance of shared feelings without judgment, explicit mention of Christian hope, prayer, an invitation to further correspondence.

4514 Moylan, David H. "Contemporary Letters of Consolation." *Pastoral Psychology* 8 (November 1957): 41–46.

A pastor offers guidance in the writing of letters in which one heart speaks to another about grief, the situation is realistically reviewed, there is understanding of feelings and an opening for further correspondence. Christian content includes a sense of the presence of God, hope and a closing prayer. Several letters are evaluated in the light of this criteria.

4515 Nouwen, Henri J. M. *A Letter of Consolation*. San Francisco: Harper and Row, 1982.

A Catholic priest and psychologist publishes a letter that he wrote to his father six months after the death of his mother. These are meditations from the author's time of retreat to a monastery for several weeks before Easter. Death is difficult for Christians who love all that is created by God, who know the value of life and are loath to abandon it. Easter is the celebration of Christ's victory over the enemy, death. Through him the paradigm for grief is "befriending death."

4516 Oates, Wayne E. *Your Particular Grief*. Philadelphia: Westminster Press, 1981.

In "A Letter to Those Who Mourn," a pastoral psychologist combines Christian comfort with psychological sensitivity in a presentation of five kinds of grief: anticipatory, sudden or traumatic, no-end, near-miss, pathological. A final chapter provides advice and encouragement on the spiritual struggles of grief and recovery. Written both for those who mourn and befriend or family member who offers comfort.

4517 Oates, Wayne E. *Pastoral Care and Counseling in Grief and Separation*. Philadelphia: Fortress Press, 1976.

A pastoral psychologist shares with the clergy his insights on various forms of grief and separation. Anticipatory grief is considered in terms of patient, family and medical and pastoral responses. Stages of separation are described, as in marriages that progressively disintegrate through unilateral decision making, mutual deception, isolation and despair, complaints to others and final separation or divorce. The variables of relationship and circumstances are considered. Pastoral rituals are briefly described.

4518 Parkes, Colin M. "Bereavement Counseling: Does It Work?" *British Medical Journal* 281 (1980): 3–6.

From a review of scientific studies of bereavement counseling an authority in thanatology concludes that professional services, professionally supported volunteers and self-help services are capable of reducing the risk of psychiatric and psychosomatic disorders resulting from bereavement.

4519 Sullender, R. Scott. *Grief and Growth: Pastoral Resources for Emotional and Spiritual Growth*. New York: Paulist Press, 1985.

A pastoral counselor presents a practical resource for clergy and laypersons in their ministries of caring. Through a readable use of his own professional experience, case studies and references to research in thanatology and psychology, the dynamics of grief are explored in relation to possibility of emotional and spiritual growth through communities of heal ing, grief rituals, the development of a relevant faith that will incorporate life and loss. Notes and bibliography.

4520 Worden, J. William. *Grief Counseling and Grief Therapy: A Handbook for the Mental Health Practitioner.* New York: Springer Publishing Co., 1982.

See 4358.

Chapter 5

CARETAKING PROFESSIONS

5.1 PASTORS, PRIESTS, RABBIS

5001 Fulton, Robert L. "The Clergyman and the Funeral Director: A Study in Role Conflict." *Social Forces*, 39(1961): 317–323.

Slightly more than a third of white Protestant and Catholic clergy returned questionnaires on the funeral. The Catholic emphasis is upon honoring the memory and body of the deceased, whereas the Protestant value of the funeral is for the peace and understanding of the survivors. Priests were more content with present-day funeral practices. Both Protestant and Catholic clergy regarded the funeral ceremony as one of their most significant rituals. There was less friction between funeral directors and priests than with Protestant ministers. Fulton suggests that a threatened loss of status influenced the Protestant ministers' antagonism.

5002 Dittes, James E. *When the People Say No: Conflict and the Call to Ministry*. San Francisco: Harper and Row, 1979.

A professor of psychology of religion makes grief a category with which a minster may understand the pains of that role and may also assist the minister in a recognition and identification with the griefs of parishioners.

5003 Linzer, Norman. *Understanding Bereavement and Grief*. New York: KTAV Publishing House, 1977.

A wide variety of papers are presented by funeral service professionals, physicians, psychologists, social workers, educators, rabbis, priest and Protestant clergy on their services, problems, goals, theoretical and practical concerns in care of the bereaved. The papers also outline current theory and research in a variety of disciplines.

5004 Shirban, John T., ed. *Coping With Death and Dying*. Lanham, Md.: University Press of America, 1985.

Those who care professionally for the dying and the bereaved are provided with a dialogue in medicine, psychology and religion that is built around the development of a model of communication between disciplines and the best way to cooperate with each other, with the patient and the family.

5005 Spilka, Bernard, *et al.* "Religion and Death: The Clerical Perspective." *Journal of Religion and Health* 20 (1981): 299–306.

Two-hundred and seventy-three clergy, Protestant and Catholic answered a questionnaire on their involvement in death work, spiritual and personal resources, satisfaction and doubts, pastoral goals and purposes, background and outlook concerning their own death. Religion as meaning and commitment was more important than the formalized concepts of theology in work with the terminally ill. Only 11% thought of funerals as a ceremony of passage from one life to another or interceding with God on behalf of the deceased. 88% favored full disclosure to a dying patient. 42% stated that they were either poorly prepared or not at all ready to deal with terminal patients and their relatives. Usually these were older clergy.

5006 Spilka, Bernard, *et al.* "The Role of Theology in Pastoral Care for the Dying." *Theology Today* 38 (1981): 16–29.

Questionnaires completed by one hundred and twenty-seven clergy who were believed to be on a liberal-conservative range within Protestantism showed the conservatives more satisfied with the aid provided by theology in the death situation, with a perception of greater personal effectiveness, more use of "other-worldly" considerations and goals, intellectual certainty about matters of ultimate concern, and an anti-euthanasia view. Conversely, conservative clergy seemed less likely to be sensitive to patients' and families needs for assistance in dealing with their feelings about an impending death.

5.2 MEDICAL AND NURSING PERSONNEL/INTERDISCIPLINARY TEAM

5007 Ackerknecht, Erwin. "Death in the History of Medicine." *Bulletin of the History of Medicine* 42 (1968): 19–23.

Medical involvement with death has historically focused upon prediction of death, fixation of movement at death, distinction between actual death and apparent death.

5008 Aldrich, C. K. "The Dying Patient's Grief." *Journal of the American Medical Association*, 184(1963): 329–331.

The loss of personal interrelations is more important than fear of dying. Implications of this thesis include the issue of who would be told about terminal illness, the way in which people express their grief with the person who is dying, the conflict of denial and acceptance and the role of physicians in care of patients and family.

5009 Alvarez, Walter C. "Care of the Dying." *Journal of the American Medical Association*, 150(1952): 86–91.

A physician presents vignettes and advice on attending the dying patient and the family from a doctor's point of view. Candor, honesty, kindness, compassion and comfort were his resources in easing the sufferings of the patients and encouraging them to have a sense of significance in the face of death.

5010 Aronson, Gerald J. "Treatment of the Dying Person." In *The Meaning of Death*, ed. by Herman Feifel, 251–258. New York: McGraw-Hill Book Co., 1959.

A psychiatrist discusses ways to help a patient as an individual human being during terminal illness. Nothing is to be said that might induce psychopathology. Hope must never die too far ahead of the patient. Be serious and tactful so that the patient will know of death from the doctor shortly before the patient is consciously aware of this possibility.

5011 Balint, Michael. *The Doctor, His Patient and the Illness*. New York: International Universities Press, 1957.

See 3118.

5012 Benoliel, Jeanne Quint. "Nurses and the Human Experience of Dying." In *New Meanings of Death*, ed. by Herman Feifel, 123–142. New York: McGraw-Hill Book Co., 1977.

The author urges direct care of dying patients as a resource against specialization, fragmentation and depersonalization in nursing service. Examples are given in a variety of settings such as intensive, emergency, recovery, chronic and terminal care. Case examples and references.

5013 Berrigan, Daniel. *We Die Before We Live: Talking With the Very Ill*. New York: Seabury Press, 1980.

From his experience as a hospice aide, a poet, priest and protester describes the dirty and serious business of dying in his experiences with a variety of patients, some of whom gained a sense of triumph over death.

5014 Brim, Orville G., Jr., Howard E. Freeman, Sol Levine, and Norman A. Scotch, eds. *The Dying Patient.* New York: Russell Sage Foundation, 1970.

See 3364.

5015 Davis, Gary and Arne Jessen. "An Experiment in Death Education in the Medical Curriculum: Medical Students and Clergy on 'Calling together.'" *Omega* 11 (1980–81): 157–166.

A clinical psychologist and a hospital chaplain developed a team approach to dying patients and their families that would utilize a medical student and a chaplain as a team. As in other courses that involve practical experience in death education, students tended to think more about their own death after the course than beforehand.

5016 Dickinson, A. R. "Nurses Perceptions of Their Care of Patients Dying With Cancer." Unpublished doctoral dissertation, Columbia University, 1966.

A study of registered nurses indicated that they were insufficiently trained to meet the religious needs of dying patients and the needs of the families of these patients.

5017 Engel, George L. "Grief and Grieving." *American Journal of Nursing,* 64 (1964): 93–98.

The grief process is related to nursing procedures both in terms of the nurse's knowledge about normal and pathological grief, and communication about death.

5018 Gammage, S. L. "Occupational Therapists and Terminal Illness: Learning to Cope with Death." *American Journal of Occupational Therapy* 30 (1975): 294–299.

Occupational therapists may assist a dying client to relinquish occupational roles. This involves listening, accepting, understanding the feelings of the dying person, the family and the medical staff.

5019 Glaser, Barney G., and Anselm L. Strauss. *Awareness of Dying.* Chicago: Aldine Pub. Co., 1965.

See 1155

5020 Group for the Advancement of Psychiatry. *Death and Dying: Attitudes of Patient and Doctor.* New York: GAP, 1965.

In a 1963 symposium, various authorities present their views on the responsibilities of a doctor to patient and appropriate means of communication concerning death.

5021 Kalish, Richard A. "Dealing With the Grieving Family." *R. N.*, 26 (1963): 81–84.

Guideposts are suggested for nurses: people need to talk, privacy is important, resentment and feelings of guilt are common, and the nurse may need to express emotion.

5022 Lifton, Robert J. *The Nazi Doctors: Medical Killing and the Psychology of Genocide*. New York: Basic Books, 1986.

In a massive historical-psychological study, Lifton explores "the healing-killing paradox": how could so many doctors participate in killing, while retaining their identity as doctors? Lifton demonstrates how "medicalized" Auschwitz was, and traces earlier euthanasia and sterilization programs which were staffed and defended by physicians. The psychological outlook was "doubling," the creation of a second, "Auschwitz self". In this way physicians accepted the "givens" of the situation and worked within them. Lifton eliminates the claim that one has to be evil to do evil things at Auschwitz. In fact, even relatively heroic persons participated in the evil of the environment.

5023 Morrissey, J. R. "A Note on Interviews with Children Facing Imminent Death." *Social Case Work* 44 (1963): 343–345.

In a pilot study of eight terminally ill children the case worker found that there was considerable concern and anxiety about illness but relief when the opportunity came for the child to discuss feelings and experiences with a sympathetic and knowledgeable adult.

5024 Quint, Jeanne C. *The Nurse and the Dying Patient*. New York: Macmillan Pub. Co. 1967.

See 3381.

5025 Rea, M. Priscilla, Shirley Greenspoon and Bernard Spilka. "Physicians and the Terminal Patient: Some Selected Attitudes and Behavior." *Omega* 6 (1975): 291–302.

One hundred and fifty-one physicians in ten medical specialties were studied. Most felt that the patient should be told of a terminal illness regardless of patient physical status, age and life-expectancy. Few drugs were employed to ease pain and there was opposition to the use of "heroic" measures. Older physicians were most negative in offering prognostic information, often disregarded the families desires, and seldom spent extra time with the patient. The authors conclude that doctors do not perceive terminality as personal failure.

5026 Schoenberg, Bernard, A. C. Carr, David Peretz, and Austin H. Kutscher, eds. *Loss and Grief: Psychological Management in Medical Practice.* New York: Columbia University Press, 1970.

See 3150.

5027 Schoenberg, Bernard. "The Nurse's Education for Death." In *Death and Bereavement,* ed. by Austin H. Kutscher, 55–74. Springfield, Ill: Charles C. Thomas, 1969.

Two extensive case histories are given of the way in which student nurses maintain intimate contact with patients who are dying and who remain accessible to their own complex of feelings during a difficult and gratifying task.

5028 Smith, Carol R. *Social Work with the Dying and Bereaved.* London: Macmillan Pub. Co., 1982.

Practical advice and a review of literature provide a text on social work for patients and relatives who are faced with death.

5029 Strauss, Anselm L. "Awareness of Dying." In *Death and Dying*, ed. by Leonard Pearson, 108–132. Cleveland, Ohio: The Press of Case Western Reserve University, 1969.

A sociologist summarizes five aspects of awareness that may be encountered between patient and staff in the process of dying and suggests procedures and attitudes by which the staff may relate to each type of awareness. See Glaser and Strauss (1155).

5030 Walborn, Karen Ann. "A Nursing Model for the Hospice: Primary and Self-Care Nursing." *Nursing Clinics of North America* 15 (1980): 205–217.

See 3408.

5031 Weisman, Avery D. "The Psychiatrist and the Inexorable." In *New Meanings of Death*, ed. by Herman Feifel, 107–122. New York: McGraw-Hill Book Co., 1977.

Professional intervention against alienation and isolation among dying patients is possible when relations are established with those who refuse treatment. Consternation can be neutralized with the help of a compassionate staff, self-esteem is established in the midst of threats to survival, anticipatory grief over inevitable loss is encouraged.

5032 White, Laurans P. "Death and the Physician: Mortuis Pivos Docent." In *New Meanings of Death*, ed. by Herman Feifel, 1–105. New York: McGraw-Hill Book Co., 1977.

A physician examines his relationship with dying persons and families in terms of open discussion of diagnosis, recognition of denial in some patients, the acceptance of anger, the consolation of religion and the security of honest discussions.

5.3 MORTUARY STAFF

5033 Kastenbaum, Robert J. and C. E. Goldsmith. "The Funeral Director and the Meaning of Death." *American Funeral Director* (April, 1963): 35–37; (May 1963): 47–48; (June 1963): 45–46.

Funeral directors become the target for displaced hostilities and anxieties of the bereaved because of the initial anxiety that surrounds death.

5034 Pine, Vanderlyn R. *Caretaker of the Dead: The American Funeral Director*. New York: Irvington Pub., 1975.

A sociologist who is familiar with mortuary practice presents the work of funeral directors within their organizations and their behavior before the public.

5035 *Professional Resources for the Funeral Director*. Milwaukee, Wis.: National Funeral Directors Association, monthly.

Books and pamphlets, videotapes and other resources are briefly described in this monthly journal. The classification of resources includes a page of monthly selections by Earl Grollman.

Chapter 6

EDUCATION FOR DEATH

6.1 CULTURAL RESOURCES

6001 Hoffmann, Frederick John. *The Mortal No: Death in the Modern Imagination.* Princeton, N.J.: Princeton University Press, 1964.

From a wide-ranging study of nineteenth and twentieth century Western literature, the author explores imaginative speculation about death in which evidences of physical dissolution have been rearranged as a transition to the spiritual life. In earlier generations, grace represented an adjustment to death by distributing our native energies between current demands and future hopes. Belief in a future life brought hope that we sin not from despair but in the expectation of a saving grace. Later, twentieth century secularism considered death in terms of violence as doctrines of grace receded. Personal violence destroyed the equilibrium between life, death and immortality. Adjustment to this violence separated humans from time and from ordinary reality. Out of this nameless violence came a third reaction to death, the search for a new basis of self-definition, as in existentialism. Insightful and erudite, despite some omissions.

6.11 LITERATURE: NOVELS, POETRY

6002 Adler, C. S.; Gene Stanford and S. M. Adler. *We Are but a Moment's Sunlight: Understanding Death.* New York: Pocket Books, 1976.

Poems, short-stories, sections from novels and autobiographies are arranged by topics: perceptions of death, process of dying, what comes after death, customs for coping with death, grief and mourning, suicide.

6003 Agee, James. *A Death in the Family*. New York: Bantam, 1969.

See 3035.

6004 Alcott, L. M. *Little Women*. New York: Grosset and Dunlap, 1947.

The heroine of this family novel from the nineteenth century dies without great show of emotion or famous last words. It is a realistic portrayal of the care of the loved one at home.

6005 Alcott, Louisa May. *Little Men*. New York: Macmillan Pub. Co., 1963.

See 6094.

6006 Ebersole, Gary L. *Ritual Poetry and the Politics of Death in Early Japan*. Princeton, N. J.: Princeton University Press, 1989.

See 1295.

6007 Falk, Walter. "Über die Bedeutung des Todes in der deutschen Literatur der achtziger Jahre." [*Concerning the Meaning of Death in German Literature of the '80's*.] In *Ars Moriendi. Erwägungen zur Kunst des Sterbens*, hrgb. von Harald Wagner. Freiburg, Germany: Herder, 1989.

Discusses such German playwrights and authors as Max Frisch *(Triptychon)*, Rainer Maria Rilke *(The Sketches of the Painter Laurid Briggs)*, Thomas Mann *(Death in Venice)*, Christoph Hein *(The Strange Friend)*, Ingeborg Drewitz *(Ice on the Elbe)*, and others, for a contemporary view of death and dying.

6008 Ferretti, V. S. and D. L. Scott. *Death in Literature*. New York: McGraw-Hill, 1977.

A selection of literature on various aspects of death are collected for high-school students. There are introductions to each section and study questions.

6009 Fiedler, L. A. *Love and Death in the American Novel*. New York: Criterion Books, 1960.

In a review of American literature from 1789 to 1960, the author finds an obsession with death and a repression of adult sexuality.

6010 Freedman, Morris. "Notes on Grief in Literature." In *Loss and Grief: Psychological Management in Medical Practice*, ed. by Bernard Schoenberg, *et al*, 339–346. New York: Columbia University Press, 1970.

A professor of English presents a brief review of aspects of death and coping with life in literature from Homer to modern novels and plays.

6011 Friedlander, A. H., ed. *Out of the Whirlwind: A Reader of Holocaust Literature*. New York: Schocken, 1976.

See 4061.

6012 Gladstein, J.; I. Knox; and S. Margoshes, eds. *Anthology of Holocaust Literature*. New York: Athenieum, 1976.

See 4062.

6013 Glasser, Ronald. *Ward 402*. New York: Braziller, 1973.

In the setting of a pediatric leukemia ward, a novelist confronts the strengths and weakness of care and wonders when doctors are giving treatment for the patient and when it is for themselves.

6014 Goodman, Lisa M. *Death and the Creative Life*. New York: Springer, 1981.

See 1138.

6015 Griffin, Jasper. *Homer on Life and Death*. London: Oxford University Press, 1983.

The poetry of the *Iliad* and *Odyssey* are reviewed for an understanding of life and death in the days of Homer.

6016 Gunther, John. *Death Be Not Proud*. New York: Harper and Row, 1949.

See 4204.

6017 Heinz, Evelyn J., ed. *Death and Dying*. Winnipeg: University of Manitoba Press, 1982.

Thirteen scholarly chapters by professors of English and linguistics, psychologists and social workers provide a wide range of intellectual interpretations of death. Some unusual selections are the treatment of death and religion in *The Rape of the Lock* and an analysis of the suicidal poetry of Sylvia Plath.

6018 Hemingway, Ernest. *The Old Man and the Sea*. New York: Charles Scribner's Sons, 1952.

The power of nature and the human spirit are combined in this insightful drama of strength and weakness before the encroachments of death.

6019 Hughes, Ann. *Hunter in the Dark*. Toronto: Clark, Irwin and Co., 1982.

A seventeen year old boy becomes seriously ill and his parents decide to hide the diagnosis of leukemia from him. The novel describes the son's discovery of the truth about his illness and the way that he coped with implication of the disease.

6020 Hart, Julian N. *The Lost Image of Man*. Baton Rouge, La.: Louisiana State Un. Press, 1964.

A theologian discusses the "iconography of death and desiccation" in modern literature.

6021 Hoffmann, Frederick J. "Mortality and Modern Literature." In *The Meaning of Death*, ed. by Herman Feifel, 132–156. New York: McGraw-Hill Book Co., 1959.

Modern literature demonstrates a different conception of death from the earlier balance of (1) fear with (2) conviction of being into eternity. Modern literature reflects a move towards the postponement of death, a reduction of belief in "superstitions" and the creation of a surrogate heaven on earth. The major terms for modern discussions of death are grace, violence and self. The footnotes are packed with choice illustrations.

6022 Lamont, C. *Man Answers Death: An Anthology of Poetry*. 2nd ed. New York: Philosophical Library, 1952.

More than 300 poems that range through many nationalities and eras are chosen to demonstrate the humanistic assertion death is the absolute end of the individual conscious personality and that the well-being of persons upon this earth is the supreme goal of life.

6023 Langer, Lawrence L. *The Age of Atrocity: Death in Modern Literature*. Boston: Beacon Press, 1978.

6024 Miller, Arthur. *The Death of a Salesman*. New York: Viking Press, 1949.

The emotional death of a person through concealment culminates in suicide.

6025 Moffatt, Mary Jane, ed. *In the Midst of Winter: Selections from the Literature of Mourning*. New York: Random House, 1982.

6026 Mojtabai, A. G. *Autumn*. Boston: Houghton-Mifflin, 1982.

This novel of bereavement in old age is a compassionate and accurate presentation of the thoughts of a widower.

6027 Morin, Edgar. *L'Homme et la Mort Devant L'Histoire (Man and Death Before History)*. Paris, France: Correa, 1951.

Curious about the crisis of individuality in the face of death, the author examines death in books (literature, poetry or philosophy), for this is the sector of civilization that deals with generalities. In them the subject of death and dying is still presented, even though it is read by people who are saturated by an atmosphere of anguish, neurosis and nihilism.

6028 Murray, Henry A. "Dead to the World: The Passions of Herman Melville." In *Essays in Self-Destruction*, ed. by Edwin S. Shneidman, 7–29. E. New York: Science House, 1967.

A professor of political psychology connects the findings of Farberow, Shneidman, and Neuringer on suicides with the concept of "dead to the world" in the writings of a 19th century New England author, Herman Melville, especially in *Moby Dick*.

6029 Poe, E. A. "A Descent into the Maelström." In Edgar Allan Poe, *The Complete Tales and Poems of Edgar Allan Poe*. New York: Modern Library, 1938.

6030 Rhode, E. "Death in Twentieth-Century Fiction." In *Man's Concern with Death*, ed. by Arnold Toynbee. New York: McGraw-Hill Book Co., 1969.

Modern writers are surveyed, from Charles Dickens, Leo Tolstoi, James Joyce and Thomas Hardy to John Hawks and Albert Camus.

6031 Right, James. *This Journey*. New York: Random House, 1982.

A Pulitzer Prize winning poet includes writings that were completed in the hospital where he died at age 52.

6032 Rosenthal, Ted. *How Could I Not Be Among You?* New York: George Braziller, 1973.

A dying poet writes about his illness in a direct fashion that has special meaning for young adults.

6033 Saint-Exupery, Antoine de. *The Little Prince*. New York: Harcourt, Brace and Co., 1943.

See 6130.

6034 Saroyan, Aram. *Last Rites: The Death of William Saroyan*. New York: William Morrow, 1982.

The son of a famous novelist describes difficulties in reaching others before, during and after the father's death from cancer.

6035 Sarton, Mary. *As We Are Now*. New York: W. W. Norton Co., 1973.

The longing and need for the loving touch of another human being is graphically portrayed in the story of a retired school teacher who can no longer take physical care for herself.

6036 Simpson, Michael A. "Death and Modern Poetry." In *New Meanings of Death*, ed. by Herman Feifel, 313–334. New York: McGraw-Hill Book Co., 1977.

A psychiatrist with an encyclopedic knowledge of thanatology (8039) discusses the return of death as a more insistent motif in modern poetry, as in other forms of literature, such as the rhetorical romanticism of the 17th century, the gloomy and smug melancholy of the 18th century, and the more personal and distinctive modern approach of poets like Emily Dickinson. Poetry is discussed in terms of war, suicide, religion, and the more intimate expression of personal distress, including psychopathology. References.

6037 Smiley, Jane. *The Age of Grief*. New York: A. A. Knopf, 1987.

A collection of short stories probe the experience of grief, with more about loss of love and hope than about physical death.

6038 Springer, Rebecca Ruter. *IntraMuros*. Forest Grove, Ore.: Booksearchers, n. d.

Before her death, an invalid woman describes the sight and sound of conversations with beloved persons who had died and visits with them during quiet walks in a heavenly park and house. The work is typical of popular nineteenth century "dreams of heaven."

6039 Stewart, Garrett. *Death Sentences: Styles of Dying in British Fiction*. Cambridge, Mass.: Harvard University Press, 1985.

Death scenes are presented in British novels from the eighteenth to the twentieth century with comments on style and language.

6040 TeBries, Peter. *The Blood of the Lamb*. Boston: Little, Brown and Co., 1969.

This novel about the life and doubts of a marginally successful man, "Don Wanderhope" centers in the last part of the death of his daughter "Carol" from leukemia. Many of the father's religious doubts are traced to his rejection of Dutch Calvinism which was rigorously taught and believed.

A moving account of the rage that a parent can feel as he tries to make sense out of the suffering of a child that he loves.

6041 Tolstoy, Leo. "The Death of Ivan Ilych." In Leo Tolstoy, *The Novels and Other Works of Leo N. Tolstoy*. New York: Charles Scribner's Sons, 1960.

See 3012.

6042 Timothy E. and Reet Mae. "Who Dies and Who Cries: Death and Bereavement in Childrens' Literature." *Journal of Communication*, 37, 4 (1987): 52–64.

See 6134.

6043 Vassein, Beth Ann. *Women and Death: Linkages in Western Thought and Literature*. Westport, Conn.: Greenwood Press, 1984.

The author demonstrates the almost automatic link between women and death in writing based upon traditional Christianity. Also, the fiction of women's fatal sexual attractions are examined. Poetic themes of women and death.

6044 Wass, Hannelore. "Thanatology Topics in Literature." In *Death Education II*, ed. by Hannelore Wass, *et al.*, 301–312. Washington, D.C.: Hemisphere Pub. Corp., 1985.

6045 Watson, Elizabeth. *Guests of My Life*. Ill. by Anne Mikolowski. Burnsville, N. C.: Sello Press, 1979.

The author spent many long evenings by the fireplace with her husband as they imagined first the lectures at Friends World College and then the book that brought them comfort from prescient phrases by great thinkers. Her comments upon their phrases are brief poems, filled with the lively and life-giving spirit of a mind that can give new meaning to the memory of a beloved daughter.

6046 Waugh, Evelyn. *The Loved One*. New York: Dell, 1948.

With absorbing detail and ferocious judgments, a novelist portrays the extremes of Hollywood burial customs.

6047 Weir, Robert F., ed. *Death In Literature*. New York: Columbia University Press, 1980.

Short sections are presented from representative literature from ancient times to the present under the following classifications: inevitability of death, death personified, personal views of dying, death scenes, children, youth, death by killing, suicide, funeral and burial customs, bereavement, immortality and the complete "Death of Ivan Ilych" by Leo Tolstoy. The author also discusses death as a literary subject.

6048 Whitaker, Agnes, ed. *All in the End is Harvest: An Anthology for Those Who Grieve*. London: Darton, Longman and Todd, 1984.

6049 Wilder, Amos N. "Mortality in Contemporary Literature." In *The Modern Vision of Death*, ed. by Nathan H. Scott, Jr. Richmond, Virginia: John Knox Press, 1967.

The literature of existentialists and others reveal the theme of death as catalyst of transcendence.

6.12 MEDIA/DRAMA/MUSIC/ART

6050 Bataille, Georges. *Death and Sensuality: A Study of Eroticism and the Taboo*. Salem, N. H.: Ayer Co. Pub., 1962.

A leader in the philosophy of the irrational that embraced the popularity of the surrealist movement after World War I uses his knowledge of art to explain the meaning of sex in relation to death taboos and investigates ritualized aspects sacrifice, murder and war. Art shows the contrast between beauty and repulsiveness in both the sexual act and in death but observations about death bring us to the inherent limits of communication and the inevitable interventions of chance.

6051 Clark, James M. *The Dance of Death in the Middle Ages and the Renaissance*. 1950. Reprint. Salem, N. H.: Ayer Co. Pub., 1976.

The death motif is explored in the Middle Ages and the Renaissance with literary and medical explorations of the dance-of-death theme. This volume also includes a reprint of Lessing's *How the Ancients Represented Death* (6059).

6052 *Death and the Visual Arts*. Salem, N. H.: Ayer Co. Pub., 1976.

Two reprints are found in this volume: James M. Clark (6051) and Gotthold E. Lessing (6059).

6053 Gallagher, Kenneth T. "Gabriel Marcel: Death as Mystery." *Humanitas* 10(1974): 75–86.

The plays of Marcel are replete with examples of the transforming power of death. Death is participation in the common fate of all people. When we recognize the uniqueness of each death, we transcend natural forces. Examples are cited from several plays.

6054 Gottlieb, Carla. "Modern Art and Death." In *The Meaning of Death*, 157–188. Ed. by Herman Feifel. New York: McGraw-Hill Book Co., 1959.

The meaning of death in art, 1850–1950, shows no contribution to the portrayal of death personified. Instead, moderns such as Gauguin may use traditional symbols of death without being specific: leafless trees, ruins, wintery scenes, coffins, vultures, slaughter, weapons. Clocks appear in such varying artists as Cezanne, Klee, Dali and Chagall. Line, shape and color (black) are non-objective expressions of death. A more realistic attitude is presented in paintings of social and political evils that suggest macabre death.

6055 Hinz, Renate, ed. *Käthe Kollwitz: Graphics, Posters, Drawings*. New York: Pantheon, 1981.

The meaning of death, grief and suffering is presented in the work of a twentieth-century artist.

6056 Holbein, Hans (The Younger). *The Dance of Death*. 1538. Reprint. New York: Dover, 1971.

In forty-one woodcuts the artist portrays a dance of life that is continually shadowed by death. There is a waiting and watchfulness in the images, for death is a reminder of the Last Judgment. Both upon the brevity of life and the depravity of humanity of all ranks and classes.

6057 Kastenbaum, Robert J., *et. al.,* eds. *Death and the Visual Arts*. New York: Arno Press, 1977.

The death motif in art is explored with selections that include the ancient portrayal of death as the brother of sleep and the horrible images of the dance of death in the Middle Ages.

6058 Lauder, Robert E. *God, Death, Art and Love: The Philosophical Vision of Ingmar Bergman*. New York: Paulist Press, 1989.

The cinematic genius of Bergman is explored through the metaphysical meanings of his movies. Chapter 4 explicates a central theme of the author that a Bergman film almost always is set against a background stained by the reality of death. The themes of various Bergman films and Bergman's comments on the films are used to support and illustrate this thesis. Some photos from films in each chapter. Judicious philosophical notes are included. Selected Bergman filmography.

6059 Lessing, Gotthold E. *How the Ancients Represented Death*. Reprinted from *Selected Prose Works of G. E. Lessing*. Trans. by E. C. Beasley and Helen Zimmern. 1879. Reprint. Salem, N. H.: Ayer Co. Pub., 1976.

Goethe was enchanted by Lessing's presentation of an ancient belief that death is the brother of sleep. This presented the possibility of portraying death in art and literature as beautiful instead of hideous. Lessing called upon artists to replace "the hideous crucifixion with ancient, serene and more becoming motif of death as restful ease. This work is contained in the same volume with Clark's *The Dance of Death in the Middle Ages and the Renaissance* (6051).

6060 Minear, Paul F. *Death Set to Music*. Atlanta, Ga.: John Knox Press, 1987.

A New Testament theologian first considers the range of attitudes toward death that characterize New Testament authors and then examines four musical works to trace the influence of these biblical attitudes on the composers' interpretation of mortality. The composers are Johann Sebastian Bach, Johannes Brahms, Krzysztof Penderecki, Leonard Bernstein. Notes.

6061 *Return to Life: Two Imaginings of the Lazarus Theme*. Salem, N. H.: Ayer Co. Pub., 1976.

From the 11th chapter of St. John and from the imaginative essay of Andreyev, *Lazarus*, and the play of O'Neill, *Lazarus Laughed*, the themes of death and resurrection are revived for the popular imagination.

6062 Ruby, J. "Portraying the Dead." *Omega* 19 (1988–89): 1–20.

In nineteenth century America, postmortem photography was socially acceptable and a subject of professional discussions by photographers. Images of the deceased were publicly displayed in wall frames and albums. The photographic portraits sought to deny death by displaying the body as if asleep or even conscious. By 1900 the deceased were photographed in a casket with increasing emphasis upon the funeral. In the 1980's, photography of the deceased is private matter that seems to be on the decline. However, counselors working with the parents of children who have died provide evidence that these images can be useful in the mourning process.

6063 Warthin, Aldred Scott. *The Physician of the Dance of Death: A Historical Study of the Evolution of the Dance Mythus in Art*. 1931. Reprint. Salem, N. H.: Ayer Co. Pub., 1976.

The author was entranced by the famous Dürer engraving "The Knight, Death, and the Devil" (1513). To his interest in art he added expertness as a medical researcher. In organizing woodcuts by woodcuts by Dürer, Rethel and others under the themes of "the danger of hubris," "death as an egalitarian leveler," "familiarity of death as an innately natural and human factor in life." His writings also discuss medieval paintings, eighteenth and nineteenth century caricatures and the question of a modern dance of death that might be impelled by the impact of World War I.

6.13 RITUALS/MORES/HOLIDAYS

6064 Aguilar, I. and V. Wood. "Therapy through a Death Ritual." *Social Work* 21 (1976): 49–54.

See 4374.

6065 Alexiou, Margaret. *The Ritual Lament in Grief Tradition.* London: Cambridge University Press, 1974.

The history of oral and literary lament and the rituals associated with it is traced as a poetic form from Homeric thought through the classical and Byzantine periods to modern times where it remains part of a living folk tradition. The three main forms were lament for men, for gods and heroes, for a city or people in distress.

6066 Conley, D. H. *Handling the Holidays.* Springfield, Ill.: Creative Marketing, 1979.

Advice is offered from a funeral director/counselor through collected suggestions from the bereaved parents and relatives for dealing with the painful emotions that holidays may evoke. Topics include dealing with feelings, making holidays acceptable for children, developing new ways to spend the holidays. Self-help groups and holiday job lists are included.

6067 Eisenbruch, M. "Cross-Cultural Aspects of Bereavement. II: Ethnic and Cultural Variations in the Development of Bereavement Practices." *Culture, Medicine and Psychiatry* 8 (1984): 315–347.

The author provides a comparative analysis of bereavement practices among various ethnic and cultural groups in the United States and finds that a cohesive group can provide bereavement procedures through a cultural code which has implications for the course of grief, detection of pathology, health-care and direction for the bereaved.

6068 Huntington, Richard and Peter Metcalf. *Celebrations of Death: The Anthropology of Mortuary Ritual.* New York: Cambridge University Press, 1979.

6069 Lamm, Maurice, and N. Eskreis. "Viewing the Remains: A New America Custom." *Journal of Religion and Health* 5(1966): 137–143.

Theological and psychological questions are raised concerning the twentieth century custom of viewing a corpse before or during the funeral.

6070 Lopata, Helena Z. "On Widowhood. Grief Work and Identity Reconstruction." *Journal of Geriatric Psychiatry* 8 (1975): 41–55.

On the basis of her research with widows, the author notes the importance of friendship and social contacts as support for women during a period of loss, but also warns against some support groups pressure grieving persons toward a return to "normal" living before the deep work of grief has been done. Personal needs and the timing of emotional expression is crucial, especially when widows feel unable to initiate contact, conform to expectations or follow the advice that is offered to them. See also Lopata (4241).

6071 Mandelbaum, David G. "Social Uses of Funeral Rites." In *Meanings of Death*, ed. by Herman Feifel. New York: McGraw-Hill Book Co., 1959.

See 4396.

6072 Pollock, George H. "Anniversary Reactions, Trauma and Mourning." *Psychoanalytic Quarterly* 39 (1970): 347–371.

Psychotherapy reveals anniversary reactions as a silent but emerging response to a "triggering" shock experience that is related to time, holidays, ceremonies, religious rituals that evoke association with traumatic events that are laden with grief, fear and depression. The symptom may be transitory or adaptive, or re-establish equilibrium but there is a continuation of regression to deeper traumatic events in the past, psychotherapy is advised, for a cluster of repressed but accumulated psychic conflicts are becoming evident.

6073 Presbyterian Church (U.S.A.). *The Funeral*. Philadelphia: Westminster Press, 1986.

See 4402.

6074 Ramsey, R. W. "Bereavement: A Behavioral Treatment of Pathological Grief." In *Trends in Behavior Therapy*, ed. by P. O. Skoden, S. Bates and W. S. Dorkans. New York: Academic Press, 1979.

From a review of various cultures, the author maintains that the bereaved are benefitted in some cultures by opportunities to review death events in a social setting and use various rituals of the culture for the healing work of grief.

6075 Salzberger, R. C. "Death: Beliefs, Activities and Reactions of the Bereaved—Some Psychological and Anthropological Observations." *The Human Context* 7 (1975): 103–116.

From a survey of various studies on grief, the author concludes that there is a deficit of ideology and ritual for grief and mourning in Western societies. For a similar criticism see Gorer (1012)

6076 Scheff, T. "The Distancing of Emotion is Ritual." *Current Anthropology* 18(1977): 483–490.

Rituals are an appropriate opportunity for individual expression of grief and group support, but the amount of emotional distance is crucial. Rituals may be overwhelming or they may lack emotional meaning for those in mourning.

6077 Taylor, Lou. *Mourning Dress: A Costume and Social History.* London: George Allen and Unwin, 1983.

The development of European funerals, the social status of widows, and the fashions of the time are reviewed from about 1600 to 1910. Specific aspects of dress are detailed.

6078 Warner, W. Lloyd. *The Living and the Dead: A Study of the Symbolic Life of Americans.* New Haven, Conn.: Yale University Press, 1959.

A sociologist with an interest in anthropology investigates the meanings and functions of symbols in one American community at mid-twentieth century. He finds that secular and religious symbols organize experiences of the dead past to provide continuity for the living members of the present. The mortality of the individual is connected to the comparative immortality of the human species through the story of heroes, political conflict, symbols of power and glory, the cult of the dead and the language of the churches.

6.14 MYTHS/FOLKTALES/DREAMS

6079 Abrahamsson, Hans. *The Origin of Death: Studies in African Mythology.* New York: Arno Press, 1977.

The most common African myths are recounted and classified according to content (such as "the message that failed") and by regions of Africa in which various symbols of death reappear. International bibliography.

6080 Becker, Howard and D. K. Bruner. "Attitudes Toward Death and the Dead, and Some Possible Causes of Ghost Fear." *Mental Hygiene* 15 (1931): 828–837.

A pioneers in the study of death attitudes compare pre-literate and civilized groups in their attitudes toward death, the dead and ghosts.

6081 Dunne, John S. *The City of the Gods: A Study in Myth and Mortality.* New York: Macmillan Pub. Co., 1965.

Various myths seek to answer the question: "If I must someday die, what can I do to satisfy my desire to live?" A Catholic priest traces answers to this questions in myths from ancient civilizations to modern existential philosophers. A central theme of death in relation to monarchy and democracy is embodied in the Sophocles, Homer, Virgil, Dante, Shakespeare. The autonomy of the person by virtue of which death becomes voluntary and free is seen in the philosophers Kant, Nietzsche, Heidegger. Ancient Greek and Roman myths presented heroic deeds as the entrance to immortality. The legend of Gilgamesh is the archetype of a human in search of immortality. See also Choron (1041).

6082 Fahs, Sophia. *Beginnings.* Boston: Beacon Press, 1950.

The wonderings of children about life and death are portrayed in selected myths from many cultures.

6083 Franz, Marie-Louise Von. *On Dreams and Death.* Boston: Shambhala, 1986.

See 3020.

6084 Freud, Sigmund. "The Theme of the Three Caskets." In *Collected Papers*, vol 4, pp. 244–256. New York: Basic Books, 1959.

The father of psychoanalysis finds a hidden preoccupation with death in literature, dreams and myths that have become symbolized in consciousness through the theme of choosing a fair lover who represents life.

6085 Henderson, Joseph L. and Maud Oakes. *The Wisdom of the Serpent.* New York: George Braziller, 1963.

See 2005.

6086 Heuscher, J. E. "Death in the Fairy Tale." *Diseases of the Nervous System* 28 (1967): 462–467.

A physician considers the challenge of death as the final crisis of life that substitutes a new pattern for a familiar old one. It is like a fairy tale in which each stage of growth plays the part of another in a series of challenges that in some fantastic way will lead to eventual success.

6087 Song, C. S. *The Tears of Lady Ming.* New York: Orbis Books, 1982.

The fable of an unjust king is used to explain Asian theology. The theme is the meaning of the death of a martyr.

6.2 COMMUNITY/PROFESSIONAL EDUCATION

6088 Morgan, Ernest. *Dealing Creatively With Death. A Manual of Death Education and Simple Burial.* Rev. ed. Burnsville, N.C.: The Celo Press, 1984.

This practical and precise guide presents resources of memorial societies in United States and Canada along with recommendations of other organizations, books and articles. As a small handbook this is an excellent guide for a one-day seminar on death and burial practices.

6089 Pacholski, R. A. and Charles A. Corr, eds. *New Directions in Death Education and Counseling: Enhancing the Quality of Life in the Nuclear Age.* Arlington, Va.: Forum for Death Education and Counseling, 1981.

Thirty-two papers from conferences of the Forum for Death Education and Counseling address issues in death, dying and bereavement at all levels of education, pre-school through college and medical-professional.

6090 Pine, Vanderlyn R. "A Socio-Historical Portrait of Death Education." In *Death Education* 1 (Spring, 1977): 57–84.

6091 Wass, Hannalore, Charles A. Corr, R. A. Pacholski, and C. M. Sanders. *Death Education: An Annotated Resource Guide.* Washington, D.C.: Hemisphere, 1980.

See 8049.

6092 Wagner, Harald. "Ars moriendi und Religionspädagogik." ("Ars Moriendi" and Religious Pedagogy.) In *Ars Moriendi. Erwägungen zur Kunst des Sterbens,* ed. by Harald Wagner. Freiburg, Germany: Herder, 1989.

Wagner examines education about death in religious instruction for children, the goals and content of such instruction and a consideration of a model school curriculum.

6.21 HOW CHILDREN LEARN ABOUT DEATH

6093 Aaron, C. *Catch Calico!* New York: Dutton, 1979.

This novel of compassion, realism and courage describes the dilemma of a fourteen year old boy who realizes that his semi-wild cat is the cause of his grandfather's fatal rabies. The grandson cares for his grandfather and also realizes that it is merciful to shoot the cat who is in growing misery.

6094 Alcott, Louisa May. *Little Men*. New York: Macmillan Pub. Co., 1963.

This lively classic about the boys in Plumfield House contains a moving episode in which death and funeral are shared by all. The publication in 1963 was unusual in the days of death denial with special secrecy around children.

6095 Aliki. *The Two of Them*. New York: Greenwillow Books, 1979.

In this picture book, short poems tell of the love between a grandfather and his granddaughter, with the events of their lives together and finally the resolution of her feelings after his death.

6096 Anthony, Sylvia. *The Discovery of Death in Childhood and After*. New York: Basic Books, 1972.

Literature, philosophy, psychoanalytic theory and Piaget's learning theories are combined in an explanation of children's responses to questions about death. Play, dreams and meditations of children illuminate their feelings about separation, aggressiveness and guilt.

6097 Bailis, Lawrence A. "Death in Children's Literature: A Conceptual Analysis." *Omega* 8 (1977): 295–304.

Of a sample of forty children's books on death, the concept of death is classified under concepts of immortality, inevitability or inherent effects. The author finds that the death in the literature for children is never presented as the permanent end of all forms of existence.

6098 Bartoli, Jennifer. *Nonna*. New York: Harvey House, 1975.

A little boy tells the story of his grandmother's death: the funeral, the next day, the first Christmas.

6099 Bernstein, J. E. and S. D. Gullo. *When People Die*. New York: Dutton, 1977.

Health, disease, accidents, disasters, murders, suicides, war, old age are discussed in this book for young children. Burial and mourning customs in different parts of the world are shown along with photographs. There is a brief discussion of grief and bereavement after the death of a loved one.

6100 Bluebond-Langer, Myra. "Meanings of Death to Children." In *New Meanings of Death*, ed. by Herman Feifel, 49–66. New York: McGraw-Hill Book Co., 1977.

From clinical experience and research studies, the author briefly considers normal children and death, terminally ill children, the inner-connection of these two and the way to talk with both normal and terminally ill children about death. References.

6101 Blume, Judy. *Tiger-Eyes*. Scarsdale, N. Y.: Bardbury Press, 1981.

See 4053.

6102 Brown, M. W. *The Dead Bird*. Ill. by R. Charlip. Reading, Mass.: Addison-Wesley, 1958.

After many years of denial, a publisher finally allowed a story about death to be printed for children. The natural inclination of children to have some ceremony about death is depicted in the burial of a dead bird. No adults are present.

6103 Carrick, C. *The Accident*. New York: Seabury Press, 1976.

A boy watches his dog killed by a truck. His grief is complicated by the decision of his parents to bury the dog without him.

6104 Cleaver, Vera and Bill Cleaver. *Grover*. Ill. by Frederic Marvin. Philadelphia: J. B. Lippincott, 1970.

After the mother of an eleven year old boy comes home from the hospital, she commits suicide because of her suffering. Although the father calls it an accident, Grover understands that it was her only way out.

6105 Coburn, J. B. *Anne and the Sand Dobbies*. New York: Seabury, 1964.

A boy experiences first the death of his little sister and then of his first dog. His father and a neighbor answer many of his questions. A complete funeral service is included by the author, Episcopal bishop of Massachusetts.

6106 Corley, E. A. *Tell Me About Death. Tell Me About Funerals*. Ill. by P. Pecoraro. Santa Clara, Calif.: Grammatical Sciences, 1973.

See 4384.

6107 Cunningham, J. *Burnish Me Bright*. New York: Pantheon, 1970.

A mute orphan boy adjusts with strength and courage as he serves for several years as apprentice to a dying man who was once the world's greatest mime.

6108 Donnelly, Elfie. *So Long Grandpa*. Trans. by A. Bell. New York: Crown Pub., 1981.

A German novel describes a young boy's relationship with his grandfather and the way it both changed and remained the same when he learned that the grandfather had cancer.

6109 Farley, C. *The Garden Is Doing Fine*. New York: Atheneum, 1975.

A high school student indulges many wishes and dreams that will keep her father from dying in a hospital. When she finally accepts the reality of her father's terminal condition, she also knows that he will continue to live on through her memories of him.

6110 Graeber, C. *Mustard*. New York: Macmillan Pub. Co., 1982.

An eight year old boy must learn to live with the increasing physical difficulties of his cat and recognized that his cat will die. Then the boy deals with the "if only" questions about death.

6111 Gordon, Audrey K. and Dennis Klass. *They Need to Know: How to Teach Children About Death*. Englewood Cliffs, N.J.: Prentice-Hall, 1979.

Two classroom teachers provide concrete guidance for parents and teachers concerning death education for children. Curricula is suggested by grade and goal with specific resources and activities. Healthcare and funeral services are considered as consumer issues.

6112 Grollman, Earl A., ed. *Explaining Death to Children*. Boston: Beacon Press, 1967.

Authorities in thanatology, anthropology, children's literature, sociology and psychology provide guidance for the love of a child in bereavement. The child's emotional stability is strengthened by trusting adults who combine a concern for spiritual, emotional and spiritual well-being of the child.

6113 Grollman, Earl A. *Talking About Death: A Dialogue Between Parent and Child*. Rev. ed. Boston: Beacon Press, 1976.

See 3089 and 4189.

6114 Grollman, Earl A. *Living When A Loved One Has Died*. Boston: Beacon Press, 1977.

For the healing of wounds during grief, a rabbi presents brief meditations and pictures that portray the ending of one chapter in life and the beginning of another.

6115 Hickman, Martha Whitmore. *Last Week My Brother Anthony Died*. Ill. by Randie Julian. Nashville, Tenn.: Abingdon Press, 1984.

This illustrated text for grade-school children to read is a straight-forward account of the events and feelings of a young child and her con-versations with her mother and her minister.

6116 Hunter, M. *A Sound of Chariots.* New York: Harper and Row, 1972.

The happiness of a favorite daughter is shattered by the death of her father. Her life continues in sorrow as she matures. Morbid reflections on time and death are dealt with in time through her desire to write poetry.

6117 Jay, Susan M., Vicki Green, Sharon Johnson, Steven Calwell, *et al.* "Differences in Death Concepts Between Children with Cancer and Physically Healthy Children." *Journal of Clinical Child Psychology* 16 (1987): 301–306.

Interviews with 32 healthy children and 32 children with cancer age 3–16 showed that the healthy children were more than likely to exhibit the concepts of immanent justice than children with cancer. Children with cancer exhibited no more advanced concepts of death than those who were physically well.

6118 Jury, Mark and Dan Jury. *Gramp.* New York: Penguin, 1976.

See 3095.

6119 Kastenbaum, Robert J. "Childhood: The Kingdom Where Creatures Die." *Journal of Clinical Child Psychology* 3(Summer 1974): 11–13.

6120 Klin, S. *The Final Mystery.* New York: Doubleday, 1974.

For readers aged 8–13 the author presents the meaning of death in different times, regions, religions. Feelings about death and fear, burial and funeral customs show the way in which people attempted to fight death, the great mystery of life.

6121 Kübler-Ross, Elisabeth. *Remember the Secret.* Ill. by Heather Preston. Berkeley, Calif.: Celestial Arts, 1982.

A book to be read to young children describes the imaginary world of a young boy and girl who find comfort in each other after the death of the girl's father. Love and affection with an older boy and girl are the center of their dreams. When the young boy is taken to the hospital, the girl cannot visit him until he comes home. Then she knows that he is sick. A week later she attends his funeral and is comforted by the thought that the two of them shared the secret of imaginary playmates. Text and illus-trations are reminiscent of the beautiful, heavenly world described in nineteenth century books of consolation.

6122 Lee, Virginia. *The Magic Moth.* Ill. by Richard Cuffari. Greenwich, Conn.: Seabury Press, 1972.

As one child in the family grows weaker and weaker, the father explains to the other children that she is going to die. They are not quite sure that she has left them, because a moth emerges from it's cocoon and flies away as they are with the sister who dies. Emphasis is upon dying at home with honest family sharing.

6123 Mallonie, Bryan and Robert Ingpen. *Lifetimes: The Beautiful Way to Explain Death to Children.* New York: Bantam Books, 1983.

With excellent illustrations this book for five to eight year olds deals with the life cycles of plants, birds and finally with people.

6124 Miles, M. *Annie and the Old One.* Boston: Little, Brown and Co., 1971.

On a Navajo Indian reservation, a grandmother announces that she will "return unto the earth" when mother completes the rug that she is weaving. The granddaughter understands that this means death for the grandmother and cannot understand why her mother continues the weaving. After the child tries several maneuvers to disrupt the weaving, the grandmother talks about the natural cycles of life and death.

6125 Mills, G., R. Riesler, A. Robinson, G. Vermilye. *Discussing Death: A Guide to Death Education.* Homewood, Ill.: ETC Pub., 1976.

A curricular guide for educators is divided in four age levels between ages 5 and 18, with curricular concepts and learning opportunities suggested for each of the four groups Considered by Corr to be flawed and oversimplified (Wass 4198, 6044).

6126 Mitchell, Marjorie E. *The Child's Attitude to Death.* New York: Schocken Books, 1967.

A child's awareness of death will usually lead to a dual response, that the child does not want to die and does not want to see loved ones die.

6127 Nagy, Maria H. "The Child's View of Death." *Journal of Genetic Psychology* 73 (1948): 3–27.

See 3059.

6128 Newman, Nanette. *That Dog!* Ill. by Margaret Hafner. New York: Thomas Y. Crowell, 1980.

For children five-eight years of age, this is a lively presentation of a boy's relationship with his dog. Eventually the dog dies. Black and white illustrations add to the underlying humor of the text.

6129 Reed, E. L. *Helping Children with the Mystery of Death*. Nashville, Tenn.: Abingdon Press, 1970.

Christian resources for children and their adult mentors are selected from the Bible, poetry, stories and prayers. Various activities are suggested.

6130 Saint-Exupery, Antoine de. *The Little Prince*. New York: Harcourt, Brace and Co., 1943.

Adults and children can read this book together or separately to receive many insights about loneliness, aloneness, gentleness, mystery, wonder, life and death. Theme: it is only with the heart that one sees rightly. A beautiful novel for all ages.

6131 Stein, S. B. *About Dying*. New York: Walker, 1974.

Younger children will appreciate this non-fiction book with very large print for young children and smaller for parents and older children. Funerals for a pet bird and for a grandfather are described along with feelings about their deaths.

6132 Sternberg, F. and B. Sternberg. *If I Die and When I Do: Exploring Death with Young People*. Englewood Cliffs, N.J.: Prentice-Hall, 1980.

A course on death for junior high school social study classes is described: how to share experiences, explore beliefs, deal with fears, humor, old age and the facing of our own death. Statements, poems and drawings by the students are interspersed among these topics.

6133 Sergent, Marilyn. *Talking to Children About Death*. Rockville, MD: U. S. Department of Health, Education and Welfare, 1979.

This brief survey of issues of death related communications with children and recommendations for adults to work with children in the solving of common problems is available as a single free copies from public inquiries, National Institute of Mental Health, 5600 Fishers Lane, Rockfield, Md. 20857.

6134 Timothy E., and Reet Mae. "Who Dies and Who Cries: Death and Bereavement in Childrens' Literature." *Journal of Communication*, 37, 4 (1987): 52–64.

From a survey of 52 books in children's literature published between 1970 and 1983 the authors found that fictional counts of death revealed stereotypes of a tearful girl and the stoic boy with little portrayal of natural grief or change of life circumstances.

6135 Viorst, J. *The Tenth Good Thing about Barney*. Ill. by Erik Blegvad. New York: Atheneum, 1971.

A little boy grieves for the death of his pet cat. Soon he is in an argument with the little girl next door. Is the cat in the ground or in heaven?

6136 Warburg, Sandol Stoddard. *Growing Time*. Boston: Houghton-Mifflin, 1969.

When a boy loses his pet dog, different members of the family help him with his grief and anger. Anger has risen because parents buried the dog before the boy was informed of his death.

6137 Wass, Hannelore, *et al*. "Books for Children." In *Death Education II*, ed. by Hannelore Wass, *et al*., 313–352. Washington, D. C.: Hemisphere Pub. Corp., 1985.

See 8052.

6138 White, E. B. *Charlotte's Web*. New York: Harper and Row, 1952.

This classic story for children ages 8–11 explains the cycle of life in the friendship of a pig and a rat for a spider. The death of the spider (Charlotte) and the birth of her children becomes the vehicle through which the author describes grief and sorrow and the ways that the memories of a friend can be kept alive in a healthy manner.

6139 Wolf, Anna M. *Helping Your Children to Understand Death*. Rev. ed. New York: Child Study Press, 1973.

With a background in child development and family dynamics, the author deals with the common questions of children and parents. Issues of faith are considered from the viewpoint of the major faiths. Also included: suicide, assassination and war, and hypocrisy.

6140 Wolfenstein, Martha and Gilbert Pliman, eds. *Children and the Death of a President*. Garden City, N.Y.: Doubleday and Co., 1965.

From questionnaires with school children, essays of junior high school students, and interviews with children ages 7–12 in a suburb of New York, an interdisciplinary team considers the reactions of children to the death of President Kennedy in 1963. In the midst of national and international mourning, adults wept more than children and children returned quickly to their usual amusements of the weekend. In adolescents the sense of disbelief and protest persisted longest. Athletic college students discussed gruesome tortures they would like to inflict on the assassin, whereas the intellectually oriented wept.

6141 Zim, H. and S. Bleeker. *Life and Death*. New York: Morrow, 1970.

A very instructive book for children aged nine and over was one of the first to discuss the biological, physical facts of life and death through the life cycle of plants, animals, and humans. Attitudes towards death in various cultures are presented along with information on the definition of medical death. Many questions are answered for young readers that are often left obscure or inaccurate by adults.

6.22 COLLEGE COURSES

6142 Eddy, J. M. and W. F. Alles. *Death Education*., St. Louis, Mo.: C. V. Mosby 1983.

Two health educators provide a handbook for teachers and a textbook for students on resources for reference both concerning methods of teaching and content of courses on bereavement, grief, suicide, mourning, euthanasia, funeral industry, hospitals and hospice.

6143 Prunkl, Peter R., and Rebecca L. Berry. *Death Week: Exploring the Dying Process*. Washington: Hemisphere Pub. Corp., 1989.

For one week a voluntary group of college students played the role of a dying person as realistically as they knew how. The experiment has evolved over a period of seven years into a model that is different from the "stage" theory of dying that was popular in the 1970's. The book is addressed primarily to teachers, researchers and practitioners in the field of death education, thanatology, death counseling, hospice care who may wish to develop simulated death and dying exercises. Journals are kept by participants in the week-long exercise and shared with other members of the group. Various emotional reactions were identified by the researchers and group so that experiences could be translated into descriptions of the process of dying that would guide individual and group in understanding and control. Appendices describe the typical reactions that could be coded. Bibliography and index.

6144 Leviton, Daniel. "Death Education." In *New Meanings of Death*, ed. by Herman Feifel, 253–272. New York: McGraw-Hill Book Co., 1977.

A professor of health education describes the development of health education programs, goals, research, qualifications of a teacher, characteristics of students, a variety of sample courses, texts, and a list of references.

6145 Meagher, D. K. and R. D. Shapiro. *Death: The Experience*. Minneapolis, Minn.: Burgess Pub. Co., 1984.

A two-hundred page spiral bound booklet in intended as a supplementary laboratory that would be appropriate for adolescents and college students. A wide range of readings, references and thirty-two death-related exercises of the paper and pencil type are included.

6146 Schmitt, Abraham. *Dialogue With Death*. Waco, Tex.: Word Books, 1976.

Through interdisciplinary courses on Death and Dying, a professor with degrees in social work and theology presents his own experience with death and excerpts from student journals on their experiences with death. The aim of his courses and seminars is existential: a death and dying journal by each participant, a confrontation of students with scenes of dying and the immediate processing of feelings in a group setting.

6147 Shibles, Warren. *Death: The Inter-Disciplinary Analysis*. Whitewater, Wis.: The Language Press, 1974.

See 1031.

6148 Shneidman, Edwin S. "The College Student and Death." In *New Meanings of Death*, ed. by Herman Feifel. New York: McGraw-Hill Book Co., 1977.

Experiences in college teaching and research on college students informed the author's brief discussion of the way that college students conceptualize death, feel about it, especially as a survivor or a victim. References.

6149 Stanford, Gene and Deborah Parry. *Death Out of the Closet: A Curriculum Guide to Living with Dying*. New York: Bantam Books, 1976.

This early book for teachers and counselors at the secondary school level offers a rationale for death education, suggest ways to deal with problems that are likely to arise, show how to organize content and survey materials and teaching strategies. Summaries and study questions for nineteen books on the subject take up almost half of the book. There are minimal references to much of the available literature of the time. The authors optimistically assume that any teacher can safely and effectively teach about death with minimal experience, preparation or training.

6150 Wass, Hannelore, *et. al.*, eds. *Death Education II: An Annotated Resource Guide*. Washington, D.C.: Hemisphere Pub. Co., 1985.

Resources include text, reference bibliographies, periodicals, audiovisuals, organizations, research instruments. Included is a hospice-training bibliography along with a discussion of thanatological topics in literature. The first edition 1980, was considered by Corr to be "an indispensable reference tool" (8009).

6.23 CHURCH AND COMMUNITY SEMINARS

6151 Bailey, Robert W. *The Minister and Grief.* New York: Hawthorn Books, 1976.

In addition to a growth group for those who grieve, clergy can also enlarge their ministry by training the membership as caregivers for those who grief. Church members can also be encouraged to keep in contact with bereaved family members. This is especially true for couples groups that include a bereaved person who has just lost a spouse. Church members can also assist in group plans for one-parent families.

6152 McBride, Alfred. *Death Shall Have No Dominion.* Dubuque, Iowa: Wm. C. Brown, 1979.

A Roman Catholic priest provides a text to be used in religious education classes for adolescents and young on death and dying who are studying death and dying. There is an emphasis upon the religious vision of death and a popular survey of psychological, social and ethical questions concerning death. The work is cohesive and systematic. A teachers manual has been written to accompany the text.

6153 Neale, Robert E. *The Art of Dying.* New York: Harper and Row, 1973.

This theological and psychological study presents questions and exercises that would be useful to people who are willing to raise their consciousness of the story of death in their own lives.

See 2143.

6154 O'Brien, Charles R. "Pastoral Dimensions in Death Education Research." *Journal of Religion and Health* 18 (1979): 74–77.

A survey of the attitudes of high school students regarding death and dying showed many implications for religious leaders. Students thought about death and wanted to talk about it, but were hesitant to discuss the subject with church leaders.

6155 Phipps, William E. *Death: Confronting the Reality.* Atlanta:, Ga.: John Knox, 1987.

A guidebook for pastors, counselors, adult discussion groups, which relates psychology and theology to definitions of life and death, life expectancy and quality of life, terminal illness, suicide, grief, funeral practices, body disposal, violent death, nuclear war, handgun control, the death penalty, how to explain death to children and theories of life after death.

6156 Wolfelt, Alan D. *Death and Grief: A Guide for Clergy.* Muncie, Ind.: Accelerated Development, 1988.

A clinical thanatologist provides information and principles of caregiving for clergy who attend those who are dying or in grief. The focus is on the psychological and social aspects of grief. Relevant case studies are provided by the author. This is an entry level text organized around the typical questions of clergy and others about death and dying. A few well chosen references are included on each topic.

6.24 PROFESSIONAL EDUCATION

6157 Benoliel, Jeanne Quint, ed. *Death Education for the Health Professional.* Washington, D. C.: Hemisphere Pub. Corp., 1982.

A professor of nursing education and colleagues provide articles on the meaning of effective care for the terminally ill. A basic background for physicians and nurses is provided through an understanding of death and dying as normal states in human existence that are profoundly influenced by social and cultural values and historical circumstances. Another foundation for professional practice is an emphasis upon ethical and legal issues, human behaviors and reactions in response to different types of death-related events and processes, teamwork in delivery of services to individuals and family, decision-making during dilemmas in clinical practice, clinical options in care of the dying. Articles consider these issues from the perspective of courses for undergraduate nursing, nurses, graduate students, a course for advanced practice, a seminar on terminal illness for medical students, humanistic health-care education in a hospice/palliative care setting. References for each chapter.

6158 Fleming, Thomas J., *et. al.,* eds. *Communicating Issues in Thanatology.* New York: MSS Information Corp. 1976.

This volume from the Foundation of Thanatology considers communication in terms of interpersonal relationships with the dying patient, reports on interpretation in the media, documentation and data bank research, death education in public and professional schools, the technical definition of thanatology and related words.

6159 Nighswonger, Carl A. "Ministry to the Dying as a Learning Encounter." *Journal of Thanatology* 1 (1971): 101–108.

A posthumous article from the chaplain at the University of Chicago hospital and clinics, who opened doors for Kübler-Ross' clinical research on the dying, reflects on the type of learning that came to theological students, pastors, chaplains during their ministry to the dying and the bereaved in a clinical pastoral education program. He credits 400 terminally ill patients with "teachers" to him and his students during the five years of the program. The pilgrimage of learning includes shock, emotion, negotiation, cognition, commitment, completion.

6160 Payne, Edmund C. "Dying: Barriers to Communication," In *Communicating Issues in Thanatology*, ed. by Thomas J. Fleming, *et. al.*, 113–119. New York: MSS Information, 1976.

In examining the growth of interest in death and dying, the author stresses the importance of communication of patients and families with physicians and nurses for a sense of physical care and security. Interprofessional communication is also essential for growth of both scientific and humanitarian aspects of thanatology.

6161 Pine, Vanderlyn R. "Communicating Issues in Thanatology: The State of the Art." *Communicating Issues in Thanatology*, ed. by Thomas J. Fleming, Austin H. Kutscher, David Peretz, and Ivan K. Goldberg, 319–334. New York: MSS Information Corp., 1976.

In concluding observations about a conference on communication, the author notes that the participants are occupationally and educationally mobile individuals. This may increase the taboo of death among them in contrast with more traditional and settled persons. Publishers, physicians and other professional persons may resist death studies for this reason.

Chapter 7

RESEARCH
AND EVALUATION

7001 Allan, Russell O., and Bernard Spilka. "Committed and Consensual Religion: A Specification of Religion-Prejudice Relationships." *Journal for the Scientific Study of Religion* (1966–1967): 191–206.

See 1202.

7002 Allport, Gordon W., and M. J. Ross. "Personal Religious Orientation and Prejudice." *Journal of Personality and Social Psychology* 5 (1967): 432–443.

See 1203.

7003 Baler, Lenin A., and Peggy J. Golde. "Conjugal Bereavement: A Strategic Area of Research in Preventive Psychiatry." *Working Papers in Community Health*. Boston: Harvard School of Public Health, 1964.

A discussion of theoretical and research implications of crises among recently bereaved widows. Extensive bibliography.

7004 Buckingham, R. W., *et al.* "Living with the Dying: Use of the Technique of Participant Observation." *Canadian Medical Association Journal* 115 (1976): 1211–1215.

Those who are caring for the dying can observe their needs and those of the family through the research technique of participant observation.

7005 Caldwell, D. and B. L. Mishara. "Research on Attitudes of the Medical Doctors Toward the Dying Patient: A Methodological Problem." *Omega* 3 (1972): 341–346.

A review of research indicates a reluctance on the part of many physicians to discuss their attitudes about death.

7006 Dee, Martin and L. S. Wrightsman. "Religion and Fears About Death: A Critical Review of Research." *Religious Education* 59(1964): 174–176.

Explanations concerning the fear of death and religiosity provide contradictory results. From a review of these contradictory reports, the authors conclude that they are overly concentrated on specialized population groups, use naive approaches in measuring fear of death, fail to take into account geo-demographic and personal variables and at times have used weak statistical procedures in the analysis of results. Since 1964, some of these methodological deficiencies have been corrected through psychometrically-developed, direct, fear-of-death measures.

7007 Dumont, Richard G. and Dennis C. Foss. *The American View of Death: Acceptance or Denial?* Cambridge, Mass.: Schenkman Publishing Co., 1972.

A chapter in this Ph.D. monograph considers "methodological problems in death attitude research," such as general shoddiness, investigator bias, deficiencies in questioning techniques, deficiencies in projective devices, overinterpretation of data, imprecise conceptualizations. See Dumont (1153)..

7008 Durlak, J. A. "Measurement of the Fear of Death: An Examination of Some Existing Scales." *Journal of Clinical Psychology* 28 (1972): 545–547.

Four different psychometric scales are examined for their validity in assessing fear and anxieties about death.

7009 Eliot, Thomas D. "A Step Toward the Social Psychology of Bereavement." *Journal of Abnormal and Social Psychology* 27 (1933): 380–390.

Various approaches to research on the problems of bereavement are outlined by a pioneer in the field.

7010 Eliot, Thomas D. "Bereavement as a Field of Social Research." *Bulletin of the Society for Social Research* 17 (1938): 4.

A shift in focus from the dead to the survivors may be necessary to promote research on bereavement.

7011 Feifel, Herman. "Attitudes Towards Death in Some Normal and Mentally Ill Populations." In *Meaning of Death*, ed. by Herman Feifel, 114–132. New York: McGraw-Hill Book Co., 1959.

In an early attempt to bring the problem and meaning of death into the domain of controlled investigation, Feifel investigated the attitudes of 85 mentally ill patients, 40 older people, and 85 persons 40 years old and younger. He found that religious persons were more afraid of death, that it was a mistake to erect psychological barriers in treatment of terminally ill patients because patients prefer honest and plain talk with their physicians, that manner of departure from death bears a definite relation to a person's philosophy of life and death. See Kahoe (1209).

7012 Fulton, Robert and W. A. Faunce. "The Sociology of Death: A Neglected Area of Research." *Social Forces* 36 (1958): 205–209.

The authors conclude that American sociologists have overlooked the area of death. A number of research topics are suggested.

7013 Godin, Andre. "Has Death Changed?" In *Death and Presence: The Psychology of Death and the After-Life*, ed by Andre Godin, 221–244. Brussels: Lumen Vitae Press, 1972.

A professor of the psychology of religion, Lumen Vitae, analyzes the sudden growth of psychological researches on death in the United States and those specialized in the scientific approach to death.

7014 Hulmes, T. H. and R. H. Rahe. "The Social Readjustment Rating Scale." *Journal of Psychosomatic Research* 11 (1967): 213–218.

See 4030.

7015 Kalish, Richard A. "A Little Myth Is A Dangerous Thing: Research in the Service of the Dying." In *Psychosocial Care of the Dying Patient*, ed. by Charles A. Garfield, 219–226. New York: McGraw-Hill Book Co., 1978.

A pioneer thanatologist considers the many books and articles that he has read on the subject to be filled with much advice but with little research criteria or clinical data that would enable professionals to evaluate the applicability of the advice. Examples of this problem are illustrated in reports on stages of dying, communication with the dying and the care of surviving relatives.

7016 Maitre, J. and A. Martins. "Sociological Statistics and Qualitative Interviews." In *Death and Presence: The Psychology of Death and the After-Life*, ed by Andre Godin, 63–68. Brussels: Lumen Vitae Press, 1972.

A hierarchical analysis of answers to religious practices, attitudes and beliefs among 1,524 French persons showed that answers varied widely between positive answers on such orthodox statements as "I believe in the resurrection of the body," and more personal statements such as "I believe that this life influences the future life" (21% for the former and 2% for the latter). The authors conclude that the deeper implications of statements concerning the afterlife will require individual interviews to show real personal significance of answers to questionnaires.

7017   Markusen, Eric and Robert Fulton. "Childhood Bereavement and Behavior Disorders: A Critical Review." *Omega* 2 (1971): 107–117.

From a survey of professional literature, the authors find four research stratagems used to determine the degree of association between childhood bereavement and later behavior disorders: observations of recently bereaved children, clinical case studies, anterospecitive (follow-up studies) and retrospective studies. Special attention is given to the methodological strengths and weaknesses of retrospective and anterospecitive studies. The authors then summarize one of their own exploratory anterospecitive studies from a very large sample relatively free of selective factors, which tentatively indicates that early parental bereavement may significantly affect adult behavior—specifically with respect to offenses against the law.

7018   May, H. J. and F. J. Breme. "SIDS Family Adjustment Scale: A Method of Assessing Family Adjustment to Sudden Infant Death Syndrome." *Omega* 13 (1982–83): 59–74.

See 4292.

7019   Richter, Kurt P. "The Phenomenon of Unexplained Sudden Death in Animals and Man." In *The Meaning of Death*, ed. by Herman Feifel, 302–313. New York: McGraw-Hill Book Co., 1979.

In an investigation of the part played by the adrenals and sympathetic nervous system in emotional states, a professor of psychobiology conducted experiments on rats which led him to conclude that their death from prolonged swimming in warm water was a reaction of hopelessness.

7020   Riegal, K. F., R. M. Riegal and G. A. Myer. "The Study of the Drop-out Rates in Longitudinal Research on Aging and the Prediction of Death." *Journal of Personality and Social Psychology* 5 (1967): 342–348.

When 380 persons above 55 years of age were retested after five years the authors concluded that previous studies had underestimated the amount of attrition in a longitudinal sample because of death or sickness.

7021 Ross, Elisabeth [Kübler-Ross]. "The Dying Patient as Teacher." *Chicago Theological Seminary Register* 57, 3 (December 1966): 1–14.

The author of *On Death and Dying* (1020) describes the clinical seminar for theological students in 1965 that became the basis for interviews by the students with two-hundred terminally ill patients and formed the basic data for *On Death and Dying* (between the publication of this article and the publication *On Death and Dying* an editor had inserted a hyphen between the maiden and married name of Ross). She describes the way in which interviews were conducted, presents excerpts from the feeling responses of theological students, describes the resistance of physicians and the divided responses of nurses. Patients were almost unanimous in accepting her clinical research project when it was explained to them. Some heartfelt examples of patient responses are given. Verbatim excerpts from the interview of Ross with several patients are given, along with her comments on the interview. The egalitarian and humane attitude of the author overcame barriers in the doctor-patient relationship. See also Pollock (4010).

7022 Shneidman, Edwin S. ed. *On the Nature of Suicide.* San Francisco: Jossey-Bass, 1969.

The first annual conference of the American Association of Suicidology (1968) included discussion among suicidologists on current issues in research on suicide. See Sheidman (3588).

7023 Templer, D. I. and C. F. Ruff. "Death-Anxiety Scale Means, Standard Deviations and Embedding." *Psychological Reports*, 29 (1971): 173–174.

See 1198.

7024 Wass, Hannelore, *et al.* "Research and Assessment of Attitudes toward Death." In *Death Education II*, ed. by Hannelore Wass, *et al*, 187–249. Washington, D.C.: Hemisphere Pub. Corp., 1985.

Very complete annotations are provided: (1) sixty research reports on death and dying, (2) 153 references to 14 selected instruments used in research on death and dying. References are included to earlier reviews of research on death and dying. An excellent resource.

7025 Worden, J. William. "Editorial: On Research and Death." *Pastoral Psychology* 23 (June 1972): 5–8.

To be worthy of the designation "scientific discipline," death research should attend to the following: systematic observation, operational concepts, integrated theory, multi-variate data analysis, interdisciplinary research teams.

Chapter 8

BIBLIOGRAPHIES

8001 *A Guide to Resources in Perinatal Bereavement.* Washington, D.C.: National Center for Education in Maternal and Child Health, 1988.

Books, pamphlets, journal articles, audio-visual selections for both the professional caregiver and the parent, sibling, relative or friend are organized around the general topics of understanding perinatal loss and providing care. A list of organizations for care and publication resources.

8002 Achenbaum, Andrew. *Old Age in the New Land.* Baltimore, Md.: John Hopkins University Press, 1978.

This study of the demographics of old age, economic dimensions and government policy in America since 1970 contains a bibliography of periodicals listed back to 1802.

8003 Adams, David W. *The Psychosocial Care of the Child and His Family in Childhood Cancer: An Annotated Bibliography.* Ontario, Canada: Dept. of Social Work Services, McMaster University Medical Center, 1979.

Title and author indexes are provided with this annotated bibliography that contains periodicals and specific chapters in books.

8004 Anglemyer, Mary, *et al. A Search for Environmental Ethics: An Initial Bibliography.* Washington, D. C.: Smithsonian Institution Press, 1980.

Selections in this annotated bibliography consider both the demonstrable decay of the environment and the roles of humans as the protectors and users of the environment. Works in science, philosophy, religion, education, literature, politics and economics are described from about 1946 to 1980 and include books, monographs, journal articles.

8005 Bernstein, Joanne E. *Books to Help Children Cope with Separation and Loss*, 2nd ed. New York: R. R. Bowker, 1983.

Annotated bibliographies are provided on books for young people and essays on helping them cope with separation and loss, death, divorce, desertion, serious illness, war, adaptation, homelessness, etc. An additional list of books (not annotated) is provided for adults. Extensive index and directory of helpful organizations.

8006 Cook, Sarah Sheets, ed. *Children and Dying: An Exploration and Selected Bibliographies*. Rev. ed. New York: Health Sciences Publishing Corp., 1974.

See 4188.

8007 Corr, Charles A. "Books for Adults: An Annotated Bibliography." In Wass, H. and Charles. A. Corr. *Helping Children Cope with Death: Guidelines and Resources*, 133–155. Washington, D.C.: Hemisphere Pub. Co., 1982.

8008 Corr, Charles A. "Bibliographies." In *Death Education II*. Ed. by Hannelore Wass, *et al.* 287–312. Washington, D.C.: Hemisphere Pub. Corp., 1985.

This annotation of bibliographies identifies and consolidates scattered resources, defines reference points for future work, and provides representative selections in the expanding subtopics of thanatology.

8009 Corr, Charles A. "Selected Texts and Reference Books." In *Death Education II*. Ed. by Hannelore Wass, *et al.* 251–286. Washington, D.C.: Hemisphere Pub. Corp., 1985.

Descriptive information and broad general evaluations are given for 23 texts and reference books published since 1979. In an introduction, the authors question the all encompassing label of a "death-denying" society and show through these annotations of texts that teaching about death and dying, caring for those with life-threatening illnesses and support for the bereaved has moved toward increasing complexity and greater sophistication. Contents, features and evaluation are offered for each review.

8010 De Pres, Terrence. "Bibliography: Original Testimony." In *The Survivor and Anatomy of Life in the Death Camps*, 249–254. New York: Pocket Books, 1977.

8011 Desai, Parimala. "The Literature–Annotated Bibliography." In *The Hospice: Development and Administration*, ed. by Glen W. Davidson, 189–204. Washington, D.C.: Hemisphere Pub. Co., 1978.

The annotations deal primarily with nursing and medical care with citations from clinically oriented journals.

8012 Edwards, Willie. M., *et al. Gerontology: A Cross-National Care List of Significant Works.* Ann Arbor, Mich.: Institute for Gerontology, The University of Michigan, 1982.

Abstracts, indexes, journals, bibliographies, directories, guides, handbooks and national conferences are listed for the United States, the United Kingdom and Canada.

8013 Farberow, Norman L. *Bibliography on Suicide and Suicide Prevention: 1987–1957; 1958–1967.* Rockville, Md.: National Institute of Mental Health, 1970.

After years of listening to cries for help and searching for new ways to provide help, an interdisciplinary team of therapists who have been associated with Suicide Prevention Center in Los Angeles discuss suicide from two viewpoints: the procedures and operations of a community center and the theoretical approaches of private practitioners (psychoanalytic, analytic psychology, Adler, Sullivan, Horney, non-directive). Extensive bibliography, 1897–1957.

8014 Fecher, Vincent John. *Religion and Aging: An Annotated Bibliography.* San Antonio, Tex.: Trinity University Press, 1982.

8015 Feigenberg, Loma. "Survey of the Thanatological Literature." In *Terminal Care: Friendship Contracts With Dying Cancer Patients,* by Loma Feigenberg, trans. by Patrick Hort, 217–256. New York: Brunner, 1980.

Important writings in the development of the field of thanatology are related to each other in terms of historical development and theme.

8016 Fulton, Robert L., ed. *Death, Grief and Bereavement: A Bibliography 1845–1975.* New York: Arno Press, 1976.

A chronological bibliography of the literature on death, grief and bereavement. Entries include journal articles and a listing of doctoral theses, 1970–1978. Indexed under subject classifications.

8017 Fulton, Robert L. *Death, Grief and Bereavement: A Bibliography, Book II, 1975–1980.* New York: Arno Press, 1981.

Over 2,000 journal articles and some books are listed along with doctoral dissertations, 1970–1978. Subject index. Cross-references.

8018 Goldstein, D. M., and L. Walters, eds. *Bioethics: A Guide to Information Sources*. Detroit: Gale Research Co., 1982.

Ethical issues arising in medicine and the life sciences are classified under organizations, general sources, dictionaries. Documents published between 1973 and 1981 compromised most of the annotations, drawn from the Bioethics Library, Kennedy Institute of Ethics, Georgetown University.

8019 Gruman, Gerald J. "An Historical Introduction to Ideas About Voluntary Euthanasia: With a Bibliographic Survey and Guide Survey for Interdisciplinary Studies." *Omega*, 4 (1973): 87–138.

See 3469.

8020 *Hastings Center Bibliography of Ethics, Biomedicine, and Professional Responsibility*. Frederick, Md.: University Publications of America, 1984.

The bibliography, with occasional annotations includes general readings on death and dying and specific topics such as definition of death, treatment of the dying, and ethical issues such as euthanasia.

8021 Kalish, Richard A. "Grief and Bereavement: A Selected Annotated Bibliography of Behavioral Science and Psychiatric Writings." In *Death and Bereavement*, ed. by Austin H. Kutscher, 343–358. Springfield, Ill.: Charles C. Thomas, 1969.

Psychological, sociological and psychiatric articles are annotated through descriptive paragraphs.

8022 Kalish, Richard A. "Death and Dying: A Briefly Annotated Bibliography." In *The Dying Patient*, ed. by Orville G. Brim, Jr., Howard E. Freeman, Sol Levine, and Norman A. Scotch., 327–380. New York: Russell Sage Foundation, 1970.

The literature of psychology, sociology and psychiatry is reviewed in relation to death and dying. Some references are from nursing, general medicine, pastoral counseling, theology, hospital administration, and anthropology. References are to English and American works, from the early 1930's until 1965.

8023 Kelly, Nathan F. *The Emergence of Roman Catholic Medical Ethics: An Historical-Methodological-Bibliographical Study*. New York: E. Mellen Press, 1979.

See 3435.

8024 Kutscher, Austin H., Jr. and Austin H. Kutscher. *A Bibliography of Books on Death, Bereavement, Loss and Grief: 1935–1968.* New York: Health Sciences Publishing Corp., 1969.

English and American titles are grouped under a variety of headings. Author Index. No annotations.

8025 Kutscher, Austin H., Jr., Martin Kutscher and Austin H. Kutscher. *Supplement 1: A Bibliography of Books on Death, Bereavement, Loss and Grief: 1968–1972.* New York: Health Sciences Publishing Corp., 1974.

English and American books are classified under a variety of headings. No annotations.

8026 Lester, David. *Why People Kill Themselves: A 1980's Summary of Research Findings on Suicidal Behavior.* 2nd ed. Springfield, Ill: Charles C. Thomas, 1983.

See 3560.

8027 MacIntosh, J. L. *Suicide among Children, Adolescents, and Students: A Comprehensive Bibliography.* Monticello, Ill.: Vance Bibliographies, 1981.

Over a thousand unannotated entries from a wide variety of indices, abstracts, and other international bibliographical sources are provided.

8028 MacIntosh, John L. *Research on Suicide: A Bibliography.* Bibliographies and Indexes in Psychology No. 2. Westport, Conn.: Greenwood Press, 1985.

More 2300 entries are given to provide materials, research and writings on many aspects of suicide: overviews, definitions and variety of self-destructive behavior, history, theories, demography and epidemiology, prevention, intervention, treatment, assessment, prediction, education, ethics, post-vention, literature for specific professions, art and literature. There is an introduction to each general topic and occasionally a citation is annotated. Although extensive, the listings are not intended to be exhaustive. They are of works published in England, primarily 1970–1984. Journals, professional associations and computer search sources are listed in the first chapter.

8029 Muldoon, M. *Abortion: An Annotated Indexed Bibliography.* New York: E. Mellen, 1980.

Over 3,000 entries, primarily from 1970 to 1980 are listed under various topics on abortion.

8030 National Center for Health Statistics. *Catalogue of Publications, 1980–88.* Hyattsville, Md.: National Center for Health Statistics, 1989.

Without annotation, the catalogue presents (1) a listing of National Center for Health Statistics Reports from 1980 through 1988, (2) articles by staff members (NCHS) that appeared in professional and scientific publications during 1988, (3) an index of selected health topics covered in Center reports.

8031 *New Titles in Bioethics.* Washington, D.C.: Center for Bioethics Library, Kennedy Institute for Ethics, Georgetown University, May 1975–monthly.

A monthly listing of books, government documents, pamphlets, serials and audio-visuals acquired by the Center for Bioethics Library includes a section on death and dying.

8032 Pacholski, Richard A. "Thanatology Topics in Literature." In *Death Education II,* ed. by Hannelore Wass, *et al.,* pp. 301–312. Washington, D.C.: Hemisphere Pub. Corp., 1985.

Sixty titles are annotated under the categories of primary materials, critical discussions of death as a literary subject, reference sources. Also included is a commentary on the thanatological content of the Bible. Eleven reference tools are included to identify literary material on thanatology.

8033 Pacholski, Richard A. "Audiovisual Resources." In *Death Education II,* ed. by Hannelore Wass, *et al.,* pp. 363–402. Washington, D.C.: Hemisphere Pub. Corp., 1985.

Eight-hundred and twenty-seven audiovisual resources include reference to appropriate age group, kind of medium, distributors, running time, publication date, topical index.

8034 Pacholski, Richard A. "Audiovisual Resources." In *Adolescence and Death,* ed. by Charles A. Corr and Joan N. McNeil, pp. 251–277. New York: Springer Pub. Co., 1986.

Audiovisual instruction units on death and dying are annotated and classified under general surveys, understanding grief, nuclear weapons and war, consciousness raising, calls to action, feature films, personal impact upon children and adolescents, caring for adolescents in dying and grief, the bereaved parent, suicide. Primarily for adolescents. Addresses of distributors.

8035 Pearson, Leonard. "Selected Bibliography on Death and Dying." In *Death and Dying,* ed. by Leonard Pearson, pp. 133–235. Cleveland, Ohio: The Press of Case Western Reserve University, 1969.

A hundred page annotated bibliography includes clinical studies, psychological and sociological research, philosophical and literary resources.

8036 Platt, Larry A. *Death and Dying*. Vol. I: *Grief and Bereavement—A Research Bibliography, 1964–1984*. Statesboro, Ga.: Georgia Southern College: The Social Gerontology Program, 1985.

A sociologist lists more than seven hundred books, scholarly journals and periodicals and professional organizations that have some research emphasis in the study of thanatology. Some bibliographies and some "this is my experience" books are also included, e. g. Kübler-Ross. Subject index.

8037 Platt, Larry A. *Death and Dying*. Vol. II: *The Anthropology of Bereavment—A Research Bibliography*. With Richard Persico. Statesboro, Ga.: Georgia Southern College: The Social Gerontology Program, 1986.

The general topic of death from a cross-cultural perspective is presented in a listing of books and articles that range from nineteenth century studies of primitive religion to twentieth century field studies by anthropologists and sociologists. Some philosophical and comparative religion studies are included in the listing of almost seven hundred references. Subject index.

8038 Prentice, Ann E. *Suicide: A Selective Bibliography of Over 2,200 Items*. Metuchen, N. J.: Scarecrow Press, 1974.

Without annotation citations are classified according to books, theses, articles (professional and popular), religious and legal journals, state legislation, medical, scientific, literary, films, tapes and recordings, 1960–1973. Index of authors and subjects.

8039 Simpson, Michael A. *Dying, Death and Grief: A Critically Annotated Bibliography and Source Book of Thanatology and Terminal Care*. New York: Plenum Press, 1987.

Annotations are provided of a wide range of books in English on death and dying from 1979 to 1987. In addition there are bibliographies on murder, terrorism, and the political uses of death, nuclear holocaust and megadeath. Author and subject index. As a pioneer in thanatology, the author is especially helpful in biomedical evaluations of literature.

8040 Simpson, Michael A. "Bibliography of Books on Nuclear Holocaust and Megadeath." In *Dying, Death, and Grief: a Critically Annotated Bibliography and Source Book of Thanatology and Terminal Care*. New York: Plenum Press, 1979.

This critically annotated bibliography and sourcebook of thanatology and terminal care is composed of several sections, the largest of which includes books by title with a subject and author index. Films, audio-visual materials, teaching materials, European literature, and key journal references make up the remainder of the volume.

8041 Sollito, Sharmon and Robert M. Veatch, comps. *Bibliography of Society, Ethics and the Life Sciences.* Hastings-on-Hudson, N. Y.: Institute of Society, Ethics, and the Life Sciences. Issued annually since 1973.

Annotated references in this annual volume include several on death and dying.

8042 Smith, Andrew J. K. and J. Kiffin Penry. *Brain Death: A Bibliography with Key-Word and Author Indexes.* Washington, D.C.: DHEW Publication No. (NIH) 73–347, 1972.

8043 *Thanatology Abstracts.* New York: Center for Thanatology Research and Education, 1986– .

A yearly abstract of articles on thanatology are prepared as a Journal and also available 5 1/4 inch disk from Roberta Halporn, Director, Center for Thanatology Research and Education, 391 Atlantic Avenue, Brooklyn, New York 1217–1701.

8044 Triche, C. W., II, and D. S. Triche. *The Euthanasia Controversy: 1812–1974. A Bibliography with Selected Annotations.* Troy, N. Y.: Whitston Pub. Co., 1975.

Books and essays are listed alphabetically along with an author index.

8045 Tyckoson, David A., ed. *AIDS.* 2nd. ed. Phoenix: Oryx Press, 1986.

See 3296.

8046 Vernick, Joel J. *Selected Bibliography On Death and Dying.* Washington, D.C.: U.S. Government Printing Office, 1969.

A variety of medical, psychological and theological periodicals primarily in English, were surveyed to provide a bibliography that covers the mid-1900's to about 1965. Author-Subject index.

8047 Walters, LeRoy, ed. *Bibliography of Bioethics.* Detroit, Mich.: Gale Research Co., issued annually since 1975.

An eclectic selection of publications are listed under topics that include death and dying. Subtopics are specifically on ethical issues such as abortion, euthanasia. A continuing series from the Center for Bioethics Kennedy Institute, Georgetown University.

8048 Wass, Hannelore and Charles A. Corr, eds. *Helping Children Cope with Death: Guidelines and Resources*. Rev. ed. Washington, D.C.: Hemisphere Pub. Co., 1984.

See 4198.

8049 Wass, Hannalore, Charles A. Corr, Richard A. Pacholski and Catherine M. Sanders. *Death Education: An Annotated Research Guide*. Washington, D.C.: Hemisphere Pub. Co., 1980.

A valuable resource for teachers in death education provides annotations of literature, some recommended texts and reference books, bibliographies and periodicals. Audiovisuals, organizational and community resources are also listed.

8050 Wass, Hannelore, Charles Corr, Richard A. Pacholski and Catherine M. Sanders. *Death Education II: An Annotated Resource*. Washington, D.C. Hemisphere Pub. Co., 1985.

The 1980 edition of Wass, *et al.* (8049) is updated and the following topics are added: hospice training bibliography, discussion of thanatology topics and literature, appendix of selected documents.

8051 Wass, Hannelore, and Cameron Forfoar. "Research and Assessment of Attitudes toward Death." In *Death Education II*, ed. by Hannelore Wass, *et al*, 187–249. Washington, D.C.: Hemisphere Pub. Corp., 1985.

See 7024.

8052 Wass, Hannelore, *et al.* "Books for Children." In *Death Education II*, ed. by Hannelore Wass, *et al.*, pp. 313–352. Washington, D.C.: Hemisphere Pub. Corp., 1985.

A hundred and fifty-five titles portray dying, death and grief in books for children that are sensitive and realistic rather than sensational and melodramatic. Honesty and specific descriptions of death are characteristic of them. The annotations are excellent.

8053 Wass, Hannelore. "Periodicals." In *Death Education II*, ed. by Hannelore Wass, *et al.*, pp. 353–360. Washington, D.C.: Hemisphere Pub. Corp., 1985.

Journals in the general area of thanatology are listed from the founding of *Omega* in 1970 to *Death Education* in 1977. More detailed information on some journals may be found in Wass (8049).

8054 Williams, M. "Changing Attitudes to Death: A Survey of Contributions in Psychological Abstracts Over a Thirty Year Period." *Humanitarian Religion* 19 (1966): 405–423.

Journal articles in 1931 and 1961 are compared on death, murder and suicide.

AUTHOR INDEX

The numbers following the citations refer to entry numbers rather than page numbers.

TITLE INDEX

The numbers following the citations refer to entry numbers rather than page numbers.

SUBJECT INDEX

The numbers following the citations refer to entry numbers rather than page numbers.

About the Compiler

SAMUEL SOUTHARD is currently Senior Professor of Pastoral Theology at Fuller Theological Seminary. He is professionally certified by the Association for Death Education and Counseling as a death educator and a grief counselor. A practitioner and teacher of counseling and pastoral theology for forty years, Dr. Southard is also the author of several books that examine various aspects of pastoral theology and ministry. In addition, he was the first director of the Hospice of Pasadena, 1979-1980.